lonely planet

Indonesia

Anthony Ham, Ray Bartlett, Jade Bremner, Mark Eveleigh, Narina Exelby, Marco Ferrarese, Paul Harding, Sarah Reid, Leyla Rose

Borobudur (p8

FROM LEFT: GILANG GEPEMOTO/SHUTTERSTOCK, KONSTANTIN TRUBAVIN/GETTY IMAGES, R.M. NUNES/SHUTTERSTOCK

CONTENTS

Plan Your Trip

The Guide

Surfing in Nusa Tenggara (p327), Bali

Pura Luhur Uluwatu (p209), Bali

Pantai Padang (p482), Sumatra

TUNATURA/SHUTTERSTOCK

Diving in Raja Ampat (p426), Papua

ZRINI4/SHUTTERSTOCK

Toolkit

Storybook

JAFARSODIK/SHUTTERSTOCK

Proboscis monkey, Kalimantan (p563)

SEKAR B/SHUTTERSTOCK

Orangutans in Tanjung Puting National Park (p556), Kalimantan

INDONESIA

THE JOURNEY BEGINS HERE

Few countries manage to straddle the divide between the wild and modern sophistication quite like Indonesia, one reason among many why I find it so strangely compelling. Wherever I go, I can't get enough of the culinary and cultural diversity, and I'm never far from a stirring wildlife encounter or a soulful and beautiful wilderness experience. I'm especially drawn to those destinations that lie beyond where the paved road ends, and this is a country that is rich in such magic, from Kalimantan to Papua to so many other places in between. Countries like Indonesia are why I travel.

Anthony Ham

@AnthonyHamWrite

Anthony searches for stories in the wild places of our planet, from the jungles of Kalimantan to the savannas and deserts of Africa to the frozen tundra of the High Arctic. He writes for the New York Times *and is also the author of two books of narrative nonfiction.*

My favourite experience is immersing myself in the rainforests of **Kalimantan** (p536), never quite knowing when an orangutan, a proboscis monkey or a clouded leopard might choose to appear. Or not. Just knowing they are there brings the forest alive.

WHO GOES WHERE

Our writers and experts choose the places that, for them, define Indonesia.

EFENDY ADA/SHUTTERSTOCK

I've visited Indonesia many times but keep coming back to Java and its incredible, mesmerizing **Kawah Ijen** (pictured; p146). The agony of getting up at midnight, the steep climb to the rim in pitch dark, the slippery descent into the crater – and then the swirling pool of blue fire that sends tendrils uphill, which is too otherworldly to describe. Afterwards, the sun finally burns off the steam to reveal the mint-green crater lake. It's priceless.

Ray Bartlett

@kaisoradotcom

Ray co-wrote the Java chapter.

PATRICKWA/SHUTTERSTOCK

South Bali is all about waves for days, in every size, shape and condition imaginable. This surfer's paradise has all the elements of an adventurous road trip, but I prefer **Nusa Lembongan** (pictured; p212) for fewer crowds and truly spectacular waves, where calm seas turn into world-class spots during the right tides. Go with a guide to score the rides of your life.

Jade Bremner

@jadeob

Jade co-wrote the Bali chapter.

As a surfer, it was difficult for me to turn my back on Mentawai's perfect waves and to concentrate instead on the sweaty interior of **Pulau Siberut** (p488), but I'll never forget my time with a Mentawaian tribal community (pictured). My traditional tattoo is a permanent reminder of some of the most hospitable people I've met in all my Indonesian travels.

SUN_SHINE/SHUTTERSTOCK

Mark Eveleigh

@markeveleigh

Mark co-wrote the Bali chapter and wrote the Sumatra chapter.

Few things are as exciting as camping near an active volcano that's been hissing smoke since 1933. And **Gunung Dukono** (pictured; p387) is exactly that – a rough trek that starts in the jungle and ends in a lunar landscape. It's dangerous and wild, and no one but the mountain itself can guarantee you'll be able to peek into its fuming crater.

SABINE_LJ/SHUTTERSTOCK

Marco Ferrarese

marcoferrarese.com

Marco co-wrote the Bali chapter and wrote the Maluku chapter.

I wasn't sure if Bali would be my kind of place. But there was something about the faded photo of my dad on a paradisiacal-looking Kuta St in 1976 that made me want to find out. It turns out I loved every minute of that first trip and I've since criss-crossed Bali and Nusa Tenggara countless times. My favourite experience is diving along the coral-encrusted walls surrounding **Pulau Menjangan** (pictured; p276).

WONDERFUL NATURE/SHUTTERSTOCK

Sarah Reid

@sarahreidtravels

Sarah co-wrote the Bali chapter.

CITTADINODELMONDO/SHUTTERSTOCK

Candi Sewu (pictured; p86) is the furthest and most serene temple in the busy Prambanan complex and, as a result, not many people go there – but go you must if you'd like to sit in peace among the stones of a 1200-year-old spiritual space. While Prambanan is known for its Hindu temples, Candi Sewu is actually the second-largest Buddhist temple complex in Indonesia.

Narina Exelby

ne-where.world

Narina co-wrote the Java and Bali chapters.

PAUL HARDING/LONELY PLANET

You have to go a long way to find truly unfettered island paradises in Indonesia, but Sulawesi has them in spades. The **Togean Islands** (pictured; p621) are a standout for me. It's hard work getting here, but after days of flights, cramped shared taxis and long-haul ferries, you arrive in a place of such tropical beauty, underwater delights and sheer relaxation that you may never want to leave.

Paul Harding

@paulhtravel

Paul wrote the Sulawesi chapter.

BIGRAIN/SHUTTERSTOCK

As the first rays of sun illuminate the glistening paddy fields around **Tetebatu** (pictured; p337) and the graceful Gunung Rinjani emerges from the darkness, you'll feel as if you're the only person around, save for a handful of farmers who've also chosen to get an early start. Take a stroll through the fields to see what's growing, followed by a morning dip in the nearby waterfall.

Leyla Rose

leylarosewrites.com

Leyla wrote the Nusa Tenggara chapter.

MYANMAR (BURMA)
THAILAND
LAOS
ANDAMAN SEA
SOUTH CHINA SEA
VIETNAM
Gulf of Thailand
Borobudur
Wander the world's biggest **Buddhist temple** (p88)
Banjarmasin
Take a boat ride to a fabulous **floating market** (p562)
Gunung Leuser National Park
Trek into the jungle in search of **orangutans** (p466)
Tanjung Puting National Park
Head upriver to observe **orangutans** (p556)
Kota Kinabalu
BANDAR SERI BEGAWAN
BRUNEI
SABAH
SARAWAK
EAST MALAYSIA
Banda Aceh
PENINSULAR MALAYSIA
Pulau Simeulue
Medan
KUALA LUMPUR
Danau Toba
Selat Melaka
Kuching
SINGAPORE
Pulau Nias
Riau Islands
Pekanbaru
Sintang
SUMATRA
KALIMANTAN
Samarinda
Padang
Pontianak
Pulau Bangka
Palangka Raya
Balikpapan
Pulau Siberut
Kerinci Seblat National Park
Jambi
Pangkalan Bun
Selat Makassar
Mentawai Islands
Palembang
Pulau Belitung
Banjarmasin
Bengkulu
Bandar Lampung
Karimunjawa Islands
JAVA SEA
Pulau Enggano
JAKARTA
Pulau Madura
Serang
Bandung
Semarang
Mataram
Lombok
Bogor
JAVA
Solo
Surabaya
BALI
Malang
Yogyakarta
Denpasar
Yogyakarta
Join street performers in Java's **cultural capital** (p76)
Ubud
Catch a traditional Balinese **dance performance** (p223)
Pura Besakih
Hike to Bali's most important **Hindu temple** (p246)
Gunung Rinjani
Climb Indonesia's second-highest **volcano** (p350)
Sumbawa
Surf the legendary left-break **Supersuck** (p304)
INDIAN OCEAN

PACIFIC OCEAN

PHILIPPINES

SULU SEA

Raja Ampat

Enjoy fairy-tale seascapes and world-class **diving** (p420)

Baliem Valley

Celebrate Papua's indigenous cultures at the **Baliem Valley Festival** (p447)

SULAWESI SEA

Manado

Pulau Halmahera

Gorontalo

Kota Ternate

Togean Islands

MALUKU SEA

Bacan Islands

Palu

Sorong

Manokwari

Pulau Biak

Kota Biak

Sarmi

Jayapura

SULAWESI

Makale

Sula Islands

SERAM SEA

Pulau Seram

Fak-Fak

PAPUA

Kendari

Watampone

MALUKU

Kota Ambon

Banda Islands

Timika

Wamena

Makassar

BANDA SEA

Kei Islands

Lorentz National Park

Aru Islands

PAPUA NEW GUINEA

FLORES SEA

Pulau Wetar

NUSA TENGGARA

Flores

Ende

DILI

TIMOR-LESTE

Tanimbar Islands

Pulau Yos Sudarso

SAWU SEA

Wasur National Park

Pulau Sumba

Kupang

Pulau Timor

ARAFURA SEA

TIMOR SEA

Banda Islands

Let your feet sink into powdery white sand of **Pulau Nailaka** (p407)

Gulf of Carpentaria

Komodo National Park

Get up close with giant lizard-like **dragons** (p306)

AUSTRALIA

ANIMAL ENCOUNTERS

Indonesia is a fabulous, world-class wildlife destination, both on land and beneath the waves. There are Komodo dragons to spot in Nusa Tenggara, and Sumatra and Kalimantan are the only places in the world (along with Malaysia) where it's possible to see orangutans in the wild. Rare sun bears, elephants, clouded leopards and tigers roam the rainforests, and there's a huge and diverse amount of bird and marine life as well.

Bird-Watching

Indonesia is a birder's paradise. More than 1700 bird species – 17% of all the world's birds – are found here and many are unique to the archipelago. Dancing birds of paradise are an unforgettable highlight.

Ethical Elephant Encounters

Sadly, we can't recommend any places where it's possible to enjoy ethical elephant encounters. If you want to see elephants, head to Sumatra's national parks.

Super Snorkelling

Don't despair if you don't have your diving certification: the snorkelling in Indonesia is awesome. Strap on a mask and fins and be astonished at the marine life.

FROM LEFT: FEATHERCOLLECTOR/SHUTTERSTOCK, JUFRISPHTR/SHUTTERSTOCK, FELINEUS/SHUTTERSTOCK

Sumatran tiger, Kerinci Seblat National Park (p497)

BEST WILDLIFE EXPERIENCES

Dive and snorkel the marine-life-rich ❶ **Raja Ampat** (p420) islands off Papua; birders also flock here for birds of paradise.

Hack through the rainforest of ❷ **Kerinci Seblat National Park** (p497) in Sumatra, home to the largest population of Sumatran tigers.

Look for orangutans and other primates, as well as elephants, rhinos and tigers, in Sumatra's ❸ **Gunung Leuser National Park** (p466).

Have an up-close encounter with orangutans at ❹ **Tanjung Puting National Park** (p556) in Central Kalimantan.

Draw near to the formidable Komodo dragon in ❺ **Komodo National Park** (p306) in Nusa Tenggara.

BEACH BLISS

With the world's fourth-longest coastline, Indonesia isn't short of beaches. Bali alone has more than 40, and there's a strip of sand somewhere in the country for everyone, whether you want to surf, snorkel, flop or party. Some beaches are wildly popular, especially in the tourist nexus of Bali, Lombok and the Gili Islands, but there are hundreds of idyllic beaches across the archipelago where your footprints might be the first of the day.

FROM LEFT: DYAH ISTIKOWATI/SHUTTERSTOCK, DUDAREV MIKHAIL/SHUTTERSTOCK, FABIO LAMANNA/SHUTTERSTOCK

When to Go

July, August and December are prime time for western Indonesia's beaches. Head to the exquisitely empty beaches of Maluku (pictured) and Papua from October to April.

Kid-Friendly

Nusa Dua and Sanur are family-friendly Bali destinations with shallow and safe beaches. Senggigi on Lombok and Gili Meno are also good family choices.

Party Beaches

Kuta, Legian and Seminyak are perennial favourites on Bali, but it's buzzy and sometimes rowdy Gili Trawangan that is Indonesia's principal party island.

Banyak Islands (p512), Sumatra

BEST BEACH EXPERIENCES

Check out the photogenic pink sand of ❶ **Pantai Merah** (p307) on Pulau Komodo in Komodo National Park.

Lose yourself on the near-deserted strips of sand that curl around Lombok's ❷ **Southwestern Peninsula** (p352).

Head to the remote and pristine ❸ **Banyak Islands** (p514) for the finest beaches in Sumatra.

Join the locals on the dozens of golden beaches spread along the coastline of ❹ **Gunung Kidul** (p94) in East Java.

Sink your feet into the powdery white sand of the tiny islet of ❺ **Pulau Nailaka** (p407) in the Banda Islands.

CLIMB A VOLCANO

Indonesia has more volcanoes than any other country on the planet, so if climbing a volcanic cone is on your bucket list, this is the perfect place to do it. Java, Sumatra and Bali are home to some of the most frequently climbed volcanoes, many of which are still active, but there are plenty of other options scattered across the country. Just make sure to check the current eruption status of the mountain before climbing.

FROM LEFT: JOAKIMBKK/GETTY IMAGES, FABIO LAMANNA/SHUTTERSTOCK, SONY HERDIANA/SHUTTERSTOCK

Spiritual Centres

Most volcanoes in Indonesia have religious significance. Some, such as Bali's Gunung Agung (pictured), are regarded as the spiritual centre of the islands over which they preside.

Supervolcano Toba

Toba (pictured) on Sumatra is Indonesia's only supervolcano – the volcanoes with the most powerful and destructive eruptions. Toba hasn't blown for 74,000 years, but it's still active.

Under the Volcano

Over five million Indonesians live close to volcanoes. While that seems an unwise choice, areas with large deposits of nutrient-rich volcanic soil are highly fertile.

Gunung Bromo (p129), Java

BEST VOLCANO EXPERIENCES

Haul yourself up the unrelenting slopes of ❶ **Gunung Api** (p408) for awesome views across the Banda Islands.

Make the pilgrimage to the crater of ❷ **Gunung Bromo** (p129) in East Java, which locals visit every year to make offerings to their traditional gods.

Marvel at the otherworldly vistas that can be seen from Lombok's ❸ **Gunung Rinjani** (p350), Indonesia's second-highest volcano.

Trek through the jungle and past waterfalls to the smoking summit of ❹ **Gunung Sibayak** (p474) in North Sumatra.

Spend the night camping on the lava flows of ❺ **Gunung Dukono** (p387), constantly active and rumbling since 1933.

DREAM DIVING

There's no better place in Southeast Asia for underwater adventures than Indonesia. It's possible to dive in just about every region of the country and the diversity and quantity of marine life is outstanding. Add in crystalline waters and vibrant reefs and it's no wonder that Indonesia is home to so many truly world-class dive sites. Novice divers will find plenty of dive schools at which to learn, while snorkellers will be in paradise, too.

FROM LEFT: VLADYSLAV LEHIR/SHUTTERSTOCK, DUDAREV MIKHAIL/SHUTTERSTOCK, SUBPHOTO.COM/SHUTTERSTOCK

Learn to Dive

Bali (pictured) and the Gili Islands are fine places to do a PADI or SSI course, with warm waters, mild currents and lots of colourful corals.

Where to Dive

Nusa Tenggara, Papua and Sulawesi offer tremendous diving, but you can dive just about everywhere in Indonesia. Kalimantan and Maluku are upcoming dive destinations.

When to Dive

April to October is the best time for diving Bali, Lombok, the Gilis and Sulawesi. Conversely, October to April is when conditions are ideal in Maluku and Papua.

Diving in Raja Ampat (p426), Papua

BEST DIVING EXPERIENCES

Access the dive sites of the ❶ **Alor Archipelago** (p318) in Nusa Tenggara, home to perhaps the most pristine reefs in Indonesia.

Dive amid huge manta rays and stingless jellyfish in the ❷ **Derawan Archipelago** (p578) off East Kalimantan, perhaps Indonesia's least-visited diving paradise.

Enjoy true ocean diving amid fabulous reefs at ❸ **Pulau Bunaken** (p632), widely considered Sulawesi's best.

Gape at the huge array of marine life and the stunning corals of Papua's paradise-like ❹ **Raja Ampat** (p420) islands.

Escape the crowds of popular Bali dive sites like Tulamben and visit ❺ **Pulau Menjangan** (p276), our favourite on the island.

SUBLIME SURFING

Surfers from around the globe flock to Indonesia in search of the perfect wave. Many are drawn by visions of empty, palm-lined beaches and perfect barrels peeling around a coral reef. The good news is that mostly those dreams are real, but be prepared to travel to more remote destinations – Nusa Tenggara and Sumatra – if you want to avoid packed lineups. Like everywhere else, Indonesia is sometimes subject to flat spells and onshore winds.

FROM LEFT: DMITRII RUD/SHUTTERSTOCK, TRUPHOTOVIDEO/SHUTTERSTOCK, PHOTOGERSON/SHUTTERSTOCK

Learn to Surf

There are surf schools at all major surf sites. The gentle waves and sandy bottoms of Bali's Kuta and Legian beaches are especially suited to newbies.

When to Surf

It's possible to surf year-round, but in western Indonesia the world-class waves mostly break from April to October, the busiest period on Bali especially.

Where to Surf

Bali is Indonesia's surf central, with excellent waves for every level of surfer. Java is less busy, while Sumatra and Nusa Tenggara have isolated but superb spots.

Surfing in the Mentawais (p489), Sumatra

BEST SURFING EXPERIENCES

Join some of the world's best surfers in ❶ **Sumbawa** (p304) as they take on Supersuck, the greatest left on the planet.

Make the journey to the ❷ **Mentawai Islands** (p489) off Sumatra's west coast for consistently brilliant waves and surf resorts.

Ride the world-famous surf of Bali's ❸ **Bukit Peninsula** (p207), home of legendary breaks and the island's largest sets.

Test yourself at ❹ **G-Land** (p151) in southeast Java, one of the world's best left-handers and a holy grail for expert surfers.

Surf where the pros do, at Papua's ❺ **Manokwari** (p431), which plays host to international events.

NATURAL WONDERS

Plunge into Indonesia's 54 national parks, six of which are also World Heritage Sites, for a taste of the huge variety of natural splendours on offer. The parks are by far the best places for wildlife spotting, with orangutans, elephants, leopards and Komodo dragons among the most notable residents. They are also home to unique birds and flora, as well as waterfalls, mountains, caves, grasslands and lots of lush tropical jungle.

Entry Fees

Many of Indonesia's national parks cost 150,000/225,000Rp for weekday/weekend entrance, but some of the most popular, such as Komodo (pictured) and Raja Ampat, charge considerably more.

Marine National Parks

Some of the most stunning national parks are offshore. There are nine marine national parks, with some of Indonesia's top dive sites within them.

Guides

Guides are compulsory in many national parks. Visitors can either hire their own or be assigned one at the park entrance.

FROM LEFT: ASIATRAVEL/SHUTTERSTOCK, AL CARRERA/SHUTTERSTOCK, GUDKOV ANDREY/SHUTTERSTOCK

Komodo dragon, Komodo National Park (p306), Nusa Tenggara

BEST NATIONAL PARK EXPERIENCES

Island-hop through the dreamy, off-grid ❶ **Togean Islands** (p621), part of the Kepulauan Togean National Park off the coast of Sulawesi.

Sail to Rinca Island in ❷ **Komodo National Park** (p306) in Nusa Tenggara, where the world's largest lizards roam.

Hope for a glimpse of a one-horned Javan rhinoceros in southwest Java's ❸ **Ujung Kulon National Park** (p175).

Take the storybook river journey through the wildlife-rich ❹ **Tanjung Puting National Park** (p556) in Central Kalimantan.

Trek through the rainforest past waterfalls and rare flora in the little-visited ❺ **Gunung Palung National Park** (p552) in West Kalimantan.

TEMPLE-HOPPING

Indonesia isn't as known for its temples as other Southeast Asian nations, yet Java and Bali have some of the most ancient and beautiful shrines in the region. Exploring the temples offers valuable insights into Indonesia's past and present, and the fact that many of them are always busy with worshippers really brings them alive.

5 4 1 3 2

BEST TEMPLE EXPERIENCES

Climb the slopes of Gunung Batukau to reach ❶ **Pura Luhur Batukau** (p260), one of Bali's holiest and most spiritual shrines.

Cross the moat to the courtyards of ❷ **Pura Taman Ayun** (p278), a former royal temple that's one of Bali's most serene spots.

Visit Bali's most important Hindu temple, ❸ **Pura Besakih** (p246), spectacularly located almost 1000m up the slopes of Gunung Agung, an active volcano and Bali's most revered peak.

Walk among the remains of 240 temples at ❹ **Prambanan** (p86), Indonesia's largest Hindu temple complex, in the Central Java plains.

Wander ❺ **Borobudur** (p88), the world's largest Buddhist temple and one of Southeast Asia's most significant sights.

FROM LEFT: SERGII FIGURNYI/SHUTTERSTOCK, KANUMAN/SHUTTERSTOCK

Dress Appropriately

Temples are sacred spaces, so visitors need to dress modestly. Some temples on Bali will offer visitors sarongs or they can be rented.

Visit During the Week

Java's most significant temple complexes – Borobudur (pictured) and Prambanan – get very busy, especially at sunrise. Avoid weekends and brave the midday heat if you want some space.

Temples Everywhere

All Bali villages have several temples, but you'll also spot shrines and temples on the slopes of mountains and volcanoes and in ricefields and trees.

TANYA KEISHA/SHUTTERSTOCK

Baliem Valley Festival (p447), Papua

FABULOUS FESTIVALS

A big range of festivals take place in Indonesia, from the religious and cultural to celebrations staged by the many indigenous peoples. Almost all festivals, including some religious ones, involve a lot of eating and partying. Joining in is a great way to get to know the locals and learn more about the country.

Religious Festivals

The largest national celebrations are religious, with the most prominent being the Muslim festivals of Idul Fitri and Idul Adha, the Hindu Nyepi festival and Chinese New Year.

Regional Festivals

There are numerous local celebrations, ranging from carnivals in Yogyakarta to coffee festivals in Sulawesi, so check if any are going on where you are.

BEST FESTIVAL EXPERIENCES

Ascend Java's Dieng Plateau for the ❶ **Dieng Culture Festival** (p125), where jazz, fireworks and strange hair-cutting rituals draw the crowds.

Join the locals celebrating the tides at the ❷ **Meti Kei festival** (p411), held every October on the most beautiful beach in the Kei Islands.

Meet writers from around the world in Bali at the ❸ **Ubud Writers & Readers Festival** (p229), Southeast Asia's most prestigious literary festival.

Party like a Dayak at the ❹ **Dayak Harvest Festival** (p543), Kalimantan's biggest Dayak celebration, staged in Pontianak and surrounding villages.

Watch reenactments of ancient tribal battles, listen to traditional music and feast on roasted pig at Papua's ❺ **Baliem Valley Festival** (p447).

UNIQUE CULTURES

With so many peoples and religions across the archipelago, Indonesia has hundreds of distinct cultures. Visitors can experience everything from traditional Balinese dance performances and historic royal palaces to Javanese shadow-puppet shows and contemporary art galleries. Plus Torajan funeral ceremonies in Sulawesi, Dayak dance-offs in Kalimantan and mock tribal battles in Papua. Wherever you are, keep an eye out for events that showcase Indonesia's unique cultures, many of which involve music and dancing.

Festivals

Local festivals offer great opportunities for experiencing indigenous cultures and some, such as the Dayak Harvest Festival (pictured) in West Kalimantan, encourage visitors to join in the fun.

Ubud

The artistic heart of Bali is Ubud, where traditional Balinese culture infuses every aspect of life. Come here to learn about Bali's extraordinary art and dance scene (pictured).

Yogyakarta

Jakarta might be the capital for now, but it's Yogyakarta that's Java's undisputed cultural centre and the place where the arts shine the brightest.

FROM LEFT: DANI DANIAR/SHUTTERSTOCK, KATIEKK/SHUTTERSTOCK, PAUL HARDING 00/SHUTTERSTOCK

Pasar Terapung Lok Baintan in Banjarmasin (p562), Kalimantan

❹ ❸ ❷ ❶ ❺

BEST CULTURAL EXPERIENCES

Catch a traditional Balinese dance or music performance at ❶ **Pura Dalem Ubud** (p223), a temple compound in Ubud with nightly shows.

Check out the superb collection of puppets at Jakarta's ❷ **Museum Wayang** (p70), which also offers free shadow-puppet performances.

Take an early morning boat ride in Banjarmasin to the busy ❸ **Pasar Terapung Lok Baintan** (p562) floating market.

Join the dancers from around Indonesia who converge on Tenggarong in East Kalimantan for the annual ❹ **Erau International Folk & Art Festival** (p571).

Hike through the highlands of Papua's ❺ **Yali Country** (p453), one of the most enduringly traditional regions of Asia.

REGIONS & CITIES

Find the places that tick all your boxes.

Sumatra

RAINFORESTS AND WILDLIFE, ISLANDS AND VOLCANOES

Indonesia's largest island has wildlife-filled rainforests, world-class waves, magical undersea worlds and dramatic volcanoes. With its national parks easier to navigate than ever before and new surf sites being discovered all the time, more travellers are embracing stunning Sumatra, a place that rewards those willing to go the extra mile.

Kalimantan

ORANGUTANS, RAINFORESTS AND RIVERS

Come to Kalimantan to leave the tourist trail behind. A rugged paradise where orangutans and other iconic wildlife roam remote national parks, much of Kalimantan is covered in thick jungle bisected by Indonesia's longest rivers. Offshore is the little-seen Derawan Archipelago, where world-class dive sites and gleaming white-sand beaches await.

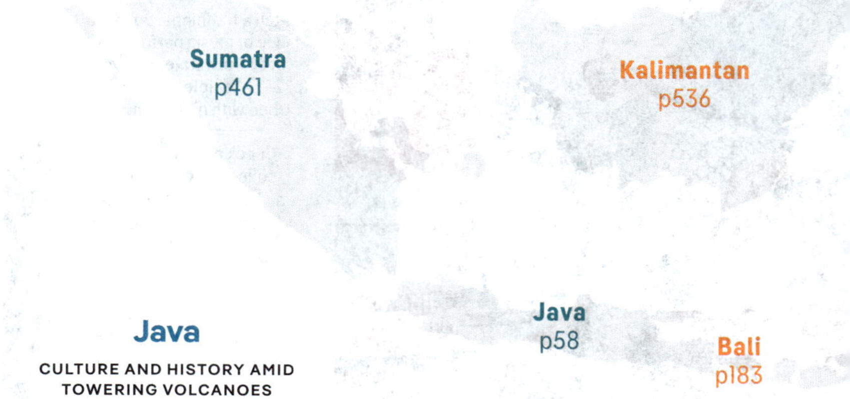

Sumatra
p461

Kalimantan
p536

Java
p58

Bali
p183

Java

CULTURE AND HISTORY AMID TOWERING VOLCANOES

Java is the most populous island on earth and it might be the most diverse, too. Overlooked by smoking volcanoes and ringed by tropical beaches, it has all the natural wonders of Indonesia, but it's also home to the capital Jakarta, a true megacity, and historic Yogyakarta, the country's cultural centre.

Bali

ISLAND OF THE GODS

Bali is Indonesia's most traveller-friendly destination for many excellent reasons. This small island has dozens of beaches, pounding surf, glowering volcanoes, serene temples, impossibly green rice terraces and, above all, truly charming people dedicated to maintaining their island's unique culture. Visit and you'll understand why there's nowhere quite like Bali.

Sulawesi

DIVE INTO INDONESIA'S MYSTERY ISLAND

With its remote highlands and islands, ancient megaliths, karst landscapes and indigenous peoples and cultures, Sulawesi offers mystery and adventure. Formed out of a sometimes-violent mashup of ethnic groups, religions and ecosystems, and flanked by waters and reefs rich in marine life, there's something for every traveller here.

Maluku

DIVING, VOLCANO HIKES AND OCEAN JOURNEYS

The remote islands of Maluku were once the world's only source of spices like nutmeg and cloves, and the fight for their control helped shape the modern world. Today, Maluku's pristine coral reefs, jungle-clad volcanoes and glorious beaches are perfect for adventures in one of Indonesia's least-visited and most idyllic regions.

Sulawesi p587

Maluku p371

Papua p416

Nusa Tenggara p286

Papua

REMOTE, WILD AND STEEPED IN TRADITION

Papua is Indonesia's final frontier, a place where roads are scarce and some people still hunt food with bows and arrows. Travel here is neither cheap nor easy, but the extraordinary wildlife, grand landscapes and charm of Papua's peoples make it a massively rewarding destination.

Nusa Tenggara

TIMELESS CULTURE, EPIC NATURE, BIG WAVES

The Nusa Tenggara archipelago is Indonesia less-trodden: a volcano-studded, mountainous land of technicolour lakes, pink-sand beaches, glassy surf breaks and traditional villages where Bahasa Indonesia is barely spoken. There are also Komodo dragons and unspoiled underwater worlds – explore this unique region while you can.

RICHARD WHITCOMBE/SHUTTERSTOCK

Shipwreck diving in Tulamben (p257)

ITINERARIES

Bali Beaches, Culture & Volcanoes

Allow: 8 days **Distance**: 189km

This Bali tour takes you from the hedonistic, surf-lined beaches of the west coast to serene Ubud – the 'other' Bali – rich in culture, history and temples. From there, head northeast to the volcanic peak of Gunung Agung, Bali's spiritual heart, before ending on the east coast at the dive site of Pulau Menjangan.

1

CANGGU ⏱ 2 DAYS

Buzzing **Canggu** (p188) is as much a state of mind as an area. This strip of Bali's west coast is lined with beaches, some great for surfing, such as black-sand Echo Beach (pictured), and there's a growing number of boutique stays, villas, creative cafes and hip restaurants. Make sure to do the Canggu Beach Walk, taking you from Batu Belig Beach to Echo Beach in a couple of hours.

2

UBUD ⏱ 2 DAYS

Head inland to unique **Ubud** (p218), where a few days on holiday might tempt you to extend your stay for weeks. Easily explored on foot or bicycle, Ubud is Bali's artistic heart: catch a traditional dance performance (pictured) or tour the art galleries and museums. This is also spa and yoga central, while cycling to the surrounding villages through lime-green ricefields is simply magical.

FROM LEFT: UMIKEM/SHUTTERSTOCK, KATIA TITOVA/SHUTTERSTOCK

3

GUNUNG AGUNG ⏱ 2 DAYS

Drive north of Ubud for 10km to see the photogenic Ceking rice terraces before veering due east to **Gunung Agung** (p245; pictured), an active volcano that is Bali's highest and most revered peak. If it's not erupting and you're fit, you can climb the steep, forested slopes for sweeping views, or explore **Pura Besakih** (p246), a complex of 23 temples that is Bali's most important Hindu site.

4

PULAU MENJANGAN ⏱ 2 DAYS

While the rest of the world heads in convoy to Tulamben, divers in the know make their way to **Pulau Menjangan** (p276), widely considered to offer the best diving in Bali. The gateway town is the relaxed town of Pemuteran, and you'll wonder if you've left Bali behind altogether, so quiet are these dive sites.

FROM LEFT: GEKKO GALLERY/SHUTTERSTOCK, DUDAREV MIKHAIL/SHUTTERSTOCK

ITINERARIES

The Java Jaunt

Allow: 10 days **Distance**: 865km

Loop through West and Central Java, taking in Indonesia's teeming capital Jakarta, the historic and cultural centres of Yogyakarta and Solo, and the awesome temples of Borobudur and Prambanan. Head to the cool air of the Dieng Plateau, where there are photo-friendly tea plantations and mountain lakes.

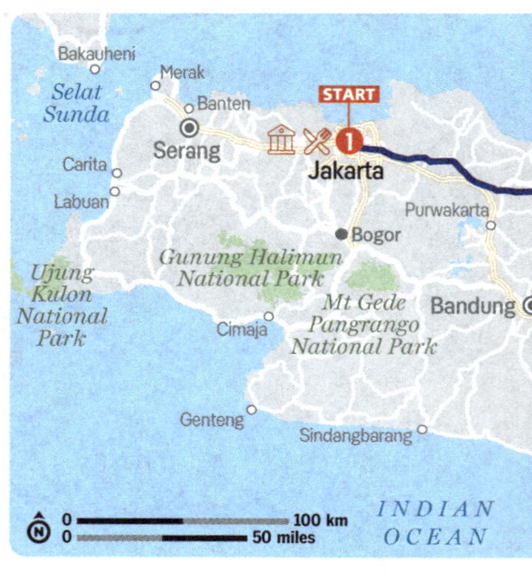

1 JAKARTA 2 DAYS

Wrap your senses around the sights and sounds of **Jakarta** (p64), Indonesia's megalopolis of a capital. Explore the museums and colonial buildings of Kota Tua (pictured), Jakarta's old town, and climb Monas, Indonesia's national monument, for spectacular views across the city. Then plunge into the famed malls and markets, followed by a meal at Loewy, one of Jakarta's fine-dining destinations.

2 YOGYAKARTA 2 DAYS

Hop the train to **Yogyakarta** (p76), Java's cultural capital and one of Indonesia's most appealing cities. Tour the Kraton (pictured), the 18th-century sultan's palace, check out Yogya's art scene and, in the evening, join the street performers on Jl Malioboro, the city's main drag. Take a day trip to the must-see majestic temple complex of Borobudur.

3 SOLO 1 DAY

Tack northeast to **Solo** (p96), stopping along the way at amazing Prambanan (pictured), Indonesia's most significant Hindu temple complex. Historic Solo is one of the heartlands of Javanese identity and is known for its distinctive batik, so it's a great place to shop as well as to catch traditional music and shadow-puppet performances.

FROM LEFT: RICHIE CHAN/SHUTTERSTOCK, ADITYA_FRZHM/SHUTTERSTOCK, SAIKO3P/SHUTTERSTOCK

4

DIENG PLATEAU ⏱2 DAYS

Head northwest into the land of the clouds and the 2000m-high **Dieng Plateau** (p120), where the views are drop-dead gorgeous. There are scenic tea plantations, mountaintop lakes, waterfalls, isolated villages and ancient temples to explore, while an increasing number of accommodation and eating options make this a great place to kick back and enjoy the sublime sunrises.

5

SEMARANG ⏱1 DAY

It's time to experience the charms of Java's north coast, and **Semarang** (p111) is one of the island's loveliest towns. Blending the decaying echoes of the Dutch colonial era with modern Indonesian culture and great food, Semarang is an atmospheric place to get to know provincial Javanese culture away from the tourist crowds.

6

KARIMUNJAWA ⏱2 DAYS

You've barely time to get airborne after taking off from Semarang before landing in **Karimunjawa** (p117), a little-known gem of an archipelago. The 27 islands here are perfect: think palm trees, idyllic beaches and pristine reefs. Start with two days to get a taste. But you may want to stay forever.

ITINERARIES

Beaches & Dragons

Allow: 8 days **Distance**: 680km

Island-hop through Nusa Tenggara from east to west. Start in Labuan Bajo on Flores and cruise to Komodo National Park to see the namesake dragons and wonderful marine life. Then fly to Lombok and traverse the southwest and south coasts, before catching a boat to Gili Trawangan, Indonesia's party island.

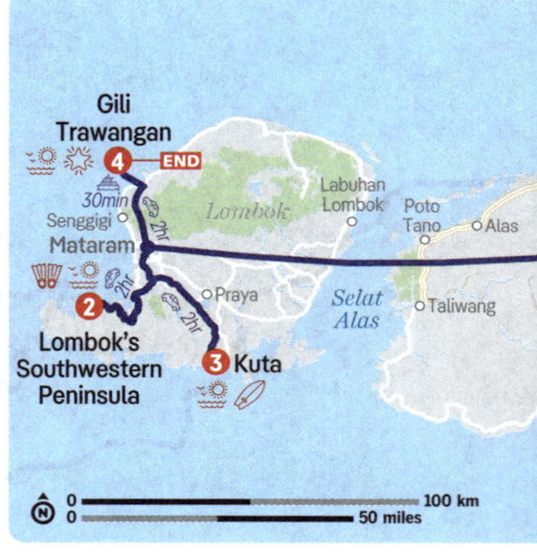

1

KOMODO NATIONAL PARK 2 DAYS

Set sail from Labuan Bajo on Flores for a two-day, one-night cruise to **Komodo National Park** (p306). Visitors are virtually guaranteed to get as close to a formidable Komodo dragon (pictured) as is sensible on tours of Rinca Island, home of the lizards. The cruises also take in some of the excellent snorkelling and diving spots.

2

LOMBOK'S SOUTHWESTERN PENINSULA 2 DAYS

Fly from Flores to Lombok and travel down to the **Southwestern Peninsula** (p352), where there are deserted white-sand beaches and unspoiled islands for superb snorkelling. Boatmen offer day trips to the pristine, marine-life-rich reefs, while on the mainland there are surf breaks, sleepy villages and a growing number of stylish resorts. Some people stay for weeks.

FROM LEFT: MIROSLAV CHYTIL/SHUTTERSTOCK, SONY HERDIANA/SHUTTERSTOCK

3

KUTA ⏱2 DAYS

Cut inland to reach **Kuta** (p332) on Lombok's south coast. Wonderful white-sand beaches lapped by azure water curve around crescent- and horseshoe-shaped bays, all backed by lush hills. The blinding, sugar-white sands of Selong Belanak (pictured), west of Kuta, might be the most fabulous beach on the island. There's outstanding surf all along the coast, a great spread of accommodation and a burgeoning dining scene.

4

GILI TRAWANGAN ⏱2 DAYS

It's time to party. A short boat ride connects Lombok's west coast with **Gili Trawangan** (p356), now one of Southeast Asia's top playgrounds for travellers. But there's more to the island than beach parties and raucous bars. There's also amazing snorkelling, spas and yoga, lots of notable restaurants and, if you have the time, this is one of the best places to learn to dive.

FROM LEFT: KHAFIDMUKRIYANTO/SHUTTERSTOCK, DANIEL WILHELM NILSSON/SHUTTERSTOCK

EDLOSA MEDIA/SHUTTERSTOCK

Gunung Sibayak (p474), Berastagi

ITINERARIES

Sumatra Wildlife, Volcanoes & Lakes

Allow: 7 days **Distance**: 245km

North Sumatra's extraordinary wildlife and landscapes are the focus of this tour. Trek into the rainforest to look for orangutans and other primates, enjoy the mountain air of hilltop retreat Berastagi, climb one of Indonesia's most accessible volcanoes and end by relaxing on the shores of Southeast Asia's largest lake.

1

BUKIT LAWANG 3 DAYS

The traveller-friendly village of **Bukit Lawang** (p466) offers access to Gunung Leuser National Park, the most likely place to see orangutans (pictured) in Sumatra. Most people opt for a two-day trek in the park, spending one night in the jungle, which increases the chances of seeing the apes. But hikes of a few hours are also possible and there's the option of rafting or tubing the Sungai Bohorok (Bohorok River).

2

BERASTAGI 1 DAY

Due southeast of the national park is **Berastagi** (p474), a mountaintop market town established during the Dutch colonial era as an escape from the lowland heat. At 1300m above sea level, the cool air is a great relief and there are stunning views of two nearby volcanoes. Walk into the surrounding Karo Highlands to find villages where the indigenous Karo Batak culture is alive and well.

FROM LEFT: SNAPTPHOTOGRAPHY/SHUTTERSTOCK, WINGKYPAPA/SHUTTERSTOCK

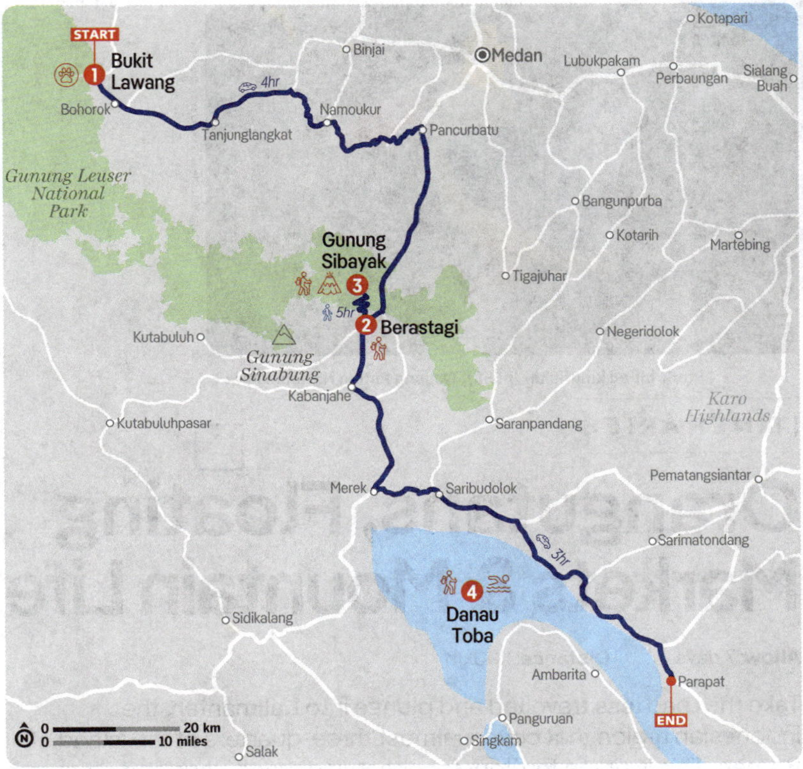

START
1 Bukit Lawang
Bohorok
4hr
Tanjunglangkat
Binjai
Namoukur
Medan
Lubukpakam
Perbaungan
Kotapari
Sialang Buah
Pancurbatu
Gunung Leuser National Park
Bangunpurba
Kotarih
Martebing
Gunung Sibayak
3
5hr
2 Berastagi
Tigajuhar
Negeridolok
Kutabuluh
Gunung Sinabung
Kabanjahe
Karo Highlands
Kutabuluhpasar
Saranpandang
Pematangsiantar
Merek
Saribudolok
3hr
Sarimatondang
4 Danau Toba
Sidikalang
Ambarita
Parapat
END
Panguruan
Singkam
Salak
0 20 km
0 10 miles

3 GUNUNG SIBAYAK 1 DAY

Berastagi is the starting point for treks to the smoking summit of **Gunung Sibayak** (p474), one of Indonesia's easiest volcanoes to climb. A reasonably fit person should get up and down the cone in five hours. Camp overnight if you want to get to the top for sunrise. On the way back to Berastagi, stop off at the hot springs in Semangat Gunung to revive those tired muscles.

4 DANAU TOBA 2 DAYS

Directly south of Berastagi is **Danau Toba** (p476), a vast sea-blue expanse of water surrounded by dramatic volcanic peaks. This is the largest lake in Southeast Asia and the setting and views are magnificent. Toba is a great spot to kick back for a few days: the lake is fine for swimming, while there are many opportunities for hikes and bike rides in the surrounding area.

FROM LEFT: PAV-PRO PHOTOGRAPHY LTD/SHUTTERSTOCK, JAVAISTAN/SHUTTERSTOCK

HARI GOPALAKRISHNEN/SHUTTERSTOCK

Stork-billed kingfisher (p558), Tanjung Puting National Park

ITINERARIES

Orangutans, Floating Markets & Mountain Life

Allow: 7 days **Distance**: 1100km

Take the road less travelled and plunge into Kalimantan, the Indonesian region that covers almost three-quarters of the island of Borneo. This is prime territory for observing orangutans and other rare wildlife, but there are also vibrant riverine cities with floating markets to explore and bucolic villages for a taste of country life.

1

BANJARMASIN 1 DAY

Let **Banjarmasin** (p560), Kalimantan's liveliest city, be your gateway to Borneo. Make an early start and travel upriver to the city's photogenic floating markets before exploring Banjarmasin's bustling riverfront, lined with stilted houses and impressive mosques (Mesjid Raya Sabilal Muhtadin pictured; p560). Detour to the Martapura market and nearby diamond fields, then end your day with a bowl of *soto Banjar*, the tasty local soup.

2

SEBANGAU NATIONAL PARK 2 DAYS

Drive north into the Kalimantan heartland, passing through an increasingly rural landscape. Bypass Palangka Raya and head deep into **Sebangau National Park** (p554). It's a terrific place to look for wild orangutans, either from the river or on foot as you make brief trekking forays into the jungle. The park has more orangutans – 6000! – than any other park on earth. Watch for primates and birdlife as you go.

FROM LEFT: SONY HERDIANA/SHUTTERSTOCK, RIDHAMSUPRIYANTO/SHUTTERSTOCK

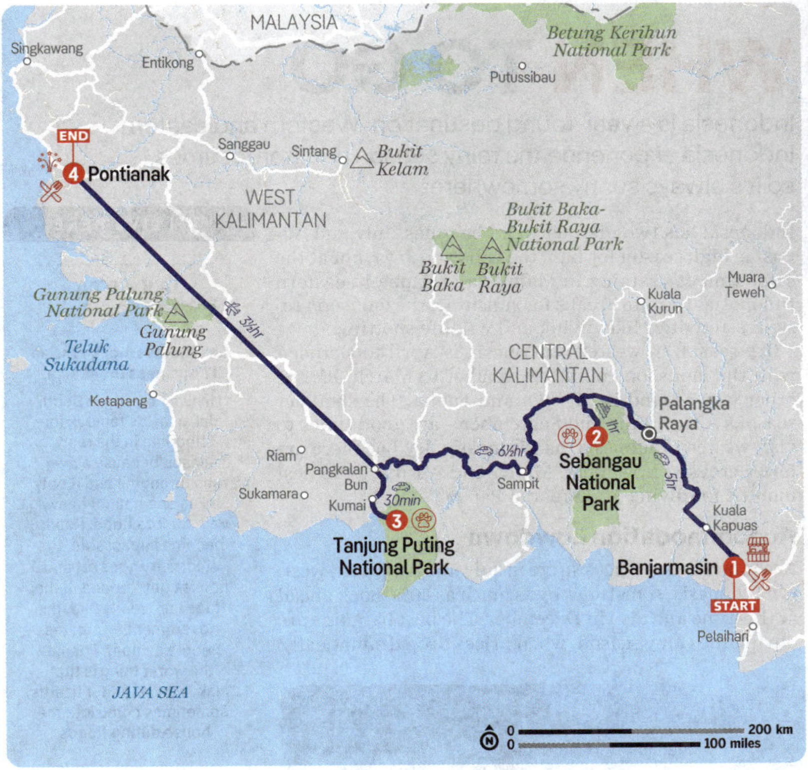

MALAYSIA
Singkawang
Entikong
Betung Kerihun National Park
Putussibau
END
4 Pontianak
Sanggau
Sintang
Bukit Kelam
WEST KALIMANTAN
Bukit Baka-Bukit Raya National Park
Bukit Baka
Bukit Raya
Gunung Palung National Park
Gunung Palung
Teluk Sukadana
3½hr
Muara Teweh
Kuala Kurun
CENTRAL KALIMANTAN
Ketapang
Palangka Raya
1hr
2 Sebangau National Park
6½hr
Riam
Pangkalan Bun
Sukamara
Kumai
30min
Sampit
5hr
3 Tanjung Puting National Park
Kuala Kapuas
Banjarmasin 1
START
Pelaihari
JAVA SEA
0 200 km
0 100 miles

3

TANJUNG PUTING NATIONAL PARK 3 DAYS

The drive from Sebangau brings you to the port of Kumai, from where houseboats head upriver into **Tanjung Puting National Park** (p556), the best place to observe orangutans (pictured) in Kalimantan. On a three-day, two-night cruise you're almost certain to see Asia's only great ape in action, as well as many other primates, rare birds and maybe even the odd crocodile.

FROM LEFT: ARIKBINTANG/SHUTTERSTOCK, ARIYANI TEDJO/SHUTTERSTOCK

4

PONTIANAK 1 DAY

It's an easy 30-minute drive from Kumai to Pangkalan Bun, from where you fly to multicultural **Pontianak** (p542), the capital of West Kalimantan. Sitting right on the equator, Pontianak has ethnic Chinese and Dayak populations and an atmospheric riverfront. Check out Kampung Beting, a historic community of stilted houses, tuck into Indonesian-Chinese cuisine and sample the thriving cafe culture. The Dayak Harvest Festival is celebrated here every May and is one of Kalimantan's best parties.

WHEN TO GO

Indonesia is a year-round destination. Western and eastern Indonesia experience the rainy season at different times, so it's always sunny somewhere.

Indonesia has two distinct weather zones. July and August is high season for Bali, the Gilis and Java, but at the same time it's raining in Maluku and Papua in eastern Indonesia. Despite breaks for sunshine, the monsoon restricts activities like diving and wildlife spotting.

Dry season in western Indonesia is April to October, with the monsoon coming November to March. It's the other way around in Maluku and Papua. The shoulder seasons – May, June and September – are good times to visit western Indonesia, as it's mostly dry but there are fewer crowds. November, March and April are the best months for diving Maluku and Papua.

Accommodation Lowdown

Accommodation prices surge in July and August in western Indonesia, sometimes by as much as 50%. Book ahead at this time and also in December. The best bargains are during the rainy season, when prices drop dramatically.

I LIVE HERE

JAKARTA FLOODS

Sesillia Overbeek runs an IT business in Jakarta.

I live in Kemang in South Jakarta. It's famous for flooding in the rainy season because a river runs through it and it only takes one hour of heavy rain for it to flood. Roads become impassable, the electricity goes off and houses get flooded. If the floods are really bad, the government evacuates people by boat. For me, the worst thing is that snakes and monitor lizards sometimes come into the house during floods.

FROM LEFT: MAHARANI AFIFAH/SHUTTERSTOCK, GANI_PRASTOWO/SHUTTERSTOCK

Dieng Culture Festival (p125), Java

MONSOON SEASON

Indonesia's rainy seasons are determined by the northeast monsoon, which impacts western Indonesia, and the southwest monsoon, which hits eastern Indonesia. Western Sumatra, Java, Bali, Kalimantan and Sulawesi get the most rainfall.

Weather Through the Year – Jakarta

JANUARY	FEBRUARY	MARCH	APRIL	MAY	JUNE
Avg daytime max: **31°C**	Avg daytime max: **31°C**	Avg daytime max: **32°C**	Avg daytime max: **32°C**	Avg daytime max: **33°C**	Avg daytime max: **32°C**
Days of rainfall: **19**	Days of rainfall: **17**	Days of rainfall: **16**	Days of rainfall: **11**	Days of rainfall: **9**	Days of rainfall: **7**

IT CAN GET COLD

Despite Indonesia's generally hot and humid climate, it does get cold at altitude. The coolest regions are the highlands of Papua, Sulawesi, Sumatra and Java. Kota Mulia in West Papua is officially Indonesia's coldest town, with temperatures dipping below 10°C at night.

Nationwide Festivals

Indonesia's large ethnic Chinese community commemorates **Chinese New Year** in style. The most extravagant celebrations are in cities with big Chinese populations, such as Singkawang (p546) in West Kalimantan. **January/ February**

Ramadan isn't exactly a festival, but the ninth month of the Islamic calendar, when Muslims fast from dawn to dusk, is the major religious event in Indonesia. Many shops and restaurants close during this period. **February/ March**

Vesak Day, also known as Waisak, is Indonesia's biggest Buddhist holiday. Monks, pilgrims and visitors flock to Borobudur (p88), the world's largest Buddhist temple, to take part in celebrations. **May**

Independence Day is marked by parades and events across the archipelago. Visitors will see school kids practising their marching in the prior weeks. **17 August**

Weird & Wonderful Festivals

Nyepi (p210) is Bali's most important Hindu festival. Everyone stays at home in an effort to convince malevolent spirits that Bali is uninhabited, but the night before sees celebrations across the island. **March/April**

The unique **funeral ceremonies** (p612) in Sulawesi's Tana Toraja region are festival-like, as Torajans from around Indonesia return home for celebrations and rituals. **July/August**

Taking place 70 days after the end of Ramadan, **Idul Adha** sees hapless goats tethered to posts across the country. Individuals or communities buy them to be sacrificed, with the meat distributed to the poor. **Date varies**

Traditional music and dance performances are a big feature of the **Dieng Culture Festival** (p125), held on Java's Dieng Plateau. The celebration includes hair-cutting rituals, should you need a trim. **August**

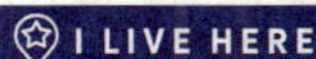

I LIVE HERE

UNDER THE VOLCANO

Rice farmer Purwati Setyorini lives 15km from Java's Gunung Merapi, Indonesia's most active volcano.

We're exposed to volcanic ash during large eruptions, when anyone living within 20km of Merapi has to evacuate. But actually the eruptions are good, because they make the land fertile. We also get a lot of tourists, which is good for local businesses. I'm not worried about living so close to the volcano. I've never thought about moving. I like the air and the views.

Gunung Merapi (p92), Java

CLIMATE CHANGE

As an island nation, Indonesia is regarded as extremely vulnerable to climate change. The World Bank considers the archipelago to be at risk from rising sea levels and temperatures, as well as extreme events such as floods and droughts.

JULY	AUGUST	SEPTEMBER	OCTOBER	NOVEMBER	DECEMBER
Avg daytime max: **32°C**	Avg daytime max: **33°C**	Avg daytime max: **33°C**	Avg daytime max: **33°C**	Avg daytime max: **32°C**	Avg daytime max: **32°C**
Days of rainfall: **6**	Days of rainfall: **5**	Days of rainfall: **6**	Days of rainfall: **8**	Days of rainfall: **12**	Days of rainfall: **14**

FROM LEFT: YONGTICK/SHUTTERSTOCK, ATLASPIX/ALAMY

Hiking near Gunung Rinjani (p350), Nusa Tenggara

GET PREPARED FOR INDONESIA

Useful things to load in your bag, your ears and your brain.

Clothes

Light, loose-fitting clothes These will be most comfortable in the tropical heat. Bring a jacket that can double as a raincoat and keep you warm at higher elevations and on air-conditioned buses. Bring something smart for fine dining in Jakarta or Bali. Almost all clothing, including from Western brands, is widely available and reasonably cheap, but finding bigger sizes can be challenging.

Footwear Flip-flops and sandals are standard on and off the beach, but wear shoes or trainers for high-end places or if doing a lot of walking (hiking boots if you're trekking).

Hats The tropical sun is intense, even when there's cloud cover. Wearing a wide-brimmed hat (and sunscreen) is a good idea.

Manners

Smile Indonesian culture values harmony. Getting angry and arguing are considered a loss of face. Whatever situation you're in, it's always best to smile.

Relax Life runs at a different pace in Indonesia. Slow down and go with the flow.

Religion Hindu-dominated Bali is the exception in Indonesia. Visitors should remember that Islam plays a central role in everyday life across much of the country.

READ

Man Tiger (Eka Kurniawan; 2015) The first Indonesian novel long-listed for the Man Booker Prize, it mixes fantasy, horror and societal realism.

This Earth of Mankind (Pramoedya Ananta Toer; 1980) The first of a quartet of acclaimed novels about Indonesia starting in the late 19th century.

Love and Death in Bali (Vicki Baum; 1937) Considered a classic novel for its portrayal of Bali under Dutch rule.

Kopi Dulu (Mark Eveleigh; 2022) A superb journey of discovery through Indonesia, including 50 of Indonesia's islands, by one of Lonely Planet's own.

Words

Salam Hello.

Selamat tinggal Goodbye (if leaving).

Selamat jalan Goodbye (if staying).

Apa kabar? How are you?

Kabar baik, anda bagaimana? I'm fine, and you?

Permisi Excuse me.

Maaf Sorry.

Silahkan Please.

Terima kasih Thank you.

Kembali You're welcome.

Ya/tidak Yes/no.

Bapak Mr/Sir.

Ibu Ms/Mrs/Madam.

Nona Miss.

Siapa nama anda? What's your name?

Nama saya... My name is...

Bisa berbicara Bahasa Inggris? Do you speak English?

Saya tidak mengert I don't understand.

Berapa harganya? How much is it?

Saya mau beli... I'd like to buy...

Di mana (stasiun)? Where's (the station)?

Jam berapa (bis yang berikutnya)? What time is (the next bus)?

Saya cari (hotel) I'm looking for (a hotel).

Ada (peta daerah)? Do you have (a local map)?

Ada (kamar kecil)? Is there (a toilet)?

Boleh saya (masuk)? Can I (enter)?

Saya (sudah punya booking) I have (a reservation).

Saya perlu (dibantu) I need (assistance).

Saya minta (daftar makanan) I'd like (the menu).

Saya mau (sewa mobil) I'd like to (hire a car).

WATCH

The Act of Killing (Joshua Oppenheimer; 2012; pictured) Oscar-nominated documentary about the 1965 slaughter of alleged communist sympathisers.

The Raid (Gareth Evans; 2011) Police hunt a crime lord in the Jakarta slums. A rare Indonesian movie that achieved international success.

What's Up With Cinta? (Rudy Soedjarwo; 2002) Popular girl falls for the school bad boy in this hugely successful, Jakarta-set teen romance.

Impetigore (Joko Anwar; 2019) Among the best in the new wave of Indonesian horror films that are conquering the world's streaming platforms.

LISTEN

Bintang di Surga (Peterpan; 2004) Alt-rock classic and one of the best-selling Indonesian albums of all time.

Best of the Best (Iwan Fals; 2001) Retrospective album from one of Indonesia's most influential modern songwriters.

Lagu Terbaik (Lesti Kejora; 2023) Very popular collection from Lesti Kejora, the current top *dangdut* diva.

The Best of Inul Daratista (Inul Daratista; 2015) Retrospective album from the provocative queen of *dangdut* music.

SLOWMOTIONGLI/SHUTTERSTOCK

Sumatran tigers

TRIP PLANNER

WATCHING WILDLIFE

Indonesia offers unique wildlife-watching opportunities. Orangutans, Komodo dragons, elephants and tigers are the stars, but there are many other species endemic to Indonesia, including birds of paradise, bears and dolphins, to say nothing of fanged frogs, walking sharks and 50cm-long stick insects. The sheer diversity of wildlife is astounding. Prepare to be amazed.

Plan Your Trip

WHERE TO GO

National parks and wildlife reserves are the principal places to see Indonesia's fauna. Some parks remain threatened by deforestation (both legal and illegal), farming and resource extraction, but there's still plenty of protected land in Indonesia. Certain parks are associated with specific species – Tanjung Puting and Gunung Leuser for orangutans, Komodo for the namesake dragons, Way Kambas for elephants – which makes it easier to identify where to go, but visitors are almost certain to see other wildlife, especially birds and primates, roaming the parks as well. The longer you spend in a park, the higher the chance of seeing rare animals, but some species are extremely elusive. Few travellers can say they've seen a Sumatran tiger in the wild.

WHEN TO GO

National parks are open year-round, but flooding can make access an issue during western Indonesia's November–March rainy season. As a general rule, wildlife becomes much harder to spot during the monsoon, whether on land or underwater, because food is plentiful and they're able to disperse more widely.

There are some more specific considerations. The shoulder-season months of April and May are the best times to see

MARINE LIFE

The incredible spread of animals on land is matched by the astonishing diversity of Indonesia's marine life. There are close to 5000 different species of fish in Indonesian waters, including 118 varieties of shark, as well as almost 600 species of coral. Divers can encounter hundreds of different species of fish in one dive at famed sites such as the Raja Ampat Islands. There's also an increasing number of manta rays. A 2022 study found more than 1000 reef manta rays in Komodo National Park alone, making it one of the world's top locations for rays.

orangutans, as those times are mostly dry and the apes are hungry and moving about. The high-season months of July and August coincide with the mating season for Komodo dragons, when it's much more of a challenge to spot the lizards.

GUIDES

Guides are compulsory in many of the most-visited national parks, but even if one isn't required, they're well worth considering. A good guide will be attuned to the local habitat and the animals within it. Good guides are adept at spotting wildlife – they'll see that orangutan high up in the tree before you – and they'll know where the animals are most likely to be, which can depend on the season. Guides will also keep you safe – an important consideration. The only recent attack by a Komodo dragon on a human was in 2017, when a Singaporean tourist wandered off on his own without a guide.

SERGEMI/SHUTTERSTOCK

Manta rays in Komodo National Park (p306), Nusa Tenggara

BEST PLACES TO WATCH WILDLIFE

Derawan Archipelago (p578)
A top diving and snorkelling destination. Expect to see manta rays, sea turtles and huge shoals of barracuda.

Gunung Leuser National Park (p466)
Sumatra's main orangutan-spotting destination, but there are elephants, rhinoceroses and tigers here as well.

Komodo National Park (p306)
The only place in the world where the dragons can be seen. There's great diving and snorkelling, too.

Meru Betiri National Park (p151)
East Java park with a big range of wildlife, including leopards, giant squirrels and the biggest pythons on the planet.

Raja Ampat (p420)
A diving and snorkelling paradise, with an almost unimaginable diversity of marine life and corals.

Gunung Palung National Park (p552)
Remote West Kalimantan park with orangutans, gibbons, proboscis monkeys, sun bears, clouded leopards, crocodiles and rich birdlife.

Tangkoko-Batuangas Dua Saudara Nature Reserve (p637)
Giant-eyed tarsiers are the main draw at this Sulawesi reserve, but look for cute cuscuses – possum-like marsupials.

Tanjung Puting National Park (p556)
The best place in Indonesia to observe wild and semi-wild orangutans, as well as many other primates.

Wasur National Park (p455)
Papua park with birds of paradise and rare parrots and pigeons. Also home to crocodiles, kangaroos and wallabies.

Way Kambas National Park (p532)
There are thought to be around 250 Sumatran elephants living here; it's your best chance of seeing these animals in the wild.

FABIO LAMANNA/SHUTTERSTOCK

Kei Islands (p409), Maluku

TRIP PLANNER

BEACHES & ISLANDS

The promise of palm-fringed white-sand beaches, transparent turquoise waters and glorious sunsets lures millions of visitors to Indonesia's beaches and islands. But with more than 17,000 islands in the archipelago, finding the right one for you can be at once challenging and deeply pleasurable. Here are a few tips to help decide.

Pick Your Beach

THE PRICE OF PARADISE

The personality of a beach or island depends in part on the prices. Bali's Kuta, Legian and Seminyak beaches are home to midrange resorts, so there are lots of package tourists, tour groups and nightlife. Head to Ungasan on Bali's south coast, though, and it's a much more exclusive scene, with hidden-away high-end resorts, clifftop villas and far fewer bars and clubs. Generally, the more popular an island or beach, the fewer budget accommodation options there will be. If you want to hit Indonesia's best-known islands on the cheap, head for their less-visited areas or go during low season.

SEARCHING FOR SOLITUDE

It can seem like half the world is on Bali, Lombok and the Gili Islands during peak season, but Indonesia has so many beaches and islands that it's easy to escape the crowds. East Nusa Tenggara islands such as Flores, Sumba and the Alor Archipelago all have sugar-white beaches that are the stuff of dreams and you might be the only person on them. The same applies to the 31 islands of the Derawan Archipelago in East Kalimantan, or some of the outer islands beyond Raja Ampat, in Papua. Venture to Maluku and you're in real Robinson Crusoe territory: the Kei Islands and Pulau Morotai are good choices if you want to stroll empty strips of sand. Many beach-

STAY SAFE

Drownings are common on some Bali beaches. Pay attention to red and yellow flag warnings and beware of riptides and strong currents. A number of tourists have also drowned on Bali rafting trips in recent years – don't raft in the rainy season.

When swimming watch out for Jet Skis, long-tail boats and speedboats coming into the shore. Don't expect them to see you.

Island roads are often in poor condition and/or poorly constructed, and gradients can be very steep. Inexperienced motorcycle riders should cut their speed and stick to main roads. Always wear a helmet.

GAUDILAB/SHUTTERSTOCK

es on the bigger islands also see few foreigners, such as the pretty ones at Gunung Kidul, south of Yogyakarta on Java.

ISLAND-HOPPING

While it's easy and quick to move between Bali, Lombok and the Gilis, island-hopping elsewhere often involves a flight or lengthy boat journey. But there are a number of island chains where you can jump between islands on a short speedboat or long-tail-boat ride. The Banda Islands and Kei Islands in southern Maluku are compact and a breeze to travel among, while it's also easy to move around the Karimunjawa Islands off Java, the Togean Islands off Sulawesi, the Banyak Islands off Sumatra and Raja Ampat off Papua. In some areas, it's even possible to kayak between islands.

SANATANA/SHUTTERSTOCK

Pulau Menjangan (p276), Bali

THE IMPACT OF TOURISM

Tourism infrastructure on Indonesia's most popular islands and beaches is increasingly being stretched to the limit, especially during the peak months of July, August and December.

Rampant development threatens ecosystems as more big hotels and resorts line beaches, Jet Skis and tour boats buzz across bays, and islands struggle to maintain adequate freshwater supplies and to dispose of waste without negatively impacting the environment. Water pollution and large numbers of visitors can have a deleterious effect on coral reefs especially.

Visitors can play their part in reducing the impact of overtourism:

- Visiting lesser-known islands, such as those of East Nusa Tenggara or Maluku, may take more time, but it relieves the pressure on the most-touristed islands, and travellers are rewarded with far fewer people, pristine beaches and Jet Ski–free seas.
- Travel out of high season. Overtourism issues aren't just caused by travellers flocking to the same destinations; it's the fact that so many people visit them at the same time.
- Check the eco-credentials and safety records of tour operators and dive outfits before booking.
- Dispose of garbage carefully and minimise your use of plastic: in 2022 over a million tonnes of plastic waste piled up on Bali alone.
- Take care when diving and snorkelling. Make sure that neither you nor your equipment touches reefs or corals.

PAUL HARDING/LONELY PLANET

Nasi campur

THE FOOD SCENE

It's worth travelling to Indonesia just for the cuisine, which reflects the huge diversity and gloriously tangled history of this immense nation.

To eat in Indonesia is to savour the essence of the country. The abundance of rice reflects Indonesia's fertile landscape, the spices recall a time of trade and invasion, and the fiery sambal (chilli) echoes the passion of the people. Chinese, Portuguese, colonists and traders have all influenced the ingredients and dishes that appear at the Indonesian table, and the cuisine has been further shaped by the archipelago's diverse landscapes, peoples and cultures.

Food is a communal experience in Indonesia. Meals are traditionally eaten in company, often sitting on the floor rather than around a table, and using fingers rather than utensils. Fish and seafood is a favourite and there are distinct flavourings: coriander, cumin, chilli, lemongrass, coconut, soy sauce and palm sugar are all common ingredients.

But the beauty of the food scene is that there is no one Indonesian cuisine, apart from a few staple dishes. Instead, each region has its own distinct variations, making eating out a real adventure. We hope you're hungry.

Indonesian Classics

The closest thing to a national dish is *nasi campur,* which is essentially the plate of the day. Served at warung (food stalls) and restaurants, it's always a combination of rice and many side dishes and flavours. At warungs, you often choose your own combination from the dozens of items on offer.

Best Indonesian Dishes

BABI GULING
Roasted pig stuffed with chilli, turmeric, garlic and ginger. A Bali speciality.

BEEF RENDANG
Sulawesi dish of slow-cooked beef simmered in spiced coconut milk.

BUBUR AYAM
Rice porridge topped with shredded chicken and more. A breakfast favourite.

Sate (skewered meat), nasi goreng (fried rice), *mie goreng* (fried noodles) and gado gado (vegetables with peanut sauce) are other dishes that can be found everywhere. Some soups, such as *coto Makassar* (beef soup) and *soto Banjar* (chicken noodle soup), have transcended their regional origins to become popular across the country.

Vegetarians & Vegans

Tempeh and *tahu* (tofu) are available in abundance, sold as chunky slabs of *tempe penyet* (deep-fried tempeh), *tempe kering* (diced tempeh stir-fried with sweet soy sauce) and *tahu isi* (deep-fried stuffed tofu). Finding fresh veggies requires more effort. Look for Chinese establishments; they can whip up *cap cai* (mixed vegetables).

Vegetarian fried rice or noodles can be found at many eateries. And there's always the iconic gado gado. Many places offer rice with a variety of sides, so skip the meat options and go for things such as tofu, tempeh, jackfruit dishes, egg dishes and leafy veggies.

Sambal

Sambal, a hot chilli paste of Javanese origin, is *the* crucial condiment in Indonesia. It comes in myriad forms and can be the best part of a meal if you're a spice fan. Insist on the real deal – ask for *sambal lokal* or 'local sambal' – which will have been prepared fresh in the kitchen from some combination of ingredients that can include garlic, shallots, chilli peppers in many forms, fish sauce, tomatoes and more.

Tempeh dish

FRUIT DELIGHTS

Indonesia has some amazing fruit.

Belimbing (star fruit; pictured above) is cool and crisp; slice one to see how it gets its name.

Jambu air (water apple) is a pink bell-shaped fruit with crisp and refreshing flesh.

Manggis (mangosteen) is a small purple fruit with white fleshy segments and fantastic flavour.

Nangka (jackfruit) is an enormous, spiky fruit that can weigh over 20kg. Inside are segments of yellow sweet flesh with a slightly rubbery texture.

Rambutan is a bright-red fruit covered in soft spines; inside is a delicious white fruit similar to lychee.

Salak is recognisable by its brown 'snakeskin' covering. Peel it off to reveal segments somewhere between an apple and a walnut.

Sirsak (soursop or zurzak) is a green-skinned fruit with a white, pulpy interior and a slightly lemonish taste.

GADO GADO

The Indonesian 'salad': veggies, bean sprouts and peanut sauce dressing.

KETOPRAK

Noodles, bean sprouts and tofu with soy and peanut sauce.

NASI GORENG

Fried rice with meat and vegetables. Found everywhere.

SATE AYAM

Grilled marinated chicken served on a skewer.

SOTO BANJAR

Soup of shredded chicken and noodles flavoured with cinnamon.

Regional Variations

Bali

Many restaurants offer the hugely popular *babi guling* (spit-roast pig stuffed with herbs and spices) on a day's notice, but look out for the warungs that specialise in it. Also popular is *bebek betutu* (duck stuffed with spices, wrapped in banana leaves and coconut husks, and cooked in embers). The local *sate lilit* is made with minced, spiced meat pressed onto skewers.

Nusa Tenggara

You'll eat less rice in dry East Nusa Tenggara and more sago, corn, cassava and taro. Fish is popular; try Sumbawa's *sepat* (shredded fish in coconut and mango sauce). The Sasak people of Lombok like spicy *ayam* Taliwang (roasted chicken served with a peanut, tomato, chilli and lime dip). Also recommended is *sate pusut* (minced meat or fish *sate*, mixed with coconut and grilled on sugarcane skewers).

Sumatra

West Sumatra is the home of spicy Padang food, among the most ubiquitous of Indonesian cuisines. In North Sumatra, the Acehnese love their *kare* or *gulai* (curry). South Sumatra's culinary capital is Palembang, famous for *pempek* (deep-fried fish and sago dumplings). South Sumatra is also home to *pindang* (spicy fish soup with soy and tamarind) and *ikan brengkes* (fish in a spicy durian-based sauce).

Kalimantan

The Banjar people's famed soup, *soto Banjar*, is now eaten across the archipelago. Also popular is *pepes ikan* (spiced fish cooked in banana leaves with tamarind and lemongrass) and *ayam masak habang* (chicken cooked with large red chillies). Kandangan town is known for *ketupat Kandangan* (fish and pressed rice with lime-infused coconut sauce). Dayak food is varied but one top choice is *sayur asem rembang* (sour vegetable soup).

Sulawesi

Ikan bakar (grilled fish) is a South Sulawesi favourite, as is *coto Makassar* (a beef and offal soup). You can easily find *pa'piong*, which is meat or fish cooked in bamboo tubes with spices. Also look for *pamarasan*, a spicy black sauce used to cook meat. If a North Sulawesi dish – normally fish or chicken – has the name *rica-rica*, it's prepared with a paste of chilli, shallots, ginger and lime.

Papua

Papua is one of the country's most traditional societies and there are refreshingly few culinary concessions made for tourists. Indonesian and Chinese migrants to the region brought their cuisines with them and charcoal-grilled and barbecued fish (*ikan bakar*) is a staple; be sure to try the local variation, *ikan gabus* (snakehead fish). Bat can be found on menus in Wamena.

JAVANESE CUISINE

The cuisine of the Betawi (the original inhabitants of the Jakarta region) is known for its richness. Gado gado (vegetables with peanut sauce) is a Betawi original, as is *ketoprak* (noodles, bean sprouts and tofu with soy and peanut sauce) *Soto Betawi* (beef soup) is made creamy with coconut milk. There's also *nasi uduk* (rice cooked in coconut milk, served with meat, tofu and/or vegetables). West Javan specialities include *karedok* (salad of long beans, bean sprouts and cucumber with spicy sauce), *soto Bandung* (beef-and-vegetable soup with lemongrass) and *ketupat tahu* (pressed rice, bean sprouts and tofu with soy and peanut sauce).

Central Javan food is sweet, including curries such as *gudeg* (jackfruit curry), while fish is popular in East Java, especially *pecel lele* (deep-fried catfish served with rice and peanut sauce). This region is also known for Madurese dishes such as *soto Madura* (beef soup with lime, pepper, peanuts, chilli and ginger) and *sate Madura* (skewered meat with sweet soy sauce).

Specialities

Everyday eating in Indonesia can challenge your palate. We dare you to try these.

Ikan kuah assam (tamarind fish soup) is a sensational, mildly astringent dish popular in East Nusa Tenggara. It's basically a fish steak, or half a fish (bones often included), steamed and swimming in a spicy and oily tamarind broth. It's simple and life affirming and might turn out to be a favourite dish of your trip.

Durian has a serious image problem. Its spiky skin looks like a Spanish Inquisition torture tool, and opening it releases the fruit's odorous power. Most people form a lifelong passion – or aversion – on their first taste of the sulphury, custardy fruit. Try the strangely alluring *tempoyak* (fermented durian).

Siobak is a Balinese speciality featuring minced pig's head, stomach, tongue and skin cooked with spices. We promise you that it tastes better than it sounds.

Durian

Avocado juice is made by blending avocado with ice and condensed milk (or chocolate syrup). Indonesians don't consider this strange, as the avocado is just another sweet fruit.

Papeda is the pulped-up pith of the sago palm (the starchy, staple food of the lowlands of Papua) mixed with water to create a kind of gluey paste usually eaten with fish. Some locals also eat the sago beetle grubs found in rotting sago palms.

MEALS OF A LIFETIME

Warung Bu Jero (p249) This simple Padangbai eatery serves exceptional grilled seafood. The best prawns in Indonesia?

Terra (p334) Fully vegan and gluten-free eatery in Kuta (Lombok), with a focus on wellness and desserts.

Depot Se'i Babi Aroma (p314) Wood-smoked pork belly with a unique flavour at this Kupang (West Timor) restaurant.

Maruba (p480) Family-run place on the shores of Sumatra's Danau Toba (Lake Toba); serves authentic and delicious Batak food.

Spiegel (p113) In a colonial-era Semarang building, with sublime smoked duck carpaccio.

Warung Novi (p563) *Soto Banjar* may have conquered Indonesia, but it's best at the source; locals swear by this simple place.

THE YEAR IN FOOD

FEBRUARY

Rice planted in the autumn – the rainy-season crop – is harvested in January and February. The dry-season crop is planted in February and March and harvested May to June.

JULY

Indonesians are addicted to coffee, drinking it at all hours, and the country produces some of the world's finest beans. July is the start of the harvest season in Bali, Java, Sulawesi and Sumatra.

SEPTEMBER

Locals love their mangoes (pictured). Mango season in Indonesia runs from June to December, but September is when the fruit is just right. This is also a good month to try star fruit and *sirsak*.

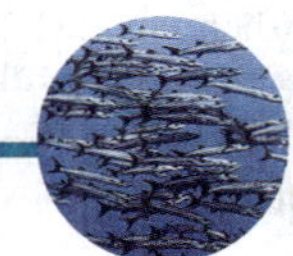

OCTOBER

This month is when the seas are teeming with barracuda (pictured), mahi mahi, snapper and yellowfin tuna. If you're in Bali at this time and you see these fish on the menu, you can bet it'll be fresh.

TOP: COLEONG/GETTY IMAGES; FROM LEFT: HELZA NITRISIA/SHUTTERSTOCK, EM FAIES/SHUTTERSTOCK, ANDRI WAHYUDI/SHUTTERSTOCK, TETIANA PHOTOS/SHUTTERSTOCK

FROM LEFT: ELIZAVETA GALITCKAIA/SHUTTERSTOCK, KKSHXT/SHUTTERSTOCK

Ubud (p218), Bali

THE OUTDOORS

Indonesia is a tremendous country for outdoor adventures, with endless opportunities for hiking and cycling. The snorkelling is out of this world.

Indonesia's supreme land and seascapes lend themselves to just about every outdoor activity. Inland, there are vast swathes of jungle to trek through and rushing rivers for rafting or tubing, as well as the chance to rock climb and canyon. Less strenuous, but equally satisfying, are bike rides through emerald-green ricefields and around volcanic lakes and ancient temples. Offshore, snorkel through some of the planet's most beautiful corals and reefs, or you can hire a kayak and paddle perfect bays.

Hiking

Setting off on foot in Indonesia offers the chance to leave civilisation behind. Travellers can ascend volcanic peaks for celestial dawn views or trek deep into the jungle, but there are also magical rice terraces and waterfall-riven hills and valleys to amble through, as well as traditional villages and stunning lakes to see.

Just about every area of the country lends itself to hiking. Serious trekkers can head to Kalimantan's remote rainforests, where the hardy can attempt the serious (and seriously rewarding) expedition that is the Cross-Borneo Trek, or climb into the highlands of Papua for grand mountain scenery and unspoiled villages. You could also spend months walking the lush landscapes of Sulawesi's Tana Toraja region, or the jungle and coffee plantations around Bengkulu in Sumatra. In most places,

BIRD-WATCHING
Head to Kalimantan's **Kutai National Park** (p574), home to several hundred rare species of birds and orangutans.

CANYONING & CLIFF JUMPING
Adrenaline fiends should make tracks for **Green Valley** (p174) in West Java for canyoning and cliff jumping.

KAYAKING
Rent a kayak to explore the pristine waters of **Raja Ampat** (p420).

FAMILY ADVENTURES

Sign up teenagers for a **surf school** (p199) along **Kuta Beach in Bali**, where gentle waves are ideal for newbies.

Spend a day exploring **Taman Mini Indonesia Indah** (p73) in **East Jakarta**, a massive theme park with bird and reptile enclosures and 16 museums.

Spot dolphins and flying fish at North Sulawesi's **Pulau Bunaken** (p632), one of the finest snorkelling and diving sites in the world.

Swim in a volcanic lake at Sumatra's **Danau Toba** (p476) and then tour the surrounding villages by bicycle.

Set out for the crater of Java's **Gunung Bromo** (p129), an easy and safe hike that lets kids experience one of Indonesia's most storied volcanoes.

Take a houseboat into Kalimantan's **Tanjung Puting National Park** (p556) and get up close with orangutans and proboscis monkeys.

you can choose between short walks and strenuous multiday treks, and just about anything in between.

Diving & Snorkelling

You don't have to be a diver to experience Indonesia's aquarium-like seascapes. The archipelago abounds in super snorkelling spots, where travellers can be amazed by brightly coloured corals and reefs teeming with fish. Snorkellers can get up close with bigger marine life, too. Manta rays, reef sharks and sea turtles can all be seen at close range looking down from the surface.

There are top diving and snorkelling sites in every region. In North and East Bali, you can just swim off the beach to find them, while the little islands off Java, Sulawesi and Sumatra all have easily accessible snorkelling spots. But the best sites are in Nusa Tenggara, especially off Lombok's southwestern coast, in Komodo National Park, the Banda Islands in Maluku and East Kalimantan's Derawan Archipelago.

For diving, there are many choices, including Alor Archipelago in Nusa Tenggara, Maratua Atoll in Kalimantan's Derawan Archipelago, Pulau Bunaken in Sulawesi and Raja Ampat in Papua. In Bali, the wreck off Tulamben is a fine dive site but can become impossibly crowded – try Pulau Menjangan instead.

Sea turtle

Cycling

Indonesia has experienced a cycling boom in recent years, with growing numbers of locals taking to the roads and hills. For visitors, hiring a bicycle for a day or joining a cycling tour is an excellent way of getting off the beaten track and seeing Indonesia in a sustainable way.

While certain cities in Java – Yogyakarta and Solo – are cycling hot spots, bikes are generally best for exploring rural areas and major temple complexes such as Borobudur and Prambanan. Bali has tonnes of scenic and gentle routes around Ubud, as well as many bike tour operators.

KITESURFING
Pantai Lakey & Hu'u (p304) on east Sumbawa is one of the world's top kitesurfing spots.

SURFING
Take your board to Bali's world-renowned **Bukit Peninsula** (p207), for some of Indonesia's best waves.

RIVER TUBING
After trekking in the jungle around Sumatra's **Bukit Lawang** (p466), tube the river rapids back to town.

WHITE-WATER RAFTING
Combine jungle-trekking and wildlife-watching with rafting around **Loksado** (p564) in South Kalimantan.

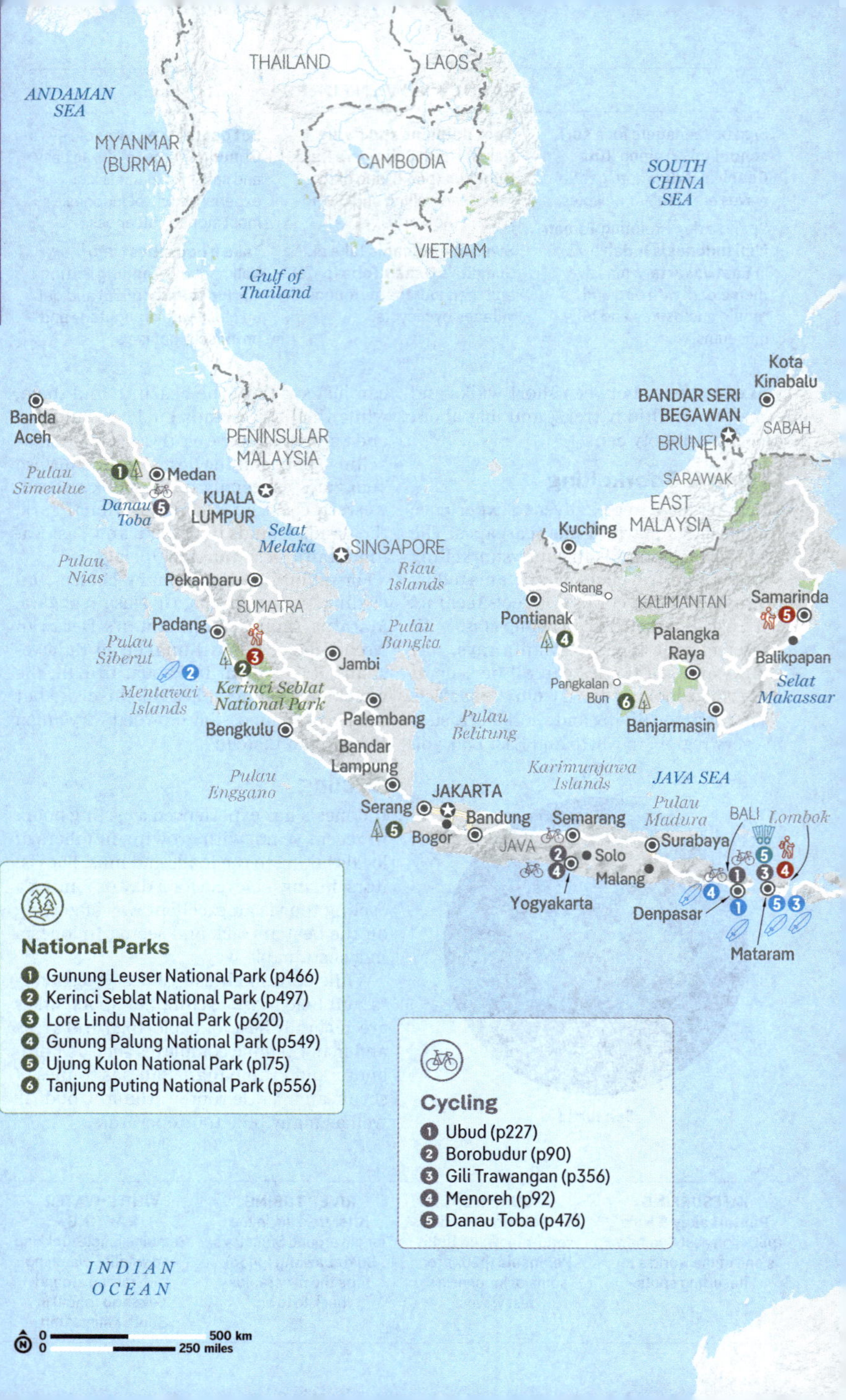
ANDAMAN SEA
MYANMAR (BURMA)
THAILAND
LAOS
CAMBODIA
VIETNAM
SOUTH CHINA SEA
Gulf of Thailand
Banda Aceh
Pulau Simeulue
Medan
Danau Toba
KUALA LUMPUR
PENINSULAR MALAYSIA
Selat Melaka
SINGAPORE
Riau Islands
Pulau Nias
Pekanbaru
SUMATRA
Padang
Pulau Siberut
Mentawai Islands
Kerinci Seblat National Park
Jambi
Pulau Bangka
Palembang
Bengkulu
Bandar Lampung
Pulau Belitung
Pulau Enggano
Serang
JAKARTA
Bogor
Bandung
JAVA
Semarang
Solo
Yogyakarta
Malang
Surabaya
Karimunjawa Islands
JAVA SEA
Pulau Madura
BALI
Lombok
Denpasar
Mataram
Kota Kinabalu
BANDAR SERI BEGAWAN
BRUNEI
SABAH
SARAWAK
EAST MALAYSIA
Kuching
Sintang
KALIMANTAN
Pontianak
Samarinda
Balikpapan
Palangka Raya
Selat Makassar
Pangkalan Bun
Banjarmasin
National Parks
1 Gunung Leuser National Park (p466)
2 Kerinci Seblat National Park (p497)
3 Lore Lindu National Park (p620)
4 Gunung Palung National Park (p549)
5 Ujung Kulon National Park (p175)
6 Tanjung Puting National Park (p556)
Cycling
1 Ubud (p227)
2 Borobudur (p90)
3 Gili Trawangan (p356)
4 Menoreh (p92)
5 Danau Toba (p476)
INDIAN OCEAN
0 500 km
0 250 miles

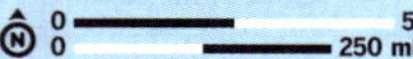

ACTION AREAS

Where to find Indonesia's best outdoor activities.

Walking/Hiking

1. Baliem Valley (p450)
2. Tana Toraja (p616)
3. Danau Gunung Tujuh (p496)
4. Gunung Rinjani (p350)
5. Cross-Borneo Trek (p576)

Snorkelling/Diving

1. Raja Ampat (p420)
2. Derawan Archipelago (p578)
3. Togean Islands (p621)
4. Komodo National Park (p306)
5. Gili Islands (p359)

Surfing

1. Bukit Peninsula (p207)
2. Mentawai Islands (p489)
3. Sumbawa (p304)
4. G-Land (p151)
5. Lombok (p335)
6. Manokwari (p431)

INDONESIA

THE GUIDE

Chapters in this section are organised by hubs and their surrounding areas. We see the hub as your base in the destination, where you'll find unique experiences, local insights, insider tips and expert recommendations. It's also your gateway to the surrounding area, where you'll see what and how much you can do from there.

Kampung Warna Warni (p131), Malang, Java

DENIS MOSKVINOV/SHUTTERSTOCK

Researched by
Narina Exelby & Ray Bartlett

Java

CULTURE & HISTORY AMID TOWERING VOLCANOES

Featuring all of the best aspects of Indonesia, Java has soaring volcanoes, dramatic waterfalls, compelling history and ancient culture – along with a dash of megacity glitz.

Java is not only the world's most populated island, it's also among the most magnificent. It's the heart of life in Indonesia and has everything the country is famous for – and so much more.

Towards the west of the island is Jakarta, the nation's current capital, which pulses with energy and life. It has a reputation for congested roads and smog-laden skies, but this dynamic megacity offers travellers far more than first impressions suggest: here, between shimmering skyscrapers and enormous shopping malls, you'll find intriguing pockets of history, rich cultural layers, a thriving creative scene and a diverse, much-celebrated culinary landscape.

Just 60km south of Central Jakarta is Bogor, home to a presidential palace and one of the most beautiful botanic gardens on the planet, while to the south, Yogyakarta is recognised as the cultural centre of not only Java, but all of Indonesia.

Dozens of active volcanoes form the skeleton of the island, from Gunung Merapi (one of the world's most dangerous) to constantly smoking Gunung Bromo, which attracts thousands of visitors every week. Further south lies the sulphuric lake of Kawah Ijen; its 'blue fire' is an incredible sight to behold.

JOEL CARILLET/GETTY IMAGES

The island of Java has it all. Its waterfalls, smoking volcanoes, teeming jungles and dreamy tropical beaches sit alongside glass-shrouded skyscrapers, making it perhaps the most diverse island on the planet.

THE MAIN AREAS

JAKARTA
Indonesia's vivacious capital city. p64

YOGYAKARTA
Cultural centre with historic temples. p76

SOLO
Rich batik tradition and gateway to Gunung Lawu. p96

SEMARANG
Captivating old town, close to idyllic islands. p111

For places to stay in Java, see p180

SETYOBUDIU/SHUTTERSTOCK

Left: Taman Fatahillah, Kota Tua (p68), Jakarta; Above: Borobudur (p88)

DIENG PLATEAU
Home to the highest village in Java. p120

MALANG
Doorstep of incredible Gunung Bromo. p129

BOGOR
World-renowned botanical gardens. p153

Ujung Kulon National Park, p175

Java's finest reserve sets the stage for trips by boat and on foot.

Jakarta, p64

The Indonesian capital hums and vibrates with an energetic, modern feel melded with a colonial past, and a dynamic food and coffee culture.

Bandung, p164

Striking Art Deco architecture dots the lively walkable centre, which is packed with restaurants and bars.

Bogor, p153

A quick train ride from Jakarta, the highland city has one of Indonesia's finest botanical gardens.

Pangandaran, p170

Head south for lovely beaches and a national park crisscrossed with trails, plus canyoning adventures inland.

PLANE

Jakarta is the main entry and exit point for international flights in Java. Other points include Surabaya, Yogyakarta, Solo, Semarang and Bandung. Domestic flights are cheap and, with most major cities having domestic airports, flying is a good way to get around if you're in a hurry.

CAR

Java has a network of motorways and tollways that run from Jakarta to other major centres, yet congestion can be a problem in some areas of the island. Links with ferries to Bali and Sumatra make the roads a popular choice.

TRAIN

Jakarta has a high-speed rail service connecting with nearby Bandung. The train is also a popular option to get as far afield as Yogyakarta, Surabaya and even Banyuwangi in the far east. Different classes of travel are available; be sure to book ahead.

Semarang, p111
This charming coastal city – with the idyllic Karimunjawa islands nearby – seamlessly blends Dutch colonialism with modern ingenuity.

Malang, p129
Gateway to the fascinating moonscape of Gunung Bromo and one of the best experiences found in Java.

Solo, p96
Laid-back Solo is the entry point to the stunning highlands, plantations and waterfalls around majestic Gunung Lawu.

Banyuwangi, p144
The spectacular Kawah Ijen is close to this port city, which is flanked by world-class national parks and remote, isolated beaches.

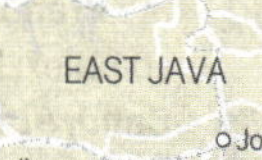

Yogyakarta, p76
The Special Region of Yogyakarta is the cultural and artistic soul of Java, and home to breathtaking ancient temples.

Find Your Way

With most of Java's major cities linked by rail, travelling by train is a fantastic way to experience the island's stunning landscapes. The buses are comfortable too, and you can expect a better public transport network on Java than on most Indonesian islands.

Plan Your Time

Jakarta has a lot to keep you busy, but beautiful Yogyakarta cannot be missed. Prefer to get out the cities? Hiking up Gunung Bromo and Kawah Ijen are once-in-a-lifetime experiences.

RICHIE CHAN/SHUTTERSTOCK

Jakarta Cathedral (p67)

If You Visit Just One Place

- **Yogyakarta** (p76) is a thriving cultural centre and its **Kraton** (p78), **royal garden** (p79) and numerous **museums** (p78 and p82) paint vivid pictures of the Special Region's traditions and past. Begin a morning with a **street-food tour** (p80), try your hand at **making batik** (p80), stroll down **Jl Malioboro** (p79) and sample a sizzling *kopi joss* (p80), then unwind in the evening at **Alun Alun Kidul** (p81).

- Plan ahead as you'll need to advance-book your visit to **Borobudur** (p88), and don't miss the **Prambanan** (p86) temple complex. Nearby is 1200-year-old **Candi Plaosan Lor** (p85); come to this royal temple to escape the crowds and soak up a deeply spiritual atmosphere. If you have time, travel to or from Yogyakarta by **train** (p74) and enjoy Java's stunning landscapes.

Seasonal Highlights

Java's natural wonders come to the fore in the wet season. The dry midyear is dominated by festivals and the tourism high season.

FEBRUARY

Ramadan falls around February and, during this holy month, it can be difficult to find places to eat during the day. Come evenings, though, markets and food halls around this Muslim-majority island come alive.

MARCH

Nyepi, Bali's sacred day of silence, is honoured at the Bromo-Tengger-Semeru National Park and park access is closed for 24 hours. It also closes for the Eid-ul-Fitr holiday, which falls close to Nyepi.

APRIL

As the dry season sets in, so does the best time to surf **Batu Karas** (p174). Offshore winds and southerly swells make for ideal conditions here.

Cities, Gardens & Beaches in 10 Days

- Begin in **Jakarta** with a tour of **Kota Tua** (p68), then head to **Monas** (p64) and, nearby, the **Masjid Istiqlal** (p65), **Jakarta Cathedral** (p67) and **Museum Nasional** (p68). Watch sunset from the top of the **tallest building in the Southern Hemisphere** (p73), then indulge in **street food** (p71) or spend a sociable evening in a **food hall** (p71).

- Explore **Bogor** (p153) in a day, visiting **Kebun Raya** (p153) and **Istana Bogor** (p155), or take the high-speed train to **Bandung** (p164), visiting tea plantations and **Kawah Putih** (p168).

- Travel to **Yogyakarta** (p76) on the **Panoramic Train** (p74) and see the city before visiting **Semarang** (p111) and its compelling **Kota Lama** (p111). Then head to **Karimunjawa** (p117) for an idyllic island escape.

The Best of Java in Two Weeks or More

- Take just over a week to explore **Jakarta** (p64), **Bogor** (p153), **Bandung** (p164) and **Yogyakarta** (p76). If you haven't yet had your fill of Javanese culture then move on to laid-back **Solo** (p96) and be sure to wander through the historic lanes of **Batik Kauman** and **Kampung Batik Laweyan** (p104).

- Hike up **Gunung Lawu** (p109) or **Bukit Mongkrang** (p110) and then, for more active pursuits, make your way to **Malang** (p129). Hike on austere **Bromo's** (p129) volcanic tableaus or find pristine **southern beaches** (p170), then marvel at **Tumpak Sewu** (p142), Java's most awe-inspiring waterfall. End with **Kawah Ijen's crater of blue fire** (p147), an otherworldly sight not to be missed, before continuing to Bali by ferry or returning to Jakarta by plane or **train** (p74).

MAY

On the first full moon in May, Buddha's birthday is celebrated with **Vesak Day**, a colourful multiday celebration at Borobudur.

JUNE

June and July see the best weather of the year for travellers, with the dry season in full swing. Temperatures tend to be cooler now, too.

AUGUST

Independence Day (17 August) brings many celebrations and Indonesian colours. The **Dieng Culture Festival** (p125) is celebrated by cutting children's dreadlocked hair.

NOVEMBER

Tumpak Sewu (p142) is an incredible sight during the wet season – but be aware that the trail is slippery at this time of year.

Jakarta

ARCHITECTURE | STREET FOOD | TROPICAL ISLANDS

GETTING AROUND

Jakarta's worked hard at throwing off its reputation for congested roads, and its public-transport system generally works well. Get yourself a JakCard (p69) if you plan to use the city's budget-friendly trains and buses. Ride-hailing apps are the most convenient way to get around: use Gojek or Grab for a scooter or car, or Blue Bird or Green SM for cars (Green SM uses only electric vehicles). Taxis are usually of excellent standard. To explore Java outside Jakarta, consider travelling by train (p74).

Located on the northwest shoreline of Java is Jakarta, the current capital city of Indonesia (this status will shift over to Kalimantan's Nusantara, p581, in time). A megacity in its own right, Jakarta pulses and throbs in a sea of humanity, with traffic that runs day and night and slick, striking buildings that reach hundreds of metres into the sky.

The city, once known as Batavia, has a rich history with roots tangled in a cultural mix, with Chinese, Malay, Indian, European and, of course, Javanese people calling it home. It would be wrong to say that this blend of cultures has always resided in harmony, as the history of Jakarta has been marked by internal conflict, violence and atrocities – but by contrast, modern-day Jakarta is a city at peace, and a thriving one at that. From Kota Tua, the old town, to Chinatown, the capital's troubled past lies far behind, and the eclectic blend of cuisines, cultures and styles make the vibrant city what it is today.

Get a Bird's View of Jakarta

MAP P66

Visit Jakarta's National Monument

Jakarta's most famous landmark is Monumen Nasional, aka **Monas** *(instagram.com/monumen.nasional; 30,000Rp)*, the towering 132m-high obelisk that commemorates the struggle of the Indonesian people in gaining their independence. Built in 1962 under President Sukarno, Monas holds pride of place in the centre of the city in the vast Merdeka ('Independence') Square.

The highlight of a visit here is a walk around the 115m-high viewing platform, which offers outstanding views of the city and surrounds – particularly if you're lucky enough to be there on a clear day. The complex also contains a museum and a timeline of Indonesian history, displayed in scenes laid out around the large room underneath the tower.

The ticket office is located underground on the north side of the square. You'll need to pay with a JakCard (p69), which you

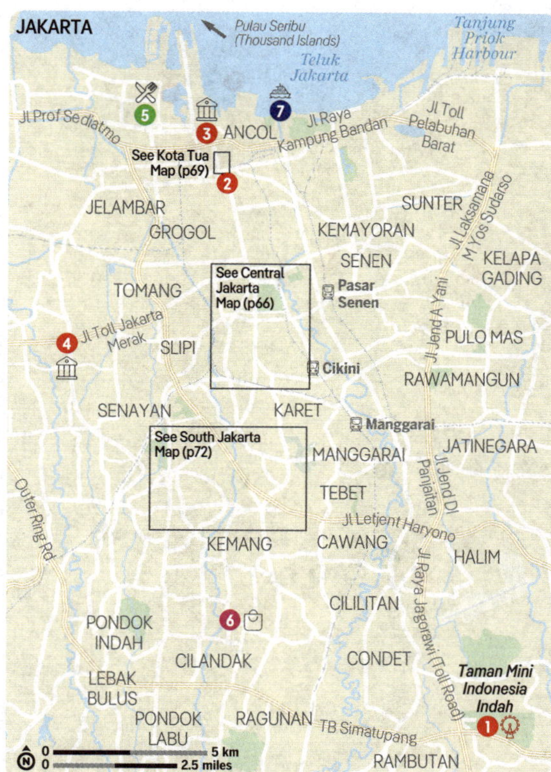

HIGHLIGHTS
1 Taman Mini Indonesia Indah

SIGHTS
2 Glodok
3 Museum Bahari
4 Museum Macan

EATING
5 Pluit Sakti

SHOPPING
6 Dia.Lo.Gue Artspace

TRANSPORT
7 Ancol Marina

can buy for 50,000Rp at the ticket office; 30,000Rp will then pay for your entry and you're left with 20,000Rp credit. The monument opens at 8am; be aware that from mid-morning onwards there are likely to be long queues (particularly on weekends) and you'll have to wait an hour or two until you're able to access the lift up the tower.

Every Saturday and Sunday evening the white monument is transformed in a rainbow of colour during the two 30-minute dancing-fountain light shows, at 7.30pm and at 8.30pm.

TOP TIP

For seamless entry when you land in Jakarta, book an airport pickup through your hotel or head straight to the Grab desk in the taxi pickup zone. There, someone in Grab uniform will help you navigate the app and will likely give you a discount code, too.

Visit Southeast Asia's Largest Mosque

MAP P66

An icon of Jakarta

Jakarta's **Masjid Istiqlal** *(instagram.com/masjidistiqlal.official)* is among the largest mosques in the world. Visitors are welcome here – free guided tours are given daily – and the 22-acre mosque has a real 'wow' factor that holds people enthralled. The mosque is vast (it can accommodate 120,000 worshippers) and the interior of the main prayer hall sparkles with reflective surfaces; much of this seriously impressive mosque is clad in marble from East Java.

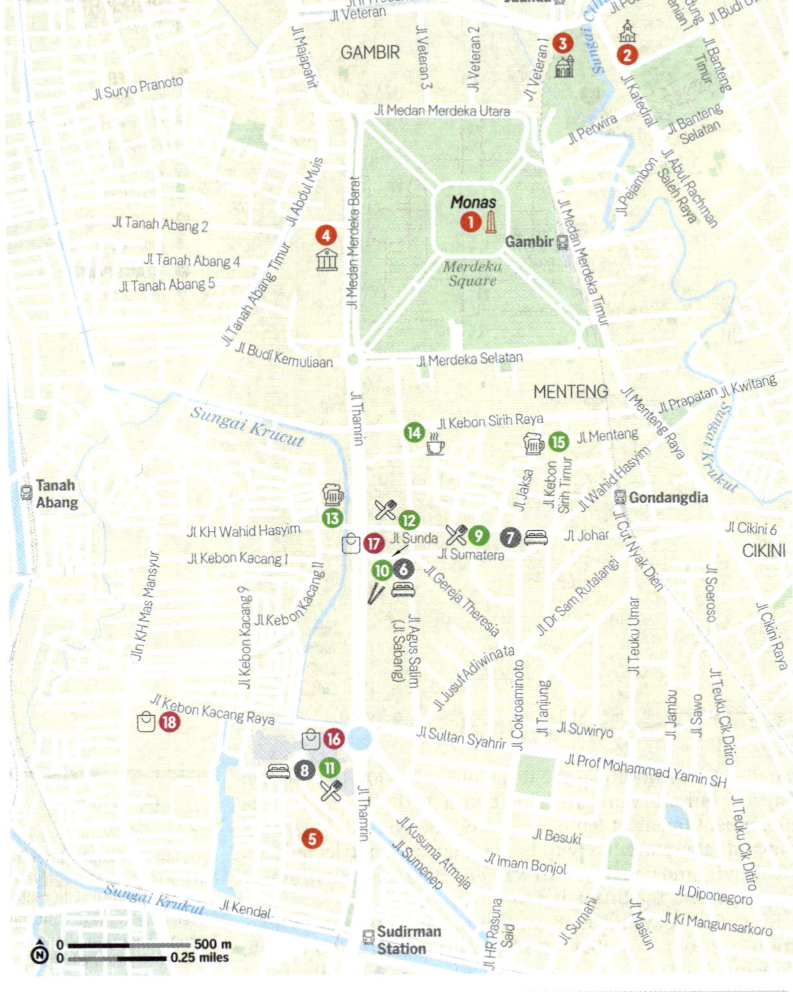

HIGHLIGHTS
1 Monas

SIGHTS
2 Jakarta Cathedral
3 Masjid Istiqlal
4 Museum Nasional
5 Up at Thamrin Nine

SLEEPING
6 Artotel Thamrin
7 Cipta Hotel Wahid Hasyim
8 Whizz Capsule Hotel Thamrin

EATING
9 Abeto
see 8 Croco by Monsieur Spoon
10 Greyhound Café Menteng
11 Pizzeria Cavalese Alta
12 Street Food Sabang

DRINKING & NIGHTLIFE
see 6 Bart Thamrin
13 Jaya Pub
14 Kawisari
15 Melly's Garden

SHOPPING
16 Grand Indonesia
17 Sarinah
18 Thamrin City

The name Istiqlal comes from the Arabic word for independence, and the mosque was opened by Sukarno, Indonesia's first president, in 1978 to commemorate Indonesian independence. Designed by Frederich Silaban, a Christian architect from North Sumatra, Masjid Istiqlal is directly over the road from the Jakarta Cathedral – which, Indonesians will tell you, demonstrates their acceptance of religious diversity.

Free guided tours depart from the office at the mosque's main entrance every 30 minutes from 10am until 4.30pm (although there are no tours at 12pm, 12.30pm or 3.30pm). You'll need to have your legs and arms covered and will be given a sarong if necessary. Non-Muslim women are not required to cover their heads.

Visit Jakarta Cathedral

MAP P66

Seat of the archbishop

The beautiful **Jakarta Cathedral** *(katedraljakarta.or.id)* is another iconic symbol of the city and, with three wrought-iron spires (two of which reach 60m in height) and its neo-Gothic design, it is instantly recognisable. The cathedral is built in the shape of a cross, and while the exterior looks like it's constructed from stone, the cathedral is actually built from red brick, and plaster gives it a stone-like appearance. The interior of the cathedral is beautiful, with the high, arched teak ceiling presiding over the 60m-long central aisle, and 5m-long wings on either side of the main altar. Officially called Gereja Santa Maria Pelindung Diangkat ke Surga, or Church of Our Lady of Assumption, the Roman Catholic church was first constructed in 1829; the building collapsed in 1890 and the new cathedral was consecrated in 1901.

Jakarta Cathedral is open to visitors throughout the day, but be aware that this is a fully operating place of worship, and services are held regularly; it is also used for weddings.

Explore Jakarta's Museums

MAPS P66 & P69

Historical and cultural artefacts

Jakarta's rich past has been captured beautifully in the city's various museums. Most are easy to access, and provide a captivating insight into what makes Jakarta and Indonesia the places that they are today.

The best place to begin is at Kota Tua's **Jakarta History Museum** *(instagram.com/museumkesejarahan; 50,000Rp).*

HOW TO DECODE JAKARTA

Famega Syavira Putri is a journalist who leads walking tours in Jakarta. *@cyapila*

To understand Jakarta's past, present and perhaps its future, explore **Kota Tua** (p68). To see how people live between the ruins of the past, walk from Taman Fatahilla to **Museum Bahari** (p71). Climb the tower to view the old port, colonial-period buildings and canal. You'll see Kampung Akuarium, an apartment complex built on what was an informal settlement; it's now owned and managed by the residents. Head to historic **Glodok** (p68) for a snack, then the **Museum Nasional** (p68). End up at trendy **Blok M** (p71) to sample 'fancy viral food' like matcha and overpriced donuts, or indulge in hearty Javanese food.

Be sure to try Soto Batawi, a Jakarta speciality.

EATING AROUND JAKARTA: OUR PICKS

MAP P66

Abeto: Embark on a culinary journey at this atmospheric, contemporary-style restaurant serving dishes from across Nusantara. *11am-10pm* $$

Kawisari: This cafe's decor is inspired by its namesake, a historic coffee plantation. Enjoy unusual cocktails, like a lemon, wasabi and mint mojito. *8am-11pm* $$

Pizzeria Cavalese Alta: Indulge in slow food at fast-paced Jakarta's Grand Mall. Revered for its pizza, Cavalese also does steak, salmon and soup. *10am-10pm* $$

Greyhound Café Menteng: 'Thai food with a twist' is the claim to fame, but there's also Western and Indonesian food. *11am-10pm Sun-Thu, to midnight Fri & Sat* $$

WHAT'S IN A NAME

At the centre of Kota Tua is **Taman Fatahilla**. This vibrant plaza carries the name of the 16th-century military commander from the Sultanate of Demak (a powerful Muslim state on Java's north coast) who played a significant role in resisting Portuguese colonial expansion in Indonesia, and in establishing Islamic influence in West Java.

In 1527 Fatahillah led an attack against the Sundanese kingdom, who had signed a treaty that allowed the Portuguese to settle at Sunda Kelapa, a key trading hub. Fatahillah conquered Sunda Kelapa and renamed the settlement Jayakarta, which means 'glorious victory' (later, it became Jakarta). Indonesia today recognises Fatahillah as one of the country's 206 National Heroes.

It's housed in what during the Dutch colonial period was the City Hall (built in 1710), and the museum contains artefacts and displays that span from pre-history Jakarta right through to independence in 1945.

The impressive **Museum Nasional** *(museumnasional.or.id; 50,000Rp)* on the western side of Merdeka Square has large collections of sculptures and artefacts from all over Indonesia. There's an opportunity to pick up a novel souvenir here: have your photo taken, and a computer will identify which Indonesian ethnic group you look most like and will then blend your photograph with that of someone from that ethnic group.

In the middle of Merdeka Square, at the base of **Monas** (p64) is a museum that contains a fascinating diorama showcasing the history of Indonesia. It's worth spending time here if you're waiting for your turn to head up to Monas's viewing platform. There's a collection of excellent museums around Kota Tua, too.

Explore Kota Tua

MAP P69

Birthplace of a megacity

One of the most popular places to visit in Jakarta is **Kota Tua**, the old town. Once known as Batavia, this is the site of the original Dutch settlement in the area and enormous, grand buildings that once were government offices now stand as museums (p70), presiding over a sprawling square that once staged regular hangings and beheadings under the oppressive and volatile Dutch rule. The contrasting architectural styles of the area are captivating, and to wander around the old buildings is an experience in itself. Kota Tua is loved by locals and it really comes alive on weekends when friends and families gather around **Taman Fatahillah**, the central square; brightly painted vintage bicycles wait to be hired, and actors resplendent in costumes ranging from soldiers to princesses offer unique photo opportunities.

Trawl the Lanes of Glodok

MAP P65

Explore Jakarta's Chinatown

Kota Tua might top the list as Jakarta's most popular area for tourists, but a short walk away there's another historic neighbourhood that's arguably more intriguing. While many of Kota Tua's grand old buildings carefully protect relics of Jakarta's past, **Glodok** wears its heritage on the streets, where history echoes through the markets and busy lanes that have been

EATING IN KOTA TUA: OUR PICKS

MAP P69

Rode Winkel: The cafe in this interesting historic building lacks soul due to its incredibly high ceilings, but the coffee's good. *10am-10pm Mon-Fri, 7am-10pm Sat & Sun* $

Acaraki: Coffee tools and technologies are used to brew glasses of *jamu*, a traditional healing elixir. Coffee and meals are served, too. *8am-8pm* $

Babah Koffie: An intriguing cafe where an enormous dragon twirls through the interior. The food's as good as the decor. *7am-11pm* $$

Cafe Batavia: Soak up the languid atmosphere in this classic colonial-era-style cafe. There's live music in the evenings. *hours vary* $$

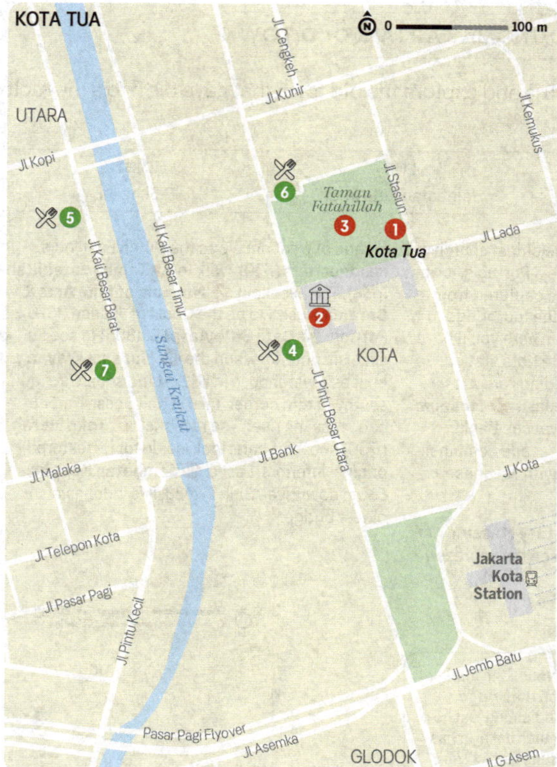

HIGHLIGHTS
1 Kota Tua

SIGHTS
2 Jakarta History Museum
3 Taman Fatahillah

EATING
4 Acaraki
5 Babah Koffie
6 Café Batavia
7 Rode Winkel

home to Jakarta's Chinese population since 1740. The city's gritty Chinatown is an important cultural and commercial hub and, over the centuries, has played an influential role in shaping Jakarta's multicultural identity.

The gateway that welcomes all to Glodok towers over Jl Pancoran a few blocks from Jakarta Kota station. Around here there are drug stores – *toko obat* – that nod towards tradition rather than science; the streets that veer off from Jl Pancoran hold family-run restaurants that are decades old, as well as market stalls where everything from fruit to electronics to festive decorations are sold. Old temples are tucked between them, providing a sense of peace amid the busyness.

You can wander the lanes of Glodok on your own (the mornings are a particularly good time to be there) or, to get a deeper understanding of the area and to track down gems like the restaurant that's been in business for a century, explore Glodok with a guide. Jakarta Good Guide *(instagram.com/jktgoodguide)* holds pay-as-you-wish walking tours in the area on Tuesday and Friday mornings.

JAKCARD FOR CONTACTLESS PAYMENTS

If you plan to use public transport and visit tourist attractions in Jakarta, consider getting a prepaid JakCard *(bankdki.co.id/digital/jakcard; 40,000Rp)*. It can be used on the MRT (underground and elevated train system), the LRT (Light Rail Transit), TransJakarta (the extensive bus network) and the Commuter Line (the rail system). It can also be used for entry to some bigger attractions, like **Monas** (p64), **Taman Mini Indonesia Indah** (p73) and some museums.

JakCards are sold at most stations, at the ticket counters to attractions, and in some convenience stores. One JakCard can be used for group entry to attractions, but individual cards are required for public transport.

A STROLL AROUND JAKARTA'S OLD TOWN

Walk the streets of Kota Tua and explore the old town that gave birth to a megacity.

START	END	LENGTH
Gereja Sion	Jembatan Kota Intan	2.3km; 1hr

Set off from 1 **Gereja Sion**, the oldest church in Jakarta. Sometimes called Gereja Portugis, it was built in 1695 for enslaved people captured from Portuguese trading ports. Use the footbridge to reach 2 **Museum Mandiri**; from here you'll have a good view of the iconic Jakarta Kota station, which opened in 1929. Both buildings are Art Deco in style. Next to the museum is 3 **Museum Bank Indonesia**, the old De Javasche Bank building completed in 1909; its facade combines neo-Renaissance architecture with Javanese ornaments.

Entrance to the 4 **Jakarta History Museum** (p67) is along the street, but to see the impressive facade of what once was the Dutch East India headquarters (1710), walk to 5 **Taman Fatahillah** (p68). The excellent 6 **Museum of Fine Arts & Ceramics** used to be the Court of Justice (1870). Pop into 7 **Café Batavia** (p68; 1805) to see its exquisite interiors, and the 8 **Museum Wayang**, built as a warehouse in 1912. At the square's southwestern corner, take Jl Kali Besar Timor 5 and cross the river. The red-brick 9 **Toko Merah** (1730) houses a cafe; look inside for its restored original interiors. Last is 10 **Jembatan Kota Intan**, 530m downriver. Built in 1628, it is Indonesia's oldest bridge.

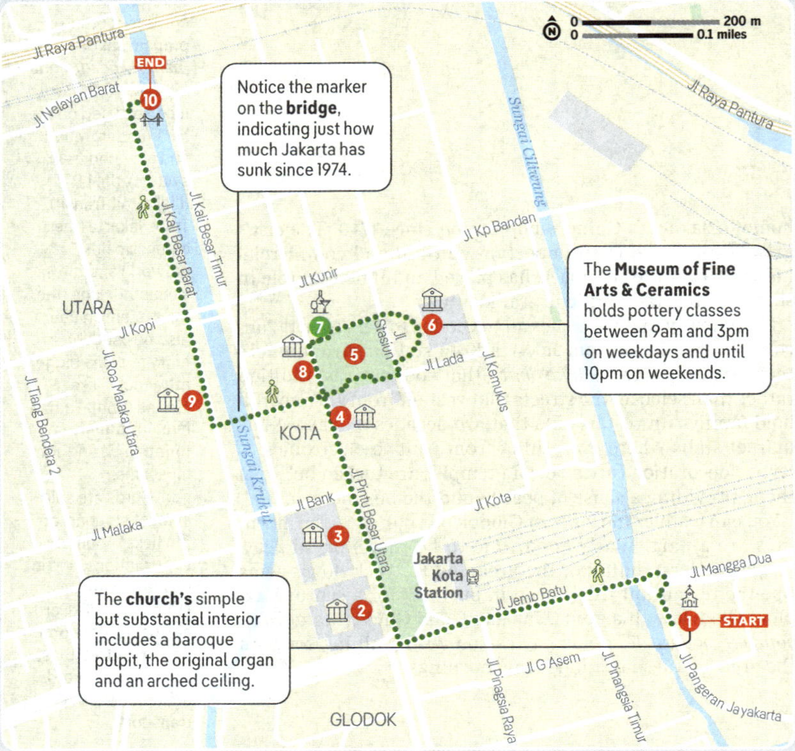

Notice the marker on the **bridge**, indicating just how much Jakarta has sunk since 1974.

The **Museum of Fine Arts & Ceramics** holds pottery classes between 9am and 3pm on weekdays and until 10pm on weekends.

The **church's** simple but substantial interior includes a baroque pulpit, the original organ and an arched ceiling.

Connect with Jakarta's Maritime History

MAP P65

Spend time around Sunda Kelapa port

Jakarta's history is deeply rooted in maritime trade, and for centuries traders from across Southeast Asia, India, China, Arabia and Europe have shaped the city's rich multicultural heritage. You can trace this history, along with seafaring traditions from across the Indonesian archipelago, at the **Museum Bahari**, or Maritime Museum *(50,000Rp)*, which is set in 17th-century spice warehouses beside the historic port of Sunda Kelapa. Wander through halls with displays that detail the types of ships that have docked at the harbour and the explorers and traders who have impacted history here; you will also see a variety of colourful boats that are specific to different islands around Indonesia.

Book a tour with **Delta Antariksa** *(deltaantariksa@gmail.com; 600,000Rp)* and you can take your maritime exploration a step further by puttering out into the port on a sampan (flat-bottomed wooden boat), and stepping onto one of the *pinisi* (traditional wooden ships) docked there. It's an enlightening way to connect with Jakarta's maritime legacy – and to get a different perspective on the city. The museum is closed on Mondays and Delta conducts his tours on weekends.

Sample Jakarta's Street Food

MAP P72

Indulge in delicious local food

Indonesia is famous for its street food, and in Jakarta you will find delicious food across the city, especially as the sun begins to set. In the late afternoon street-food carts, chairs and tables appear in many places where once there were barren pavements, and as night falls people gather to feast on their favourite fare, often until well past midnight. One of the better-known places to eat is on **Jl Sabang** (the name widely used for Jl H Agus Salim), on the section that's just north of Jl KH Wahid Hasyim. Here, come 5pm, outdoor seating is set up and smoke begins to fill the air as everything from delicious *sate ayam* (chicken skewers) to *soto Betawi* (creamy beef soup – a Jakarta special) to *lele goreng* (fried catfish) is cooked up and served to street-side diners. Other good places for street food include the very popular **Blok M** (good for day and night), the streets of **Glodok** (p68) (best in the morning) and, on weekends, the streets of **Kota Tua** (p68).

Jakarta's Famous Shopping Scene

MAPS P66 & P72

From glittering malls to local shopping

Jakarta is famous for its shopping scene: glitzy malls are to the city as beach clubs and cafes are to Canggu, and there are more shopping centres than you could wave a credit card at.

One of the biggest is **Grand Indonesia** *(instagram.com/grandindo)*, which features two malls – East and West – that are connected by a multistorey 'bridge' across Jl Teluk Betung. With eight floors and 200 stores, it's virtually impossible

DON'T MISS THESE CULINARY HOT SPOTS

Culinary storyteller **Ade Putri Paramadita** on three of Jakarta's best foodie spots. *@misshotrodqueen*

Glodok (p68) The narrow alleyways are full of sizzling woks, steaming dumplings and the smell of garlic and soy sauce. Many food stalls have been here for generations, so you're getting a taste of history.

Pluit Sakti Low-key, but packed with some of Jakarta's best Chinese-Indonesian food. Many have been run by the same families for decades, serving everything from legendary fried *kwayteow* to bowls of vibrant iced jellies.

Blok M Buzzes with nostalgic charm and fresh, creative energy. You'll find classic warungs (food stalls), *izakaya* (informal Japanese bars), trendy coffee shops and modern Indonesian food spots.

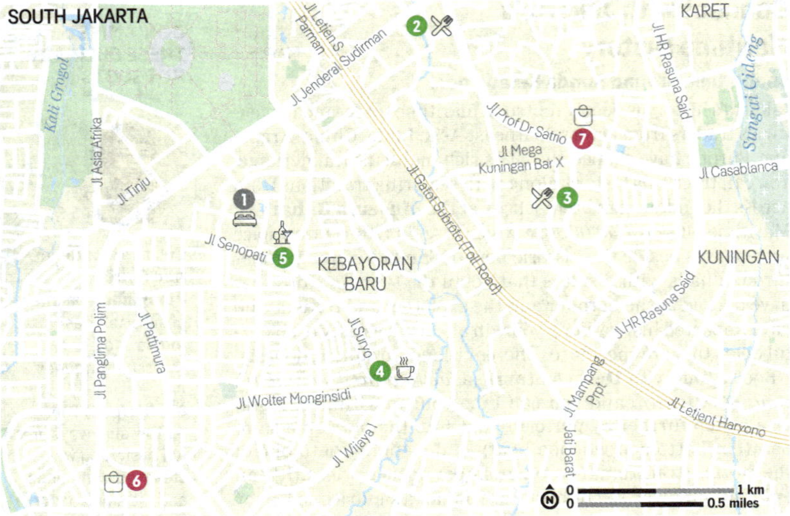

SOUTH JAKARTA

● **SLEEPING**
1 Langham

● **EATING**
2 Kembang Goela
3 Loewy
4 RUCI Art Space & Cafe
see 1 Tom's by Tom Aikens

● **DRINKING & NIGHTLIFE**
5 Pantja

● **SHOPPING**
6 Blok M
7 Mall Ambasador

not to get lost inside. Almost next door is Plaza Indonesia *(plazaindonesia.com)*, and if you're searching for exclusive brands, this is where you'll find them. There's even a luxury-car showroom inside the mall. Both Grand Indonesia and Plaza Indonesia are open from 10am to 10pm.

Half a kilometre down the road is **Sarinah** *(sarinah.co.id)*, which launched as Jakarta's first department store in 1966 and is open from 10am to 10pm. Here you'll come across boutique shops and quality souvenirs that you're unlikely to find in the local markets – it's brilliant for batik fashion. For an even more local experience, try **Thamrin City** *(instagram.com/thamrincity_jkt)* near Grand Indonesia, open 9am to 8pm. It's famous for its batik and local Indonesian cultural-dress shopping. For electronics and tech supplies, **Mall Ambasador** *(instagram.com/mal_ambasador)* – 'Ambass' – is the place to go from 10am to 9pm. You'll find shops specialising in laptops of every make and model, and phones, cameras and gadgets of every description.

EATING AROUND JAKARTA: OUR PICKS

MAPS P66 & P72

Loewy: A classic bistro and bar serving delicious Paris- and New York–inspired food, plus Asian dishes. *8am-midnight Mon-Fri, 9am-midnight Sat & Sun* $$

Croco by Monsieur Spoon: This cafe, loved for its delicious pastries, has both air-con and street-side dining. Close to the Grand Indonesia mall. *8am-10pm* $$

Tom's by Tom Aikens: A refined, contemporary restaurant with gorgeous views, serving British- and French-inspired cuisine. *hours vary* $$$

Kembang Goela: A high-end Indo-Dutch restaurant with a wide menu. Try the *ayam mevrouw lintje* (grilled chicken with coconut curry). *11am-10pm* $$$

Swing High Over Jakarta

MAP P66

Experience the city from above

Take in views of Jakarta from the top of – and, if you dare, swing over the edge of – Autograph Tower, the tallest building not only in the city, but the whole southern hemisphere. Looming up from the Thamrin Nine super-block in Central Jakarta, Autograph Tower is the 383m-high skyscraper that is three times the height of Jakarta's iconic **Monas** tower (p64). It tops the charts on a number of lists: world's highest outdoor swimming pool, Indonesia's highest swing and also the country's tallest observatory deck. You'll find access to **Up at Thamrin Nine** *(up-thamrinnine.com; 140,000Rp)* on the 2nd floor of Agora Mall. From there it's an ear-popping elevator ride up to the 100th floor of Autograph Tower, where you can step out onto a glass-bottomed observatory deck, pay an additional fee *(60,000Rp)* to take another elevator up another nine floors, or pay another 75,000Rp and strap yourself into a seat that swings over the edge of the building. Up at Tamrin Nine opened in June 2025; at the time of research a cafe, restaurant and outdoor pool were yet to be opened.

Explore Taman Mini Indonesia Indah

MAP P65

A theme park for everyone

Indonesia comprises more than 17,000 islands and spans more than 5000km from east to west – to travel across it would take far longer than your regular visa-on-arrival would allow but, at an enormous theme park in East Jakarta, you could simulate this epic journey in a day. **Taman Mini Indonesia Indah** *(tamanmini.com; 35,000Rp)* celebrates the culture and history of Indonesia through an astounding collection of museums (15 in all) as well as traditional-style buildings that represent the architecture, clothing and culture of the archipelago's provinces.

The park is vast (it covers 150 hectares) and, even if you have the best intentions, it's unlikely you'll be able to see and do everything in a day. A good way to tackle it is to pick up a map at the entrance, then do a loop around the entire park on one of the free electric shuttle buses – you'll then know what to expect (and see what's open), and can plan which places you'd like to stop off at on your next loop around. If you'd prefer to travel independently, you can hire a bicycle, e-bike, buggy or electric scooter near the entrance; there's also a cable car that spans the length of the park.

CREATIVE SPACES AROUND JAKARTA

Leslie Tanujaya, chief concierge at the Oddbird *(25hours-hotels.com)*, shares his recommendations:

Jakarta's creative scene is thriving, and the city has become a very vibrant hub for artists. One of my favourite places to recommend is **Dia.Lo.Gue Artspace** *(dialogue-artspace.com)*, a creative hub that combines art, indie goods and a cafe in one place. Another favourite is **Ruci Art Space** *(instagram.com/ruci.art)*, a dynamic modern gallery and cafe that spotlights fresh Indonesian artists in a minimalist setting. And of course, there's **Museum Macan** *(museummacan.org)*, Jakarta's world-class museum for global contemporary art. It has some permanent and some rotating exhibitions, and the cosy cafe is worth a stop.

DRINKING AROUND JAKARTA: OUR PICKS

MAP P66 & P72

Melly's Garden: A relaxed spot styled on a Balinese courtyard garden. The cocktail menu is extensive, and there's live music every night. *6am-2am*

Pantja: This elegant bar pays homage to classic cocktails – and does so beautifully. Ranked 27th in Asia's 50 Best Bars 2024. *11am-midnight Sun-Thu, to 1am Fri & Sat*

Bart Thamrin: Enjoy laid-back vibes on the rooftop of the artsy Artotel, close to Sarinah mall. There's live music on weekends. *5pm-1am*

Jaya Pub: A classic 1970s pub with a vintage vibe, serving good food at reasonable prices. There's live music here, too. *6pm-1am Mon-Sat*

TRAIN TRAVEL IN JAVA

Many cities in Java are connected by rail, and the trains (operated by KAI; *tiketkai.com*) offer a comfortable – and scenic – option for getting around the island. Tickets can be booked at station counters (sometimes only from two hours before departure) or ticket machines (foreign credit cards aren't accepted, so download the Dana app to pay). You can also book via online platforms like Traveloka and 12go.asia, as well as KAI's website.

The Panoramic Train, a luxury 38-seater carriage with swivel chairs and oversized windows, leaves from Jakarta's Gambir Station and makes for an unforgettable departure from the city. You can ride it all the way to Yogyakarta but will need to book one ticket to Bandung, and another onwards to Yogya.

Your entrance fee covers most of the museums (which cover transportation, science, communication and even stamps), but if you're wanting to visit the bird garden, insect museum, reptile park or Komodo museum you'll need to pay extra. You can buy tickets online, or pay at the gate.

Take a Trip to Pulau Seribu

MAP P65

An idyllic tropical getaway

The perfect antidote for the frenetic pace of city life is to escape to a peaceful island – and it's possible to get your fix of azure tropical waters and lazy palm trees less than an hour's boat ride from Jakarta's traffic jams. Pulau Seribu ('Thousand Islands') is a cluster of 342 islands that stretch northward from the city, and they're so close to Jakarta that they comprise one of the city's municipalities. Only 36 of the islands are designated to tourism, but that's still more than enough to find a spot that suits you, whether you want to snorkel, dive, kayak, explore or simply relax. The general rule of thumb is, the further the island is from Jakarta, the quieter it tends to be – just keep in mind that Pulau Seribu is a popular weekend getaway for Jakarta's residents.

AMADEUSTX/SHUTTERSTOCK

Jakarta skyline

Cheaper, slower boats leave from Pelabuhan Muara Angke, but most people take the faster, more comfortable boats that leave from **Ancol Marina**. The boats depart at 8am and the ticket office, which is opposite Dermaga (dock) 16, opens at 7am. Return tickets cost from 260,000Rp (cash only); the price varies depending on your destination and you must give your return date when you buy your ticket, and it will be valid for that date only. The boats leave Pulau Seribu in the early afternoon.

On weekdays you can buy your ticket at the office, but for a weekend departure it's best to buy your ticket online. You can book a one-day visit or overnight stay on one of the islands via Sea Leader Marine *(sealeadermarine.com)*, who also have an office opposite Dermaga 16.

The easiest way to get to Ancol Marina is to take a taxi – use Dermaga 16 Marina Ancol as your destination address – and note that you'll have to pay 35,000Rp per person to enter the marina area.

OUR PULAU SERIBU ISLAND PICKS

Pulau Onrust: Home to Pulau Seribu's only museum, Onrust also has the remains of a Dutch fortress and other colonial-era remnants.

Pulau Payung: Beside an impossibly turquoise lagoon is Asha Beach Club and Resort *(instagram.com/asha.resort)*, popular for its glamping tents.

Pulau Macan: Home to a gorgeous eco-resort with wooden stilted bungalows. Reserve at least a month ahead *(pulaumacan.id)*.

Pulau Genteng Kecil: Open only to overnight guests, this peaceful island *(instagram.com/pulaugentengkecil)* is mostly covered by forest.

Pulau Pelangi: This private island with powder-white beaches is brilliant for snorkelling *(instagram.com/pulaupelangi.id)*.

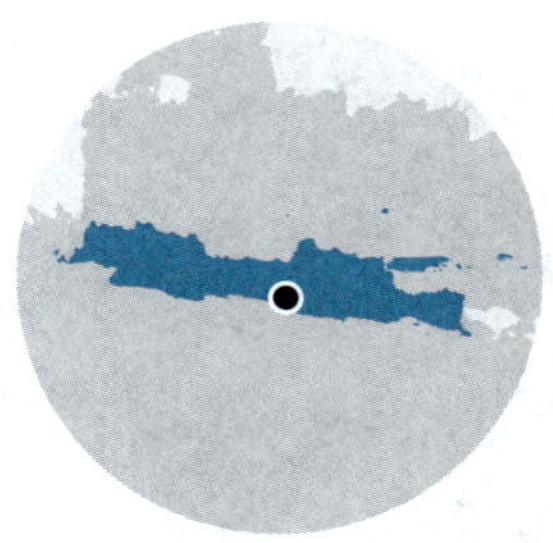

Yogyakarta

RICH CULTURE | HISTORIC TEMPLES | DIVERSE LANDSCAPES

GETTING AROUND

In the city centre, many of the most popular sights are located around Jl Malioboro and the Kraton, and can easily be reached on foot. You can also take a becak (bicycle-rickshaw) or *andong* (horse-drawn passenger cart). If you're on a tight budget, use the bus network (pop into the tourist information office on Jl Malioboro for details); if you're looking for the most convenient transport, use the Grab or Gojek apps, or MaxRide (the ride-hailing app for tuk-tuks).

TOP TIP

Yogyakarta is a popular weekend getaway destination. Its major sights tend to be crowded on Saturdays and Sundays, and are closed on Mondays – plan to be in the city between Tuesday and Friday if you can.

Yogyakarta – Yogya or Jogja, as it's affectionately known – has long held a special place in the hearts of the Javanese people. It's widely considered to be the arts and culture capital of the island, a reputation the city holds onto with pride and dedication.

Yogyakarta was once a seat of power in the Mataram kingdom; today it is the only Indonesian city still ruled by a monarchy, and it presents visitors with an authentic look into the past, melded with a modern and thriving city. Here you will find an abundance of art galleries, batik workshops and stores, and excellent museums that trace and celebrate Javanese culture and traditions. Wonders such as the ancient temples of Borobudur and Prambanan draw visitors from far and wide, and places like the Kraton and Taman Sari provide a glimpse of royal life in a sultanate.

Visit Tugu Yogyakarta

Learn about Yogya's Cosmological Axis

A traffic circle might seem like a strange tourist destination, but in Yogyakarta there's one that makes for a very logical first stop for anyone who wants to gain a basic understanding of the city. At the intersection of Jl Jenderal Sudirman, Jl Pangeran Diponegoro and Jl P Mangkubumi stands the immensely symbolic **Tugu Yogyakarta**, a white, 25m-high monument that forms part of the sacred Cosmological Axis of Yogyakarta (p78). The monument itself is a popular tourist site (read: selfie spot), but don't just snap a pic there – take some time to look around the scale city layout that stands on one corner of the intersection, and to read the highly detailed information boards that explain the symbolism and various aspects of the Cosmological Axis. Go early in the morning or later in the evening, when the temperature is pleasant and you can endure spending time on the side of the road – the information is excellent, and time spent here really is worth it.

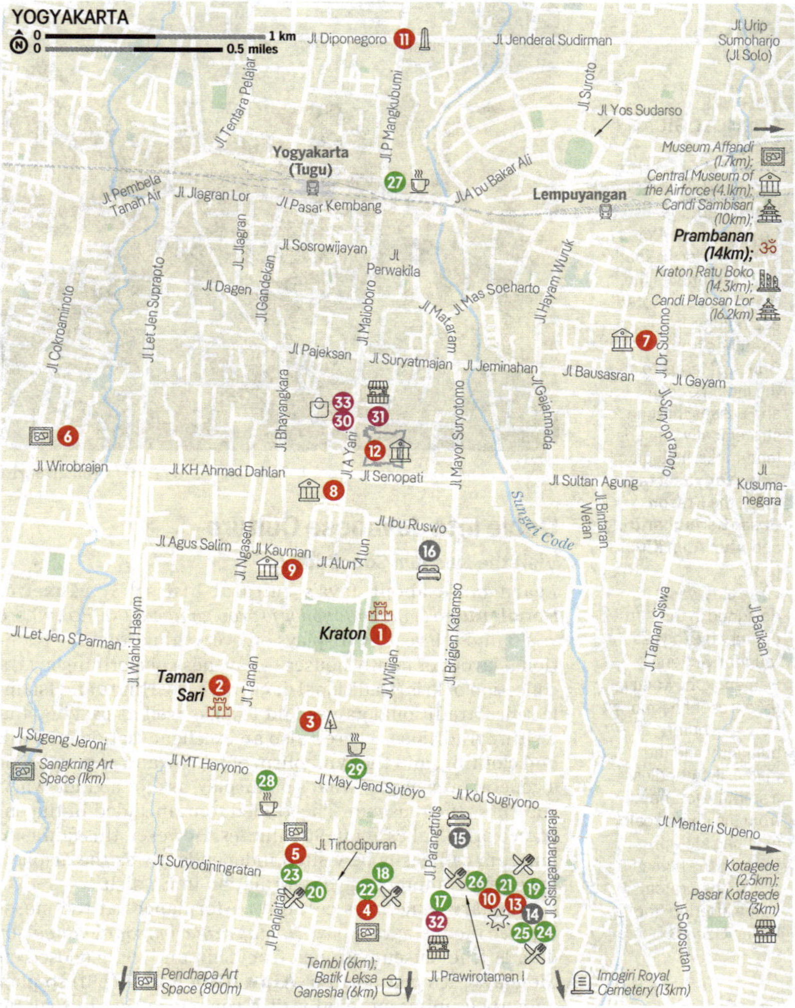

YOGYAKARTA

0 — 1 km
0 — 0.5 miles

HIGHLIGHTS
1 Kraton
2 Taman Sari

SIGHTS
3 Alun Alun Kidul
4 Batik Seno
5 Cemeti Institute for Art and Society
6 Jogja National Museum
7 Museum Batik Yogyakarta
8 Museum Sonobudoyo
9 Museum Wahanarata
10 Prawirotaman
11 Tugu Yogyakarta
12 Vredeburg Fort Museum

ACTIVITIES
13 Via Via Travel

SLEEPING
14 Adhisthana
15 Good Karma Hostel
16 Snooze

EATING
17 Black Forest Cafe
18 Chicken Shack
19 Easy Groovy
20 House of Chocolate Monggo
21 La Contrada
22 Mediterranea Restaurant by Kamil
23 Nanamia
24 Ng'laras Coffee & Gelato
25 Sellie Coffee
26 Till Drop
see 13 Via Via
see 14 Warung Lawas

DRINKING & NIGHTLIFE
27 Pak Hendrix
28 Space Roastery 1890
29 Tadasih

SHOPPING
30 Hamzah Batik
31 Pasar Beringharjo
32 Pasar Prawirotaman
33 Teras Malioboro 1

YOGYA'S COSMOLOGICAL AXIS

Yogyakarta's UNESCO World Heritage–listed Cosmological Axis is a symbolic north–south line that reflects the region's deep-rooted cosmology. It stretches from Gunung Merapi to the Indian Ocean and passes through strategically placed landmarks, including **Tugu Yogyakarta** (p76), the **Kraton**, **Pasar Beringharjo** and **Alun Alun Kidul** (p81).

The axis was designed in the 18th century by Yogya's founder, Sultan Hamengkubuwono I, to represent harmony between nature, humanity and the divine. It embodies a spiritual journey from the divine realm (Gunung Merapi) through the human world (the Kraton) to the afterlife (the Indian Ocean).

MARIUS DOBILAS/SHUTTERSTOCK

Taman Sari

Delve into Javanese Culture

Visit the Museum Sonobudoyo

Learn more about Java's cultural history at **Museum Sonobudoyo** *(sonobudoyo.jogjaprov.go.id; 20,000Rp)*, where you'll find interesting displays on everything from the traditional layout of family houses to Javanese performing arts, a collection of kris (traditional daggers), early Hindu and Islamic relics, traditional games and toys, as well as carving and writing traditions. There's also an excellent section on batik and clothing, and the symbolism of fabrics and patterns. For a general overview of what's on display, ask for a guide when you enter the museum. The guided tour, included in the entrance price, takes about 90 minutes. However, this fantastic museum can easily be visited independently as the displays have very comprehensive information in English.

There are sometimes cultural performances at the museum; see the Instagram page *(instagram.com/sonobudoyo)* for details. The museum is open from 8am until 9pm (closed on Mondays); it's just north of **Alun Alun Kidul** (p81) so plan an early evening museum visit if you're wanting to soak up Alkid's festive evening atmosphere.

Discover History at the Kraton

Insights into royalty

The **Kraton** *(kratonjogja.id; 70,000Rp)* is the royal palace of the Sultan of Yogyakarta. It is located in the very centre of Yogya and, while it's still a fully functioning palace, the walled complex is also open to the public as a living and breathing museum. A visit here provides an enthralling glimpse into the lives of a fully functioning Indonesian monarchy.

The original Kraton building, constructed in 1756, stands at its centre and is the focal point of the palace, facing directly north towards Gunung Merapi; its south side faces towards the Indian Ocean, paying homage to the mythical Queen of the South Sea. The original central pavilion has been added to by successive sultans, becoming a much larger complex. Many of these buildings are now museums housing historical pieces and artefacts.

Your entry fee will include the cost of a guide, so ask someone at the ticket office to point you in the direction of where to find one. It's well worth doing so as the Kraton is exceptionally rich in symbolism and a guide will point out so many things that you'll miss should you walk through the complex independently. The Kraton is open from 8.30am to 2.30pm daily, but is closed on Mondays.

Visit Taman Sari

Relics of a sultan's playground

Enchanting **Taman Sari** *(adult/child 25,000/20,000Rp)*, a once-splendid refuge for Yogya's royal family, is a short becak ride west from the Kraton. According to Javanese cosmology, a royal garden is considered to be the imitation of heaven, and Taman Sari is a wonderful complex of old walls, an orchard, bathing pools and tunnels.

The original 10-hectare Taman Sari complex was built between 1758 and 1765. Much of the complex still stands intact today, but many of its 57 buildings were damaged during a major earthquake in 1867. Instead of restoring the complex, the sultan invited people whose homes had been destroyed to live on the grounds, and the descendants of this original community continue to live there today.

You are welcome to explore the Taman Sari grounds on your own, but guides (who work on a tip basis) are available and it's worth taking a walk with one of them. Most of the guides are from the community here and their family history is deeply connected with the palace; they will regale you with stories of days gone by, taking you on a journey through life in a sultan's royal playground. Much like a visit to the Kraton, a visit to Taman Sari provides a unique glimpse into the daily lives of sultans past.

Shop on Jl Malioboro

Spend time on Yogya's iconic street

Jl Malioboro is Yogya's most iconic street and it pulses with life almost 24/7. It stretches down the city's cosmological axis and is a popular destination for shoppers, as malls (including **Teras Malioboro 1**), multistorey stores and restaurants line the street. It's a good place for those shopping on a budget, too: just up from the **Vredeburg Fort Museum** is **Pasar Beringharjo**, a traditional market that's popular especially for its range of affordable batik. Another favourite batik (and souvenir) store on Jl Malioboro is **Hamzah Batik**, where you'll find authentic batik and can witness it being created. Jl Malioboro is busy by day, but really comes into its own in the evenings, when people gather to socialise, snack and soak up the atmosphere.

MUST-VISIT MARKETS

Arnovi Putty Febriani has worked as a tour guide in Yogyakarta since 2007. *viaviajogja.com*

Pasar Beringharjo offers a glimpse into Yogya's authentic culture. Batik, clothes and traditional crafts are sold in the front; it's good for souvenirs. Spices and fresh produce are at the back, and there are legendary warungs (food stalls) in the food court.

Pasar Kotagede is Yogya's oldest market. In the mornings it sells spices, old batik, cool antique stuff; in the afternoon you'll find traditional snacks.

Pasar Prawirotaman is a mix of old and new. The traditional market is on floors one to three. On the 4th (rooftop) floor there's a communal space for coworking, meeting and broadcasting, and a food court offering local and international delicacies.

FIND BATIK AROUND YOGYAKARTA

Diah Nur Matin (Nunung) is an artist who teaches batik classes at her home in Kotagede. *@batiktuliskotagede*

To learn about the history of batik, visit the **Kraton** (p78) or **Sonobudoyo** (p78) museum in central Yogya; the **Ullen Sentalu Museum** (p93) is a bit further away, but it also has some batik. To shop for batik products go to **Hamzah Batik** (p79) on Jl Malioboro. It has a wide variety of batik and the prices here are good. At **Batik Leksa Ganesha** in Tembi village you can watch women making batik in an authentic setting, and make your own, too. There is a batik gallery here, which is interesting to see. **Batik Seno** also has a really nice gallery of modern batik art, and holds workshops, too.

Create Your Own Batik

Yogya's living tradition

Batik, a textile created with wax-resistant dyeing techniques, is synonymous with Yogyakarta and you'll find echoes of the traditional patterns all across the region, from the clothing people wear to business logos, storefront decorations and even manhole covers. The painstaking and intricate traditional process of creating batik, which was once done only in the Kraton, has been inscribed on UNESCO's Intangible Cultural Heritage list. To create batik the artisans draw or stamp delicate, often symbolic, patterns onto fabric with hot wax before dyeing the cloth, and they repeat the process multiple times, depending on the colours and shades required.

While various shops and studios around Yogya offer short batik-making classes, one very memorable place to try your hand at the artform is in the home of **Diah Nur Matin** (aka Nunung). Nunung (*instagram.com/batiktuliskotagede; 400,000Rp*) teaches batik classes in the front room of her family home in Kotagede and you can either create your own design or base your batik on a pattern she has already created. It's a lovely, personal experience, into which Nunung integrates a short walking tour of the historic neighbourhood, guided by her father.

Eat Your Way Around Yogya

Set off on a food tour

Perhaps the best way to connect with contemporary and traditional Yogya is to walk its streets while sampling local dishes. Head out with **Jogja Food Tour** (*jogjafoodtour.com; 500,000Rp*), which specialises in taking guests to off-the-beaten-track eateries (and those cherished by locals), and you'll experience more than just a food tour; you'll gather intriguing cultural insights, too.

You'll find out about *nasi kucing* (which translates as 'cat rice', but are actually small, snack-sized portions of rice designed for the city's busy student community) and enjoy the sweet sizzle of *kopi joss,* a unique Yogya tradition where a red-hot coal is dropped into a glass of coffee.

Pace yourself, because you're likely to eat in six or seven different venues, including historic eateries and roadside favourites. While most food tours run after dark, Jogja Food Tour also leads one in the early morning (*300,000Rp*), which offers something quite different – and will be a delight to anyone with a sweet tooth.

Learn about Indonesia's Healing Drink

Brew your own *jamu*

Stop by any traditional morning market in Java and you're likely to come across 'Mbok Jamu', a woman carrying a basket jam-packed with bottles of liquid in an astounding array of yellows. *Jamu* is a traditional herbal drink that has its roots deep in Javanese culture; it was originally crafted in the island's royal courts by palace healers to promote health and beauty, and these days it is still a regular part of people's wellness routines across the island.

Jamu is made from a blend of spices, roots and bark and is typically prepared with turmeric (hence the yellow colour), ginger and tamarind. Every *jamu* maker is likely to have their own secret recipes crafted to ease ailments ranging from digestive problems to menstrual pain, fertility issues and weight loss – and in Yogyakarta you can try your hand at making your own. **Via Via Travel** *(viaviajogja.com; 450,000Rp)* offers a *jamu* tour that begins with a visit to the herbal section of a traditional market (where the wide variety of ingredients used to make *jamu* are sold), then continues on to a '*jamu* bar' that's been serving a range of traditional elixirs since 1950, and that ends up with a class where you learn how to brew up your own *jamu*.

Yogya's Coffee Culture

Sample Yogya's speciality brews

You can be sure that, as a city located almost dead-centre in an island celebrated for its coffee, Yogya has its fair share of speciality coffee shops. The bold brew is usually enjoyed in the late afternoons when people begin to socialise, so many cafes and coffee stalls open only later in the day – including **Pak Hendrix**, a warung on Jl Margo Utomo that's known for its *kopi joss*. This Yogya speciality is simply a glass of sweet black coffee served with a lump of red-hot charcoal in it – which, some say, neutralises the coffee's acidity.

If you're serious about coffee then plan ahead and put **Tadasih** *(tadasih.com)* on your itinerary. This coffee haven has a real speakeasy vibe: it has no sign and to gain access you must produce the QR code you'll receive when you book your slot. The owner-barista introduced booking-only admission when his place started to get too busy; he restricts access so that patrons can have time and space to appreciate their brew. The coffee menu is updated monthly, and only coffee roasted on site is served.

At **Space Roastery 1890** *(spaceroastery.com)* there is a tasting table with about 20 different blends available for you to sample before you place your coffee order or buy a bag of beans. With tasting notes ranging from floral to chocolate to various fruits, there really is an exceptional variety. This cafe is worth a visit if not for the excellent coffee then for the historic building the cafe is located in. It was built by the sultan in 1890 as a wedding gift for one of his sons – and if you peek behind the green velvet curtain hanging behind the bar you'll see the lavishly decorated *senthong*, a traditional space for newlywed couples.

Make Your Wish Come True

Hang out at popular Alkid

Just a few blocks behind the Kraton is **Alun Alun Kidul**, or Alkid, an open square that transforms by night into one of Yogya's most vibrant gathering spots. At its heart, two large banyan trees stand about 25m apart. According to local legend,

MUST-TRY YOGYA DELICACIES

Kalika Ratna leads food tours in Yogyakarta. *jogjafoodtour.com*

Sate klathak is goat meat seasoned only with salt; the skewer is metal, which helps cook the meat evenly. It's usually served with a light curry-like soup.

Mie lethek are cassava-flour noodles. The texture's a bit rough; the flavour is earthy and savoury. You can have it stir-fried or in broth, usually with vegetables, shredded chicken and egg. It's a humble dish, but filling.

Jajan pasar is the term for traditional market snacks. Some are sweet, some savoury, and they come in many colours and shapes. Try *klepon*, glutinous rice balls filled with palm sugar, or *arem-arem*, small rice rolls filled with vegetables or minced meat.

SPECIALITY MUSEUMS IN YOGYA

Vredeburg Fort Museum: A colonial fortress turned local-history museum. Exhibits focus on Indonesian independence and Dutch colonial rule.

Museum Wahanarata: Yogya's Royal Carriage Museum displays the many types of horse-drawn carriages used by the city's sultans.

Central Museum of the Airforce: This museum showcases Indonesian aviation history with a wide variety of aircraft, including fighter jets, on display.

Museum Batik Yogyakarta: Make batik and learn about the history and traditions surrounding the fabric.

Merapi Volcano Museum: The displays here give visitors insight into the geological makeup of **Gunung Merapi** (p92) and surrounds.

if you can walk blindfolded between them without veering off course, your wish will come true. To add to the challenge, you need to walk from about 50m away from the trees and to be spun around three times first. The square is accessible anytime, but it truly comes alive after dark when friends and family gather; there's a lot of street food, a festival-like atmosphere and no shortage of becak adorned with neon lights.

Walk the Streets of Kotagede

Explore Yogyakarta's oldest quarter

Kotagede (the deceptively named 'Big Town') is a small neighbourhood about 5km southeast of the city centre – and it's here that Yogyakarta began. It was the first capital of the Mataram kingdom, founded in the late 16th century by an ancestor of Yogya's current sultan way back when the area here was predominantly forest. It's said that one of the trees from that time remains: the enormous fig tree that grows outside the neighbourhood's historic Gedhe Mataram Mosque.

The mosque and its ancient bathing pools (still in use today) are two of the destinations on the **Kotagede Heritage Trail** *(instagram.com/kotagedeheritagetrail; 320,000Rp)*, which is run by local guides. The walking tour weaves in various aspects of the neighbourhood, from historic and traditional buildings to local legends, the Kotagede market, fun facts about the neighbourhood, and also a stroll through the residential area, where you can visit the workshops of the traditional silversmiths Kotagede is known for.

Soak Up the Traveller Vibes

Spend time around Prawirotaman

Wander the streets around **Prawirotaman** in the early evening and soak up the traveller vibe that has earned this cosmopolitan neighbourhood the nickname Kampung Bule – 'Foreigner Village'.

Jl Prawirotaman, the neighbourhood's main street, is where you'll find a wide assortment of restaurants, cafes and some bars. Stop in at one that grabs your attention, pick a streetside table and enjoy some people-watching. There are souvenir-type shops too, and tucked into the surrounding streets are more cafes, the offices of travel companies and many small guesthouses and boutique hotels that were established in what, until around the 1980s, were batik workshops.

The pumpkin ravioli is delicious!

EATING AROUND PRAWIROTAMAN: OUR PICKS

Via Via: Popular among travellers for its range of wholesome, healthy options, including smoothies, Thai papaya salad and eggs Benedict. *8am-11pm* $$

Easy Groovy: Pop in for a happy-hour drink, then stay for a meal. The menu covers Mexican, Indonesian and Western dishes. *11am-1am* $$

Warung Lawas: Generous servings at this tucked-upstairs restaurant. Excellent nasi goreng (fried rice), and other Indonesian favourites. *7am-10pm* $$

La Contrada: Indulge in pizzas, pastas, soups and salads – as well as international wines – at this laid-back Italian resto. *11am-11pm* $$

GANESSATYA/SHUTTERSTOCK

Alun Alun Kidul (p81)

Look carefully at the street corners on either end of Jl Prawirotaman and you'll see, often hidden behind food carts, the statue of a soldier. This refers to Prawirotaman's initial function: the neighbourhood served as a residential area for the Prawiratama soldiers. The plaque at the base of the statue explains (in Bahasa Indonesia) how the neighbourhood name came about: *prawira* is derived from the Kawi (an old form of Javanese) word for brave or soldier, while *tama* means expert or clever – indicating that the soldiers were expected to be brave and wise in war.

Learn to Cook Javanese Cuisine

Experience village life and cooking

Tembi is a traditional art and farming community on the southern outskirts of Yogyakarta, and its inspiring community is finding innovative ways to maintain its traditions through sustainable tourism initiatives. Batik classes (with natural dyes) are offered here, and there are some homestays, too. One very memorable way to experience village life is to take a cooking class *(instagram.com/hanungyogatama; 300,000Rp),* which offers so much more than simply time spent in a kitchen.

PROMINENT ART GALLERIES

There are scores of galleries across Yogya; here are five not to miss:

Jogja National Museum: Showcases work by contemporary Indonesian artists; exhibits change regularly.

Cemeti Institute for Art and Society: Yogya's oldest contemporary art space. Exhibitions, talks and workshops are held here frequently.

Museum Affandi: Celebrates the life and work of Affandi (1907–90), Indonesia's revered Expressionist painter.

Pendhapa Art Space: A dynamic venue hosting exhibitions as well as experimental and contemporary performances.

Sangkring Art Space: A prominent gallery that calls itself 'an experimental space for all circles and artists'.

EATING AROUND PRAWIROTAMAN: OUR PICKS

Till Drop: This bar/resto might have only burgers on the menu, but it's a groovy place to chill out with cold beer and live music. *9am-1pm* $

Sellie Coffee: The speciality coffee is excellent, and the snacks (french fries, *pisang goreng*) are cheap as chips. *8am-11.30pm Tue-Sun* $

Ng'laras Coffee & Gelato: This street-corner cafe does basic meals, but its focus is on sweet treats and good coffee. *9am-midnight* $

Black Forest Cafe: The meals here are 100% vegan, and outstanding value, from pizzas and burgers to Indonesian faves. *8am-11.30pm* $

SPECIAL REGION OF YOGYAKARTA

Yogyakarta and its surrounding area are officially recognised as a Special Region, and have existed as a state since 1755, when the Treaty of Giyanti divided the Mataram Kingdom.

The eastern half went to Pakubuwono III (the Mataram king and a Dutch ally) who established the Surakarta Sultanate; the west went to his uncle, Prince Mangkubumi, who established the Yogyakarta Sultanate as Sultan Hamengkubuwono I. The sultan opposed the Dutch and, three decades after his death, Yogya was the seat of military power during the Java War (1825–1830). During Indonesia's War of Independence Yogya stood as the country's capital for two years and in 1950, it was granted Special Region status.

MUSTAFA AMMAR/SHUTTERSTOCK

Kraton Ratu Boko

The two- to three-hour session begins with a walk around Tembi so that you can learn more about local agriculture (which ranges from rice and sugarcane to medicinal plants) and livestock (everything from brahmin cattle to catfish). The community prides itself on empowering local women, and the cooking class is usually led by one of the village's older women, who are renowned locally as skilled chefs. Whether you learn to cook *ikan pepes* (fish baked in banana leaf), *gudeg nangka* (a jackfruit dish special to Yogya) or Javanese-style *mie goreng* (fried noodles), you'll cook from scratch, grinding the aromatic ingredients (shallots, pepper, chilli and a great heap of garlic) on the traditional *cobek dan ulekan* (pestle and mortar). A class here is a brilliant way to connect with the people of Tembi and to catch a glimpse of local life.

EATING ALONG JL TIRTODIPURAN: OUR PICKS

Nanamia: Prepare to be delighted by the many pizzas and pastas here. The ravioli is particularly good, with a choice of five sauces. *11am-10pm* $

House of Chocolate Monggo: Sweet-lovers heaven, with an array of indulgent pancakes, puddings, gelato and hot or iced chocolate drinks. *9am-10pm* $

Mediterranea Restaurant By Kamil: Be sure to reserve ahead for this popular restaurant serving French and Mediterranean cuisine. *8am-11pm* $$

Chicken Shack: Serving everything from pumpkin soup and tikka masala to beef pho and nasi goreng, this colourful spot appeals to all tastes. *5pm-10pm Tue-Sun* $$

Wander Around an Ancient Palace

Enjoy the serenity of Kraton Ratu Boko

Just a 10-minute drive south of busy Prambanan lie the serene hilltop ruins of **Kraton Ratu Boko** *(ratuboko.injourney destination.id; adult/child 275,000/200,000Rp)*. This sprawling compound – more royal palace than temple, although it does contain some religious elements – was 'discovered' by the Dutch in 1790. Of course, local farmers and villagers had always been well aware of the great hand-carved stones that were heaped across the hilltop.

While it's commonly known as Kraton Ratu Boko (the Palace of Queen Boko), the oldest inscription found here, which dates to 792 CE, identifies the 16-hectare complex as Abhayagiri Wihara (meaning 'Peaceful Buddhist Monastery'). In comparison with Prambanan – with its selfie-snapping crowds – Ratu Boko is a serene stroll among weathered stones with sweeping views. You'll see Buddhist inscriptions and Hindu statues but, in this land of a thousand temples, it's important to remember that this was in fact a living palace, with holy wells (for bathing), human-made caves (for meditation) and a spectacularly grand *pendopo* (audience hall).

Find Solitude among Ancient Stones

Visit quiet Candi Plaosan Lor

Just over a kilometre west of the busy Prambanan complex is **Candi Plaosan Lor** *(50,000Rp)*, a compelling, deeply spiritual place and a poignant reminder of the harmony that existed between Hinduism and Buddhism when it was built. Almost 1200 years after this royal temple was completed, Plaosan Lor still functions as a place of worship, so don't be surprised to find Hindu worshippers lighting incense in the most southerly of the two towering temples, where two of the best-preserved effigies preside. Another big temple structure, further to the north, has long since crumbled so that little more than the foundations remain. The main temple is guarded by 58 smaller temples, known as *perwara,* and 116 stupas.

Visit a Temple Excavated from Ash

Candi Sambisari, a sunken temple

One morning in 1966 a farmer was working his field near Yogyakarta when his hoe hit something solid. He noticed that the rock was carved but it was far too deep to dig it out – and it would be another 21 years before that rock – and the temple below it, now known as **Candi Sambisari** *(50,000Rp)* – was fully excavated. The 'sunken' 9th-century Hindu temple was buried layer by layer during multiple eruptions from Gunung Merapi's crater, which lies 29km to the north. The main temple is fronted by three sturdy *perwara* guardian temples, and the whole complex – complete with stone deities and male Lingga and female Yoni statues – was unusually well preserved during the centuries underground. Candi Sambisari is a 15-minute drive west of Prambanan; it's open 8am to 4pm on weekdays and 7am to 5pm on weekends.

THE ROYAL CEMETERY

On a hillside on the southern outskirts of Yogyakarta is the final resting place of the kings of the Mataram kingdom, and generations of Yogyakarta and Solo's sultans. The **Imogiri Royal Cemetery**, also known as Astana Pajimatan Himagiri, was built in 1632 by the Sultan Agung, who is buried at the centre of the cemetery complex.

It's evolved over the years, and the cemetery's layout is symbolic: the sultans of Yogyakarta are buried east of the centre, and of Solo to the west. The cemetery's three main gates represent birth, life and death; there is a set of 45 stairs, which marks the year that Sultan Agung passed away (1645); a set of nine stairs represents the nine religious leaders who spread Islam on Java.

PERFECT LAZYBONES/SHUTTERSTOCK

TOP EXPERIENCE

Prambanan

Prambanan, Indonesia's largest and most impressive Hindu temple complex, is an astounding place to visit. It was constructed in the 9th century and comprises 240 temples in total. The three main temples, dedicated to the gods Brahma, Vishnu and Shiva, tower as high as 47m and are adorned with beautifully detailed bas-reliefs of the Hindu epics Ramayana and Bhagavata Purana.

DON'T MISS

- Lumbung Temple
- Bubrah Temple
- Sewu Temple
- Ramayana Ballet
- Museum Candi Prambanan
- Kraton Ratu Boko
- Hiring a local guide

The Main Temples

The three main temples of the Prambanan complex are the most impressive, towering into the sky with their distinctive pointed construction. When approaching the temples, you will walk up a long path and stairs directly into the complex. Don't miss the billboards at the bottom of the stairs that have some information about the temples and the site. As you walk around the main temples, take note of the angles of the sun. Head away from the crowds and around to the rear of

PRACTICALITIES

● 6.30am-5.30pm ● ticket.borobudurpark.com ● adult/child 400,000/250,000Rp (buy online or at gate)

the temples, where you will find a grassed area and a couple of trees. Photos are easier here, as the sun generally doesn't cause as much backlight.

A Complete Rebuild

Much of the Prambanan complex still lies in ruins, the result of several large earthquakes over the past few hundred years. The main temples have been rebuilt, and restoration of the lesser temples is ongoing. Construction of the original temples was incredible, with no mortar or steel rods involved. Instead, every piece was carved to fit into its spot perfectly. Due to a lack of funding, only a few teams of builders and archaeologists are able to work at any one time, making the process painstakingly slow. It's estimated work on the entire complex will take over 200 years to complete.

The Prambanan Complex

Away from the main complex lie three smaller temple complexes (many visitors are not aware of this unless they have a guide): **Lumbung**, **Bubrah** and **Sewu**. Exit the main temple complex on the side opposite where you entered, and follow the paved path towards the first temple. You have a few options to get around: on foot (it'll take about 20 minutes to walk to Sewu, the furthest temple) or you can hire an electric scooter *(15min 30,000Rp),* a bicycle or tandem, golf cart, a Segway or scooter *(per person 20,000Rp).*

The last temple, Sewu, is the largest and most impressive, and is well worth investigating. Also around the complex you will find the **Ramayana Ballet**, an outdoor theatre where dances with over 200 performers are held after sunset, with the Prambanan temples as a backdrop. To learn more about Prambanan, visit the **Museum Candi Prambanan**, which is home to artefacts, statues and fossils from the area.

And, if you purchase a combined Prambanan/Ratu Boko ticket *(adult/child 675,000/450,000Rp),* don't miss **Kraton Ratu Boko** (p85); though it's not part of the complex, a shuttle service is included in the ticket price. These tickets are available at the gate, where you can also buy a combined ticket for Prambanan and Borobudur that's valid for two days *(adult/child 750,000/450,000Rp).*

The Local Legend

Local legend says that the complex was constructed by Prince Bandung Bondowoso, who fell in love with Princess Rara Jonggrang. The princess rejected his marriage proposal, and set him the impossible task of building 1000 temples in one night before she would agree. Thus he created the Prambanan complex overnight, with the assistance of demons conjured from the earth. The princess, aware of the feat, played a trick on him: she stopped him from completing his task by getting the roosters to crow early, heralding in sunrise. In anger he turned her to stone, and visitors can now see her, frozen for eternity in the image of Durga, in the north cell of the Shiva temple of Prambanan.

HIRE A LOCAL GUIDE

To get the most out of your experience, hire a local guide *(150,000Rp)* from inside the main entrance. A guide truly adds value to your visit, filling you in on the history of the temple and the stories the bas-reliefs tell. Guides know all the best spots and angles for photos, plus shortcuts between the temples and ruins – information that's absolute gold on a hot day.

TOP TIPS

- Catch the complimentary shuttle to Kraton Ratu Boko from Prambanan, included in the ticket price.
- Visit early to beat the heat. Alternatively, later in the day is cooler if you wish to see the sunset.
- For sunset, make sure you enter before 5pm, otherwise the ticket office will be closed.
- As most visitors are domestic tourists, Friday (an important mosque day) generally sees fewer visitors.
- To save money, consider purchasing a combined ticket that includes a visit to Borobudur.

Beyond Yogyakarta

The Yogyakarta Special Region packs a punch with iconic temples, sunrise and sunset viewpoints, a dramatic volcano and golden sands on far-flung beaches.

Places

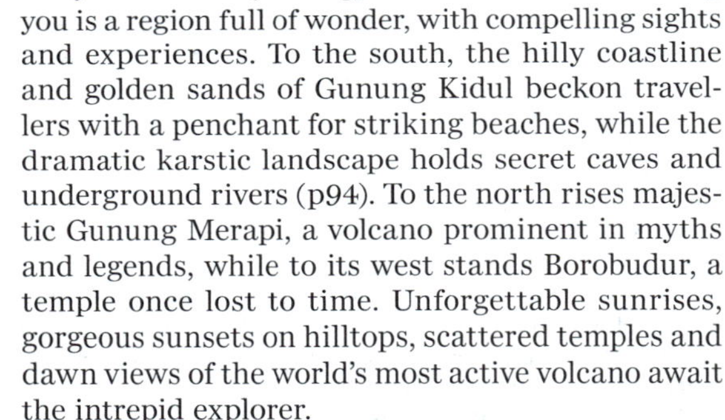

Hire a car or scooter, or find a driver and venture away from the city of Yogyakarta – because awaiting you is a region full of wonder, with compelling sights and experiences. To the south, the hilly coastline and golden sands of Gunung Kidul beckon travellers with a penchant for striking beaches, while the dramatic karstic landscape holds secret caves and underground rivers (p94). To the north rises majestic Gunung Merapi, a volcano prominent in myths and legends, while to its west stands Borobudur, a temple once lost to time. Unforgettable sunrises, gorgeous sunsets on hilltops, scattered temples and dawn views of the world's most active volcano await the intrepid explorer.

GETTING AROUND

Tour companies based in Yogya city offer day trips into the surrounding areas, and this can be a convenient way to see the sights. You can also head out to the Merapi and Gunung Kidul areas by bus (check in with the tourism office on Jl Malioboro in Yogya for route info and times). Of course you'll have more freedom if you travel independently; renting a scooter outside of Yogya can prove tricky so it's best to rent one in the city and depart from there.

Borobudur

TIME FROM YOGYAKARTA: **1¼HR**

Visit the world's largest Buddhist temple

Borobudur, the largest Buddhist temple on the planet (and now Indonesia's most popular tourist site) is a bucket-list destination that's often the sole reason travellers head to Central Java. The 8th-century temple's 72 iconic stupas, 2672 intricate reliefs and 504 Buddha statues need to be seen in person to be truly appreciated, and there's something quite momentous about walking around the temple's tiers.

Borobudur is so large (2500 sq m) and robust that it's difficult to imagine it was lost to humanity for centuries. It's believed that sometime around the 10th century much of the temple was buried in ash from an eruption of Gunung Merapi, and it was then overgrown with vegetation that thrived on the nutrient-rich soil. Subsequent Merapi eruptions caused the relocation of the Mataram kingdom to East Java, leaving the area – and Borobudur – abandoned. The temple was finally rediscovered in 1814 when Thomas Stamford Raffles (at that time the lieutenant governor of Java) sent a party into the jungle to investigate rumours of a lost religious monument. Over the years there were several attempts at restoration projects, but it wasn't until the 1970s that, with the assistance of UNESCO, major restorations were undertaken. Borobudur was eventually listed as a World Heritage site in 1991 and these days sees over two million visitors annually.

You'll need to plan a few days ahead as Borobudur operates on an advance-booking ticketing system and visitor numbers are restricted *(ticket.borobudurpark.com)*. There are two tickets available: the Temple Ground Ticket and the Temple Structure Ticket. The Temple Ground Ticket *(adult/child 400,000/240,000Rp)* will give you access to the grounds around the temple only, and you can arrive at any time (gates open at 6.30am). Try timing your visit to miss the buses and bulk of the tourists who tend to arrive as soon as the gates open; by lunchtime their numbers dwindle and there's another mad rush late in the afternoon. The Temple Structure Ticket *(adult/child 455,000/305,000Rp)* includes a 90-minute guided tour of the temple itself, as well as access to the grounds. Note that you choose your time slot when you book your ticket. Ticket options are labelled Bhumisambhara, Caitya or Mandala – these refer to how the groups are divided, and not to the tours themselves, which are all the same.

See the sunrise over Borobudur

Sunrise at the Borobudur area is a magical experience. As the first light of day spills onto misty plains, the silhouette of the ancient Borobudur temple emerges between jungled hills set against a backdrop of Gunung Merapi and Gunung Merbabu. **Punthuk Setumbu** *(punthuksetumbu.com; 50,000Rp)* is a community-run site that offers panoramic views of the Borobudur area, with the ancient temple in the distance and Gunung Merapi and Gunung Merbabu on the skyline (between June and July the sun rises directly between the two peaks). From the Punthuk Setumbu parking area it's a 500m walk along a wide, paved pathway to the viewing platform at the top of the hill. Along the way you can buy refreshments and souvenirs and, if you tire of the view, there are a few selfie spots to hold your interest.

After being closed to sunrise visitors for a few years, it is once again possible to visit the Bodobudur temple structure at dawn. Tours are limited to 100 people a day and must be booked via WhatsApp *(+62 857 2758 7800; 1,000,000Rp)*.

MY BOROBUDUR

Ika Satyawan is co-owner of Efata Homestay *(efatahomestay.com)* near Borobudur.

I was born in the Borobudur temple complex. Many visitors today don't realise that there was once a community that lived around there; we were moved out in the early 1980s when the temple was being renovated by UNESCO.

I haven't been into the temple for years because it is so expensive for us to enter, but to me it still feels like home. Borobudur was my playground when I was a child and I know the temple so well. What I love most about Borobudur is that it is a garden of peace and healing, not only a garden of tourism.

EATING AROUND BOROBUDUR: OUR PICKS

Eyoop: An airy cafe with rice-paddy views and varied dishes, from *sup buntut* (oxtail soup) and chicken schnitzel to 'nachos Javana'. *8am-9pm* $

Warung Bakmi Pak Muri: This simple warung is a huge favourite with locals – for both its value (all meals under 20,000Rp) and flavours. *5pm-11pm Tue-Sun* $

JH Corner: Grab a coffee or mocktail as well as a snack and head upstairs for a bout of people-watching from the rooftop. *24hr* $

Phuket: This popular restaurant close to Borobudur's gates is known for its vast menu of exceptionally good Thai food. *11am-9pm* $$

CYCLING TOUR

History & Tradition in Borobudur

There's more to the Borobudur area than its famed temple. Surrounded by misty hills, ricefields and vibrant villages, this region is rich in history and tradition, and the quiet neighbourhoods here reveal a slower pace of life where artisans still hand-craft pottery, make tofu and process palm sugar. This 8km cycling route is designed to connect history and tradition in Java's heartland.

1 Candi Mendut

Begin where pilgrims start their procession on Vesak Day: **Candi Mendut** *(40,000Rp)*, the Buddhist temple built in what 1200 years ago was a bamboo forest. It might be small, but Candi Mendut houses an impressive 3m-high statue of the Buddha. Stroll the tranquil grounds of the adjacent monastery. Keep your ticket for entry to Candi Pawon.

The Ride: Turn right onto Jl Mayor Kusen. Cross over Sungai Elo and, at the Soekarno-Hatta monument, turn left onto Jl Sudirman. Cross Sungai Progo then turn left onto Jl Candi Pawon.

2 Candi Pawon

Stop for a few minutes at the small Buddhist temple of **Candi Pawon**, which has relief carvings similar to those at Borobudur and Mendut, and was likely founded at the same time as these temples.

CORNELIUS KRISHNA TEDJO/SHUTTERSTOCK

Candi Mendut

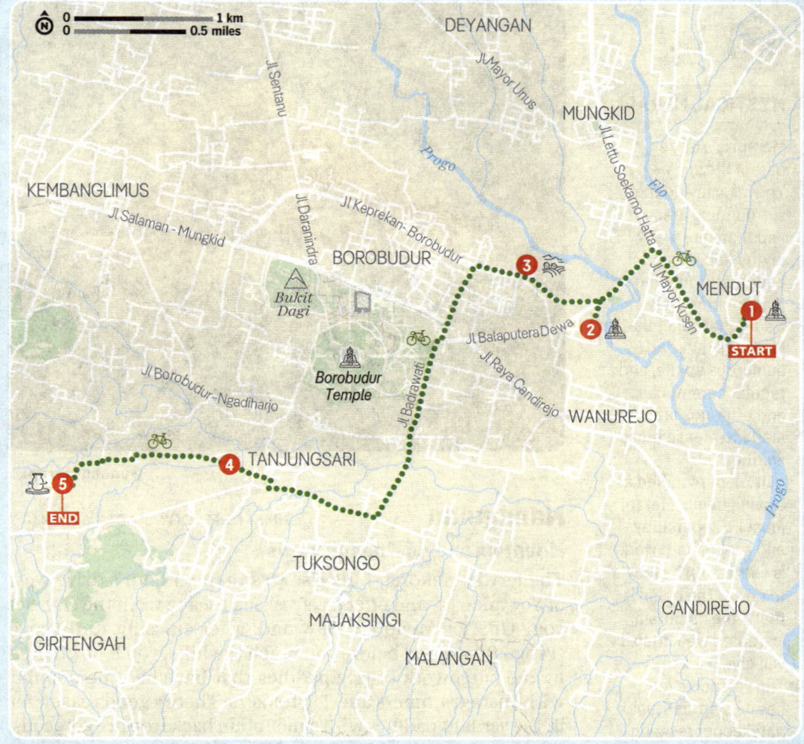

The Ride: Cross Jl Surdiman to reach Jl Keprekan-Borobudur. After 570m turn right onto the brick-paved lane opposite Toko Langsung Jaya (a furniture store). About 100m on you'll find your next destination, Pawon2.

3 Coconut Palm Sugar Home Industry

You'll likely have come across *gula Jawa* (coconut palm sugar) in Java. This is made in a few kitchens in unassuming Dusun Jligudan hamlet, and **Pawon2** is one of them. Knock on the door and you'll be welcomed into the kitchen, where a wok of syrupy liquid will be boiling. Taste some of the finished sugar for an energy boost; it's a 3.6km ride to your next stop. There's no charge to visit these home industries, but a donation of between 30,000Rp and 50,000Rp is always gratefully accepted.

The Ride: Turn right onto Jl Keprekan-Borobudur then left onto Jl Pramudyawardhani. Pass Borobudur temple and turn right onto Jl Ganjuran. Look out for Eyoop restaurant, and after 640m turn right onto the unnamed road. Take the first left and continue to Brian's Motor.

4 Tofu Home Industry

The family of **Pak Daruki** has been producing tofu in this humble workshop since the 1970s, and it's fascinating to watch the traditional process. Get here before 1pm, when the 'factory' closes up for the day. There's no sign for this family-run business, which you'll reach via the green doors of Brian's Motor.

The Ride: Turn right out of Brian's Motor and continue for 1.2km to Mbak Anik pottery.

5 Pottery Home Industry

Mbak Anik has been making pottery for more than 30 years on a traditional hand-powered stone wheel, creating bowls, planters and other functional household objects. You can watch her and her father at work, or try your hand at creating something yourself.

MYSTICAL MERAPI

Merapi is a large part of life in Yogyakarta and the surrounding areas, and there are many myths, taboos and beliefs surrounding the mountain. It is traditional belief that Merapi is guarded by numerous spirits, and regular ceremonies and offerings are made to please these spirits.

Often personified as a living being, Merapi must be kept happy, and a lot of hard work is carried out by locals to do so. The belief is that if the mountain is treated well, then it will give back in kind. The volcano even has its own spiritual gatekeeper residing on the slopes, who is in tune with the mountain and can 'talk' to it, advising and updating local authorities on the condition of Merapi.

GANI_PRASTOWO/SHUTTERSTOCK

Gunung Merapi

Nanggulan

TIME FROM YOGYAKARTA: **50MIN**

Mountain and rice-paddy views

The fertile Menoreh hills rise less than an hour's drive west of Yogyakarta, and offer a refreshing escape from the city. Set your GPS for Menoreh View and, after crossing Kali Progo (Progo River) and before you reach the hills, you'll be greeted by the patchwork of rice paddies that have become popular with Instagrammers and TikTokkers. There's good reason for it: the verdant paddies with a mountain backdrop are gorgeous.

Adjacent to the **Menoreh View** cafe (*instagram.com/menoreh.view*) you can rent an electric scooter at **Tour Sepeda Menoreh** (*instagram.com/toursepeda_menoreh; ½hr 30,000Rp*) and explore the roads between the fields that are tended by farmers who live in the area. Yogyakarta-based company Moana offers 'sustainable cycling tours' around Menoreh (*moana.id; 450,000Rp*), and combines gentle riding with the chance to witness village life.

The hills themselves are shrouded with trees (a lot of teak and mahogany, as well as coconut palms and fruit trees) and, if you set your GPS this time for Kebun Teh Misi Nglinggo (*instagram.com/kebuntehmisinglinggo*), you'll wind up and up an exceptionally steep road and eventually arrive at a cluster of small tea plantations. Information on tea production is somewhat lacking, but there are a few cafes and great photo opportunities. The elevation is 900m and the views from here, on a clear day, are absolutely astounding.

Gunung Merapi National Park

TIME FROM YOGYAKARTA: **1HR**

Visit the slopes of an active volcano

Gunung Merapi, one of the most active volcanoes in Indonesia, presides over the entire Yogyakarta region. It holds a special place in the hearts and lives of the local populace of Yogyakarta and the Javanese people; it is prominent in Javanese myths and legends (it was said to be the home of the gods, and that the volcano was cut from the mythical Mount Meru), and cultural and spiritual connections to Merapi run deep. The **Kraton** (p78), the royal palace and home of Yogyakarta's sultan, was built to face Gunung Merapi. There are many restaurants, cafes and attractions built around the volcano's lower slopes, and weekends see crowds flocking from the city to enjoy the incredible views.

You can visit **Gunung Merapi National Park** easily from Yogyakarta. Many roads lead here from the city centre and, beyond following Google Maps, all you really have to do is point your nose towards the mountain. Many of the attractions around Merapi (including the lava fields created during the 2010 eruption, which killed more than 350 people) can be visited as part of the very popular 4WD tours. These can be booked through almost every travel company and hotel in the region and follow very similar itineraries; expect a plethora of colourful vehicles and zero sense of solitude.

Hikes to the summit of Merapi have been off-limits for a few years now, but there are walking trails that will give you exceptional views of the volcano. **Vogels Trekking** has been leading hikes on and around Merapi since 1981 and has designed various routes that cater to different levels of fitness – including an early-morning hike *(300,000Rp)* that'll have you viewing Merapi's glowing lava pre-dawn, and a sunrise view of the volcano.

Learn more about volcanoes

Get to grips with the geological make-up of Gunung Merapi and its surrounding landscape by taking a walk through the **Merapi Volcano Museum** *(10,000Rp)*. While only some of the displays contain information in English, it makes for an interesting 30-minute look-around for anyone who likes to put the area they're travelling through into historical and geological context. Displays here cover plate tectonics and the different types of volcanic eruptions; there are pictures of how the volcanic landscape has changed over the years, and photographs of previous eruptions and the destruction they caused. The museum is closed on Mondays; it's open from 8am-3pm, but closes at 2pm on Fridays.

Wander through a private museum

Ullen Sentalu Museum *(ullensentalu.com; 100,000Rp)* is a carefully curated, privately owned museum on the slopes of Gunung Merapi that showcases Central Java's art and culture. It houses relics including royal batik and heirloom textiles, as well as ceremonial kris, masks and gamelan instruments, many of which belong to the royal families of Yogyakarta.

Visitors are not permitted to take photographs, and so walking through the buildings feels like stepping into a well-guarded secret. You're not allowed to wander through the museum alone and must take a guided tour (included in the entry fee); the guides are very well informed and share so much

GUSTI NURUL – A POPULAR PRINCESS

Gusti Nurul (1921–2015) was a much-loved Javanese princess and an acclaimed dancer who in 1937 sailed to the Netherlands to dance at Princess Juliana's wedding. Famously, the gamelan music for her dance was played at the Mangkunegaran palace in Solo and broadcast via radio to the wedding.

Born to the royal family of Mangkunagaran in Solo, Gusti Nurul was a fiercely independent woman who defied social norms (and turned down a marriage proposal from Indonesia's founding president Sukarno). She was admired for balancing tradition with progressive ideals, and became a symbol of modern womanhood in Java.

THE DRAMATIC LANDSCAPE OF GUNUNG KIDUL

The hilly Gunung Kidul regency southeast of Yogyakarta is carved from ancient coral reefs that once lay beneath the sea, and its dramatic landscape is a maze of jungled limestone hills, underground rivers and yawning cave systems. Its karst hills form the western part of the Sewu Mountains, which stretch for 120km along the southern coast of Java and fall within a geopark recognised by UNESCO for its unique geological formations and biodiversity.

Popular destinations around these mountains include **Jomblang Cave** (p95) and the cave and underground river systems, navigable by boat and tube, at Goa Tanding and Goa Pindul.

intriguing information about the museum pieces that you'll leave with a deeper understanding of and appreciation for Javanese culture. One special section well worth lingering in is that dedicated to Javanese princess Gusti Nurul (p93), and contains some of her poetry collection. The museum is closed on Mondays; the guided tour takes about 45 minutes.

Gunung Kidul

TIME FROM YOGYAKARTA: 1½HR

Discover hidden beaches

Spend a day or two beach-hopping around Gunung Kidul (70km south of Yogyakarta) and you'll gather a profound respect for the power of nature and the sheer diversity of Java's landscape. The south coast's craggy karstic topography contains dozens of beaches between its hills, and each one is distinctly different from the next. Some are protected by coral reefs and might be littered with enormous boulders; some are safe for swimming while the water at others is wild. More often than not, the beaches are dramatic, flanked by limestone cliffs that have been shaped over millennia by pounding Indian Ocean waves.

The best way to experience Gunung Kidul is to explore from beach to beach rather than settling on one for the day, so hop onto your scooter, open your GPS or map app and traverse the coastline. You'll tootle along roads flanked by towering teak trees, dip into valleys of terraced fields and pass through unassuming villages before happening upon a sandy cove.

What to expect? The unexpected. Every beach is different – from the Buddhist and Hindu temples at **Pantai Ngoboran**, surrounded by stalls of traditional Balinese attire (rented out for selfies), to the extensive food market at **Pantai Baron** and the fishing fleet and seafood warungs at little **Pantai Ngrenehan**, to the carnival atmosphere at **Pantai Slili** and the gleaming Santorini-inspired day club above **Pantai Jungwok**.

For surfing, head for **Pantai Wediombo**, where a two-hour lesson costs 350,000Rp *(instagram.com/wediombosurflesson)*; to paddle on a reef-protected lagoon make your way to busy **Pantai Sandranan** *(boat hire per hr from 100,000Rp)*; **Pantai Nglambor** is good for snorkelling *(gear rental 50,000Rp)*; to swim look for **Pantai Krakal**. Be aware that currents along this coastline are strong and the waves can be heavy, so always check with locals before you get into the water.

It's almost impossible to rent a scooter in Gunung Kidul, so it's best to rent one in Yogya. Check the brakes before you leave – you'll need reliable ones in the hilly coastal region.

EATING ALONG THE GUNUNG KIDUL BEACHES

De Flava Beach Bar: Spot serving Mexican-inspired food, with beanbags and day beds on an almost-private section of Pantai Krakal. *noon-6pm Tue-Sun* $$

Joglo Wediombo: Feast on a variety of delicious *ikan bakar* (grilled fish) at this laid-back restaurant just off Pantai Wediombo. *8am-7pm* $

Jungwok Blue Ocean: This might be a Santorini-inspired resort, but the food's firmly Asian – from noodle dishes to chicken and fish. *8am-8pm* $

Baron Lighthouse: The food's good (Indonesian and pizzas), as are the views at this hilltop restaurant overlooking Pantai Baron. Beer served. *8am-8pm* $

ANDANG RIANA/SHUTTERSTOCK

Fishing boats, Pantai Baron

Also, be sure to leave Yogya with cash as ATMs in Gunung Kidul are hard to come by, and keep a stash of smaller denominations handy as you'll need to pay entry fees *(per person 5000-15,000Rp)* to access various beach areas, and then a further 3000Rp or 5000Rp parking fee.

Gunung Kidul is hugely popular with the residents of Central Java, who flock to the beaches on weekends in scores of brightly coloured tour buses. On weekends the warungs and market stalls come alive; during the week you're more likely to find beaches to yourself.

Test your nerves at Jomblang Cave

Tucked into Gunung Kidul's limestone hills is **Jomblang Cave** *(goa-jomblang.com; 500,000Rp),* which offers a thrilling descent into the earth; it's perfect for travellers who have a head for heights and a love of the underground. You'll descend 60m into a dramatic cave via a rope-and-harness system powered by a team of men who lower adventure seekers down (and haul them back up again) using a network of ropes. It's a tandem drop, so solo travellers are paired with a guide. Once inside, expect muddy steps, narrow passages and the payoff: a vast chamber where beams of sunlight pierce through the ceiling in the early morning (be there between 9am and 11am to enjoy the spectacle). Entrance is limited to 80 people per day; weekends are busy, and it's best to book in advance during peak season, from June to September. If you're afraid of heights, darkness or suffer from claustrophobia, Jomblang Cave is best avoided.

THE GODDESS OF THE SOUTH SEA

Java's southern coast is the realm of a goddess called Nyai Roro Kidul, Queen of the South Sea, and any shrines or temples shrouded in green are likely to be devoted to her. Don't be tempted to wear green swimwear in the sea: locals believe that the colour invites drowning at the hands of a goddess who's always hungry for human lives.

Nyai Roro Kidul is not only found on the coast; once a year in the Kraton at Surakarta a dance is held in her honour, with nine specially trained virgin dancers. A strong breeze and the scent of flowers is a sign that the goddess is in attendance. Some guests claim to have seen not nine, but 10 dancers.

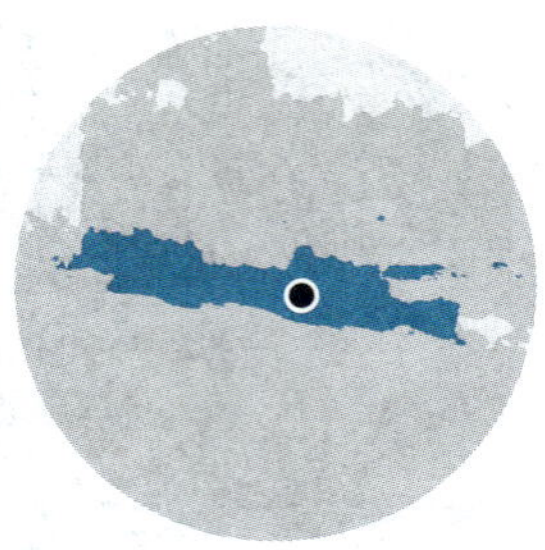

Solo

TWIN PALACES | BATIK SHOPPING | TRADITIONAL FOOD

GETTING AROUND

Solo is a relatively small city and, if you don't mind negotiating pavement that are sometimes broken and sometimes the territory of street-side markets, then walking from A to B around the Kraton area is an option. The Batik Kauman and Batik Laweyan neighbourhoods are best explored on foot, and you'll often find becak round touristy places like the Kraton, Pura Mangkunegaran and Pasar Gede. To travel further around the city, the Gojek and Grab apps are invaluable.

TOP TIP

Although Solo can easily be visited from Yogyakarta on a day trip, it is worth spending more than just a single day in the city. Give yourself at least two days to appreciate the area.

Unassuming Surakarta (better known as Solo) often falls into the shadow of neighbouring Yogyakarta, but this small city – once a thriving sultanate – has a captivating history, with its roots tangled with Yogya's in the once-powerful Mataram kingdom.

The Java Man fossil was found on the city's outskirts, and the region's deep past is of particular interest to archaeologists. Reflecting Solo's more recent history are its two palaces, both of which are still home to royal families (Pura Mangkunegaran is particularly endearing), and Solo also has a thriving batik tradition.

The pace of life here tends to be slow, and the many becak still operating around Solo are a testament to this. For travellers looking to have a more 'local' experience in Central Java and to escape the tourist-oriented side of Yogyakarta, Solo can be a welcome change.

Tour the Kraton of Solo

Visit the traditional home of the sultan

Located at the very heart of Solo is **Kraton Surakarta** *(60,000Rp)*, the traditional home of the sultan. It was established in 1745, and while the royal family still lives here, the Kraton today also acts as a museum; visitors are welcome to explore a section of the palace grounds, and a guided tour here is a fantastic introduction to the history of Solo and to the intricate traditions of Central Java.

Visitors are welcome to enter the grounds on their own, but almost no written information is given at the Kraton, so accepting the service of a guide (included in the entry fee) will add so much depth to your visit. You'll learn about how Solo and Yogyakarta came to be, how power was divided between the two kingdoms, and some of the differences that arose between the two as their traditions evolved.

There is symbolism everywhere around the Kraton; from the colour of the pillars and ceiling (blue), to the number of trees

HIGHLIGHTS
1 Kraton Surakarta
2 Pasar Gede
3 Pura Mangkunegaran

SIGHTS
4 Sheikh Zayed Grand Mosque
5 Tien Kok Sie

SLEEPING
6 De Solo Boutique Hotel
7 Doeloerkoe Homestay
8 Holabeds Hotel

EATING
9 Hidden Swargi
10 JuLi Bakery & Cafe
11 Kooken Cafe
12 Omah Lawas
13 Par Four
14 Pracimasana
15 Slari Coffee
16 Soga
17 Tirai Bamboe Restaurant
18 Wedangan Pendhopo
19 Yassalam
20 Zagladi

ENTERTAINMENT
21 Sriwedari Theatre

SHOPPING
22 Pasar Triwindu

planted in the courtyard (77), to the sand on the courtyard ground (a mix from Merapi and the south coast). Learning about these during the guided tour will give you insights into the culture of Solo and Java. You'll also see (but not enter) the tower that, until 1985, was the tallest building in Solo. It's still used today as a place of meditation for the sultan.

If you're exploring the Kraton on your own, you might be done in 15 minutes, but with a guide you'll likely spend an hour to 90 minutes wandering the grounds and rooms that hold royal carriages and various relics. The Kraton is closed on Fridays, and open from 9am to 2pm every other day. The guides are volunteers, so a tip is gratefully received; 50,000Rp would be reasonable.

TWO PALACES, ONE CITY

Solo has two royal palaces due to an 18th-century power struggle. In 1755 the powerful Mataram Sultanate (which at its height encompassed all of Central and East Java) was divided by the Dutch-backed Treaty of Giyanti, and the sultanates of Yogyakarta and Surakarta were created. The conflict didn't end there. Two years later Raden Mas Said, a rebellious prince, reached a settlement with the Dutch and was granted his own realm within Surakarta, creating the Mangkunegaran princedom. It was then that the second palace was established, alongside the main Kraton Surakarta. While the Kraton remained the dominant royal court, both institutions coexisted, and both remain culturally significant.

Wander Around a Royal Palace

Explore Pura Mangkunegaran

You'll get a solid schooling on Solo's history when you take a guided tour at the Kraton, but that doesn't mean you should pass up the chance to visit the city's second palace, **Pura Mangkunegaran** *(mangkunegaran.id; card payments only 30,000Rp)*. With gorgeous gardens and various rooms decorated with heirlooms and family photos, visiting Mangkunegaran is a completely different experience – and it's just as compelling.

Although both were initially built in the mid 1700s, the Kraton and Mangkunegaran are now, architecturally, quite different: while the Kraton is distinctly Javanese in style, Mangkunegaran is an intriguing blend of Javanese and European styles. It has a very homely feel to it – indeed, members of the royal family still live in the palace, and there's every chance you'll see the prince (the current head of the family) arriving or leaving, or his sister walking through the grounds.

Ask for a guide when you buy your ticket (there is no additional charge, but a tip is appreciated) and you'll receive a full account of the palace's history along with explanations on how each courtyard and building is used. Between 10am and noon on Wednesdays and Saturdays traditional gamelan music is performed, and on Wednesdays there are dancers, too. Mangkunegaran is open 8am to 2.30pm and is closed on Thursdays.

The elegant **Pracimasana**, one of Solo's most popular restaurants, is located on the grounds of Mangkunegaran. Prices are surprisingly affordable, and you'll need to book via Instagram *(instagram.com/pracima.mn)*.

Shop for Unusual Souvenirs

Trawl the Triwindu market

Any traveller who enjoys trawling markets should have **Pasar Triwindu** at the very top of their itinerary. The stalls at this two-floor antiques market are packed with fascinating items, from old lamps, Javanese masks and enamel coffee pots to vintage radios and telephones, travelling trunks, coins, cassettes, ceramics, hair pins and colonial-era furniture. The market has a very laid-back atmosphere – it's unlikely you'll be hassled or hustled by anyone – so shopping here is a pleasure. While not all goods sold here are museum-quality antiques (and some are 'made-to-order antiques'), they make

Don't miss the baklava.

EATING IN SOLO: OUR PICKS

Yassalam: The food is delicious and exceptionally reasonable at this modern Arabian restaurant not far from the Kraton. *9am-9pm* $

Zagladi: A simple, family-owned Arabian eatery with excellent food and big servings. The samosas and houmous are recommended. *8am-8pm Thu-Tue* $

Canting Londo Kitchen: The extensive menu features Asian fusion and imaginatively presented Western dishes. With courtyard seating. *10am-10pm* $$

Kale Locale: There's a set menu at this popular restaurant (book in advance via Instagram) set in an atmospheric old house. *noon-9pm* $$

MARIUS KARP/SHUTTERSTOCK

Pura Mangkunegaran

for unusual souvenirs. Pasar Triwindu was established in 1939; for decades it was a regular traditional market before it transitioned into antiques in the 1970s.

Visit Traditional Javanese Cottage Industries

Watch the artisans at work

The village of **Wirun**, a 15-minute drive east of Solo, is a hive of industry, especially in the mornings. It is best to arrive about 9am, when one part of the village clangs to the rhythmic hammering of gongs. These gongs – destined to be part of prized gamelan orchestras – are not being beaten as a form of entertainment. Far from it; in a ritual of flames and sparking metal that has changed little over the centuries, teams of artisans work in formidable heat as they smelt and hammer an alloy of nickel and copper into the form of traditional gongs. In Wirun you can witness the entire process involved in the production of a 12-piece gamelan orchestra (which might cost more than US$30,000).

It would be possible to visit under your own steam, but it's not just about knowing which doors to knock on; it's about understanding what is going on within. Wahyu Prapto Nugroho *(WhatsApp +62 852 2904 3477; 300,000Rp)* leads tours by motorbike, car or bicycle through several fascinating cottage industries in the Wirun area, and he knows the workers well.

Wahyu can also take you to a family-run *wayang kulit* (shadow-puppet) workshop where Mbah Merto Wirejo – a legend in the industry – has been producing traditional shadow puppets for almost six decades. The last stop is at a huge, steaming barn where around 40,000 prawn-flavoured *krupuk* (crackers made from wheat- and tapioca flour) are fried in giant woks. Take the opportunity to try the freshly made products, which are particularly delicious when still warm from the pans.

SOLO'S ARCHITECTURAL DELIGHTS

Yasinta Primastuti, a walking-tour guide, on some of the city's historic buildings. *@soerakartawalking tour*

There are beautiful and significant buildings in Solo; among the best-known are the Kraton, Pura Mangkunegaran and Pasar Gede. Masjid Laweyan in Kampung Laweyan is Solo's oldest mosque. Monumen Pers, the only remaining building of the historic Societit social club in Solo, now holds a collection of over a million newspapers and magazines. Ponten Mangkunegaran is lovely; it was once a public bathroom, and its architecture is interesting as it's similar in design to the *candi* of Central Java. Balapan is among the oldest train stations in Indonesia; the first stone here was laid in 1864.

TIEN KOK SIE TEMPLE

The very peaceful **Tien Kok Sie**, which stands opposite the bustling main entrance of **Pasar Gede**, is one of the oldest Chinese *klenteng* (temples) in Solo. It was built by Chinese immigrants around 300 years ago, and vibrantly blends together Taoist, Confucian and Buddhist elements, which can be seen in the ornate dragons, smoky incense coils and candles, and the bright-red altars and pillars.

The name of Sudiroprajan, the neighbourhood that surrounds the *klenteng*, translates roughly as 'harmony'; when the area was established, Chinese and Javanese people lived here together. This was unusual at the time, as these communities tended to be quite separate.

RENHUE/SHUTTERSTOCK

Pasar Gede

Trawl Solo's Oldest Market

Uncover history at Pasar Gede

The oldest market in Solo is **Pasar Gede** (open 24 hours), a vibrant trading place that, close on two centuries after it was founded, still attracts hordes of visitors who trawl the stalls for jewellery, fresh produce, snacks and just-made delicacies, as well as meat, home goods and batik. There's an abundance of food stalls here, and Pasar Gede is an excellent place to head to if you want to sample some of the foods Solo is known for (p103), including the deliciously sweet *dawat talasi*.

Pasar Gede's origins date back to 1745, when it was surrounded by a predominantly Chinese community – and if you look over the road from the market's main entrance you'll see, squeezed between shopfronts and behind scooters and shoppers, the **Tien Kok Sie** temple, which was founded around the same time as the market. The current market building was constructed in 1910; it was designed by Dutch architect Thomas Karsten (who designed many buildings around Java) and is notable for ergonomic features like the raised platforms that allow seated traders and walking shoppers to interact on the same level, and the gentle pitch of the ramps that makes it easier for porters to carry goods between floors.

EATING IN SOLO: OUR PICKS

Soga: A cool, contemporary restaurant serving Asian and Western fare. It's right beside the House of Danar Hadi. *10am-10pm* $$

Par Four: Expect cold beer, good music and delicious meaty meals (including pork) at this Texas-themed bar-restaurant. *4.30pm-midnight Tue-Sun* $$

Tirai Bamboe Restaurant: This buffet-style restaurant is great for families or those wanting to try varied local foods. *7am-9pm Mon-Thu, to 10pm Fri-Sun* $$

Épice Restaurant: Located in the lobby of the Alila hotel, this is an upmarket place for those wanting to try local food. *6am-10pm* $$

There is much more to the market (and the neighbourhood) than meets the eye, and the best way to uncover it is to go on a two-hour walkabout with **Soerakarta Walking Tour** *(instagram.com/soerakartawalkingtour; 250,000Rp)*; the small company has knowledgeable local guides who peel back the layers of the area's rich history.

Sunset at Sheikh Zayed Grand Mosque

Visit Solo's impressive new mosque

Solo's **Sheikh Zayed Grand Mosque** *(instagram.com/masjidzayedsolo)* is a stunning symbol of Islamic architecture and cultural harmony – and it's open to all. Inspired by its namesake in Abu Dhabi, this smaller (but still very impressive) replica was a gift of friendship from the United Arab Emirates. It was completed in early 2023 at a cost of some US$20 million, and the mosque's gleaming white domes and elegant minarets form a captivating landmark, particularly after sunset when its blue lights are turned on. While structurally it resembles the mosque in Abu Dhabi, Solo's Sheikh Zayed Grand Mosque has batik designs on the floors, carpets and ceilings, a feature that blends the mosque's architectural style with local cultural traditions.

The mosque can accommodate 10,000 worshippers, and it's open to people of all religions from 3am until 9pm. A particularly evocative time to visit is in the evening, when the muezzin proclaims the Adzan Maghrib, the sunset call to prayer. To enter the mosque you must be modestly dressed, and women need to wear a *jilbab* (headscarf).

Watch a Traditional Javanese Performance

Spend an evening at the Sriwedari Theatre

Six nights a week at Wayang Orang Sriwedari, the **Sriwedari Theatre** *(instagram.com/wayang_orang_sriwedari; 50,000Rp)* puts on captivating displays of Javanese culture and storytelling through *wayang orang*, or human puppet theatre. This traditional dance-drama brings to life ancient epics like the Ramayana and Mahabharata, which are performed with elegant (sometimes overstated) movement, vibrant costumes and live gamelan music. The performances blend dance, drama and humour, reflecting moral values and classical heroism – and giving visitors a vibrant glimpse of traditional Javanese culture.

VISITING SOLO'S GREAT MOSQUE

Rifat Sungkar is the manager of Doeloerkoe Homestay. *@doeloerkoe_homestay*

We're proud of our Sheikh Zayed Grand Mosque and are happy when foreigners visit. To ensure you act respectfully, please note the following:

Men and women can visit the outer patios and alcoves together – but at the main prayer hall, women should enter from the right and men from the left.

Women should cover legs, arms and head (no hair showing). Men should wear long trousers; any shirt besides a vest is fine.

There is no need to cover up tattoos.

This is not a fixed rule, but unless you're a Muslim, it would be considered more respectful to leave the prayer hall during prayers.

EATING AROUND SOLO: OUR CAFE PICKS

Omah Lawas: Friendly service, homely decor and interesting bric-a-brac add to the magic of this unassuming cafe. *9am-5pm Wed-Mon* $

Slari Coffee: This student hangout has three floors of balcony seating. Good coffee, and shelves of books about Indonesia, too. *8am-midnight* $

Saudagar: This cafe in the shady garden of an old merchant's house has immense romantic appeal. *8am-11pm Mon-Thu, 8am-midnight Fri-Sun* $

JuLi Bakery & Cafe: A tiny, carefully considered neighbourhood cafe serving exceptional pastas, pastries and sourdough bread. *7am-9pm* $

WHAT IS WEDANG?

On the menu at restaurants and warungs around Yogyakarta and Solo you'll see a section dedicated to *wedang* – if you do, be sure to try it because you're in for a treat. *Wedang* is a traditional drink (served hot or with ice) made from herbal ingredients like ginger, lemongrass and spices. It's commonly drunk in the afternoons and evenings, and is known for healing properties. Common ingredients include:

jahe ginger
gula Jawa palm sugar
kencur aromatic ginger
sereh lemongrass
daun pandan pandanus leaf
cenkeh cloves
kayu manis cinnamon
jeruk nipis lime
lada hitam black pepper
kapulaga cardamom
daun jeruk kaffir lime leaves

The performances usually take around two or three hours – but, as they're in Javanese, it's unlikely foreigners will feel compelled to sit through all of it. And that's okay. Members of the audience duck out from time to time to fuel up on the snacks and drinks sold at the warungs just outside the theatre, and it's not frowned upon if you decide to leave early. A very brief outline of what's happening on stage is given via words on a projector (in Bahasa Indonesia and English). You can buy tickets at the door; the ticket office opens at 6.30pm and the show starts at 8pm. There is no show on Sundays.

Visit the Home of Java Man

Explore Sangiran Museum

Back in 1891 near Sangiran village, in what are now the outskirts of Solo, a Dutch physician found the skullcap, tooth and femur of what became known as Java Man. At that time

The coffee and sparkling tea are as good as the aesthetics.

EATING AROUND SOLO: OUR CAFE PICKS

Kooken Café: Pose for selfies in the cute plant-shrouded alley beside this cafe, or nip in for a refreshing iced coffee. *8am-7pm* $

Geger Geni Coffee & Roastery: Slow coffee is taken seriously at this small speciality cafe, where beans are roasted on site. *8am-midnight* $

Wedangan Pendhopo: An atmospheric cafe selling traditional hot drinks made from herbs and spices, plus snacks. *3pm-10pm Mon-Sat* $

Hidden Swargi: This cool contemporary cafe has a wonderful shady terrace area and is a popular gathering place for friends. *9am-midnight* $$

PAK_SUN/SHUTTERSTOCK

Hominid fossils, Museum Manusia Purba Sangiran

they were the oldest hominid fossils ever found, and the area has since become one of the world's most important sites for studying human fossils.

The **Museum Manusia Purba Sangiran** *(30,000Rp)* is located very close to the site where Java Man was found, and it's a fantastic place to learn about the history and evolution of early humans. The museum is a lot larger than you might expect; it comprises multiple rooms with excellent and informative displays on the geology of the area and the fossils found there, including an impressive 3m-long tusk of an elephant. The museum also has displays about the origins of the universe, and geological information on the Ring of Fire (the Pacific Ocean's volcanic zone), which had a big hand in shaping the islands of Indonesia.

Be sure to ask for a guide when you buy your ticket – they are exceptionally knowledgeable and have lived all their lives in the area.

There are four other smaller museums nearby; all are connected with the geology and archaeology of Sangiran, but unless you have a very specific interest, the main Museum Manusia Purba Sangiran is the one to see. The guides will be able to arrange a visit to the other museums, should you wish. The museum is open from 8am to 4pm and is closed on Mondays.

TASTE TRADITIONAL SOLO CUISINE

Solo has a thriving food scene. While you're in the city try the following:

***Timlo Solo*:** A clear, savoury broth that usually contains shredded chicken, egg and *sosis*. Served with rice and fried shallots.

***Nasi liewt*:** Rice cooked in chicken broth, coconut milk, bay leaves and lemongrass, with egg, shredded chicken and vegetables.

***Serabi Solo*:** A thick pancake made with rice flour, coconut milk and palm sugar.

***Dawet talasi*:** Sweet, sticky rice, chia seeds, coconut milk, palm-sugar syrup and *cendol* (a green jelly made with pandanus leaves).

***Selat Solo*:** A Dutch-inspired meal of sliced beef braised in a broth of garlic, vinegar, sweet soy sauce and Worcestershire sauce.

WALKING TOUR

Explore Solo's Batik Areas

Solo, one of Java's great batik centres, is a living gallery for Indonesia's iconic textile art. In the Batik Kauman and Batik Laweyan neighbourhoods, centuries-old methods are still practised in family-run workshops, where artisans use traditional wax-resistant dyeing techniques to create intricate patterns on fabric. Use a taxi or *ojek* (motorcycle that takes passengers) to travel between neighbourhoods, then wander the alleys and learn more about Indonesia's famous fabric traditions.

1 House of Danar Hadi

House of Danar Hadi (*danarhadibatik.com; 45,000Rp*) is a renowned family-run batik producer and museum with more than 700 valuable batik pieces; an exceptional starting point for your textile journey. During the 45-minute tour you'll learn about the cultural and regional influences on Solo's batik styles, and see how batik is made.

The Drive: Hail a taxi for the trip to Pasaw Klewer and save your energy for wandering around the enormous multistorey market.

2 Pasar Klewer

In contrast to the priceless fabrics at Danar Hadi, the batik at **Pasar Klewer** are cheap-cheap. There's always a lot going on at Solo's large textiles market and you'll find everything from formal shirts to dresses and trousers – all in wonderful printed batik. Be prepared to bargain.

The Walk: Walk around Masjid Agung Keraton to Jl Cakra, to the iron gateway welcoming you to Kauman. This is Jl Cakra, location of your next stop.

RADITYA/SHUTTERSTOCK

Batik tulis

❸ Batik Gunawan Setiawan

To try your hand at the batik process, head for **Batik Gunawan Setiawan** (*instagram.com/batikgunawansetiawan_official*). This respected batik producer, which has an extensive store and a museum, offers drop-in workshops *(100,000Rp)*.

The Walk: Take time to wander around Batik Kauman. On the wall outside Kooken Café, notice the labelled examples of batik patterns.

❹ Kampung Batik Kauman

Kampung Batik Kauman is one of Solo's two historic batik neighbourhoods, and as you wander the narrow streets you'll come across family-owned shops selling batik fabrics and clothing. The evocative neighbourhood is a delight to explore – particularly along Jl Wijaya Kusuma, where some studios have cafes. Arrive before 3pm to see artisans at work.

The Drive: Hail a taxi to Saudagar cafe. This will put you on the fringe of the Batik Laweyan neighbourhood.

❺ Kampung Batik Laweyan

Kampung Batik Laweyan is Solo's other batik neighbourhood. The narrow streets, decorated with murals and lined with potted plants, are enchanting; as much a delight to explore as the family-run batik shops you'll find along them. Stop in at Saudagar cafe to appreciate the old architecture.

The Walk: Ignore the maps and follow your nose – this neighbourhood is best discovered on foot. Head in a westerly direction from Saudagar to your final stop.

❻ Batik Mahkota Laweyan

By now you'll have a trained eye when it comes to batik, so head to **Batik Mahkota Laweyan** *(batikmahkotalaweyan.com)* for something different. This studio specialises in high-quality production of abstract patterns – and it offers workshops, too.

Beyond Solo

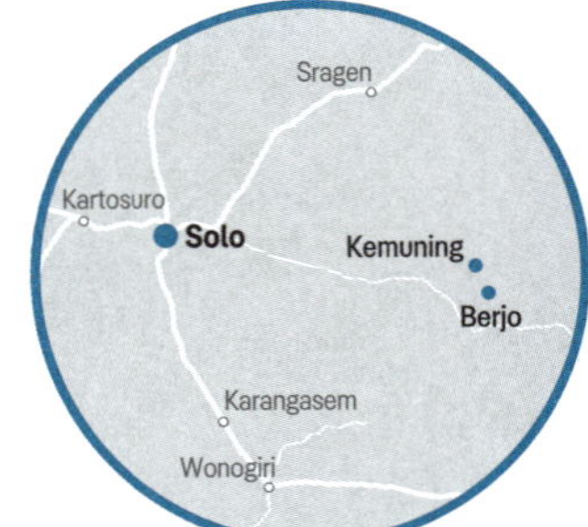

Beyond Solo, the holy peak of Gunung Lawu maintains its vigil over peaceful tea plantations, popular waterfalls and centuries-old temples.

Places

As you move east from Solo, the city transitions into swathes of verdant rice paddies; the land then rises into steep hillsides of tea plantations and strawberry fields before stretching up to the imposing peak of Gunung Lawu, which dominates the skyline. Lawu is a sacred mountain of the Hindu faith, and it only makes sense that there are ancient temples to be found upon its slopes. Climbing Gunung Lawu is a popular activity not restricted to those on religious pilgrimages, with the panoramic views from its peak famous far beyond Central Java. Gorgeous tea plantations, plummeting waterfalls and intriguing temple complexes make this part of Java irresistible.

GETTING AROUND

Experiences in this area tend to be close to each other, and can be combined to form a fulfilling day trip. It's difficult to navigate public transport away from Solo, so consider either hiring a car and driver for the day or driving yourself by car or scooter. Note that the hills are very steep and you'll need a powerful scooter with good brakes. There are not many places in Solo to rent scooters, but Doeloerkoe Homestay *(doeloerkoe.com)* can assist with these and private car hire.

Kemuning

TIME FORM SOLO: **1¼HR**

Enjoy a cool mountain town

A wonderful day trip from Solo is to the village of Kemuning, which sits at the base of Gunung Lawu; the temperatures here are a lot cooler than in Solo, and the air is crisp and clean. The village sees a lot of visitors, and several tourist-oriented attractions have sprung up around the area. Blessed with ideal growing conditions, Kemuning is the perfect place to see picturesque tea plantations, like those found in the Dieng Plateau and other similar regions of Central Java. The plantations here are large, with panoramic views, and they're also set up to entertain tourists: selfie spots and viewpoints are seemingly everywhere, and activities such as paragliding and 4WD tours are also available.

Tucked into a crease in the village landscape is Kalimas *(5000Rp)*, a quaint, riverside gathering spot that's peppered with colourful umbrellas, woven mats beneath them and flanked by small warungs. The river burbles down over collections of rocks that create a few cascades, and towering tree ferns provide some shade. It's a pretty place to chill for a while and take a break from exploring the area, and is popular with families whose little ones splash about in the river.

Capture gorgeous tea-plantation views

The highlands around Kemuning are packed with lofty teahouses offering selfie spots and gorgeous views – and while many live up to the hype, none can compete with the photo ops presented around **Kemuning Sky Hills** *(instagram.com/kemuningskyhills; 30,000Rp)*. Here, a tempered-glass bridge stretches a dramatic 120m over a hillside tea plantation; at its highest point the bridge towers 60m above the ground. While the views are sublime, the walk along the glass bridge can, for many, be quite a mental challenge.

On the hill and just 'behind' the bridge is **Kemuning Sky View** *(instagram.com/kemuningskyview)*, another place to up your social-media game. Buy an 'all-in' ticket *(50,000Rp)* and you'll have access to five places that promise sublime photo opportunities. There are the white bicycles on a zip line above the tea plantation, a white rope bridge leading to an ornate bandstand, a swing (of course), a lookout post and a ski-lift chair system that will transport you – with feet dangling in the breeze – above the plantation.

You'll need to pay 10,000Rp to enter the Kemuning Sky Hills and Kemuning Sky View area, and pay 3000Rp for parking, so be sure to carry smaller denominations with you. On weekends a number of warungs operate along the road leading to the selfie spots.

Visit a mountainside temple

At the foot of Gunung Lawu, not too far from Kemuning, is **Candi Cetho** *(50,000Rp)*, a 15th-century Hindu temple built in a completely different style to nearby Candi Sukuh. It's striking to look at, resembling the Hindu temples found in Bali, and its six tiers are accessed by long staircases and *candi bentar* (split gateways) that open onto each separate part of the complex – much like Bali's iconic Pura Besakih temple (p246). On a clear day, the views from Candi Cetho are lovely (and a popular drawcard on weekends especially), and all levels of the temple can be accessed by visitors unless there is a ceremony taking place.

There are two other, lesser-known sacred sites within the Candi Cetho complex. Pay an additional 7000Rp to enter and follow the signs to unassuming Candi Kethek; it's a few hundred metres further up the hill, and you'll likely pass hikers returning from Gunung Lawu (see p109). On the way back towards Candi Cetho, be sure to stop off at pretty Puri Saraswati, the site of a sacred spring.

THE FALL OF A KINGDOM

The two Hindu temples located around Kemuning and Berjo are a clear indicator to historians that the region, and in particular Gunung Lawu, held a prominent place in the Majapahit kingdom.

The temples, constructed towards the end of the kingdom's rule, are also believed to be connected to the disappearance of Brawijaya V, the last king of Majapahit. King Brawijaya V is believed to have resided and meditated on the lower slopes of Gunung Lawu, a belief that is supported by the existence of the prominent temples. At the end of his reign, during a war with the Kediri kingdom in 1478, Brawijaya is believed to have fled to the mountain instead of facing defeat, living out his days as a hermit.

EATING AROUD GUNUNG LAWU: OUR PICKS

Kebun Hanoman: Enjoy a wide range of Indonesian meals in a peaceful garden setting. This is a good place to sample *wedang*, too. *11am-7pm* $

Tenggir Coffee & Eatery: Enjoy a coffee or tea while relaxing beneath towering trees, close to Candi Sukuh. It's cool and peaceful up here. *10am-5pm* $

Bridge Coffee & Eatery: There's plenty of space (and selfie spots) at this popular resto. The views are gorgeous, too. *10am-10pm Mon-Fri, 9am-10pm Sat, 9am-9pm Sun* $

Ndoro Donker: Tea plantation views with old-world charm. This is one of the most popular places in town. *10am-9pm* $$

HINDU TEMPLES IN JAVA

When visiting Java you will notice almost immediately that the dominant faith is Islam – so you may be wondering why there are so many Hindu temples throughout the island. Some of the oldest temples in Java, including those at the Dieng Plateau and Ambarawa, as well as the Prambanan Temple in Yogyakarta, date back many centuries to when Islam wasn't the main faith here. Hundreds of years ago it was Hinduism, and the many temples left behind are a reminder of those times. They are still visited regularly by the Balinese and others who follow the Hindu faith.

Berjo

TIME FROM SOLO: 1¼HR

Wander around Candi Sukuh

Candi Sukuh *(50,000Rp)* is a small, squat and somewhat truncated pyramid-style of temple that's set high up on the slopes of Gunung Lawu, where the villages peter out. It's often compared to the temples constructed by the Mayan civilisation, and the similarities are astounding; in truth, it is a Hindu temple and, although built in the 15th century, it resembles temples that were in use 1500 years earlier.

Around the small, very carefully manicured complex there are numerous carved stone statues. While it's an interesting temple to visit, Candi Sukuh is also popular for its panoramic views. Climb to the top of the temple (via a short but steep set of centuries-old stone stairs) to take in the full layout of the temple complex and admire the mountains in the distance. If you appreciate the cooler mountain air and would like to linger longer, then go next door to well-forested Tenggir Park *(15,000Rp)*, which has a cafe (with live music on weekends), some glamping bungalows, a few short walking trails and a hillside garden where plants and trees are labelled.

Getting to Candi Sukuh can be a challenge as no public transport services the site, so you'll need to arrive by private car or scooter. It's a very steep drive to reach the temple, so before you go up make sure your brakes are working well. The temple is open from 7am to 4pm.

Relax at Jumog Waterfall

There is nothing wild or challenging about the walk to reach pretty **Jumog Waterfall** *(50,000Rp)* on the slopes of Gunung Lawu – and therein lies its appeal. It might be an easy 350m stroll along a paved pathway from the ticket office to the waterfall itself, but you could nevertheless spend an entire afternoon relaxing here.

The route is lined with warungs and riverside picnic spots marked with umbrellas and woven mats, and what makes the experience magical are the towering tree ferns that line the pretty, cascading river, filtering the dappled sunlight. If you're travelling with kids, they'll appreciate the shallow, human-made pool near the entrance to the waterfall. The waterfall area, open from 8am to 5pm, is particularly busy on weekends and public holidays.

Walk to the base of Grojogan Sewu

Grojogan Sewu *(125,000Rp)* is an impressive 81m-high waterfall that plummets over vegetated cliffs into a surprisingly small pool below. Reaching it requires a bit of effort: the main route involves descending around 1250 steps – a demanding trek for some visitors, especially when faced with the walk back up. It's an enchanting walk, though; trees tower overhead and there are usually a few mischievous monkeys around to keep you entertained. Hold tightly onto your belongings or, better still, don't carry too much stuff – these monkeys are known to steal water, food and sunglasses off visitors.

Once down there prepare to get wet if you get close to the base of the falls, particularly during rainy season when Grojogan

NUGI NATANAEL/SHUTTERSTOCK

Jumog Waterfall, Berjo

Sewu is at its most powerful; it's also at this time of year that a few other smaller misty falls tumble over the surrounding cliffs. For an easier route to the waterfall head to 'Grojogan Sewu Loket 2', the second entrance, which is on the opposite side of the valley. The waterfall is open from 8am to 4pm.

Catch sunrise on Gunung Lawu

Straddling the border between Central Java and East Java, **Gunung Lawu** (3265m) is considered one of the holiest mountains on Java. It's also known for the spectacular views from the peak, and the stratovolcano (which last erupted in 1885) is popular with hikers who tackle the well-used trails to catch sunrise from the summit.

There are three routes to the peak. The 9.2km hike from **Candi Cetho** (p107) is the most popular route as it passes across a fair amount of savanna. The other two trailheads, Cemoro Kandang and Cemoro Sewu, are just a few hundred metres apart near Gondosuli village. The route from Cemoro Sewu is shorter but steeper and the path is quite rocky, while the route starting at Cemoro Kandang is longer in distance but takes a shorter time (it'll take around seven hours to reach the summit).

If you want to go up and return on the same day (*tek-tok*, Indonesians say) then you must leave the trailheads by 5am in order to make it back before dark; another possibility is to leave later in the morning and camp along the trail and then climb the summit before sunrise the following morning. The trails are well worn and you can hike independently – but a guide is useful, particularly if you'd like assistance with setting up logistics and renting hiking or camping gear. It'll cost around 800,000Rp to walk with a guide and 1,000,000Rp if you'd like someone to carry your gear. Agus Susanto *(WhatsApp: +62 896 1060 9190)* has guided on Gunung Lawu (as well as other mountains in Java, Lombok and Sulawesi) for many years; he can help to arrange a guide and set up all logistics.

MYTHS & LEGENDS

Gunung Lawu is the centre of many myths and legends. Some are old, while others live on to the present day, passed between climbers of this famous mountain.

One of these is the legend of the Devil's Market, an occurrence claimed to have been witnessed by many hikers, with the sounds of a crowded marketplace apparently clearly distinguishable upon the slopes. Of course, nothing is visible, and only the sounds have been reported. Another local warning is to avoid wearing the colour green when you climb Gunung Lawu. Green is often associated with the Queen of the South Sea (p95), whose influence extends from the ocean to other mystical places.

LOCAL CUSTOMS & EXPERIENCES

Central Java can be a very conservative area and it is essential that local customs and religious practices are respected. This is especially noticeable in smaller towns and mountainous areas where there isn't as much tourism. Many places you may visit around Central Java will see very few foreigners. You will not find much alcohol, if any at all; Western food may not exist, and only small food carts and warungs will be available. But it's in these areas that you will really be able to soak up the local life – so eat at a warung, buy food on the roadside and chat with people who live in the villages. These experiences often make the best memories.

NOER CUNGKRING/SHUTTERSTOCK

Bukit Mongkrang

Hike up Bukit Mongkrang

Immediately south of Gunung Lawu is **Bukit Mongkrang** *(instagram.com/bukitmongkrangofficial_; 10,000Rp)*, a peak surrounded by strawberry farms and streaked with pockets of forests. The popular, relatively easy hiking trail to its summit (2194m) offers uninterrupted views of **Gunung Lawu** (p109) – particularly captivating early in the morning and at sunset. It's a short but steep hike to the top, taking around 1½ hours for those of average fitness to cover 3km; the trail is well worn (warning: slippery when wet), so you won't get lost and can easily walk it without a guide. You will, however, need to register at the trailhead and leave some form of identity there while you hike. If you're hesitant to leave your passport, an ID card or driver's licence will do. The office is open from 7am to 10pm on weekdays and 24 hours on weekends.

If you want to catch sunrise from the peak during the week, you'll need to camp overnight at one of the designated areas along the route. Take water and snacks with you; there are occasionally one or two warungs that open along the trail, but don't rely on them being open. From the trailhead the route is 6km in total (you return on the same path) but you'll need to first walk 700m from the parking area, making the total distance 7.4km. If you walk at a comfortable pace and take a few breaks along the way, you can walk the trail in 2½ to three hours. Hiking poles can be useful if you descend in the morning, when the trail is still wet from dew.

Semarang

COLONIAL HISTORY | ISLAND GETAWAYS | ANCIENT TEMPLES

Claiming a strategic position on Java's north coast is the captivating city of Semarang. It often flies under travellers' radars, which is surprising given that this major port city (which happens to be the capital of Central Java) is steeped in intriguing history. It has a wonderfully atmospheric old town that is an absolute delight to explore, and is also an access point for Karimunjawa, a cluster of idyllic tropical islands.

Semarang's history harks back to the Dutch colonial era when it was a key port for the Dutch East Indies and the main hub for the Dutch East Indies Railway. Much of the city's architecture stands today as a reminder of that time. Several of Semarang's most prominent landmarks have recently been fully restored, and along with the city's nostalgic and vibrant Kota Lama (old town) are centres of tourism on weekends and holidays in particular.

GETTING AROUND

While the old town is best explored on foot, it's most convenient to get around the rest of the city with the Gojek or Grab apps. Semarang is well connected via its airport (Jenderal Ahmad Yani Airport) and Semarang Tawang train station (trains are affordable, reliable and very comfortable). Well-respected shuttle services like Joglosemar Executive Shuttle Bus *(joglosemarbus.com)* and Daytrans *(daytrans.co.id)* also run between the major regional centres.

TOP TIP

Consider travelling between Semarang and Jakarta by train, as the route is very scenic and seats are spacious. To buy a ticket at Semarang Tawang station you'll need the DANA app installed and connected to your credit card.

Nostalgic Kota Lama

Stroll through a bygone era

Kota Lama, Semarang's romantic old town, should not be missed on a trip to the city. The neighbourhood's streets and buildings date back to the Dutch colonial era in the 17th century, and visitors are surrounded by striking neoclassical and Art Deco architecture as they stroll through this timeless part of the city. Kota Lama is more than just a classic European setting in the heart of Semarang. It is an event that springs to life in the evenings, and an unmissable experience for any visitor to Semarang.

For decades the area withered away as Semarang focused its spending on flashy new malls and developments, but in recent years enough buildings in the historic Kota Lama area have been renovated to make it a popular destination, particularly in the evenings. As the sun sets behind the red dome of the iconic **Gereja Blenduk** church, and as historic lamps light up the pavement, the streets teem with people soaking up Kota Lama's ambience and capturing selfies with evocative

ICONIC BUILDINGS OF KOTA LAMA

Discover the architectural gems of Semarang's old town. Check the buildings' front doors for QR codes; these link to information in English on their history.

START	END	LENGTH
Kantor Pos Semarang	Kota Lama Museum	1.5km; 45min

Begin at 1 **Kantor Pos Semarang**, one of the oldest post offices in Indonesia, and head for 2 **Bank Mandiri**. This building, completed in 1908, influenced the Tropical Modernism style. Over the street is the beautiful 3 **Djakarta Lloyd building**. On the next street right is 4 **Rumah Akar** ('root house'), the facade of an abandoned tobacco house that's now strangled by roots. The iconic 5 **Gereja Blenduk** (p111), Central Java's oldest church, is around the corner.

Walk behind the church to Peek House, built in the neo-Renaissance style in 1886; it's now the 6 **Semarang Contemporary Art Gallery** (p113). On the corner of Jl Lejgen Suprapto and Jl Gelatik is photogenic 7 **Gedung Marba**, one of the first buildings in Semarang with its facade angled on a street corner. Opposite is 8 **Spiegel** (p113), once a luxury-goods store and now an elegant bar.

Around the corner on Jl Cendrawasih is another bar/restaurant, 9 **Marabunta** (p113). Originally the Schouwberg Building, it was built as a theatre; the stained-glass windows show characters from fairy stories. The renovated interiors are fascinating. Wind up with a basic introduction to the area's history at the 10 **Kota Lama Museum**.

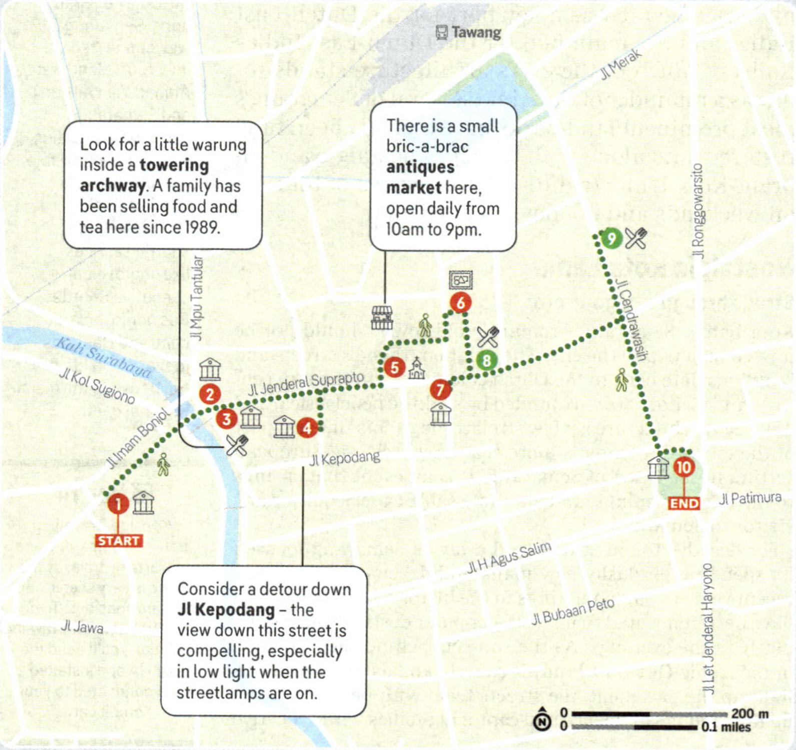

Tawang
Jl Merak
Look for a little warung inside a **towering archway**. A family has been selling food and tea here since 1989.
There is a small bric-a-brac **antiques market** here, open daily from 10am to 9pm.
Jl Ronggowarsito
Jl Mpu Tantular
Kali Surabaya
Jl Kol Sugiono
Jl Jenderal Suprapto
Jl Cendrawasih
Jl Imam Bonjol
Jl Kepodang
START
END
Jl Patimura
Jl H Agus Salim
Jl Bubaan Peto
Jl Jawa
Consider a detour down **Jl Kepodang** – the view down this street is compelling, especially in low light when the streetlamps are on.
Jl Let Jenderal Haryono
0 200 m
0 0.1 miles

backdrops. There are some atmospheric bars and restaurants and while in the evenings these might appeal to Semarang's higher-income residents, a wander through the streets in the mornings will reveal very basic warungs that sell tea and *bakso* (meatball soup) to builders and becak riders.

The most peaceful time to explore the streets and appreciate the architecture of Kota Lama is before 7am, when the light is soft and motorbikes and cars aren't zipping through the old town – but be sure to spend some time here during opening hours (roughly 10am to 8.30pm) too, as the **Semarang Contemporary Art Gallery** *(instagram.com/semaranggallery)* and **Asem Kawak**, a small antiques market, are worth visiting, too. The gallery is closed on Mondays.

Climb the Tower at the Grand Mosque

Take in a view of Semarang

A good place from which to put Semarang into perspective (and to get your bearings) is from the top of the **Asmaul Husna Tower** *(10,000Rp)* at the Grand Mosque of Central Java on Jl Gajah Raya. The imposing tower stands 99m high (to represent the 99 names of Allah) and from the viewing platform at the top you'll have 360-degree views far beyond the city limits. There are a few coin-operated telescopes up there, so take some 1000Rp coins if you'd like to use them. Late afternoon and early evening up here are particularly lovely. The tower is open from 8am to 9pm daily, but closed from 11.30am to 12.30pm and 5pm to 6.30pm. On Fridays the tower is closed from 11am to 1pm.

Get Lost in Lawang Sewu

The building with a thousand doors

Lawang Sewu *(30,000Rp)* is the most recognisable historic building in Semarang and, located as it is in the heart of the city at one of the main roundabouts, it is almost impossible to miss. This grand colonial-era building was opened in 1907 as the head office for the Dutch East Indies Railway, and earned its nickname Lawang Sewu ('thousand doors') for all the doors it contains. The number is exaggerated, but the building is extremely large and has so many archways, corridors and rooms that it isn't impossible to get lost inside.

Over time the building fell into a bad state of disrepair, but it was eventually restored and reopened 2011. Wander through and you will find many rooms filled with nothing

A HAUNTING HISTORY

Lawang Sewu has a violent and bloody past, and it's said to be one of the most haunted places in Indonesia – this may come as no surprise once you learn about the dark history of the building. Originally the headquarters of the Dutch East Indies Railway Company, Lawang Sewu was repurposed during the Japanese occupation of WWII, when it reportedly served as a prison and site of torture and executions.

One well-known, horrific episode occurred in 1945 when a fight broke out on the premises and bodies from the resulting casualties were buried in the building. Years later they were moved to a cemetery. Perhaps more infamous are the cells in the basement, which were the scene of many grisly tortures, and worse.

The kopi susu Kota Lama is delicious.

EATING IN KOTA LAMA: OUR PICKS

Sedjenak Koffie: Pop into this quiet, atmospheric and out-the-way cafe for excellent coffee and a simple meal. *10am-10pm Mon-Fri, to 11pm Sat & Sun* $

Red Soul Coffee & Bistro: Find many Asian favourites here, from Korean spicy chicken wings to *nasi Bali* (rice dish with side dishes). *11am-midnight* $$

Spiegel: With its grand colonial-era style, artisanal cocktails and eclectic menu, dining at Spiegel feels more like an occasion than simply a meal. *10am-1am* $$

Marabunta: There's live music every night in this historic ex-theatre. Come for dinner and a drink – the cocktail list is extensive. *11am-1am* $$

WHY I LOVE SEMARANG

Narina Exelby,
Lonely Planet writer

I was completely captivated by Semarang the moment I walked through Kota Lama (p111). The old town is packed with character and it's a compelling juxtaposition of grand, beautifully renovated Art Deco and neoclassical buildings alongside ones that are gently being lost to time.

My most memorable morning in Semarang unfolded when I took a dawn stroll from the old town along the canal, and into the Chinese neighbourhood. It's here that you'll find Gang Lombok and its famous *lumpia* warung, as well as the Tay Kak Sie temple, which dates to 1746. Chat with locals over coffee in a small warung and you've the makings of an unforgettable morning.

but the invisible memories of the past. Some areas are set up with a timeline of the history of the railway, and the histories surrounding the building and the company that constructed it. Be aware that most of the signs, posters and information displayed are in Bahasa Indonesia, so you'll want to have Google Translate at the ready. One corridor contains some souvenir shops and there are some food places around the courtyard. Lawang Sewu is open from 8am to 8pm weekdays and to 10pm on weekends; it will take around an hour to explore this building including time to snap photographs.

Pay Tribute to a Revered Admiral

Visit Semarang's oldest temple

Sam Poo Kong *(adult/child 40,000/20,000Rp)* is a striking temple complex that is part shrine, part historical site and, these days is celebrated as a crossroad of cultures and a gathering place for visitors of all religions. Its origins can be traced back to the early 15th century, when Chinese Muslim admiral Zheng He (also known as Cheng Ho) is believed to have landed here during one of his legendary maritime voyages and used a nearby cave as a place for prayer. The original temple was apparently destroyed by a landslide in the early 1700s; a new cave was created by the area's Chinese community and the site has since evolved to include five temples that blend Chinese and Javanese styles. Aside from the impressive red and green tiered structures with soaring roofs, highlights of the site include a large relief panel that tells the story of Zheng He (there are explanations in English), and the large statue of the revered admiral.

An Evening at Simpang Lima

Fun for all the family

Simpang Lima, located in the centre of Semarang, consists of a large field of green grass situated at the intersection of five main arterial roads. It basically acts as a massive roundabout – but come evening time Simpang Lima is much more than this; it springs to life and families from all over the city gather here for a fun evening out. The footpath surrounding the large field lights up with flashing, colourful, neon-covered electric scooters and carts (elaborately decorated with unicorns, dinosaurs and other images) for hire.

EATING IN SEMARANG: OUR PICKS

Kuliner Simpang Lima: Set among the warungs around Simpang Lima, this popular spot offers generous servings of Indonesian dishes. *4.30pm-midnight* $

Lumpia Gang Lombok: For decades this family-run warung has been known for its delicious *lumpia. 7am-4pm Mon-Thu, to 5pm Fri-Sun* $

Gion – The Sushi Bar: There's an overwhelming choice of beautifully fresh sushi and other Japanese dishes at this slick resto in DP Mall. *10am-9pm* $$

Silverspoon Restaurant & Bar: Delicious Western and Indonesian food in luxurious surrounds with top-tier service. *hours vary* $$

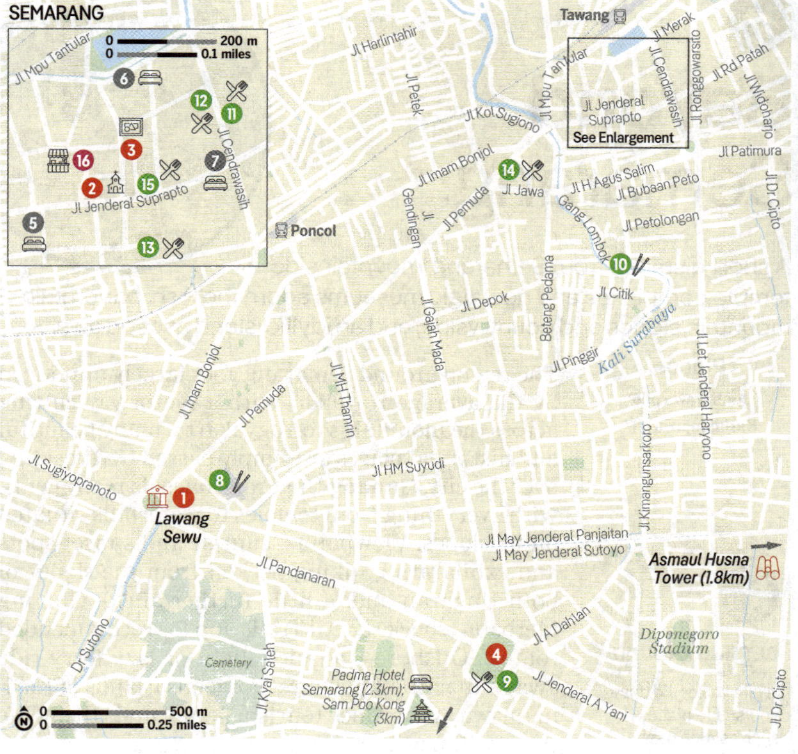

Within the massive grassed area there are numerous activities to keep children entertained. Everything from poster painting to a mini motordrome for kids is designed to make your evening one that the family will remember. Across the road warungs sell every kind of local dish you could think of.

Simpang Lima is easy to find as it is right in the heart of the city. Surrounding the square are five-star hotels, towering apartment complexes and glittering shopping malls. You could even be forgiven for assuming that the city itself had been specifically designed around Simpang Lima.

Beyond Semarang

A short distance from Semarang, mountainside temple complexes and nostalgic museums adorn the lush, panoramic mountain slopes and countryside, and an idyllic island escape awaits.

Places

The region around Semarang goes largely unnoticed by the average traveller. With a motorway cutting across the mountains to Yogyakarta, many beautiful and historical places are simply passed by. Presiding over the city, Gunung Ungaran conceals many gems, with everything from temples to waterfalls situated on its slopes. Viewpoints, sunrise and sunset spots and exhilarating hiking beckon from the slopes of both Ungaran and, a little further afield, Gunung Merbabu (check the All Trails app for recommended routes). Offshore – a quick flight or lazy ferry ride away – the little-known yet gorgeous islands of Karimunjawa await. Once tourism finally finds them, life there will never be the same.

GETTING AROUND

While you could drive yourself to places such as Ambarawa, it can be quite a hassle to rent a car or vehicle, so your best bet is to find a friendly taxi driver who'll agree to drive you for a day rate. For Karimunjawa, catch the ferry from Jepara on the coast north of Semarang; the schedule is irregular, so check with your accommodation for current departure days. The regular ferry takes about five hours, while the fast boat takes around two hours. Susi Air *(susiair.com)* flies between Semarang and Karimunjawa (40 minutes) on Mondays, Fridays and Sundays.

Ambarawa

TIME FROM SEMARANG: **1HR**

Hike around Candi Gedong Songo

Candi Gedong Songo *(instagram.com/pesona_kabsemarang; 75,000Rp)* is an ancient Hindu temple complex located high on the hills near Ambarawa. The temples here were built around the 8th century and, along with the strikingly similar temples at Dieng, are believed to possibly be the oldest Hindu temples in Java – older even than Yogyakarta's impressive Prambanan.

It's said that Candi Gedong Songo originally consisted of nine temple clusters; today, however, only five remain and it's thought that stone ruins of the other temples might exist higher up, beyond temple number five.

The temple complex is 1200m above sea level and to reach Candi 5, the temple furthest from the entrance, involves walking a paved, well-maintained trail over a couple of steep hills. The effort is worth it, though, as the area has clean air, the temples are incredible and the panoramic views amazing. It's about 2.5km from the entrance to Candi 5, and if you're daunted by the prospect of walking this you have two other options: once you've reached Candi 5 you can take a shorter, steeper

Karimunjawa

route back down (this will cut about 1km off the whole route, and bypasses all of the temples) or you can visit the temples on horseback *(250,000Rp)*. The docile horses, which are stabled close to the entrance, are well looked after and you'll be led by a groom (who's on foot) the whole way.

Ride a vintage train

Ambarawa's nostalgic **Museum Kereta Api Ambarawa** *(instagram.com/wisata.museumkeretaapiambarawa; 30,000Rp)* is a recommended stop for anyone who has a love of trains. It's set in a beautifully preserved station that was in use as far back as the time of the Dutch East Indies Railway, and more than 20 original steam locomotives – all lovingly cared for – are housed here. Also on display around the railyard are several other engines, the original ticket office and station structures, and a complete timeline of the area's rail history. The best time to visit is on Fridays, Saturdays or Sundays, when you can take a scenic ride on the vintage diesel-powered train that runs from the station a few times a day. Find departure times on the museum's Instagram page; tickets are 125,000Rp.

Karimunjawa

TIME FROM SEMARANG: **30MIN**
TIME FROM JEPARA: **2HR/5HR**

Escape to an island paradise

Kick off your flip-flops, shift down a gear and settle into the tropical paradise of Karimunjawa. This gorgeous 27-island archipelago comprises powder-white beaches fringed with palm trees and reefs flourishing with stunning coral gardens. The main island, Karimunjawa, holds the key to exploring this utopia and is where you will find budget-friendly accommodation, low-key eateries and local services.

AN OLD DUTCH FORT

Benteng Fort Willem I, located in the town of Ambarawa, was constructed in 1835 by the Dutch not as a defensive structure, but as a a logistics and storage depot. It was capable of housing up to 12,000 troops, as evidenced by the style of its construction, which features many windows, staircases and living quarters. During the Japanese occupation of the area in 1942, the fort was used as a prison for Dutch and local citizens who rejected the new regime. Many atrocities occurred here at this time, and many of the prisoners died within these walls. At the end of 2025 the fort reopened as a restaurant and shopping centre *(instagram.com/bentengambarawa)*.

EXPLORE KARIMUNJAWA BY SCOOTER

Get to know the beaches and viewpoints of Karimunjawa on this scooter tour. This route is best done as a full-day trip.

START	END	LENGTH
Pantai Bobby	Sunset Beach	46km; 1 day

Begin early morning at popular 1 **Pantai Bobby**, a powder-white, palm-fringed beach where you can snap sunrise photos. Take the coastal road through town then up the west coast. For selfie ops or an elevated ocean outlook, head to 2 **Bukit Love** viewpoint.

Continue around the coast for 6km, until you see the *candi bentar* (split gateway) on your right. Drive through the gates and uphill; from the parking area *(2000Rp)* it's a 120m walk to an important Muslim pilgrimage site, the 3 **Makam Sunan Nyamplungan** (grave of Sunan Nyamplungan). Back on the main road, after 2.5km, follow the sign for 4 **Pantai Alano**. You'll reach a well-kept beach; it's a wonderful place to swim and relax, and there's a small warung.

Continue 'up' the island to the national park's 5 **Tracking Mangrove** site. A boardwalk loops through the mangroves; climb the tower for good views. Drive another 9km to scout 6 **Laendra Sunset Beach** as a potential sunset spot, then stick to the coastline and head to 7 **Pantai Mrican**, where seaweed is cultivated and dried, and 8 **Pelabuhan Wetan** to watch boat-builders at work. Retrace your tracks to the *candi bentar*; after 2.5km follow the signs to 9 **Sunset Beach**. You'll have a choice of epic (and very popular) sunset spots around here.

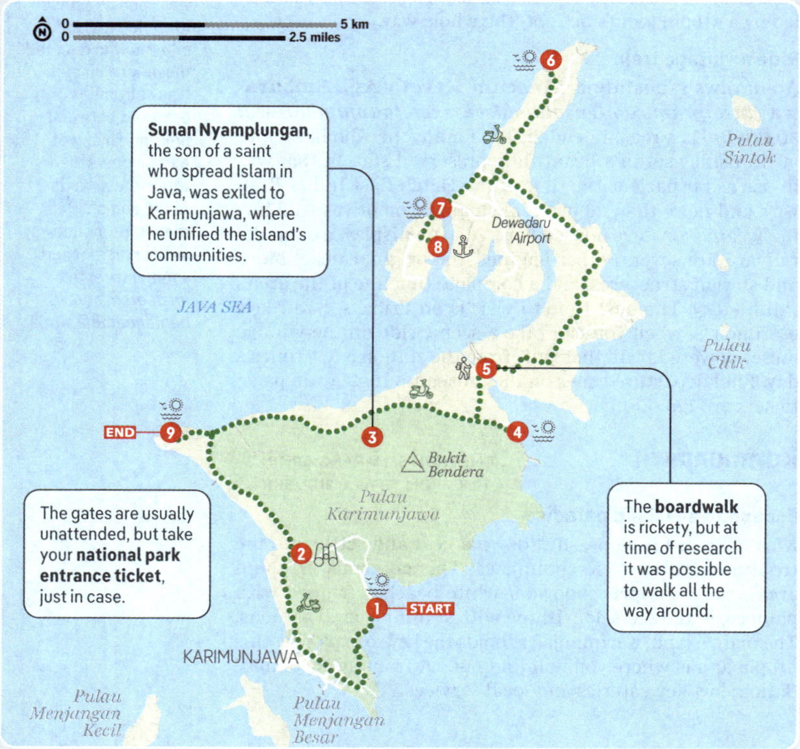

Sunan Nyamplungan, the son of a saint who spread Islam in Java, was exiled to Karimunjawa, where he unified the island's communities.

The gates are usually unattended, but take your **national park entrance ticket**, just in case.

The **boardwalk** is rickety, but at time of research it was possible to walk all the way around.

0 5 km
0 2.5 miles
JAVA SEA
Dewadaru Airport
Pulau Sintok
Pulau Cilik
Bukit Bendera
Pulau Karimunjawa
KARIMUNJAWA
Pulau Menjangan Kecil
Pulau Menjangan Besar
START
END

The pace of life here is slow and relaxed, and it's tempting to commit all your time to lying in a beachside hammock – but don't leave Karimunjawa without taking a day to go island-hopping and snorkelling; there's an abundance of marine life and the archipelago has some truly astounding coral gardens. You'll pay around 250,000Rp if you join a group trip or 2,000,000Rp for a private boat (lunch usually included), and you can set this up through your accommodation.

Beach- and sunset-hunting are other favourite pastimes, and you'll need to rent a scooter (about 100,000Rp a day) to get around. Be sure to carry cash as there are entrance fees to some beaches, usually 5000Rp or 10,000Rp; it's money well spent as these beaches are cared for (unfortunately there's often a lot of plastic on the unattended ones). If you'd like to get some exercise there's a waterfall you can hike to (ask your accommodation for a guide) and **Floating Paradise** *(floatingparadise.id)* offers yoga classes and kayaking sessions, too.

Post-sunset, **Alun Alun** Karimunjawa (the town square) is the place to be for street food and fresh seafood. In the high season from June to September the education-focused non-profit Kejora *(kejorakarimunjawa.com)* arranges cultural evenings at Bukit Love, where local dancers and musicians showcase their talents. Karimunjawa has the only private observatory in Indonesia, and scanning the night skies from **Deepsky Villa** *(deepsky-villa.com; 100,000Rp)* is an unforgettable – and mind-blowing – way to spend an evening.

When planning your trip keep in mind that weekends are busy with domestic tourists. There is an ATM on Karimunjawa but it's best to arrive with cash on hand as when you reach the ferry port or airport you'll be ushered to the national park desk to pay the 150,000Rp (cash only) park entrance. Keep these tickets on you at all times.

A Susi Air *(susiair.com)* light aircraft flies to Karimunjawa three times a week (Friday, Sunday, Monday) from Semarang and from Yogyakarta. Online bookings open mid-month for the following month. If you fly in, ask your accommodation to arrange a pickup for you as there are no taxis at the tiny airport.

KARTINI, A NATIONAL HEROINE

Pioneering journalist Raden Adjeng Kartini, recognised as one of Indonesia's National Heroes, was raised in Jepara, the gateway to Karimunjawa. Known for advocating fiercely for women's rights, Kartini believed education was the key to liberating women from oppression, and her ideals laid the groundwork for Indonesia's women's movement.

Through her short lifetime Kartini wrote extensively about topics including politics, education and public welfare; after her death aged 25 (four days after giving birth), these letters were published in a book titled *Door Duisternis tot Licht (From Dark Comes Light)*. In 2025 UNESCO inscribed Kartini's letters in its Memory of the World Register. Indonesia celebrates Kartini Day on the anniversary of her birthday, 21 April.

EATING AROUND KARIMUNJAWA: OUR PICKS

Eco Casa Resto: This beachside restaurant serves healthy meals and smoothie bowls plus Indonesian and Italian fare. *7am-9am, 11.30am-2.30pm & 5pm-9pm* **$$**

Kalinda Bakery: Indulge in freshly baked cakes and pastries a short walk from the port, and pop into neighbouring Karimunjawa Coffee Shop for coffee. *7am-10pm* **$**

Amore Cafe: Serving seafood, snacks and drinks, this cafe is a fantastic sunset option in Karinumjawa town. *10am-11pm* **$**

Sabar by Alam Kita: Enjoy a gorgeous ocean view alongside a tasty lunch. The small menu features absolutely delicious Indonesian food. *11am-8pm* **$$**

Dieng Plateau

SPECTACULAR VIEWS | SULPHUROUS LAKES | UNIQUE CULTURE

GETTING AROUND

Local minibuses are available from the town of Wonosobo to the village of Dieng. From here you can walk to many of the most popular sites with a reasonable level of fitness and trusty footwear.

The best way to get around the Dieng Plateau is by private car or scooter. Travelling by large tour bus may limit the places you can visit, as roads are steep and at times narrow. Also reconsider 4WD tours, as many of the places they will take you are accessible with your own vehicle or by foot for a lot less money.

The gorgeous and scenic panoramas found at the Dieng Plateau cannot be missed if you are travelling through Central Java. At over 2000m high, this volcanic plateau offers incredible views, serene tea farms, bubbling volcanic craters and placid mountaintop lakes. With the mosques, the terraced ricefields, the oxen and buffalo, there's a decidedly different vibe here that's well worth checking out if your itinerary has the time.

Hindu temples, among the oldest in Java, dot the plateau, though they pale in comparison to those in places such as Prambanan or Borobudur. Many Javanese long to visit if only for one goal: to feel cold for the first time. It gets chilly up here.

Be aware that, as in many parts of Java, men and women travelling together may need to attest they have a marriage certificate before sharing a room.

More than Matcha

Green tea, coffee and dreamy panoramas

The Dieng Plateau has many examples of responsible tourism, with its natural resources being brought to the fore. One example of this is evident at the area's tea plantations. These were originally owned by the Dutch, but after independence were quickly purchased by the local government, which has since gone to great lengths to preserve them and the traditional ways in which they are operated. The carbon footprint of the Dieng Plateau stays extremely low, with handpicking operations favoured over machinery, and the tea farms themselves produce far lower carbon emissions than modern, mechanised industry.

At the farms, local residents have also been able to turn one of their most prolific resources into tourist destinations. To do this they added a few viewpoints and a coffee shop or two, and simply opened the fields up with welcome signs. In a nutshell, visitors love it. Tea farms, with their beautifully

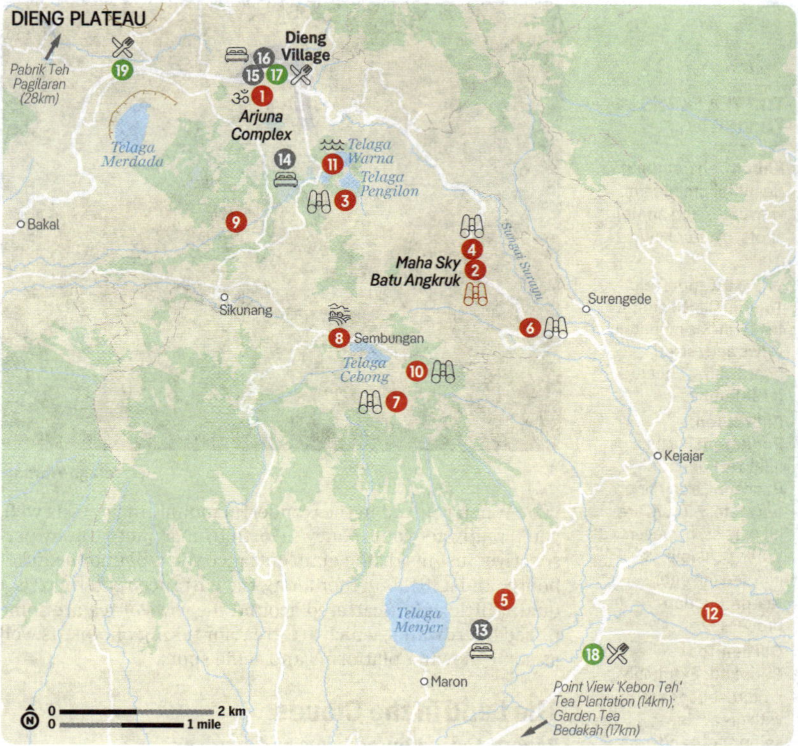

DIENG PLATEAU

HIGHLIGHTS
1 Arjuna Complex
2 Maha Sky Batu Angkruk

SIGHTS
3 Batu Pandang Ratapan Angin
4 Bukit Awan Sikapuk
see 1 Candi Sembadra
5 Kebun Teh Panama
6 Pintu Langit
7 Puncak Seroja
8 Sembungan Village
9 Sikidang Crater
10 Sikunir Hill
11 Telaga Warna
12 Wisata Kebun Teh Tambi

SLEEPING
13 Agora Home
14 Fifa Homestay
15 Green Savanah
16 Homestay Cemara

EATING
17 Kedai Ongklok Dieng 2
18 Opor Entok Pak Zen
see 14 Syra
19 Waroeng Pass

ENTERTAINMENT
see 1 Dieng Culture Festival

manicured leaves, rows of neatly trimmed bushes and orderly style, are a dream for photographers, both professional and amateur. In Dieng, most of them also have a backdrop of mountains, clouds or both. The brilliant green colours set against the bright blue sky look incredible, and it's no wonder these locations see a constant stream of visitors.

There are plenty of places to choose from around the Dieng Plateau, so you will certainly be spoilt for choice. Most will just appear alongside the road while you are out exploring, and visitors almost always drop in to them spontaneously. One of our favourite tea farms is **Kebun Teh Panama** *(instagram.com/kebuntehpanama; 10,000Rp)*. A little away from the main road, this one has the added bonus of partially overlooking a

TOP TIP

Aside from bringing a sweater, carry cash in small notes. Every viewpoint, car park and attraction will cost you money, and cash is king in Dieng. Hang on to entry tickets as they may allow access to more than one place (see p123).

TOP TEA FARMS TO VISIT

Kebun Teh Panama: Beautiful green farm with cafes and photo spots, overlooking a lake.

Wisata Kebun Teh Tambi: This beautiful tea farm has mountain views and raised boardwalks. Located on Jl Tambi.

Pabrik Teh Pagilaran: Further afield is Pabrik Teh Pagilaran, a working tea factory. Tours are hit or miss, however. When possible, you can see the entire tea-production process.

Garden Tea Bedakah: Extremely picturesque tea farm with great views, selfie spots and coffee.

Point View 'Kebon Teh' Tea Plantation: For a more authentic tea-farm experience, without the tourist selfie spots and crowds.

ALEXANDERSTEVE80/SHUTTERSTOCK

Telaga Warna

lake. When you add in the wonderful mountain views as well, you'll really get your money's worth from a photography perspective. Just inside the main entrance you will find the ticket booth, and a little further along the entrance road there is a quaint little cafe. Scattered around the rows of tea are some raised boardwalks, which are great for taking photos, as well as some viewing platforms and selfie spots.

The Land in the Clouds

Panoramas, coloured lakes and sunrises

The Dieng Plateau is famous throughout Java for its amazing panoramas. Just a simple drive into the highlands will open up views so extraordinary that you will find yourself constantly scanning the road ahead for a place to stop. It was always inevitable that a place such as Dieng would begin to build cafes and restaurants commanding views of the surrounding valleys, as well as viewpoints on the highest peaks; especially once word spread and tourists began trickling in. However, Dieng has done a wonderful job with this, giving weary tourists plenty of opportunities to pull over to snap photos, and to take a well-earned rest at the same time. Note, however, that for this reason, traffic in the area can be slow and the driving can become tiresome.

EATING ON DIENG PLATEAU: OUR PICKS

Syra: A one-stop restaurant popular with bus tours, with great views, tasty food and friendly service. Some English spoken. *7.30am-9pm* $

Kedai Ongklok Dieng 2: One of several in a local chain, this branch is the best to try Dieng's speciality, *mie ongklok*, a special noodle dish. *8am-9pm* $

Waroeng Pass: Great cheap eat that can box food for takeout, with simple tables for those who eat in. *24hr Fri-Wed* $

Opor Entok Pak Zen: Duck *soto* (soup) and other specialties make this spot popular, though it's a bit out of town. *10am-8pm* $

There are plenty of amazing viewpoints around Dieng. You will spy them from far below, and they will pop up ahead as soon as the road begins to ramp up sharply. Places such as **Maha Sky Batu Angkruk** *(15,000Rp)* stand out, with a myriad of brightly coloured selfie spots scattered across viewing platforms overlooking the valleys far below. It sounds gimmicky, and in reality it is, but it also has some of the best views in the area, and has the added bonus of easy accessibility for the elderly or mobility restricted, with no walking or climbing required.

There are many places to stay along the same road with incredible views as well. New homestays and B&Bs seemingly appear every week in Dieng. Here you can certainly see why the area is known as the 'Land in the Clouds', with constant banks of cloud drifting lazily past, wafting in and around the viewpoints, cafes and homestays.

Most of Dieng's viewpoints are topped with cafes, and those that are not will usually have a nominal entry and parking fee. One such place is **Batu Pandang Ratapan Angin** *(15,000Rp)*, located on a peak overlooking the popular, bright-green **Telaga Warna**. The best views of this lake are from this viewpoint, which also offers near-360-degree panoramas from multiple spots.

The most famous viewpoint in Dieng by far is **Sikunir Hill** *(15,000Rp)*. Popular mostly for sunrise, it can get clouded in and even wet and rainy later in the day, depending upon the time of year. Sikunir Hill isn't really easy to get to, as the road climbs high and becomes very narrow and broken. Best access is probably by scooter or small 4WD; however, it is definitely passable, and many make the trek before dawn every day. One interesting thing to note is that the road to Sikunir Hill will also take you through **Sembungan Village**, recognised as the highest village in Java.

BEST PLACES TO SEE THE VIEWS

Sikunir Hill: The most popular sunrise point in Dieng; it can get very crowded, but in a party kind of way. Also quite chilly in the wee hours.

Pintu Langit: Sunrise spot on the road up to Dieng, with viewing platforms and selfie spots. Similar to Sikunir in terms of cold.

Maha Sky Batu Angkruk: Bridges and viewing platforms overlook panoramic views popular for sunsets.

Bukit Awan Sikapuk: Not far from Maha Sky, this simple viewpoint has outstanding sunrise views. Less crowded.

Puncak Seroja: Beautiful lake views from a viewpoint accessible via a hike up from the car park.

Ancient Hindu Temples

Local history and culture

One of the most visited attractions around the Dieng Plateau is the group of temples at the **Arjuna Complex** *(50,000Rp)*. It's worth noting that the **Sikidang Crater** (p124) can be viewed with the same ticket. (So hang onto it; and currently, it's an easily lost strip of thermal paper!)

Arjuna Temple is on Jl Arjuna Barat, with the car park right alongside the main road. Google Maps tends to be a little problematic in this area, and a lot of the temples simply do not exist in the locations marked on the app. But enter Arjuna Temple or **Candi Sembadra** (or just ask people) and you will be directed to the correct place. Right beside the car park you will find one temple, but the main complex is a couple of hundred metres down the footpath. Midway you will find the ticket booth.

The Arjuna Complex isn't large, and only really consists of several small structures, set next to each other amid a grassy area where (incongruously) you may find buskers dressed up

MISSING TEMPLES

The Dieng Plateau temples are famous for being among the oldest in Java. The Arjuna Complex houses the best examples of the incredible temple architecture. In total, there are nine temples preserved at Dieng, though Dutch histories recorded up to 117 temples in the area. Today, though faint remains of structures and scattered artefacts are still being found, there are no signs of these other temples. What happened to them is a mystery, although the widespread belief is that they were raided by locals, who used the stones for road construction. In 1807 restoration began on the remaining temples in Dieng, and by 1830 the complex was opened to the public.

IRENE ISKANDAR 41/SHUTTERSTOCK

Sikidang Crater

as Teletubbies or Disney characters. It's hard to argue that adds anything to the ancient mystique, but it certainly is a quirk of visiting, and families with young kids may appreciate that there's a bit of entertainment for the toddlers.

The interesting thing about these temples is that they date back to about the 8th or 9th centuries, making them among the oldest Hindu temples in Java. Once you finish strolling around them, there are exits in two directions. Make your way out the same way you came if you parked at the car park, otherwise you might end up in a totally different spot.

Boil, Boil, Toil & Trouble

A volcanic crater you can get close to

Sikidang Crater *(50,000Rp)* is a highly volcanic area, and the pit is constantly boiling, causing an ever-present steam cloud to emanate from it. Behind it, a hillside is polka-dotted with yellow crust from sulphur gas, and it's worth noting you may find it hard to breathe at times if the wind blows into your face. Those with breathing issues such as asthma may want to just look from afar rather than venture down into the crater.

If you arrive from **Arjuna Temple** (p123), scan the barcode on your combined ticket at the turnstiles; otherwise, purchase a ticket and keep it for visiting Arjuna next. From the entrance you simply have to follow the boardwalk to the crater, detour to the hillside, and then continue following it to the exit. There isn't much else to see at Sikidang; however, it does give you a good insight into the volcanic nature of the area. You will also get the opportunity to have some local snacks or to stock up on souvenirs as you leave past all the shops and local warungs.

Disappearing Dreadlocks & Much More

Jazz performances, fireworks and haircutting

The **Dieng Culture Festival** *(festivaldieng.id; 1-/2-day 300,000/350,000Rp)* is held in August every year on the Dieng Plateau. The initiative started in 2010, with the purpose of promoting cultural tourism in the region. Although the event hasn't been running very long, it has rapidly grown in popularity. One of the main reasons for this revolves around the local phenomenon of the children of Dieng and their dreadlocked or *gimbal* hair.

From an early age, the children of Dieng grow hair that forms dreadlocks of its own accord. Locals believe that the children have been chosen by the ancestors to accept the gift of their *gimbal* hair, and they must live with it until the children themselves ask for it to be cut off. To remove the hair without the blessing of the child is believed to bring bad luck not just upon the parents and family of the child, but upon the entire village in the form of sickness or disaster.

When a child requests the removal of their hair, they accompany the request with a wish that the parents are obliged to fulfil. If the wish is too extravagant for this to be possible, then it is decided that the child is not yet ready to have their hair shaved. The hair-shaving ceremony is a big event in the lives of the children of Dieng, and is held during the Dieng Culture Festival each year. In front of the main temple at the Arjuna Complex, the children come one by one to have their hair removed. The hair is then taken to the lake, where it is submerged in the waters as a symbol of sending it back to their ancestors.

While this ceremony (usually on the last day) is a large part of the Dieng Culture Festival, there is a lot more to the event as well. There's a jazz event held on one night, usually in freezing or sub-zero temperatures. Called Jazz above the Clouds, it is becoming a widely anticipated event each year. Just remember to bring warm clothes if you plan to attend. During the day, traditional art and dance performances can be enjoyed, and at night-time there are fireworks displays.

One of the other big drawing cards over the years has been the traditional release of lanterns into the night sky. This has been cancelled in the past due to environmental concerns, and although still on the schedule for future events, there is no guarantee that it will occur.

Accommodation in Dieng gets booked out months or even longer in advance for the festival. Get in early, or search for options further afield. Public transport can be caught to nearby Wonosobo; from there you can catch a minibus to Dieng.

ONOMATOPOEIA ONGKLOK

Mie Ongklok is the regional speciality here, a hearty soup with thick broth and chewy noodles, usually served with bean sprouts, scallions and other veggies, as well as a skewer or two of beef *sate* (thin morsels of beef roasted to perfection). The *sate* can often be swapped for chicken, or left off entirely if you're avoiding animal-based protein. For vegans this dish can be tricky – the broth is often made with chicken, anchovy, shrimp or beef stock, so it's best to check first before ordering. The name comes from the sound made by the noodle basket being dipped into the broth repeatedly, making a *klok...klok* sound.

Beyond Dieng Plateau

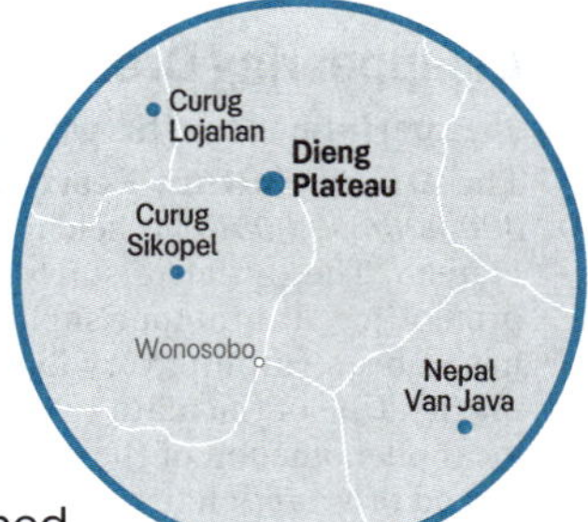

Those venturing beyond Dieng will find untamed jungles, plummeting waterfalls and villages high on the sides of ancient volcanoes.

Places

The regions around the Dieng Plateau are a rolling, many-peaked conglomeration of volcanic hills and troughs that define the land and the people who reside upon it. At this altitude there are only a few villages and even fewer small towns dotted across the landscape, laced with tea plantations, tobacco and potato farms. Those who dare to venture here, far beyond Java's well-trodden trails, will find a wealth of natural treasures hiding in the remote wilderness. Tackling long treks through difficult terrain and pushing transport to the limit will reward you with rarely seen views and memories to cherish.

GETTING AROUND

The mountainous region around Dieng is best navigated by private vehicle. A rented car and driver would also suffice; however, some viewpoints and places such as Nepal Van Java are difficult to access without a scooter, motorbike or 4WD. Public transport is scarce, except small minibuses between major towns such as Wonosobo and Dieng. Plan your time and prepare well, as services are few and far between away from the few small towns in this region.

Nepal Van Java

TIME FROM DIENG PLATEAU: **2½HR**

Visit a colourful village

Nepal Van Java is a brightly coloured village in Central Java, high up on the slopes of Gunung Sumbing.

Even though the village still operates in its traditional agricultural capacity, it is also a popular tourist destination. This came about after several local students made the decision to brighten up their village by painting the houses in loud, very bright colours. The result was an instant home run for tourism in the town, something that barely existed before.

Locals in the village are amazing and friendly. They love that visitors come to see their little town, and although the tourist spending here goes a long way, they never push for you to spend your money. This approach is a breath of fresh air, and one reason visitors keep returning.

One important tip for visiting Nepal Van Java is to use a strong, reliable vehicle or scooter to get here. The hill leading up to the village is very steep, and once here even many locals have to park at the bottom of the hill, as access to the village itself is very difficult. Try to visit on weekdays, as weekends and holidays can get very crowded, and parking, while ample, can fill up fast.

M DZ FAHMI/SHUTTERSTOCK

Nepal Van Java

Curug Sikopel

TIME FROM DIENG PLATEAU: 1HR

Extreme waterfall chasing

If you are around the Dieng Plateau and have had enough of plantations and views, then why not opt for a good old-fashioned waterfall adventure? There are a couple of fantastic waterfalls in the area, and both are reasonably close to the Dieng village centre. However, both of these waterfalls can take some getting to – quite a challenge that may not be for the faint-hearted.

The first of these is **Curug Sikopel**. This 30m-tall monster can really turn it on when there's been a lot of rain. It's powerful and strong, so you won't want to venture too close, but the view and experience of just being near it are amazing. To get to Curug Sikopel involves a lot of up-and-down mountains and hills with some sketchy roads that have big drops on either side. Make sure you have a vehicle that's in good condition and can handle some steep inclines, with competent brakes for the road back down. Once at the waterfall, expect to navigate a lot of stairs before you actually reach the bottom. If you're here during the wet season, you will also be rewarded with several other waterfalls that spring to life along the way.

VAN JAVAS

Nepal Van Java got its nickname due to the resemblance the village houses had to those in Nepal, bearing the same 'stacked' appearance. Dusun Butuh (Butuh Hamlet) is certainly more of a mouthful than Nepal Van Java, and no surprise, other spots in Java have adopted this nomenclature as well.

Paris Van Java is the nickname of Bandung, and a section of road heading to Dieng – with its alpine-like mountains and verdant valleys – is Swiss Van Java. One can imagine that as the 'Van Java' craze catches on more cities, towns and villages will hop on the bandwagon, but for now anyway, it's just those three.

EATING & DRINKING BEYOND DIENG

Payung Teduh Coffee Shop: The beautiful view is why people stop for a cup of *kopi susu* (coffee) here. *6am-6pm* $

Warung Makan Lombok Ndeso: Colourful spot with a simple garden, with fried Indonesian specialties, smoothies and drinks. *8am-6pm* $

Warung Mak E: Sit on the floor or outside on benches and enjoy simple, home-cooked Indonesian food, with instant coffee or *teh* (tea). *7am-9.30pm* $

Warung Makan Bang Jaya: In the middle of the hive of houses, this spot has an overlook that's perfect for sipping simple instant noodles and *kopi susu*. *6am-midnight* $

FOUNTAIN OF YOUTH

When visiting Curug Sikopel, you might want to be aware of the local myths and legends that surround it. The locals consider the pool of water at the base of the falls sacred. Usually this would mean you'd be forbidden to touch or swim in such waters. At Curug Sikopel, though, it's exactly the opposite. The waters are believed to have the ability to preserve youth and beauty. Swimming is encouraged, and locals can even be seen taking the water away in large bottles and jars. Another legend is about a mythical creature that resides behind the falls. This has never been confirmed, but visitors are always on the lookout!

WAHYU KURNIAJI/SHUTTERSTOCK

Curug Lojahan

It's possible to visit Curug Sikopel and nearby **Curug Lojahan** in a single day if you have a private vehicle. Tell someone where you're going before you head to either waterfall, as staff here don't keep track of visitors. When arriving, park somewhere safe, where you see people around. Wear sturdy hiking shoes, take plenty of water and snacks, protection from sun and rain, and a first-aid kit if you have one. Phone service might be nonexistent, but a local SIM card is still good to have.

Curug Lojahan

TIME FROM DIENG PLATEAU: 1HR + 2HR

More captivating cascades

Another impressive waterfall near the Dieng Plateau, and one not to be taken lightly, is **Curug Lojahan**. This is one of the tallest waterfalls of the Dieng area, and is a captivating sight to behold. To see it takes a lot of effort, though. The drive to get here, which isn't too well signposted, is only a small part of the battle. Once the drive ends, you will have a trek of around two hours through thick jungle to reach the falls. Along the way you will encounter swarms of bugs, wildlife and possibly overgrown conditions.

This really is a remote waterfall, and the trek will be considered extreme for many. Children are prohibited due to the difficult access, and it is not recommended for anyone that has mobility issues. If you're afraid of heights, then this also might not be the trek for you, as the final approach to the waterfall is via a climb down into the gorge using a long wooden ladder and a rope that literally hangs down a cliff. After trekking for two long hours, you'll want to be certain you'll be able to tackle these final challenges in order to reach the waterfall. The end result is worth it, though, with one of the most extraordinary waterfalls in Central Java awaiting.

Malang

VOLCANO | TOWERING WATERFALLS | THEME PARKS

Malang is a quieter town and an ideal place to base yourself for visiting the best natural attractions around East Java. Surrounded by mountain peaks, it has a cooler climate than the steamy coastal cities – a welcome change when you're travelling in Java. The city itself feels leafy and green, with several wide boulevards standing in stark contrast to the crammed, concrete-only streets of some other Indonesian cities. Locals take pride in Malang, and places such as Alun Alun and the famous colourful village set it apart from other Indonesians centres.

The majority of visitors to Malang aren't here for the city itself, though. From here, you can visit such wonders as nearby Gunung Bromo and the incredible Tumpak Sewu. Only a short drive up the road is Batu, its theme parks, waterfalls and museums filling the city to bursting every weekend and public holiday.

GETTING AROUND

Most visitors get around Malang by private vehicle or via the Gojek and Grab apps – cheap options, especially around the city centre. Local forms of transport include *angkot* (minibus) and *mikrolet* (small taxi), but some local knowledge is needed to navigate their routes and the drivers don't speak English. The city centre has a free tourist bus on weekends, and traditional becak (bicycle-rickshaws) are available for short distances. *Delman*, the horse-drawn buggies, are a fun vanity option for anyone travelling with kids.

Climb a Live Volcano

An exhilarating experience

Visiting **Gunung Bromo** *(bromotenggersemeru.id; 255,000Rp)* is one of the most unique activities not only in Java, but possibly all of Indonesia. There is a good reason that this epic spot features on most of the tourism brochures, banners and websites for the country. Bromo, essentially, is an active volcano. However, it is a lot easier to access than most volcanoes, as reaching the summit only involves a short hike. In this regard, standing on the rim of a live volcano and feeling its raw power is an experience no longer limited to those extremely fit hikers who are able to summit nearby Semeru or Yogyakarta's Merapi.

Taking a trip to Gunung Bromo is usually done by 4WD from Malang, or even from Surabaya. Most tours will start at around midnight with a pickup from your hotel, transferring to 4WD along the way, and then a drive into Bromo-Tengger-Semeru National Park under the cover of darkness. The first stop for many is the ever-popular sunrise point (although this is a bit

of a misnomer, as there isn't really just one sunrise point, but many stretched out along the ridgeline above the road). On a typical morning, 4WD vehicles will be lined up for kilometres in each direction, full of visitors that have all come for the same reason – the incredible panorama provided by a Bromo sunrise.

Once the sun has risen, you will head back down the hill in your 4WD into the sandy, barren Bromo wasteland, and cross to the foot of the volcano itself. After the 4WD parks a couple of kilometres away, it is then up to you to trek across the remaining sand, and up a couple of hundred stairs to the rim of the Bromo crater. For most people, standing at the

> **TOP TIP**
>
> Give yourself a couple of days to fit in a tour of Bromo. Most start with a hotel pickup at midnight, and finish at noon the next day. You will want to stay another night in the hotel to rest and recover from a full night without sleep.

top of Gunung Bromo is one of those experiences that only comes around once in a lifetime. The noise that emits from the throat far below sounds not unlike a jet engine, and only hints at the incredible power that resides right under your feet. After the trek back to the 4WD, your tour ends with the drive back to your hotel, possibly with a couple of stops at scenic viewpoints along the way.

Getting to Bromo is easy with the various tours readily found online. Private tours range in price, depending on the number of people in your party and what extras you opt for. Group tours are also available for the more budget-conscious. Any visitors are required to register online; there is a quota of fewer than 3000 people per day, so register early if you're not going as part of a tour.

GO IT ALONE

If you would like to tackle a trip to Gunung Bromo on your own, and really cut down on costs, then consider seeking accommodation locally in Cemoro Lawang, the closest village to Bromo. To get here, you will have to find your way to Probolinggo and then source local transport in a bemo (minibus).

Once in Cemoro Lawang you can simply hike to the crater, the sunrise point and other viewpoints around the area. Be aware, though, that there are entrance and parking fees, so going it alone is still not completely free *(park entry foreigners/locals 255,000/79,000Rp)*, even if it does avoid the costs of a tour.

Visit the Colourful Village

A village's incredible transformation

One of the most popular attractions in Malang is a local village in Jodipan, actually made up of three small *kampung* (villages), known simply as the **Colourful Village**. But life wasn't always so bright in Jodipan. Once, not so long ago, the entire area was a riverside slum. In fact, it was one of the most unattractive and unsanitary places on the entire island of Java; so much so that the local government made the decision to demolish it and relocate the residents. It was at this point that a group of university students formulated a plan to save the village. They proposed to paint the village in bright colours, and thereby transform it into a tourist destination. The government agreed to the plan, and with the assistance of a local paint company, they set to work. The result was amazing, turning the slum into one of the most attractive and popular villages in Java. The locals have an entirely new form of income, and enjoy having visitors wander down their streets, taking photos and stopping for a chat.

The first of the *kampung* to undergo this transformation was **Kampung Warna Warni** *(instagram.com/kampung_warna_warni; 5000Rp)*, which is a good place to start your visit. Once you enter you are free to wander the streets as you like. Expect to find many places to take photos, stop for a cold drink, or simply rest and take in the amazing little spot and its residents. Even though the *kampung* is small, you'll likely spend more time here than you expected as you explore the tiny network of streets and alleys. All the streets in

DRINKING IN MALANG: COFFEE SHOPS

mmmm Cafe: A spotless coffee shop with wood floors, earthy tones, and a variety of options such as drip, pour over, and espresso. *7am-5pm Tue-Thu*

Java Dancer Coffee: This small and intimate coffee shop decorated in traditional style offers a variety of local coffees. *7am-1am*

Bukit Delight: A little outside of Malang, located on top of a hill with nice views and a romantic atmosphere. *24hr*

Ijen Kopitiam: A local favourite, with good prices and nice food right in the centre of town. *6am-midnight*

THE BROMO LEGEND

Bromo-Tengger was named after a Mataram princess, Roro Anteng, and her husband, Joko Seger, who made the Bromo area their home in the 1400s. Their lives were idyllic, except for the fact that they couldn't have children. Deciding to pray to the gods at the rim of Gunung Bromo, they were granted their wish to bear offspring. The one catch was that they had to sacrifice their last-born to the mountain. Trying to get out of the agreement, they had 25 children, before they were forced to sacrifice the 25th after the gods became angry. A demand was then made of the people to perform an annual ceremony to appease the gods. This event is still held, and is known as the Kasado Ceremony.

DENIS MOSKVINOV/SHUTTERSTOCK

Kampung Warna Warni run downwards, and eventually you will find yourself at the river. Even here, the transformation is incredible. Gone is the sewerage-choked waterway, and in its place is a clean, free-flowing stream that rings with the sounds of children swimming, diving and playing. Above the river stretches a bright-yellow footbridge sparkling in the sun. Take the stairs beside the river, and cross the bridge to the next *kampung*.

This second *kampung* is **Kampung Tridi** *(instagram.com/kampung_tridi; 5000Rp)* and after the success of their neighbours Kampung Warna Warni, they followed suit and completely revamped themselves as well, with similar results. A little further down the river, on the other side of the road bridge, is a third colourful *kampung*, **Kampung Biru Arema** *(instagram.com/kampungbiruarema; by donation)* painted completely blue in honour of their local football team.

There are several entries to Kampung Warna Warni from the local streets. There's limited street parking and access available along Jl Ir H Juanda – if you're arriving by private vehicle, you may have to get creative to find parking. In major streets there may be local parking attendants to assist you. Visitors fees to these *kampung* are paid to locals at the entries.

EATING IN MALANG: OUR PICKS

Toko Oen: Eat delicious Indonesian food at this famous local restaurant, which has been serving since 1930. *8am-9pm* $$

Javanine Resto: A spiffy spot for dining in the heart of the city, with Western and Indonesian food, often with live music or karaoke. *7am-10pm* $$$

La Regina Restorante Italiano: Centrally located, with tasty (if smallish) pizzas, pastas and Italian desserts for really good prices. *10am-10pm* $$

SaigonSan Restaurant & Rooftop: Vietnamese/Thai restaurant serving tasty food in rooms ranging from kitschy to stoic. *11am-11pm Tue-Sun* $$

Colourful Village (p131)

An Evening on the Town

Live music with heritage vibes

In the centre of the city of Malang you will find the **Kajoetangan Heritage Village** *(kajoetanganheritagevillage.com; 5000Rp)*. This area has been turned into a tourist attraction, reminiscent of what was done in the nearby Colourful Village, and it is a great place to go strolling, taking in the unique atmosphere and admiring the architectural styles.

Essentially it is a residential area, with most of the older-style houses, schoolhouses and other buildings now converted into galleries and shops. The main attraction of the area is the main street. Dubbed the 'Malioboro of Malang', **Kayutangan Heritage Street** *(free)* is indeed very similar to famous Jl Malioboro in Yogyakarta (p79). From the heritage street lamps lining the street to the general atmosphere and vibe, Kayutangan Heritage Street is the place to be.

Kajoetangan Heritage Village is generally open all day. If you are after the vibes of the main street, you are best to come late in the afternoon and stay into the evening. This is when the cafes are all open, live music kicks off along the pavement and the crowds arrive.

SEE THE TOWN FOR FREE

Visitors to Malang can now view the entire heritage area of the city from the comfort of the free **Macito Tour Bus**. This open-air bus seats 18 to 20 people, and there are currently four of them touring the city. They run every day except Fridays, and the majority of the buses are equipped with disabled access.

To ride the bus, download the Macito app on your phone and register, then book your desired trip and schedule, selecting your seat and filling in other options. Then bring your booking code to the meeting point at Jl Majapahit on the day of your tour.

Take a Walk on the Creative Side

Art, culture and more

Opened in 2023, the **Malang Creative Center** *(mcc.or.id; event costs vary)* has rental and performance space, and lots of events throughout the year. Dance troupes, artist showings, open mics, visiting lecturers, medicinal healing demonstrations – there's something for just about anyone. The catch? It's mostly geared towards an Indonesian-speaking audience. Some visual arts (such as painting and sculpture) are readily accessible without much need for translation. If you're in town for a while and have some local friends to depend on, this is a great way to dive into the art and culture scene.

Beyond Malang

Surrounded by mountains, Malang holds the key to incredible volcano tours, waterfall treks and fun-filled theme parks.

Places

Malang is the perfect place to base yourself to see the very best of what the rest of East Java has to offer. The amazing Tumpak Sewu waterfall is right on the doorstep of Malang – a sight that's never to be matched. Nearby, the village of Lumajang also has several incredible, towering waterfall experiences.

Closer to Malang, the mountainside tourist town of Batu is home to several theme parks attracting thousands of visitors every weekend and public holiday. The waterfalls, tea plantations and nostalgic museums bring in busloads of people from all over Java, making Malang one of the best tourism hubs on the island.

GETTING AROUND

Public buses are available to reach Batu from Malang; however, once within Batu you may require the Gojek or Grab apps to reach your final destination. Hiring a scooter is by far the best way to get around the hilly Batu area. To reach places further afield, such as Lumajang and Tumpak Sewu, hire a car and driver to negotiate the dubious road conditions, or book yourself on an organised day tour.

Batu

TIME FROM MALANG: **40MIN**

Waterfalls, ATVs and outdoor fun

Batu, a city in East Java only a short distance from Malang, is located in a slightly cooler, more elevated setting on the lower slopes of the mountains. It's no wonder that it's become a local favourite for getaways and family holidays, with plenty of natural attractions around the area. Waterfalls, in particular, draw visitors year-round, especially during the wet season. Places like **Coban Talun** *(instagram.com/coban_talunofficial; 12,000Rp)*, a powerful, towering waterfall, also offer side activities such as 4WD tours, camping and a flower garden to keep you entertained. Paragliding, fruit picking and theme parks are also on offer.

Coban Rondo *(instagram.com/cobanrondo.econique; 40,000Rp)* is another waterfall site that has been transformed into a day full of activities. At over 80m tall, Coban Rondo is spectacular in itself, and despite being a half-hour drive out of town, locals and tourists flock here every day. This has a lot to do with the activities that are available around the entrance to the complex. A massive hedge maze is an instant favourite, and will keep you occupied for some time as you navigate your way around its twists and turns. There's

DENIS MOSKVINOV/SHUTTERSTOCK

Hedge maze at Coban Rondo, Batu

no need to worry though, as there are platforms that allow you to cheat if you truly get lost. There's also archery, ATVs (all-terrain vehicles), bicycling, a zip line and even strawberry picking here – there are so many options you may forget that you actually came to see a waterfall.

To reach the falls themselves will require you to continue driving further into the complex. Coban Rondo has a beautiful setup. The walk in is along a path through a nicely maintained garden area. Closer to the falls you will encounter monkeys, playing and swinging through the trees above you. They will mostly steer clear of visitors, but have been known to be mischievous, so be sure to keep your eye on them.

Coban Talun and Coban Rondo are only two of the dozen waterfalls within easy driving distance of Batu.

THE COBAN RONDO LEGEND

A legend surrounding Coban Rondo claims that unmarried couples who visit the waterfall together are destined to break up. The myth comes from a story involving a Javanese woman, Dewi Anjarwati, who fell in love with a man named Raden Baron Kusumo. They quickly married, and a few days later decided to visit the house of Dewi's parents. Along the way they met a foreigner named Joko Lelono, who immediately fell in love with Dewi. He challenged her husband to a duel, and Dewi went to hide behind the waterfall while the men fought. But both men died in the duel, and it's said that Dewi's ghost can be seen at the waterfall's base at night, crying and still awaiting his return.

A world of theme parks

The mastermind behind turning Batu into a tourism hot spot is the company Jawa Timur Park Group. The company's three parks here receive thousands of visitors every day, and have become the main reason that families in particular love spending their vacations in Batu.

Jawa Timur Park 1 *(jtp.id/jatimpark1; from 115,000Rp)* is an amusement park chock-full of rides that will keep everyone in the family entertained. The best thing about the Jawa Timur parks is that they are not just about mindless fun on rides and roller-coasters. Each of the parks has an actual theme, and they concentrate on education as much as they do on entertainment. In Park 1 this theme is science, which provides a great opportunity for parents to have fun with their kids while watching them learn something new at the same time.

Jawa Timur Park 2 *(jtp.id/jatimpark2; from 125,000Rp)* occupies a huge area, and here the theme is animals, with an emphasis on African species. The massive zoo includes Tiger Land, Monkey Island and Baby Zoo. One of the highlights is a

MUSEUM ANGKUT - GOOD TO KNOW

Buy Online: Tickets usually cost 110,000Rp, but you can find them online with special deals at tiket.com.

Combined Tickets: You can get combined tickets to visit other Jawa Timur Park Group attractions in Batu for an additional fee.

Shows & Parades: There are several shows throughout the day, including the driving display and costume parade in the main street area.

Formula One: For an additional cost you can dress as an F1 driver and have your photo taken in an F1 car.

Food: There are cafes and eating places inside the park.

Avoid Crowds: Arriving later in the day you miss the crowds, but give yourself at least two to three hours to see the large park.

STOCK HIGH ANGLE VIEW/SHUTTERSTOCK

Madakaripura Waterfall

glass-sided tunnel that allows you to stroll right through the middle of a replica savanna. It's a similar experience to walking through a tunnel at an aquarium. Families with younger kids will likely find this particularly enjoyable, as most children love getting to see the various animals. That said, while the zoo is well kept and clean, those with objections to keeping animals for display may want to skip this one.

Jawa Timur Park 3 *(jtp.id/jatimpark3; from 140,000Rp)* concentrates on dinosaurs, with some incredibly realistic displays. Keeping with the realism theme, the park also has a Madame Tussauds-style museum called 'The Legend Stars', where you can pose alongside models of some of your favourite celebrities.

And let's not forget **Jawa Timur Park 4** *(batulovegarden.jtp.id; 50,000-165,000Rp)*, more commonly known as the Batu Love Garden. Great for couples or families, this is a feast of colours and easy activities. There's a rainbow slide, a ferris wheel, as well as more sedentary attractions like choo-choo trains and colouring stations.

To visit any of these parks is easy, as they're all located right in the heart of Batu. Prices are rather cheap for theme parks, and become even more attractive with the option to purchase combined tickets for admission to other attractions in the area.

Immerse in the history of transport

Museum Angkut *(museumangkut.jtp.id; 110,000Rp)*, a transport museum in Batu, is an absolute must-visit for anyone who loves automobiles. The range of cars on display is seriously impressive, and even those with only a passing interest can find themselves enthralled for hours. Probably the only place with more vintage vehicles in pristine condition is the island of Cuba.

The museum takes most visitors by surprise. The exterior isn't exactly impressive, and even when lining up at the ticket office you don't really have much idea of what to expect. But step inside and you'll find the entrance hall filled with cars, vintage motorcycles, a helicopter and even a tank.

You could be forgiven for thinking this is all that the museum has to offer, such is the impressiveness of the display. However, up the stairs from the entrance hall is a whirlwind of displays that just keep coming, one after another, until you seriously begin to doubt that there could possibly be this many makes, models and styles of cars in the world. From a Formula One Ferrari to the trusty Studebaker, and from the Model T Ford to the Holden Camaro, Museum Angkut has it all, and everything is in pristine, showroom condition.

Around halfway through the museum you will come across an open street lined with diners, souvenir shops and parked cars. Live performances take place in this section of the museum. Check the showtimes before you visit to make sure you don't miss them. The driving displays are sensational, and the skills of the drivers are impressive.

Beyond this street, the museum becomes a series of showrooms dedicated to every major country or city in the world that can lay claim to any automotive success. England, Italy, Germany and the US all hold their own pride of place, with displays of their legendary, and not so legendary, cars.

The museum's exit is through a series of train carriages, which is a novel idea, and the perfect way to wrap up a day at a transport museum.

A TOUR OF MADAKARIPURA

A smart and safe way (with vastly less bargaining) to visit Madakaripura Waterfall is on a guided tour. Many tour companies offer this, often combining the waterfall visit with a trip to nearby Gunung Bromo, which makes for a very attractive deal. Alternatively, you can create your own tour by hiring a car and driver to take you there; this is also a popular option. The proximity of the waterfall to Probolinggo, Malang and even Surabaya make visiting it on a day tour possible from several different directions.

Madakaripura Waterfall

TIME FROM MALANG: 1¾HR

Experience spectacular falls

Madakaripura Waterfall *(55,000Rp; guide fees vary)* is one of Java's, indeed Indonesia's, most spectacular sights. It's the tallest waterfall in Java, topping out at an incredible 200m, which also makes it the second-tallest waterfall in Indonesia; yet this waterfall is often missed by visitors to East Java.

Located near Probolinggo, it's on the north side of the island, well away from other tourist hot spots, such as the famous Tumpak Sewu near Lumajang. However, a recent rise in popularity, and the addition of a couple of tours stopping at Madakaripura, has seen these amazing falls featuring more and more on social media. Bucket lists have been updated and more visitors are starting to arrive. And with good reason, too. While Madakaripura is a seriously impressive waterfall, its beautiful, iconic location and the trek to reach it turn a simple visit here into a memorable experience.

From the entry gate and ticket booth, the trek into Madakaripura is straightforward but stunning. An easy hike, it is still worth taking one of the guides with you (you'll need to bargain for a price; aim for 100,000Rp), as they know all the tips and tricks along the way for snapping the best photos and taking the easiest path. That said, you might be put off by the hard-sell tactics (to buy helmets, plastic ponchos, and even to pay for the guides). If you're looking for a waterfall that feels a bit less of a Wild West, anything-goes place, consider **Tumpak Sewu** (p142) instead.

TIPS FOR VISITING THE WATERFALLS

Visiting Batu's waterfalls can be a challenge, with the remoteness and mountainous topography hindering access at times, so be prepared:

Hire a good scooter. An NMAX is better than a Vario for getting two people up the bigger hills and down mountain paths.

Bring a poncho to stay dry, as the weather can change many times a day in the mountains.

Fill up with petrol in town, as you may not find many options to do so near the waterfalls.

Carry snacks and drinking water with you.

Plan ahead. Give yourself enough time to visit then get back to Batu, or at least back onto the main road before dark.

There are five waterfalls along the path, each as impressive as the last, and anywhere else it would be worth spending time to investigate each of them. But up ahead, the real Madakaripura awaits.

The trek to the main waterfall is up a canyon that could be right out of a *Jurassic Park* movie. The walls, clad in lush, green foliage, close in on either side. Gusts of spray spin crazily in the air, and smaller waterfalls appear out of nowhere as they crash down around you. The gorge twists and turns, and with a dramatic sense of theatre at the penultimate moment opens up to reveal Madakaripura in all of its glory. Nothing will prepare you for the sight of this huge waterfall crashing down the cliff face, framed beautifully by a natural amphitheatre. You really have to see it to believe it.

To visit Madakaripura, you can drive or ride here yourself. It is easily located on Google Maps, but the roads can be rather sketchy, and a wrong turn can leave you in the middle of nowhere. Remember to take care: this area has only recently become popular with visitors, and with increased traffic on already deteriorating roads, conditions can change as quickly as the weather.

Lumajang

TIME FROM MALANG: **2HR**

A waterfall lover's dream

Lumajang in East Java has some of the most beautiful, powerful and incredibly photogenic waterfalls in the country, and possibly the world. There's a good reason that people travel from all over to experience them.

Tumpak Sewu (p142) is among the most famous of Indonesia's waterfalls, and is definitely the most impressive. The name Tumpak Sewu means 'Thousand Waterfalls', and with hundreds of falls cascading over a huge semicircular cliff, it's easy to understand how it got its name.

If located anywhere else, the other incredible waterfalls around Lumajang would be world famous in their own right. As it is, they dwell in Tumpak Sewu's considerable shadow, and don't attract the crowds of visitors that they deserve. This is great news for waterfall seekers, and those that have the time to seek them out, as these falls can be experienced in much less crowded circumstances.

The first of these falls is **Kapas Biru**. This powerful waterfall plummets down the face of a beautiful, orange-coloured cliff surrounded by thick jungle. The impressive sight has become very famous on social media, though not many people actually

EATING IN LUMAJANG: CHEAP EATS

Warung Pondasi: Indoor seating off the town square with *nasi, mie,* and *ayam* at street-food prices; the best of both worlds. *7am-9pm Mon-Sat, 6am-1pm Sun* $

Lumajang Central Park: This town square has dozens of food carts, from *soto ayam* (chicken soup) to Japanese *okonomiyaki* (savoury pancakes). *24hr* $

Soto Ayam 'Pak Yadi': Absolutely the best *soto ayam* in all of Java, served out of a food cart at the intersection of Jendral Sutoyo and Cokro Sujono. *6am-9pm* $

Piranti Bake: Satisfy that sweet tooth with cake or cookies from a tiny shop you can find (probably) just by following your nose. *8am-8pm Mon-Sat, to 5pm Sun* $

LANDSCAPEMANIA/SHUTTERSTOCK

Gunung Semeru

realise where the falls are located. Only a short distance from Lumajang, and not far from the main road, Kapas Biru only takes about 30 minutes to reach after a fairly easy hike. Like most waterfalls in Indonesia, you will need a basic to moderate level of fitness to get here, and the hike back is uphill. You also may come across a dodgy bridge or ladder along the way.

Beyond Kapas Biru, if you walk along the same path for another 20 to 30 minutes, you will reach yet another waterfall, by the name of **Coban Sriti**. This is a hidden treasure that possibly rivals Kapas Biru for its beauty and power. Not many visitors to Kapas Biru are aware of this second waterfall only a short hike further along, so make sure you give yourself enough time to check them both out.

Another unmissable waterfall near Lumajang is **Kabut Pelangi**. A seriously impressive cascade down into mossy, foliage-covered rocks, Kabut Pelangi is one of the most photogenic waterfalls you will find in Indonesia. Still not very well known, a place as beautiful as this will likely not stay hidden for much longer. You can reach Kabut Pelangi after about 45 minutes of hiking. There are a couple of other, smaller waterfalls to be seen along the route, and you will cross a couple of streams and get your feet wet, so wear appropriate gear. The hike back is also a lot harder than the hike to the waterfall, with some serious uphill stretches.

Gunung Semeru

TIME FROM MALANG: 1½HR

Test your fitness on a volcano

At 3676m above sea level, **Gunung Semeru** *(bromotengger semeru.id; per day 200,000Rp)* is the tallest mountain in Java. By default, it is also the highest volcano. This makes it a very popular goal for many hikers and mountain climbers visiting Indonesia. In fact, around 140,000 hikers attempt the peak every year.

ARE WEDDING BELLS RINGING?

Lumajang is one of many spots in Java where strict Muslim sharia law is followed, and many hotels and guesthouses will require couples sharing a room to sign a waiver saying that they have a marriage certificate. They may check the document, though many hotels don't. This should not be taken lightly or laughed off; while it's unlikely you'll be arrested, the potential is there and Indonesia has lately veered into stricter enforcement of religious laws. Avoid problems by either having a document to show if needed, or by budgeting enough that you can, if needed, stay in separate rooms.

GUNUNG SEMERU: NEED TO KNOW

Booking is required with the Bromo-Tengger-Semeru National Park *(bromotenggersemeru.id)* before climbing Gunung Semeru. There is a limit of just 200 people per day, so avoid disappointment by booking well in advance.

Due to increased volcanic activity in 2025, at the time of research all hiking was suspended.

A 'fit-to-climb' letter has to be obtained from a clinic or doctor a day before climbing in order to be able to register.

As of 2025, hikers are required to obtain and wear a radio-frequency identification (RFID) tracking device.

ALBERT LIMANSASTRO/SHUTTERSTOCK

Pantai Ngudel

That said, this mountain should not be treated lightly. It's one of Java's heaviest hitters, an extreme climb that requires experience and the understanding that this climb could be your last. In December 2021, a sudden eruption killed over 50 people, and the mountain has remained active with several significant events since then. It remained closed to hiking until 2025, and after reopening for limited use it erupted again. At the time of research it remained closed to all hiking.

When it is open, it is highly recommended that you hire a guide or join a tour. Whether they're a local guide or part of a professional guided hiking expedition is up to you. Gunung Semeru has claimed the lives of many visitors in the past, and having an experienced guide drastically reduces the chances of mishaps, getting lost or being stranded on the slopes of this live volcano.

Most hiking tours to Semeru begin in Malang and generally take two to three days. The hike itself begins at the base camp, located in the village of Ranupane, which is also your last chance to stock up on supplies and equipment. The Semeru hike starts with some wonderful views of green meadows and lush rainforests, but then the real struggle begins at around 2700m, as the hike to the summit is hard. Should hiking to the summit reopen, the final ascent begins after midnight from the overnight basecamp, when hiking conditions and temperatures are most favourable. The climb here is tough, and a decent level of fitness is required in order to tackle the loose, scree-covered slopes. The crater rim presents an incredible panorama of nearby Gunung Bromo and surrounding peaks, with views that seemingly go on forever. As beautiful as it is, directly below you lies the open mouth of the Semeru crater, which often emits clouds of poisonous gas that have been the demise of more than a few unfortunate hikers in the past. Using extreme caution is vital, and pay close attention to any tips or suggestions from park staff or your guides.

Pantai Selok to Pantai Bajulmati

TIME FROM MALANG: 2HR

Hit the beaches

Take a drive south from Malang and you will reach Java's stunning southern coastline. This is where the Malang regency really turns it on, with a string of beaches sporting pearly white sand, blue waters and hardly a soul to be seen. As with those at Gunung Kidul, Malang's beaches are not to be missed, though high surf and currents can make swimming a 'for-experts-only' affair. Ask before diving in. Nominal parking fees *(10,000-15,000Rp)* often apply.

To reach these beaches, you'll need your own transport. Some of them are harder to reach than others, but even though they are well off the international-tourism radar, local roads are still fairly good in most areas. Local and domestic tourism also means that you will find basic facilities at many of the larger and more popular beaches.

One of the first beaches to visit from Malang is **Pantai Selok**. A relatively 'new' beach, it has incredible golden-yellow sands, serene conditions and some beautiful, photogenic rock formations in the water.

A short drive to the east is **Kondang Merak Beach**. This calm, remote beach offers conditions that are perfect for snorkelling, with plenty of rocks and coral to explore. Camping is available locally, and the beautiful white sands are the perfect place to relax and watch some of the best sunsets in the area.

For something a little bit different, take a drive down to **Balekambang Beach**. The road can be a bit sketchy, so be careful if you are on a motorcycle. The drive is worth it, though, with the scenic location playing host to a beautiful temple built on a small island just offshore. Reminiscent of Bali's Tanah Lot, this temple can still be reached during high tide via a small pedestrian bridge.

Travelling further east you find another popular beach, **Pantai Ngudel**, which has facilities for camping and is very popular for sunsets. With a collection of nice warungs, a clean white strip of sand and nice places to chill in the shade under the trees, it's no wonder Ngudel is a local favourite.

Probably the most popular beach in the area, though, is **Pantai Bajulmati**. This 1km-long stretch of sand not only has the best beach facilities you will find in the area, but there's even a search-and-rescue team here, something that is very rare. At the eastern side, known as **Pantai Ungapan**, a river and lagoon offer calm, brackish playtime, as well as stunning eroded limestone islands just offshore.

Sempu Island and the mainland fishing port just next to it are also worth a stop. You can hire boats to take you around the island *(150,000-400,000Rp)*, or just watch the fishermen hurling ice and rocks into their skiffs before setting off for the day.

ESSENTIAL TREKKING TIPS

Bring mountain gear, including trekking boots, a poncho/raincoat, warm clothes and a torch/headlamp.

Take protection for your camera equipment, as the weather can change rapidly.

Climb at night for the best conditions and to see sunrises.

Take a local guide at places such as Gunung Semeru, where the wrong path can lead to fatal consequences.

Never get too close to the rim of a volcano, as they are unstable and disasters can happen. Be aware of toxic gases and sulphur clouds that can suddenly appear.

Carry plenty of snacks, energy food and water.

Always climb in company, and don't attempt treks unless you are in good condition physically and mentally.

ALVAROELEZ/SHUTTERSTOCK

TOP EXPERIENCE

Tumpak Sewu

A once-in-a-lifetime experience, Tumpak Sewu in East Java is not to be missed. The hundreds of waterfalls, pouring off the edge of a 120m-high semicircular cliff into a canyon lost in the mists far below, must be seen to be believed. Tumpak Sewu is an adventure you are guaranteed to remember for life.

DON'T MISS

- Tumpak Sewu viewpoint
- The waterfall hike
- Goa Tetes waterfalls
- The base of Tumpak Sewu waterfall
- Waterfall swimming
- Goa Tetes caves
- Coban Sewu

The Viewpoint

Visiting Tumpak Sewu from above is easy. Park near the entrance, pay the fee at the ticket booth, then follow the footpath to the viewpoint. This is the most popular spot to view the waterfall, and you can take some spectacular photos here. Early morning is the best time, with the clouds of mist rising from the canyon below making for some really eerie effects.

There's a small track leading outside the viewpoint, offering unobstructed photos. We do not advise going here as it

PRACTICALITIES

● airterjuntumpaksewu.com ● 100,000Rp ● 7am-5pm

is extremely dangerous, with slippery footholds and a long, long drop if you fall.

If you have a drone, this viewpoint is the best place to launch it from, and will allow you to get amazing photos with the falls and Gunung Semeru in the background.

Accessing the Canyon

As wonderful as the view is, the true joy of visiting Tumpak Sewu is the hike to the falls' base. Note that this hike can be tough going. Wear sturdy shoes and follow the path to the left of the viewpoint area. The hike begins along a muddy track and stairs, turning quickly into steel gantries, wooden walkways and ladders. About two-thirds of the way down, the ladders end and you'll find yourself holding a rope as you make your way down a rocky slope with a rushing waterfall all around you. You'll get very wet, but the end result is worth it.

Waterfalls & Caves

In the canyon, follow the trail towards Tumpak Sewu Waterfall. At some point you will pay an extra fee as you move into a new village area. Reaching the base of the falls is a memorable experience: the raw power, with gusts of spray soaking you, and the falls plummeting from above are unforgettable.

Following the canyon back in the other direction you will reach the **Goa Tetes waterfalls**. These are another set of beautiful falls flowing down an orange cliff face, forming pools at the base that you can swim in. If you follow the track further, and are careful enough, you will find yourself climbing up above the falls and into the **Goa Tetes caves** in the cliff face.

Coban Sewu

If you're travelling here from Malang, you will first come across signs pointing to **Coban Sewu**. This is actually the same waterfall as Tumpak Sewu, but seen from the western side instead of the east.

It's worth paying the entrance fee to enter from the Coban Sewu side, simply to see the falls from a different angle. It's less crowded here too, as only locals tend to visit Coban Sewu.

While you can also access the base of the falls from this Coban Sewu viewpoint, it is not advisable as the track and ladders are extremely dangerous compared with those on the Lumajang side.

Exploring the Area

Getting around is best via private transport or on a tour. The Batu area is close to Malang, but moving around between attractions is easiest with your own vehicle or on a scooter. To reach far-flung places such as Lumajang or Tumpak Sewu will take two to three hours by road.

WHEN TO VISIT

The rainy season in Java runs from November to April and can be the most spectacular time to visit Tumpak Sewu. More water flowing over the falls makes for an extraordinary sight. However, if you have a sense of adventure, the best way to see the falls is by hiking the canyon to the base. Note that the trail may be closed if there's been too much rain.

TOP TIPS

- Wear waterproof hiking shoes or sandals.
- A local guide is not necessary here.
- Don't miss the base of the falls.
- Carry a small amount of cash for extra fees.
- Bring snacks and drinking water.
- Be prepared to get wet, both on the climb down into the canyon and at the base of the falls.
- From the Goa Tetes caves you can continue following the trail up and out of the canyon.
- Do *not* try to enter the canyon from the Coban Sewu side.
- Get here early to avoid the crowds and enjoy the best conditions.

Banyuwangi

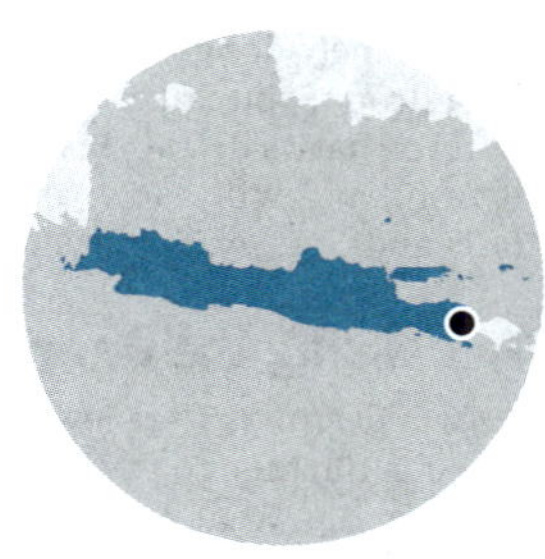

VOLCANO HIKES | SECLUDED BEACHES | NATIONAL PARKS

Most visitors think of Banyuwangi as no more than a simple stopping-off point for continuing on to nearby Bali. The city is much more than this, though, and is now gaining deserved recognition as the gateway to the many spectacular sights that, until recently, lay hidden in far East Java.

The majority of travellers to Banyuwangi come for the incredible experience of the night-time climb of Kawah Ijen. The famous and unique 'blue fire' phenomenon has made the mountain famous worldwide, and helped spark tourism to the region. This influx of visitors has not only been a boost to the Banyuwangi township, but also to the outlying areas.

National parks with diverse scenery from savanna to thick jungle, towering dormant volcanoes and remote isolated beaches await those that seek adventure in this region of Java.

GETTING AROUND

You can reach Banyuwangi by train from Surabaya via Jember, by ferry from Bali's Gilimanuk, or by road from within Java. If you're staying centrally, you can get around in the city by walking or using a *bentor,* the local motorised version of the traditional becak, which is widely available around the city centre.

To reach locations further out, such as homestays and even Kawah Ijen, consider using Gojek or Grab. Hiring your own scooter is another great way to get around.

The Ends of the Earth...or Java, Anyway

Coffee and spectacular views

Banyuwangi is Java's easternmost city, a port on the shores of the Bali Strait. Many visitors come not from the Java side, but by ferry across the strait from Bali, often to visit **Kawah Ijen** (p146) on an overnight excursion. It's the area's prime attraction, but by no means the only thing to do here. Visitors from Bali might find the first thing they notice that's 'different' is how many mosques there are here, versus relatively few in mostly Hindu Bali.

Many people just enjoy Banyuwangi for its delightful fresh air, its shoreline and seaside views, and its relaxed feel. In fact, the name 'Banyuwangi' roughly translates to 'ocean fragrance', and indeed, the air here smells fresh and salty. You can see Bali just across the strait, and watching the ferries go back and forth between the islands is a fun pastime. Cormorants and seagulls glide in the updrafts, and while it's not exactly the beach bliss of some of the other Indonesian islands, it's got a charm all of its own.

TOP TIP

If you're in town to climb Kawah Ijen and don't have your own transport, you can utilise the Grab app for ridesharing or to have food delivered to your accommodation.

HIGHLIGHTS
1 Kawah Ijen

ACTIVITIES
2 1911 Cafe & Resto Kalibendo

SLEEPING
3 éL Hotel Banyuwangi
4 Hotel Santika Banyuwangi
5 Juda Homestay
6 Sandy's Homestay

Tours to Kawah Ijen often end the trip with a stop at one of the nearby coffee plantations, but you don't have to combine that with a volcano trip – the plantations are interesting in their own right. A visit to **1911 Cafe & Resto Kalibendo** *(instagram.com/1911cafeandrestokalibendo; 105,000Rp)* offers great coffee tours, where you'll be given some insights and history about coffee in Java, learn about the different varieties, walk along the rows of plants and see how the cherries are prepared before roasting. You'll also get to sample some, which some feel is the best part!

Staying overnight in Banyuwangi is the most popular option, and homestays are a dime a dozen, with wonderful hosts that can answer any enquiry you might have about the mountain and surrounds. If you're already in Java, then consider catching the train from Surabaya to Banyuwangi. After your hike, you can explore further around the eastern end of Java, including the incredible national parks and surfing locations. Otherwise, Banyuwangi is the perfect jumping-off point to head to Bali, via the simple one-hour ferry transit.

THANK YOU, THANK YOU, THANK YOU

No expression is more vital for a traveller than 'thank you' in the local language. ('Where's the bathroom?' is the obvious runner up, with 'Can I get a beer, please?' a close third.)

In Java though, learning *'terima kasih'* ('thank you' in Bahasa Indonesia) only just suffices. It gets you by, but many locals prefer to hear their own region's version.

In Yogyakarta, for instance, you'll be coaxed to say *'matur nuwun'*.

In Bandung, where Sundanese rules, it's *'hatur nuhun'*.

Banyuangi's local language is Osingese, so gain points by saying *'kesuwon'*.

DENIS MOSKVINOV/SHUTTERSTOCK

TOP EXPERIENCE

Kawah Ijen

Kawah Ijen is gorgeous by day, with a milky green lake surrounded by yellow and white cliffs that, even on a bad day, will take your breath away. But it's in the darkness that the crater's secret comes alive: burning sulphur gas sends rivers of blue flames uphill, a phenomenon that can be seen in only one other place in the world.

DON'T MISS

- The blue fire
- Sunrise from the rim
- The Rim Trail
- Kawah Ijen by day

On Your Mark, Get Set...

Whether you arrive on your own or as part of an organised tour, the initial process involves getting your wristband and meeting your guide. A zoo of other hikers will be milling around, often waiting an hour or more, sipping coffee and chatting. If you have last-minute shopping needs (such as plastic ponchos or bananas at prices that make robbery seem kind) this is your only chance to get them. While a few stops along the way have food and drinks, provisions are best either brought or bought here before starting.

PRACTICALITIES

- tiket.bbksdajatim.org
- admission 150,000Rp; insurance 5000Rp
- 2am-noon, closed every first Friday of the month

Go! The Ascent to the Rim

At 2am sharp, entry to the park is allowed and the hordes begin hiking. It's chaos at first, but the steep grade soon tires out all but the serious hikers, and the crowd thins substantially. You'll want your headlamp on to avoid rocks and puddles, but the trail is well marked and impossible to get lost on. It's very steep at times. Your guide can tell you how close to the rim you're getting.

Take a Lamborghini

If you're feeling tired (or if you're looking at the trail and going 'no way!' from the start), you can always take a Lamborghini: at least, that's the affectionate nickname for the cushioned wheelbarrows that teams of locals will whisk you to the top in, without you lifting a finger or breaking a sweat. It costs about 800,000Rp round trip.

Into the Crater

Once you reach the rim you'll have to descend a slippery, rocky trail for 30 or so minutes to reach the fire. This is for many the most hazardous part, and irritatingly, many tourists jostle and push as they go down, disrespectful of the safety of others. Be slow, meticulous and kind. It's everyone's mountain, and a twisted ankle or broken leg will bring your visit to an unhappy end.

The Mesmerising Blue Fire

Congratulations: you made it. Before your eyes is a swirling, dancing, absolutely unearthly scene. The blue fire. It swirls around in a pool on the ground before rising up the hillside and eventually burning itself out some 20m or 30m away. You'll need to wait your turn for a selfie and photos, and if you haven't already, get your gas mask out and have it around your neck – the wind often changes, sending choking sulphuric acid clouds into the crowd. Those with a mask just pop it on and squeeze their eyes shut, but you'll hear screams and panic from the careless (or clueless) who thought a volcano visit was just a walk in the park.

Sunrise

Many visitors, exhausted, head back down the moment they come back to the rim, finishing the hike in darkness or bare glimmers of morning sun. But it's worth it to hang around the (often chilly) rim and watch the sun rise. When it burns off the steam covering the lake surface you're in for a treat: the mint Oreo-coloured water surrounded by the jagged cliffs is stunning. A trail leads partway around the rim and is a good spot for lake overlooks.

WHEN TO VISIT

Kawah Ijen is open year-round, but is fickle at best. Larger gas eruptions have closed the crater for weeks, and weather (such as heavy rains) can make the trail slippery or even impassable. The dry season (after March) is often recommended, but even then, recent changing weather patterns have made the rains less predictable.

TOP TIPS

- If possible, time your visit to not fall on an Indonesian public holiday or a weekend, as those are the most crowded.
- Keep your gas mask at the ready at all times, musty though it may be.
- Bring plenty of water and snacks, as the prices on the mountain are hilarious.
- There are no ATMs at the park entrance, and mobile phone service is very spotty. Bring plenty of cash and plan on being off the grid for a while.
- Sulphur carvings will be confiscated at airport security (even if in checked luggage), so don't plan on bringing these souvenirs back home.

Beyond Banyuwangi

Jangkar
Baluran National Park
Banyuwangi
Gilimanuk
Meru Betiri National Park
Pulau Merah
De Djawatan Forest
Pantai Wedi Ireng
Grajagan
Alas Purwo National Park

National parks full of wildlife await in all directions, along with stunning beaches that remain isolated from the presence of humans.

Places

Venturing out from Banyuwangi provides a glimpse into a seldom explored area of East Java. Soaring mountains and smoking volcanoes slope away into heavily forested coastlines, lined with pristine, unspoiled beaches.

In this region of Java usually bypassed by tourists, natural wonders abound. Three major national parks await, each with its own personality and mysterious past. Ancient temples lie hidden in thick jungles, green sea turtles venture onto remote beaches and world-class surf crashes along beaches where tigers are rumoured to prowl. Meanwhile, in the villages and towns, local culture thrives.

GETTING AROUND

Public transport barely exists away from Banyuwangi.

Hire a car or scooter to get you further afield, or a private car with a driver for day trips. Amang *(javaprivatedriver.com; WhatsApp +62 822 4443 6333)* can set up car hire and has connections throughout Java if needed.

If you're surfing, consider speaking to local fishermen to hire fishing boats as transport between beaches.

Pulau Merah

TIME FROM BANYUWANGI: **2HR**

Sun, surf and island views

Pulau Merah, also known as **Red Island**, is one of those pockets of paradise that are becoming few and far between in the modern world. Far enough from the main tourist route that it manages to escape attention, Pulau Merah provides the shrewd travellers who seek it out with just reward for their efforts.

At Pulau Merah you can still stroll along a perfect strip of white sand and leave the only set of footprints. It's a place where you can watch the sunset in peace, and where half a dozen people sharing a morning surf is considered crowded. With 4km of pristine white sand, amazing island views and a dreamy palm-lined beachhead, here you could be forgiven for thinking you'd been dropped into paradise. You wouldn't be alone in this thought – most of the locals already believe it and the majority of visitors leave vowing that it is true.

Surfing is a popular pastime here and most guesthouses have a board or two you can borrow or rent, usually for a nominal fee *(around 100,000Rp)*. The surf is best on the far left side of the beach, though it depends a bit on the swell direction. It's all sand, so beginners will find it a friendly and forgiving

MIKAIL ARVIN/SHUTTERSTOCK

Pulau Merah

place to have a go. Three-hour lessons run about 300,000Rp, and you can set them up from any of the on-site surf shops there at the beach. Rips do occur, however, so pay attention to any signs or warnings, be sure you listen to the instructor's advice, and never paddle into something you can't swim out of should you and your board get separated.

Pulau Merah isn't easy to get to. There's no public transport, so a bit of ingenuity will be required. This might be in the form of renting your own car or scooter, or hiring a car and driver for the day. If you're comfy with rides from strangers, chances are you'll be offered a ride the moment you stick out a thumb. Getting here is worth it, though. If you are seeking a peaceful beach getaway with quiet, unspoiled surf, empty beaches and a sleepy community that still charges local prices in its restaurants, then you will find it here.

The only word of warning before you venture to Pulau Merah is not to expect five-star resorts. In any case, given that small, mostly untouched pockets of Indonesia such as this are rare, most visitors don't mind roughing it a little in a friendly two-star homestay for a night or two, especially for all the peace and seclusion Pulau Merah provides. Those who want a bit more snazz can find it at the **Java Turtle Lodge** (p181) *(javaturtlelodge.com)* about 30 minutes away.

SURFING AT THE NATIONAL PARKS

National parks in East Java cost between 150,000Rp and 205,000Rp per person to enter. This fee is payable at ticket offices upon entry.

If you are heading to **G-Land** (p151) only to day surf, the price of accommodation within the park and the park-entrance fee can be avoided by accessing the surf spot directly by boat. Local boats can be hired from Grajagan, about 20km away, across the bay.

Pulau Merah has its own surf camps, and if you're staying here you can take a morning boat around to G-Land to test your skills on the advanced waves.

EATING & DRINKING IN PULAU MERAH

Yogi Cafe & Resto: Any closer to the beach and your feet would be wet, with Indonesian faves like *mie ayam* and nasi goreng. Can be slow. *8am-8pm* $$

Wisma Pulau Merah: Youthful, funky vibe at this bar-restaurant-coffee shop that's only a five-minute walk from the beach. *7am-11pm* $

Tepi Sawah Caffe Resto: Quite a ways out of town, but worth it for the creamy lattes, well-pulled espressos and spotless decor. *8am-10.30pm* $

Warung Mama: Set back a bit from the beach, this spot has tasty Indonesian food at rock bottom prices. *7am-8pm Mon-Fri, 6am-9pm Sat & Sun* $

PANTAI WEDI IRENG: LOCAL TIPS

Park at the warung and walk to the beach. This car-park warung is great for snacks.

Carry a small amount of cash to tip the warung owner for watching your vehicle.

Due to the track's condition, do not attempt to ride a scooter to the beach unless you are very confident.

Take plenty of drinking water, sunscreen and a hat.

Wear good walking shoes.

Take some rain protection for the hike in wet season.

ROBY KURNIAWAN/SHUTTERSTOCK

Pantai Wedi Ireng

Pantai Wedi Ireng

TIME FROM BANYUWANGI: **2HR**

Your own private beach

Not too far from Pulau Merah is a beach that not many people know about. The reason for this is that it is quite remote, even if geographically it's only a stone's throw from Pulau Merah. It is also one of the most beautiful little beaches that you will find in all of Java – and that's saying something.

Pantai Wedi Ireng is hard to find, and takes a bit of effort to get to. For this reason, many just hire a boat from Pulau Merah, and the captain will whisk you there and take you back at the end of the day. But this isn't the only option. While there is no real road to the beach, and it takes some local knowledge to locate the track that does lead here, there are signs if you keep a look out for them. The first is halfway between Pulau Merah and **Pantai Lampon**. Turn to the right and follow the road until it turns left, then take the first right. Cross a couple of small bridges and when you see a red hand-painted sign that says 'Wedi Ireng', turn left. At the end of the road you can park near a small warung.

Pantai Wedi Ireng doesn't give up its charms cheaply. Once you've parked your car, you still have a long, hot walk ahead of you, to the tune of about 4km in each direction. Make sure you stock up on drinking water before you set off. Note that a lot of locals will ride their scooters to Pantai Wedi Ireng. This isn't advisable, especially during wet season, as the track can get very sketchy and in the rainforested area it can become very slippery.

Once you reach Pantai Wedi Ireng, you will be greeted by a rather small beach with brilliant white sand and calm, crystal-blue waters overlooking a sheltered lagoon with island views. To say that it is possibly the perfect place to spend a day would be an understatement. You will very likely also have it all to yourself...though that may change once it's in a guidebook – *cough, cough*.

Unusually for such a remote location, there are now a few facilities at Pantai Wedi Ireng, including a lone warung with simple offerings and a toilet. Dotted along the beachhead are a couple of small *bale*-style huts offering shelter, and some nice bench seats under the trees that also provide some shade from the sun.

Alas Purwo National Park

TIME FROM BANYUWANGI: **1½HR**

Explore the national parks

There are three major national parks around the coastlines at the far end of East Java, with each of them offering completely different experiences.

Perhaps the most famous for international visitors is **Alas Purwo National Park** *(nationalparksassociation.org/indonesia-national-parks/alas-purwo-national-park/; 205,000Rp)*. Located on the very southeastern tip of Java, this lowland area is dominated by dense forests and mangroves. The surfing hot spot of **G-Land** is located on the southwestern shoreline of the park, and the consistent world-class waves have it ranked as one of the best left-handers on the planet.

Alas Purwo has a very spiritual connection with the people of Indonesia. The name itself means 'first forest' and legends recognise the area as the first land to appear from the seas at the dawn of time. For this reason, there are many temples to be found throughout the forests, and caves around the area are considered sacred places, with many people making pilgrimages to spend days and weeks praying and meditating inside them.

Meru Betiri National Park

TIME FROM BANYUWANGI: **2HR**

Explore the Javan tiger's last home

West of Alas Purwo lies wildlife-rich **Meru Betiri National Park** *(205,000Rp)*, considered to be the last home of the Javan tiger, now believed to be extinct. The park itself is under constant threat from gold miners in the area, and the thick jungles hamper efforts to stop illegal hunters. Despite this, tourism is on the rise mostly thanks to **Sukamade Turtle Beach**, where green sea turtles can be found laying eggs at night. Local guides are available to take you to the beach, and in the spawning season from October to April you are almost guaranteed to see turtles. For this experience, consider staying at **Java Turtle Lodge** (p181), which runs guided tours.

Baluran National Park

TIME FROM BANYUWANGI: **1HR**

See wildlife on a savanna

A third national park lies in the northeast corner of the island. **Baluran National Park** *(205,000Rp, plus nominal vehicle fee for private vehicles)*, despite having a large, dormant volcano dominating much of it, is famous for its incredible savanna landscape. In scenes reminiscent of Africa, bulls, water

WHY I LOVE JAVA

Ray Bartlett, Lonely Planet writer

I've travelled through many different parts of Indonesia and adore that each island has such uniqueness; its own character, it's own customs and dialects and discoveries to make. But of all the islands, I think Java fits me the best, as it has so much of what mesmerises me about travel: the natural wonders are unparalleled, the people are kind and generous, I'm constantly questioning my preconceptions...and the food, oh, the food. There are pristine beaches worthy of any magazine cover, smouldering volcanoes to gawk at, mosques that look like giant Fabergé eggs...it gets better the longer I stay here.

THE ELUSIVE JAVAN TIGER

There are many who believe the Javan tiger still exists. Officially recognised as extinct since the 1970s, this tiger once resided all over the island, and existed in such numbers that in the 1800s it was actually branded as a pest and a bounty was issued to hunt it. It didn't take long for the tiger to begin retreating, finding refuge in the most remote forests and unsettled jungles of East Java.

The last confirmed sightings of the Javan Tiger were in Meru Betiri National Park. Despite several expeditions, no confirmed evidence has been found proving the continued existence of the tiger. Locals, however, believe it is still out there, prowling East Java's beaches and jungles.

HABS PHOTOGRAPHY/SHUTTERSTOCK

Horse-drawn *andong*, De Djawatan Forest

buffaloes, small deer, eagles and even peacocks can be seen here. You can arrange for a tour from most hotels in Banyuwangi, or hire a 4WD driver *(up to 6 people 700,000Rp)* at the entrance. From the entrance, there are only a few roads within the park, and most visitors drive around for a few hours looking for wildlife, then return to Banyuwangi. Hikers and overnight campers will need to arrange for this at the office beforehand.

De Djawatan Forest

TIME FROM BANYUWANGI: **1HR**

Get lost in a tree forest

De Djawatan Forest *(20,000Rp plus parking)* was once a train depot, but its giant trees remained off the logger's list long enough for it to be turned into a gorgeous, lush, incongruous park. It's just off the main road, yet most passersby don't even realise that it exists, which is a real shame. Created over 100 years ago, it consists of hundreds of trembesi trees that really have to be seen to be believed. The twisted and gnarled branches of these massive trees seemingly intertwine with each other to plait a canopy overhead. Along the huge, curving branches grow orchids that drape down, making the place a perfect spot for wedding photos and selfies.

As with any such touristy place in Indonesia, there are several other activities attached that you can try out if you like. Archery, ATVs and horse-drawn *andong* (horse-drawn passenger cart) rides around the perimeter are very popular. Around the back there are also a few small warungs offering refreshments. Don't miss the treehouse in one of the large trees just inside the main entry, along with a couple of cool little bridges that offer nice photo opportunities.

Bogor

GARDEN STROLLS | CAFE CULTURE | MOUNTAIN VIEWS

'A romantic little village' is how Sir Thomas Stamford Raffles described Bogor when he made it his country home during Java's brief period of British rule. As an oasis of unpredictable weather – it's credited with 322 thunderstorms a year – cool, quiet Bogor was the chosen retreat of colonials escaping the stifling, crowded capital.

Things have changed a little since then, and today the long arm of Jakarta reaches all the way to Bogor, meaning this satellite city experiences the overspill of the capital's perennial traffic and air-quality problems. Despite the relentless pull of 'development', the world-class botanical gardens that sit right in the heart of the city have lost none of their beauty. Indeed, deep in forested sections of the gardens, the chatter of insects and twitter of birdsong drowns out the hum of traffic circling the gates. The city also has a lively Chinatown, which is dotted with cafes and restaurants within walking distance of the gardens.

GETTING AROUND

Traffic is heavy in town and it's often quicker to get around on foot. *Angkot* minibuses shuttle around, particularly between the bus terminal and train station. Angkot 03 does a counterclockwise loop of the botanical gardens on its way to Jl Kapten Muslihat, near the train station. Bogor has frequent train services to and from Jakarta Kota Station, with trains making the hourlong journey every 15 minutes or so.

Tropical Plants & Birdsong

Exploring Bogor's verdant botanical gardens

At the heart of Bogor covering 87 hectares is the city's green lung, the fabulous **Kebun Raya** *(kebunraya.id; weekday/weekend 15,000/25,500Rp)*. Everyone loves the Orchid House with its exotic and delicate blooms, but there are more than 15,000 other species of plants here, including 400 different kinds of palm (don't miss the footstool palm, which tops out at an impressive 25m). While some of the gardens are meticulously manicured, other sections have a feeling of verdant wilderness, so keep an eye out for colourful birds, butterflies and massive, fruit-eating flying foxes.

TOP TIP

To avoid the infamous thunderstorms, visit the botanical gardens as early in the day as you can, allowing a half-day to enjoy them (and the excellent on-site restaurant). Crowds flock here on weekends, but the gardens are otherwise quiet.

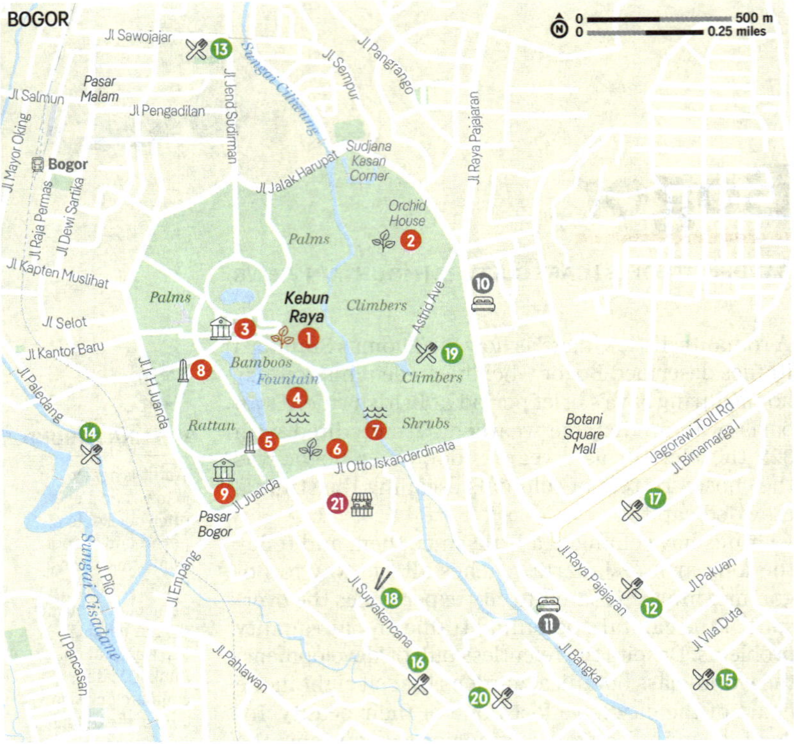

BOGOR

HIGHLIGHTS
1 Kebun Raya

SIGHTS
2 Griya Anggrek
3 Istana Bogor
4 Kolam Bulat
5 Memorial to Olivia Raffles
6 Mexico Gardens
7 Sungai Ciliwung
8 Tomb of DJ de Eerens
9 Zoological Museum

SLEEPING
10 Hotel Grand Savero
11 Rion Bogor Hostel

EATING
12 De' Leuit
13 Doea Tjangkir
14 Gumati Resto
15 Medja
16 Mr Yos
17 Raindear Coffee & Kitchen
18 Resto Kencana
19 Resto Raasaa
20 Soto Mie Agih

SHOPPING
21 Pasar Baru Bogor

EATING IN BOGOR: OUR PICKS

De' Leuit: The multistorey favourite does exciting variations of *sate*, mixed rice, fried fish and chicken, as well as local veggie dishes. *10am-8.30pm* $$

Resto Kencana: Feast on satisfying Chinese fare in an elegant dining room fronted by red paper lanterns and full of vintage photos of Bogor. *10am-7pm Tue-Sun* $$

Soto Mie Agih: Specialising in *soto mie* (noodle soup), this simple place does such a roaring trade you may have to queue. *8am-7pm Mon-Fri, to 8pm Sat & Sun* $

Mr Yos: A great place for a pit stop while exploring Suryakencana, this delightful bakery and cafe has flaky pastries and many other temptations. *7am-10pm* $

The main entrance gate is at the south (somewhat eastern) end of the gardens. Nearby, you can hire scooters or bicycles. A good landmark to get your bearings is the small **memorial** erected in memory of Governor-General Raffles' first wife, Olivia Raffles, who died in 1814 and was buried in Batavia (now Jakarta). Keep following the main path to reach a lotus-filled pond, with **Istana Bogor** in the background. This presidential palace is an obligatory photo stop for every visiting Indonesian. Keep your eyes to the ground to spot *kenari* nuts, the tropical almonds that grow readily in Maluku. Veer left to visit a small, peaceful cemetery, which has a few Dutch headstones, including the **tomb of DJ de Eerens**, a former governor-general. From here, you can plunge into the shadowy world of bamboo, amid towering species like the 30m-high Bambu Raksasa.

Heading straight south from here, you can take a detour through the **Zoological Museum** *(separate admission charge weekday/weekend 15,000/25,00Rp)*, which is full of taxidermised creatures from across Indonesia. At the main entrance you'll walk beneath a massive blue-whale skeleton harvested from a specimen that washed onto a West Javan beach in 1916. Inside the galleries you can get your fill of glorious insects, from the leaf-mimicking *Kallima paralekta* to the massive *Attacus atlas* moth; contemplate the mournful loss of the last rhinoceros from Preanger, shot in 1914; and see numerous species of monkeys, birds and big cats. There's even a replica of the early human ancestor *Pithecanthropus erectus,* aka 'Java man', the oldest hominid ever found at the time of its discovery in 1894.

Emerging back into the gardens, find your way over to the **Kolam Bulat** ('round pool'), which is dotted with *Victoria regia* waterlilies – the largest on the planet – and backed by a venerable banyan tree. Next up are the **Mexico Gardens**, with prickly cacti and overabundant agave looking rather out of place in this damp landscape. Follow the sounds of rushing water to reach the edge of the fast-moving **Sungai Ciliwung**. A suspension bridge gives a fine vantage point over the water.

You may want to take a break at **Resto Raasaa** *(WhatsApp +62 811 9711 5927)*. The beautifully set space has sweeping views down to the waterlily ponds and there's a good variety of Indonesian and Western fare plus drinks (mocktails, with no alcohol). It's open from 9am to 8pm during the week and from 7am on weekends. Afterwards, finish your garden tour at the impressive **Griya Anggrek** (Orchid House).

QUINTESSENTIAL SUNDANESE DISHES

West Java is worth visiting for the food alone. Sundanese cooking is celebrated in Indonesia, and you'll find flavour-packed greens and many healthy but rich combinations. Try these dishes:

Karedok: Salad of long beans, bean sprouts and cucumber with peanut sauce.

Soto Bandung: Beef-and-vegetable soup with lemongrass; *ayam* (chicken) is also popular.

Ketupat tahu: Pressed rice, bean sprouts and tofu with soy and peanut sauce.

Nasi liwet: Rice cooked with coconut milk and spices.

Colenak: A dessert of roasted cassava with coconut sauce.

Uli: Another dessert, made of roasted sticky rice with peanut sauce.

EATING IN BOGOR: BEST ATMOSPHERE

Doea Tjangkir: This classy place has well-made Javanese dishes like *karedok* and *soto ayam* plus steaks and roast duck. *11am-8pm Tue-Sun* $$

Gumati Resto: Enjoy fabulous views over town with delicious Sundanese food, including a reputable *sup ikan bambu* (fish and bamboo soup). *7am-10pm* $$

Raindear Coffee & Kitchen: A spotless Euro-style cafe with Indonesian and Western mains, sandwiches and canned coffees to go. *10am-10pm* $$

Medja: A beautiful atrium space with fountains and shrubbery whips up good Indonesian fare served family-style (big plates for sharing). *11am-9pm* $$

ONWARD TRAVEL FROM BOGOR

If you're not travelling to or from Jakarta, leaving Bogor can be a little complicated. Several bus companies, including Maya Graha Indah, make the trip to Bandung from Baranangsiang bus terminal, and there are also smaller shuttle buses leaving from behind Bogor Trade Mall (like Sinar, Aragon and Lintas).

On weekends, when traffic is at its worst, it may be faster to take the train north to Jakarta, disembark at Stasiun Gondangdia, hop on an *ojek* or walk the 1.2km to Stasiun Gambir and catch the train from there to Bandung. If you're aching for the coast, two buses a day head to Pangandaran, including with Bus Budiman, with an evening overnight departure arriving at around 5am.

TEGUH JATI PRASETYO/SHUTTERSTOCK

Lotus-filled pond, Istana Bogor (p155)

Produce Emporium

The frenetic energy of Pasar Baru

Jl Suryakencana, steps from the botanical gardens' gates, is a whirlwind of activity as shoppers spill en masse from within the byzantine concrete halls of **Pasar Baru** and the Plaza Bogor onto the street. Inside, the morning market is awash with all manner of produce and flowers, meat and fish, secondhand clothes and more. Hot, sweltering and fragrant with spices and overripe fruit, it's a place of pure sensory overload. Dive into the barter and trade for an authentic slice of Bogor, or just walk around marvelling at the cacophony and frenetic energy of the colours, the aromas and the voices.

Beyond Bogor

Bogor
Gunung Halimun Salak National Park
Cimaja

Escape the bustling streets and enter a world of nature, with wildlife-filled forests, photogenic tea plantations and a dramatic coastline.

Flower-filled gardens aside, one of the best features of Bogor is its proximity to some truly inspiring scenery. Gunung Halimun Salak National Park is worth the effort to reach – this pristine swathe of nature has mist-shrouded mountains and opportunities for outstanding hikes. The mixed-use park is also home to several plantations, such as Nirmala Tea Estate, where you can see every shade of green imaginable. Further south, the road passes rice paddies and rolling hills before ending around Cimaja, a picturesque stretch of shoreline that attracts a handful of surfers who come for the fine but not particularly well-known waves. It's also a serene nature escape even if you're not here to surf.

Places

GETTING AROUND

One waterfall-filled section of the park is easily reached by *angkot* from Bogor. For other areas, you'll need your own transport unless you're on a tour. The usual access is through Cibadak on the Bogor–Pelabuhan Ratu road, from where you turn off to Cikidang, then on to the Nirmala Tea Estate. For Cimaja, catch one of several daily buses in Bogor to Pelabuhan Ratu. From there, *angkot* continue on to Cimaja. Here, locals hire out motorbikes and you'll even find surfboard racks.

Gunung Halimun Salak National Park

TIME FROM BOGOR: **1HR**

Waterfalls and zip lines

Stretching across some 400 sq km, **Gunung Halimun Salak National Park** *(200,000Rp)* is home to two impressive mountains, which are often cloaked in clouds along with the lush valleys below. The park's best feature is the rich montane forest in the highland regions around Gunung Halimun (1929m), its tallest peak. The scenery is ravishing and there's a lot of wildlife (though most of it is hard to see), including langurs, gibbons and birdlife.

If you're seeking a quick nature escape, the easiest access to the national park is the area surrounding **Curug Nangka**, whose name means 'jackfruit waterfall'. Not one cascade but rather a series of them, this much-loved getaway features easy-going paths (mostly paved with steps) that lead past the rushing mountain stream as it tumbles over slick wet boulders against a background of ferns, mosses and palms. The tallest of the falls, **Curug Kaung**, plunges from a height of about 17m and makes a refreshing spot for nature's finest shower after the 20-minute walk from the park entrance. Just below it, **Curug Daun** feeds into a small plunge pool, which is better for a full immersion.

HOMEGROWN SURF LEGEND

Born in Cimaja in 1985, Dede Suryana used to watch foreign surfers with envy as a young boy. When first given the opportunity to surf, he plunged in, tackling waves at the age of six. He soon became obsessed with the sport. His parents, who were farmers, initially frowned on his hobby – until the sponsors came knocking. At the age of 18, in 2003, he made history, beating world champion Kelly Slater in the Todd Chesser Memorial Contest in Hawaii. He's since gone on to win a number of championships while running a surf shop and **guesthouse/restaurant** that's an easy walk to the beach.

You're almost sure to see the long-tailed macaques that frequent this section of the park. There are warungs inside, as well as a camping area, and you can hire a tent and sleeping pad *(200,000Rp)* to stay the night.

For something slightly more adventurous, head up to **Bogor Treetop Zipline Adventure** *(bogortreetopzipline.com; weekday/weekend online bookings 150,000/250,000Rp, walk-in bookings 160,000/260,000Rp)*. Located just above the main park entrance, a series of zip lines crisscrosses the canyon, yielding dramatic views as you soar high above the forest and waterfall on one of Indonesia's longest zip-line tracks. There are eight different lines totalling 2.1km; completing the course takes about one hour. The resort also has a restaurant with panoramic views, well-equipped A-frame cabins and camping.

You can get here by *angkot;* these depart from opposite the BTM mall at the southwest corner of Bogor's botanical gardens. Look for those with 'Ciapus' or 'Faten' written on the windshield. The drive takes you to a stop near the **Highland Park Resort Hotel** *(thehighlandparkresortbogor.com)*, from which it's a pleasant 1.3km walk to the park entrance gates.

Hiking in the national park

A good half-day hike is to **Kawah Ratu** *(20,000Rp)* the so-called Queen Crater, with its alien landscape of steaming turquoise pools, craggy smoke-spewing rock formations and the scent of sulphur tinging the air. Several different trails lead up to this area. The best approach starts at the **Cidahu entrance gate** (1108m) in the south (near the Javana Spa) and heads up the 5km trail to the crater. Elevation gain is moderate (around 250m), and it typically takes around four hours to get there and back. Along the way, you'll pass various streams, an abandoned helipad and a few HM (hectometre) signs marking the route. These were once found every 100m or so but most have disappeared over the years. Note that it's best to have lunch before (or after) you reach Kawah Ratu, to avoid lingering amid the sulphurous smells.

More ambitious, well-prepared hikers can take this trail and turn off at Bajuri before reaching Kawah Ratu to make the ascent up **Gunung Salak** (2211m). It gets quite steep in places, with ropes tied between trees giving assistance in some of the tougher stretches. The park recommends allowing around eight hours (one way) to reach the top, though fit hikers can make the climb in about five hours. If you run out of light before arriving at the summit, **Pos Bayangan** is a good open camping spot.

EATING & DRINKING IN CIMAJA: OUR PICKS

Nurda's: A restaurant and guesthouse with a large deck overlooking the beach and gardens; very popular for non-surfing day drinkers. *8am-5pm* $$

Cimaja Square: A hotel restaurant with excellent breakfasts and Indonesian lunch and dinner options served until (relatively) late. *9am-9pm* $$

Olelo: Grab coffee or simple pastries at this clean, well-lit shop that's not far from the turn to the beach. *8.30am-10pm Mon-Fri, 7.30am-11pm Sat & Sun* $

Dede Suryana Place: A one-stop surfer's dream, with hearty meals, great coffee, surf advice and rentals. It's a central spot for the community. *7am-9pm* $$

For a one-day summit up Salak, the trail to climb begins near the **Cimelati trailhead office**, southeast of the mountain. It's a steep but fairly direct climb starting from 800m elevation. The walk leads you through forest, with a fair bit of manoeuvring around roots, rocks and mud, and there are drop-offs in some sections so tread carefully. The canopy thins out as you near the end. If the clouds disperse, you'll have magnificent views over the southern reaches of Bogor as well as the peaks of Gunung Gede and Pangrango off to the east. Allow about four to five hours to reach the top and another four hours to descend, plus time on the summit.

A third option for the ascent begins near the **Pasir Reungit entrance station**, on the northwest side of Salak. This trail takes you up through wet and muddy sections, so good waterproof shoes are essential. Keep an eye out for leeches as well.

Cimaja

TIME FROM BOGOR: **4HR**

Seek southern swell

Cimaja, pronounced *chee*-mah-jah (and spelled Tjimadja on Google), is an attractive, low-key surf resort some 100km south of Bogor, with a good choice of accommodation and several decent and reasonably unfrequented surf spots (though none attain the epic standards found elsewhere in the archipelago). It's also just a cool, off-the-map place to hang out. After a long sunset surf session, as you wander back through the ricefields along the canals, board under your arm, you'll hear the ethereal calls to prayer filter through the palms and feel far away from Java's teeming, cosmopolitan cities, even though the spot is only a few hours south of Jakarta. The slow pace and oceanic air make for an exhilarating change that will appeal to non-surfers, too. To get here, you have to pass through the large, unlovely resort of Pelabuhan Ratu; Cimaja is 8km further west.

In general, the wave quality isn't as high as Indonesia's more famous surf areas, but as every surfer knows, even an average Indonesian surf spot is probably 10 times better than your home break! Some of the better-known waves include **Cimaja Point**, which is a long, walled-up right point with rare cover-up sections. It's the most consistent and crowded wave. **Indicator Point**, just outside Cimaja Point, fires at high tide when there's a big swell, but it's only for experienced surfers. **Pantai Karang Haji** has a sectioned beach break that's good for beginners. There are other spots tucked away along the coastline either side of Cimaja, such as **Loji**, a large left-hander. Some of these are very good waves indeed.

Surf lessons start at about 500,000Rp for two hours, with boards available from 100,000Rp. Diving, fishing, rafting and motorcycling trips can also be organised through one of the area's guesthouses. If you're feeling the need to rest your weary bones in some hot water, consider hopping over to the hot springs of **Cisolok** *(55,000Rp)*, a mostly-for-locals spot where you can soak in mineral-laden water, view a steaming geyser, munch snacks and inexpensive warung meals, and enjoy. It's open 8am to 5pm.

WATERFALL REJUVENATION

Tom Arinto Soetomo, Bogor local guide and Tom's Homestay owner, shares a favourite nature retreat.

It's wonderful to go to Curug Nangka early in the morning. Catch a 4am *angkot*, and you can reach the waterfall before sunrise when no one else is there. The water comes from the high mountains and is full of minerals and perhaps healing qualities. It's like a kind of purification bathing in the waterfall, and it's a good way to release any negativity from your body. Afterwards you can walk up to a lookout nearby (where the zip lines cross the valley) and watch the sunrise over the forested mountains. This is an amazing and rejuvenating way to start the day.

Gunung Gede Pangrango National Park

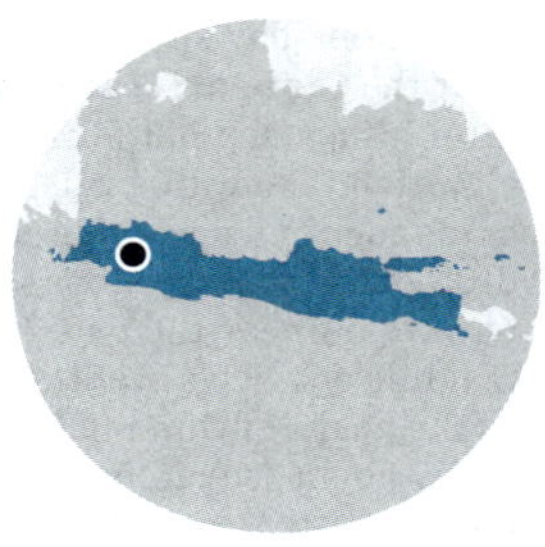

TREKKING | WILDLIFE WATCHING | NATURE ESCAPES

GETTING AROUND

The town of Cibodas is the main gateway to the park. Frequent *angkot* run from town to the entrance to the Kebun Raya Cibodas. If you're accessing more remote trails, it's easiest to go by *ojek* or taxi to your intended departure point. Note that on weekends and holidays the traffic along this route is almost gridlocked. Plan your excursions here for midweek to avoid wasting the day in traffic.

Named after two towering volcanoes that rise above the slopes of western Java, Gunung Gede Pangrango National Park is an extraordinary biological refuge – one that was named a UNESCO World Biosphere Reserve back in 1977. An impressive array of plant and animal life inhabits the diverse ecosystems encompassing lowland, mountain and subalpine forests, as well as mountain grasslands. Rare and endemic animal species include leaf monkeys, Javan leopards, silvery gibbons and the diminutive mouse deer, along with some 250 bird species. Given the park's relative proximity to Jakarta, this biodiversity is all the more astonishing – and faces ongoing threats owing to pollution and forest degradation.

Most people come here for a nature escape and to hike the park's rewarding trails, which lead past lakes, waterfalls and dramatic overlooks. Chief bragging rights go to those who make the challenging (but not technical) climb up Gunung Gede (2958m) or the Pangrango summit (3019m).

TOP TIP

On arrival at Gunung Gede Pangrango National Park register for the climb and obtain your permit (a steep 300,000Rp for foreigners) from the PHKA office just outside the entrance to the Kebun Raya Cibodas. The office has an information centre and pamphlets on the park.

Climbing Gunung Gede

West Java's second-highest peak

The thick, jungled slopes of the 2958m volcano **Gunung Gede** offer one of the most exciting and challenging treks in West Java. The terrain encompasses surprising variety, with a sparkling lake, waterfalls, hot springs, an otherworldly crater and a lush high-elevation meadow. Wildlife, birding and botanic wonders are all part of the allure.

The park is noted for its alpine forest and birdlife, including the rare Javan eagle, one of those 'life list' species that many birders come here specifically to see. If one is soaring above, they're not even that hard to spot; you just have to be lucky. Officially, guides to the summit have to be hired here *(2-day round trip 500,000Rp)*, though the main trail is relatively easy to follow. Gunung Gede is closed to hikers during

HIGHLIGHTS
1 Gunung Gede

SIGHTS
2 Cibeureum Falls
3 Gunung Pangrango
4 Kandang Badak
5 Suryakencana Meadow
6 Telaga Biru

ACTIVITIES
7 Hot Springs

stormy weather, between January and March, and usually in August, too.

Be aware that the 10km (one-way) hike right to the summit takes at least 12 hours there and back, so you should start as early as possible and take food, water, a torch and warm clothes (night temperatures can drop to 5°C). Some hikers leave by 2am to reach the summit in the early morning, before the mists roll in. That's wise, because once the mists *do* start coming, your incredible views may vanish and you won't be able to see more than 10ft in front of you. From Cibodas, the trail quickly passes **Telaga Biru**, a beautiful blue-green lake. The **Cibeureum Falls** (one hour away) lie just off the main trail. Most picnickers only go this far, though some continue on to the **hot springs**, 3½ hours from the gate. Treks to the falls alone are possible for just 150,000Rp plus the entry fee.

The trail continues to climb for another 1½ hours to **Kandang Badak**, where a hut has been built on the saddle between the peaks of Gunung Gede and **Gunung Pangrango** (3019m). Take the trail to the right for a hard three-hour climb to Pangrango. Most hikers turn left for the easier, but still steep 1½-hour climb to Gede, which has more spectacular views (again, assuming the clouds don't obscure it). The Gede Crater lies below the summit, and you can continue on to the **Suryakencana Meadow**.

The park attracts its share of weekend warriors, which is not surprising given its close proximity to Jakarta (it only takes around 2½ hours to get to the park information centre at Cibodas on good days). This can be annoying, if you're the type to want the trail all to yourself, but it can also be a great way to meet new friends, as many of the locals will be excited to chat with a traveller. You may even find that you're the centre of a selfie or two.

REPLANTING THE FOREST

One of the more ambitious environmental projects in West Java is the reforestation of a degraded area on Gunung Gede Pangrango National Park's periphery. It was launched in 2008 by Conservation International (CI) to address the increasing threat to endemic species, the expansion of logging and the destruction of a vital watershed.

CI involved a local community in the project, providing a more sustainable source of income and transitioning people away from farming. In all, some 120,000 trees have been planted across the 300-hectare Green Wall. Though small in scale, the project has positively impacted both the national park and the community, and there are hopes that it could be a model for other parts of Indonesia.

Beyond Gunung Gede Pangrango National Park

After adventures in the national park, immerse yourself in the abundant greenery of this region by exploring gardens, ricefields and tea plantations.

Places

GETTING AROUND

The turnoff to Cibodas is on the Bogor–Bandung Hwy, a few kilometres west of Cipanas. Buses running between these two cities will drop you off at the turnoff. The gardens – the undisputed highlight of Cibodas – are 5km from the main road. *Angkot* run from the roadside in Cipanas up to the gardens and the entrance to the Gunung Gede Pangrango National Park.

At the foot of the forested mountain park, the town of Cibodas has absorbed the encroaching urbanism of nearby cities, though it still retains elements of its former days as a prosperous yet simple tea and market town. The big draw is its famous botanical garden, a manicured spot with greenhouses, fountains and lots of grassy lawns.

Weekending urbanites come for the cool air and natural attractions (though gridlocked traffic is a constant). East of here, the market town of Cianjar is enveloped by shimmering green paddy fields, which produce some of Java's finest rice. Urban sprawl diminishes the charm, but the area is a gateway to walking trails, hillside villages and attractive countryside.

Kebun Raya Cibodas

TIME FROM GUNUNG GEDE PANGRANGO NATIONAL PARK: **10MIN**

Lush gardens

The stunning gardens of **Kebun Raya Cibodas** are an extension of the botanical gardens at Bogor (which makes sense, when you consider that altitude and temperature make a vast difference in where certain plants are able to grow). Spread over the steep lower slopes of Gunung Gede and Gunung Pangrango at an altitude of 1300m to 1440m, these lush gardens are among the dampest places in Java. The Dutch tried to cultivate quinine here (its bark is used in malaria medication), though the East Javan climate proved more suitable.

You'll find an outstanding collection of ferns, palms, 65 species of eucalyptus and Mexican mountain pines, as well as glasshouses bursting with cacti and succulents. A road loops around the gardens, passing the **Sakura Garden** with its cherry trees, and there are also paths leading through forests of bamboo to the impressive **Cismun waterfall**. In general, the gardens here have more of a wild and unkempt look than those found in Bogor – and it's well worth seeing both if you have the time.

Kampung Budaya Padi Pandan Wangi

TIME FROM GUNUNG GEDE PANGRANGO NATIONAL PARK: **30MIN**

Views over the rice paddies

If you're looking for that perfect panorama over ricefields with the mountains in the backdrop, it's hard to top the setting at this so-called cultural village southwest of Cianjar. At **Kampung Budaya Padi Pandan Wangi** *(10,000Rp)*, raised wooden platforms wind past the fields, where farmers at work are happy to chat with visitors (though you'll likely need some Javanese). We say 'so-called' because while it is certainly an experience, it's hard to claim that it has the same depth of information and the educational qualities most foreigners expect from a 'cultural' tour. Being able to get up and close to the incredible latticework (known as *anyaman bambu*) that adorns the walls of the huts is a treat. The practice of making walls like this is slowly dying out, but these walls regulate airflow, providing much needed ventilation, as well as give a house a distinct pattern. The village, which is open to visitors from 7am to 5pm, remains a fun day trip out of Bogor or a diversion from hiking in Gunung Gede if you're based on the mountainside.

Riung Gunung

TIME FROM GUNUNG GEDE PANGRANGO NATIONAL PARK: **30MIN**

Strolling through a tea plantation

The main road from Bogor heading east towards the Cibodas turnoff corkscrews its way along as it reaches **Puncak Pass**, a mountain pass that tops out at 1500m. Resorts, gardens and tea plantations dot the road, which has been a popular highland getaway since the early 20th century. A worthwhile place to stop is **Riung Gunung** *(10,000Rp)*, a rolling tea plantation scenically set against the mountainous backdrop. Vendors sell hot drinks and food out of pushcarts, there's car and motorcycle parking, and if you're lucky you'll see paragliders soaring around in the breeze. The tea itself is beautiful, offering meditative wanderings through the cool, often misty paths. Arrive in the morning and you might see harvesters with baskets on their backs gathering leaves.

KOPI LUWAK

One of the most expensive coffees in the world, *kopi luwak* is made from coffee beans that have been eaten and defecated by the *luwak* (Asian palm civet), with small producers found in West Java, Sumatra and Bali. According to connoisseurs, the partial fermentation of the beans after passing through the animal's gastrointestinal tract cuts down the acidity of the bean and makes for a rich, earthy taste, with a noticeably smoother finish.

Critics, meanwhile, cite the inhumane conditions *luwak* are often subjected to – confined to small cages, the animals experience a life without access to the outdoors or proper nutrition. Even if your pocketbook allows the luxury, most animal rights activists encourage visitors to give the coffee a miss.

Bandung

ART DECO ARCHITECTURE | SUNDANESE COOKING | URBAN EXPLORING

GETTING AROUND

Bandung is a fiendishly difficult city to negotiate on public transport, and few travellers bother as taxi rates are reasonable. Stick to ever-reliable Bluebird taxis, as well as Uber, Grab and Gojek.

The main train station is about 1km west of lively Jl Braga. Most travellers arriving by high-speed train from Jakarta disembark at Padalarang Station, 17km northwest of the centre, and change to the free feeder train to Bandung Station.

City (Damri) buses run from west to east down Jl Asia Afrika to Cicaheum bus terminal, and from Bandung train station to Leuwi Panjang bus terminal.

Bandung's energy is palpable, with teeming markets, thriving cafes in reclaimed colonial Dutch relics and a vibrant arts-and-culture scene. At an elevation of 768m, Bandung has cooler temperatures than Jakarta and a mountainous backdrop, though like its bigger sibling to the northwest, heavy traffic (and smog) is no small consideration in this city of 2.5 million.

You'll have to use your imagination to see 'the Paris of Java', a moniker bequeathed in the early 20th century when Bandung was a resort city for tea-plantation owners, and the streets were dotted with European-style boutiques, luxury hotels and upscale restaurants. The post-WWII period brought explosive growth that uprooted much of Bandung's historic core to create office towers, malls and banks. Though not an obvious choice for a getaway, Bandung has lots going on, with ambitious museums, striking architecture and an impressive dining scene – all of which make for a rewarding two-day visit.

Exploring Prehistoric Wonders

Bandung's Geological Museum

Even if the thought of gazing at rock samples puts you to sleep, this sizeable **museum** *(museum.geologi.esdm.go.id; locals/foreigners 5,000/25,000Rp)* makes for some fascinating exploring owing to its diverse collections set in a historic building from the 1920s. You'll get a sense of the great creatures that once roamed the earth by checking out the towering skeletons – including an 85%-intact skeleton of a 165,000-year-old elephant found in Blora. There are also replicas of mystifying human skulls, like that of the famous 'Java man' unearthed on the island in the 1890s. Another hall displays meteorites; the biggest is the 156kg Jatipengilon found in East Java in

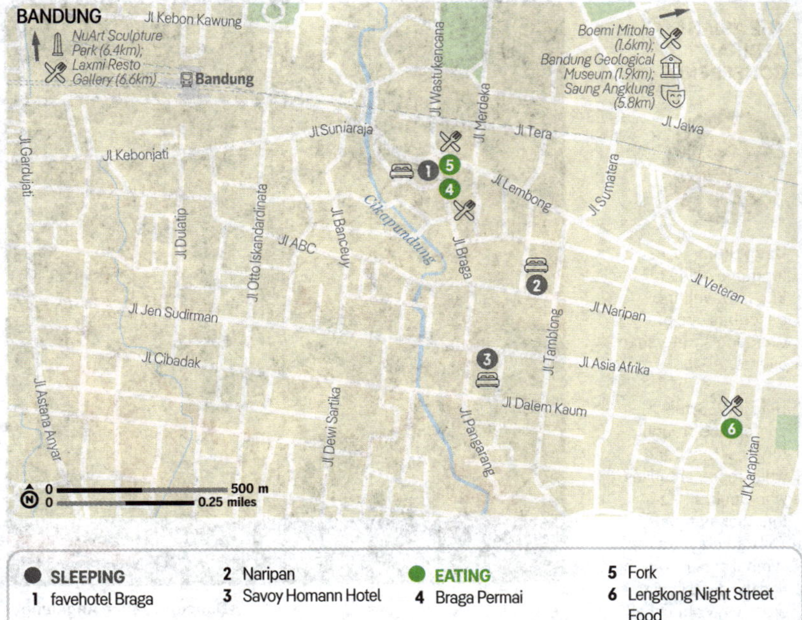

1884. Don't miss the displays that delve into the geological evolution of Java, from its volcanic origins to the first humans that settled in the Bandung area. Be aware that much of the information is in Bahasa Indonesia.

Discovering New Art

Imagination at work at the NuArt Sculpture Park

Spread across four hectares northwest of the centre, **NuArt Sculpture Park** *(nuartsculpturepark.com; 50,000Rp)* features the works of Nyoman Nuarta among others, a renowned Balinese artist whose art has appeared in exhibitions around the globe. Over 100 of his works fill the space, which encompasses two storeys of gallery space and verdant gardens, with waterfalls, walking trails, ponds and forest glens, with the art intermixed throughout. A regular lineup of performing-arts events such as dance performances, concerts and art exhibitions happens in the amphitheatre, and you can also munch on Balinese cuisine at **Laxmi Resto Gallery** *(+62 22-201 7815)*. Both are closed on Mondays.

TOP TIP

A few steps from Alun-Alun Bandung, the well-run **Pusat Informasi Pariwisata** (tourism office) has helpful English-speaking staff. Nearby, you'll find the stop for the Bandros, an open-sided bus that does a one-hour circuit; it gives a fine overview of the city.

THE ASIAN-AFRICAN CONFERENCE

Usep Sunarto, a longtime guide for Enoss Travellers, describes one of Bandung's watershed events.

Held in 1955, the conference brought together Black and white representatives who would sit together as equals. The gathering was a symbol against racism and the old colonial order. Only about half of the countries that participated were actually independent, and in many ways, the summit would be a catalyst for those unfree nations to gain their sovereignty. Places like Indonesia would help Malaysia get its independence, which came in 1957. People from Bandung are rightly proud of the Asian-African Conference, and it's an event children learned about in school – not only here in Indonesia but all across Asia.

HENI YULIANI/SHUTTERSTOCK

Dancers, Saung Angklung

Hypnotic Traditional Music

Performances at Saung Angklung

Around 10km northeast of the city, the arts centre **Saung Angklung** *(angklung-udjo.co.id; weekday/weekend foreigner 100,000/120,000Rp)* hosts enjoyable *angklung* (bamboo musical instrument) performances. Here you can also catch periodic dance events and ceremonial processions, assuming you can find the schedule. Check with a local guide or your hotel as a start.

EATING IN BANDUNG: OUR PICKS

Braga Permai: Bandung hub with a terrace, Dutch architecture and standout Indonesian and Western fare. *8am-midnight Mon-Fri, from 7am Sat & Sun* $$

Boemi Mitoha: This bustling Indonesian buffet restaurant serves tray upon tray of delicious foods; as in many parts of Java, you eat with your hands. *10am-10pm* $

Fork: An atmospheric 24-hour place for indulging in sizzling brisket, pizzas fired up in a wood-burning oven, or pastries and coffee. *24hr* $$

Lengkong Night Street Food: Four blocks of Lengkong become a nightly foodie extravaganza with everything from char-grilled chicken to durian ice cream. *6pm-midnight* $

STROLLING HISTORIC BANDUNG

See some of Bandung's most historic and iconic sites on this easy walking tour.

START	END	LENGTH
Alun-Alun Bandung	Wiki Koffie	1.5km; 1-2hr

Central Bandung is awash with striking architecture, buzzing streets and well-placed terrace cafes for watching the passing people. Start at 1 **Alun-Alun Bandung**, a prime meeting spot. Towering overhead are the 81m minarets of the aptly named 2 **Grand Mosque (Masjid Raya) of Bandung**, which can hold 13,000 worshippers. Nearby, the 3 **Asia Africa Monument** features a large globe atop a monument with the names of all the countries that participated in the Asian-African Conference.

Carefully cross busy Jl Asia Afrika and go inside the former office of the 4 **Dutch Trading Company NHM**. Now housing a bank, the interior is beautifully preserved, with stained-glass windows and a swirling frieze. Delve deeper into the famous conference at the 5 **Museum Konferensi Asia Afrika**, which has vintage photos of Sukarno, Nasser and other leaders. Stop at one of the city's finest Art Deco hotels, the 6 **Savoy Homann** (p181). Next, stroll 7 **Jl Braga**, Bandung's most photogenic street, packed with restaurants, cafes and bars. The excellent 8 **Grey Art Gallery** features works by Bandung greats like the late Jeihan Sukmantoro. Across the street, find 9 **Wayang Golek Bapak Ramdan**, a shop with a variety of Indonesian puppets. End your walk at 10 **Wiki Koffie**, a charmingly old-fashioned spot for coffee and snacks.

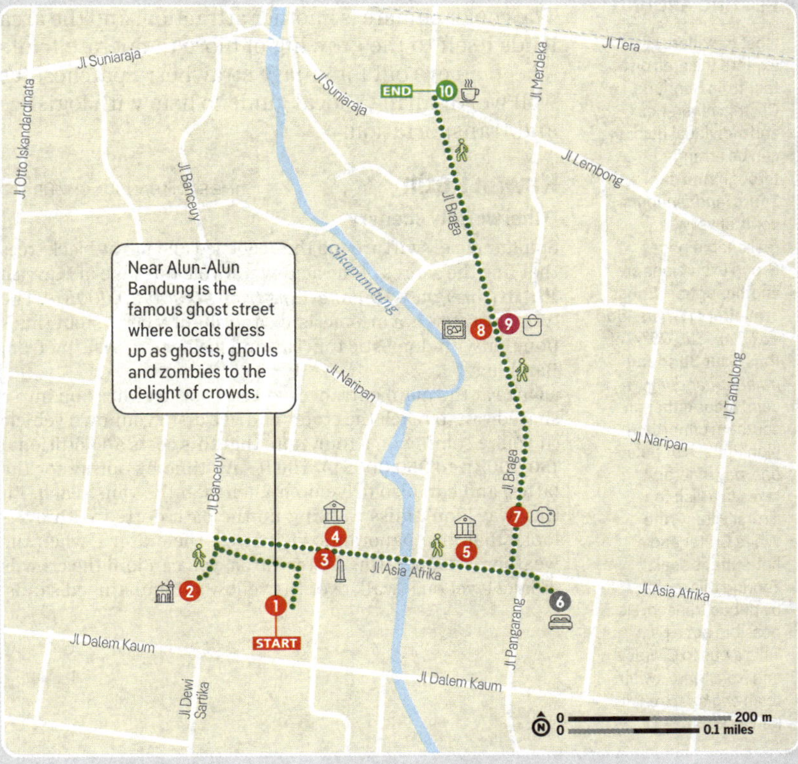

Near Alun-Alun Bandung is the famous ghost street where locals dress up as ghosts, ghouls and zombies to the delight of crowds.

Jl Suniaraja
Jl Tera
Jl Merdeka
END 10
Jl Otto Iskandardinata
Jl Lembong
Jl Banceuy
Jl Braga
Cikapundung
Jl Naripan
Jl Tamblong
Jl Asia Afrika
START
Jl Dalem Kaum
Jl Pangarang
Jl Dewi Sartika
0 200 m
0 0.1 miles

Beyond Bandung

Outside the urban bustle, you'll find verdant hillsides covered in tea plantations, smoking volcanic lakes and enticing hot springs tucked into a valley.

Places

GETTING AROUND

Most travellers explore the area on a tour from Bandung. Custom itineraries and individual guiding can be arranged through **Andriani Tours** *(andrianitours.com)*, at very reasonable prices. Group excursions are another option. **Enoss Travellers** *(WhatsApp +62 896 5380 0077)* or **Raja Tour Bandung** *(rajatourbandung.com)* focus either on southern or northern highlights. A popular one-day itinerary takes in a visit to a rural village, the White Crater and a hot-springs soak. Touring this region by public transport is possible but a pain. Take a bus to Ciwidey, and from there switch to an *angkot* to reach Kawah Putih.

One of the best reasons for visiting Bandung is to use the city as a launchpad to explore some exceptional scenery. Nearby, you'll find a rolling evergreen landscape of neatly cropped tea bushes, clumps of tropical forest and misty hilltops. Volcanic activity sits just below the surface, which you can experience on walks to the edge of smoke-spewing crater lakes, followed by some downtime in steaming hot springs. The cooler climate is another attraction, and the area lends itself to the growing of more temperate fruits – keep an eye out for village strawberry patches. It's well worth hiring a local guide to help with logistics and transportation.

Kawah Putih

TIME FROM BANDUNG: 1½HR

Otherworldly scenery

Sulphur mists swirl around the deadened and burnt-black trees that line the shores of the acid-water volcanic lake of **Kawah Putih** *(foreigners/Indonesians from 90,000/30,000Rp)*. The 'White Crater' is a mesmerising and slightly eerie sight that's popular with domestic tourists and well worth visiting from Bandung.

Once at the main entrance, you can opt to either hop into a shared van to reach the crater or drive up in your own vehicle (if you're coming on a tour, note that this costs an additional 150,000Rp to 250,000Rp). You'll save time by opting for the latter, and can also drive up higher than the vans reach. Either way, don't miss walking up the path dotted with overlooks that give panoramic views over the crater – when the weather is cooperating. Afterwards, you can join the crowds at lake level on a walk over the yellow sulphur-tinged sands.

RIZKY RAHMAT HIDAYAT/SHUTTERSTOCK

Suspension bridge, Kawah Rengganis

Kawah Rengganis

TIME FROM BANDUNG: 1½HR

Bask in hot springs

Lovely **Kawah Rengganis** (also known as Kawah Cibuni) is a pretty, isolated river fed by hot springs and surrounded by billowing steam from volcanic vents. It was once something of a local secret, with several holy Muslim graves where visitors would pay their respects while also undergoing a bathing purification ritual. These days the site has been developed into an attractive **complex** *(30,000-100,000Rp)* that includes pools of varying temperatures (the hottest is second from the bottom), as well as small cascades where you can sit down and let the warm water envelope you. It's open from 7am to 5pm.

At the entrance, you also have the option to pay for a walk across the suspension bridge, which yields fine views over the steaming valley below – or you can save a few rupiah and simply head straight to the pools, taking the unpaved path downhill. This is a great spot to linger, and there's also an area where you can enjoy some DIY mud treatments – just grab a bucket, collect the mud and apply as desired. Let it dry then rinse off in the steaming pools.

BANDUNG & SURROUNDING ATTRACTIONS

Neni Andriani, local guide and owner of AndrianiTours.com, shares sightseeing tips.

If you're in Bandung, I recommend a ride on the Bandros bus even if you don't speak Bahasa Indonesia. It's a great way to see the city. Then visit some ghosts by taking a walk on Asia Africa street. You should also have traditional Sundanese food at **Boemi Mitoha** (p166) restaurant, and if you like geology or have young children, visit the **Geological Museum** (p164). The Great Mosque is also stunning, well worth a visit even if you're not Muslim. Be sure to go to **Kawah Putih**: a guide can easily arrange the trip for you. If you like mountains you can visit Kawah Rengganis.

Pangandaran

BEACHES | FOREST WALKS | FRESH SEAFOOD

TOP TIP

Pangandaran's beach is wide and long, and often pummelled by a heavy swell that doesn't make for great swimming; watch out for dangerous rips. But it is a great place to get out on a board and to learn how to ride (surf lessons are easily arranged).

Situated on a narrow isthmus, with a broad stretch of sand on either side and a thickly forested national park on the nearby headland, Pangandaran is West Java's premier beach destination. It's built up, especially towards the south end, where a jumble of concrete-block towers stand shoulder to shoulder across the channel from the national park. Yet for most of the year, Pangandaran is a quiet, tranquil place to enjoy walks along the beach or through the forest. Of course, on weekends and during peak holiday times the place gets packed with visitors.

The city is also the gateway to an impressive national park, which takes up the entire southern end of Pangandaran. Within its boundaries live porcupines, *kijang* (barking deer), hornbills, monitor lizards and various species of monkey. Small bays within the park also enclose pretty, tree-fringed beaches, perfect for a refreshing swim after a hike.

GETTING AROUND

It can be frustratingly slow and complicated to get to Pangandaran. The nearest train station is in Sidareja, 41km away, which has direct services from Jakarta, Bandung and Yogyakarta. Most express buses to Jakarta and Bandung leave from the main bus terminal, 1.5km north of the beach and tourist centre. Pangandaran's becak start at around 10,000Rp and require heavy negotiation; expect to pay around 20,000Rp from the main bus terminal to the main beach area. Grab and Gojek rideshare taxis and motorbikes offer the cheapest and most reliable options in Pangandaran. Bicycles can be rented for 30,000Rp per day, and motorcycles for around 100,000Rp per day.

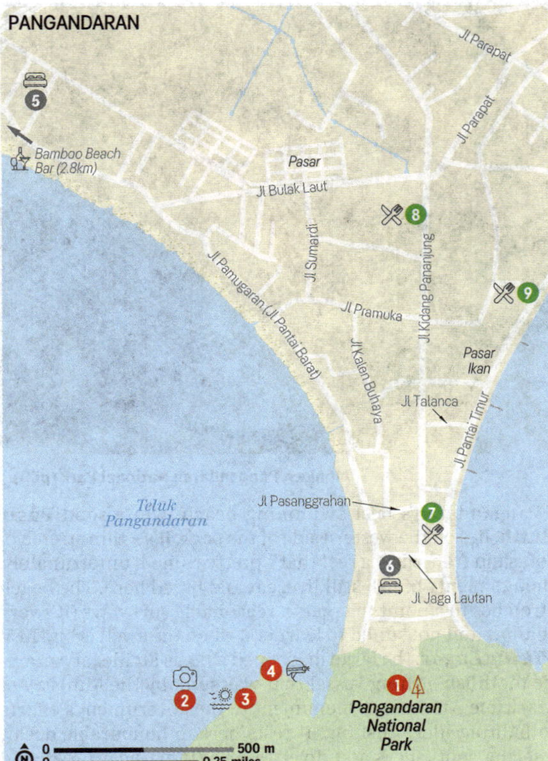

HIGHLIGHTS
1 Pangandaran National Park

SIGHTS
2 MV *Viking Lagos*
3 Pasir Putih

ACTIVITIES
4 Gua Jepang

SLEEPING
5 Mini Tiga Homestay
6 Nyiur Indah Beach Hotel

EATING
7 Chez Mama Cilacap
8 Green Garden Cafe
9 Karya Bahari

Forests, Caves & Beaches

Exploring Pangandaran National Park

Pangandaran National Park *(weekday/weekend 210,000/310,000Rp)* and an adjoining forest reserve occupy the entirety of a box-shaped peninsula attached to the mainland by a narrow isthmus. Inside this well-protected 15-sq-km expanse is dense forest that's home to porcupines, *kijang*, hornbills, monitor lizards and various monkey species. It's hard to think of a better ending to a hike than a refreshing swim at the beaches in the small bays within the park.

Well-maintained paths crisscross the park, passing small caves (including **Gua Jepang**, used by the Japanese in WWII), the remains of Hindu temple Batu Kalde and a scenic beach on the eastern side. There are two main park entrances, where you'll also find authorised English-speaking guides. Paying for a guide for a two-hour excursion is not much more expensive and well worth it to get the most out of a visit here. Longer hikes are also possible and guides can take you on a moderate hike on forested slopes to several waterfalls.

PANGANDARAN NATIONAL PARK TIPS

Iwan Kurniowan, a guide with over 20 years' experience, shares his tips for making the most of a park visit.

There are many mosquitoes in the park, so be sure to bring insect repellent. Long trousers and walking shoes are also a good idea. And don't forget water.

Experienced guides can help you get more out of your experience, taking you off the beaten trail to places where you'll have a better chance of spotting wildlife.

If you just want to hang out on the beach, boat operators can take you from Pantai Pangandaran to Pasir Putih for 150,000Rp per person (round-trip), but you still need to pay the park-entrance fee. Pay this not to the boatman, but to the park staff after arriving.

TOBIAS KAETER/SHUTTERSTOCK

Monkey, Pangandaran National Park (p171)

Pangandaran's best swimming beach, white-sand **Pasir Putih**, lies on the western side of the park. It's a thin stretch of soft sand fronted by a reef that's pretty ruined, unfortunately, though plenty of fish still live, eat and breed here. The beach stretches to a point that gets a reasonable surf wave (it's very shallow and not suited to learners) when the swell is big. **MV *Viking Lagos***, the large marooned ship, is an illegal Antarctic toothfish-fishing vessel that was sunk by the Ministry of Maritime Affairs as a monument to the government's efforts in fighting illegal fishing. It rests here in honourable decay, offering snorkellers and divers a nice (if artificial) reef, and a stately photo op or two for those on shore.

You may find that even on grey days there's a lovely vibe here, with the waves breaking, the MV *Viking Lagos* looking forlornly over the waves, and the wrapping peninsula of the park off to the left. It's easy to sit here, read a book, dip toes in the water or the waves and wonder if you really need to keep on going elsewhere.

EATING & DRINKING IN PANGANDARAN: OUR PICKS

Green Garden Cafe: Welcoming owners Asep and Rini serve local specialities like *pindang gunung* (fish soup), plus seafood barbecue by night. *7am-10pm* $$

Bamboo Beach Bar: Around 4km west of town is this unrivalled spot for a sundowner, offering cold beer and a varied Indonesian/Western menu. *8am-1am* $$

Karya Bahari: At this famous seafood place, you select your fish, prawns or squid and choose your sauce and cooking method. *9am-10pm* $$

Chez Mama Cilacap: This spot serves a huge range of Indonesian specialities, but it's most famous for its fresh seafood. *8am-10.30pm* $$

Beyond Pangandaran

Enjoy some downtime in beachside Batu Karas or get active on canyoning adventures in the Green Valley and Green Canyon.

Places
Green Canyon p173
Green Valley p174
Batu Karas p174

The scenic coastline around Pangandaran has some lovely beaches offering decent surf, plus fishing communities and one of the most appealing seaside villages in West Java. Heading inland, the scenery is a mix of ricefields and forests, fringed by sleepy but hard-working settlements. Locals here survive on the land, growing fruits and vegetables, producing palm sugar and harvesting coconuts.

Along with beachside relaxation, this is a prime destination for eco-tourism adventures: you can hike through forest and scramble around waterfalls, then take a scenic float down a river in the aptly named Green Valley. Opportunity for adventure is equally impressive in the Green Canyon, a photogenic waterway, where a boat trip leads to breathtaking waterfalls and dripping, fern-covered cliffs.

Green Canyon

TIME FROM PANGANDARAN: **45MIN**

Travel a verdant wonderland

The top tour from Pangandaran is an excursion to **Green Canyon**, where, as the name suggests, green comes in 50 shades. Boats buzz up the jungle-fringed, emerald river to a waterfall and a beautiful canyon where there's swimming (though the current is often strong) as well as the chance to leap from a lofty boulder. This is a good place to have a waterproof camera to capture the canyon's beauty, just a short swim from where the boats drop you off.

Locals take good care of the river and you won't see any plastic rubbish; keep an eye out to spot monitor lizards en route. Boatmen work on a return-trip schedule of just 45 minutes, which only gives you about 15 minutes to swim and explore the narrowest and most beautiful part of the canyon. If you want to motor further upstream or stay any longer, you'll have to pay an extra 100,000Rp for each additional 30 minutes.

GETTING AROUND

This is a great area to explore by motorbike. Various guesthouses in Pangandaran can set you up with one, including **Mini Tiga Homestay** (p181). If you prefer a guided trip (a good idea if you have limited time), Mini Tiga also runs excellent full-day outings that include visits to the Green Valley, Green Canyon and stops at rural villages.

SURF IN BATU KARAS

Batu Karas is one of the best places in Indonesia to learn how to surf. It's also a classic longboard spot. **The Point** (at the end of the main surf beach) is perfect for beginners and longboarders, with paddle-in access from the beach, and has slow, peeling waves over a sandy bottom. Its sheltered position means it needs a fairly decent-sized swell to even start showing.

Other waves include **the Reef**, a faster, more consistent and slightly more hollow right-hander a 10-minute walk up the beach from the Point; and **Bulak Benda**, a more challenging right-hander in the open ocean that's a 40-minute ride away by motorbike or boat.

Many tour operators in Pangandaran run trips here for around 500,000Rp and include 'countryside' excursions to make a full-day tour.

To get here yourself, arrange transport (by motorbike, *ojek* or taxi) to the Green Canyon river harbour (where you can hire a boat) on the highway, located 1km before the turnoff to Batu Karas. The entrance is clearly signposted at several points along the highway.

Green Valley

TIME FROM PANGANDARAN: **45MIN**

Canyoning adventures

Reached by a rough inland road from the village of Cipinda (8km from Pangandaran) is a small but beautiful gorge called **Green Valley** (it involves an easy riverside walk from a dam to the gorge). You can swim at Green Valley and there are cliff jumps for the brave (or foolhardy).

Sign up for a tour such as Green Canyon Indonesia *(greencanyon.id; 600,000Rp)* from Pangandaran for a more adrenaline-fuelled adventure. You'll walk through the forest then enter the river upstream, clambering over and around small waterfalls, peering in caves hidden along the riverbanks, and then swim a final stretch along the jade-green waterway.

Batu Karas

TIME FROM PANGANDARAN: **1HR**

Surfing and relaxing in a seaside village

The idyllic fishing village and surfing hot spot of **Batu Karas**, 32km west of Pangandaran, is one of the most enjoyable places to kick back in West Java. It's as pretty as a picture – a tiny one-lane fishing settlement with two beaches separated by a wooded promontory. Come for the day and you may find yourself sticking around longer than you expected. A growing number of expats have fallen in love with the place and put down roots here.

The main surfing beach is the smaller one, and it's a striking bay tucked between two rocky headlands. The other is a long, arcing black-sand number packed with pontoon fishing boats that shove off each night looking for fresh catch in the tides. There's good swimming, with sheltered sections that are calm enough for a dip, but many visitors are here for the breaks, and there's a lot of surf talk. On weekends, however, it can become inundated with domestic tourists. The best time to surf and relax here is midweek.

Ujung Kulon National Park

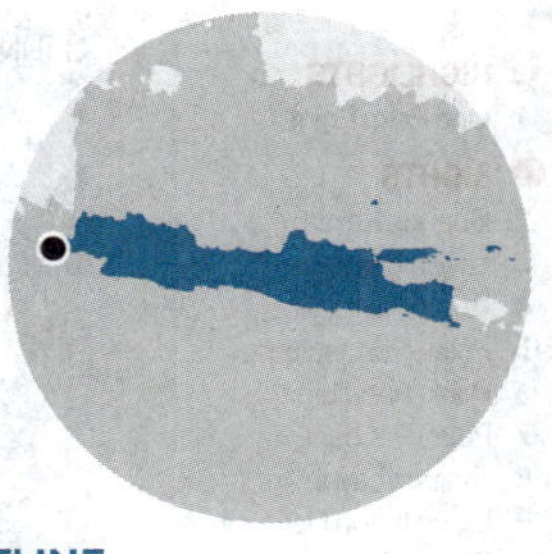

WILDLIFE WATCHING | TREKKING | VIRGIN COASTLINE

The UNESCO World Heritage–listed **Ujung Kulon National Park** *(ujungkulon.net; 205,000Rp)* is an outpost of prime rainforest, untouched wilderness, beaches and coral reefs. Though difficult to reach, it's one of the most rewarding parks in Java.

The park also includes the island of Panaitan (where Captain James Cook anchored HMS *Endeavour* in 1771) and the offshore islands Peucang and Handeuleum. Much of the peninsula is dense lowland rainforest and a mixture of scrub, grassy plains, swamps, pandanus palms and stretches of sandy beach on the west and south coasts.

Most people visit Ujung Kulon on a tour organised through an agency (day trips from Jakarta are the most popular way to go), but organising tours out of Labuan or Tamanjaya is doable, too.

TOP TIP

The Labuan PHKA Office is a useful information source. Pay your entry fee when entering the park, at the Tamanjaya park office or on the islands. Hikers should try to pick up the excellent (but rarely available) *Visitor's Guidebook to the Trails of Ujung Kulon National Park* from the park office.

Hikes & Island Bases

Top destinations in the park

A three-day hike across to the west coast via beaches and river crossings and on to **Pulau Peucang** is very popular, but there are decent alternatives, including a route taking in coastal scenery and the lighthouse at **Tanjung Layar**, mainland Java's westernmost tip. For wildlife viewing you can take day hikes in Tamanjaya.

GETTING AROUND

From Labuan there's a daily direct bus to Tamanjaya, departing usually around noon. There are also hourly *angkot* as far as Sumur until around 4pm. From Sumur, you can hop on an *ojek* to Tamanjaya. The road between Sumur and Tamanjaya is usually in very poor shape, particularly during rainy season.

English-speaking guide Hendi *(WhatsApp +62 877 7215 8455)* offers customisable tours, with day-trekking trips to Ujung Kulon starting at 2,700,000Rp per person, including transport to and from Carita or Labuan.

You can charter a boat to get here from Carita, Labuan or Sumur. Given the long stretch of open sea, it pays to fork out for a decent one. Speedboats are double the price of the wooden relics but worth it. Surf tours use their own transport.

HIGHLIGHTS
1 One Palm Point

SIGHTS
2 Gunung Raksa
3 Legon Bajo
4 Legon Haji
5 Pulau Handeuleum
6 Pulau Panaitan
7 Pulau Peucang
8 Tanjung Layar
9 Ujung Kulon National Park

EATING
10 Naksan Padang
see 10 Pondok Makan

RHINOS & OTHER WILDLIFE

The one-horned Javan rhinoceros was once the most widespread Asian rhino species. Due to persecution, poaching and habitat loss, it's now one of the world's most critically endangered large mammals. There are estimated to be only between 60 and 70 remaining, all inside Ujung Kulon National Park.

Numbers are thought to be stable and the rhinos are breeding; however, they're extremely rare. Don't expect to see one. You're far more likely to see banteng (wild cattle), wild pigs, otters, deer, squirrels, leaf monkeys, gibbons and monitor lizards. Leopards also live in the forest and crocodiles dwell in the river estuaries. Green turtles nest in some bays and the birdlife is excellent.

Pulau Peucang, only reachable by chartered boat, is one of the park's more popular destinations thanks to its good accommodation. Peucang also has beautiful white-sand beaches and coral reefs on its sheltered eastern coast (bring snorkelling gear).

Pulau Handeuleum, ringed by mangroves, is less commonly visited. It has some Timor deer but lacks Peucang's attractions. Canoes can be hired for the short cruise up a jungle river.

Large **Pulau Panaitan** has some fine beaches and hiking. It's a day's walk between the PHKA posts at **Legon Bajo** and **Legon Haji**, or you can walk to the top of **Gunung Raksa**.

You can arrange tours with Krakatau Tour *(krakatautour.com; prices vary)* or with Hendi *(WhatsApp +62 877 7215 8455; prices vary)*. These are custom, individual trips, not group tours. You may not embark on these without proper admission and a guide.

Legendary Surf

Admiring Java's most powerful wave

The best known surf break on Pulau Panaitan is infamous **One Palm Point**. This mesmerising left-hander, which barrels in perfect form for hundreds of metres down the side of the island, appears to be the world's most perfect wave. Yet most of the time there's barely another surfer around, and that's because this beauty comes with a very severe sting in its tail. Even at high tide, the wave breaks over razor-sharp live coral in water depths that can be measured in centimetres. The wave itself is so long and fast that it's almost impossible to outrun it, with the result being that you will get violently thrown across the reef. This is one surf spot that is reserved only for absolute experts and even then most people wear full wetsuits and helmets for safety. There are other waves here as well, but almost all of them are equally unforgiving. Do not even consider coming here to surf unless you are of a very high standard.

Beyond Ujung Kulon National Park

Follow the coast to Carita, launchpad for trips out to the Krakatau volcano, or continue to Merak for the journey to Sumatra.

If you've made the trip out to this remote corner of West Java, there are a handful of other worthwhile sights in the area. The star of the region is the infamous volcano of Krakatau, which has experienced massive volatility over the years and even affected the world's climate after a particularly powerful eruption in 1883. Various outfitters run boat trips out to where you can have a look at the still-smouldering crater, and you can combine this with a multiday excursion to Ujung Kulon.

Further north lies the rather unappealing port town of Merak, which is the hop-off point for ferries heading to the island of Sumatra. Nearby are several islands, which remain remarkably undeveloped.

Places

GETTING AROUND

From the Ujung Kulon park office in Labuan it's about 30 minutes' ride by *angkot* to Carita, the main departure point for trips to Krakatau. If you're coming from Tamanjaya, expect a rough, slow journey (of about 3½ hours), with one bus running daily between Tamanjaya and Labuan. If you're heading to Sumatra by ferry, 24-hour boats run between Merak and Bakauheni in Sumatra. The journey takes about two hours (45 minutes by fast boat).

Carita

TIME FROM UJUNG KULON NATIONAL PARK: **30MIN**

Beach getaway

Carita feels like a different world from the sprawl of Jakarta and other massive West Java urban areas. Here you'll find a region of rising jade hills clumped with palms and laced with green rivers. The sandy beach of **Karang Bolong** has one small (and very inconsistent) surf break, and the area is popular with weekenders from Jakarta. Most travellers are here only to arrange trips to Krakatau or Ujung Kulon National Park, though there are some pleasant places to stay overnight for a bit of a beach break.

If you're not in a rush, about 2km from Carita over the rice paddies you will find the village of **Sindanglaut** (End of the Sea), which is where the giant Krakatau tsunami of 1883 ended its destructive run.

A DEVASTATING ERUPTION

Regarded by early mariners as a mere nautical landmark, Krakatau sprang to life in the late 19th century. On 27 August 1883 it erupted so violently that on the island of Rodriguez, more than 4600km away, a police chief reported hearing the booming of heavy guns. Krakatau sent up a column of ash 80km high and emitted nearly 20 cu km of rock. Ash fell on Singapore 840km to the north and on ships 6000km away.

Even more destructive were the great ocean waves Krakatau triggered. Coastal Java and Sumatra were devastated, with 165 villages destroyed and more than 36,000 people killed. The eruption affected weather worldwide: ash clouds circled the earth for three years.

Anak Krakatau

TIME FROM UJUNG KULON NATIONAL PARK: **2HR**

Boat tours of the famous volcano

Virtually everyone in Carita is peddling a Krakatau tour. Keep in mind the weather conditions, as well as volcanic activity, which will of course cause any tours to be cancelled. Check your boat first as waves can be rough, and make sure it has a radio and life jackets on board.

A typical itinerary involves travelling across Sunda Strait to **Anak Krakatau** (meaning 'child of Krakatau'; a newer formation rising some 500m above the waterline). The ride here takes about 90 minutes by fast (double-engine) and possibly deafeningly loud boat. From here, you'll go around the island, taking in views below the rim of the volcano. You'll dock at the beach and head off on foot for a hike across the barren landscape. The steam wafting out of the crater and the nefarious-looking sulphur lakes appear all the more surreal given the seaside backdrop. There are plenty of unusual photo ops, and guides can point out other islands in the Krakatau archipelago.

Back on the beach, you'll reboard the boat and continue to the island of **Rakata** (aka Greater Krakatau), the largest and southernmost of the volcanic islands. The least-destroyed of the islands, Rakata is currently less active than Anak Krakatau, and the island periphery is a fine spot for snorkelling, with the chance to spot colourful sea life amid the coral reefs. Afterwards you can eat lunch in the shade on Rakata beach, have a swim and perhaps a snooze. The daylong tour gets you back to Carita by mid-afternoon – in time to catch a bus back to Jakarta if you're just coming for the day, though it'll be a rather long one as this tacks on another three hours each way to the trip.

There's also good diving in the area. Special dive trips can take you to some of the unusual volcanic scenery under the water. Located near Rakata, **Legon Cabe** is a popular spot with hard and soft corals and towering pinnacles – living records of past eruptions.

EATING IN & AROUND UJUNG KULON: OUR PICKS

Nyeniel: A tasty warung in Labuan with a varied array of dishes. You point to what you want and they either serve it to go or for eating at the small tables. *9am-9pm* $

Pangrango Restaurant: This upscale Tanjung Lesung beach spot has Western and Indonesian dishes. Wear bug spray. *7am-10pm* $$

Pondok Makan: A rare dining spot in Ujung Kulon. Simple Indonesian foods (think *mie ayam* and nasi goreng), served with a smile. *6am-8pm* $

Naksan Padang: Another inexpensive Ujung Kulon option, based on the Padang style food (lots of plates). Pull up a plastic chair and enjoy! *8am-8pm* $

KEMARRRAVV13/SHUTTERSTOCK

Anak Krakatau

With another day at your disposal, you can spend the night camping on one of the islands. Guides typically set up tents on the beach at Anak Krakatau, and you'll barbecue fish over a wood fire to cap the day's activities. Have more time? Keep going on a multiday trip that continues on to Ujung Kulon for rainforest walks, with canoeing up the Sungai Cigenter and an overnight stay at a lodge on Pulau Peucang.

If your time is limited, it is possible to visit Krakatau on a one-day tour from Jakarta. Most outfits will pick you up from your hotel at around 5am or 6am and reach Carita around three hours later. You'll then have breakfast and depart by boat from Carita Beach. In the afternoon, at around 4pm or so, you'll arrive back in Carita, and then hop back in the car for the drive back to Jakarta.

Among the many outfitters, **Krakatau Tour** *(krakatautour.com; per person 10,500,000Rp)*, based on Carita Beach, has a good reputation and offers a wide range of tours. These include one-day volcano experiences departing from Jakarta, camping trips, visits to tribal villages, diving tours and trips to Ujung Kulon National Park. Local English-speaking guide Hendi *(WhatsApp +62 877 7215 8455)* is also recommended, with customisable tour options starting around 6,000,000Rp.

ONWARD TO SUMATRA

Located 140km west of Jakarta, the rather gritty port town of Merak is the departure/arrival point for ferries to Bakauheni in Sumatra. Boats to Bakauheni depart every 30 minutes, 24 hours a day, with the journey taking about two hours. Fast boats (45 minutes) also make this crossing, but they don't operate in heavy seas.

Frequent buses make the run between Merak and Jakarta (taking 2½ hours). Most go to the capital's Kalideres bus terminal, but buses also run to/from Jakarta's Pulo Gadung and Kampung Rambutan. Other buses run all over Java, including to Bogor and Bandung.

There are also infrequent trains to Jakarta, which have economy-class carriages only.

Places We Love to Stay

$ Budget $$ Midrange $$$ Top End

Jakarta

MAPS p66 & p72

Whizz Capsule Hotel Thamrin $ Clean, comfortable and very convenient location in the busy Thamrin district.

Cipta Hotel Wahid Hasyim $$ An old hotel – but it's centrally located and the rooms are neat and clean. All rooms are for smokers.

Artotel Thamrin $$ This lovely, small hotel has comfortable rooms and a rooftop bar. It's a short walk from Jl Sabang, great for streetfood.

Langham $$$ Among the most lavish hotels in the city, the Langham is perfect for discerning travellers who want to stay near Jakarta's glitzy malls.

Yogyakarta

MAP p77

Good Karma Hostel $ Good budget option, away from the centre but close to popular Jl Prawirotaman for bars and cafes.

Snooze $$ The decor is lovely at this carefully considered hostel, and lots of care has been taken to make it feel homely. There are dorms and double rooms, all with shared bathrooms.

Adhisthana $$ This small boutique hotel (with a pool) offers excellent value for money. It's close to good restaurants in the Prawirotaman neighbourhood.

Beyond Yogyakarta

Ama Awa Resort $$ Set atop a hill between Pantai Baron and Pantai Kukup, this small hotel (with jungly, Insta-inspired rooms) is a good base for exploring Gunungkidul beaches.

Baron Lighthouse Cottage $$ The incredible view over Pantai Baron from the rooms, restaurant and swimming pool is worth the drive up a particularly bad road.

Solo

MAP p97

Holabeds Hotel $ A centrally located and comfortable place for backpackers. There are single and double rooms, with private bathrooms.

Doeloerkoe Homestay $ The exceptionally helpful staff will arm you with insights on Solo and surrounds, and help arrange travel plans.

De Solo Boutique Hotel $$ There's a lovely vintage charm to this small, quiet hotel in central Solo.

Zigna Kampung Batik $$ Enjoy a touch of luxury (and a swimming pool) at this glitzy hotel on the edge of Kampung Batik Lewayan.

Alila Solo $$$ Regarded as Solo's finest hotel, the rooftop bar at this Alila property also has one of the best views in the city.

Gunung Lawu

Kebun Hanoman Villa $$ A handful of wooden villas are tucked into a verdant garden of flowers and fruit trees. This is a peaceful base from which to explore the Kemuning and Gunung Lawu areas.

Semarang

MAP p115

Bobopod Kota Lama $ This quirky, clean capsule hotel in Kota Lama is within walking distance of the train station. Shared bathrooms.

Raden Patah Heritage $$ Centrally located in Semarang's old town, this excellent value for money boutique hotel is set in an historic building just a short walk from bars and restaurants.

Manon Boutique Hotel $$ Contemporary comforts meet Art Deco chic at this striking little hotel in Kota Lama. It's conveniently close to the train station.

Padma Hotel Semarang $$$ Possibly the best hotel in Semarang, with wonderful mountain views, friendly staff and a great pool for kids.

Karimunjawa

L'Isola Che $ There are dorm beds and double rooms at this vibrant hostel close to the port.

Alam Kita $$$ A quiet, dreamy island escape that offers yoga and meditation as well as various activities around the island.

Dieng Plateau

MAP p121

Green Savanah $ Homey place right in the middle of Dieng, close to restaurants and other facilities.

Fifa Homestay $ Cosy cabins centrally located, with hot showers. Can be chilly at night.

Agora Home $$ Very comfortable new villas with views of the mountains in front and tea plantations at the rear. Local breakfast is included.

Homestay Cemara $$ Clean and comfortable homestay, with a very nice, helpful owner who makes you feel instantly at home.

Malang

MAP p130

Huize Jon Hostel Malang $ Very homely hostel only a few minutes' walk from the centre and Alun Alun. Welcoming and very attentive family and staff.

De'Corner Guest House $ Clean and simple accommodation that's high quality for a low price. Located in the centre, walking distance from everything.

Swiss-Belinn Malang $$ Nice hotel accommodation with small rooms but everything you'll need. The location near the university keeps food prices low.

Hotel Tugu Malang $$$ Enchanting and unique, Hotel Tugu will captivate you with its charm, cultural heritage and artistically decorated rooms.

Banyuwangi

MAP p145

Juda Homestay $ A basic but comfortable place with a wonderful owner in a perfect location for visiting Ijen. Good breakfasts included in the price.

Sandy's Homestay $$ A spotless room awaits, with TV and shower, in a house with a fountain and super-helpful owner.

Hotel Santika Banyuwangi $$ Large clean rooms and a beautiful sunny pool. Staff at the hotel are very friendly, polite and accommodating.

éL Hotel Banyuwangi $$ A nice option at a midrange price, with a fantastic pool. Western and Indonesian breakfast options are a welcome touch.

Meru Betiri National Park

Red Beach Homestay $ Basic homestay accommodation a short walk from Red Island Beach. A friendly, proactive owner and home-cooked breakfasts.

Java Turtle Lodge $$ Upscale spot with tidy wooden cabañas, not far from the entry to Meru Betiri National Park and Sukamade beach.

Bogor

MAP p154

Rion Bogor Hostel $ About 1.3km south of the gardens, Rion Bogor is a good-value guesthouse with tidy rooms, friendly hosts and a small swimming pool.

Hotel Grand Savero $$ Looming over the botanical gardens, this upmarket hotel has classic, well-maintained rooms and good service.

DIONNASIUS ADITYA/SHUTTERSTOCK

Artotel Thamrin, Jakarta

Cimaja

DSP Guesthouse $ The guesthouse side of Dede Suryana's Place, with surfer-friendly rooms, showers and of course, all the surf accessories you need.

Cimaja Square $$ Attractive thatched roof cottages, all of good size and built over the rice paddies, make this a tranquil and endearing choice.

Gunung Hanimun Salak National Park

MAP p161

Lodges Ekologika on Portibi Farms $$ On the slopes of Gunung Salak, this organic farm has lovely bungalows, outstanding home-cooked meals and magnificent views.

Bandung

MAP p165

Naripan $ The exterior is bland, but rooms are comfy and modern at the Naripan – one of the best budget options near Jl Braga.

Savoy Homann Hotel $$ Dating back to 1921, this historic place has a palm-tree-filled atrium restaurant, impressively large, bright rooms and communal areas with Art Deco details.

favehotel Braga $$ You can't beat the location of this reliable chain hotel with polished rooms, right in the heart of Braga's dining and nightlife.

Pangandaran

MAP p171

Mini Tiga Homestay $ Long-standing and superb-value backpacker favourite with spacious, tidy rooms and artfully decorated common areas for chatting with fellow travellers.

Nyiur Indah Beach Hotel $$ Low-rise boutique hotel with a lovely palm-fringed pool and handsome rooms with shuttered windows and wood furnishings.

For places to stay in Bali, see p284

HEIKONEUMANNPHOTOGRAPHY/SHUTTERSTOCK

Above: Pura Besakih (p245); Right: Snorkelling, Pemuteran (p270)

THE MAIN AREAS

CANGGU AREA
Buzzes with a youthful energy. p188

SEMINYAK AREA
Sunsets, spas and world-class restaurants. p194

ULUWATU
Iconic waves, cliff bars and a temple. p207

NUSA LEMBONGAN
Surfing, diving and a chilled island scene. p212

Researched by
Sarah Reid, Jade Bremner, Narina Exelby, Marco Ferrarese and Mark Eveleigh

Bali

ISLAND OF THE GODS

The mere mention of Bali evokes thoughts of an island paradise. It's more than a place; it's a tropical state of mind.

Impossibly green rice terraces, pulse-pounding surf, enchanting Balinese Hindu temple ceremonies, mesmerising dance performances, ribbons of beaches and truly welcoming people: there are as many images of Bali as there are flowers on the ubiquitous frangipani trees.

This small island – roughly 150km by 110km – looms large for any visit to Indonesia. Arguably, no place is more visitor-friendly. Accommodation ranges from simple seaside homestays to sybaritic retreats in the lush mountains. The shopping, from locally made home decor to Bali-born fashion labels, will tempt you to increase your luggage allowance. You can dine on local dishes bursting with fresh flavours at a traditional warung (food stall) or let a world-class chef take you on a culinary journey at an elegant restaurant. From a cold Bintang beer at sunset to an epic night of clubbing, your social whirl is limited only by your own fortitude. When it comes time to relax, you can lose yourself in an all-day spa.

DUDAREV MIKHAIL/SHUTTERSTOCK

But small doesn't mean homogeneous. The family-friendly resorts of Kuta and Seminyak segue into trend-chasing Canggu. The artistic swirl of Ubud is a counterpoint to misty treks amid volcanoes and lush waterfalls. Lo-fi beach towns such as Amed, Pemuteran and Medewi offer mellow alternatives to the teeming tourist hubs of south Bali, and just offshore are laid-back Nusa Lembongan, Nusa Ceningan and Nusa Penida.

UBUD
Bali's cultural heart. **p218**

SIDEMEN
Ricefield walks and views. **p242**

AMED
Great diving and volcano views. **p254**

PEMUTERAN
Amazing diving and snorkelling. **p270**

0 — 20 km
0 — 10 miles

Pemuteran, p270

Refreshingly relaxed town on a sandy bay. Close to the underwater wonders of Pulau Menjangan, with Bali's best dive sites.

Lovina, p265

Beach town for travellers who want nothing trendy. Timeless guesthouses and a narrow beach are close to waterfalls, hikes and historic Singaraja.

BALI SEA

Prapat Agung Peninsula
Pulau Menjangan
Gunung Prapat Agung
Banyuwedang
Pemuteran
Ketapang
Labuhan Lalang
Gilimanuk
Bali Barat National Park
Cekik
Gunung Sanglang
Gungung Kelatakan
Gunung Merbuk
Gunung Musi
Celukanbawang
Seririt
Pengastulen
Rangdu
Mayong
Lovina
Mundu
JAVA
Melaya
Pupu
Pujungan
Selat Bali
Negara
Mendoyo
Perancak
Medewi
Antosari

Munduk, p258

This enchanting town surrounded by plantations is the heart of Bali's best trekking area and an ideal base from which to explore the volcanic highlands.

Canggu Area, p188

Bali's storied hangout is packed with trendy cafes, cocktail bars, yoga studios, nameless beer shacks and pulsing clubs. Everyone watches surfers offshore.

MOTORBIKE

Motorbikes – everything from small mopeds to retro cafe-racers – are easily hired. Congested roads and manic residents on their own motorbikes can be overwhelming for inexperienced riders. Get rides on motorbikes via apps or by hailing.

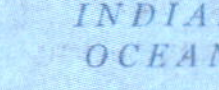

Seminyak Area, p194

Seminyak's golden beaches are lined with bars and clubs, and the streets with boutiques, cafes and enticing spas. Kerobokan boasts world-class restaurants.

CAR

Taxis are common, and the ride-hailing apps Grab and Gojek make booking a ride a breeze. Hiring a car and driver for a day or week is a popular way to see the island.

BOAT

Fast boats link Nusa Lembongan and Nusa Penida with Sanur and other coastal towns on Bali, as well as the Gilis off Lombok. Boats for dive trips and excursions are found all along the coast.

Find Your Way

Although small in size, Bali's population and number of visitors mean that roads are often filled to capacity, especially in the south, where a short journey can take a long time.

Plan Your Time

Traffic aside, Bali's compact size means you can fit more of its wonders into your days of exploration. Best of all, there's always another temple, cafe or beach at which to take a break from driving.

NICOLA PULHAM/SHUTTERSTOCK

Pura Taman Ayun (p278)

Pressed For Time

- Start south, at a cliffside perch above the famous waves of **Uluwatu** (p207) on the busy but beautiful Bukit Peninsula. Be mesmerised by a Kecak dance performance at **Pura Luhur Uluwatu** (p209).

- Head north to work your way around the surf breaks, beach clubs, cafes and restaurants of youthful **Canggu** (p188). Drive north to magnificent **Pura Taman Ayun** (p278), the core temple of Bali's UNESCO-recognised *subak* (irrigation) system.

- Next, go west to **Ubud** (p218) to immerse yourself in Balinese culture. Spoil yourself – stay in one of Ubud's many hotels with views across ricefields and rivers. Spend your time touring Ubud's temples, relaxing at its spas, browsing its excellent galleries and boutiques and enjoying memorable meals.

Seasonal Highlights

Bali has two seasons: the rainy season (October to April) and the dry season (May to September).

FEBRUARY

The rainy season pours, and Bali starts to hum again after the January pause that follows the holiday high season. West Bali National Park is lush and green.

MARCH

As the rainy season ends, the sacred Balinese day of **Nyepi** (p210) shuts down the island (even the airport) for 24 hours. Silence is expected from everyone.

APRIL

Bali soaks up the sunshine in the dry season. In Ubud, the **Bali Spirit Festival** celebrates yoga and music. Beaches are mostly cleared of rainy-season debris.

One Week to Travel Around

- Seven days will fly by on this trip that covers Bali's top-drawer sights. Start at a beachside hotel in **Seminyak** (p194) or **Canggu** (p188), shopping the streets and spending time at the beach. Make a day trip to the monkey-filled temple at **Uluwatu** (p209) and chill on a nearby beach, such as **Pantai Padang Padang** (p208).

- Head to seaside **Sanur** (p203) for a fast boat to **Nusa Penida** (p217) for a day of island exploration. Make the quick hop to the tropical idyll of **Nusa Lembongan** (p212) for great waves, snorkelling and diving, and chilled island vibes.

- Return to Bali and blast up to **Ubud** (p218) for a few nights of rice-terrace walks, dance performances and indulgent dining experiences.

With Two Weeks

- Do everything in the one-week itinerary and then continue from Ubud into the lush mountains and waterfalls at **Munduk** (p258.

- Head to the island's northwest corner and **Pemuteran** (p270), where the low-rise hotels and resorts define relaxation. Dive or snorkel right offshore or at the wonderful nearby **Pulau Menjangan** (p276), renowned for its sheer coral-encrusted wall, in West Bali National Park.

- Follow the coast east to **Amed** (p254) for more diving and snorkelling, yoga and relaxing in the shadow of Bali's largest volcano, Gunung Agung.

- Continue south, leaving ample time to explore the cultural diversions of **Amlapura** (p251) and the old palace at **Klungkung** (p238) on the way.

JUNE

Experienced surfers descend on the Bukit breaks for peak surfing season, and crowds watch from the cliffs. The premier cultural event, the **Bali Arts Festival** (p206), begins in mid-June.

AUGUST

The busiest time in Bali sees huge numbers of visitors, especially Australians fleeing winter. Warm, dry weather and big waves make Bali an ideal escape. **Indonesian Independence Day** is celebrated on 17 August.

OCTOBER

The skies darken with seasonal rains, and crowds thin a little. The **Ubud Writers & Readers Festival** (p229) draws book lovers and famous authors for four days of literary conversations.

DECEMBER

Visitors rain on Bali ahead of the Christmas and New Year holidays. Most hotels and restaurants are booked out, and the south is in party mode, with big-name DJs hitting the decks at beach clubs.

Canggu Area

SURFING | DINING OUT | HEALTH & WELLNESS

GETTING AROUND

The traffic around Canggu is notorious. On Jl Raya Canggu, it can take more than an hour to travel 10km in a car. Your quickest option to get from A to B in the Canggu area is to use a scooter from ride-hailing apps Grab or Gojek – and if you want to go further (say, to Ubud or Uluwatu), then book one of their cars. Your hotel can also help you source a private car and driver, if you prefer. Hiring a standard scooter *(per day 100,000-120,000Rp)* isn't recommended for beginner or unlicensed riders.

TOP TIP

Beat the traffic by walking on the beach between Berawa, Canggu and Pererenan. You can then use Grab or Gojek to hail a scooter to take you to your destination.

Surfers put Canggu on the map, but during the last two decades, this once low-key stretch of Bali's coastline has evolved into the island's most cosmopolitan beach area.

Centred on Jl Batu Bolong, Canggu is also a catch-all term for the area between Seminyak and Cemagi, including Berawa and quieter but rapidly developing Pererenan, which flank Canggu to the east and west, respectively. Each of Canggu's three main areas houses a heady mix of bars and eateries, hotels and villas, boutiques and wellness offerings. There's also the surf, with breaks suitable for beginners to seasoned surfers, as well as a beach club for every mood.

While Canggu old-timers bemoan the continuing retreat of the area's once-abundant rice paddies – not to mention its ever-increasing traffic – travellers can't seem to get enough. Join the daily migration of gym-buffed bodies to the beach at sunset and you'll begin to understand why.

Surf Canggu's Iconic Waves

Find your perfect break

Batu Bolong might fall short of Indonesia's finest surf spots, but Canggu's main beach break is one of the most popular longboarding waves in the country. Also known as Old Man's (for the party venue just back from the beach), it's a beginner-friendly ride that tends to break further out before reforming again.

Northwest of Batu Bolong is **Echo Beach**, home to several barrelling breaks better suited to intermediate and advanced surfers. Echo Beach Left or Stairs is a powerful left-hander breaking over a shallow reef. Sandbar is the middle section of the beach break, and River Mouth is a reef break.

Southeast of Old Man's, **Pantai Nelayan** is popular with kitesurfers (although not for beginners). Beginner surfers may also find some gentle waves here. Further southeast,

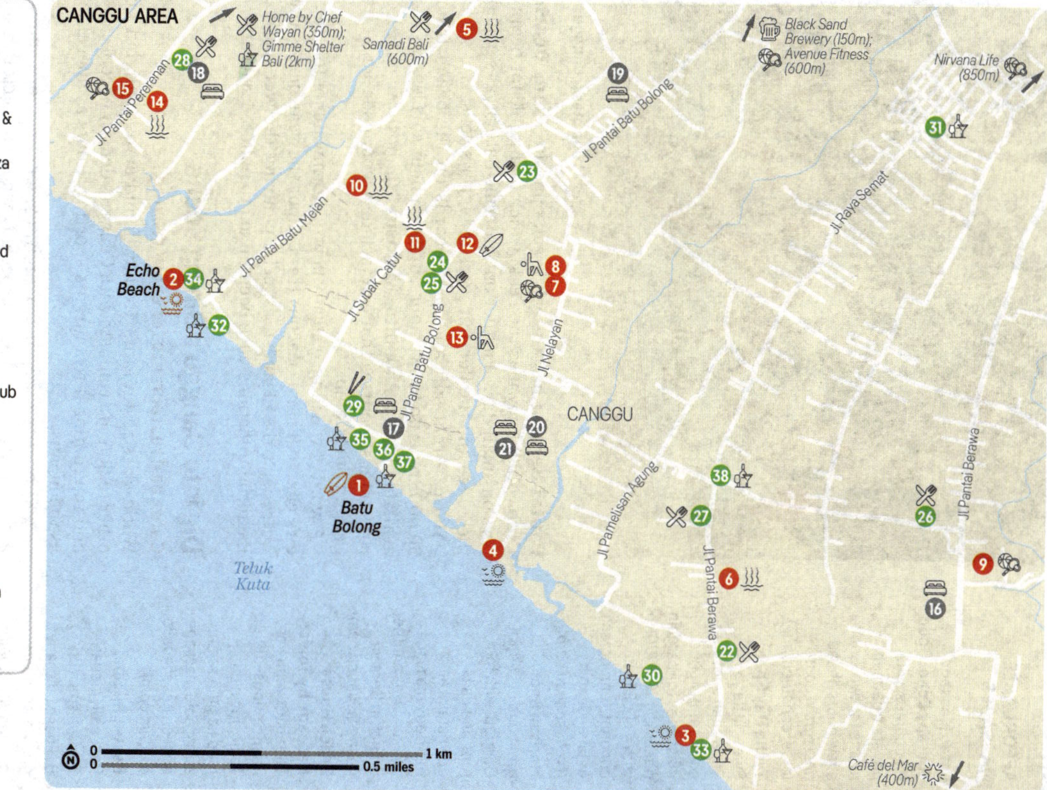

HIGHLIGHTS
1 Batu Bolong
2 Echo Beach

SIGHTS
3 Pantai Berawa
4 Pantai Nelayan

ACTIVITIES
5 Beach House Massage by Tonic
6 Beautyful Spa
7 Body Factory Bali
8 BWork Yoga
9 Finns Recreation Centre
10 Lotus Massage Therapy Echo
11 Marissa Spa
12 Mojosurf
13 Practice
14 Tyche Day Spa
15 Wrong Gym

SLEEPING
16 Guru Canggu
17 Hotel Tugu Bali
18 Kayu Village
19 Melati Bali Homestay
20 Serenity
21 Zin Canggu

EATING
22 Ghost Kitchen & Record Bar
23 Luigi's Hot Pizza
24 Masonry
25 Meimei
26 Milk & Madu
27 Neighbourhood
see 20 Serenity
28 Shelter
29 Yuki

DRINKING & NIGHTLIFE
30 Atlas Beach Club
31 Bar Souvenir
32 COMO Beach Club Canggu
33 Finns Beach Club
see 17 Ji Terrace
34 La Brisa
35 Lawn
36 Motel Mexicola
37 Old Man's
38 Shady Pig

AFFORDABLE MASSAGES

Lotus Massage Therapy Echo: Good for couples, with private treatment rooms for two. Book a few hours ahead. *(instagram.com/lotus_echotheraphy)*

Tyche Day Spa: Sweet little Pererenan spot with consistently good massages for bargain prices *(1hr 190,000Rp)* with a choice of coconut, lemongrass or lavender oil. *(tychespabali.com)*

Marissa Spa: A great find in central Canggu, with foot rubs and nails downstairs and full-body massages upstairs. Has another branch in Berawa. *(marissaspabali.com)*

Beach House Massage by Tonic: The sister venue of Palm Springs–styled Tonic down the road has the same affordable massage prices. *(beachhousebytonic.com)*

Beautyful Spa: Peaceful, modern Berawa spa with Balinese massages *(instagram.com/beautyfulspa.bali)*.

NICOLEEEEKM/SHUTTERSTOCK

Yoga class, Canggu

Pantai Berawa has a beach break opposite **Finns Beach Club** (p193) known as the Peak, which is suitable for beginners on small days. Further out, intermediate breaks called the Ledge and the Bommie work in bigger swells.

You can rent soft and hard boards on the beach from 50,000Rp for up to two hours, and two-hour surf lessons are available from 350,000Rp. **Mojosurf** *(mojosurf.com)* also runs intense courses that can include accommodation at its Canggu Surf Camp.

A word of warning: a steady flow of stormwater onto Canggu's charcoal-sand beaches throughout the year means the water isn't the cleanest, especially during the wet season. Bacterial infections have been linked to polluted seawater.

Dig into Canggu's Dining Scene

Cafes and restaurants for every craving

World-class restaurants are now found across Bali, but no other region can compete with Canggu's density of cool cafes and international restaurants sporting fitouts as appealing as the menus.

Food quality (and, increasingly, hygiene) is high, and so are the prices – for Bali – especially when you factor in the 12% government tax and service charge (usually 5% to 10%)

The lasagne with 'nduja is decadently rich.

EATING IN THE CANGGU AREA: BEST RESTAURANTS

Home by Chef Wayan: You haven't tasted Indonesian food until you've dined at the lauded Balinese chef's relaxed Pererenan restaurant. *11am-10pm* $$

Shelter: Superb Mediterranean fare served in an airy garden *bale* (open-side pavilion), with a special menu for vegans. *noon-midnight* $$

Ghost Kitchen & Record Bar: Simple dishes are supercharged with flavour at this Berawa neighbourhood bistro. *noon-midnight Fri-Sun, from 3pm Mon-Thu* $$

Meimei: The team behind excellent local Japanese restaurant Yuki is onto another winner with this sizzling Southeast Asian barbecue spot. *5pm-2am* $$$

added to your bill. With an increasing number of venues also charging for card payments (usually 2% to 3%), your sushi degustation at **Yuki** *(yuki-bali.com)* or a contemporary feast at **Masonry** *(masonrybali.com)* can end up costing a lot more than the price listed on the menu. And yet the bill is still likely to total less than many international visitors would pay for the same meal at home.

It's not just the food that makes dining out in Canggu a joy, but the good-times energy that permeates the photogenic venues. Most local restaurants accept walk-ins, but it's a good idea to book at the most popular places. Meanwhile, it can feel like a new cafe opens every day in Canggu, most with Australian-standard (read: high) coffee and decadently flaky pastries to rival the bakeries of Paris. Perennial favourites include **Neighbourhood** *(neighbourhoodfood.co)* in Berawa and **Milk & Madu** *(milkandmadu.com)*, with branches in Berawa and Canggu.

Begin (or Deepen) Your Yoga Practice

Find a class that suits your vibe

Ubud (p218) might be revered as Bali's yoga heartland, but manic Canggu doesn't fall too far behind with its own growing offering of yoga studios. There is something for everyone here, from beginners to lifelong yogis, and hippies to hipsters. Near Pantai Nelayan, family-owned, permaculture-based **Serenity** (p284) *(serenitybali.com)* is a down-to-earth yoga resort offering nine 90-minute classes a day, including aerial yoga *(nonguest/guest 130,000/110,000Rp)*. Stay for a meal at Serenity's vegan restaurant, or check into the guesthouse.

You can't stay overnight at **Samadi Bali** *(samadibali.com)*, but you can spend all day there. Up to 15 classes ranging from one to two hours *(155,000Rp)* take place throughout the day, and Samadi also offers a series of retreat packages for women.

In a breezy bamboo pavilion atop the BWork coworking hub on Jl Nelayan, **BWork Yoga** *(bwork.id/empoweredyoga; classes 165,000Rp)* specialises in power yoga, but there's also yin, Hatha and flow. Classes run from 60 to 75 minutes.

On Jl Pantai Batu Bolong, traditional Hatha yoga is king at the **Practice** *(thepracticebali.com)*. Classes run for 75-90 minutes *(150,000Rp)*.

DESTINATION GYMS

Body Factory Bali: Sweat it out at a kickboxing class and then chill by the pool with a collagen shake in Berawa. *(bodyfactorybali.com)*

Wrong Gym: The sleek Pererenan mega-gym comes complete with a 'booty room' dedicated to lower body building. *(wronggym.com)*

Nirvana Life: Takes a more holistic approach with its class schedule, heroing movement and breathwork. *(bali.nirvanalife.com)*

Finns Recreation Centre: A major renovation was underway in 2025, with the new centre set to include multiple training spaces, a 25m indoor lap pool and a recovery area. *(finnslifestylevillage.com)*

Avenue Fitness: The cheapest of Canggu's full-service gyms has a limited class schedule and no pool, but there's an ice bath, sauna and hot tub. *(avenuefitnessbali.com)*

Great spot to escape the sunset crowds.

DRINKING IN THE CANGGU AREA: BEST BARS

Bar Souvenir: The mid-century minimalist interior allows the cocktails and natural wine to shine. In Berawa. *7pm-midnight Mon-Sat*

Ji Terrace: Sip classic and house cocktails (including a good piña colada) as you soak up the sunset views over Batu Bolong Beach. *noon-11pm*

Black Sand Brewery: Craft brews and pub grub in an airy, industrial-style space with a breezy beer garden and daily specials. *noon-midnight*

Motel Mexicola: Begin your night with tacos and happy-hour margaritas at the colour-popping Canggu outpost of the Seminyak institution. *11am-1am*

Find Bali in Canggu

A slice of old Indonesia

Canggu is a cosmopolitan, ever-changing neighbourhood that nowadays feels distinctly un-Balinese, but there is one special enclave that stands as a bastion of tradition and culture. **Hotel Tugu Bali** (p284), a boutique hotel owned by an Indonesian art collector, connects travellers with the history and traditions of the archipelago. Simply walking into the antique-filled property tucked behind Pantai Batu Bolong is an evocative journey into the Indonesia of old, and experiences like Balinese dance, cooking or *jamu*-making classes (*jamu* is a turmeric-based elixir), ceremonial dinners and spa treatments rooted in beauty traditions offer an opportunity to experience Balinese culture. Balinese feasts fit for royals *(700,000Rp)* are served in the Bale Puputan, housing an extensive collection of artefacts from Bali's 1906 **Puputan War with the Dutch** (p238).

Hit the (Beach) Club

Find your groove

Beach clubs have exploded across Bali, with more than 50 of these day-to-night party palaces dotting its coastlines at last count. There's a beach club for every mood in the Canggu area. Bounce between 11 bars and three pools at pulsing party spot

EATING & DRINKING IN CANGGU: SPOTS FOR A NIGHT OUT

Luigi's Hot Pizza: Start with a pizza and stay for the party, with DJs hitting the decks on Mondays and Thursdays. *4pm-midnight* $$

Gimme Shelter Bali: A rock-'n'-roll bar in Pererenan with a mini skatepark, open-mic Mondays and live music on Wednesdays and Saturdays. *7pm-3am*

Old Man's: Canggu's original beach bar pumps until late. Kick on at next-door Sandbar until 3am. *noon-1am or 2am*

Shady Pig: DM the venue on Instagram *(instagram.com/theshadypigberawa)* for the password to enter this clandestine Berawa cocktail bar. *7pm-4am Tue-Sun*

DAVIDPHOANDRA/SHUTTERSTOCK

Finns Beach Club

Finns Beach Club *(finnsbeachclub.com)* in Berawa, which gets rowdier as the evening progresses. Next door to Finns, **Atlas Beach Club** *(atlasbeachfest.com)* has family-friendly spaces and ample room to spread out, while **Café del Mar** *(cafedelmarbali.co.id)* offers a slice of the Balearics in Berawa.

Heading north from Finns, surfer-chic **Lawn** *(thelawncanggu.com)* spills onto Pantai Batu Bolong at sunset, **COMO Beach Club Canggu** *(comohotels.com)* is popular with well-heeled families, and **La Brisa** *(labrisa-bali.com)* resembles a sprawling bohemian castaway village overlooking Echo Beach.

Hike 'Bali's Camino'

Uncover the real Bali

Slow down and connect with Bali's verdant ricescapes and ancient culture on the **Astungkara Way** *(astungkaraway.com)*, a 135km guided hiking experience crossing the island from south to north. Designed to support regenerative agriculture, the experience offers a meaningful opportunity to immerse yourself in local culture in an authentic, responsible way.

Beginning at Cemagi, northwest of Pererenan, the full coast-to-coast experience *(15,900,000Rp)* takes 10 days and ends at Seririt Beach in North Bali. Everything is included, with wholesome meals showcasing farm-fresh produce, and camping accommodation in traditional Balinese family compounds and picturesque farms. With profits supporting free training, micro-financing and market access for regenerative rice farmers, it's an ultra-feel-good hike.

If you don't have the time (or the stamina), shorter four- and six-day sections of the trail are also offered *(four-/six-day 6,100,000/8,900,000Rp)* along with overnight experiences *(from 2,400,000Rp)*. Check Facebook *(facebook.com/astungkaraway)* for updates on spots on upcoming departures.

SURF 'N' ZOOM

Canggu has become one of the world's most popular hubs for digital nomads. While there are some positives – remote workers have created economic benefits for some locals, particularly hospitality businesses – the influx of digital nomads has partly driven a boom in villa construction that is contributing to the strain on Bali's infrastructure. Canggu alone has nearly a dozen coworking spaces.

With a mission to create a sustainable future for the local community through its impact program, **Zin Canggu** *(zin.world)* resort offers a free coworking space next to its cafe, which fills up early. Note that Indonesian law prohibits travellers on standard tourist visas from conducting remote work.

Seminyak Area

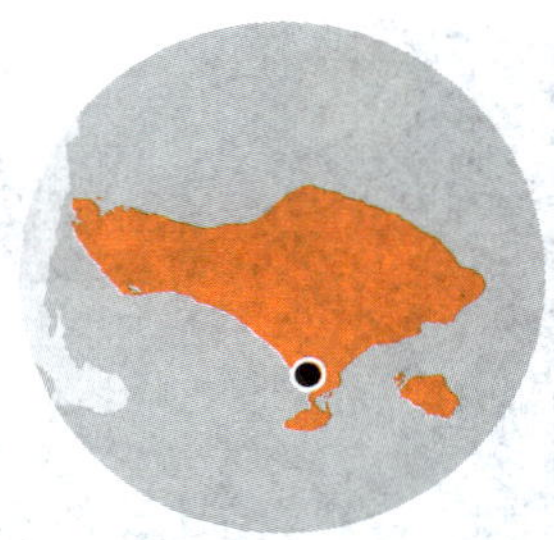

BEACH BARS | SUMPTUOUS SPAS | SHOPPING

GETTING AROUND

Seminyak's pavements are generally in decent condition, so walking is a great way to get around and explore the area, particularly for shoppers. Much of Seminyak's beach is lined with a boardwalk, and you can stroll along the paved walkway from here right through to Kuta. Scooters are readily available for rent, but it may be more convenient (or safer, if you're planning on a big night) to use the ride-hailing apps Grab or Gojek than to drive yourself. Allow an hour for airport transfers.

Seminyak blends luxury with a laid-back beach vibe, and this busy neighbourhood is a magnet for those seeking a fusion of fun, style and relaxation. While its waves are no match for those of Canggu or Kuta, Seminyak's wide stretch of golden beach is arguably southwest Bali's nicest. Sunset is a busy time, when beanbags are hauled out, and strings of lights are hung beneath umbrellas, ready for the revellers.

Seminyak has long been an alluring destination for shoppers with its mix of designer boutiques, homeware emporiums, and cheap and cheerful clothing shops. Northeast of Seminyak, more industrial Kerobokan is a home decor heaven. The Seminyak area isn't short on dining options either, with everything from Australian-style cafes to haute Indonesian fare served up – or you can learn how to cook it yourself. You'll find every type of accommodation here, too.

A Feast for the Senses

Learn to prepare Balinese cuisine

Bali's tropical climate and fertile volcanic soils yield an astounding range of fruits, vegetables, herbs and spices, and enrolling in a cooking class provides you with an excellent opportunity to explore not only how these ingredients shape Balinese cuisine, but also to be immersed in a multilayered experience that really is a feast for the senses.

At **Nia Cooking Class** *(niacookingclass.com; adult/child 600,000/475,000Rp)*, which is based on the edge of the flea market on Jl Kayu Aya, the morning evolves as you set about making the various elements of iconic Balinese dishes, like spice pastes and the delicately flavoured minced fish mix for *sate lilit ikan* (minced fish satay). The class ends with a delicious feast.

HIGHLIGHTS
1 Desa Potato Head
2 Ku De Ta
3 Nia Cooking Class
4 Pura Petitenget

ACTIVITIES
5 Bodyworks
6 Jari Menari
7 Lamora Spa
8 Spring Spa

SLEEPING
9 Grandmas Plus Hotel Seminyak

EATING
10 Fed by Made
11 Livingstone Cafe & Bakery
12 Pasar Kerobokan
13 T&T Chindo's Cuisine
14 Warung Babi Guling Pak Malen
15 Warung Balung Tianyar Mudah
see 3 Warung Nia

DRINKING & NIGHTLIFE
16 Alila Seminyak
17 District 1
18 La Plancha
see 1 Potato Head Beach Club

SHOPPING
19 Bali Tailor
20 Drifter Surf
see 3 Flea Market
21 Home Basket
22 Kara Home Living
23 Kim Soo
24 Lulu Yasmine
25 Magali Pascal
26 Mercredi
27 Uma & Leopold

Seminyak's Beach Allure

Spend all day on the sand

Seminyak's stretch of golden beach lies halfway along the gentle arc that sweeps from the airport south of Kuta up almost to Tanah Lot, and it morphs from the umbrella-cluttered sand at Legian's Double-Six resort through more umbrellas and beach clubs to calmer Batu Belig Beach.

TOP TIP

With its lovely wide beach, decent footpaths and plentiful resorts, Seminyak has long been a popular option for families looking for a stylish stay within striking distance of the airport. Foodies will find the dining options a cut above those of Kuta and Legian.

The northern section of Seminyak's beach tends to be quieter, flanked by big hotels and beach clubs like **Ku De Ta** *(kudeta.com)*, **Alila Seminyak** *(hyatt.com)* and **Desa Potato Head** , while the southern section, between Double-Six and the small inlet near Noku Beach House, draws the crowds. Here, you can rent a sunlounger and activate holiday mode.

Get Inspired to Tread Gently

Go on an enlightening waste tour

Desa Potato Head *(seminyak.potatohead.co)* is a village-like complex (*desa* means 'village') integrating its **Potato Head Beach Club** with six restaurants and bars and two luxury hotels. The brand is driven by the ethos 'good times, do good', and from the moment you arrive, you're made aware of how your footprint will be reduced.

Learn more on the free 90-minute Follow the Waste Tour, which starts at 11am daily. From seeing where and how Potato Head's waste is sorted, you learn about the steps taken to reduce waste through the supply chains and how the plastic is recycled and shaped into furniture, beads and containers for Potato Head's amenities. And that's just the beginning. It's an incredibly inspiring tour that showcases what can be done when creativity meets responsibility, and at the end, you get to make your own recycled waste item.

Rejuvenate Body & Soul

Spa-hop across Seminyak

You never need to walk far to find a spa in Seminyak. Its spa scene offers a harmonious fusion of traditional Balinese healing techniques and contemporary wellness practices. Spas cater to every budget, from budget salons where a 60-minute massage costs under 200,000Rp – try **Lamora Spa** *(lamora spa.com)* – to ultra-luxurious destination day spas that are a sanctuary of indulgence and wellbeing.

At **Bodyworks** *(bodyworksbali.com)*, you might be tempted to come just for the gorgeous Morocco-inspired design, but the luxurious treatments are even better. Contemporary **Spring Spa** *(springspa.com)* offers urban views with many of its treatments, while **Jari Menari** *(jarimenari.com)* is famous for its excellent massages given only by men.

SEMINYAK'S FOOD SECRETS

Chef Wayan Kresna, who helms Desa Potato Head's Kaum Restauran, dishes on the dynamic local food scene. *@chefwayan*

Local chefs hang out at **T&T Chindo's Cuisine** *(instagram.com/tandtbali)*, where chef Renaldy makes an amazing pork noodle soup. Chef Made Danu at **Fed By Made** *(fedbymade.com)* is also really talented; he uses local produce to create simple, modern dishes bursting with flavour.

You can find *babi guling* (suckling pig) everywhere, but **Warung Balung Tianyar Mudah** is one of the only places you can find *babi balung* (braised pork-rib soup). **Pasar Kerobokan** is great for tropical fruit and *jaje Bali* (sweet snacks), and family-run **Warung Nia** makes an excellent Balinese *rijsttafel* (multiple dishes and condiments).

EATING & DRINKING IN SEMINYAK: OUR PICKS

Fed by Made: Three Bali-born, Melbourne-trained friends joined forces to open this excellent modern bistro. Go for the set menu. *6-11pm* $$

Livingstone Cafe & Bakery: Prides itself on its croissants, but also serves a deliciously smoky carbonara. The light-filled dining area has air-con. *7am-10pm* $$

La Plancha: Beanbags on the beach and lights strung under umbrellas make this one of Bali's most colourful sunset spots. A DJ plays from 5pm. *10am-11pm*

District 1: Expertly crafted cocktails are the name of the game at this moody hidden speakeasy. *5.30pm-1am Mon-Sat, to midnight Sun*

Potato Head Beach Club

DICKADIPRTM/SHUTTERSTOCK

Guardian Temple

Admire traditional Hindu architecture

Standing guard on Seminyak's busy beachfront is **Pura Petitenget** *(50,000Rp),* one of Bali's six sea temples built to protect the island from evil spirits. Its name translates loosely as 'magic chest' and relates to the time, according to legend, the Hindu priest Dang Hyang Nirartha transformed Buto Ijo, a malicious beast, into the guardian of the nearby village.

As Nirartha exorcised evil spirits from the area, he captured them in wooden chests, which were kept under the watch of Buto Ijo. With the iconic *candi bentar* (split gateway) flanked by *naga* (mythical snake-like creature) statues at its entrance, *meru* (a multitiered shrine) and the intricate stone carvings on the walls and around doorways, Pura Petitenget is a fantastic example of Balinese temple architecture.

Get It While It's Crispy

Get a taste for *babi guling*

Cafes in Bali's trendy traveller hubs are fast growing their offering of vegan dishes, but *babi guling* remains an unapologetically carnivorous indulgence. Prepared with infusions of coriander seeds, turmeric, lemongrass and other herbs and spices, it's a delicacy on the island. Many warungs specialise in *babi guling* (you'll recognise them from the image of the skewered pig that hangs outside), but **Warung Babi Guling Pak Malen** *(instagram.com/babigulingpakmalen)* on Jl Sunset is a great place to try it in Seminyak.

KEEP BALI BEAUTIFUL

Bali often receives harsh media coverage because of the trash that washes up on the beaches. Some visitors assume that the beaches are permanently filthy, but they're like this particularly during the rainy season, when the rivers carry the trash accumulated along their banks during the dry months into the ocean.

One of the organisations working hard to alleviate the island's plastic problem is Sungai Watch *(sungai.watch),* which focuses on removing plastic from the island's rivers. Permanent teams clean the rivers daily, but Sungai Watch also organises river cleanups for volunteers; the schedule is on its website. Another leader in the plastic war is Desa Potato Head.

ALL ABOUT *ARAK*

Once considered backstreet hooch, *arak* (colourless, distilled palm wine) now features on many of Bali's trendy cocktail menus. Not to be confused with Middle Eastern *arak* (made from grapes and anise), Bali's *arak* can be tapped from more than a dozen different trees, most commonly the aren palm.

Non-alcoholic *tuak* is the juice that is first collected. Once fermented, the potent *arak* has about 40% alcohol content. You might also come across *brem* (sticky rice simmered with yeast and then fermented). *Arak* and *brem* are commonly used in the offerings placed on the ground for Bhuta Kala (the low spirits). Take care when consuming *arak* produced in village stills, as cases of methanol poisoning (leading to blindness and death) have been reported.

I MADE RAI YASA/SHUTTERSTOCK

***Arak* (colourless, distilled palm wine)**

Indulge in Retail Therapy

Shop up a storm in Seminyak

Seminyak is Bali's original shopping destination, and while an outpost of nearly every brand born here can now be found in Canggu and beyond, it's still a great place to shop.

The main shopping streets include Jl Kayu Aya and Jl Petitenget. Jl Kayu Aya houses the flagship stores of Bali brands, including **Drifter Surf** *(driftersurf.com)* and womenswear label **Magali Pascal** *(magalipascal.com)*, along with branches of **Uma & Leopold** *(umaandleopold.com)* and **Lulu Yasmine** *(luluyasmine.com)*. At the big bend in the road, the **flea market** has affordable clothing and souvenirs.

The retail cavalcade continues on Jl Petitenget. Notable shops include **Kim Soo** *(kimsoo.com)* and **Mercredi** *(instagram.com/mercredi.home.bali)* for designer homewares, and the **Bali Tailor** *(thebalitailor.com)* for leather footwear.

Neighbouring Kerobokan is great for homewares, with top stops including **Kara Home Living** *(instagram.com/karahomelivingstore)* and **Home Basket** *(homebasketbali.com)*.

Kuta & Legian

BEACHES | LOW-KEY CROWD | GOOD SURF

Bali's original tourist hub may be dated, but Kuta still has its draws. If you've been lured to its golden beaches for sunshine, cocktails and cheap spas, you've come to the right place – and you'll find a dose of culture here too, among the shrines and temples (Buddhist and Hindu) and in the early morning market that has changed little over the last century. While Seminyak and Canggu sprawl quite widely, Kuta's long-established community has retained a town centre that is still walkable. The beach strip is lined with bars and a pleasant promenade, and a handful of newish hotels make the beachfront more appealing than ever.

Kuta merges into Legian at Jl Benesari. A hybrid of its neighbours, it blends the low-key vibe of Kuta with a touch of Seminyak style. The dining scene is a cut above Kuta's, and it's a short hop to Seminyak for a fancier night out.

GETTING AROUND

The urban sprawl and traffic jams make walking the best (and often fastest) way to explore Kuta and Legian. *Ojeks* (motorbike taxis) are the quickest way to nip around. **Kura-Kura Bus** *(kura2bus.com)* runs a service between Kuta and Ubud. **Perama** *(peramatour.com)*, which has an office on Jl Legian, also runs shuttles to Ubud, Sanur, Amed, Lovina and elsewhere. For longer trips, consider hiring a car and driver.

Wave of the Day

Where to surf around Kuta

Kuta has drawn surfers in ever-increasing numbers since Bob Koke – Kuta's first hotelier – had his boards shipped here from Hawaii in the early 1930s, and these days, with rental boards available by the hundreds and surf instructors by the score, **Pantai Kuta** (Kuta Beach) is one of the best places in Bali to learn how to surf. You simply need to approach one of the board-rental kiosks on the beach to set up a lesson; expect to pay about 250,000Rp for an hour-long private session. Or engage the expert coaches from the **Rip Curl School of Surf** *(ripcurlschoolofsurf.com; two-hour lessons from 722,500Rp)*, which has booths in Kuta (inside the **Mamaka by Ovolo** hotel) and Legian (on the boardwalk south of Jl Arjuna).

Offshore winds combined with a decent swell see surfers with more experience beeline for breaks further out, including the left-hander at **Kuta Reef**, off **Pantai Jerman**, where you might think that you're out in open ocean if it weren't for

TOP TIP

The pavements in Kuta and Legian are generally in good condition, which means they make convenient bypass routes for scooter drivers who are frustrated by slow-moving traffic. Look both ways before you step out from between stationary vehicles or onto the pavement.

HIGHLIGHTS
1 Pantai Kuta
2 Waterbom Bali

SIGHTS
3 Memorial Wall
4 Pantai Jerman
5 Pantai Legian
6 Vihara Dharmayana Temple

ACTIVITIES
7 Kuta Reef
8 Kuta Skate Park
9 Rip Curl School of Surf

SLEEPING
10 De Puspa Residence
11 Mamaka by Ovolo
12 Poppies Bali
13 Puri Damai

EATING
14 Crumb & Coaster
15 Fat Chow
16 Made's Warung
17 Warung Kampung

SHOPPING
18 Pasar Kuta
19 Pasar Pagi Desa Adat Legian

TRANSPORT
20 Kura-Kura Bus
21 Perama

the planes booming down just over your head. South of Kuta Reef, **Airport Lefts** and **Airport Rights** break either side of the rocky promontory at the end of the international runway.

Boatmen can always be found on Pantai Jerman to shuttle you out to reef breaks *(return per person from 100,000Rp)*. The price drops if you buddy up with other surfers. Arrange a pickup time and then simply look for the boat.

A Wild Watery Adventure

Slip down the slides at Waterbom

One of the island's most popular family tourist attractions since 1993, **Waterbom Bali** *(waterbom-bali.com; adult/child 370,000/325,000Rp)* is a seriously impressive waterpark. Spiralling, spinning, shooting and splashing across 5.1 hectares of carefully landscaped tropical gardens are 26 slides and attractions, and their names alone – Smashdown 2.0, Fast n Fierce, Constrictor and Climax – might convince you that Waterbom is for adrenaline junkies. But its strength lies in its appeal for 'kids of all ages'.

There are lagoon pools with sunbeds and VIP gazebos, and an enduringly popular lazy river, which provides sufficient excitement in the form of bridges, cascades and water jets. In 2025, Waterbom opened Zuluu Hill, an adventure zone just for kids with six slides across two levels. Those who prefer to relax can enjoy a massage, and seven bars and dining options replenish your energy. Run on 100% renewable energy, Waterbom has also implemented water-saving initiatives.

A Night to Remember

Watch the sunset on Kuta Beach

West-facing **Pantai Kuta** (p199) and **Pantai Legian** are famous for dramatic sunsets, and you could write an entire book about the activity that unfolds on this action-packed swatch of sand. Along here, it's all about people-watching, so order a Bintang beer or a fresh coconut from a beachfront vendor and settle in for the show.

Watching the sunset here can also become a static spa and shopping spree. Without having to move from your seat, you could have your hair braided, get a fake tattoo and enjoy a manicure and a back massage, all at the same time. In Kuta, there's also a **skate park**, open 8am to 10pm, that has become a favourite meeting place for kids of all ages, with skateboards available for hire *(per hour 50,000Rp)*. It's floodlit after dark.

MEMORIAL WALL

The bombing attack of 12 October 2002 is regarded as one of the darkest days in Bali's modern history. Just after 11pm a bomb exploded at Paddy's Pub, a Kuta bar popular with backpackers, and as revellers fled to apparent safety on the street, another (bigger) bomb was detonated over the road, just outside Sari Club.

The blasts killed 202 people, among them 38 Indonesians, 88 Australians and 23 Britons. There is now a **memorial wall** for those who lost their lives on Jl Legian, just metres from where the Sari Club once stood. The victims' names are listed, and family and friends still bring flowers and photos to honour the memory of those who were killed.

EATING IN KUTA & LEGIAN: OUR PICKS

Try the sweetcorn fritters.

Warung Kampung: This airy eatery serves all the popular Indonesian dishes. Tasty meals at budget-friendly prices. *10am-10pm* $

Crumb & Coaster: Kuta's coolest cafe spills out of an industrial space, with breakfast served until 6pm. A wider menu is available from lunchtime. *7.30am-11pm* $$

Fat Chow: Delicious Asian fusion dishes include a refreshing caramelised pork-belly salad with shredded mango. On Jl Poppies II. *10am-10pm* $$

Made's Warung: Turning out some of Kuta's best Balinese food since 1969, with an additional location in Seminyak. *10am-9pm* $$

BALI'S STRIKING SPLIT GATEWAYS

If you enter Pantai Legian from Jl Melasti, you walk through an ornate split gateway (called *candi bentar*), the same sort of architectural structure you see at entrances to temples, palaces and other sacred sites around Bali. These traditional gateways serve as important cultural and spiritual symbols and consist of two symmetrically shaped pillars connected by a central opening, which creates a striking entryway.

The gates are typically adorned with intricate carvings and decorative motifs, and represent the division between the profane world and the sacred realm, signifying the transition from the mundane to the divine. The inside edge of the gates is always smooth, some say to cleanse the mind upon entry.

GEKKO GALLERY/SHUTTERSTOCK

Vihara Dharmayan Temple

To Market, To Market

Start your day in real Bali style

Kuta and Legian might feel like a long way from 'traditional' Bali, but a trip to a morning market reveals a slice of life that's remained almost unchanged for generations.

Two morning markets in the area are worth a visit: the popular Legian morning market (known officially as **Pasar Pagi Desa Adat Legian**) and the even more timeless **Pasar Kuta** (at the junction of Jl Raya Kuta and Jl Pantai Kuta). The most lively sections of both markets are the fruit and vegetable stands and the wonderfully colourful stalls that sell a mind-boggling selection of traditional offerings. Go early.

Unexpected Serenity

Reset at a Chinese Buddhist temple

Dating from 1876, colourful **Vihara Dharmayan Temple** is possibly the most calming place in Kuta.

A bright red-and-yellow entrance gate opens into the main courtyard, where the *baktisala* (main prayer hall) is strung with large Chinese lanterns and supported by giant crimson pillars wrapped with menacing dragons. Incense swirls around the moodily lit interior.

Sanur

SPACIOUS RESORTS | TRANQUIL BEACH | WATERFRONT PROMENADE

Sanur's waterfront promenade is laid-back compared with the beachfront bustle of Bali's southwest beaches and draws a different crowd – families and older travellers gravitate to the luxury resorts or humble homestays here. A peaceful, shaded walkway connects several kilometres of bars, restaurants, shops, leafy resorts with huge swimming pools and some surprisingly quiet stretches of beach, all protected by an offshore reef.

The area's intriguing history (a Chinese ship wrecked on the reef here ultimately brought about the ritual suicide of the royal family) has become barely a footnote in the ongoing tourism business, yet traditions continue to play out on the water, where you'll see fishers in colourful *jukung* (outrigger fishing boats) decorated with goggle-eyed swordfish faces zipping between the fast ferries.

Sanur borders Denpasar on its west side, and everything in the sprawling capital is just a short drive away.

GETTING AROUND

Given Bali's notorious traffic, this is not an island where cycling is generally recommended as a method of transport; however, Sanur's excellent beachfront promenade is an exception, and pedal power can be the best way of getting around, as most of the promenade has a dedicated cycle lane.

For trips around the Sanur area, use Gojek or Grab to hail a car or motorbike taxi. For travel beyond Sanur, consider upgrading to a taxi – the speedy traffic on the fast-flowing Ngurah Rai Bypass can be unnerving for anyone unused to motorcycle transport. Kura-Kura Bus services connect Sanur with Kuta and Ubud.

Cycle the Coastline

Ride Sanur's beachfront promenade

Alongside **Sanur Beach**, there is a paved, almost 6km-long **promenade**, and a leisurely cycle along it provides an idyllic opportunity to explore the coastline of one of Bali's most family-friendly beach towns.

The bicycles available for hire are comfortable cruisers *(per hour 20,000Rp),* most of which have baskets in front and a bell that should be gently pinged when you're approaching pedestrians from behind. The Sanur beachfront promenade has been designed with bicycles in mind, and along much of it, there is a dedicated bike lane. (Cyclists must stick to the inland side of the path.)

HIGHLIGHTS
1 Sanur Beachfront Promenade
2 Sindhu Night Market

SIGHTS
3 Museum Le Mayeur
4 Pantai Mertasari
5 Sanur Beach

ACTIVITIES
6 Baby Reef
7 Rip Curl School of Surf

SLEEPING
8 Kubu di Kayla's
9 Puri Mesari
10 Tandjung Sari Hotel

EATING
11 Fisherman's Club
12 Seagrass by the Beach
13 Soul on the Beach
14 Titie's Warung

DRINKING & NIGHTLIFE
15 Byrd House Beach Club
16 Casablanca
17 Costa by Monsta
18 Shotgun Social

SHOPPING
19 Icon Bali Mall

TRANSPORT
20 Sanur Harbour

TOP TIP

Plan your beach activities according to the tide, as the reef-protected shoreline is almost dry at low tide. Surfers need to get beyond the barrier reef, and it's a hell of a paddle, but boat rides are always available for a fee if you want to catch uncrowded waves.

On your ride, there are many places to stop for a coffee, a massage, lunch, an ice cream or even a spot of designer shopping. The chic **Icon Bali Mall** *(iconbalimall.com)* has an entrance right off the beach and houses designers from Calvin Klein to Ted Baker.

The promenade runs from just south of **Sanur Harbour** south to the car park at **Pantai Mertisari**, and there are pockets of bike-hire places all along here; many have small bikes for children, too. The bikes are usually available for hire from around 7am. The quieter early mornings make for the most carefree cycling.

Night Street-Food Sampling

Trying tasty Indonesian dishes

Sanur's atmospheric **Sindhu Night Market** (sometimes called Senggol Market) might at first glance appear small, but its food stalls are a hive of activity and offer a fantastic opportunity to sample a wide variety of tasty traditional Indonesian fare from about 25,000Rp a dish. Many stalls are retro in appearance and are very photogenic; each specialises in something different, and most of the food is prepared while you wait.

Try everything from *sate ayam* (chicken satay), *bakso* (meatball soup) and *lumpia* (similar to spring rolls) to *nasi campur* (rice with a choice of side dishes). The tables belong to the stalls near them; if you want to sit down, be sure to use one belonging to the stall you buy from. Leave some room for treats like doughnuts, *pisang goreng* (banana fritters) and *onde-onde* (sweet rice-cake balls filled with palm sugar), which are sold from a cart near the entrance to the market.

Sanur's Barrier Reef

Watersports fun

Sanur's tranquil coastline is protected by a barrier reef that stretches for 7km and creates a series of waveless beaches, a real novelty on Bali's south-facing coastline. Even at high tide, the crystal-clear water in this 'lagoon' is rarely much over waist-level, making it an ideal playground for kayaking and stand-up paddleboarding (SUP). SUPs and kayaks can be rented from about 100,000Rp per hour all along the beachfront promenade.

Those looking to surf have a decent paddle (between 500m and 1km from shore) to get to the waves, but schools along the beach, including **Rip Curl School of Surf** *(ripcurlschoolofsurf.com; 2hr lessons 850,000Rp),* offer boat rides with boards and lessons to the various reefs in the area, complete with insurance (a rarity in Bali). **Baby Reef** is suitable for beginners and intermediates. Boats are typically traditional outrigger *jukung* (unique in this part of the island), which are adorned with long swordfish 'noses' and staring eyes painted on the bows.

Discover the Museum Le Mayeur

Tour an artist's home

Artist Adrien-Jean Le Mayeur de Merprès (1880–1958) arrived in Bali in 1932 and married Legong dancer Ni Polok three years later, when she was just 15. They lived in the compound that now houses the **Museum Le Mayeur** back when Sanur was still a quiet fishing village. Later, the Balinese-style compound became a museum featuring many of Le Mayeur's works. Paintings from his early period in Bali are romantic depictions of daily life and beautiful Balinese women – often Ni Polok.

The museum was under refurbishment at the time of research, but you can peer into the grounds to admire the stunning architecture.

BALI KITE FESTIVAL

During the windy season, Bali's sky is dominated by kites that are flown not only as a pastime, but also as a thanksgiving message to the gods for abundant harvests. For a few days, all eyes turn to Sanur (Galak or Mertasari Beach), the hub of the Bali Kite Festival, as teams compete to get the most spectacular – and the most gigantic – kites soaring on the thermals.

This colourful festival usually takes place in July or August; the exact dates vary to capitalise on the favourable windy conditions that are needed to get the enormous kites (which sometimes measure more than 4m wide by 10m long) into the air. Check Bali Tourism's Instagram *(instagram.com/balitourismauthority)* for dates.

EATING IN SANUR: ALONG THE BEACHFRONT

Titie's Warung: A good budget option on the beach, Titie's serves up Indonesian classics, as well as sandwiches and snacks. Cash only. *8am-6pm* $

Soul on the Beach: This breezy cafe is a beachfront fave. It has an international menu with a focus on fresh, healthy meals. *7am-11pm* $$

Seagrass by the Beach: Laid-back beachfront restaurant with pizzas, tacos, seafood platters and superb Indonesian curries. *7am-11pm* $$

Fisherman's Club: A classy seafood resto on Sanur's promenade, with comfy seating on the shady beach. Has a kids menu. *11.30am-11pm* $$$

CELEBRATE BALI'S ARTISTIC HERITAGE

For one month every year, Denpasar erupts into an extravaganza of colour and costumes as Bali's rich artistic heritage is celebrated. The **Bali Arts Festival**, which usually takes place in June and July, serves as a platform to showcase and preserve the island's vibrant traditional art forms.

Dance, music, visual arts and literature take centre stage, and each day performances, competitions and workshops are put on at the **Taman Werdhi Budaya Art Centre** *(03-6122 2776)*, the home of the festival. If you only see one thing, make it the opening-day parade, an absolute highlight of the festival when performers wearing intricate costumes and traditional dress take to the streets of Denpasar.

ALEKSANDAR TODOROVIC/SHUTTERSTOCK

Museum Negeri Propinsi Bali

Dip into Denpasar

Bali's main museum and market

Sanur segues into the urban sprawl of Bali's busy capital to the west, making it a great base for exploring Denpasar's key attractions. The **Museum Negeri Propinsi Bali** *(Bali Museum; adult/child 100,00/50,000Rp)* has a fascinating collection of relics, including daggers, religious objects, art, coins and effigies. These are housed throughout four striking pavilions in a building with pretty courtyards and gardens.

A pre-booked local guide can help to put everything into perspective. The ones who approach you tend to offer little value; instead, try **Bali Walking Tours** *(WhatsApp +62 895 3580 51932; prices vary by group size)*, which offers multihour walking tours of historic Denpasar, each with an introduction to Balinese culture and a history lesson of the city.

A short walk to the west, **Pasar Badung** (Badung Market) is the largest traditional trading place on the island. In and around the imposing three-storey building, there's always something being traded, and while shopping is serious business for those who work here, it's a fun and lively place to visit, especially before 10am when the market is in full swing.

DRINKING IN SANUR: OUR PICKS

Byrd House Beach Club: This elegant 'beach house' sprawls beneath towering palms; there's a relaxed atmosphere and views of Mt Agung. *6.30am-11pm*

Shotgun Social: With 16 craft beers on tap, an extensive cocktail menu and a large garden and play area, this hip restaurant is great for families. *9am-11pm*

Costa by Monsta: Mediterranean vibes on the beach, with white linen seats, fairy lights at night and international wines and cocktails. *9am-10pm*

Casablanca: No-frills restaurant in the evening, vibey dive club later at night, with live music (usually cover bands), sports and happy-hour specials. *5pm-1am*

Uluwatu

CLIFFTOP VIEWS | DRAMATIC BEACHES | WORLD-CLASS SURF

For many, Uluwatu is more a life choice than a holiday. In the five decades since the epic waves at 'Ulus' were first ridden, its name has echoed around the world, and surfers continue to descend on its iconic left-handers in big numbers. Plenty of others come to watch from the seaside cliffs.

It's hard to imagine today that the dry Bukit Peninsula at Bali's southern tip was once, apart from a small community that cared for Pura Luhur Uluwatu (Uluwatu Temple), almost uninhabited. The region's tiny lanes and infrastructure can't keep up with the mushrooming population – expect streets clogged by water tankers and scooters. Yet Uluwatu can be a dream beach-holiday spot, whether you seek surf, wellness, partying, fresh seafood or lounging by the sea. The sunsets are sublime, and Uluwatu Temple sets the stage for an exhilarating evening dance performance.

TOP TIP

The monkeys around Uluwatu and the Bukit Peninsula might seem quirky and cute, but they can be malicious and are renowned for stealing food, drinks and mobile phones. Sometimes, they take sunglasses right off people's heads. Keep a safe distance, secure your belongings and be aware that monkey bites can transmit diseases.

Surfing Uluwatu

Bali's best-known waves

With its consistent peeling waves, Uluwatu is considered one of the best places in the world to surf, and the cliffs here provide exceptional vantage points from which to watch the action. It's hard to beat the view from **Single Fin** *(singlefinbali.com)* and the cluster of cliffside cafes at **Pantai Suluban**.

GETTING AROUND

The notorious traffic jams (especially around the all-important sunset peak hour) are enough to convince most visitors to travel by motorbike rather than car, and the Gojek and Grab ride-hailing apps are convenient and tend to offer quick responses.

Walking can be perilous along the peninsula's small, traffic-clogged lanes, which have blind bends, often no pavements and little street lighting. If you have to walk at night, carry a light visible to traffic, but catching a ride is often much safer.

Motorbikes and scooters are also widely available. Wear a helmet and be aware that you can be fined for not wearing one or not having an International Driving Permit.

HIGHLIGHTS
1 Pantai Suluban
2 Pura Luhur Uluwatu

SIGHTS
3 Pantai Bingin
4 Thomas Beach

ACTIVITIES
5 Padang Padang

SLEEPING
6 Mû Bungalows Boutique Resort
7 Temple Lodge
8 Uluwatu Surf Villas

EATING
9 Seed
10 Single Fin
11 Warung Local

DRINKING & NIGHTLIFE
12 Dugong Lounge & Bar
13 La Terrazza

Five peaks comprise what is affectionately referred to as Ulus; none are suitable for beginners, but neighbouring **Thomas Beach** and nearby **Padang Padang** *(adult/child 15,000/10,000Rp)* have smaller waves. The former is better for newbies and the latter for intermediate surfers. Boards can be rented at most beaches for about 150,000Rp, and locals on the beach offer lessons for about 500,000Rp. Expect crowds.

If you're an experienced surfer, paddle out from the famous cave at Pantai Suluban, the entry point to Ulus, to reach **Racetracks**. This is the fastest section with the steepest walls and the roundest barrels; at mid to lower tides, you can score some of the world's most perfect tubes.

EATING & DRINKING AROUND ULUWATU: OUR PICKS

Warung Local: This super-popular warung in the backstreets of Bingin has an array of delicious Indonesian dishes on offer. *8am-10pm* $

Seed: Chilled spot in Bingin for beautifully presented French-Asian food. Creative small plates have bodacious flavour combos. *7.30am-11pm* $$

Dugong Lounge & Bar: Look out over a curved infinity pool and across the ocean above Pantai Padang Padang with a wine, cocktail or juice. *7.30am-11pm*

La Terrazza: Italian food and drinks on the cliff at Uluwatu. Book ahead to nab one of the best sunset views on the Bukit. *8am-9pm Mon-Thu, to 10pm Fri & Sat*

Just south of the cave is the **Peak**, which is best avoided around low tide when it can be uncomfortably shallow. It's not for the fainthearted, but the Peak has a forgiving take-off point. **Outside Corner**, where the swell can rise to triple overhead, is where the 'Balinese Pipeline' starts to work some real big-wave magic. It breaks beyond the Peak and fires right across the line of Racetracks. South of Outside Corner (and breaking even further out) is the **Bombie**, which can reach 12m and should be avoided unless you're a big-wave charger of note.

If you're looking for a quiet wave, then head for **Temples**, a relatively fickle spot south of the Peak that can break on smaller days; the longer paddle also helps to keep crowds to a minimum. For an excellent guide to the surf breaks around the Bukit Peninsula, see indonesiansurfguide.com.

FIRST TO SURF ULUS

In 1971, film director Albert Falzon's crew was filming footage for the iconic surf movie *Morning of the Earth* when they stumbled upon the now-legendary freight-train left-handers breaking off the cliffs at Uluwatu.

That was almost four decades after surfing was first introduced in Kuta (thanks to Bob Koke, p199), and the other waves of the Bukit Peninsula had barely been discovered yet.

Australian surfer Stephen Cooney (just 15 years old at the time, and who later told his story in his book *Unearthed*) was filmed catching the first wave ever ridden at Ulu. Within a few years, Wayne 'Rabbit' Bartholomew and Hawaiian legend Gerry Lopez were photographed shooting the barrel at Ulu.

Clifftop Temple Spectacle

Visit Pura Luhur Uluwatu

According to ancient Balinese scripts, the 11th-century **Pura Luhur Uluwatu** or Uluwatu Temple *(adult/child 50,000/30,000Rp)* is a magical portal that has the potential to transport those who set eyes on it directly to heaven. Even the casual observer can feel its significance through the architecture and its dramatic location atop 70m-high cliffs.

Dedicated to Shiva Rudra, Uluwatu Temple is one of Bali's six holiest temples. Statues of deities and notable figures abound. An inner temple is guarded by statues of Ganesha. Only Hindu worshippers can enter the prayer courtyard, but anyone can peer in. A long, fortified concrete pathway runs along the cliffside. Watch out for the resident monkeys, adept at snatching visitors' belongings.

As the sun begins to slip below the Indian Ocean, the air around the temple reverberates with the hypnotising 'chak-chak-chak' chant and Kecak (pronounced ke-chak) performers mesmerise an audience that's gathered to watch what has become one of the most iconic displays of Balinese culture. With the majestic Uluwatu cliffs as a backdrop, the dancers enact tales from the Ramayana (one of the great Hindu holy books), and their traditional attire, the flickering flames, and rhythmic sounds and movements create a real spectacle.

Queue from 4.30pm for tickets *(150,000Rp)* for both the 5.45pm show and the second 7pm show. Or you can avoid the queues and buy your ticket online at least 24 hours in advance *(kecakdancebali.com; 200,000Rp)*.

Beyond Uluwatu

The hot and arid Bukit Peninsula is revered for its sunset views, languorous beaches, famous surf breaks and clifftop hotels.

Places

It's a bizarre fact that the Bukit Peninsula, which hangs off the southern tip of Bali, is markedly less well known than Uluwatu at its tip. On early Dutch maps, the peninsula was marked as Tafelhoek (Table Corner), and the Bukit (pronounced 'book-it' and translating simply as 'hill') was barely inhabited thanks to its lack of permanent rivers.

These days, the Bukit coastline and its luxury-resort enclave of Nusa Dua host some seriously dreamy beach clubs and hotels. You'll find accommodation to suit every budget (from US$10 dorms to Raffles' US$3500 a night villas), and beaches are incredibly varied; every kind of traveller will find their ideal piece of paradise here.

GETTING AROUND

Even the main roads in the central part of the Bukit Peninsula are winding country lanes (often covered in potholes). Roads in Nusa Dua are newer, wider and of much better quality, and its sprawling green areas offer a break from the chaotic traffic noises in other parts of the peninsula. At busy times (particularly around sunset), it can take forever to travel by car.

Jimbaran

TIME FROM ULUWATU: **35MIN**

Walk among giants

The beginning of the Balinese year, according to the Saka calendar, is Nyepi, a remarkable time to be on the island, a day when Bali descends into silence. The night before, however, pandemonium reigns as enormous effigies of monsters and demons from Balinese mythology are paraded through the streets. The effigies, called ogoh-ogoh, are astounding pieces of art, often standing more than 3m tall before they're burned in a shower of sparks.

Jimbaran's well-curated **Saka Museum** *(sakamuseum.org; adult/child 200,000/100,000Rp)* delves into this cultural phenomenon and houses a collection of enormous ogoh-ogoh, designed and made by the most revered artists in every one of Bali's nine regencies. Save time for the 3rd floor's Saka Auditorium, which shows 360-degree films of Bali scenes in a tented dome theatre.

Central Bukit

TIME FROM ULUWATU: **25MIN**

Visit Indonesia's tallest statue

One of the first things you see as you fly into Bali is the Garuda Wisnu Kencana statue in **GWK Cultural Park** *(gwkbali.com;*

150,000Rp), which depicts the Hindu god Vishnu riding the mythical bird Garuda. It towers over the Bukit Peninsula, standing almost 120m high. It was designed by renowned Balinese sculptor Nyoman Nuarta and comprises 3000 tonnes of copper and bronze.

It is a feat of art, science and engineering, and it's worth paying the extra fee *(350,000Rp)* for the 45-minute tour inside the statue to see the far-reaching views of Bukit. There's also a glass-bottomed walkway and excellent displays sharing details on the design, engineering and construction of the statue.

Tuck into a seafood feast

Pantai Jimbaran is famous for the scores of seafood restaurants that line the 4km bay and spill out onto the golden sand, and an evening spent here allows you to indulge in exceptionally fresh locally caught fish that's barbecued while you soak up the laid-back tropical ambience.

As evening falls and strings of lights begin to twinkle, aromatic smoke from the restaurants' grills swirls through the air, and meandering musicians serenade diners seated at tables on the sand. Along Jimbaran's sweeping 4km beach are three groups of restaurants. All sell the fish by weight (snapper is about 150,000Rp per kilogram at Pantai Muaya). The price includes rice and vegetables, and platters and set menus are available, too.

Nusa Dua

TIME FROM ULUWATU: **45MIN**

Witness the ocean's power

The exclusive resort enclave of Nusa Dua, with its manicured lawns, calm beach and luxury hotels, flanks the northeastern peninsula of the Bukit. And it has its own little peninsula, **Nusa Gede Island** (sometimes called Peninsula Island), which has been tamed into a park called the **Garden of Hope**, fringed by dramatic, ragged limestone edges that provide a stark contrast to its manicured surroundings.

On the east side of this peninsula is the natural phenomenon of **water blow** *(25,000Rp)*, where powerful waves crash against a slab of dangerously jagged rocks, and the water is forced up through steep, tight gaps in the limestone, creating dramatic water eruptions up to 10m high. A concrete walkway takes you safely over the rocks and close to the blowhole. The gate opens at 9am, a pity as sunrise here would be epic.

BYE-BYE, BINGIN

With its lovely strip of white sand framed by steep limestone cliffs, **Pantai Bingin** was one of Bali's most beautiful beaches. Hanging out in its cliffside cafes and watching the surf has been a quintessential Bukit Peninsula experience for decades, so it came as a shock to tourists and locals when local government officials descended on Bingin in July 2025 with an army of demolition workers and began tearing down more than 35 'illegal' buildings on the cliff face, effectively reducing the cliffside to rubble.

The cleanup is expected to continue through 2026, with a redevelopment plan set to include a stage for cultural performances. You can still surf here, but the Pantai Bingin you may have been lucky enough to know has gone.

EATING & DRINKING BEYOND ULUWATU: OUR PICKS

Le Bleu by K Club: Chic spot on Nusa Dua Beach with an impressive raised weaved roof, chilled beats and fine international cuisine. *10am-11pm* **$$$**

Rumari: Indulge in a fine-dining experience at Raffles in Jimbaran, where the seven-course menu is inspired by the Indonesian archipelago. *6-10pm* **$$$**

Rock Bar: Decks jut out over the rocks, south of Jimbaran, and it's spectacular for sunset drinks. Book in advance *(ayana.com)*. *4pm-midnight*

El Kabron: Adults-only clifftop beach club with a Mediterranean vibe and stunning ocean views. Extensive drinks menu. *11am-midnight*

Nusa Lembongan

EPIC SURF | GOOD DIVING | MANGROVE FORESTS

GETTING AROUND

Boats to Nusa Lembongan leave from Sanur, Benoa and Serangan harbours, and a variety of companies offer fast-boat services, which take 30 to 40 minutes, depending on weather and ocean conditions. Find and compare prices at baliferries.com.

Grab and Gojek apps don't operate in Nusa Lembongan, but 'taxis' (in the form of canopied pickups) ply the streets. Most visitors tend to hire a scooter (available from ferry stations) since distances are minimal. Beware, though, that maintenance might be lax (compared with the mainland) and many lanes are badly potholed.

Easily reachable from Bali by fast boat, but a world away from the mainland, Nusa Lembongan offers a step back in pace from the often-hectic beach towns of South Bali. The car-free island (aside from mini taxis) is rich with Hindu culture and dramatic landscapes of wave-pounded cliffs, plus quiet mangrove forests, but most visit for its superb and uncrowded surf spots and vibrant marine life.

The 2km stretch of white sand off Pantai Jungutbatu must be one of the few beaches where you can snorkel over a coral reef just 100m from surfers who are riding perfectly formed waves. Numerous surf shops and dive centres offer easy access to its ocean bounty. The island is also the launch pad for Nusa Ceningan and Nusa Penida, but for an island of its size, about 8 sq km, it has more variety and activities than your typical beach holiday.

Explore the Underwater World

Dive or snorkel around the islands

The reefs surrounding Nusa Lembongan (along with neighbours Nusa Ceningan and Nusa Penida) are home to beautiful coral gardens and an abundance of marine life. These waters were declared a marine protected area in 2010, and there are said to be some 300 species of coral and 575 species of fish here. Don a mask and snorkel and you'll likely see schools of colourful reef fish, curious turtles and majestic manta rays gliding with the currents. Between July and October, it's also possible to spot *mola mola* (ocean sunfish) here.

The visibility for diving is good year-round (it averages 20m, although often it can be up to 30m), and the warm water makes for pleasant snorkelling. The three islands boast more than 15 dive sites – **Manta Point** in Nusa Penida, with its cleaning station, is a highlight for many – with trips leaving directly from Lembongan and Penida. Many sites are accessible for snorkellers, too.

NUSA LEMBONGAN

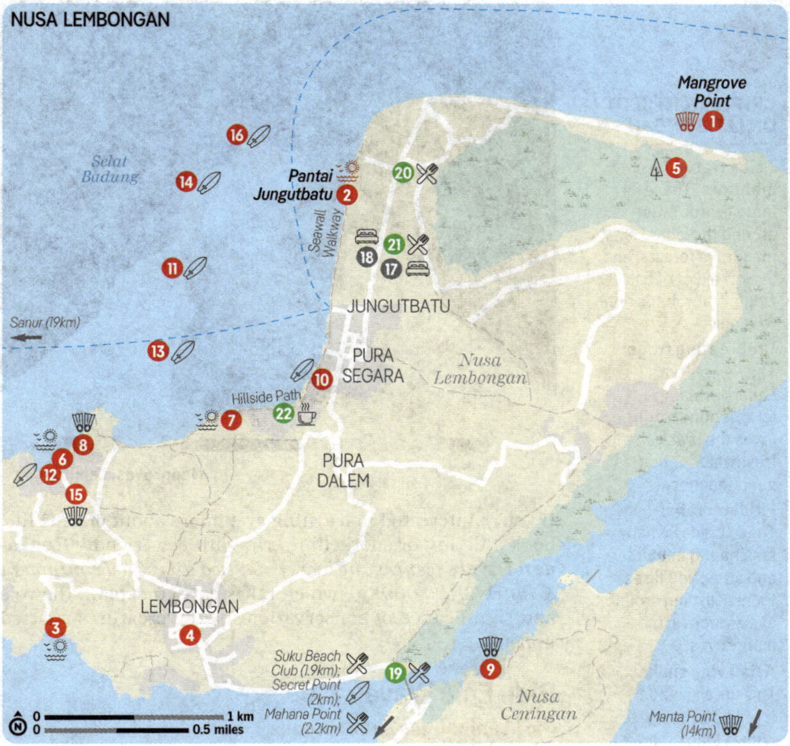

Mangrove Point
Selat Badung
Pantai Jungutbatu
Seawall Walkway
JUNGUTBATU
Sanur (19km)
PURA SEGARA
Nusa Lembongan
Hillside Path
PURA DALEM
LEMBONGAN
Suku Beach Club (1.9km); Secret Point (2km); Mahana Point (2.2km)
Nusa Ceningan
Manta Point (14km)
0 1 km
0 0.5 miles

HIGHLIGHTS
1 Mangrove Point
2 Pantai Jungutbatu

SIGHTS
3 Dream Beach
4 Gala-Gala Underground House
5 Mangroves
6 Mushroom Bay
7 Song Lambung Beach

ACTIVITIES
8 Bali Hai
9 Ceningan Divers
10 Eddy Surfboard Hire
11 Lacerations
12 Nusa Islands Surf School
13 Playgrounds
14 Razors
15 Scuba Center Asia
16 Shipwrecks

SLEEPING
17 Isla Indah Retreat
18 Pondok Jenggala

EATING
19 Alponte Ristorante
20 Curry Traders
21 Kayu Lembongan

DRINKING & NIGHTLIFE
22 Deck Café & Bar

Setting up a boat-based snorkelling or diving trip from Lembongan is easy. Dive shops abound, and most homestays and guesthouses also sell trips. Expect to pay from about 200,000Rp for a three-stop snorkelling trip, including an excellent drift at **Mangrove Point**.

For diving, **Bali Hai** *(balihaicruises.com; two dives incl equipment from 1,800,000Rp)* and **Scuba Center Asia** *(scubacenterasia.com; two dives incl equipment from 1,700,000Rp)* arrange everything, including boat transfers and a basic lunch.

TOP TIP

Pack light and be prepared to get a little wet when getting on and off the boats. While departures from mainland Bali are via jetty, fast boats and ferries moor off the beach at Nusa Lembongan, meaning wading through the shallows and carrying your luggage a short distance across the beach.

CRITTERS TO SPOT ON LEMBONGAN

Asian water monitors: These large lizards swim around the island's mangrove forests, and live off a diet of fish, frogs, crabs, birds and rodents.

Crab-eating frogs: The *Fejervarya cancrivora* (crab-eating frog) loves the brackish freshwater ponds near beaches.

Fiddler crabs: These come in many fascinating colours and sizes; you'll see them scuttling around everywhere in the mangroves.

Asian vine snakes: This green slender reptile can be up to 1.8m in length and camouflages itself as a vine. It's mildly venomous.

Monkeys: Long-tailed macaques do live in Nusa Lembongan, but they're more chilled out than in other areas of Bali.

ANNA ZHELUDKOVA/SHUTTERSTOCK

Mangroves, Lembongan

If you're interested in learning even more about marine life, book a diving or snorkelling trip with eco-friendly **Ceningan Divers** *(ceningandivers.com; two dives incl equipment & lunch 2,400,000Rp)*, which takes care to explain the role and significance of conservation for the creatures spotted underwater.

Ride Epic Waves

Surf Lembongan's reef breaks

Spectacular **Pantai Jungutbatu**, a 2km-long west-facing stretch of Lembongan's coast, has three offshore reefs that catch good, consistent surf, including occasional barrelling overhead waves.

Playgrounds is the southernmost – and most popular – surf spot accessible from **Song Lambung Beach** *(board rental per hour 150,000Rp)*. **Lacerations** is just a 150m paddle to the north, and **Razors** is another 150m north again, with a lovely left-hand peeling wave suited to longboarders in smaller swells. Although some surf schools do bring their students to Lacerations, it might be the intimidating name that keeps the crowds away, but beautifully peeling waves break both

EATING & DRINKING IN NUSA LEMBONGAN: OUR PICKS

Kayu Lembongan: Relaxed setting in a lush tropical garden, serving sustainable, organic, healthy eats, including colourful breakfasts and salads. *7am-10pm* $$

Curry Traders: Quite unexpected, this dreamy restaurant is as much a feast for the eyes as it is for the taste buds. *5-11pm* $$

Alponte Ristorante: With gorgeous views of the Yellow Bridge and Nusa Ceningan, this alfresco-style restaurant serves Italian faves. *8am-10pm* $$

Deck Café & Bar: Set above Pantai Jungutbatu, the views are a big drawcard. Beer on tap, a good gin selection and interesting cocktails. *7.30am-10pm*

left and right, allowing for an easy paddle with the current back around the edge of the reef. In larger swells, Lacerations is not safe for beginners. Beware of surfing these breaks and powerful **Shipwrecks** further north at lower tides, as the reef can become very shallow.

Boatmen can take you out and pick you up at an arranged time for 150,000Rp. **Eddy Surfboard Hire** at the southern end of Pantai Jungutbatu has a good selection of boards for all conditions, and **Nusa Islands Surf School** *(nusaislands.com; two-hour lesson from 450,000Rp)* on Mushroom Beach runs well-prepared classes for all levels.

Secret Point is the only surf spot on neighbouring Nusa Ceningan. Ideal for experienced surfers, it is reached via **Mahana Point**, a bar and grill with two high-tide cliff-jump boards, or via the beach below at **Suku Beach Club** (p217).

Kayak Through Mangroves

Glide through brackish waters

The northeastern corner of Lembongan is wrapped in an immense tangle of **mangroves**, and exploring these waterways is probably the most peaceful way to experience the island. Shady tunnels that wind through trees offer respite from the sun and – despite the shrill sounds from cicadas – the world here feels quiet, still and cool. Hire a boatman to pole you through the waterways *(30min about 150,000Rp)* or rent a kayak and explore on your own, or go on a one-hour guided kayak tour *(about 175,000Rp)*.

E-Bike Adventure

Pedal Lembongan

Bali E-Bike Tours *(baliebiketours.com; 4hr tour per person 600,000Rp)* has strung together a 23km route that makes for a fun way to get to know the island.

The tour starts at **Mushroom Bay**. The first stop is **Dream Beach** and the rugged wave-pounded chasm known as Devil's Tears. You'll then visit the unusual **Gala-Gala Underground House**. A cycle across the narrow Yellow Bridge puts you on Nusa Ceningan to meet with a family of seaweed farmers. Other stops include one of the oldest and most beautiful traditional family compounds on Lembongan, a death temple and the **mangroves**.

GIVE BACK AS YOU TRAVEL

The density of trash on Indonesia's beaches – Nusa Lembongan's included – often correlates with the seasons and tides, and the rainy season (usually November through February) can be a particularly upsetting time to be on the beaches, in the surf or exploring the region's underwater world.

Lembongan's community regularly holds beach cleanups. Lembongan Surf Team *(instagram.com/lembongansurfteam)* leads a cleanup every Thursday, while French Kiss Divers *(instagram.com/frenchkissdiverslembongan)* arranges one every Tuesday. Ceningan Divers *(instagram.com/ceningandivers)* holds village cleanups every Monday.

To get involved, check their social media pages for updates. On Nusa Penida, Penida Colada beach bar (p217) *(penidacolada.com)* gives one free fresh coconut for every bag of trash collected.

Beyond Nusa Lembongan

Places

Nusa Penida and the little sliver of Nusa Ceningan have lovely beaches and an even more laid-back and local feel.

Barely 1km wide, the coral outcrop that is Nusa Ceningan (sandwiched between Nusa Lembongan and Nusa Penida) offers surprisingly varied landscapes with forested hilltops, sprawling mangrove forests, dramatic cliff views and gorgeous beaches. It's connected to Nusa Lembongan via the narrow Yellow Bridge, accessible to scooters, bikes and foot traffic only.

A short boat ride away is hilly and largely arid Nusa Penida, the largest of the three islands. It has remained relatively undeveloped in terms of tourism, yet hordes of tourists come on organised day trips to snap photos of its gorgeous views. At times, the tour-car traffic is unbearable. Those who stay longer can avoid the peak visiting hours and settle into the wonderfully slow island pace.

GETTING AROUND

On Ceningan, you can rent a scooter or walk around. Boats from Nusa Penida run from the Yellow Bridge *(per person from 50,000Rp)* and have no fixed departures; they leave between 6.30am and 5pm when there are more than 10 passengers. The same applies at beach port Toya Pakeh in Penida (expect to wade a little to get on and off the boat).

From Bali, you can take a boat from Sanur *(baliferries.com)*. Penida doesn't have car hire or public transport, so book a local driver or rent a scooter *(per day from 100,000Rp)*. Roads are particularly bad in the southwest, and there can be a lot of traffic.

Nusa Ceningan

TIME FROM NUSA LEMBONGAN: **5MIN**

Observe seaweed farming

A beguiling patchwork of **seaweed plantations** blankets the shallow, 600m-wide channel between Lembongan and Ceningan islands, making for intriguing photos. A visit to the farms also lets you learn about the incredibly hard work of planting, harvesting and drying that's involved in farming this submarine crop, which sustains a considerable proportion of the island's population.

You get a better understanding of the complexities of seaweed farming if you visit with a guide, as some farmers only speak Bahasa Indonesia. Most hotels and homestays can arrange tours *(per person about 200,000Rp)*.

Nusa Ceningan's seaside bars and restaurants, including **Sea Breeze** *(instagram.com/seabreezeceningan)*, are great places to watch the sun set behind the seaweed farms.

Nusa Penida

TIME FROM NUSA LEMBONGAN: **15MIN**

Temple beneath the earth

Deep within a beachside hill in Nusa Penida's Suana district is a rather unusual temple. **Pura Goa Giri Putri** *(20,000Rp donation expected)* is located in a cave, and reaching it is an adventure in itself. After wrapping a sarong *(rental 10,000Rp)* around you, you climb 110 steps from the car park before you are blessed by a Hindu priest in a short purification ritual.

An important place of pilgrimage for Balinese Hindus, the temple is entered by crouching and wiggling through a narrow gap (which larger people will struggle with) between boulders that form its gateway. The entrance can be claustrophobic, but once inside, there's no more squeezing – the ceiling reaches the size of a three-storey house in places, and the cave's size is astounding, with several chambers connected in a natural cave system. Electric lighting has been fitted here, but it can still be dark and spooky in parts while you walk past atmospheric stations of prayer, which echo around the cave.

Epic views, beaches and bays

Among Penida's scenic spots drawing ever-larger crowds is **Kelingking** on the west coast, a picture-perfect rock covered in greenery that looks like a *T. rex* jutting off the mainland. It's offset by turquoise waters and ivory sands. To get to the beach, descend about 1000 steep steps (it takes roughly two hours to do the return hike). Come at mid-tide or high tide for a good stretch of sand. Hopefully by the time you read this, a 182m illegally built glass lift to the sand will have been demolished.

To the east, **Diamond Beach** *(45,000Rp)* offers a similarly dramatic view with two diamond-shaped rocks off the coast, but it's less crowded. It's all about the viewpoint here – for sunbathing and swimming, head to the next-door **Atuh Beach**.

Lined with warungs and umbrellas, **Crystal Bay** is a popular snorkelling and diving spot with shallow reefs and a chance of glimpsing *Mola mola* (ocean sunfish). **Broken Beach** has a big natural archway that wraps around the bay. At high tide, it's possible to avoid the heavy local traffic and charter a boat to it. Ask at the harbour.

TRADITIONAL WEAVERS AT WORK

In the hills of remote southeast Nusa Penida is the village of Tanglad, which is revered for its weaving traditions. The skills and knowledge have been passed down through generations, and textiles made here end up in clothes worn by many politicians and celebrities.

Tanglad resident Ngurah Hendrawan is an acclaimed dyer who uses only natural ingredients to colour his threads. He makes red from the root bark of his *mengkudu* trees (*Morinda citrifolia*), and browns from mahogany bark. His wife weaves textiles on a backstrap loom next to their **Ngurah Gallery shop** *(instagram.com/ngurahcepuktenun alami)* in the village, where you can buy their wares. If you'd like to see his dying process, Ngurah will gladly show you.

EATING & DRINKING ON PENIDA & CENINGAN: OUR PICKS

Three Island Bar: Enjoy budget Indo classics like *sate ayam* (chicken satay) and nasi goreng with cold drinks and Nusa Ceningan coast views. *9am-7pm*

Suku Beach Club: The chicest spot in the area, with a large pool and cliff-edge views, fancy cocktails and imported steaks. *8am-9pm* **$$$**

Penida Colada: Eco-conscious Nusa Penida beachfront cafe with a broad menu of healthy foods and excellent cocktails. *8am-11pm* **$$**

Cactus Beach Club: In Nusa Penida, chill beside the pool or in the breezy cafe, and feast on Asian-influenced Mediterranean dishes. *11am-10pm* **$$**

Ubud

ART & CULTURE | NATURE | FOODIE DELIGHTS

TOP TIP

To avoid the worst of the traffic coming from Denpasar, drive to Ubud via Canggu's Pererenan using the back road Jl Raya Tangeb to Mengwi. Continue east on Jl Raya Puspa Resti and north on Jl Raya Mambal Semana to access Ubud's western side.

A few days in Ubud can easily turn into a stay of weeks, months – even years for some. Carefully developed over the decades, the town's reputation for art and culture is well deserved. This is a place where Balinese traditions imbue every waking moment, where colourful offerings adorn the streets and where the hypnotic strains of gamelan are an ever-present soundtrack to everyday life. It's also somewhere that is relentlessly on trend – a showcase of sustainable design, mindfulness, culinary inventiveness and personal development, be it through yoga or a more esoteric pursuit.

Ubud is also popular, suffocatingly so. Ubud draws people with creative visions from across Bali and the world. But there's always an escape into a gallery, a hidden cafe or along a rice-field path. Come here for relaxation, rejuvenation and self-fulfilment, and revel in all Ubud has to offer.

Visit Ubud's Palace

Wander amid glitter and sculpture

The modest **Ubud Palace** *(free)* and **Puri Saren Agung** *(free)* temple share a compound in the heart of Ubud. Most of the structures were built after the 1917 earthquake, and the local royal family still lives here. Despite the name, this sprawling compound is not palatial or excessively ornate. Rather, it's a warren of courtyards and traditional Balinese buildings that extend well beyond the limited area open to visitors.

GETTING AROUND

From South Bali, Ubud can be reached by various routes via Denpasar or Sanur. Expect the trip from the airport to take from 90 minutes to two hours or more, depending on traffic. Most visitors arrive in a hire car.

Much of central Ubud is walkable, and walking is one of the top local activities. For trips further afield, local taxi drivers hold up signs at roadsides, but negotiations can be a costly hassle, and rides are not metered. The ubiquitous Gojek and Grab apps provide easy access to motorbike and car rides.

PIKKTEE/SHUTTERSTOCK

Pura Taman Saraswati

Stone carvings are a highlight. Many are by notable Ubud artists such as I Gusti Nyoman Lempad (1862–1978) and can be easily appreciated on a brief visit. At night, the palace's main courtyard is a popular and evocative venue for dance performances. One way to gain access to the inner sanctum is to stay in one of two midrange guest rooms hidden inside (search for 'Istana Saren Kauh Ubud' on Airbnb). This way, you can rise with the roosters in the morning, feel the rhythms of the royal compound and observe traditional Balinese life.

Enjoy Sacred Masterpieces

Visit Ubud's evocative temples

Ubud has dozens of temples. Most are closed to visitors, but there are some noteworthy exceptions. **Pura Taman Saraswati** *(Ubud Water Palace; ubudwaterpalace.com; adult/child 35,000/25,000Rp)* is the most picturesque. Right off Jl Raya Ubud, it provides a welcome relief from the crowded pavements. Waters flowing from the rear of the large site feed a pond in front, overflowing with lotus blossoms. Carvings honour Dewi Saraswati, the goddess of wisdom and the arts, who clearly blesses Ubud. Regular dance performances are staged at night.

Only 100m to the east, quiet **Pura Desa Ubud** *(free)* is the main temple for the Ubud community. It's often closed, but it comes alive for the extravagant ceremonies and processions for which Ubud is known. Stop by to see if something is on.

From Pura Desa Ubud, it's a 10-minute walk west along Jl Raya Ubud and the start of Jl Raya Campuan to **Pura Gunung Lebah** *(free)*, which sits on a jutting rock at the confluence of two tributaries of Sungai Cerik (*campuan* means 'two rivers'). One of Ubud's oldest temples, it's thought to date from the 8th century. The setting, far below street level in a lush gorge, is magical: listen to rushing waters while admiring the impressive *meru* and a wealth of elaborate carvings.

UBUD'S NEIGHBOURHOODS

Central Ubud: The original heart of Ubud is easily walkable and flush with businesses and attractions.

Padangtegal & Tebesaya: Conveniently located, these two areas blend into central Ubud to the west.

Sambahan & Sakti: North of Jl Raya Ubud, with rolling rice terraces and expat villas.

Nyuhkuning: A popular and quiet area just south of the Monkey Forest.

Pengosekan: South of the centre and an extension of Jl Hanoman.

Campuan & Sanggingan: Two communities strung out along a namesake road west of the centre.

Penestanan: Sitting on a plateau above Campuan, this area of cafes, guesthouses and ricefields can be a long walk to the centre.

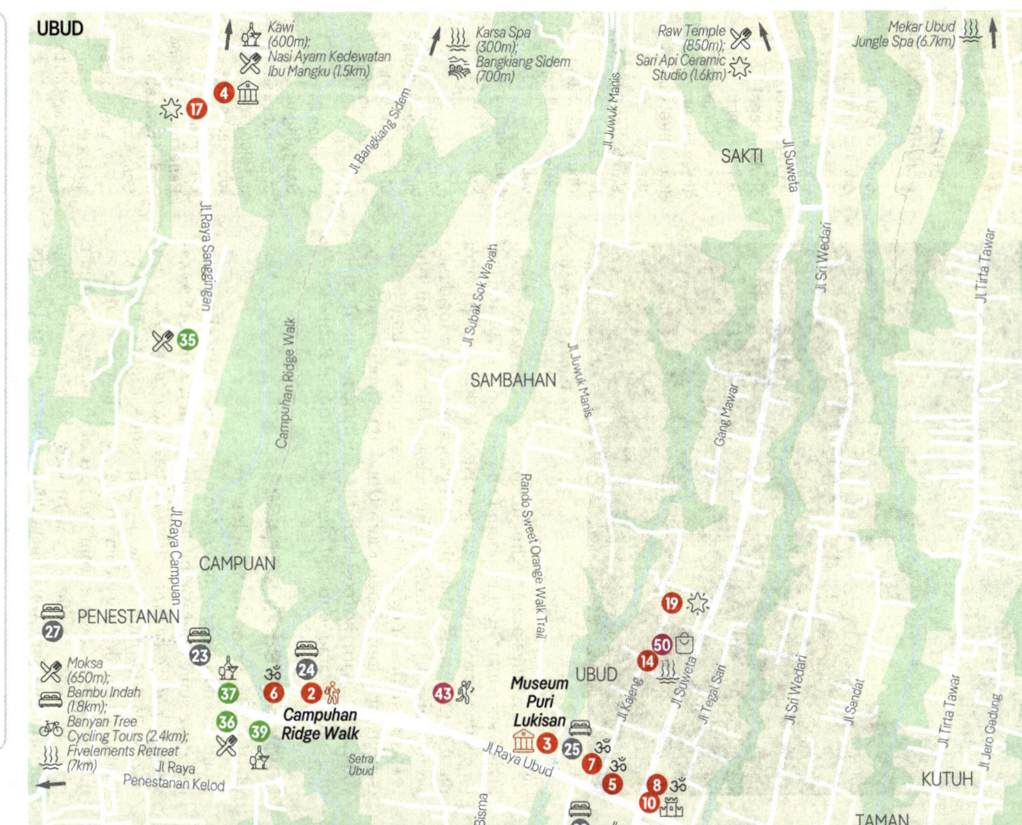

HIGHLIGHTS
1 Agung Rai Museum of Art
2 Campuhan Ridge Walk
3 Museum Puri Lukisan

SIGHTS
4 Neka Art Museum
5 Pura Desa Ubud
6 Pura Gunung Lebah
7 Pura Taman Saraswati
8 Puri Saren Agung
9 Ubud Monkey Forest
10 Ubud Palace

ACTIVITIES
11 Bali Swasthya Yoga Centre
12 Cafe Wayan Cooking Class
13 Casa Luna Cooking School
14 Golden Hands Therapeutic Massage
15 Jaens Spa Center
16 Radiantly Alive
17 Room4Dessert
18 Studio Perak
19 Ubud Botany Interactive
20 Ubud Story Walks
21 Yoga Barn

SLEEPING
22 Arjuna Homestay
23 Hotel Tjampuhan
24 Ibah
25 Puri Saraswati Dijiwa Bungalows
26 Three Win Homestay
27 Villa Nirvana

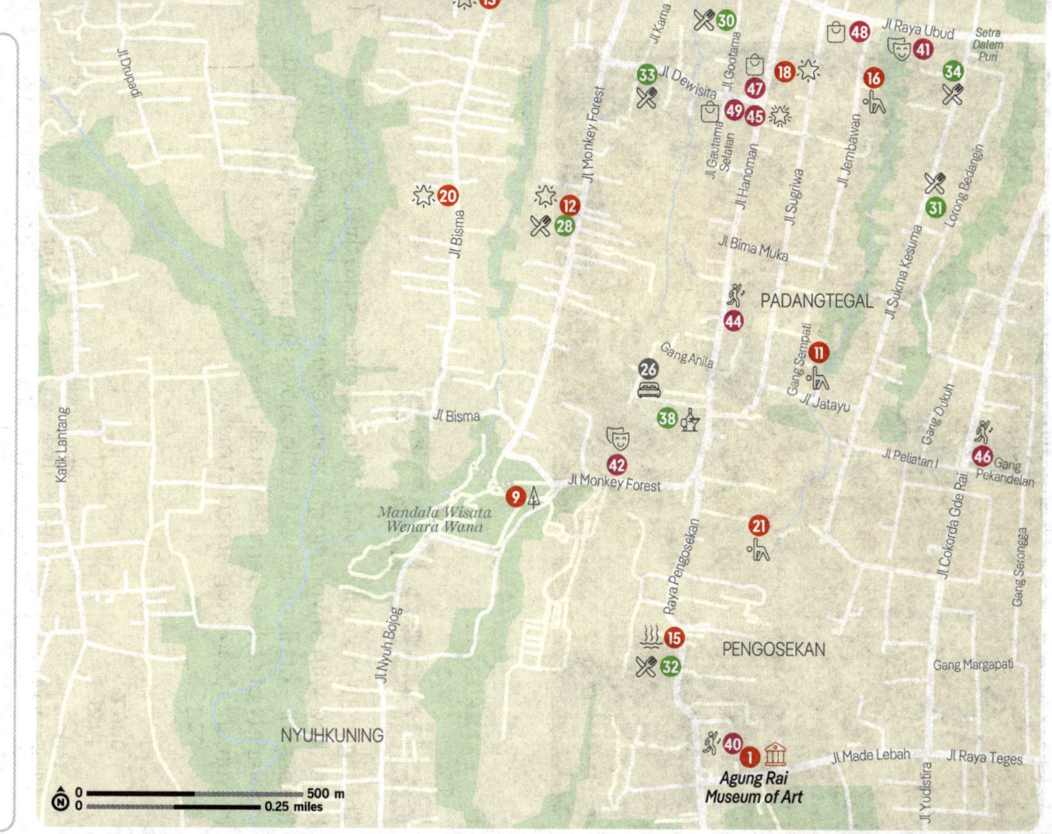

EATING

28 Honey & Smoke Open Fire Bistro
29 Hujan Locale
30 In Da Compound Warung
31 Mama's Warung
32 Merlin's
33 Nusantara
34 Sayuri Healing Food Cafe & Academy
35 Warung Pulau Kelapa
36 Zest

DRINKING & NIGHTLIFE

37 Boliche Bar
38 Ibu Susu Bar & Kitchen
39 Lair

ENTERTAINMENT

40 ARMA Museum & Resort
41 Bali Culture Workshop
42 Pondok Bamboo Music Shop
43 Pura Dalem Ubud
44 Pura Padang Kerta
45 Pura Penataran Kloncing
see 7 Pura Taman Saraswati
46 Puri Agung Peliatan
see 10 Ubud Palace
see 40 Ubud Village Jazz Festival

SHOPPING

47 Above the Clouds Natural Wear
see 47 Ananda Soul
48 Ganesha Bookshop
49 Kado by Saraswati Paper
see 49 Kevala Home
50 Threads of Life
51 Ubud Art Market

MARK WOLTERS/SHUTTERSTOCK

Legong dancers

TOP EXPERIENCE

Balinese Dance

The highlight of an Ubud visit, Balinese dances like the Legong and Kecak flow with a hypnotic grace as performers tell stories rich with the essence of Hindu lore. Multiple shows are staged nightly in Ubud, in a variety of styles. Gamelan music played on bamboo and bronze instruments is an integral part of many.

DON'T MISS

Look for the following troupes:

- Semara Ratih
- Gunung Sari
- Semara Madya
- Tirta Sari
- Cudamani

Kecak Dance

Probably the best-known dance for its spellbinding, hair-raising atmosphere, the Kecak features a 'choir' of men and boys who sit in concentric circles and slip into a trance as they chant and sing 'chak-a-chak-a-chak', imitating a troupe of monkeys. Sometimes called the vocal gamelan, it's the only music to accompany the dance reenactment from the Hindu epic Ramayana, a love story about Prince Rama and Princess Sita. The tourist version of Kecak was developed in the 1960s. The

PRACTICALITIES

● Ubud Palace performances start around 7pm ● General admission is 100,000Rp

Semara Madya troupe *(facebook.com/kecaksemaramadya)* is famous for its hypnotic chants and performs at **Puri Agung Peliatan** on Thursdays at 7pm.

Barong & Rangda

The Barong and Rangda dance rivals the Kecak as Bali's most popular performance for tourists. The show is a battle between good (the Barong) and bad (the Rangda).

The Barong is a good but mischievous and fun-loving shaggy dog-lion, with huge eyes and a mouth that clacks away. Because this character is the good protector of a village, the actors playing the Barong (who are utterly lost under layers of fur-clad costume) emote a variety of winsome antics. The Barong is a sacred character, and you'll often see one in processions and rituals.

There's nothing sacred about the Barong's buddies – monkeys that often steal the show. Actors are given free rein, the best aiming a lot of high jinks at the audience. Meanwhile, widow-witch Rangda is bad through and through. The Queen of Black Magic, the character's monstrous persona, can include flames shooting out of her ears.

The story features a duel between the Rangda and the Barong, whose supporters draw their kris (traditional daggers) and rush in to help. The long-tongued, sharp-fanged Rangda throws them into a trance, making them stab themselves. It's quite a spectacle. Thankfully, the Barong casts a spell that neutralises the power of the kris so it cannot harm them.

Legong Dance

Characterised by flashing eyes and quivering hands, this most graceful of Balinese dances is performed by young girls. Their talent is so revered that in old age, a classic dancer is remembered as a 'great Legong'. The stylised and symbolic story involves two Legong girls dancing in mirror image. They are elaborately made up and dressed in gold brocade, relating a story about a king who takes a maiden captive and consequently starts a war, in which he dies.

Some noteworthy Legong dance troupes include **Semara Ratih** *(semararatih.org)*, which also has great gamelan musicians; pioneer **Gunung Sari** *(peliatan.com/gunungsari)*, founded in 1926; and **Tirta Sari**, performers of both Legong and Barong dances. Catch Gunung Sari at **Puri Agung Peliatan** on Saturdays at 7.30pm.

Kecak Fire Dance

This dance was developed to drive out evil spirits from a village. A male dancer or boy in a trance dances around and through a fire of coconut husks, riding a coconut palm 'hobby horse'. There are many variations of this dance, which are often included as a dramatic, flaming add-on at the end of other performances.

TOP DANCE VENUES

Ubud Palace
Magical setting with a glittering, ornate backdrop.

Pura Dalem Ubud
A temple compound with a flame-lit, carved-stone backdrop.

Pura Taman Saraswati
Beautiful temple setting with water features.

ARMA Open Stage
(p225)
Hosts top troupes.

Puri Agung Peliatan
Village hosting serious troupes.

Pura Padang Kerta and **Pura Penataran Kloncing**
Convenient venues on Jl Hanoman.

TOP TIPS

- Most performances begin at about 7pm or 7.30pm. Arrive at least 20 minutes beforehand to get a good seat or space on the floor.
- Touts sell tickets around town, but you can also buy tickets at the venue entrance.
- Snacks, water and beer are often sold inside the venue.
- Performances last about 90 minutes.
- Holding up a bright phone screen to take photographs is distracting to spectators sitting behind you. Resist the urge.
- Leaving in the middle of a performance is extremely rude and an insult to the performers.

UBUD'S ARTFUL HISTORY

Late in the 19th century, Cokorda Gede Agung Sukawati established a branch of the Sukawati royal family in Ubud and began a series of alliances and confrontations with neighbouring kingdoms.

In 1900, with the kingdom of Gianyar, Ubud became (at its own request) a Dutch protectorate and was able to concentrate on its religious and cultural life. The Cokorda descendants encouraged Western artists and intellectuals to visit the area in the 1930s, most notably Walter Spies, Colin McPhee and Rudolf Bonnet. They provided an enormous stimulus to local art, introduced new ideas and began promoting Balinese culture worldwide.

As mass tourism arrived in Bali, Ubud became an attraction not for beaches or bars, but for the arts.

Try Ubud's Quintessential Hike

Strike out on the Campuhan Ridge Walk

Walking through green hills, lush river valleys and rolling ricefields is a top Ubud activity. Surprises abound, from finding idiosyncratic artists at work in a trailside hut to a sensational little juice stand where everything's organic.

A classic Ubud walking route is the **Campuhan Ridge Walk** *(campuhanridgewalk.com; free)*, which is easy and gives a good taste of what you'll enjoy on future perambulations. Following this paved trail along a ridge between two rivers is a popular sunrise and sunset activity, but it can be enjoyed at any time of the day. Pick up the trail by the driveway of the **Ibah** hotel and follow the walk signs, bearing left where the walkway crosses the Sungai Wos (Wos River), and passing the tranquil **Pura Gunung Lebah** (p219).

Continue north on the concrete path, climbing up onto the Campuhan Ridge between the Wos and Cerik Rivers. Fields of elephant grass, traditionally used for thatched roofs, slope away on either side of the path, and you can see the ricefields above Ubud in all of their lush green majesty. Continue uphill past ricefields to the village of **Bangkiang Sidem**, passing little warungs and low-key vendors and artists along the way. Avoid retracing your steps or braving the narrow road by summoning a ride with the Grab or Gojek apps.

See an Overview of Balinese Art

Works amid gardens at Museum Puri Lukisan

The modern Balinese art movement started in Ubud when artists abandoned religious and royal themes for scenes of everyday life. Of the various local art museums, **Museum Puri Lukisan** *(purilukisanmuseum.com; adult/child 95,000Rp/free)* is the most enjoyable, even if your interest in art is limited. Its tiered gardens, replete with water features, are lovely.

Four buildings display works from all schools and periods of Balinese art, with a strong focus on modern masters, including I Gusti Nyoman Lempad, Ida Bagus Made Poleng and I Gusti Made Kwandji. Artworks are labelled in English, and QR codes link to excellent additional info. Immediately east, a river path takes you to ricefields behind the museum.

Visit an Indonesian Arts Cultural Hub

Admire Ubud's finest masterpieces at ARMA

Agung Rai Museum of Art *(ARMA; armabali.com; adult/child 150,000Rp/free)* is a must-see museum next to the resort of the same name. Founder Agung Rai built his fortune selling Balinese artwork to foreigners in the 1970s, and during his time as a dealer, he acquired one of Indonesia's most impressive private collections of art. Highlights displayed include the wonderful 19th-century *Portrait of a Javanese Nobleman and His Wife* by Javanese artist Raden Saleh (1807–80).

The complex also has a hotel and a cafe, and is a venue for dance performances.

Marvel at a Balinese Art Enthusiast's Collection

Sculptures and paintings at the Neka Art Museum

On Jl Raya Campuan, the **Neka Art Museum** *(nekaart museum.com; adult/child 150,000/75,000Rp)* offers an excellent introduction to Balinese art, with a top-notch collection displayed in a series of pavilions and halls. During your one-hour visit, don't miss the multiroom **Balinese Painting Hall** showcasing *wayang* (puppet) style and European-influenced Ubud and Batuan styles introduced in the 1920s and 1930s. Also notable are works by the master I Gusti Nyoman Lempad in the **Lempad Pavilion**, and the **East-West Art Annexe**, where the artistic prowess of Affandi (1907–90) and Widayat (1919–2002) impress.

Check Out a Shadow-Puppet Show

An evening of Indonesian light artistry

Look for *wayang kulit* (shadow-puppet performances) in Ubud, attenuated to a manageable 90 minutes or less. Watching this low-tech artistry in action makes for an enthralling evening. **Bali Culture Workshop** (*baliculture workshop.com; 100,000Rp*), inside the central Oka Kartini BnB, stages popular evening shows at 8pm on Wednesdays, Fridays and Sundays. Reserve tickets in advance.

Short programmes are also performed on Mondays and Thursdays at 8pm at **Pondok Bamboo Music Shop** (*WhatsApp +62 36 197 4807; 100,000Rp*), at the southern end of town.

Learn Something New

Courses in art, dance and culture

Ubud is the perfect place to develop your creative skills, discover your inner artist and plunge into the wonders of Balinese culture.

ARMA Museum & Resort *(armabali.com/cultural-workshops; from 100,000Rp)* is a veritable college of Balinese culture and creativity. Classes include painting, silver jewellery, woodcarving, gamelan (traditional Javanese and Balinese orchestra) and batik, as well as Balinese dance and offering-making. **Museum Puri Lukisan** *(purilukisanmuseum.com/museum-puri-lukisan-workshop.html; from 100,000Rp)* and **Neka Art Museum** *(nekaartmuseum.com; from 100,000Rp)* offer similar courses.

INDONESIA'S TRADITIONAL SHADOW-PUPPET PLAYS

Much more than sheer entertainment, *wayang kulit* has been Bali's candlelit village cinema for centuries. Embodying the sacred seriousness of classical Greek drama, traditional performances were long and intense, lasting six hours or more and often not finishing before sunrise.

Originally used to bring ancestors back to this world, shows feature painted buffalo-hide puppets believed to have great spiritual power. The *dalang* (puppet master and storyteller) is an almost mystical figure, sitting behind a screen and manipulating the puppets while telling the story, often in dialects. Stories are chiefly derived from Hindu epics like the Ramayana. Find shortened performances nightly in Ubud.

EATING IN UBUD: BEST WARUNGS

In Da Compound Warung: Behind a family guesthouse on Jl Goutama. Bargain-priced dishes burst with flavour, and bunnies hop about the garden. *11am-10pm* **$**

Mama's Warung: Expect spicy Indo classics redolent with garlic. The satay peanut sauce is silky smooth, and the fried sambal is superb. *8am-10pm* **$**

Nasi Ayam Kedewatan Ibu Mangku: The star of this Bali version of a roadhouse is *sate lilit* (minced chicken grilled on skewers). *7am-9pm* **$**

Warung Pulau Kelapa: Huge menu of Indonesian dishes. Sensational sambals. For real spiciness, ask for dishes 'local style'. *10am-11pm* **$$**

UBUD'S FAMOUS PAINTERS

I Gusti Nyoman Lempad (1862–1978): A giant of Balinese art, known for ink drawings conveying movement in a *wayang* style suggestive of shadow puppets.

Ida Bagus Made Poleng (1915–99): Won international competitions in the 1930s. Renowned for his softly coloured depictions of everyday life.

Murni (1966–2006): Famed for her stark, even whimsical depictions of serious issues facing local women.

Walter Spies (1895–1942): This German painter played an important role in promoting Bali's artistic culture in the 1930s.

Arie Smit (1916–2016): Ubud's best-known Western artist. He came to Bali in 1956 and influenced the 1960s Young Artists school of painting in Penestanan.

EBRUANITA RACHMAWATI/SHUTTERSTOCK

Sambal varieties, Nusantara

Threads of Life *(threadsoflife.com; from 670,000Rp)* transports students from their exquisite Jl Kajeng shop to their nearby studio to learn the traditional techniques of creating batik with natural dyes. The non-profit is renowned for its work preserving age-old textile skills from across Indonesia. Personalised training in ceramics at an open-air workshop and kiln is offered at the long-running **Sari Api Ceramic Studio** *(sariapi.com/classes; 15-hour intensive course 4,500,000Rp)*, while **Studio Perak** *(WhatsApp +62 81 2365 1809; three-hour lesson 250,000Rp)* specialises in Balinese-style silversmithing courses. During the lesson, expect to make at least one finished piece; classes can be geared towards children.

Learn how to combine and refine locally grown plants and herbs into healthful potions and lotions during a botanical workshop at **Ubud Botany Interactive** *(ubudbotany.com; from 300,000Rp)*. It also offers tours exploring Ubud's flora.

Cultivate Culinary Creations

Learn how to recreate Balinese flavours

Ubud cooking classes often start at the local produce morning market, set deep within the modern **Ubud Art Market**. You'll learn about the huge range of fruits, vegetables and other foods that are part of the Balinese diet.

Go for the chargrilled lamb skewer.

EATING IN UBUD: TOP-END RESTAURANTS

Nusantara: Boldly flavoured, highly spiced dishes by the legendary Locavore team. *noon-2.30pm & 6-9.30pm Tue-Sun, 6-9.30pm Mon* $$$

Hujan Locale: Chef Will Meyrick serves creative Indonesian in an open-air dining room. Passion fruit cocktails are addictive. *noon-3pm & 5.30-10pm* $$$

Merlin's: Immersive dining experience paired with magic: draw tarot cards to find which food 'chooses you'. Reserve ahead. *2-11pm* $$$

Honey & Smoke Open Fire Bistro: Flatbread to veggies, everything is flame-grilled using Ottoman fire-smoke techniques. *noon-11pm* $$$

Casa Luna Cooking School *(casalunacookingschool.com; from 450,000Rp)* has a full menu of classes. Half-day courses have a different theme each day and cover a range of dishes.

The basics of Balinese spices and cuisine are the focus of two-hour courses at long-running **Cafe Wayan Cooking Class** *(cafewayan.com/cooking-classes; 450,000Rp)*. The lesson plan varies each day, and you get to eat your work for lunch.

Or learn from master Balinese chef Wayan Manis in her home kitchen, preparing iconic dishes for a dinner feast using traditional ingredients and a wood stove. Book through travelingspoon.com. For the sweet-toothed, the lauded fine-dining restaurant **Room4Dessert** *(room4dessert.com)* hosts 'pastry bootcamps' and other culinary classes.

Choose Your Wellness Journey

Take your pick of spas and yoga classes

Ubud is known around the world for its holistic and spiritual side, and enjoying a massage, wellness treatment or yoga course is at the top of most visitors' lists.

It's hard to beat **Golden Hands Therapeutic Massage** *(instagram.com/ubudspa.goldenhands)* or **Jaens Spa Center** *(jaensspashanti.com)* for a good massage that won't break the bank, while visitors looking for more sumptuous spas with longer treatment menus would be wise to book a day of bliss at the likes of **Karsa Spa** *(karsaspa.com)*, **Fivelements Retreat** *(fivelementsbali.com)* and **Mekar Ubud Jungle Spa** *(kclubgroup.com/mekar)*.

For yoga, the ever-popular **Yoga Barn** *(theyogabarn.com)* offers a vast range of classes and also has upper and whole body treatments at its Kush Spa. **Radiantly Alive** *(samyama.com)* is another central yoga centre appealing to students looking for a mix of drop-in and long-term yoga classes in various disciplines, while the **Bali Swasthya Yoga Centre** *(instagram.com/baliswasthyayoga)* is the place to go for Balinese-born instructors who eschew trends.

Embrace a Guided Adventure

Join an Ubud walking or biking tour

Spending a few hours exploring with a local expert is a fabulous way to savour Ubud and its region.

Perhaps the best two to three hours you'll spend locally is on a remarkably detailed and entertaining tour covering Balinese culture and history with **Ubud Story Walks**

TODAY'S TOP BALINESE ARTISTS

Nyoman Masriadi (b 1973): Born in Gianyar, Bali's current painter superstar is renowned for his sharp-eyed observations of Indonesian society.

Made Djirna (b 1957): Ubud's Djirna critiques the relationship between ostentatious money and modern Balinese religious ceremonies.

Agung Mangu Putra (b 1963): His works decry the impact of Bali's tourist boom and its unequal spread of benefits.

Wayan Sudarna Putra (b 1976): Ubud native Putra uses satire to question the absurdities of contemporary Indonesian life.

Gede Suanda Sayur (b 1980): Sayur questions the pillaging of Bali's environment. He helped create an installation in a ricefield that spelt out 'not for sale'.

EATING IN UBUD: VEGETARIAN & VEGAN

Sayuri Healing Food Cafe & Academy: Japanese chef Sayuri Tanaka promotes raw-vegan food culture at this restaurant and cooking academy. *8am-11pm* $$

Zest: Peaceful bohemian cafe with a delightful forest view serving global foods made from farm-to-table fine plants. *8am-10pm* $$

Raw Temple: Self-proclaimed raw vegan sanctuary serving inventive, uncooked dishes – from pizzas to burritos – and detox juices. *9am-11pm* $$

Has weekly music and transformative experiences.

Moksa: In a bucolic setting on a permaculture farm, Moksa creates extraordinary meals with simple vegetables. Many dishes are raw. *10am-9pm* $$

BOOKISH UBUD

Art-rich Ubud is also renowned as one of Southeast Asia's few literary towns. For starters, it is the home of Bali's best place for the printed word: **Ganesha Bookshop** *(ganeshabooksbali.com)*, founded in 1986, sells an impressive selection of Indonesia- and Bali-focused titles, plus a well-curated selection of new and used books.

Since 2004, the town has hosted the **Ubud Writers and Readers Festival** *(ubudwritersfestival.com)* in October, now one of Southeast Asia's (and possibly the world's) largest and most significant literary events. Founded by Australian Janet DeNeefe and her Balinese husband as a healing cultural response to the 2002 Bali bombings, the festival hosts up to 170 international writers, readings and workshops each year.

(ubudstorywalks.com; from 350,000Rp). Learn about Ubud's past and present, the unsung wonders of temples in Pejeng, the works of legendary artist I Gusti Nyoman Lempad, and more.

You could also spend the early morning exploring old villages and landscapes before sunrise with Agung Rai, founder of his namesake art museum **ARMA** (p224), on a three-hour Golden Hour Tour *(armabali.com/product/golden-hour; 1,340,000Rp)*. It usually starts at 5.45am when guests set off in Rai's car to some of his favourite spots: rice paddies, quiet villages, streams and temples bathed in ethereal morning light provide a choreographic backdrop for the art collector's explanations of Balinese cultural nuances.

Ubud native Dewa Rai of **Bali Nature Walks** *(balinaturewalks.net; from 400,000Rp)* conducts three- to four-hour nature walks through jungle and ricefields around Ubud.

Whizz downhill on day-long tours led by the popular **Banyan Tree Cycling Tours** *(banyantreebiketours.com; from adult/child 920,000/580,000Rp)* to remote villages near Ubud where you can interact with villagers.

DRINKING IN UBUD: BEST COCKTAILS

Boliche Bar: On the site of Cantina Rooftop, this stylish, top-end cocktail bar draws on local flavours for offbeat drinks. *8pm-2am Thu-Sat*

Kawi: Means 'poet' in Sanskrit. Inventive drinks use local ingredients like *arak* and dried bananas. Narrow bar, chill garden. *7pm-midnight Mon-Sat*

Lair: Look for the boho sign pointing down at Campuhan Bridge. Within earshot of the flowing river, with primitive decor, sophisticated drinks and snacks. *7pm-midnight*

Ibu Susu Bar & Kitchen: Excellent, well-presented cocktails like pomelo negroni, fusing Southeast Asian tastes with international mixology. *noon-midnight*

TATIANA POPOVA/SHUTTERSTOCK

Ubud Monkey Forest

Enter the Monkey Forest

If you dare

With its flashy theme-park-like entrance near the south end of the eponymous road, you'd be hard-pressed to realise that the **Ubud Monkey Forest** *(monkeyforestubud.com; adult/child 100,000/80,000Rp)* was once merely a shady expanse housing three temples and a resident troop of more than 1000 well-fed and light-fingered monkeys. It's now a top destination for day-trippers from across Bali, though you can escape the crowds by visiting early and late in the day. You can't miss the grey-haired and greedy longtailed Balinese macaques – they can bite, and rabies is present in Bali, so be careful and watch all your belongings (and children).

Ubud's Fashionable Heart

Shop for stylish wares made in Bali

Within a few hundred metres of where Jl Dewi Sita meets Jl Hanoman, you can find some of Ubud's most interesting and stylish shops. **Above the Clouds Natural Wear** *(abovethe clouds.store)* sells casual linen and cotton clothes designed and sewn in villages around Ubud; quality and service are both tops. Proceeds from locally designed and produced jewellery and a small line of resort wear sold at **Ananda Soul** *(anandasoul.com)*, a shop with a heart, support disadvantaged Balinese.

Kado by Saraswati Paper *(saraswatipapers.com)* sells journals, cards, prints and other high-end goods for creative pursuits. Everything is made from recycled paper and produced in Bali. Next door, slick **Kevala Home** *(kevalaceramics.com)* sells stylish, locally made ceramic and porcelain.

UBUD'S BEST EVENTS

Ubud Writers & Readers Festival: Southeast Asia's major literary event draws writers and readers from around the world for a five-day celebration in October. *(ubud writersfestival.com)*

Ubud Open Studios: Two-day celebration in March, with more than 70 local artists opening their studios to visitors. Many special events. *(ubud openstudios.com)*

BaliSpirit Festival: A popular yoga, dance and music festival in May, with hundreds of workshops and concerts. *(bali spiritfestival.com)*

Ubud Village Jazz Festival: Annual two-day jazz festival in late July featuring an international lineup of performers. *(ubudvillagejazz festival.com)*

Ubud Food Festival: Diverse and delicious Indonesian cuisine takes centre stage at this three-day festival in late June or July. *(ubudfoodfestival. com)*

Beyond Ubud: North

The action of the south melts away as you move upslope from Ubud. It's a lush land with ancient sites.

Places

North of Ubud, Bali becomes cooler and greener. Fascinating sights and natural beauty abound in this hilly countryside. One easy route from Ubud, northeast towards Gunung Batur, passes through Tegallalang (home to the touristy Ceking rice terraces) and continues via Tampaksiring, passing the ancient sites of Gunung Kawi Sebatu, Gunung Kawi and Tirta Empul. The scenery on this route is verdantly picturesque – you'll see farmers working in their fields, colourful flags fluttering in the wind and plenty of rice terraces and roadside shrines. Hillside villages such as Taro remain good spots to observe Balinese life.

GETTING AROUND

Having your own wheels is the only way to explore north of Ubud. The relentless uphill climbs make it a challenge for all but the most dedicated cyclists – rent a scooter. Otherwise, given that returning to Ubud is all downhill, you can get a ride one-way and cycle back downhill. Use apps for taxi rides and consider hiring a car and driver for a day out to the top sights.

Tegallalang

TIME FROM UBUD: **30MIN**

Busy rice terrace views

Heading north from Ubud, the stupendous views of the **Ceking Rice Terraces** from Tegallalang's main road are marred by the vast tourist circus, replete with competing Instagram swings and a barrage of cafes whose viewing terraces now obscure most of the views from the cliffside.

Still, this is one of Bali's most scenic rice terrace panoramas. Take it all in from somewhere like **Alas Harum** *(alasharum.com; 50,000Rp)*, a coffee plantation replete with restaurant, zip line, giant swings and large cliff-hanging pools.

If that's not your scene, access the terraces from the trails that descend into the lush valley. You'll be charged 25,000Rp, plus an occasional toll levied by some farmers.

Alternatively, visit the terraces by bike on an organised, supported tour with the likes of **Jegeg Bali Cycling** *(jegegbalicycling.com; adult/child 400,000/300,000Rp)* or **Love Bali Bike Tours** *(lovebalibiketours.com; adult/child 500,000/350,000Rp)*.

Kedewatan

TIME FROM UBUD: **30MIN**

Take to Ubud's rushing river

The Sungai Ayung (Ayung River) is Bali's most popular river for white-water rafting. You start north of Ubud and end in

MARKUS GEBAUER PHOTOGRAPHY/GETTY IMAGES

Rice terraces, Tegallalang

Sayan to the west. Depending on rainfall, the river can range from sedate to thrilling. Of the numerous companies offering trips – all similar – pioneering operator **Mason Adventures** *(masonadventures.com; from 795,000Rp without transport)* still offers the longest rafting trip, at 12km. It was the first rafting company here three decades ago.

Transport is usually provided from hotels and resorts in Ubud and South Bali (the departure from Nusa Dua can be very early) to a starting point off the main road north to Kintamani. Protective gear and beverages are provided. Some rafting packages include lunch at tourist-group-oriented restaurants, and additional options include short treks in the lush river valley and ecologically damaging ATV rides.

Tampaksiring

TIME FROM UBUD: **40MIN**

Visit an iconic water temple

Immediately east of the **presidential palace**, **Pura Tirta Empul** *(tirtaempultemple.com; adult/child 75,000/50,000Rp)* dates from 962 CE (although little remains from then). This water temple is believed to have magical powers, and the holy springs bubble up into a large pool and gush out through waterspouts into a *petirtaan* (bathing area). The site is always thronged with Balinese and visitors performing the *melukat* ritual cleansing, which is meant to assure a better future.

For a more serene setting, go downstream about 500m and take a long flight of steps down to **Pura Mengening** *(free)*, a temple with a freestanding *candi* similar in design to those at **Gunung Kawi** (p232). This towering stone structure is thought to be more than 1000 years old.

COFFEE LUWAK CONCERNS

Coffee luwak (*kopi luwak*) is ubiquitous and overhyped in tourist areas north of Ubud. It's named after the cat-like civet (*luwak)* indigenous to Sulawesi, Sumatra and Java, which eats ripe coffee cherries. Entrepreneurs initially collected the intact beans found in the nocturnal civet's droppings and processed them to produce a supposedly extra-piquant brew.

However, once the profit potential of exploiting coffee luwak was realised, outlets proliferated. With interest in coffee luwak exceeding all reason, trouble abounds. There is no certification that your expensive cup of coffee was brewed from beans that passed through the gut of a civet. Reports of mistreatment of caged civets on factory farms are common.

MORE WATER TEMPLES

Besides Pura Tirta Empul, check out **Pura Ulun Danu Bratan** (p264), which appears to float on Lake Bratan, and **Pura Taman Ayun** (p278) in Mengwi, an important part of the UNESCO World Heritage–listed *subak* water irrigation system.

MYSTERIOUS GUNUNG KAWI

Uncertainty and myth surround the founding of **Gunung Kawi**, believed to have been built in 1080 CE by King Anak Wungsu, the third son of Bali's landmark historical figure, King Udayana. The five *candi* on the eastern riverbank are probably dedicated to King Udayana, Queen Mahendradatta and their sons Airlangga, Anak Wungsu and Marakata. While Airlangga ruled eastern Java, Anak Wungsu ruled Bali.

The four *candi* on the western side are, by this theory, dedicated to Anak Wungsu's chief concubines. Another theory is that the whole complex is dedicated to Anak Wungsu, his wives, concubines and, in the case of the remote 10th *candi*, to a royal minister.

Explore a remarkable ancient site

One of Bali's oldest, holiest and most important monuments, the stunning river-valley complex of **Gunung Kawi** *(adult/child 75,000/50,000Rp)* consists of 10 huge, 8m-high *candi* cut out of rock faces. Each is believed to be a memorial to a member of 11th-century Balinese royalty. Legends relate that the whole group was carved out of the rock in one hardworking night by the mighty fingernails of the legendary giant Kebo Iwa.

Groups of *candi* (shrines) and monks' cells carved into cliff faces are found throughout this area that was once encompassed by the ancient Pejeng kingdom; it stretched south along the Pakerisan River to **Goa Garba** (p234) and beyond.

Arrive in Gunung Kawi as early as possible for the best experience. Start making your way down the 250 steps by 7.30am to observe residents going about their morning ablutions and cleaning of ceremonial offerings in the streams. You'll also still have cool air when you start the hike back up the steep staircase.

Sebatu

TIME FROM UBUD: **45MIN**

Purification at a temple to Vishnu

Coming from the west by the hilly road, you'll spot **Pura Gunung Kawi Sebatu** *(gunungkawisebatu.com; adult/child 50,000/25,000Rp)* set in a lush gorge below.

The temple is dedicated to Vishnu, the supreme Hindu god who protects the cosmic order, and is used for purification rituals. Inside, spring-fed pools are set against a lush green backdrop. Behind an ornate wall, you'll find two ritual bathing pools fed by water spouting from carved heads, where you can take a dip in the cool, clear water.

In the surrounding small village of **Sebatu**, look for shops run by woodcarvers who create intricate decorative items from fine-grained, light albesia wood.

Taro

TIME FROM UBUD: **1HR**

Experience tranquil village life

The air is noticeably cooler in the hillside village of Taro, 18km north of Ubud. It's compact, easily visited on foot, and the local community runs a useful website *(desawisatataro.com)* filled with info about the village, including homestay options.

Start at **Pura Agung Gunung Raung** *(free)*, the large temple in the centre with statues of *lembu putih* (white cows, a local icon) at its entrance. The temple dates from the 17th century and is named after Gunung Raung, the active volcano in East Java, where its founding priests hailed from.

EATING NORTH OF UBUD: OUR PICKS

Heliostar: Tropical concept cafe in a quiet villa outside Petulu, with well-curated food and a working space upstairs. *8am-8pm* $

Mimpi Manis: Cosy, boho-chic restaurant in Sebatu offering a range of flavourful beef and fish steaks, Indonesian mains and live music. *8am-11pm* $$

Warung Umah Bali: Hearty servings of Indonesian mains like nasi goreng and satay in a relaxing garden setting, west of Tegallalang's scrum. *10am-10pm* $$

Semara Ratih Delodsema Village: The viewing platforms above the jungle make this international and Indonesian restaurant in Taro stand out. *8am-6.30pm* $$

Beyond Ubud: South

Villages of artisans, astonishing ancient sites and plenty of places to shop for handicrafts dot the lands south of Ubud.

A remarkable artefact more than 2000 years old is but one of the highlights of the adjacent villages of Pejeng and Bedulu, once the centres of a great kingdom. The legendary Dalem Bedaulu ruled the Pejeng dynasty from here and was the last Balinese king to withstand the onslaught of the powerful Majapahit from Java in the 14th century. They are but two of the villages dotting the drier and flatter countryside running to the coast.

The roads are lined with little shops that make and sell handicrafts. Many visitors shop here as they head to and from Ubud. Places like Mas, Blahbatuh, Sukawati and Batubulan are renowned for the quality and craftsmanship of their goods.

Places

Pejeng

TIME FROM UBUD: **15MIN**

See an astounding relic

The village of Pejeng, 5km east of central Ubud, was the capital of the Balinese Pejeng kingdom for a short period between Javanese invasions. It collapsed in 1343 when the Majapahits defeated King Dalem Bedaulu. Today, it is home to one of the region's most extraordinary but least-visited sights.

Founded in 1266, **Pura Penataran Sasih** *(free)* was once the state temple of the Pejeng kingdom. In the inner courtyard is a more remarkable treasure: a huge bronze drum known as the **Moon of Pejeng**, thought to date back as far as 300 BCE. The hourglass-shaped drum is 186cm high and is the largest single-piece cast drum in the world. The bronze alloy and casting technique have been traced to the Dong Son people of ancient Vietnam, revealing a previously unknown trade route.

Visit intriguing temples

There are several other fascinating sites near Pura Penataran Sasih. **Pura Pusering Jagat** *(free)* was built in 1329 and is popular with young couples who pray at the stone lingam and yoni – Hindu symbols of the male and female sexual organs, life force of the universe – in hopes of fertility. Also in the

GETTING AROUND

The towns and villages south of Ubud lie along roads that get ever busier the further south you go. Cycling here is tough (even if it's relatively flat) because you dodge traffic along the narrow roads. Having your own motorbike or car (with or without a driver) is the way to go, as it allows for greater flexibility. Pejeng and Bedulu are easily reached by taxi from Ubud.

EXPLORING SOUTH OF UBUD

Khana Putri Pertiwi, a tour guide and archaeology major, shares her tips for visiting the area south of Ubud.

Don't skip **Batuan**, 30 minutes from Ubud. This historically rich village holds great significance as it's where the renowned American anthropologist Margaret Mead conducted most of her research on Balinese culture.

On Sundays, guests can visit **Studio Gelombang** *(instagram.com/studiogelombang)* and watch the local artist Made Griyawan conducting a traditional art class for neighbourhood kids.

Nature lovers can take a refreshing dip in either of the nearby waterfalls, **Air Sumampan** or **Air Uma Anyar**. In the late afternoon, it's fun to walk along Sukawati's **jogging track** through ricefields, where residents watch the sunset from a wide open space.

SHARON WILDIE/SHUTTERSTOCK

Goa Gajah

grassy compound is a large stone urn with elaborate carvings of gods and demons searching for the elixir of life in a depiction of the Mahabharata tale *Churning of the Ocean of Milk*.

Pura Kebo Edan *(20,000Rp)* translates as 'Crazy Buffalo Temple', and although it's not an imposing structure, it is well known for its much-weathered 3m-high Giant of Pejeng statue. Thought to be approximately 600 years old, the statue is generally covered, but one peek at its midsection and you'll see that the giant moniker is apt.

Across two rivers further east, lesser-known **Goa Garba** *(adult/child 30,000/15,000Rp)* is an ancient rock-hewn meditation enclave set deep into a ravine on the banks of the Pakerisan River. The quiet, atmospheric site echoes the rock carvings of **Gunung Kawi** (p232) to the north. Niches in the cliffs known as hermit's alcoves are thought to date to the 11th century.

Admire ancient treasures

Many of the region's oldest treasures have been unearthed by farmers while ploughing their fields. Admire a range of artefacts at the **Museum Gedung Arca** *(free)*. Exhibits in several small buildings at the archaeological museum include sarcophagi dating from as early as 300 BCE and some of Bali's first pottery from near Gilimanuk. **Ubud Story Walks** (p227) runs an excellent tour of the main Pejeng sites *(ubudstorywalks.com/the-myth-of-pejeng; 300,000Rp)*.

Bedulu

TIME FROM UBUD: **20MIN** 

Mysterious cave temple

The demonic mouth of the incense-wafting **Goa Gajah** *(Elephant Cave; adult/child 50,000/25,000Rp)* is one of Ubud's most recognisable sights. Its origins are uncertain: myth says that legendary giant Kebo Iwa sculpted it with his fingernail. It likely dates from the 11th century in the early Majapahit era and was probably named after the nearby Petanu River, once known as Elephant River – Bali never had the pachyderms.

Inside are fragmentary remains of a lingam, the phallic symbol of the Hindu god Shiva, and its female counterpart, the yoni, as well as a statue of Shiva's son, the elephant-headed god Ganesha. Outside, two square bathing pools have waterspouts held by six female figures.

Visit a hidden Hindu hermitage

Set amid rice terraces, under-appreciated **Yeh Pulu** *(adult/child 30,000/15,000Rp)* is a 25m-long carved cliff face next to the Pakerisan and Petanu Rivers. It is believed to be the remnants of a 14th-century hermitage. Even if your interest in carved Hindu art is minor, the site is compelling, and you're likely to have it all to yourself. Apart from the figure of Ganesha, the nine scenes depict everyday life 600 years ago. There are good walks here through the surrounding ricefields. Ask for directions to **Goa Gajah**.

Mas

TIME FROM UBUD: **20MIN**

Discover art and commerce

Woodcarving is the principal craft in this village south of Ubud. Shops and galleries line the main road of Jl Raya Mas, and workshops are located both here and alongside the streets. West of the village, dramatic and modern gallery **Ubud Diary** *(ubuddiary.com; free)* is a labour of love by a collector of Indonesian art, with an emphasis on celebrating the Ubud school of painting.

A world of serious make-believe

One of the best museums in the Ubud area, **Setia Darma House of Masks and Puppets** *(maskandpuppets.com; free)* is home to more than 7000 ceremonial masks and puppets from Bali, other parts of Indonesia, Asia and beyond. All are beautifully displayed in a series of renovated historic buildings in a rural compound. Among the many treasures, look for the amazing Barong Landung puppets and the Kamasan paintings.

Visit some artsy spots

One of the premier galleries in the Ubud area, **Tonyraka Art Lounge** *(tonyraka.com)* shows top-notch Balinese tribal and contemporary art. Come to browse, buy and enjoy the cafe.

Learn how to make your own stencils and prints at **Black Hand Gang** *(bhgstudio.id)*, a creative compound that also features the Toko Hands shop. Recalling the hip Japanese outpost Tokyu Hands, it's filled with irreverent T-shirts designed by local artists.

Blahbatuh

TIME FROM UBUD: **30MIN**

Visit vital temples

Blahbatuh is known for its association with Kebo Iwa, the legendary strongman and minister to the last king of the Bedulu kingdom. A massive statue depicting him in full warrior mode adorns a roundabout on the main road between Blahbatuh and Gianyar.

BAMBOO REVOLUTION

Opened in Abiansemal in 2008, **Green School** *(greenschool.org)* enjoyed immediate hype for its unorthodox curriculum and flamboyant bamboo architecture. A passion project of Canadian expat John Hardy (of the namesake international jewellery mega-brand) and his wife, Cynthia, the school's sinuous and soaring bamboo trusses were soon repeated by Hardy in his own home.

From there, the look spread across Bali, from beach clubs in Canggu to upscale restaurants amid Ubud's ricefields to housing projects in Denpasar.

Intrigued by the style and sustainable promise? **Bamboo U** *(bamboou.com)*, a project that includes Hardy's son Orin, offers online training in bamboo design and construction. Ibuku *(ibuku.com)*, the architecture firm of Hardy's daughter Elora, creates bamboo structures worldwide.

VILLAGE ARTISANS

In small villages throughout the Ubud region, especially in the south, you'll see signs – often near the local temple – for artists and craftspeople. As one resident told us, 'Our village is only as rich as our art'. It is for this reason that the creators behind the ceremonial costumes, masks, kris, musical instruments and other beautiful aspects of Balinese life and religion are accorded great honour.

It's a symbiotic relationship, with the artist never charging the village for the work and the village, in turn, seeing to the welfare of the artist. Many artists are often in residence because of the shame entailed in needing to procure a sacred object from another village.

TRAVEL-FR/SHUTTERSTOCK

Pura Puseh Batuan

An 11th-century carved head of Iwa can be admired in the village's major temple, **Pura Puseh Desa Blahbatuh** *(free)*. Just north, **Pura Kahyangan Jagat** *(free)* has Bukit Dharma (Dharma Hill) as a backdrop. Climb the hill to reach a shrine featuring a stone statue of the six-armed goddess of death and destruction, Durga, killing a demon-possessed water buffalo.

Learn about traditional textiles

A symphony of click-clacking looms greets visitors to **Pertenunan Putri Ayu** *(tenunputriayu.com)*, which produces colourful batik and woven ikat fabrics (including Bali's much-prized *endek* style) using age-old methods. Staff show you through the workshop and explain the process. Fabric and clothes are for sale.

Batuan

TIME FROM UBUD: **50MIN**

See 1000-year-old temples

Batuan's recorded history goes back 1000 years. In the 17th century, its royal family controlled most of southern Bali. The decline of its power is attributed to a priest's curse, which scattered the royal family to different parts of the island.

The twin temples of **Pura Puseh Batuan** and **Pura Dasar Batuan** *(free)* are among Bali's oldest. They're accessible studies in classic Balinese temple architecture. The former is renowned for the quality of its sculptures and its Javanese-influenced water garden.

Sukawati

TIME FROM UBUD: 1HR

A village of arts and crafts

Once a royal capital, Sukawati is now known for its sprawling **Art Market**. Look for local workshops marked *tukang prada*, where you'll find temple umbrellas beautifully decorated with stencilled gold paint.

To the west, artisans in the villages of **Puaya** and **Singapadu** specialise in high-quality leather shadow puppets and masks for Topeng and Barong dances. On the main street, look for workshops where local artisans both make and sell ceremonial items for dance performances. **Nyoman Ruka** *(instagram.com/nyoman_rukaartshop)* runs a studio famous for its Barong masks.

Batubulan

TIME FROM UBUD: 1¼HR

Explore a village of stone carvers

Stone carving is Batubulan's main craft. Workshops are found along the road to Tegaltamu, with another batch further north around Silakarang. The village is the source of the stunning temple-gate guardians seen all over Bali, made with a porous grey volcanic rock resembling pumice called paras. Soft and surprisingly light, it also ages quickly, meaning 'ancient' artworks may be years rather than centuries old.

By night, the village is a hub of Balinese dance, making it an attractive option for visitors from the south who don't want to go all the way north to Ubud. Depending on the night, Kecak, Barong and fire dances are performed in the village's large **Sahadewa**.

Klungkung

ROYAL RESIDENCES | HISTORIC ARCHITECTURE | MARKETS

GETTING AROUND

Klungkung is best reached with your own wheels. The main road along the east coast runs only 4km south of the centre, so it's an easy detour. It's also convenient for Gianyar, Bangli, Pura Besakih and Sidemen.

Klungkung is compact, so it's convenient to walk everywhere. Stashing a car or motorbike is not hard; street attendants will collect a small fee. The town can be reached in an hour or less from both Ubud (via Gianyar) and Sanur (via the coast road).

TOP TIP

Despite its sights, Klungkung is not a tourist town, so don't expect to find many eating and drinking options. However, the market is great for fruit, especially before noon.

Officially called Semarapura but commonly known by its traditional name Klungkung, this district capital is home to the historically significant Puri Agung Semarapura (Klungkung Palace), a relic of the days of Klungkung's rajas, the Dewa Agungs. Once the centre of Bali's most important kingdom, the busy town retains the palace compound from its royal past, with a market opposite. East of the palace, the main road crosses one of Bali's largest rivers, Sungai Unda. Throughout the area, there are also large temples and mosques.

It's easy to spend a couple of hours here exploring the remains of the palace and the local market. Klungkung is a hub of roads, so it's easy to visit other areas of the south from here, or stop off as part of a larger itinerary.

Honouring Ritual Suicide

A monument to sacrifice

Klungkung was the last Balinese kingdom to succumb to the Dutch (in 1908). The sacrifice of its royal family, who died by *puputan* (ritual suicide) rather than surrender, is commemorated in the towering **Puputan Monument** *(Semarapura City Tour ticket adult/child 50,000/25,000Rp)*. In its base are 16 reliefs that showcase important historic events, including a battle led (unusually) by a woman (p241). There's also a sculpture of Ida I Dewa Agung Jambe, who founded the Klungkung kingdom in 1686. The monument is the logical starting point for exploring Klungkung, as the same ticket gets you into the **Puri Agung Semarapura** complex across the road.

The Puputan Monument is on the northeastern side of the **Patung Kanda Pat** monument, honouring the four spiritual siblings that the Balinese believe accompany us through our lifetimes. It stands at the intersection of Jl Untung Serapati and the road to Besakih.

FOTOS593/SHUTTERSTOCK

Kertha Gosa

Step Back in Time

Visit Klungkung's historic palace

Stroll around the **Puri Agung Semarapura** *(Semarapura City Tour ticket adult/child 50,000/25,000Rp)* compound and you'll catch a glimpse of the Klungkung palace as it was in 1710 when it was completed for the Dewa Agung dynasty. At that time, this was the most powerful of Bali's royal families. The original compound was laid out in a square and featured courtyards, gardens, pavilions and moats. Most of it was destroyed during the Dutch attacks in 1908, and all that remains is the carved **Pemedal Agung** (the impressive gateway on the south side) and two pavilions.

The open-sided **Kertha Gosa** pavilion was the supreme court of the Klungkung kingdom, where disputes and cases that couldn't be settled at the village level were brought. A superb example of Klungkung architecture, its ceiling is covered with 20th-century paintings in the local Kamasan style that depict the Garuda story among scenes related to karma. The ceiling of the **Bale Kambang** 'floating pavilion' in the centre of the compound also features Kamasan paintings. The first row is based on the astrological calendar, the second on the folktale of Pan and Men Brayut and their 18 children, and the upper rows on the adventures of hero Sutasona.

On the compound's western side, a colonial-era building houses the **Museum Semarajaya**, also included in the palace admission price. Displays include traditional weapons, costumes and cherished ceremonial items alongside old photos of the royal court. Scan QR codes for information in English.

KLUNGKUNG'S BLOODY HISTORY

In 1849, the rulers of Klungkung and Gianyar defeated a Dutch invasion force at Kusamba. Before the Dutch could launch a counterattack, a peace settlement was brokered.

For the next 50 years, the South Bali kingdoms jostled for supremacy until the raja of Gianyar petitioned the Dutch for support. When the Dutch finally invaded, the king of Klungkung had to choose between a *puputan* (ritual suicide) or an ignominious surrender. He chose the first option.

On 28 April 1908, as the Dutch surrounded his palace, the king led hundreds out to certain death from Dutch gunfire or the blades of their own kris.

Beyond Klungkung

From wild beaches to one of Bali's oldest villages, the lands around Klungkung combine beauty, sacred meaning and cultural interest.

Places

Travellers are spoiled for day trips and adventures around Klungkung. Look for scenic surprises along the lovely roads linking towns like Bangli and Gianyar, and further on around the hills towards Sidemen.

This region presents an authentic introduction to Indonesia's textile heritage, and you can pop into a decades-old *endek* (a single-ikat fabric) workshop in Gianyar to watch weavers at work or stop at the Masa Masa cultural centre to admire beautiful antique fabrics and other cultural artefacts. For a peek at a traditional Balinese village, visit Penglipuran. The coastline beyond Klungkung is lined with moody black-sand beaches, known for pounding surf and few crowds. Gunung Agung looms large to the north.

GETTING AROUND

This region is a good area to rent a scooter and set off on a random adventure: you can never get too lost, and there's always a waterfall, view, temple or village around the corner to surprise.

Ubud and Sanur are easy day trips by taxi. Negotiate with the driver to stick around for your return trip, given that picking up another ride via one of the ride-hailing apps can be a challenge.

East Coast

TIME FROM KLUNGKUNG: **30MIN**

Connect with Indonesia's cultural heritage

For a peaceful introduction to Indonesia's cultural heritage, visit **Masa Masa** *(instagram.com/masamasabali)*. It has a beautifully curated gallery of Indonesian antiques – handwoven fabrics mostly, as well as jewellery, *kebaya* (the elegant tops that Balinese women wear) and other artefacts.

There's also a shop selling batik fabrics, clothing and handmade goods.

Explore the beaches

The coastal motorway between Sanur and Kusamba runs alongside a swathe of black-sand beaches for more than 20km – almost every road heading towards the coastline ends up at a beach. The shoreline is striking if somewhat sombre, with beaches in various shades of volcanic grey pounded relentlessly by waves. At high tide, the beach is swallowed up, and waves pummel the breakwater. The entire coast has great religious significance, and oodles of temples are scattered along it.

Some beaches have warungs and cafes, while others have nothing at all. Few are crowded. **Pantai Keramas** and **Pantai Ketewel** are known for their surf breaks. You can night-surf at Keramas for a fee – book at **Hotel Komune** *(komuneresorts.com)*. Keep in mind that swimming along this stretch of coastline is dangerous.

Go wine or beer tasting

Right off the coastal motorway, **Sababay Winery** *(sababaywinery.com; tasting 484,000Rp)* produces wine that hits above its weight, given that many consider winemaking and tropical climates to be mutually exclusive. Grapes are grown on Bali's north coast, but the wine is produced close to Pantai Keramas, and it's here that you can indulge in a wine-and-cheese tasting experience. There are a few on offer, but the 'Wine Down in the Garden' experience pairs vino with local cheese.

If beer's more your thing, **Breman Brewery** *(bremanbrewery.com)*, near Pantai Keramas, produces lagers and offers a brewery tour with beer tasting.

STATUE OF A HEROINE

On Bali's east coast, where Jl Rama (from Klungkung) intersects with the coastal motorway, a statue of a woman faces east. She is standing defiantly, with a *lontar* (a type of palm tree) in her left hand and her right hand pointing upwards in command.

The woman depicted is **Ida I Dewa Agung Istri Kanya**, a Balinese heroine celebrated for leading the Klungkung army to victory in the battle against the Dutch at Kusamba in 1849. It was in battle that General AV Michiels, the temporary commander of the Royal Dutch East Indies Army, was killed.

Gianyar

TIME FROM KLUNGKUNG: **20MIN**

Watch *endek* being produced

Gianyar was once known for its factories producing the vibrantly patterned *weft ikat*, which is called *endek* and originated in Bali in the Klungkung regency. Although many have closed in recent years, two notable holdouts remain.

Pertenunan Setia Cap Cili *(instagram.com/setiacapcili)*, said to be Gianyar's oldest weaving factory, was founded by a couple in 1948 and at one point employed 200 people from surrounding villages. These days it's run by the third generation and is vastly smaller (the number of employees is in the single digits), but there's still a large showroom where you can buy exquisite fabric and find women weaving out back.

You'll have a similar experience about 500m west at **Cap Togog** *(instagram.com/gallerytogog)*, founded in 1953. Here you can see how the entire *endek* production process works, beginning with the dyeing of the thread.

Bangli

TIME FROM KLUNGKUNG: **45MIN**

Stay in a traditional village

Settled in the 14th century, the village layout of **Penglipuran** *(penglipuran.com; adult/child 50,000/30,000Rp)* is very traditional. It's organised into family compounds branching off a long, grass-lined pedestrian avenue. Visitors are welcome to step through gateways into most of the compounds, where many buildings are still made from bamboo – scan the QR code near its entrance for information. Near the top end of the village, don't miss the 500m-long boardwalk running through a bamboo forest.

Penglipuran is now a popular tourist attraction, welcoming thousands of visitors each day. If you prefer an experience that goes beyond the crowds, book into a village homestay via the village website.

Sidemen

PADDY WALKS | EXTRAORDINARY VIEWS | TRADITIONAL ARTISANS

GETTING AROUND

You need to find your own way to Sidemen, and, once here, you're on your own regarding transport - ride-hailing apps don't cover this area. However, it's easy to source a scooter to rent, and you'll likely enjoy having your own wheels to explore the area: the rural roads are a delight. Walking is always an option, but cafes and restaurants are quite spread out.

In Sidemen (pronounced si-da-men), a walk in any direction is a communion with nature. Winding through one of Bali's most beautiful river valleys, the road to this village offers marvellous rice-terrace scenery, a delightful rural character and, when the clouds over the mountain clear, extraordinary views of Gunung Agung, which looms large to the northeast.

People looking for a sense of space flock to Sidemen for day walks through the paddies and to revel in the lush, luxuriant countryside while relaxing in quiet homestays, low-key guesthouses and boutique hotels. There are some delightful cafes too, many of which use fresh produce sourced from the fields around Sidemen.

Travellers who've known Bali for decades sometimes compare Sidemen with Ubud as it was 30 years ago. While tourism is developing and new hotels are vying for those sought-after paddy views, it seems, for the time being at least, to be moving forward in a manageable way.

Paddies, Forests & Volcano Views

Trek through rural Sidemen

Sidemen's rural charm is its biggest drawcard - many happy hours can be spent exploring paddies, gardens and forests surrounding the town. Every hotel, homestay and guesthouse can hook you up with a local guide to lead you on a trail through valley gardens and share insights into Bali's farming traditions and UNESCO-listed *subak* system. For a greater physical challenge, ask your guide to take you to **Pura Bukit Tageh** *(free)*, the shrine at the highest point of the hill rising on Sidemen's west side. The four-hour return hike rewards you with gorgeous views of Agung and the ocean on clear days (as the crow flies, Sidemen is just 10km from the coast).

On Sidemen's western fringe, over the Sungai Telaga Waja, is **Sidemen Rice Terrace** *(instagram.com/sidemenriceterrace; 25,000Rp)*. A community organisation manages this circular,

TOP TIP

Sidemen's weather can be quite unstable in the afternoons, so it's best to hike in the mornings. Evenings can be unexpectedly chilly.

well-signposted, 3km-long trail, which can easily be walked on your own; guides *(per hour 100,000Rp)* are available if you're keen to learn more about the area. The trail is paved to start, but soon transitions into a regular paddy path running along the narrow walls of irrigation channels.

About 800m from the start point is **Panorama Sidemen** *(instagram.com/panoramasidemen)*, a restaurant with lovely valley views. About 500m further is **Warung Made**, a simple trail-side shelter well worth a stop, where young Made sells delicious locally harvested coconuts.

Watch Weavers at Work

Support traditional artisans

Sidemen is renowned for the beautiful handwoven textiles produced in the area, particularly *endek* and *songket* (a type of brocade, often with silver and gold threads woven in). This makes it an ideal place to shop for fabric. It can be a bit hit-and-miss finding workshops where you can watch weavers at work, but one reliable place to head to is **Pelangi Traditional Weaving** *(instagram.com/cedut_pelangi)*, at the entrance to Sidemen village from the Karangasem road. You're welcome to take a look around the workshop where women weave (there's a tip box near the door) and peep upstairs to see men and boys tie designs onto the threads.

Sample Sidemen's Tipple

Visit a backyard *arak* distillery

Arak (p198) is an alcoholic drink made from the fermented sap of palm trees. It's used as an offering in religious ceremonies and as a base for cocktails in tourist bars. In recent years, it has begun to enjoy more attention, and while there are some commercial brands and emerging boutique producers, the Sidemen area has always had a reputation for producing some of the island's best *arak*. It's typically distilled in a *pondok* (hut) in family homesteads – if you ask around in Sidemen, you'll be directed to a house where it's made and likely be offered some to sample.

It's best to go with a guide who can explain the process. If you don't buy a bottle, it's considered polite to leave a gratuity for the family whose home you've just visited. Only drink *arak* from a reputable producer vouched for by your guide.

WHY I LOVE SIDEMEN

Narina Exelby,
Lonely Planet writer

A trip to Sidemen brings an opportunity to exhale. Time slows down here and, particularly after dealing with traffic in the south of the island, you're presented with a wonderful opportunity to live days at walking pace and explore on foot.

The area is known for its rice-terrace trails (an absolute must), but the village itself is a treat to explore, too. With every twist and turn in the road, there's a different view to be had. Gunung Agung, so often hidden by clouds, also makes unexpected appearances – you could sit down at a rooftop cafe, and before you've finished your coffee, the clouds might have cleared and the majestic mountain returned to take centre stage.

Beyond Sidemen

Sidemen's enchanting surroundings present beautifully peaceful views and spiritual places, plus exhilarating opportunities to get active.

Places

Carefully tended by farmers for centuries, the quiet hills and verdant valleys around Sidemen are absolutely exquisite, particularly when explored in the early morning light and the sun's rays filter through the trees. Tucked into forested valleys are hidden waterfalls and tumbling rivers.

Always in the distance, brooding over the landscape, is mighty Gunung Agung (3142m). This volcano is the most holy of Bali's mountains and also the island's highest. On clear mornings, keen hikers are rewarded with superb views across Bali from the rim. On the southeastern slopes of Agung, you'll find Pura Besakih, Bali's 'mother temple', also a starting point for a challenging trek to the summit of the volcano.

GETTING AROUND

You can't rely on public transport or ride-hailing apps to explore around Sidemen: you need to have your own set of wheels. Your accommodation in Sidemen can almost certainly assist with setting something up, be it a private driver or scooter rental.

If you're driving yourself, be aware that bigger roads are frequented by large trucks transporting rocks and sand down towards the coastline.

Rendang

TIME FROM SIDEMEN: **20MIN**

Raft the Telaga Waja River

Whoop and cheer your way through East Bali on an exhilarating rafting journey down the Sungai Telaga Waja. While rafting the Sungai Ayung (p230) near Ubud has you slipping between the walls of a canyon flanked with jungle, rafting the Telaga Waja takes you through a more open landscape, past paddies, towering trees and waterfalls gushing tributaries into the river. You'll also shoot down invigorating rapids and weirs – this fast-flowing river is graded Class III+.

The Telaga Waja can be rafted all year, but the best time is usually the dry season (April to October) when the rapids are at their most exciting. Various companies offer rafting trips: **Bali Sobek** *(balisobek.com; adult/child 1,200,000/800,000Rp)*, established in 1989, pioneered rafting in Bali, and **BCR** *(Bukit Cilli Rafting; bcrrafting.com; from 1,200,000Rp)* also has a good reputation. Two- to three-hour trips often include lunch. The endpoint is usually about 20 minutes north of Sidemen.

Gembleng Waterfall

TIME FROM SIDEMEN: **25MIN**

Frolick in a cascading waterfall

Bali has many spectacular waterfalls, but when it comes to a view *from* rather than *of* the cascading water, **Gembleng Waterfall** *(instagram.com/gemblengwaterfall; entry by donation)* tops the charts.

A steep five-minute walk up 130 well-maintained steps leads you to Gembleng's biggest drawcard: a collection of terraced rock pools with a view through palm trees onto a fertile, farmed valley. There are some picture-worthy (but less spectacular) rock pools on the way up, and you'll know you've reached *the* ones when the path crosses the stream – or, when you bump into the queue of people waiting their turn to slip into the pool and pose.

Continue a short way up the steps from these pools, and you'll reach **Gembleng Waterfall Restaurant**, with impressive views. Prices are surprisingly reasonable given its location.

It takes about 25 minutes to reach the parking area from Sidemen. Access to the waterfall trail opens at 7am. If you're looking for a peaceful experience, arrive early.

Besakih

TIME FROM SIDEMEN: **35MIN**

Summit Bali's highest mountain

Bali's highest and most revered mountain, the spiritual centre of the island, is 3142m **Gunung Agung**. Scaling the imposing volcano is one of Bali's most physically challenging adventures, but watching sunrise from up here is a profound experience.

The two most popular routes are from **Pura Pasar Agung Sebudi**, on Agung's southern slope, and **Pura Besakih** (p246), on the southwestern slope. The Pura Pasar Agung Sebudi route is the shortest and most direct; count on about four or five hours to ascend to the summit from here. It takes six or seven hours on the much tougher Pura Besakih route.

While the majority of hikers set off before midnight to summit in time for sunrise, some choose to leave from Besakih in the afternoon and camp on Agung for the night – sunsets up here are gorgeous – before departing to reach the top before dawn; **Raja Rimba Adventure** *(instagram.com/rajarimba_adventure; from 1,600,000Rp)* offers this option. Whichever way you go, be prepared for cold temperatures and a tough climb that's very steep in parts.

Most of the places to stay in the region can recommend climbing guides (you cannot climb Agung without one). Two experienced guides are **Wayan Tegteg** (*WhatsApp +62 813 3852 5677; instagram.com/tegtegwayan*) and **I Ketut Uriada** (*WhatsApp +62 812 364 6426; ketut.uriada@gmail.com*).

SUCH GREAT HEIGHTS

Wayan Tegteg has worked as a trekking guide since 2000 and has summited Gunung Agung more than 1000 times. *@tegtegwayan*

My preferred starting point for an Agung trek is the Pasar Agung temple. It's at a higher altitude than Pura Besakih, and while on that route, you can choose the ending: either a lower point at 3000m or, if conditions allow, the more challenging route to the peak of Agung.

If you leave from Pura Besakih, you can reach only the highest peak, and that route is very long.

Anyone wanting to trek Agung needs to come prepared with long trousers, good hiking shoes, wind-protection layers and gloves. The other equipment needed – like headlamps and trekking poles – is often provided by guides.

TOP EXPERIENCE

Pura Besakih

Bali's most important temple, Pura Besakih, stands on the southwestern slope of Gunung Agung. It is a vast complex of 23 temples that form a landing complex for the gods on Bali (*besakih* is derived from the Sanskrit word for 'sanctuary'). Constant processions of village groups arrive for ceremonies and blessings and to take holy water back to their own temples.

PHRAISOHN SIRIPOOL/SHUTTERSTOCK

TOP TIPS

- You may receive offers to 'come pray with me'. Visitors who take this chance to enter a closed temple risk facing extortionate demands.
- If you accept offerings from someone, you'll be expected to pay for them. A sign in the ticketing area lists prices.

PRACTICALITIES

- besakih.org
- 7am-6pm
- 150,000Rp

Find the Best Views

Bali's oldest and most important temple, **Pura Penataran Agung Besakih**, stands in the middle of the Besakih complex. Although you can see into the temple area from various angles, it is not always open to visitors. For an exquisite view of scores of jet-black *meru* soaring towards the sky – a dramatic sight on misty mornings – follow the path behind **Pura Penataran Pande Besakih** (the clan temple for the island's blacksmiths, goldsmiths and silversmiths) to the back of Pura Besakih. For a fantastic view over Bali, head up to **Pura Gelap**, surrounded by intricately carved walls.

Make an Offering

You can enter some of the temples if you wish to pray, but you must take offerings with you. Women sell these throughout the complex; a noticeboard at the ticket desk details the prices (20,000Rp to 70,000Rp).

Get the Most from Your Visit

The quality of local guides included with entry varies greatly. Get more from your visit by asking lots of questions, and ask them to take you to Pura Gelap. You will invariably be asked for a tip at the end.

Padangbai

BEACHES | DIVING & SNORKELLING | FERRIES

While there are a few dive spots in the area, most travellers head to Padangbai to get away. The town's busy port connects Bali with Lombok, the Gilis and Nusa Penida. Later in the day, when the boat traffic diminishes, Padangbai takes on a more mellow mood, with visitors wandering the waterfront and hanging out at backpacker cafes and simple restaurants, many fronting the beach. When the moon reflects off the bay, it's almost romantic.

Accommodation ranges from hostels to guesthouses to a few resorts focused on diving. By day, avoid the transiting mobs by hitting nearby beaches to dive and snorkel. Take a short walk around the headland to Pura Silayukti, the place where Empu Kuturan – who introduced the caste system to Bali in the 11th century – is said to have lived.

GETTING AROUND

Padangbai town is small and easily walkable. Its port is a hub for ferries fast, slow and otherwise. Government-run ferries for Lombok and Nusa Penida leave from **Pelabuhan Padangbai**; these are the ones for people who want to take their motorbikes. Fast boats to Lombok and the Gilis depart from the **Fast Boat Pier**, a separate, crowded pier to the east. Buy tickets at pier entrances. For tips on navigating the port, see p249.

Underwater Adventures

Dive into East Bali's underwater delights

Padangbai is one of Bali's main centres for diving and snorkelling. There's good diving on local coral reefs, but the most popular local spots are **Blue Lagoon** and **Jepun**, with a range of soft and hard corals and varied marine life, including sharks, turtles and wrasse. Blue Lagoon boasts a 23m wall.

Snorkellers: instead of snorkelling from **Blue Lagoon Beach** (p249) (which is not recommended), head out to sea with one of the former fishing boats that ferry tourists to snorkelling spots from **Padangbai Beach**.

Find dive centres, including **OK Divers** *(okdiversbali.com)*, on Jl Silayukti, past the fast-ferry pier. Many operators offer trips to nearby **Gili Tepekong** and **Gili Biaha**, just off Teluk Amuk, as well as Tulamben (p255) and Nusa Penida (p217).

TOP TIP

Need a beach read? **Wayan Bookstore** *(9am-6pm)* has an excellent selection of secondhand novels in English and books in other languages. It's set just off the road opposite the Bamboo Paradise guesthouse – follow the signs.

HIGHLIGHTS
1 Bias Tugal
2 Blue Lagoon
3 Jepun

SIGHTS
4 Blue Lagoon Beach
5 Padangbai Beach

ACTIVITIES
see 7 OK Divers

SLEEPING
6 Bloo Lagoon
7 OK Divers Resort & Spa
8 Padang Bai Beach Homestay

EATING
9 Martinis
10 Topi Inn
11 Warung Bu Jero
12 Zen Inn

SHOPPING
13 Wayan Bookstore

TRANSPORT
14 Fast Boat Pier
15 Pelabuhan Padangbai
16 Ticket Office

Hit the Beach

Chill beside the sea

On the far side of Padangbai's eastern headland, about a 500m walk from the town centre (turn left as you begin to climb uphill), is **Blue Lagoon Beach**. Tucked in a small bay, it has a few warungs and sunloungers, which you can rent for 25,000Rp per day.

The other (more appealing) option is to walk southwest from the ferry terminal to **Bias Tugal**, a lovely cove with powder-white sand and warungs, making it a pleasant base for a day. Be careful in the water because currents can be strong. Access the beach on foot via the rough pathway adjacent to the Bamboo Paradise guesthouse, or if you're on a scooter, continue up the hill and follow signs to Bias Tugal (also known as Pantai Kecil or 'Little Beach'). There are some warungs at Bias Tugal, and it's a pleasant beach at which to base yourself for a day. Be careful in the water as it's subject to strong currents.

TIPS FOR PADANGBAI PORT

Slow government-owned passenger and vehicle ferries run 24/7 from **Pelabuhan Padangbai** (p247). Tickets are cheap; buy them at the **ticket office** in the ferry terminal.

Fast boats usually leave between 8am and 1pm and return in the afternoon. If you have time to spare, shop around for a fast-boat ticket from one of the many offices around the **Fast Boat Pier** (p247). Or buy your ticket online – 12go.asia is a reliable platform to use.

Piers can get manic, so try to travel light. Anyone who carries your luggage on/off a boat expects to be paid. Agree on the price first; expect to pay from 20,000Rp (it's luggage-dependent) and remember: a little extra from you can make a big difference to a porter.

EATING IN PADANGBAI: OUR PICKS

Martinis: This three-table warung at the fast-boat pier serves large Indonesian dishes (plus seafood and sandwiches) at affordable prices. *7am-10pm* $

Warung Bu Jero: Super-affordable seafood and Indonesian fare. You'll be dreaming of its succulent prawns long after you leave. *9am-10pm* $

Zen Inn: Come here for the pasta or playlist – both are well worth it. The menu includes Indonesian and international staples. *7am-10pm* $

Topi Inn: Meals use chemical-free ingredients whenever possible. The overwhelmingly large menu includes apple crumble and brownies. *7am-10pm* $$

Beyond Padangbai

Uncover beautiful water gardens, laid-back beach towns and, in quiet villages, surprises for travellers with a penchant for food.

Places

The coastline around Padangbai is a green, rocky ribbon backed by steep hills, and the narrow roads that wind their way up here through farmlands and forests are a delight to explore.

Kusamba is the last of the flatlands to the west and mixes traditional work with the sacred. Around Amlapura, you'll find striking temples, gorgeous water gardens and quiet royal residences, while seaside Candidasa charms with mellow waterfront stays in a quiet strip of hotels. The beach at Pantai Pasir Putih makes up for the lack of sand elsewhere in the area with a long, brilliant white strand that's the envy of other Balinese beaches.

Kusamba

TIME FROM PADANGBAI: **20MIN**

Discover the 'Bat Cave Temple'

One of Bali's small but striking directional temples is **Pura Goa Lawah** *(instagram.com/penataran_goa_lawah; 30,000Rp)*, established in the 11th century. An unconfirmed legend says the cave leads all the way to **Pura Besakih** (p246), some 19km away.

Set against an oceanside cliff, the temple is full of fruit bats (said to be guardians of the temple) and tour groups. These bats provide sustenance for the legendary giant snake, the deity Naga Basuki, also believed to live in the cave. Across the road from Pura Goa Lawah, there is an impressive bat-cave statue in the rest area. There are some warungs around here, too.

GETTING AROUND

The main coast road east and west of Padangbai is busy with traffic. If you're a nervous driver, your accommodation can hook you up with a driver (scooter or car). If you're heading away from the coast (and you must – it's beautiful in the hills), you need a scooter with sufficient power to get you up the steep hills and reliable brakes to get you safely down.

Tenganan

TIME FROM PADANGBAI: **35MIN**

Visit historic Bali Aga villages

North of Candidasa, Tenganan is home to the Bali Aga (p253). Often spoken of as one village, there are two in fact: Tenganan Pegringsingan (east) and Tenganan Dauh Tukad (west), separated by a small valley. A visit to either is an opportunity to learn about Bali Aga traditions. Both are car-free and laid out as they have been for centuries, with homes leading off a central walkway.

The two villages offer quite different visitor experiences. **Tenganan Pegringsingan** *(entry by donation)* has a small pavilion at its entrance displaying beautiful photographs. Many residents erect tables outside their homes and demonstrate *prasi* (the art of decorating *lontar* palms) or display *kamben gringsing*, the double-ikat cloth traditionally woven in Tengenan. Scan the QR code at the front office beside the pavilion for a PDF detailing village food, traditions and crafts.

In smaller **Tenganan Dauh Tukad** *(entry by donation)*, you're greeted by someone from the village at the entrance who shows you around and accompanies you to a homestead where *kamben gringsing* are made and sold. You can also buy a *lontar* calendar with your name written on it.

Jungutan

TIME FROM PADANGBAI: **50MIN**

Delightful museum

Run by the local community, the **Samsara Living Museum** *(samsarabali.com; 100,000Rp)* offers an engaging and well-curated window into Balinese culture and daily life. Volunteers take visitors through the 14 important ceremonial events in Balinese life and then offer hands-on demonstrations of topics such as gamelan instruments, *arak* distillation and offering making.

Amlapura

TIME FROM PADANGBAI: **1HR**

Step into a royal palace

The tranquil **Puri Agung Karangasem** *(instagram.com/puriagungkarangasem; 30,000Rp)* is still home to descendants of the royal family, but visitors are welcome to wander around a lovingly kept part of it. Entry to the royal palace is past beautifully sculpted panels and an impressive multi-tiered gate.

Inside, admire architectural influences from Bali, Europe and China. The main building in the 19th-century compound is **Maskerdam**, the raja's residence, built as a gift by the Dutch as a reward for the Karangasem kingdom's acquiescence to Dutch rule. It houses furniture and photos from that time. A highlight of the lovely, manicured grounds is the **Bale Kambang**, an ornate floating pavilion surrounded by a large pond.

THE ROYALTY OF KARANGASEM

Amlapura's royal family ruled its regency of Karangasem with savvy and guile. In the 19th century, they led the domination of Lombok just across the channel, which brought them great wealth.

As the 1890s wore on and the colonial Dutch consolidated their grip on Bali and the region, the royal family cut deals with the Dutch that saw the Europeans treat the region as a protectorate (they even built the palace **Puri Agung Karangasem** as a gift) instead of a conquered foe.

Before the royals were replaced by a republic, the last king of Karangasem, I Gusti Bagus Jelantik (r 1908–50), used his riches to build the lavish water palaces.

RICHIE CHAN/SHUTTERSTOCK

Pura Penataran Lempuyang

A captivating water garden

Wander between pretty ponds dotted with stone statues and home to hundreds of koi fish at **Tirta Gangga** *(instagram.com/tirtagangga.bali; adult/child 90,000/45,000Rp)*, an exquisite and very popular water garden north of Amlapura. Built in 1946 for the last raja of Karangasem, it has fountains, flowers, bridges, stepping stones and even a small pool that you can bathe in. The garden's ponds, fed by a natural spring, are considered to be holy, hence the garden's name 'Sacred Water of the Ganges'.

A small **museum** in the southeast corner of the property displays a collection of the royal family's heirloom *keris* (ornamental or ceremonial dagger), and in the upstairs pavilion, a statue of the king and lovely views of the garden and neighbouring rice paddies. Tirta Gangga gets incredibly busy – arrive early (gates open at 6am) to enjoy the peace here.

Stroll the grounds of Taman Ujung

South of **Tirta Gangga**, the **Taman Ujung** *(instagram.com/tamansoekasadaujung; 100,000Rp)* water palace was built by the last king of Karangasem and dates from 1919. Taman Ujung is simpler than Tirta Gangga, but it's the geometry of the design here that makes it so striking, particularly when the water of its three large ponds is still, perfectly reflecting the garden's bridges and pavilions.

An earthquake largely destroyed Taman Ujung in 1979. It's mostly been restored, but on the western side of the complex, evocative ruins of Bale Kapal (an old pavilion) remain. From here, you have a view over the water palace to the sea.

See Bali's 'gates of heaven'

Pura Lempuyang is the place to get *that* iconic photo – with a mirror reflection of the *candi bentar* (split gates) in front of majestic Gunung Agung. The scene makes a striking photo, but there's far more to this sought-after picture than a clever illusion. The *candi bentar*, which serves as a spiritual threshold between the outside world and a sacred space, marks the entrance to one of Bali's important directional temples.

Pura Lempuyang *(70,000Rp)* is a complex of seven temples perched on the steep slopes of Gunung Lempuyang (1058m), a 'twin' of neighbouring Gunung Seraya. The largest and most easily accessible temple is **Pura Penataran Lempuyang**, where visitors queue for hours to be photographed.

From a second temple, 2km uphill, the calf-punishing stair climb begins: it's 1700 steps from here to the highest temple, **Pura Lempuyang Luhur**. Visiting all seven temples takes at least four hours and involves a breathtaking 2900 steps.

Pura Lempuyang is open to visitors from 5am. In the car park, you need to pay 50,000Rp for the shuttle that takes around eight minutes to transport you up the steep, winding hill to the entrance. Upon paying the admission fee, you're given a ticket number to have your pic taken between the gates.

A gourmet feast

The farming village of Gelumpang, just outside of Amlapura, is where Australian chef Penelope Williams runs **Bali Asli** *(baliasli.com.au)*, which offers a world-class culinary experience. *Asli* is the Balinese term for something created in the traditional way, and there's much that's traditional here – the Balinese menu changes daily, dictated by what's fresh at the local *pasar* (market) or has been harvested in the restaurant's garden. By day, there are cooking classes and rice-terrace hikes.

BALI AGA

The Bali Aga are the descendants of the original Balinese who inhabited the island before the arrival of the Majapahit in the 11th century. Bali Aga villages, which include Tengenan and Trunyan, are mostly in the mountains around East Bali and tend to be very traditional, with strict social rules and unique traditions.

Ancient customs include an unusual, old-fashioned version of the gamelan known as the *gamelan selunding*. Girls dance an equally ancient dance known as the Rejang; a good time to see this is during the **Usaba Sambah Festival**, honouring gods and ancestors. The festival is famous for its contest of *perang pandan* (ritual combat using thorny stalks made of pandan leaves), usually taking place in June or July.

Amed

EXCELLENT DIVING | DRAMATIC VIEWS | COASTAL SCENERY

GETTING AROUND

This small area packs a lot in. To make the most of your time, rent a scooter (your accommodation can point you in the right direction for hiring one) to explore the coastline. Roadworks are ongoing as the coastal road is upgraded. Motorists should check before booking accommodation that parking is available – space for four-wheel vehicles can be hard to find.

TOP TIP

At the time of research, plans were apparently underway to build a pier servicing fast boats to Lombok and the Gili islands. Do some research into this if your travel plans include a trip to these other islands.

Stretching from Amed village to Bali's easternmost tip near Kusambi, the semi-arid coast generically called 'Amed' draws visitors with its succession of small scalloped bays. Fishing boats lined up like multihued sardines colour grey-sand beaches, and the area revels in its relaxed atmosphere, boho vibe, and very enjoyable diving and snorkelling.

Resorts, flush cafes and open-air restaurants dot the 15km-long coastline, and overnight options cover most price points, tastes and interests: find dive resorts, health and meditation retreats, plus dozens of hotels, guesthouses and homestays. Amed village and Jemeluk are dining hot spots – vegetarian and vegan options are as common as offers to head out to sea on a *jukung*. Many people come to Amed for a day or two and end up staying for much longer. It's also a popular base for diving at nearby Tulamben.

Explore a Striking Coastline

Go beach-hopping around Amed

For such a compact area, the beaches and bays along the Amed coastline are surprisingly different in character – beach-hopping makes for an interesting break from time spent underwater. Some, like **Pantai Lean** and **Pantai Bunutan**, are predominantly working beaches, more practical than pretty, that tend to be a hive of activity around 8am when fishing boats return to shore.

Others, such as **Pantai Selang** and **Pantai Lipah**, are good options for snorkelling, despite the fair number of fishing boats lining the sand. Tucked in a well-protected bay, **Pantai Jemeluk** sports many beachfront restaurants and is popular for snorkelling and swimming. At more than 2km long, **Pantai Amed** is popular for walking and, with its striking black sand, makes for dramatic sunrise and sunset photos.

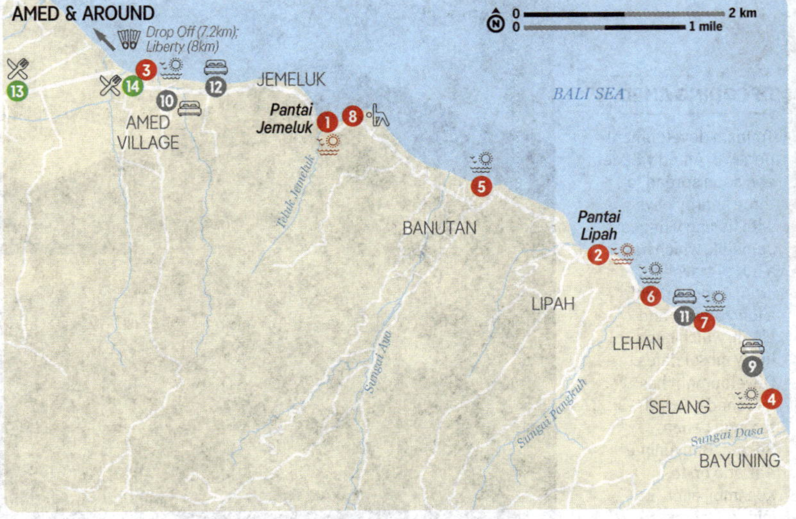

HIGHLIGHTS
1 Pantai Jemeluk
2 Pantai Lipah

SIGHTS
3 Pantai Amed
4 Pantai Banyuning
5 Pantai Bunutan
6 Pantai Lean
7 Pantai Selang

ACTIVITIES
8 Blue Earth Village
see 1 Ocean Prana
see 1 Teluk Jemeluk

SLEEPING
9 Aquamarine Beach Villas
10 Kirana Homestay
11 Life in Amed
12 Solaluna Beach Homestay

EATING
see 8 Blue Earth Village Restaurant
13 Good Stuff Cafe
14 Sweet Harmonia
see 2 Vienna Café

Experience Amed's Underwater Paradise

Dive and snorkel the east coast

The Amed area is revered for its clear water and abundant marine life – the reason so many travellers linger here. Snorkelling is excellent: **Teluk Jemeluk** (Jemeluk Bay) is a protected area where you can admire live coral and plentiful fish within 100m of the beach, while the coral gardens and colourful marine life at **Pantai Selang** are highlights. The much-hyped sunken Japanese fishing boat off **Pantai Banyuning** is little more than a few bits of wooden debris, but it's still a popular spot for snorkellers.

Diving is obviously excellent too, and there are many dive shops and centres along this stretch of coastline. Dive sites off beaches **Pantai Jemeluk**, **Pantai Selang** and **Pantai Lipah** feature slopes and drop-offs with soft and hard corals, and abundant fish; some are accessible from the beach, while others require a short boat ride. Tulamben's **Liberty** (p257) wreck is 13km north of Amed; count on 20 minutes by car or scooter.

DECODING AMED

Tourism development began in Amed village and soon spread to three nearby bays with fishing villages: Jemeluk, which has a buzzy travellers strip; Bunutan, with a long beach; and Lipah, which has a lively mix of cafes. Development has marched onward through Lehan, Selang, Banyuning, Aas and on to Kusambi, each a minor oasis at the base of the arid hills. The entire area is now collectively known as Amed.

For accommodation, you need to choose between the villages and the sunny headlands in between. The former puts you right on the sand and offers a small amount of community life, while the latter gives you sweeping vistas and isolation.

Bend & Stretch

Amed's yoga offerings

It was only a matter of time before chilled-out Amed became a haven for the yoga crowd. Among the most popular places to practise is **Blue Earth Village** *(blueearthvillage.com)* with two dreamy yoga spaces in a hillside resort overlooking Jemeluk Bay. Daily classes at 8am and 5pm include yin, vinyasa and medicinal yoga. Book a day in advance.

Ocean Prana *(oceanprana.com)*, a 'freedivers' village' in Jemeluk, offers daily classes in a poolside yoga space at 5pm. Classes (book before 3pm) are popular with freedivers who use the disciplines to regulate their breathing. Consider signing up for a freediving course while you're here.

If you're just here for the yoga, also check out **Life in Amed** *(lifebali.com)*, a beachfront boutique hotel in Lehan that sports a lovely elevated yoga shala with a garden and ocean view for multiday retreats and also classes most days (drop-ins welcome). Contact reception for the class schedule.

EATING IN AMED: OUR PICKS

Sweet Harmonia: Come here for plate-licking-good Asian fare. The menu also covers vegetarian and vegan options. *11am-10pm* $

Blue Earth Village Restaurant: Begin a day in Jemeluk with coffee, juice, a healthy breakfast and a peaceful view of Gunung and the ocean. *7.30am-10pm* $

Good Stuff Cafe: Smoothie bowls, cold-pressed juices, kombuchas, mouthwatering burgers, steaks and more – all eco-sourced. *7.30am-10pm* $$

Vienna Café: Tropical-style cafe on Lipah Beach with seafood, Asian and continental options; gluten-free and allergy-friendly dishes. *7.30am-10pm* $$

HENRI VAN KALKEREN/SHUTTERSTOCK

View of Gunung Agung (p245) from the Amed coastline

Watch Sunset From The Sea

Take a late-afternoon boat ride

While Amed's coastline has some spectacular sunset spots, it's hard to beat the late-afternoon view of Gunung Agung from the ocean. As the sun lowers, it brings the outline of both Bali's tallest peak and smaller Gunung Batur into sharp view.

The beaches and bays around Amed are jam-packed with *jukung*, and you'll easily find someone willing to take you out for a sunset jaunt. Many guesthouses and restaurants work with at least one boatman and can set up your trip as little as an hour or two in advance. Expect to pay about 300,000Rp for two people for a 1½-hour sunset trip.

Dive a WWII Wreck

Explore the *Liberty*

The wreck of the ***Liberty*** in nearby Tulamben is among Bali's most popular dive sites and has transformed a fishing village into a resort town based on diving. Even snorkellers can easily swim the 50m out to explore the wreck. You'll see the stern rearing up from the depths, 5m below the surface. It's heavily encrusted with coral and swarming with colourful fish – and divers most of the day. The ship's hull is broken into sections – the most interesting parts are between 15m and 30m deep. Entry to the site from the road is 25,000Rp per person (included with organised dives).

Close by, **Drop Off** is another popular dive site; look out for electric 'disco' clams. Some Tulamben dive centres offer free transport for divers staying in Amed.

THE WRECK OF THE *LIBERTY*

In 1942, the US military cargo ship *USAT Liberty* was torpedoed by a Japanese submarine near Lombok while sailing from Australia to the Philippines. It was beached at Tulamben so that its cargo of rubber and railway parts could be saved.

The Japanese invasion prevented this, and the ship sat on the beach until the 1963 eruption of Gunung Agung, which broke it in two and sank it just off the shoreline, much to the delight of divers and snorkellers.

The *Liberty* was built in 1918 for service during WWI. More than 125m long, it had a globe-spanning career before WWII. (And for the record, it was not a WWII Liberty-class freighter.)

Munduk

SPECTACULAR HIKING | ICONIC TEMPLES | EXCEPTIONAL VIEWS

GETTING AROUND

Munduk town and the surrounding hillsides are best explored on foot. Motorbikes are available for rent if you want to explore further afield – you can get to the north coast in about 30 minutes. Cars with drivers are easily organised through any hotel, and the best drivers also serve as informative guides.

Long before the Dutch took advantage of Munduk's blissful climate to establish a hill station here about 130 years ago, these pretty highlands had been settled by the early Balinese (some say the Bali Aga) who, according to legend, were escaping a plague of ants. Whatever the case, Munduk and the exquisite surrounding highlands make for an idyllic escape, even today.

The views across hillsides of plantations of clove, nutmeg, coffee and cacao trees – all the way to the ocean – are astounding, and some special lodges and homestays are tucked in between the trees. The hills and UNESCO-protected terraces of this quiet region are laced with tracks and walking trails, and while it's possible to explore some solo, Munduk has an established network of experienced guides who share anecdotes, legends and the enthralling culinary and medicinal traditions that are still an integral part of the unique highland culture.

The Road Least Travelled

Take the scenic route to Munduk

The journey up to Munduk is as much part of the adventure as time spent actually hiking in the Central Highlands. A stunning introduction to the area is to take the Antosari road that leads from Pantai Soka on the West Bali coast up to Pupuan, sweeping you past spectacular rice terraces, palm trees and tumbling bougainvillea.

For an even more memorable route, turn right in the village of **Pujungan** onto Jl Gunung Batukaru and follow the winding lanes to Munduk. It's a magnificent journey along small rural roads that will have you ogling spice plantations, fruit orchards, jungle ravines and countless flower-decked temples.

TOP TIP

People who dress for the beach are often surprised – nighttime temperatures in the highlands can drop to 12°C. Pack warm layers, especially if you plan on getting up for a sunrise hike. July to September are the coldest months.

HIGHLIGHTS
1 Bali Botanic Garden
2 Danau Tamblingan
3 Jatiluwih Rice Terraces

SIGHTS
4 Banyumala Twin Waterfalls
5 Melanting Waterfall
6 Pujungan
7 Pura Jero Taksu
8 Pura Luhur Batukau
9 Pura Luhur Besikalung
10 Pura Luhur Pucak Petali
11 Red Coral Waterfall

SLEEPING
12 Puri Lumbung Cottages
13 Terrasse du Lac Munduk

EATING
14 Botanist
15 Jatiluwih Resto
16 Munduk Farm House
17 Munduk Moding Plantation

MYSTERIOUS TEMPLES OF BATUKARU

Established in the 11th century, **Pura Luhur Batukau** (often written Batukaru) stands at the end of a lonely road on the slopes of Gunung Batukaru. Hindu worshippers invariably stop first at **Pura Jero Taksu**, which serves as a spiritual and literal gateway to Batukau – it's believed that only if you pray there first will your Batukau prayers reach the gods.

Batukau was historically said to be a lair for bandits, and 2km from the old temple is the almost-forgotten **Pura Luhur Pucak Petali**. Dedicated to Sang Hyang Maling ('God of Thieves'), this temple, along with **Pura Luhur Besikalung** nearby, is said to have been the place to pray if you wanted to become adept at 'the thieving business'!

WONDERFUL NATURE/SHUTTERSTOCK

Bali Botanic Garden

A Scented Trail

Hike through Munduk's spice plantations

Munduk is surrounded by paddies, plantations and spice forests. Travellers seeking to connect with nature gravitate to this small town to hike through the region's densely forested hills and cascading waterfalls. While the area has virgin forests, the woodland more often consists of working plantations of clove, nutmeg and cinnamon, with coffee and cacao thriving under the shade of the canopies. A network of trails connects hamlets, markets and homesteads. The blissful highland temperatures – typically 20°C to 25°C – make this idyllic hiking country. It's possible to walk some trails independently from Munduk – around town, you'll see signs indicating paths to some of the area's waterfalls – but for fascinating insights into local history and lifestyles, hire a guide. Ketut Darma *(WhatsApp +62 822 3657 6149; walking tours per day 700,000Rp)* is highly respected.

To the uninitiated observer, the wooded valleys might appear as pristine jungle, but you'll learn that almost everything seems to be either edible, medicinal or of folkloric spiritual value. A guide can add interest to your walk by telling you about the intricacies of ancient spice crops, as well as the complicated methods of preparing staples like cassava, taro, palm sugar and *arak*. You can learn about the cultivation of coffee, cacao and vanilla (which is pollinated entirely by hand). You can walk set routes, but guides (easily arranged through any hotel) can also tailor treks to suit your interests.

Explore a Sacred Forest

Trek around Danau Tamblingan

Shrouding the rim of the caldera that forms **Danau Tamblingan** (Tamblingan Lake) is an ancient, sacred rainforest that for centuries has been a source of plants for traditional medicine. It's an enchanting place, with towering nettle trees and magnificently tangled ficus trees (some more than 600 years old) growing as pillars of a lush ecosystem entangled with ferns, orchids and vines.

Walking trails vary from a short hour-long stroll to extended hikes through the forest, returning across the lake by motorised canoe. Since it's a community project, a guide is obligatory, and you're assigned one when you arrive at the ranger office at Danau Tamblingan. Entrance to the protected forest is 100,000Rp per person, plus the rate for the walk, which varies depending on the length of the trail you do.

There are also tents for rent for those who wish to sleep on the lake shore, an experience that's equally unforgettable for the star-studded nights as for the moody mist that rises off the lake at dawn. Kadek Sandiana is an experienced and highly knowledgeable guide *(WhatsApp +62 877 8436 7848).*

Discover Indonesia's Botanical Riches

Visit Bali's beautiful garden

Indonesia is the world's second-most biodiverse country (after Brazil), and **Bali Botanic Garden** – known locally as Kebun Raya Bali *(kebunraya.id; weekday/weekend 15,500/25,500Rp)* – showcases some of its most spectacular floral riches.

You could spend an entire day wandering around the collection of themed gardens, but if time is short, hire an e-scooter, electric moped, e-bike or bicycle from the ticket office at the entrance *(10,000-100,000Rp)*. These vehicles are rented out in half-hour blocks, but to do justice to these extensive gardens takes at least an hour.

Highlights include the **Cactus Greenhouse**, featuring 68 species, and the **Rhododendron Garden**, with more than 100 varieties. The **Orchid Garden** – at its most colourful when many specimens are flowering around July and August – is mind-blowing, and **Taman Usada** has more than 300 plants used by traditional healers.

Sprawling across almost 160 hectares, Bali Botanical Garden boasts 2400 species of plants in total. Bird-watchers are also drawn here by an estimated 79 resident and migrant bird species.

MUNDUK'S WONDERFUL WATERFALLS

Ketut Darma, a senior trekking guide and traditional healer, describes some of his favourite waterfalls. *WhatsApp +62 822 3657 6149*

Red Coral: This waterfall is easy to access, so it's a good one to visit for older people and those travelling with small children. You'll walk through plantations of coffee, cloves, avocados and vanilla to get there.

Melanting: Not many people go to this waterfall; it's one of Bali's tallest and is really pretty. You need to go down about 500 steps, and it can be slippery in the wet season.

Banyumala: The 'twin waterfall' is a great option if you want to swim. There is a wonderful, clear pool at the bottom, and it's never too crowded.

EATING AROUND MUNDUK: RESTAURANTS WITH VIEWS

Munduk Moding Plantation: Book a table and tuck into local produce and homegrown coffee while gazing over the infinity pool all the way to Java. *10am-9pm* $$

Desa Seni: Irresistible offerings on a changing menu that invariably features organic local vegetables and delicious regional produce. *10am-8pm* $$$

Munduk Farm House: Enjoy cosy evenings in front of the log fire, dining on the best beef *rendang* (coconut curry) and sipping perfectly crafted Irish coffee. *8am-9pm* $$

Botanist: Seasonal vegetables, smoothies, excellent burgers and chilled playlists, overlooking a jungle-clad ravine at Desa Eko Glamping. *8am-10pm* $$

GODDESS OF RICE

The paddy fields of **Jatiluwih** are decorated with intricately sculpted shrines. According to Balinese farmers, water and the fertile volcanic soil are only two of the facets that make up this uniquely rich agricultural system – without the all-important offerings to Dewi Sri, the goddess of fertility, the harvest would assuredly fail.

Bali can achieve up to three rice harvests a year (a rarity elsewhere), but then Balinese *petani* (farmers) point out that other areas fall short because nowhere else is Dewi Sri worshipped. These are intensely sacred landscapes, and signs have been placed along Jatiluwih's paddy field trails requesting that visitors respect these shrines and not encroach within 1m.

Fingerprints of the Gods

Walk among terraced ricefields

With elegantly stepped terraces curving like enormous fingerprints, the paddy landscapes of **Jatiluwih Rice Terraces** are postcard-perfect. This 195-sq-km area is protected by UNESCO, and it's here that the island's *subak* tradition – a complex irrigation system that dates from the 9th century – remains deeply rooted. It's easy to explore the area on your own, and a good starting point is **Jatiluwih Resto**, a small restaurant that faces a paved track with a signboard listing marked trails (ranging from 1.5km to 5.5km).

UN Tourism recognised Jatiluwih as one of the Best Tourism Villages of 2024, and the trails are busy from about mid-morning (despite a 75,000Rp fee for every international tourist to enter the area). For a more sedate paddy experience, arrive in the afternoon, enjoy sunset from a cafe terrace and stay overnight. This way, you can enjoy the spellbinding solitude of a sunrise walk through the paddies when this unique landscape is saturated with colours: the vibrant neon green of young rice shoots; the mirror-like, sky-blue sheen of flooded paddies; and the swaying golden sheaves of the harvest.

Cloud Forest Adventure

A long trek across jungle highlands

Allow at least seven hours to complete the 16km jungle-bashing route from an ancient, sacred rainforest on the rim of **Danau Tamblingan** (Tamblingan Lake) (p261) to Jatiluwih's UNESCO-protected **rice paddies**; and this trek should not be attempted without a guide.

The forest is home to barking deer, porcupine, mongoose, flying foxes, lutung monkeys, macaques and civets, but it's the vegetation that's really jaw-dropping: towering fig trees, tree ferns and tangled lianas. Orchids and bromeliads hang from every tree.

Carry plenty of water and wear long trousers and long sleeves to protect yourself from leeches, itchy nettles and thorny *tunggu sebentar* (wait-awhile) bushes. Tamblingan-based jungle guide **Kadek Sandiana** *(WhatsApp +62 877 8436 7848)* charges 800,000Rp per person, including a substantial picnic lunch.

Beyond Munduk

With its lake, smouldering peak and extensive black lava fields, Gunung Batur is one of Indonesia's geological marvels.

The volcano you see today rises from within a caldera formed during an eruption some 30,000 years ago. The town of Kintamani spreads around the southern rim, overlooking a crater lake and barren black lava fields, and onto the lower slopes of the relatively 'new' (still spectacularly active) volcano. It's here that hundreds of visitors arrive in the early hours of each morning, eager to climb its slopes and catch a view of the sunrise with mighty Gunung Agung in the distance.

This area is as captivatingly stark as Munduk is lush, and the atmosphere here – possibly fuelled by the earth's fiery forces – is instilled with a rugged sense of adventure.

Places

Gunung Batur Area

TIME FROM MUNDUK: **2¼HR**

Geology and spirituality

Gunung Batur stands as the centrepiece of the **Batur UNESCO Global Geopark**, a 370-sq-km area renowned for its unique geological and cultural significance. It is encircled by a vast caldera, the remains of a 3000m-high volcano that erupted 30,000 years ago, and within it, the rugged lava fields from various eruptions are flanked by a lake, clustered with houses, and tamed pockets of farmlands.

Just off the southern rim of the caldera is the imposing **Batur Geopark Museum** *(adult/child 50,000/30,000Rp)*, which serves as a portal to the geological and spiritual heritage of the area. Its exhibits showcase the fascinating history of volcanic eruptions, the evolution of the landscape and, in the upstairs section, the deep-rooted relationship between regional culture and the fiery surroundings. An hour at the museum, open 8am to 4pm, adds a rich layer of understanding to the time you spend exploring this dramatic landscape.

GETTING AROUND

To trek Gunung Batur or Gunung Abang, you need a guide. Most hotels and homestays can help, and guides usually arrange transport to and from your accommodation. Most people come here for the sunrise Batur walk only, and tour companies include an early-morning pickup (often around 1am or 2am) from most tourist centres on the island in their prices.

If you're staying longer, explore the surrounding area by renting a scooter, but if you're going to be carrying a pillion passenger, opt for a more powerful bike (an N-Max or similar).

ONE OF BALI'S MOST ICONIC TEMPLES

Beautiful lakeside **Pura Ulun Danu Bratan**, which was built around 1634 CE, is one of the most important places of worship for Balinese Hindus. It honours Dewi Danu, the goddess of water, and ceremonies take place here to ensure a sufficient supply of water in the *subak* system for the island's rice farmers.

Images of the temple – with its striking *merus*, formally landscaped garden and stunning backdrop mountain reflected in the still water of the lake – have become iconic of Bali, and the temple attracts busloads of tourists every day. While it remains a functioning temple, tourism here is big business, so expect souvenir stalls lining the parking area, cash machines, a childrens playground and lakeside restaurants.

A volcano sunrise trek

A sunrise trek up Gunung Batur has long been one of Bali's most popular excursions, with up to 300 people setting off every morning for a dawn rendezvous. Spectacular as the view might be, it is hardly a spiritual experience. Neighbouring **Gunung Abang** (2151m) is Bali's third-highest mountain, reaching just below the level of Gunung Batukaru and almost 1000m below mighty Gunung Agung. Abang offers exceptional sunrise views all of its own, and a poignant solitude that is at odds with the crowds on Batur.

As with Batur, the Abang hike typically starts at 2am if you want to catch sunrise at the summit, although a daylight hike through the gorgeous cloud forest has a thrill all of its own. You need a local guide, and **Bali Sunrise Trekking and Tour** *(balisunrisetrekkingandtour.com; from 900,000Rp)* can arrange the entire package, including transfers from your hotel. Even relatively fit hikers take up to three hours to reach Abang's summit, and it's a challenging trek, particularly after heavy rain.

Once on the peak – with just a handful of other hikers – you have unspoiled sunrise views to the summit of Agung to the east, and to the west a view of Batur across the mirror-like expanse of the crater lake. In the distance, you'll see Rinjani (Lombok), Batukaru (Bali), and even Arjuna on distant Java.

Trunyan

TIME FROM MUNDUK: **3HR**

Sky burial cemetery

Trunyan is the only community in Bali to use what are sometimes referred to as 'sky burials' for their dead. The unique cemetery on the eastern shore of Danau Batur is accessible only by boat. Eleven bodies at a time are laid to rest here, covered only by slatted bamboo frames, known as *ancak-saji*. When new bodies arrive, the oldest of the 11 is relegated to the heap of bones and collection of skulls piled under the sacred *taru menyan* tree, which is said to neutralise the odour so that there's no discernible smell from the decomposing bodies.

Pak Donal is one of several reliable local guides who can arrange boat trips to the cemetery *(WhatsApp +62 812 3879 5153; tours up to six people from 450,000Rp)*.

EATING IN KINTAMANI: OUR PICKS

The authentic beef rendang has become famous among locals.

Toteme Restaurant: Chic, open-sided Indo restaurant that's charmingly laid out. Grab an armchair and enjoy excellent coffee and cakes. *7am-11pm* **$$$**

O Club By Oculus: This avant-garde restaurant has a rooftop terrace with spectacular views of Batur, the lake and lava fields. *5am-10pm* **$$**

Ritatkala Cafe: The best among a parade of cafes with views towards Batur mountain, serving everything from fish and chips to massaman curry. *6am-6pm* **$$**

Rumah Makan Pitopang Jaya: Kintamani's newest, best and most affordable warung serves excellent buffet-style Padang cuisine. *10am-6pm* **$**

Lovina

QUIET DAYS | QUIET NIGHTS | MELLOW BEACHES

Lovina is at its best when the setting sun nears the horizon, setting off a brilliant display of fiery colours. Otherwise, 'relaxed' is how most people describe this strip of fishing villages and rather dated beachside development. Low-key, low-rise, low-priced Lovina is the antithesis of Canggu. The waves are calm, the beach is thin and Insta-ready poseurs are far and few between.

A highlight every afternoon at fishing villages such as Anturan is watching *prahu* (traditional outrigger canoes) being prepared for night fishing. When sunset reddens the sky, the boats flicker to life as dozens of points of light move across the horizon.

Lovina is not overstocked with sights, but it's close to various temples, soaring waterfalls and the urban charms of Singaraja, about 10km to the east.

TOP TIP

Touts are more active in Lovina than in other areas of Bali and can be pushy. Beware that the hotel prices they quote include a kickback.

Dolphin Watching

Early-morning aquatic adventure

Sunrise (6am) boat trips to observe and 'swim' with dolphins (typically spinner dolphins) are Lovina's much-hyped tourist attraction, with prices for the two-hour excursions fixed by the boat-owners' cartel *(viewing only/with swimming 100,000/225,000Rp)*. The swimming part sees you don a snorkel and hang onto a bar dangling from the curved boom of the

GETTING AROUND

Depending on the traffic gods and your route, the trip to Lovina can take three to five hours over the central mountains from south Bali. Descending the fertile hillsides of north Bali brings alluring verdant scenery and opportunities to stop at waterfalls. Most people use their own wheels or line up a ride through their accommodation at either end of the trip.

Alternatively, you can reach Lovina from the coasts to the east or west, which takes considerably longer than from the south, but which also allows for stops along the way. A few tourist shuttles run from the south.

SIGHTS
1 Dolphin Monument

SLEEPING
2 Frangipani Beach Hotel
3 Funky Place

DRINKING & NIGHTLIFE
4 Drinks Vendors Zone

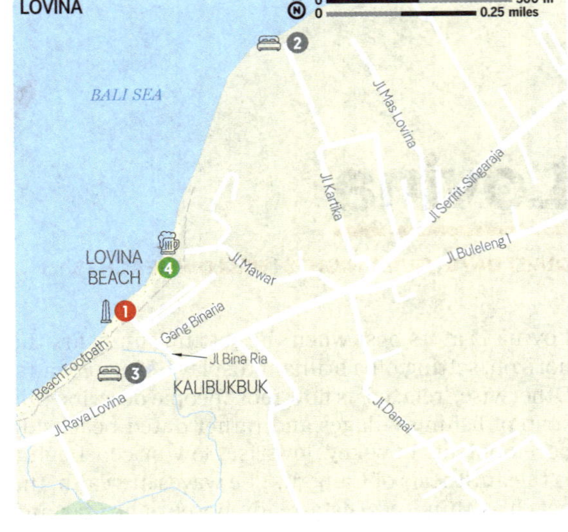

DECODING LOVINA

The Lovina tourist area stretches over 8km, and one fishing village seems to blend into the next. Kalibukbuk is the centre of the action, particularly along Jl Bina Ria and Jl Mawar. Going east, Jl Pantai Banyualit is an area dense with modest rental villas.

Some 3km northeast of the centre, a few tiny side tracks and Jl Kubu Gembong lead to lively little Anturan, which is a real travellers hangout. Further along, quiet Tukad Mungga feels removed from the rest of Lovina. To the west, Kaliasem is good for simple warungs and older waterfront lodging. Most Lovina hotels are budget-focused, as are the no-frills cafes and restaurants.

small outrigger as it moves. For an extra 75,000Rp you can add a snorkelling session at Lovina's reef on the way back, making it a three-hour excursion.

The ocean can get pretty crowded with dozens of roaring motorised outriggers chasing the dolphins around, and there's debate about how this affects the animals, which, amazingly, continue to cruise Lovina in huge pods. The later (7am) tour generally has fewer boats, but for us, it was too many.

Spectacular Sunsets

Lovina's free show

Don't miss sunsets from the waterfront when the western sky becomes a beautiful show of orange and crimson. The best place for viewing is the **drinks vendors zone** about 150m northeast of Kalibukbuk's **Dolphin Monument**. Enjoy cheap drinks on the mixed bag of chairs, loungers and reclining pillows on the sand, shaded by trees.

Diving & Snorkelling

Explore Lovina's reefs

Because dynamite fishing has damaged most of Lovina's reefs, the snorkelling and diving here aren't spectacular. The best spot for snorkelling is 1.3km west of the centre, a few hundred metres offshore, which most people visit as part of a dolphin-watching tour. Even though the reef isn't in great shape, there are still plenty of tropical fish to admire. Local dive centres take most divers to **Pulau Menjangan** (p276). The boat dock is 62km (about 1½ hours) west, so it's a long day out.

Beyond Lovina

Hike through luxuriant landscapes and discover urban culture in Singaraja, plus explore intriguing temples, waterfalls and natural springs.

Waterfalls, waterfalls everywhere! That's the glorious truth about the verdant landscape south of Lovina. Impossibly green mountainsides are cleaved by gorges and sprayed by pounding cascades of water. Hiking here is a delight, with evocative scents in the air, ripe fruit hanging from trees and magical vistas in every direction. The hills behind Lovina also reveal other treasures, including a rare Buddhist temple in Bali and a hot spring bubbling up out of the jungle.

The city of Singaraja embodies Balinese history in its museums and architecture, in particular at the old port. Throughout the region are temples core to Balinese beliefs, and many have surprising features in their ornamentations. The Bali Sea laps this reef-protected coast.

Places

GETTING AROUND

Singaraja is served by long-distance buses from Java via Gilimanuk, as well as occasional large buses from Denpasar. Generally, it's best to have your own wheels as the lands around Lovina reward free exploration.

Taxis are not common, but you can arrange rides (and motorbike hire) through your accommodation. Expect to pay 400,000Rp for a lift to Pemuteran and 9000Rp per day for a motorbike. Guides usually provide transport for days out.

Lovina's Hinterland

TIME FROM LOVINA: **20MIN**

Immerse yourself in a hidden hot spring

Hot springs percolate amid lush tropical plants at **Air Panas Banjar** *(45,000Rp)*. Eight fierce-faced carved stone *naga* (mythical snake-like creatures) pour water from a natural hot spring into the first bath, which then overflows (via the mouths of five more *naga*) into a larger pool.

In a third pool, water pours from 3m-high spouts to give you a pummelling massage. The water is slightly sulphurous and pleasantly steamy (about 35°C). You must wear swimwear.

Tour a rare Buddhist temple

Bali's only Buddhist monastery, **Brahma Vihara Arama** *(35,000Rp)* is a fascinating place to explore, with a lofty location that affords great views down across the ricefields to the north coast and manicured gardens brimming with frangipani and bougainvillea. Highlights include a miniature version of **Borobudur** (p88), the famous Buddhist temple and UNESCO site in Java. Statues of Buddha and lotus ponds abound.

THE HISTORIC GATEWAY TO BALI

In the 18th century, the colonial Dutch became the main purchasers of enslaved Balinese people. In the 1840s, the Dutch tried to make treaties with Balinese rajas to assert their control over the island before other colonial powers. But ultimately, the Dutch resorted to force and seized control of much of the island in 1849.

Singaraja became the centre of Dutch power in Bali and remained the administrative centre for the Lesser Sunda Islands (Bali to Timor) until 1953. Until the Denpasar airport in south Bali became the main means of arrival after WWII, most visitors arrived on steamships at Singaraja.

KASAKPHOTO/SHUTTERSTOCK

Sekumpul Waterfalls

Singaraja & Around

TIME FROM LOVINA: **20-40MIN**

Historic waterfront

Singaraja (which means 'lion king') is Bali's second-largest city and the capital of Buleleng Regency, which covers much of the north. It's worth exploring the tree-lined streets for a couple of hours; most people stay in nearby Lovina.

At the sleepy waterfront north of Jl Erlangga, you'll find the atmospheric old harbour, once Bali's main port before WWII. A modern pier juts out over the water with a couple of simple warungs, and old men play chess in a shady waterfront park.

Across the car park, look for some old Dutch shipping company buildings. One now houses the small but interesting **Museum Soenda Ketjil** *(12,000Rp; closed Sat & Sun)*. It covers the colonial era of Buleleng with displays in English. Other exhibits include early European contact, the role of the royal family and Bali's multicultural mix (Balinese, ethnic groups from across the archipelago, Chinese, Indians, Arabs and Europeans).

Nearby is the vibrantly red Chinese temple **Ling Gwan Kiong** *(entry by donation)*, which dates from 1873, and a few old canals. Walk up Jl Erlangga to see the Art Deco lines of late-colonial Dutch buildings.

Splash around in a natural waterpark

North Bali's answer to Kuta's **Waterbom** (p201), Aling-Aling is a natural waterpark made for adrenaline junkies. Thundering down through the jungle, **Air Terjun Aling-Aling** is the tallest of four waterfalls you can view on a loop trail *(20,000Rp)* that takes about 30 minutes from the ticket booth; factor in some steep stairs.

Like Sekumpul, there are also 'trekking' options. Short trekking *(1½ to two hours 125,000Rp)* includes a chance to swim, slide and jump into three of the four waterfalls of various heights on the main trail and a local guide to show you the safest way to do so (of course, it's not without risk).

Visits to a picturesque local rice terrace and the Blue Lagoon, a natural pool with an idyllic turquoise hue, are added to the medium trekking package *(three to four hours 250,000Rp).*

Long trekking *(five to six hours 500,000Rp)* also includes lunch and visits two additional waterfalls upriver. With a restaurant next to the **ticket office**, you can make a whole day of it in the lush hills above Singaraja.

Easy waterfall walks

Powerful **Air Terjun Gitgit** *(45,000Rp)* is on the main road to south Bali, about 12km south of Singaraja's waterfront. An 800m path from the parking area leads to impressive 40m-high falls that produce refreshing mists.

With more time, you can lose the crowds 2km further up the hill, where the multitiered **Air Terjun Bertingkat** *(20,000Rp)* waterfall is about 600m off the western side of the main road.

Sekumpul

TIME FROM LOVINA: **1HR**

Marvel at the Sekumpul cascades

Collectively known as the **Sekumpul Waterfalls**, the collection of cascades that pour over cliffs in a verdant valley is up to 80m high and ascends a green gorge that's almost mystical in its beauty. Trees, including clove, cacao, jackfruit and mangosteen, scent the air. Trails wind through the valley from one cascade to another, and it's easy to spend a day here revelling in the splendour.

Approaching from the north coast road, there's a car park and a ticket booth at the intersection of Jl Air Tejun and Jl Lemukih. There are three main entrance options: viewing only from a scenic **lookout** *(20,000Rp),* medium trekking *(150,000Rp)* and long trekking *(250,000Rp).* A guide is included in trekking prices along with a plastic bottle of water; it's best to bring your own reusable bottle instead.

If you opt for trekking, an *ojek* ride to the lookout is included. Otherwise, it's a 20- to 30-minute walk to the lookout point, or you can ride your own motorbike (turn left at **Spice Warung** and follow the steep and winding path).

Facing Sekumpul's main **Twin Waterfalls**, with **Fiji Waterfall** visible to the right, the view from the lookout is magical, with several simple warungs perched on the cliff side offering an opportunity to linger. From here, trekkers follow steep stairs down to **Hidden Waterfall** (not visible from the lookout) and then onto Twin Waterfalls. The 'long' trek continues to the base of Fiji Waterfall. Allow at least 30 minutes for the medium trek and an hour for the long trek. Expect to get soaked by the spray even if you don't swim at the base of any of the falls; water shoes are advisable.

It's also possible to access the falls from **Warung Fiji** in Lemukih Village to the south. Access to the trails to the bottom of the falls is 20,000Rp, but a guide isn't currently required. Beware of scam ticket booths along the approach to Sekumpul from south Bali.

LESSER-KNOWN TEMPLES

Pura Maduwe Karang: Look for the relief depicting a man riding a bicycle, thought to be a Dutch artist who, in 1904, brought the first bike to Bali. In Kubutambahan.

Pura Ponjok Batu: Legend holds that it was built to provide spiritual balance to all the temples in the south; it's 7km east of Yeh Sanih.

Pura Beji Sangsit: Dedicated to the goddess Dewi Sri. Sculptured panels feature demons; in Sangsit.

Pura Dalem Sangsit: This temple of the dead 500m from Pura Beji shows scenes of punishment in the afterlife.

Pura Dalem Jagaraga: Small temple with sculptured panels. Look for a vintage car, a steamer at sea and an aerial dogfight; in Jagaraga.

Pemuteran

UNDERWATER ADVENTURES | RELAXATION | CHEAP EATS

TOP TIP

With the exception of live music in the early evening at beachfront Dimpil and the odd Balinese dance performance at Pondok Sari resort, Pemuteran doesn't have a nightlife scene to speak of. If you want to party, head elsewhere.

One of Bali's most delightful beach towns, Pemuteran is northwest Bali's tourism hub, but it's still refreshingly relaxed. Peaceful resorts mix with welcoming homestays, all set back from a black-sand bay. The beach is calm, thanks to its location protected by coral reefs, and is never crowded. Most people spend at least some time viewing the undersea wonders offshore from Pemuteran and at nearby Pulau Menjangan, while others delight in days of relaxation on a sunlounger under a shady tree.

The busy Singaraja–Gilimanuk road is the town's spine, and many businesses aimed at visitors can be found along it. While noise can be distracting along the main road, numerous good cafes and restaurants line it. Most guesthouses are tucked back in the side streets. Despite its increasing popularity, Pemuteran's community and tourism businesses have forged a sustainable vision for development that should be a model for the rest of Bali.

Under the Sea

Reefs and human-made surprises

Strap on a snorkel and head straight out from the beach in front of the **BioRock Indonesia info booth** to explore more than 100 metal **structures** (including a long, twisting dragon) adorned with corals and anemones and swarming with fish.

GETTING AROUND

Pemuteran is a four- to five-hour drive from south Bali, either over the central mountains or around the west coast. Hotels at either end of the journey can arrange a car and driver; expect to pay about 1,000,000Rp to and from Canggu. Lovina is about an hour's drive to the east. Pemuteran is on the Gilimanuk–Lovina–Singaraja public bus run; just flag one down. Tourist buses generally do not serve the area.

You can get around all of Pemuteran by walking. Expect to pay 50,000Rp to 150,000Rp per day for motorbike rental to explore further afield.

HIGHLIGHTS
1 BioRock Reef
2 Proyek Penyu

ACTIVITIES
3 Garden of the Gods
4 Reef Seen

SLEEPING
5 Arjuna Homestay
6 Mango Tree Inn
7 Taman Sari

EATING
8 Dimpil Beachbar & Resto
9 Lakawi
10 Mantra Sari
11 Warung D'Bucu

INFORMATION
12 BioRock Indonesia Info Booth

Pemuteran's reefs, accessed by boat, aren't nearly as spectacular as those of **Pulau Menjangan** (p276), but the macro life makes them worth a dive, particularly **Napoleon Reef**, where we saw a good variety of anemone shrimp and nudibranchs.

Also accessed by boat is the **BioWreck** dive site, featuring an artificial ship and a turtle that's popular for beginners and night dives. On the seafloor about 400m off the beach in front of the **Reef Seen** *(reefseenbali.com)* dive centre, the **Garden of the Gods** dive site isn't as popular, owing to the lack of coral growth.

Support Baby Turtles

Visit Pemuteran's turtle hatchery

Run by the beachfront Reef Seen Divers' Resort since 1992, the nonprofit **Proyek Penyu** purchases turtle eggs found by locals and looks after them here until they're ready for ocean release.

You can visit the small **hatchery** *(reefseenbali.com; 40,000Rp)* to see eggs incubating and adorable hatchlings (green, hawksbill and/or olive ridley) in small pools, which are typically full during the nesting season (January to May).

Another pool holds Buddy, a 25-year-old hawksbill turtle surrendered to the hatchery in 2010. Time your visit for the 4.30pm feeding time, when the baby turtle tanks come alive with tiny flapping flippers. If there are juveniles available for release, it happens locally between 10am and 11am.

GROWING A NEW REEF

By the early 1990s, dynamite and cyanide fishing, along with a warming ocean, had bleached and damaged large parts of Pemuteran's reef. Facing this threat to the area's growing tourism, a group of local hotels, diving operators and community leaders hit upon a novel solution: grow a new reef using electricity.

The idea had already been floated by scientists internationally, but Pemuteran was the first place to implement it on a wide – and hugely successful – scale. Three decades on, the project, called **BioRock Indonesia** *(biorock-indonesia.com)*, is being adopted across the archipelago. Learn more at an **info booth** (p270) (generally open 9am to 3pm) on the beach by Pondok Sari.

JUDITH LIENERT/SHUTTERSTOCK

Pura Pulaki

The Other Monkey Temple

See Pemuteran's sea temples

Flanked by a pair of tiger sculptures, **Pura Pulaki** *(entry by donation)* at the east end of Pemuteran is home to a large (and intimidating) troop of monkeys. Dating from around the 16th century, it's one of Bali's auspicious sea temples, but the metal cage around the inner sanctum to keep the monkeys out detracts from the ambience.

About 150m across the busy road, a subsidiary temple, **Pura Pabean** *(entry by donation)* has a lovely location on a waterfront knoll. Its unusual Chinese-accented architecture is a legacy of traders who once lived here.

EATING IN PEMUTERAN: OUR PICKS

Warung D'Bucu: This no-frills family warung gets our vote for Pemuteran's most flavoursome *ikan bakar* (grilled fish). *11am-10pm* $

Lakawi: Bali's best burgers? Served with house-made fries, they sure hit the spot after a day's diving. *noon-10pm* $$

Mantra Sari: Dishes including a standout *nasi campur* are beautifully presented on miniature *jukungs*. *11am-10pm* $$

Dimpil Beachbar & Resto: Come for a sundowner and stay for tasty seafood and Indo mains. *11am-10pm* $$

Beyond Pemuteran

Bali's best snorkelling, diving and bird-watching draw visitors to the island's only national park to the west. But wait, there's more...

Occupying the island's western tip, West Bali National Park (Taman Nasional Bali Barat) is the main attraction, a place where you can enjoy Bali's best diving at Pulau Menjangan; hike, bike or drive through forests in search of birds and wildlife; explore coastal mangroves by kayak; and discover untrodden white-sand beaches. The mangrove-lined cove of Banyuwedang, east of the national park, offers both easy access to the park and a pleasant hot spring, though many use Pemuteran as a base for exploring the park.

East of Pemuteran is a clutch of vineyards forming part of Bali's first winery, complete with cellar-door tours and tastings.

Places

West Bali National Park

TIME FROM PEMUTERAN: **30MIN-1HR**

Lace your boots

Most visitors to West Bali National Park are struck by the mellifluous sounds emanating from the birds darting among the rustling trees. Some 300 species can be spotted here, along with wildlife including leaf monkeys, macaques, rusa and barking deer, wild pigs, squirrels, buffalo, iguanas, pythons and green snakes. The park *(200,000Rp)* covers 190 sq km of the western tip of Bali, including almost 70 sq km of coral reef and coastal waters. Together, this represents a significant commitment to conservation on a densely populated island.

From a trail west of the **Labuhan Lalang park entrance** (the main access point to Pulau Menjangan), a two- to three-hour hike exploring the fringe of **Teluk Terima** (Terima Bay) begins at the mangroves and monsoon forest. Another two-to-three-hour hike allows you to explore the savanna area at the heart of the park. There are many more hiking options, including a longer hike up 698m **Gunung Kelatakan**. Note seasonal variations: in the dry season, vegetation is brown and sparse, which aids animal spotting. In the wet season, the park gets green and lush, but animals also have plenty of cover.

GETTING AROUND

West Bali National Park can be reached from North Bali or via the busy road to the Java ferries in Gilimanuk, which runs west from South Bali. The closest tourist centre is Pemuteran. You can either arrange rides with your accommodation or use your own wheels.

Walking and hiking are major reasons to visit the park, but most excursions require the services of a park guide.

CENDRAWASIH PANJI/SHUTTERSTOCK

Bali starling

Guides, who can be found at the various park gates and who are required for tours, are of variable quality. Recommended guides include Ketut Suliastra *(WhatsApp +62 813 3778 4500)*, Komang Mastika *(+62 852 5371 5022)* and Muhamad Idriss *(WhatsApp +62 823 4018 5768)*. Hiking prices are more or less set (there's a rate sheet in the rundown information centre at the Labuhan Lalang gate) and aren't cheap, with the standard monsoon forest hike costing 850,000Rp for one or two people. At 300,000Rp for every extra person, it's more affordable if you split the cost among a group.

The sunset views from here are magnificent.

EATING & DRINKING BEYOND PEMUTERAN: OUR PICKS

Warung Makan Sri Ayu: Simple, great-value warung near Banyuwedang Hot Spring with nasi goreng for 30,000Rp. *2-11pm* $

Mangroove Bay Cafe: Great selection of Indo and international dishes (including house-made ravioli for dinner) in a serene, modern setting. *7.30am-10pm* $$

Sunset Beach Restaurant: On the water in Banyuwedang, with a good range of Asian dishes and the usual pizzas and pasta. *7am-11pm* $$

Bali Tower Bistro: Buy a drink to enjoy superb views over West Bali National Park from a 5th-floor tower at the Mengangin hotel. *7.30am-3pm, to 11pm May-Oct*

Spot Bali starlings

Previously tightly guarded, the **Bali Starling Breeding Centre** *(entry by donation)* is home to scores of the critically endangered Bali starling, a brilliant white bird with cobalt highlights around the eyes. Once collected to the point of extinction, the starling has made an incredible comeback, largely thanks to breeding programmes here and elsewhere in Bali. On a half-hour visit, the staff explain the facility and talk about the birds. It's 200m from a park entry gate near Sumber Kelompok; you need to pay the park admission.

An easy place to see wild Bali starlings is at a starling feeding station directly to the left of the **Labuhan Lalang park entrance** (p273). You don't need a guide.

A temple to Bali's Romeo

Jayaprana, the foster son of a 17th-century king, planned to marry Layonsari, a woman of humble origins. The king, however, also fell in love with Layonsari and had Jayaprana killed. Layonsari learned the truth of Jayaprana's death in a dream and killed herself rather than marry the king.

This *Romeo and Juliet* story is a common theme in Balinese folklore, and Jayaprana's grave is regarded as sacred. A 10-minute walk up stone stairs brings you to the monkey-filled temple built atop the grave, **Pura Jayaprana** *(free)*.

Sanggalangit

TIME FROM PEMUTERAN: **25MIN**

Taste Bali Wine

The vineyards east of Pemuteran may surprise those lulled by the ricefields that cover so much of Bali. Yet the island has a burgeoning wine scene that has been developing for two decades. One of the pioneering vineyards is Hatten Wines, which, like East Bali's **Sababay Winery** (p241), creates white, rosé, red, sparkling and fortified wines. Sample the wares with a tour and tasting at **Hatten Wines Vineyard Visitor Centre** *(hattenwines.com; 100,000Rp)*.

WHY I LOVE NORTH BALI

Sarah Reid, Lonely Planet writer

North Bali flies under the radar, and that's exactly why I love it. Hidden behind a mountain range, the region's isolation has helped places like Pemuteran retain a wonderfully relaxed Balinese beach town vibe now rare on the island. And the wall diving at Pulau Menjangan? Wow. And I've dived all over the world.

Then there's the waterfalls – the first time I set eyes on Sekumpul, it seemed too beautiful to be real. And you could spend months visiting the many temples in this region.

People often ask me why I return to Bali, year after year. Sure, I'm partial to a fancy Canggu restaurant meal (p190). But North Bali feeds my soul.

DUDAREV MIKHAIL/SHUTTERSTOCK

TOP EXPERIENCE

Pulau Menjangan

The home of Bali's best diving and snorkelling, uninhabited Pulau Menjangan is ringed by more than a dozen superb dive sites. The experience is excellent – iconic tropical fish, vibrant hard and soft corals, great visibility (usually), caves and spectacular drop-offs. Huge gorgonians (branching soft corals) provide both texture and hiding spots for small fish that form a colour chart for the sea.

DON'T MISS

- Eel Garden
- Bat Cave
- Dream Wall
- Anchor Wreck
- POS 2
- Coral Garden
- Pura Gili Kencana

Diving Menjangan

Most of Menjangan's dive sites are walls that meet the sandy bottom at various depths and are suitable for open-water-certified divers; advanced divers can explore deeper, more challenging sites. If conditions allow, operators typically aim for a dive at **Eel Garden**. After exploring a coral-encrusted wall, you pass a sandy patch dotted with garden eels. Other popular sites include **Bat Cave**, **Dream Wall**, **POS 2** (all with stunning walls) and **Anchor Wreck**, named for the rusting

PRACTICALITIES

- park entrance fee per day 200,000Rp

anchor of a mysterious 19th-century boat that lies about 7m below the surface. The remains of the wreck lie on the sandy bottom beside the reef at about 30m; you can get a good look from about 25m (advanced divers only).

The highlight of diving in Menjangan is its splendid walls covered in soft, hard and whip corals and lacey gorgonian fans. Keep your eyes peeled for anemone shrimp, frogfish, crocodile fish, pygmy seahorse, electric clams, nudibranchs and lionfish. Among the 'big stuff' you might see are turtles, eagle rays, grouper, barracuda, giant trevally, dogtooth tuna, reef sharks and even the odd whale shark.

A standard dive trip from Pemuteran includes two dives and lunch, and gets you back to town about 4pm. Most boats dock at a jetty at the southwestern end of the island for a lunch break between dives; there are shaded sitting areas, toilets, curious rusa deer and a small beach. Some operators use a smaller jetty at the southeastern end of the island instead, near Pura Gili Kencana.

Snorkelling Menjangan

There's good snorkelling all around the island. Depending on the conditions, operators typically take you to several spots along the southern side of the island (including **Mangrove Point**) to admire colourful corals, anemones and myriad reef fish in the shallows, or snorkel along the edges of the drop-offs that extend along the southern side of the island for better chances of spotting 'big stuff'. You might see bubbles rising from divers below.

If conditions allow, you also get a chance to snorkel on the northern side of the island; **Coral Garden** is a fine spot. Snorkelling boats also use both of the island's jetties for lunch breaks.

Exploring the Island

Uninhabited Pulau Menjangan has what is thought to be Bali's oldest temple, **Pura Gili Kencana**, dating from the 14th century and about 300m from the pier of the southwestern jetty. It has a huge Ganesha (the elephant-headed Hindu deity) carved from brilliant white stone at the soaring arched entrance.

An easy trail circles the low island. It's 6km in length, and a circuit takes about 1½ hours (divers won't have enough time to reach the temple during a lunch break). On the way, you pass small temples, mangroves and some thin but lovely beaches on the northwest side. Having a picnic lunch here is one of the good reasons to arrange for your own boat with a skipper amenable to a flexible schedule.

GETTING THERE

Most dive operators (which also run snorkelling trips) are based in Pemuteran; dive trips include transport to the boat dock at Labuhan Lalang. Dive centres in Banyuwedang also accommodate snorkellers.

Independent snorkellers can arrange trips at the Labuhan Lalang boat dock for about 650,000Rp per person, including gear, depending on the number of people.

TOP TIPS

- Factor in a one-hour return boat trip to Palau Menjangan.
- Arranging a snorkelling trip ad hoc at the Labuhan Lalang boat dock is more cost-effective for larger groups. Trips take three to four hours, including transit time.
- If your guide adds to your experience, tip accordingly.
- The Biosphere Foundation (jointhevoyage.org) undertakes stewardship projects in the national park; support its work with a donation.
- Leave no trace on the island, including food scraps (don't feed them to the deer), and consider bringing a rubbish bag to collect marine debris you encounter.
- Wear reef-safe sunscreen to help protect the delicate coral.

Tabanan & Mengwi

UNMISSABLE TEMPLE | UNIQUE STAYS | RICEFIELDS

GETTING AROUND

Useful public transit is nonexistent, with self-driving the quickest and most rewarding way to explore the Tabanan region. You can get around the heart of Tabanan and Mengwi towns on foot, but otherwise, you'll want your own wheels to explore villages and beaches beyond, driving the backroads and discovering views, workshops and temples.

Making up the best part of the less-travelled hinterland between Ubud and northern Canggu, rural Tabanan and Mengwi see little tourist traffic beside a trickle of van-hopping day-trippers. Like most regional capitals in Bali, Tabanan is a large, well-organised place with a central temple next to a huge banyan tree. The verdant surrounding fields are emblematic of Bali's rice-growing traditions and are part of its UNESCO recognition of the *subak* system of irrigation. The magnificent temple Pura Taman Ayun celebrates this, together with the renovated Tabanan's Mandala Mathika Subak (Subak Museum).

You need your own transport to drive the fecund back roads north of Tabanan, with opportunities to experience idiosyncratic and interesting places to stay while passing ricefield vistas around almost every turn.

The Tabanan regency stretches down through productive ricefields to the coast and sweeps west from Nuanu Creative City to Balian Beach and beyond.

Visit One of Bali's Most Alluring Temples

Beautiful Pura Taman Ayun

One of the most rewarding temples to visit on the island, **Pura Taman Ayun** *(30,000Rp)*, is a beautiful place of enveloping calm. This huge royal water temple, northeast of Tabanan in Mengwi, is surrounded by a wide, elegant moat. It was the main temple of the Mengwi kingdom, which survived until 1891, when it was conquered by neighbouring kingdoms. The complex was built in 1634 and extensively renovated in 1937.

The first courtyard is an open, grassy expanse. The *jeroan* (inner courtyard) is screened by a low wall, which, unusually for Bali, allows easy viewing of the thicket of evocative *meru* within. The canal-bordered walk around the perimeter of the *jeroan* is a sublime treat.

TOP TIP

To avoid traffic, stay off the main Gilimanuk–Denpasar road and access Tabanan using the well-paved back roads connecting Pererenan Beach to the west of Ubud. Secondary roads are always more scenic and less jammed up.

HIGHLIGHTS
1 Pura Taman Ayun
2 Pura Tanah Lot

SIGHTS
see 4 Aurora Media Park
3 Mandala Mathika Subak
4 Nuanu Creative City
5 Ogoh Ogoh Bali Museum
6 Pantai Balian
7 Pura Batu Bolong

SLEEPING
8 Pondok Pitaya
see 6 Surya Homestay
see 6 Secret Bay
see 8 Tekor Bali

EATING
see 6 Deki's Warung
see 6 Mojo Balian

DRINKING & NIGHTLIFE
see 4 Luna Beach Club

Just west of the temple complex, the **Ogoh Ogoh Bali Museum** *(20,000Rp)* celebrates the huge and outlandish papier-mâché monsters that have become a part of Nyepi celebrations. The market area immediately east of the temple has good warungs for lunch.

Learn about Bali's Ancient Irrigation System

Visit a *subak* museum

To learn about UNESCO-inscribed *subak*, a social-agrarian institution deeply tied to Balinese culture since the 9th century, head to the **Mandala Mathika Subak Museum** *(adult/child 15,000/10,000 Rp)*, also known as the Water Museum, located in Tabanan city, approximately 8km west of Pura Taman Ayun.

It was renovated and reopened in 2024, expanding its scope beyond the traditional Balinese irrigation system to include water management from other parts of Indonesia and the world, all explained with decent English-language placards.

A Seaside Temple Fantasy

Side-step the crowds at Pura Tanah Lot

A hugely popular tourist destination, the sea temple **Pura Tanah Lot** *(adult/child 75,000/30,000Rp)* is closely associated with the Majapahit priest Nirartha and has great spiritual significance

SEEING SEA TEMPLES

The legendary 16th-century priest Nirartha is credited with introducing many of the complexities of Balinese religion to the island, as well as establishing its chain of *pura segara* (sea temples). These sacred coastal spots both honour the sea gods and protect Bali from sea demons. Each was intended to be within sight of the next, and several have dramatic locations.

In addition to the famous **Pura Luhur Uluwatu** (p209) on the island's southwest tip and the lesser-known **Pura Pulaki** (p272) near Pemuteran on the north coast, the sea temples are most heavily concentrated in West Bali. Notable examples include **Pura Tanah Lot** (p279), **Pura Rambut Siwi** and **Pura Gede Perancak** (p283).

to the Balinese. Because of its floating illusion at high tide, when the rock on which the temple stands seems to be drifting on the waves, Tanah Lot is also one of Bali's most visited and photographed temples, especially for the overhyped sunsets.

You can walk to the temple at low tide, but non-Balinese are not allowed to enter. Two sacred snakes are said to live in the innermost sanctum. Follow the pathways in the gardens along the overlooking clifftop to escape the crowds and enjoy a somewhat more contemplative atmosphere. **Pura Batu Bolong** is connected to land by a natural bridge.

To reach Tanah Lot, you normally follow walkways from the vast car parks through a mind-boggling sideshow of tatty souvenir shops, unsustainable animal attractions and other schlock down to the sea. Clamorous announcements screech from loudspeakers. Note that during the pre- and post-sunset rush, traffic is awful, with backups stretching for many kilometres. The secret to enjoying Tanah Lot is to arrive before noon: you beat the crowds, and the vendors are still asleep.

See the Future in Bali

Explore Nuanu Creative City

South of Pura Tanah Lot, **Nuanu Creative City** *(nuanu.com; adult/child 50,000Rp/free)* feels like a wellness theme park with its serene spa complex, butterfly garden, alpaca park and tranquil hotel. But this futuristic and still-evolving 44-hectare development (the Balinese word *nu-anu* means 'in the process') has a bit of something for every curious visitor. Take art classes, admire surreal light installations at the **Aurora Media Park**, party beneath Burning Man–esque sculptures at **Luna Beach Club** and even enrol your kids at an international school. Quirky? Certainly. But Nuanu is never boring.

Chase Waves in Balian

A surf town in the making

Ever more popular, **Pantai Balian** is a rolling area of dunes and knolls that overlooks pounding surf. It attracts both surfers and those looking to escape the bustle of South Bali. The sand is right at the mouth of the wide Sungai Balian (Balian River); it's 800m south of the town of Lalang-Linggah.

Behind the beach, there's a small village of cafes, tourist businesses and guesthouses where travellers band together for drinks, talk surf or watch the sunset. The surf break is a reliable walled-up clean left shoulder; other activities include yoga and bodysurfing.

EATING IN BALIAN: OUR PICKS

Tekor Bali: Airy cafe set under a breezy awning, with coffee, house-made pastries and international food, plus good wi-fi. *7am-10pm* $$

Mojo Balian: Coworking space and cafe with all-day breakfast, good coffee and healthy dishes like smoothie bowls. *7am-9.30pm* $$

Deki's Warung: Breakfast, burgers, pizzas and Indonesian dishes are served at this warung with impressive beach views. *7am-9pm* $$

Secret Bay: Lovely beachside seafood restaurant on a cape overlooking secluded Mejan Beach. *7.30am-10.30pm* $$

Jembrana Regency

RICEFIELDS | FISHING BOATS | SEASIDE TEMPLES

Bali's most sparsely populated district, the Jembrana Regency is also one of the largest, hemmed by mountains to the north and a long coast of nearly empty, dark-sand beaches to the south. Most travellers come here for Medewi Point, a popular left-hand point break. To the east are Pulukan Beach and Pekutatan village, where one can experience local culture in the form of sunset walks with the region's rare pink buffalo.

Less experienced surfers can paddle out further west at paddy-field-backed Pantai Yeh Sumbul, which offers a more forgiving sandbank. Even further west, the lonesome sea temple **Pura Rambut Siwi** is a worthy stop on the way to the inlet of Perancak, just south of the regional capital Negara, where beautiful *selerek* fishing boats, one of the world's most extravagant fleets, await keen photographers on the way to the port of Gilimanuk and ferries to Java.

TOP TIP

Base yourself midway along the coast, either in Medewi or Pantai Yeh Sumbul, and take day trips to the surrounding sites. A rental scooter gives you the freedom to explore and hop between your accommodation and the surfing beaches.

Catch Waves at All Levels

Surfing at Medewi Point and Pantai Yeh Sumbul

The Jembrana Regency's main tourist draw is a top surf break, **Medewi Point**, with a much-vaunted long left-hand wave that makes rides of 200m to 500m common. Spectators view the action out on the water from the point, most likely seated at

GETTING AROUND

The Jembrana Regency is best toured with your own wheels or by leaving the driving to someone else. Distances are far; don't expect to walk much. Whether transiting to Java or taking the coastal route to north Bali and West Bali National Park, you have to negotiate the main Gilimanuk–Denpasar road with its impatient strings of jockeying cars and trucks. You could hop on and off any of the buses plying the distance between the ferry port of Gilimanuk and Denpasar, but it's often a long and sweaty walk to any of the accommodation where you can rent a scooter.

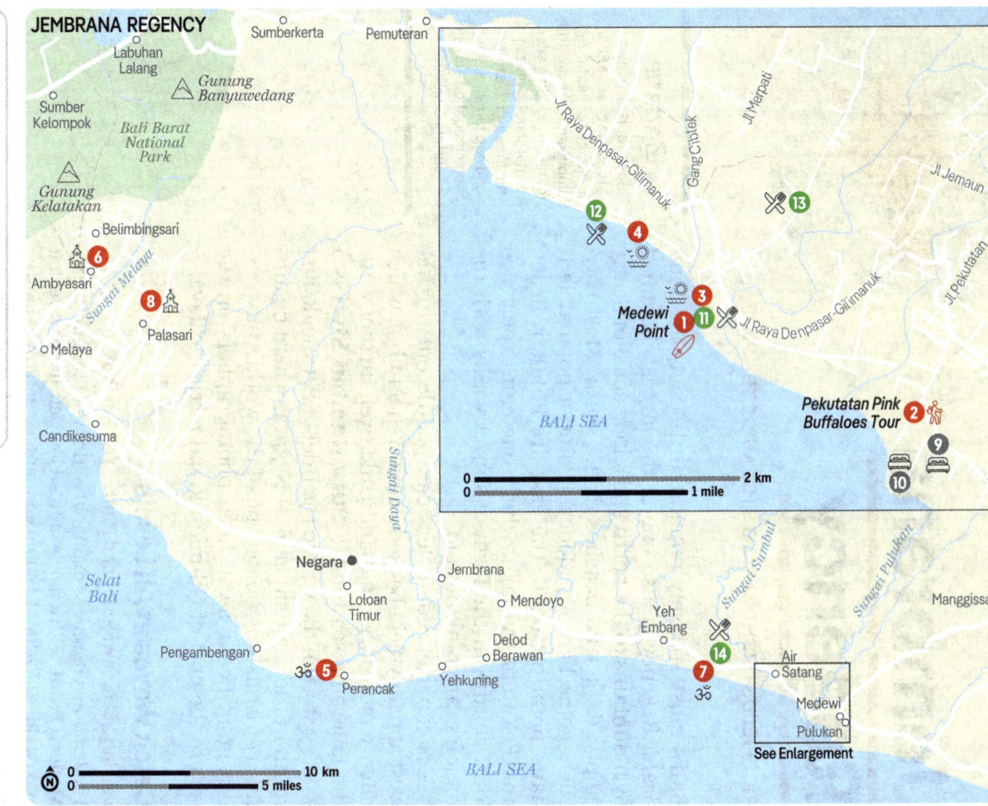

HIGHLIGHTS
1 Medewi Point
2 Pekutatan Pink Buffaloes Tour

SIGHTS
3 Pantai Medewi
4 Pantai Yeh Sumbul
5 Pura Gede Perancak
6 Pura Gereja
7 Pura Rambut Siwi
8 Sacred Heart Catholic Church

SLEEPING
9 Asri Villas
10 Puri Dajuma Cottages

EATING
11 Bombora Medewi Wave Lodge
12 Holy Tree Kitchen
see 5 Lesehan Ikan Bakar New Muara Indah
13 Rasta Cafe
see 11 Umadewi Surf & Retreat
14 Warung Negaora Ikan Bakar & Nyatnyat

either **Bombora Medewi Wave Lodge** *(bomboramedewi.com)* or **Umadewi Surf and Retreat** *(umadewi.com)*, two plush beachside resorts with restaurants, coffee and loungers. The immediate beach, **Pantai Medewi**, feels less touristy and has a stretch of huge, smooth grey rocks interspersed among round black pebbles – think of it as free reflexology.

Just west, **Pantai Yeh Sumbul** is another long swath of grey-sand beach with less dangerous rocks, more suitable for less-experienced surfers. It has a sufficient number of guesthouses and cafes, yet feels much more like its own secluded village. At sunset, the ricefields just beyond the beach get washed in ethereal shades of light.

Walk with Bali's Rare Pink Buffalo

Bovine encounters in Pekutatan

West Bali's rare pink buffaloes are endangered because of sacrifices and *makepung*, the brutal buffalo chariot races held in the paddies south of Negara. In Pekutatan village, farmer Pak Saudana has tailored a two-hour conservation-driven **walking tour** *(westbali.net/experience-medewi; adult/child 200,000Rp/free)*, taking guests along as he herds his three animals along the beach. Saudana's son, Komang, speaks good English and assists with translations.

Colour & Culture by the Sea

Visit the fishing village of Perancak

Some 10km south of the regional centre of Negara, the fishing village of Perancak is the site of Nirartha's arrival in Bali in 1546, commemorated by the limestone sea temple **Pura Gede Perancak**. It's on a wide river inlet, between mangroves and the ocean, at the end of which is the lettering sign Ujung Muara.

Look for the colourful fishing boats called *perahu selerek*. They are always moored in pairs, believed to be husband and wife. A string of humble cafes near the oceanfront point has sunset drinks, fresh seafood and boatmen happy to take you out for a closer look at the boats. At sunset, the wide black beach to the south fills with locals flying kites.

CHRISTIAN BALI

Discouraged by the secular Dutch, Christian evangelism via sporadic missionary activity in Bali resulted in few converts, many of whom were subsequently rejected by their own communities. In 1939, they were encouraged to resettle in two communities in the wilds of West Bali. The two communities are examples of the hidden multiculturalism of the island.

Palasari boasts the huge **Sacred Heart Catholic Church**, largely made from white stone and set on a large town square. It's a peaceful, off-the-beaten-path spot with gently waving palms. Nearby Belimbingsari was established as a Protestant community and now has the largest Protestant church, **Pura Gereja**, on the island. It has Balinese details such as a *kulkul* (hollow tree-trunk drum) instead of a bell.

EATING IN MEDEWI & PERANCAK: OUR PICKS

Rasta Cafe: This beloved vegan-focused Medewi cafe has a range of curated curries and rice-based dishes. *noon-10pm* $

Holy Tree Kitchen: Right on Pantai Yeh Sumbul, with good coffee, healthy breakfasts, tasty lunches and addictive views. *7am-9.30pm* $$

Warung Negaora Ikan Bakar & Nyatnyat: Excellent *mujair* fish (tilapia) or chicken served grilled or in sweet-sour *nyatnyat* sauce. *10am-8pm* $$

Lesehan Ikan Bakar New Muara Indah: Eat grilled fish in a relaxing seaside garden looking over the *selerek* boats. *8am-10pm* $

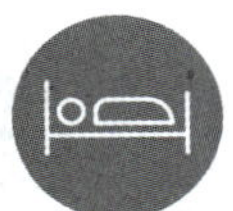

Places We Love to Stay

$ Budget $$ Midrange $$$ Top End

Canggu Area

MAP p189

Serenity $ An eco-friendly guesthouse and yoga resort close to Pantai Nelayan, with a distinctly bohemian vibe.

Melati Bali Homestay $$ Lovely traditional wooden rooms are surrounded by a tropical garden. The property is small but private and full of character.

Guru Canggu $$ This quiet boutique hotel has a small pool and garden. Each room is different.

Kayu Village $$ Twelve cosy but charming traditional-style wooden bungalows face off in a lush garden.

Hotel Tugu Bali $$$ A hotel with lots of character and Indonesian antiques; it has many activities on offer, too. Brilliant place to connect with Balinese culture.

Seminyak

MAP p195

Grandmas Plus Hotel Seminyak $$ Rooms are compact and contemporary, and it's a convenient base from which to explore Seminyak.

Desa Potato Head (p196) $$$ Uber-stylish sites and studios, and a huge, inspiring emphasis on minimising waste. There is always something happening, from sunrise yoga classes to DJ events.

Kuta & Legian

MAP p200

De Puspa Residence $$ This small homestay is tucked into a side street off Jl Arjuna. The location is excellent – on the doorstep of the beach, shops, spas and restaurants.

Puri Damai $$ Built around a garden of frangipani trees close to Double-Six Beach, this well-cared-for accommodation has an old Balinese atmosphere and apartment-style rooms.

Poppies Bali $$$ Operating for over 50 years, this peaceful boutique hotel is a tropical-oasis escape tucked in the heart of built-up Kuta.

Sanur

MAP p204

Kubu di Kayla's $ Sanur's best-value budget rooms offer no frills but easy access to the beach, an eight-minute walk away.

Puri Mesari $$ Spacious, cosy rooms surround a pool and gardens with walkways intersected by fish ponds. It's a five-minute walk from Mertasari Beach and has a casual restaurant.

Tandjung Sari Hotel $$$ Family-owned boutique hotel built in the 1960s by an Indonesian-Dutch artist. It's on the beach and comprises cottages surrounded by a verdant garden.

Uluwatu & Bukit Peninsula

MAP p208

Temple Lodge $$ Dreamy, eclectic suites with a surf-and-yoga vibe and sea views from Uluwatu to Kuta.

Uluwatu Surf Villas $$$ Family favourite clifftop resort with modern villas and ocean views. A skate park and yoga shala add appeal.

Mû Bungalows Boutique Resort $$$ This laid-back boutique-style resort is perched atop a cliff. Has a bohemian feel and stunning views from the pool and restaurant.

Nusa Lembongan

MAP p213

Pondok Jenggala $ Offering excellent value, this small guesthouse has large, simple rooms set around a deep pool.

Isla Indah Retreat $$ A tropical, midrange chic boutique just off Pantai Jungutbatu. There is a yoga space, a surf shop and a good cafe on-site.

Ubud

MAP p220

Arjuna Homestay $ Basic rooms in a super-central house with its own temple in the courtyard, perfect for backpackers.

Three Win Homestay $ The family offers five modern guestrooms in their compound off Jl Hanoman. Get one with a spacious balcony.

Hotel Tjampuhan $$ Overlooks two rivers. Artist Walter Spies lived here in the 1930s, and his former home is part of the hotel.

Puri Saraswati Dijiwa Bungalows $$ Centrally located, with lovely gardens that open onto beautiful Pura Taman Saraswati and attractive bungalow-style rooms.

Villa Nirvana $$ Serene retreat by a river in Penestanan. Modern villas set in garden surrounds, many with pools.

Bambu Indah $$$ This eco-resort near the Ayung Valley has 100-year-old Javanese wooden houses and extraordinary bamboo structures.

Keramas

Nirmala Guest House Surf $$ With spacious rooms and bungalows surrounded by a garden, this is a good option for those who enjoy a sense of space. Short walk to the beach.

Padangbai

MAP p248

Padang Bai Beach Homestay $ This peaceful homestay, close to the fast-ferry pier, has simple rooms set around a garden with a swimming pool. Great value.

OK Divers Resort & Spa $$ Built around a pool shrouded with palms, this small hotel feels very boutique-y. It's beside the fast-ferry pier.

Bloo Lagoon $$$ Set atop a headland with gorgeous ocean views, this eco-village has 25 individually decorated villas.

Sidemen

Uma Agung Villa $$ Beautiful views, spacious balcony rooms and a glistening pool – you get more than you pay for here.

Samanvaya $$$ This adults-only retreat is absolutely dreamy. Think stunning stone or bamboo villas, gorgeous paddy and mountain views, infinity pools, and swinging chairs.

Amed

MAP p255

Kirana Homestay $ Large rooms are actually cottages with their own small kitchens, and verandas with daybeds.

Solaluna Beach Homestay $$ Enjoy direct access to Amed Beach (and views of Agung). It has a wonderful pool. For a treat, book a beachfront room.

Aquamarine Beach Villas $$$ Each large villa has a kitchenette and a veranda with comfy couches and sea views.

Munduk

MAP p259

Terrasse du Lac Munduk $ Only four rooms and – thanks in part to the romantic log fires – they book up fast. Also an appealing dining room overlooking **Danau Tamblingan** (p261).

Puri Lumbung Cottages $$ A lovely mountaintop resort with a variety of rooms. An ideal base for a range of activities from hiking to medicinal-plant workshops and dance classes.

Kintamani

Tamalia House $ While the farmlands around the western shore of Danau Batur are plagued by flies, this family-run property is an affordable highland escape.

Lakeview Hotel $$ This solid old hotel has a range of rooms. The standard ones are basic, while the more luxurious deluxe rooms are worth the upgrade.

Lovina

MAP p266

Funky Place $ Rollicking hostel in Kalibukbuk with dorms and a treehouse, and proximity to the beach.

Frangipani Beach Hotel $$ A clutch of spacious, traditional rooms face off in a lush garden in Anturan. Beach access, with pool and restaurant.

Pemuteran

MAP p271

Mango Tree Inn $ One of Pemuteran's best budget stays, with canopy beds and alfresco showers. Set in a lush garden.

Arjuna Homestay $$ Also the home of Dive Concepts, this lovely hotel's 2nd-floor rooms have balconies overlooking the leafy pool.

Taman Sari $$ Traditional-style bungalows with intricate carvings and traditional artwork. Beachfront location.

Balian Beach

MAP p279

Surya Homestay $ One of a dozen excellent local homestays. Owners are charmers; the basic rooms are close to the surf.

Pondok Pitaya $$ Beachfront property fronted by a swimming pool, a popular restaurant, spa and a yoga shala.

Medewi

MAP p282

Asri Villas $ Comfy budget guesthouse with large bungalow-style rooms, shared kitchen and pool.

Puri Dajuma Cottages $$ Suites, cottages and villas have private gardens, hammocks and walled outdoor baths. Most have ocean views, too.

Puri Lumbung Cottages, Munduk

Researched by
Leyla Rose

Nusa Tenggara

TIMELESS CULTURE, EPIC NATURE, BIG WAVES

Welcome to a more remote part of Indonesia, home to rumbling volcanoes, Komodo dragons and animist culture.

Spreading west from the Wallace Line that divides Asia from Australasia, the Nusa Tenggara archipelago is Indonesia less-trodden: a verdant, volcano-studded, mountainous land of technicolour volcanic lakes, pink-sand beaches, limitless surf breaks and barrels, and traditional villages that continue to resist Balification.

On Flores, far away from crowds bristling with selfie sticks, you'll encounter Komodo dragons, unspoiled underwater worlds teeming with creatures, hidden waterfalls, hot springs and steep volcanic slopes that throw down a gauntlet to intrepid hikers, challenging them to race to the top to watch the sun rise.

West Timor, Sumba and the smaller islands will make you forgo creature comforts as you leave the main towns behind and venture inland to explore traditional villages with soaring thatched roofs. This is where the spirits of the ancestors reside side-by-side with the living and where Bahasa Indonesia – the nation's lingua franca – is little spoken.

To the west, the island of Lombok beckons with its impressive bays, the archipelago's second-highest peak and an increasing number of enticing places to stay and dine. Surfers flock to the southern half of the island for highly lauded waves, while trekking enthusiasts traverse the north-central region to Gunung Rinjani: an active volcano that climbs up to 3726m above sea level. People with less intense hobbies find themselves somewhere in between, typically with their toes in powdery-soft sand.

MUHD FUAD ABD RAHIM/SHUTTERSTOCK

THE MAIN AREAS

FLORES
Diving, dragons, volcanoes and villages. p292

WEST TIMOR
Traditional villages and ikat-weaving. p310

SUMBA
Indigenous culture, ikat and epic surf. p320

KUTA
Traveller hub near beaches and surf. p332

SENGGIGI
Longstanding resorts and quieter shores. p340

For places to stay in Nusa Tenggara, see p368

GUDKOV ANDREY/SHUTTERSTOCK

Left: Hiker near Gunung Rinjani (p350); Above: Komodo dragon, Komodo National Park (p306)

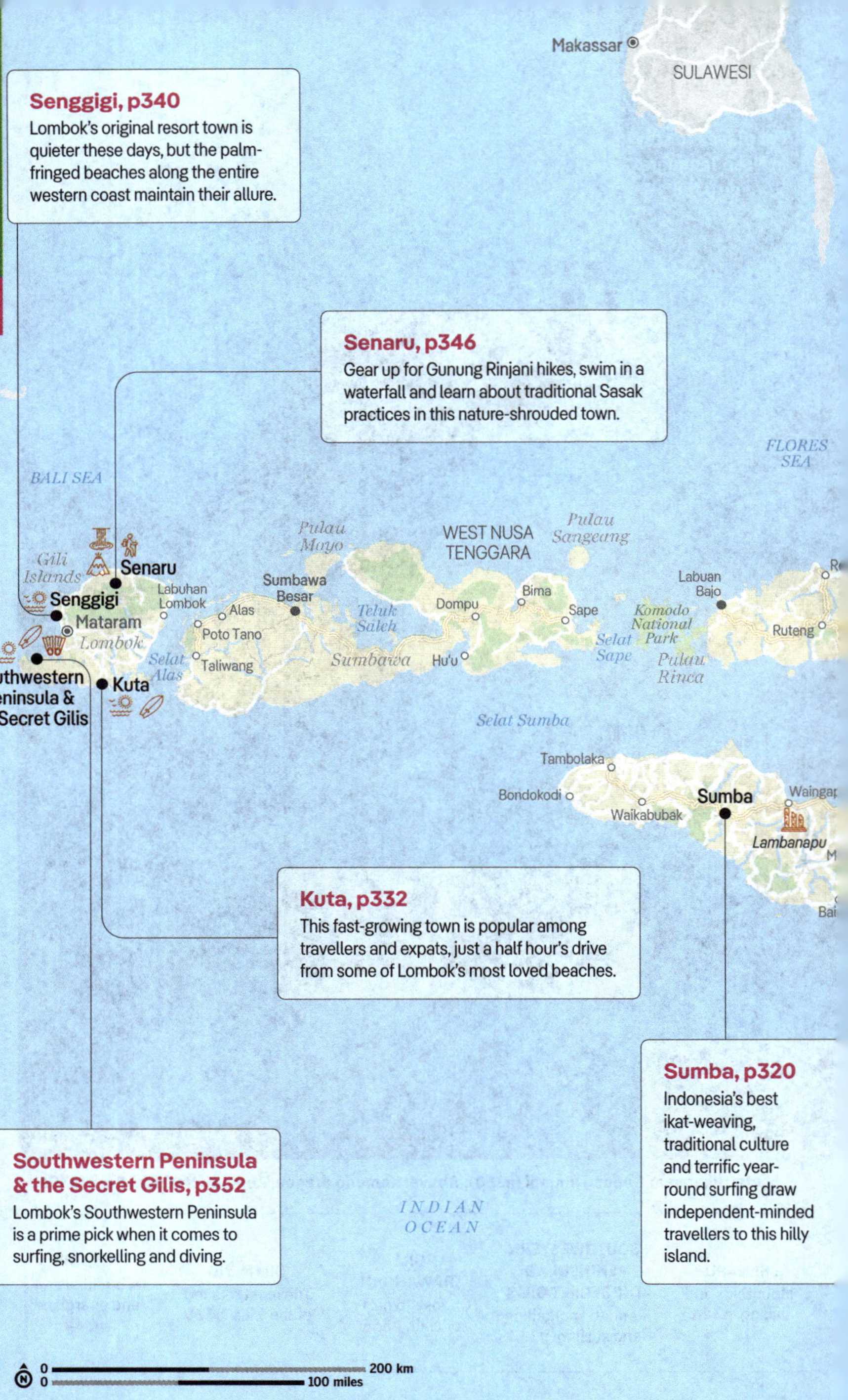

Senggigi, p340

Lombok's original resort town is quieter these days, but the palm-fringed beaches along the entire western coast maintain their allure.

Senaru, p346

Gear up for Gunung Rinjani hikes, swim in a waterfall and learn about traditional Sasak practices in this nature-shrouded town.

Kuta, p332

This fast-growing town is popular among travellers and expats, just a half hour's drive from some of Lombok's most loved beaches.

Southwestern Peninsula & the Secret Gilis, p352

Lombok's Southwestern Peninsula is a prime pick when it comes to surfing, snorkelling and diving.

Sumba, p320

Indonesia's best ikat-weaving, traditional culture and terrific year-round surfing draw independent-minded travellers to this hilly island.

Find Your Way

Nusa Tenggara (both East and West) comprises more than 800 islands and accounts for a substantial chunk of Indonesia. We've picked the places that best capture the region's history, culture and natural landscapes.

Flores, p292

Hike up volcanoes, explore rice terraces and visit traditional villages before going island-hopping, diving and snorkelling from this all-rounder island.

West Timor, p310

Chew betel nut with royalty in traditional settlements, visit the village of former headhunters and seek out intricately woven ikat.

ON FOOT

On the smaller islands, walking is still the best way to get around. For instance, the perimeter of Gili Trawangan can be walked in less than two hours – even less for the neighbouring islands.

BUS, CAR & MOTORBIKE

Overland travel always takes longer than you think it will. Main roads are decent and surfaced, but minor roads can be rough. Trucks and buses connect main towns; for everything else, rent a car or motorbike.

BOAT & AIR

An extensive and slow ferry network connects Nusa Tenggara's islands to each other, to Bali and beyond. Rough seas cause cancellations, particularly during the rainy season. Several airlines cover inter-island routes, many of which start in Denpasar, Bali.

Plan Your Time

For Komodo dragon encounters and volcano treks, prioritise Flores. Culture vultures should head for Sumba or West Timor, while Lombok's finest beaches deserve at least a few days to a week (or longer).

YUSUF MADI/SHUTTERSTOCK

Hiking, Gunung Rinjani (p350)

Pressed for Time

- If you're a diver, explore the teeming underwater world of **Komodo National Park** (p306), part of the species-rich Coral Triangle, with diving outfits from **Labuan Bajo** (p304). Go for the day or dive more spots on a multiday liveaboard trip.

- Is Komodo dragon-spotting a must do? See the legendary lizards on a **speedboat day trip** that includes bouts of snorkelling, often with manta rays, between October and March.

- For immersion in Sumbanese indigenous culture, fly to **Tambolaka** (p329), then spend a couple of days visiting the traditional villages around **Wanokaka** (p324) and **Waikabubak** (p326). Shop for beautiful Sumbanese ikat while you're travelling around.

Monthly Highlights

The dry season is ideal for trekking, diving and snorkelling. Many flock to the Gilis in March for the Balinese holiday of Nyepi.

JANUARY TO MARCH

Expect rain. Keep a raincoat within reach and don't plan any big treks – Gunung Rinjani routes are closed. Watch warriors on horseback engage in combat during Sumba's **Pasola festival** (p325).

APRIL & MAY

The occasional rain shower lingers but the shoulder season is a good time to score travel deals across Nusa Tenggara before the high season begins.

JUNE

As rains abate, hike up the volcanoes in Flores. Ride Nusa Tenggara's epic barrels in Rote and Sumbawa, and search for Komodo dragons on Komodo Island.

One-Week Sampler

● Within just one week, you can experience the duality between Lombok's stunning coastlines and the impressive mountainous region. Using **Kuta** (p332) as your base for the first four days, you can surf, swim and snorkel the surrounding beaches – including the **Southwestern Peninsula** (p352) if you're feeling more adventurous.

● When you're ready for something different, head up to the mountains for hiking on and around **Gunung Rinjani** (p350) and the **Sembalun Valley** (p349). Swim in waterfalls, feast on fresh produce and enjoy the lush surrounds.

● Stay longer in the mountains or pop over to **Gili Air** (p364), **Gili Meno** (p360) or **Gili Trawangan** (p356) for some post-hike relaxation on your idyllic tropical island of choice.

Two Weeks to Travel Around

● After two days of exploring **Komodo National Park** (p306) above and below the water from **Labuan Bajo** (p292) in Flores, head into the mountains to visit the traditional villages of **Wae Rebo** (p296) and **Bena** (p297) before ascending **Kelimutu** (p302) from Moni.

● Fly to **Kupang** (p310) in West Timor and spend two days visiting the traditional villages of **Tamkesi** (p313) and **Boti** (p315). Or, if you're a diver, proceed directly to the **Alor Archipelago** (p318). Chasing waves? Make for **Rote** (p319) instead.

● Tack on a visit to **Sumba** (p320) if time permits, where more traditional villages and waves await, along with waterfalls and ikat shopping opportunities.

JULY & AUGUST

The dry season is ideal for exploring Komodo National Park on day trips or from Labuan Bajo, or the underwater worlds of the Alor archipelago from a liveaboard.

SEPTEMBER

If you're a surfer, make the most of the end of the dry season in southwest Sumba, Rote, Sumbawa and southern Lombok. Experience Nusa Tenggara's low-key charm between downpours.

OCTOBER

Dry season is on its way out, but there are still plenty of sunny days (and waves) in October. Join the Gavi ceremony festivities at Sa'o Ria on Flores, marked by four days of dancing, *arak* drinking and buffalo sacrifices.

NOVEMBER & DECEMBER

Rainy season begins and the islands become greener every week. December is a great time to see manta rays in Komodo National Park before the rainy season really impacts visibility.

Flores

SPECTACULAR NATURE | TRADITIONAL VILLAGES | DIVING

GETTING AROUND

The Trans-Flores Hwy is a beautiful paved drive that'll always take longer than Google Maps estimates. Secondary roads range from narrow and paved to shocking, with the latter only accessible by 4WD or motorbike.

Most hotels and guesthouses rent motorbikes and scooters *(per day 80,000-100,000Rp)*. Car rental is available in Labuan Bajo and Ende. Many travellers hire a car and driver *(per day 800,000-1,200,000Rp)* – the price depends on English-speaking and tour-guiding capabilities. Guides can arrange detailed, island-wide itineraries.

Regular buses run between Labuan Bajo and Maumere. More comfortable air-con public minibuses link major towns.

Pass through a succession of diverse topographies as you follow the serpentine 670km Trans-Flores Hwy, which follows the spine of Nusa Tenggara's longest, equally sinuous island. Appropriately, the original name references snakes rather than the flowery title that 16th-century Portuguese colonists bestowed upon it.

In the west, buzzy Labuan Bajo is the destination du jour of divers and dragon-seekers, and the gateway to the pink-sand beaches and gin-clear waters of Komodo National Park. Heading into the jungle-covered mountains, you pass through the highland towns of Ruteng and Bajawa, fringed by rice terraces, volcanic cones, hot springs and traditional villages. Further north, Riung and its offshore archipelago are another draw for divers, while east of Bajawa, rainforest gives way to verdant, vertiginous hills, white sand, beaches and busy ports. There is also the mountain town of Moni, from where you summit Kelimutu volcano with its emerald lake, and can seek out ikat (woven textiles) and Lio culture in nearby villages.

Lounge Around Labuan Bajo

Explore Labuan Bajo's terrestrial attractions

Its glossy marina and ever-expanding number of restaurants aside, the jumping-off point for **Komodo National Park** (p306) and its famous dragons is a smidgen short on sights. Everything you need is on one-way Jl Soekarno Hatta, from Western restaurants and local *rumah makans* (eating houses) to coffee shops, accommodation, travel agents, ATMs and dive shops.

Head up to a centrally located spot on Jl Ande Bole, a block from the waterfront, for terrific sunsets. If you want to explore further afield, rent a motorbike or scooter *(per day 100,000Rp)* from numerous outlets along Jl Soekarno Hatta, and head south of Labuan Bajo to **Gua Batu Cermin** (Mirror Stone

LEE RISAR/SHUTTERSTOCK

Labuan Bajo

Cave; *entry/plus guide 50,000/100,000Rp*), 5km east of town. You'll need a torch to check out the large grotto with stalactites and stalagmites, while squeezing through tight spaces lets you see a fossilised turtle. To get to the more popular **Gua Rangko** *(50,000Rp)*, an ocean cave famed for its sunlit turquoise water (visit in the afternoon for the best light), drive 12km northeast from Labuan Bajo to Rangko village, then pay around 350,000Rp for a boat to take you there. An hour or two should be plenty of time to explore each cave.

Hang with Hobbits

Encounter tiny human remains

The Manggarai have long-told folktales of *ebo gogo* – hairy little people with flat foreheads who once roamed the jungle. Nobody paid them much attention until September 2003, when archaeologists made a stunning find.

Excavating the limestone cave at **Liang Bua** *(30,000Rp)*, archaeologists unearthed a skeleton the size of a three-year-old child but with the worn-down teeth and bone structure of an adult. Six more remains confirmed that the team had unearthed an entirely new species of human, who reached around 1m in height. The species was named *Homo floresiensis* and nicknamed 'hobbit'.

Commandeering an *ojek* (motorbike taxi) in Ruteng, you can travel 12km north past flooded rice paddies, and visit the vast stalactite-filled overhang looming above a small vegetable garden. Local guides, whose service is included in your entry fee, will meet you at the cave's entrance, explain why Liang Bua is considered sacred and point out the excavation site where the bones of at least eight more 'hobbits' were found. The small adjacent museum tells the story of the findings (in English and Bahasa Indonesia), displays a replica 'hobbit' skeleton, explains the theories of *Homo floresiensis* evolution and, of course, quotes Tolkien.

THE MYSTERIOUS ORIGINS OF THE FLORES 'HOBBIT'

An Australian study in 2017 supposedly disproved the prevailing theory that the 'hobbits' were descendants of *Homo erectus* (who spread from Africa to Asia around two million years ago).

A new study analysing *Homo*-related bones and dental samples from multiple countries found the two had vastly different structures. *Homo floresiensis* could be even more ancient than *Homo erectus*, most likely evolving from a common African ancestor.

Anthropologists suggest that the Flores find could represent *Homo sapiens* (who travelled between Australia and New Guinea 35,000 years ago) that suffered from microcephaly – a form of dwarfism. But a 2018 study refuted any link between the 'hobbit' and *Homo sapiens*.

TOP TIP

Visit traditional villages with a local guide to bypass the language barrier, learn about indigenous beliefs and avoid making embarrassing faux pas. Visitors must sign the guestbook in each village and make a donation.

FLORES

HIGHLIGHTS
1 Gunung Inerie
2 Kelimutu National Park
3 Liang Bua
4 Seventeen Islands Marine Park

SIGHTS
5 Bajawa
6 Bena
see 2 Inspiration Point
7 Koanara
8 Luba
9 Pulau Bakau
10 Pulau Laingjawa
see 9 Pulau Ontoloe
11 Pulau Rutong
see 11 Pulau Tembang
see 10 Pulau Tiga
12 Sa'o Ria
13 Sopi Lontar Aimere
14 Spider Web Rice Fields
15 Tololela
16 Wae Rebo
17 Wae Rebo trailhead
18 Wolotopo

ACTIVITIES
19 Air Panas Malanage
20 Air Panas Soa
21 Gua Batu Cermin
22 Gua Rangko
23 Kanha Liveaboard
24 Komodo Kayaking
25 Manta Rhei
26 Neren Diving Komodo
see 23 Scuba Junkie Komodo
27 Uber Scuba Komodo
28 Wunderpus Liveaboard

Labuan Bajo

Jl Binongko
Airport
Jl Mutiara
Jl Soekarno Hatta
Jl Opseter Maun
Jl Bandara
Jl Soekarno Hatta
Pulau Palue
0 500 m
0 0.25 miles

Seventeen Islands Marine Park
Ngara
Tonggu Rambang
Mbay
Wewaria
Olaia
Wulabhara
Kamubheka
Ranga
Seso
Kelimutu National Park
Wolowea
Air Terjun Ogi
Bajawa
Ende
Wolotopo
See Gunung Inerie Enlargement
Witurombaua
Podenura
Puutara
Boba
Pulau Ende

Gunung Inerie

Gunung Inerie
Luba
Bena
Tololela
Gurusina
0 2 km
0 1 mile

SLEEPING
- see 5 Arnolds Family Homestay
- 29 Bintang by Tobias Lodge
- 30 Blasius Monta Homestay
- 31 Kelimutu Crater Lakes Ecolodge
- 32 Mama's Homestay Ruteng
- 33 Seaesta Komodo Hostel

EATING
- 34 Alma
- 35 Buso Izakaya
- see 32 Café Agape
- 36 Café Del Mar
- see 36 Café Rico Rico
- 37 Copper Bonnet Bistro
- see 29 Good Moni
- see 40 Istana Sehat
- see 5 Kartini Restaurant
- see 28 Komodough Artisan Bakery & Coffee
- see 28 La Cucina
- see 35 Le Bajo Flores
- see 5 Milonari Restaurant
- see 29 Mopi's Place
- 38 Pari Koro Resto
- 39 Pasar Malam
- see 36 Pato Resto
- see 36 Rutong Café
- see 32 Spring Hill Restaurant
- see 34 Taman Laut Handayani

SHOPPING
- 40 Ikat Market

CACI WHIP FIGHTS

Every November, as part of the Penti harvest festival, Manggarai villages such as Wae Rebo stage **Caci** – a ritual whip fight between pairs of men. One man plays the role of aggressor and the other is the defender. The aggressor tries to hit the defender's bare upper body with a rattan whip while the defender blocks with a buffalo-hide shield.

At the beginning, the participators run towards each other to raise the tension. If the defender is struck on the back, it's considered a good sign, with the blood anointing the earth and promising bounteous harvest. The aggressor and defender switch roles after every whiplash, with a new pair stepping up after four strikes.

ROSSIAGUNG/SHUTTERSTOCK

Wae Rebo

Wander to Wae Rebo

Visit a traditional Manggarai village

The most intact of traditional Manggarai villages, **Wae Rebo** is only accessed on foot, via a 5km hike from the **trailhead** at the end of a cratered narrow road leading north from the village of Denge. The footpath climbs relentlessly up the jungle-covered mountain slope for around 3km before the greenery opens up and you catch a glimpse of the valley, Denge's tin roofs and the blue of the Savu Sea. Shortly thereafter, past the lookout tower from which you glimpse the cone-shaped houses of your destination, the trail flattens out and you descend gently to the clearing, with robusta coffee thickets, banana trees and taro plants signifying human habitation, before the much-photographed clearing with its horseshoe of conical houses comes into view.

Sitting on the woven mat of the main house, you take in the hearth in the centre, the smoke from the cooking permeating the interior; the curtained-off living quarters – one room per each of the eight families that live here – and the ceremonial gongs. You're welcome to wander around, taking in village life – children playing amid darting chickens, women pounding husks of rice in giant pestles, men returning from their plots of land come sundown. The only place that's off-limits is the raised ceremonial ground in the centre, where ritual sacrifices are made.

EATING IN LABUAN BAJO: OUR PICKS

La Cucina: Popular Italian-owned spot reminiscent of an authentic trattoria, with handmade pasta and a long list of pizzas. *7am-11pm* $$

Buso Izakaya: Authentic Japanese food and creative cocktails in gorgeous interiors that open up onto a jetty. *5-11pm* $$

Pasar Malam: Smoky, lamp-lit waterfront stalls cook up fresh fish, prawns, squid and crab from sunset on. Wash it down with BYO Bintang. *6-11pm* $$

Taman Laut Handayani: Fish steamed in banana leaf and seafood dishes served with a side of sunset views await at this lofty outdoor restaurant. *10am-10pm* $$

The hike is best made early in the morning before the heat; simple meals of rice, cassava, tempeh and vegetables can be arranged through your guide, and you can stay overnight on a mattress on the floor in the *mbaru tembong* (traditional house) turned guesthouse *(per night incl meals 500,000Rp)*, or retrace your steps before sunset. Hire guides via guesthouses in Denge or bring them with you from Labuan Bajo or Ruteng.

Summit Gunung Inerie

Tackle Flores' highest volcano

A breathtakingly beautiful, spectacularly jagged cone of a volcano looming above Bajawa, **Gunung Inerie** (2245m), 10km south of town, throws down a gauntlet to intrepid would-be climbers. The ascent is relentless but not quite as daunting as the steep sides suggest. Guided ascents are possible outside the wetter months; with an English-speaking guide and transport from Bajawa, expect to pay about 1,000,000Rp for one and 1,200,000Rp for two people. Bring plenty of water and a sun hat, since beyond the sparse eucalyptus forest at the volcano's base, the cone is shadeless. Beyond the treeline, you zigzag up its north flank to the summit; many guides prefer to do the ascent in the predawn dark, starting around 3am and arriving in time for sunrise. Depending on your fitness levels, the round-trip hike takes roughly seven hours.

Explore Bajawa's Traditional Villages

Immerse yourself in Ngada culture

Perched at 1100m above sea level, framed by forested volcanoes and blessed with a cooler climate, **Bajawa** is a laid-back, predominantly Catholic hill town, and a great base from which to explore dozens of surrounding Ngada villages.

One of the most traditional is **Bena**, resting on the flank of Gunung Inerie, 19km south of Bajawa *(return trip by ojek 120,000Rp)*. Though all villagers are now officially Catholic, traditional beliefs and customs endure. Sacrifices are held three times each year, and village elders still talk about a rigidly enforced caste system that prevented 'mixed' relationships, with those defying the *adat* (traditional law) facing serious consequences.

Bena is home to nine clans, and its houses with high, thatched roofs line up in two rows on a ridge. They're interspersed with ancestral totems, including megalithic tombs, *ngadhu* (thatched parasol-like structures – the bases of which are

THE NGADA PEOPLE

More than 60,000 Ngada people inhabit the upland Bajawa plateau and the slopes around **Gunung Inerie**. Most practise a fusion of animism and Christianity, worshipping Gae Dewa, a god who unites Dewa Zeta (the heavens) and Nitu Sale (the earth). The Ngada are matrilineal, meaning that kinship passes through the female line.

The most evident symbols of Ngada traditions are the pairs of *ngadhu* (male) and *bhaga* (female) structures, each associated with a particular family within a village. Some structures were built over 100 years ago to commemorate ancestors killed in battle. The *ngadhu* is a parasol-like structure about 3m high, consisting of a carved wooden pole and thatched 'roof', while the *bhaga* is a miniature thatched-roof house.

EATING IN LABUAN BAJO: OUR PICKS

Copper Bonnet Bistro: Come for the meze, noodle bowls, Cobb salad and BBQ ribs and linger over craft beer on the terrace. *8am-11pm* $$

Komodough Artisan Bakery & Coffee: A cosy bakery serving a range of pastries, cakes and hot and cold drinks, perfect for breakfast or a light lunch. *6am-10pm* $$

Alma: Mediterranean fare with tapas and plenty of fresh seafood options, with harbour views. *8am-11pm* $$

Le Bajo Flores: Grilled meats and seafood, burgers and pasta in this all-day eating spot right on the jetty. *11am-11pm* $$

SPIDERWEB RICEFIELDS

Scramble to the viewpoint *(25,000Rp)* up the hill near Cara village, 20km west of Ruteng, and an extraordinary sight awaits: vast **ricefields** in the shape of spiderwebs.

This is the last surviving vestige on Flores of the traditional communal agriculture of the Manggarai, whereby the *lingko* (land) is divided by the village headman among the village's families. During the allocation of each segment, a buffalo sacrifice takes place at the *lodok* (ceremonial ground) in the centre of the web.

The more resources the family has, the bigger its slice of the web, with choice sections owned by the headman's family. When the head of a family dies, the land segment is re-allocated.

splattered with animal blood from sacrifices), *bhaga* (miniature thatched-roof houses), and small sacred houses where significant relics are kept. Most houses have male or female figurines on the roofs, while doorways are decorated with buffalo horns and pig jawbones – more remnants of ritual sacrifice. Look out for wood carvings at the base of each house: roosters symbolise greatness; horses, hard work and abundant harvest; while serpents protect the inhabitants from evil powers.

After paying the entrance fee *(25,000Rp)* you're given a purple scarf to wear for the duration of your visit, and as you walk around, you'll see cash crops of cloves, vanilla pods and candlenut drying on the ground. It's possible to stay the night for 150,000Rp per person, which includes meals of boiled cassava and banana, but if you want a more intimate experience, walk several hundred metres uphill to the village of **Luba**.

Luba is home to four welcoming clans, a baker's dozen of houses and a handful of Catholic graves silhouetted against Gunung Inerie. You'll see four *ngadhu* and *bhaga*, and houses decorated with depictions of symbolic horses, buffalo and snakes. Leave a donation of 25,000Rp.

Alternatively, a mere 4km trek from Bena, or a short drive south via Gurusina, brings you to **Tololela**, a seldom-visited Ngada settlement *(donation per person 25,000Rp)* consisting of three linked traditional villages.

Soak in the Hot Springs

Bajawa's mineral waters

Unofficially staffed by friendly locals and featuring basic changing rooms, the natural **Air Panas Malanage** hot springs *(20,000Rp)* are 6km south of **Bena** (p297). At the base of one of the many volcanoes in the area, two streams – one hot (up to 50°C), one cold – mix together in a temperate stream. Soak amid the greenery-covered boulders and flitting dragonflies, and don't be surprised if you're joined by locals who take the opportunity to wash their clothes while they bathe.

If you're making the journey from Bajawa to Riung along the rough road northeast of town, **Air Panas Soa** *(10,000Rp)* is another option. The most-serviced hot springs in the region consist of two manufactured pools (one an invigorating 45°C; the other a more pedestrian 35°C to 40°C) and one natural pool (25°C to 30°C), and can get rather busy, particularly on weekends.

EATING IN RUTENG & BAJAWA: OUR PICKS

Café Agape: Simple but homey place in Ruteng selling a mix of Western and Indonesian meals, snacks and desserts. *8am-9pm* $

Spring Hill Restaurant: Indonesian classics with vegetarian options, set among beautiful gardens in Ruteng. *11.30am-9pm Mon-Sat, 8.30am-9pm Sun* $$

Milonari Restaurant: Tempeh and tofu dishes alongside chicken and rice combos, sweet-and-sour fish, good coffee and pancakes. In Bajawa. *9am-10pm Mon-Sat* $

Kartini Restaurant: Extensive menu of Western and Indonesian dishes with generous portions and outdoor seating, next to a park in Bajawa. *10am-10pm* $$

EDUARDO CABANAS/SHUTTERSTOCK

Fruit bats, Seventeen Islands Marine Park

Snorkel the Seventeen Islands

Boat-tripping off Flores' north coast

Lapped at by turquoise waters and fringed with white-sand beaches, the 23 islands that make up the misnamed **Seventeen Islands Marine Park** (government authorities decided on the number 17 as a convenient tie-in with Indonesia's Independence Day, 17 August) are a worthwhile detour. The park is accessed via a three-hour bumpy drive from Boawae, or a four-hour bone-shaking bus ride via a bumpy (but improving) road from Bajawa, or a four-hour bus journey along an arid coastal road from Ende to the laid-back, coconut-fringed little fishing town of Riung – the islands' gateway.

Standard day trips tend to include lunch, snorkelling and four island stops, the first almost always being the mangrove-fringed **Pulau Ontoloe**, home to a massive colony of fruit bats and a few Komodo dragons. This is typically followed by snorkelling over the shallow reef near **Pulau Tiga**, **Pulau Laingjawa** and **Pulau Bakau** – the park's coral was impacted by the El Niño bleaching of 2002, so there are patches where the reef hasn't recovered. However, the visibility is up to 15m, and you're likely to spot a variety of reef denizens, from parrotfish and clownfish to the venomous lionfish. Stops on **Pulau Rutong** (for the viewpoint) and **Pulau Tembang** (for picture-perfect white sand) are also popular.

BIRD-WATCHING IN FLORES & BEYOND

Clichéd as it may be to say this, the Lesser Sunda Islands are a bird-watcher's paradise, with hundreds of feathered species spotted across varied habitats, including over 70 endemics – some very rare.

Yovie Jehabut *(jagarimba.id)* is a well-regarded Flores-based bird-watching guide who specialises in custom-made trips in the Wallacea bioregion (Lesser Sunda Islands, Sulawesi and Maluku).

He can arrange itineraries to suit you, whether you want to scour the Flores lowlands for the Flores crow, the Flores green pigeon and the critically endangered Flores hawk eagle, hunt for the Timor friarbird and Timor figbird in woodlands near Kupang, or spot Sumba's apricot-breasted sunbird and the Greater Sumba boobook by night in Langgiliru National Park.

EATING IN MONI & ENDE: OUR PICKS

Mopi's Place: Start the day in Moni with local coffee, then come back for live reggae, *tapa kolo* (coconut rice) and *arak* cocktails. *hours vary* $$

Good Moni: With a friendly chef-owner and misty hill views, this open-air restaurant does Indonesian staples and the Moni potato croquette. *8am-9pm* $

Istana Sehat: Fresh and healthy local and Indonesian dishes, plus freshly caught seafood, with views of the beach in Ende. *6am-10pm* $

Pari Koro Resto: Free-range chicken rubs shoulders with sauteed pumpkin shoots and water spinach with papaya flower. In Ende. *10am-10pm Mon-Sat, to 11pm Sun* $$

IKAT TEXTILES

Ikat textiles are not just for aesthetic appeal – they hold cultural significance across Flores and other islands in Nusa Tenggara. These fabrics are used in everyday life and always present at births, weddings and funerals. They're often used as dowry, with exclusive types of ikat such as *kikir kobar* priced at the same amount as a horse.

In the past, the motifs indicated status and social ranking. The *patola* ikat (introduced to Flores by Gujarati traders) could only be worn by nobility or community leaders. It's common for old and sacred ikat cloths to be passed down as family heirlooms through generations. The women of the village are responsible for creating ikat textiles – girls start learning as young as 10 years old.

To arrange your boat trip, hang out by the boat dock, where in high season you're likely to find fellow travellers to split day-trip fares with. Prices depend on how many people you're with, but the going rate is between 600,000Rp and 800,000Rp for a boat, which includes a guide, snorkelling gear and lunch. Alternatively, organise a guide via your guesthouse; Al Itchan, owner of **Café Del Mar**, comes recommended. Before going to the islands, sign in and pay the 100,000Rp per person entrance fee at a separate booth by the dock.

Take the Ikat Trail to Moni & Ende

Go in search of fine textiles

The mountain villages east (around Jopu) and northeast (around Lio) of the gritty port town of Ende – and around the appealing mountain town of Moni, which is fringed by ricefields and greenery-clad volcanic peaks – are still renowned for their ikat and sarong weavings, with distinctive regional patterns of triangular motifs made of continuous lines. In Ende, a block inland from the waterfront, visit the daily **ikat market**, where there's a good selection of ikat from the region and beyond; bargaining is acceptable. Alternatively, catch an *ojek* up the rough road from Ende to the village of **Wolotopo** to observe the weaving process right in front of weavers' houses and buy directly from the source.

Accessed from Moni, weaving is practised in the villages of Koanara, Jopu and further afield, in Wolonjita and Nggela. A 10-minute drive through the rice paddies south of Moni gets you to **Koanara**, with the vivid purples, oranges and electric blues of ikat cloth hanging by the roadside and weavers working their looms.

Visit Sa'o Ria

Delve into Lio culture

A mere 10 minutes' drive south of Moni is the village of **Sa'o Ria**, just up from the bend in the road overhung by a giant ficus tree. There, you'll be able to see its *rumah adat* (traditional house) with the traditional thatched roof. If you're lucky, the headman's effusive wife, Maria, will welcome you inside the house; only other Lio headmen, their wives and visitors from outside the Lio culture are granted entry (a 20,000Rp donation is appropriate). You'll step inside the tiny doorway, decorated with intricate carvings, and sit on the springy bamboo floor inside the smoky interior while your guide translates stories of local traditions.

EATING IN RIUNG: OUR PICKS

Café Rico Rico: Grilled fish with punchy tomato sambal is the standout at this casual pier-side spot. Live music some nights, and snorkelling trips arranged. *8am-10pm* $

Pato Resto: Hoover up fried noodles with vegetables, aubergine with tomato sauce and fried squid washed down with banana juice. *7am-midnight* $

Café Del Mar: Dine on grilled catch-of-the-day with *cah kangkung* (garlicky water spinach) and arrange your snorkelling trips. *6am-11pm* $

Rutong Café: Barbecued fish, chicken satay and an array of vegetable and noodle dishes really shine with Simeon's special sambal. *8am-midnight* $$

FLORES ROAD TRIP FROM TIP TO TOE

Discover the best of Flores' villages, highlands and coastal scenery on this island-wide road trip along the scenic Trans-Flores Hwy.

START	END	LENGTH
Labuan Bajo	Larantuka	787km; 1 week

Begin in ❶ **Labuan Bajo**, a harbour town where explorations of **Komodo National Park** (p306) begin. A four-hour drive through jungled hills bring you to ❷ **Ruteng**, a highland market town ideal for visiting the **Liang Bua Cave** (p293) and detouring to **Wae Rebo** (p296). Heading east, pass a viewpoint overlooking terraced ricefields before the road skirts the coast at ❸ **Aimere**, home to several *arak* distilleries, while the volcanic cone of **Gunung Inerie** (p297; 2245m) comes into view. Ignore the hairpin bends leading directly to Bajawa, and skirt the volcano along the occasionally bumpy coastal road, via the village of ❹ **Bena** (p297), to approach ❺ **Bajawa** (p297). Detour north to ❻ **Riung** to snorkel and island-hop in the **Seventeen Islands Marine Park** (p299) before driving along the northern coast and back south through banana plantations. The scenic coastal road brings you to ❼ **Ende**, a muggy market town, with the cones of Gunung Meja and Gunung Iya looming above. Head up forested hills to reach ❽ **Moni**, gateway to **Gunung Kelimutu** (p302) and ikat-weaving villages. Passing a string of beautiful white-sand beaches at ❾ **Paga**, detour to ❿ **Sikka**, one of Flores's first Portuguese settlements, before proceeding to ⓫ **Maumere**, an urban hub backed by layered hills. A three-hour drive brings you to the port of ⓬ **Larantuka**, from which you can sail to West Timor or the Alor Archipelago.

Larantuka also has a small airport with flights to West Timor.

Take a 45-minute drive from **Aimere** to Kampung Adat Belaraghi for a wonderful, non-touristy traditional village.

Get incredible sunrise and sunset views of Gunung Inerie from Wolo Bobo peak, a half-hour drive south from **Bajawa**.

THE ART OF *ARAK* DISTILLATION

Approaching Aimere from the west, you'll pass **Sopi Lontar Aimere**, an *arak* distillery, marked by a display of plastic bottles containing different-coloured liquid – not to be confused with other displays of plastic bottles sold by the roadside (petrol = '*arak* for motorbike').

Coastal *arak* is made from the sap of a particular palm tree, with men scaling the tree and attaching a bucket for five days. On day six, the bucket is retrieved and stored in plastic vats to ferment.

The resulting juice is distilled over a wood fire, with the clear liquid slowly dripping through a bamboo pipe. The first dripping is the most potent (up to 50%) while the second and third go from 30% to 20%.

LEE RISAR/SHUTTERSTOCK

The Gavi ceremony, which accompanies the beginning of planting season in October, sees 1000 Lio from other villages come to Sa'o Ria. There are four days of dancing, imbibing of *arak* (colourless, distilled palm wine), and buffalo sacrifice. The hearts of the buffalo are cooked in the *rumah adat* and placed onto a sacred woven platform as an offering to the spirits. After the four days, the hearts mysteriously disappear. After the harvest in April, there's a two-day thanksgiving ceremony, accompanied by a pig sacrifice and the consumption of yellow rice.

Marvel at Multicoloured Lakes

Summit Indonesia's unique volcano

Waking up at 4am, you either hop on the motorbike for the solo hour-long ride from Moni to the car park near the top of **Kelimutu volcano** (1639m), or you're driven there by your guide which can be arranged through your accommodation in Moni. Pay the fee at the ticket booth at the park entrance *(weekdays/weekends 150,000/225,000Rp)*. A gentle 15-minute ramble along the pine-fringed slope followed by a climb up some steps brings you to **Inspiration Point** at the summit. This is the most common route, but if you're hiking the full loop it can take up to 8½ hours.

As the first rays of the sun crest Kelimutu's western rim, filtering mist into the sky and revealing three deep volcanic lakes, there's a collective gasp of wonder from the shivering crowd.

A sacred and extinct volcano, Kelimutu is the centrepiece of the mountainous, jungle-clad national park of the same

Kelimutu volcano

name. It is sacred to the local Lio people, who believe the souls of the dead migrate here. Young people's souls go to the warmth of **Tiwu Koo Fai Nuwa Muri** (Teal Lake); old people's souls to the cold of **Tiwu Ata Bupu** (Royal Blue Lake); and those of the wicked to **Tiwu Ata Polo** (Black Lake). If you happen to be up the volcano on 14 August, you'll witness the exuberant dancing on Lio ceremonial grounds en route to the summit – part of the annual 'Feed the Spirits of the Forefathers' ceremony, after which pork, betel nuts, rice and other valuable offerings will be left on ceremonial rocks beside the lakes. Alert your guide if you have dreams about the sacred lakes prior to your ascent – apparently, siren-like spirits have lured people to their demise, which can be avoided if the right prayers and offerings are made. Resist temptation from these will-o'-the-wisps, and don't stray beyond the two official lookouts – several hikers have perished after slipping on the loose scree.

A pre-dawn visit to Kelimutu is not the meditative, tranquil experience you may be hoping for, since it's when you'll encounter the biggest crowds. There's a risk of clouds rolling in later on, but on a fine day, you'll find Kelimutu's summit empty and peaceful, and when the sun is high, the lakes really sparkle.

On the way down, take the shortcut (you'll need to ask locals for directions) down to Moni through steep, scenic copses of eucalyptus, and through farmland rich in banana, taro and vanilla, until you reach a gorgeous waterfall and dipping pool right below the road running through Moni. Budget half a day for the 15-minute ramble up, or a full day for the full loop.

Beyond Flores

Head west of Labuan Bajo for primeval monster encounters or further west to Sumbawa for monster waves.

GETTING AROUND

There's fierce competition among Labuan Bajo's boat operators and diving outfits for day and multiday trips to Komodo National Park.

Group day trips by speedboat cost from 1,350,000Rp per person and allow for more time at each location than the cheaper slow boats.

Multiday liveaboards cater to divers and explorers. Rinca Island is accessible by private boat only *(from 1,500,000Rp)*. Fly to Bima (Sumbawa) to catch a bus to Hu'u, or take a taxi from Bima *(1,000,000Rp)* directly to Pantai Lakey.

Arguably the single biggest reason to come to Labuan Bajo is the chance to visit Komodo National Park, centred on Komodo Island and the main home of the fearsome *ora* (Komodo dragon), the world's largest monitor lizard. Dragon sightings are also common on the smaller Rinca Island, though since Rinca has been 'tamed' in recent times for cruise-ship visitors, it has become far less popular with Labuan Bajo crowds. West of Flores, the large conservative island of Sumbawa is full of natural beauty with untouched beaches and desert islands. It's never been a big tourist destination and continues to fly under the radar, save for in-the-know surfers who come for the island's powerful breaks and uncrowded waves.

Sumbawa

TIME FROM FLORES: **1HR**

Ride the waves in Sumbawa

Hollow tubes break on the reefs of the white-sand **Pantai Lakey**, attracting international championship surfers year-round. The most consistent swell is between June and August. **Lakey Peak** and **Lakey Pipe** are hallowed names, both within easy paddling distance of Lakey's string of modest beach guesthouses, all linked by a sandy path studded with bars. From August to October, the wind gusts, which turns Pantai Lakey into Indonesia's best kitesurfing destination. Firman is a great surf instructor who offers group and private lessons *(WhatsApp +62 823 4125 6400; group/private lessons 500,000/750,000Rp)*.

MAKIKISS/SHUTTERSTOCK

Pantai Lakey, Sumbawa

Grounded by reef, the A-frame Lakey Peak is the wave here, right in front of the famous tower; it's for experienced surfers only. Next to it, Lakey Pipe is a nice left-hander, best at mid-to-high tide. A five-minute drive from Lakey, less crowded **Cobblestones** is a left- and right-hander break; the gentler right-hander is good for beginners.

A short paddle from the shore, 15 minutes from Lakey, **Periscope** is a steep right-hander barrel reef-break. A similar distance away, left- and right-hander **Nangadoro** is worth seeking out at high tide, while **Nungas**, a long left-hander reef break near Lakey, is gentler than Peak or Pipe and best at low-to-mid tide, with killer sunsets from the beach.

MUNDOSEMFIM/SHUTTERSTOCK

Pulau Padar

TOP EXPERIENCE

Komodo National Park

Most visitors to Labuan Bajo have dragons on their mind. To see the world's largest lizards in their most spectacular setting, head to Komodo National Park. The best way of getting around the park is a boat trip, with most Labuan Bajo operators running a standard day trip to Komodo, either via speedboat or slow boat, and stopping in the same six locations.

DON'T MISS

- Pulau Padar
- Pulau Komodo
- Pulau Rinca
- Snorkelling
- Scuba diving
- Kayaking

Pulau Padar

The first stop on a boat trip around the park is typically the compact, vertiginous **Pulau Padar**. A steep 15-minute hike brings you to the highest of a series of viewpoints, from which you can admire the volcanic island's scalloped bays fringed with white sand, the island's mountainous spine and the surrounding marine panorama. Next up is swimming and sunbathing on one of the national park's pink-sand beaches, on the far side of Pulau Padar.

PRACTICALITIES

● komodonationalpark.org ● park entrance per day 350,000Rp; drone permit per day 2,000,000Rp ● 6am-6pm

SONY HERDIANA/SHUTTERSTOCK

Komodo dragons, Pulau Komodo

Pulau Komodo

A short boat ride away, **Pulau Komodo** awaits, its steep hillsides lush with greenery in the short wet season (December to March) and frazzled by sun to a rusty tan that makes its crystal waters pop the rest of the year. Ashore, you are paired with a ranger armed with a forked staff for keeping dragons at bay. The 1,355,000Rp entrance fee includes a choice of three walks: the short walk (1.5km, 45 minutes), which includes a stop at an artificial waterhole that attracts diminutive local deer, wild boar and of course *ora* (Komodo dragons); the medium walk (2km, 1½ hours), which includes a hill with sweeping views and a chance to see colourful cockatoos; and the long walk (4km, two hours), which includes the features of the shorter hikes and distances you from peak-season crowds.

Most boat trips also include a stop on **Pantai Merah** (Pink Beach), which gets its rosy hue from the shells of tiny marine organisms.

Pulau Rinca

After sailing past dramatically hilly, sparsely forested islets and islands, you'll arrive at the arid **Pulau Rinca**, where you're greeted with a larger-than-life statue of two Komodo dragons engaged in mortal combat.

A five-minute stroll along the wheelchair-accessible wooden boardwalk with a mandatory ranger accompaniment brings you to the excellent museum, with its detailed information on Komodo dragons, and the terrestrial and marine fauna of the national park. Directly behind the museum, you're likely to find Komodo dragons resting under the trees in the daytime heat. Get here early in the day to observe them at their most active. Besides dragons, you may see tiny Timor deer, snakes, monkeys, wild boar and birds.

DRAGON-SPOTTING

At Komodo and Rinca, your odds of seeing dragons are very good, with the exception of mating season on Komodo (June and July), when females go into hiding and males spread out on the vast island trying to find them. Peak months for sightings are September to December, when both sexes are out and about. Mating season is less of a problem at Rinca, where the dragons hang around near the museum.

TOP TIPS

- Avoid visiting the dragons during menstruation, as they can smell blood from 5 miles away.
- Stick to designated safe zones and don't go wandering by yourself – always stay with your group.
- Don't make any loud noises or sudden movements when near the dragons.
- There's not a lot of shade on the islands, so bring sun protection.
- The terrain can be uneven, so wear sturdy shoes and comfortable clothing.
- Bring cash as there are souvenir stands on the islands.
- Do not touch or step on the corals when snorkelling and scuba diving.

FUN FACTS ABOUT KOMODO DRAGONS

Believed to have originated in Australia four million years ago, Komodo dragons reside on Komodo and Rinca, and parts of north and west Flores. One toxin-loaded bite from these dragons promotes bleeding that slowly kills its prey. Komodos can eat up to 80% of their body weight in a single sitting, before retiring for up to a month to digest. An estimated 5000 dragons live in the wild today, but only a few hundred or so are egg-laying females.

Long walks or overnight stays on Rinca are no longer permitted. On request, the ranger can lead you through the mangroves and up a steep, barren slope for spectacular panoramic views of the bay.

Snorkelling

After lunch, the boat makes a snorkelling stop at the spectacular **Taka Makassar** with its diversity of healthy coral, vast shoals of reef fish and frequent sightings of sea turtles and other pelagic life. Next, you head to **Karang Makassar** (Manta Point) in search of manta rays – often reliably present. The final stop is the rather anticlimactic **Pulau Kanawa** for more snorkelling. If you have more time, a rewarding way of experiencing Komodo National Park is via three-day, two-night liveaboard boat trips, offered by some operators such as **Kanha Liveaboard** *(kanhaliveaboard.com; from 3,750,000Rp)*. Most dive companies have liveaboard options, too. A three-day trip takes in all the day trip's highlights plus less-visited spots, such as the small uninhabited **Siaba**, **Kalong** and **Bidadari** islands – excellent for snorkelling. It also means beating the crowds to Padar's viewpoint in the morning, and visiting Komodo Island earlier, when the dragons are more active.

Kayaking

Komodo Kayaking *(komodokayaking.com; 2/3 day US$590/890)* – the only Indonesian kayaking operator in Labuan Bajo – offers an active, eco-friendly way of exploring

SERGEUWPHOTO/SHUTTERSTOCK

Scuba diving with sea turtles

the park that includes dining in beachside safari tents in the evening and paddling along the coastlines of various islands during the day, stopping to snorkel and occasionally catching a glimpse of the dragons – excellent swimmers – in the water.

Scuba Diving

Komodo's submerged seamounts make for an incredible diving experience, with several dozen dive sites dotted around the national park's islands. Its vibrant, exceptionally diverse reefs teem with life and are haunted by manta rays, reef sharks and turtles; visibility is excellent.

The challenging underwater topography, combined with strong, unpredictable currents, means that some of the top diving sites are for experienced divers only, though there are calmer spots for beginners. There's tremendous competition for divers in Labuan Bajo, with dozens of scuba-diving operators based there; you can also opt for a multiday liveaboard for a more tranquil experience away from diving day-trippers. Look out for the 'DOCK' (Dive Operators Community Komodo) sticker in the window of the most conservation-minded of the diving outfits; they actively combat dynamite fishing and other harmful practices. Some also have programmes that hire and train locals and turn them into conservation ambassadors.

The best place to see Komodo's manta rays is **Karang Makassar** (Manta Point), a shallow (12m max) drift dive along a sloping rubble reed. It's a manta cleaning station and a popular feeding spot when the water is plankton-rich.

Off Pulau Komodo's northern side, **Castle Rock** is a submerged seamount, well known for its intense currents and encounters with grey, whitetip and blacktip reef sharks, as well as schooling jacks, giant trevally, tuna and huge schools of fusiliers. Another terrific site for huge shoals of fish is **Batu Bolong** – for experienced divers only due to the currents – with the shallows on the lee side of the pinnacle thick with damselfish, fairy basslets, Moorish idols, large sweetlips and sheltering lionfish, while the deep blue teems with Spanish mackerel, surgeonfish and red-toothed triggerfish.

Near Pulau Seraya Besar, **Sabolan Kecil** is great for macro diving and for beginners, with batfish, seahorses, scorpion fish and blue-spotted stingrays spotted among the gorgonian fans and barrel sponges of the sloping coral reef and sand below. The white-sand bottom of the reef on the north side of **Pulau Sebayur** (halfway between Komodo and Flores) attracts eagle rays, while the reef's ledges and overhangs house cleaner shrimp and glassfish, with hairy squat lobsters spotted between the sponge and barrel corals, and emperor fish and groupers cruising by.

LABUAN BAJO'S BEST DIVING OPERATORS

Wunderpus Liveaboard *(wunderpusliveaboard.com)* Diving and snorkelling liveaboard operator offering three- to seven-day trips, focusing on small groups, environmentally conscious tours and uncrowded dive sites.

Manta Rhei *(mantarhei.com)* Specialises in themed day trips and PADI courses. Nitrox dives and liveaboards also available.

Uber Scuba Komodo *(uberscubakomodo.com)* Offers a range of day and multiday dives, liveaboard trips and SSI courses. Also offers trips combining diving and komodo dragon visits.

Neren Diving Komodo *(nerendivingkomodo.net)* Dive centre with a focus on conservation, offering courses, daily fun dive trips plus dragon-spotting on Rinca.

Scuba Junkie Komodo *(scubajunkiekomodo.com)* Excellent range of diving and snorkelling outings, liveaboard experiences and PADI courses.

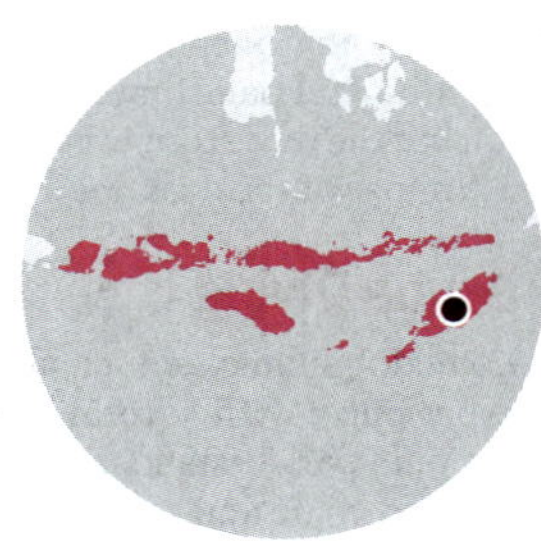

West Timor

TRADITIONAL CULTURE | IKAT | CAVE DIVING

GETTING AROUND

Bemos reach most of Kupang's spread-out attractions. A ride costs 5000Rp; clap loudly when you want to stop. Useful routes include 1 & 2 Kuanino–Oepura (past popular hotels); 5 Oebobo–Airnona–Bakunase (past the main post office) and 10 Kelapa Lima–Walikota (Terminal Kota, the Oebobo bus terminal and the Museum Nusa Tenggara Timur).

Hotels rent motorbikes and scooters for 100,000Rp per day. Buses from **Terminal Oebobo** (bus terminal), 7km from the airport, run to Soe (three hours), Kefamenanu (5½ hours) and Atambua (12 hours). You can rent a car and driver from 800,000Rp to 1,000,000Rp per day.

Fringed by vast, rice-growing plains and white-sand beaches, the greenery-clad hills and deep valleys of West Timor are as beguiling as the island's inhabitants. Smile at someone, and you're likely to get a smile in return, often with teeth stained a vampire-red from betel nut – an integral part of indigenous culture here.

It was the island's natural wealth of sandalwood that brought the Portuguese here in the early 1500s, followed by the Dutch and missionaries from both countries, who've been largely successful in Christianising the local population. Nonetheless, West Timor's ruggedly mountainous, *lontar*-palm-studded topography and centuries-old division into independent, warring kingdoms has made it possible for animist traditions to persist, alongside 14 different languages and tribal dialects. After leaving the music-thumping bemos (minibuses) of the capital Kupang, you enter the less-visited world of beehive-hut villages, whose chiefs preserve *adat* and whose artisans produce exquisite ikat.

Revel in the Sweet Sounds of Sasando

Mastering a Rotinese string instrument

Heading towards Soe, pull up outside **Tempat Pembuatan Sasando** in Oebelo and step inside. A young man clad in a *ti'i langga* (*lontar*-leaf hat with a centre plume) – traditional headgear from the island of Rote – will treat you to an unforgettable musical repertoire as his hands fly deftly over the strings of the *sasando*, Rote's traditional 32-string zither that sounds like a cross between a harp, a piano and steel pans. Used by the Rote islanders since the 17th century (though the original had bamboo or civet-gut strings rather than metal ones), the *sasando* is crafted from bamboo and teak, with a foldable palm leaf 'sail' for resonance. After the son of locally renowned Rotinese musician Pak Pah finishes

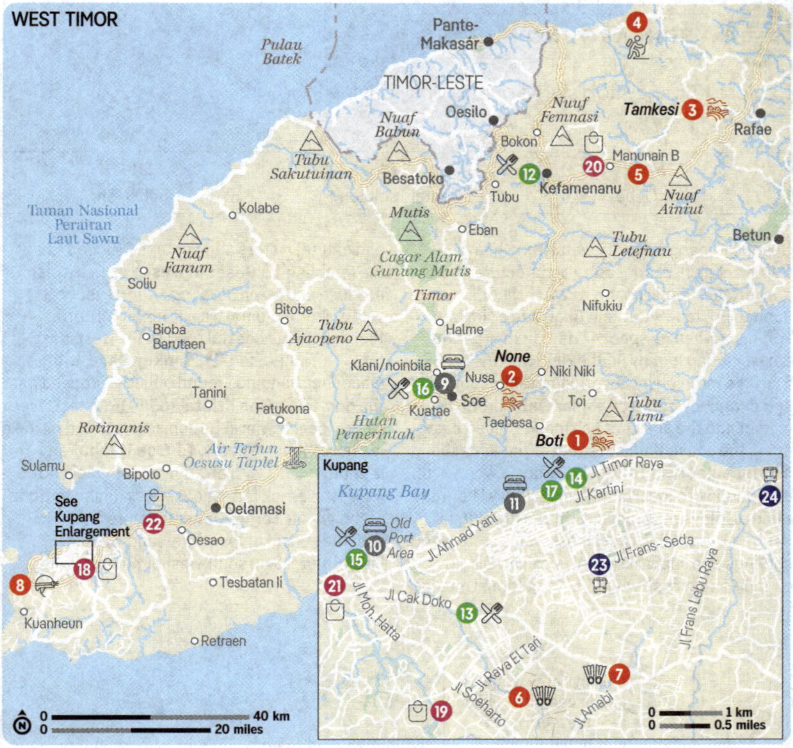

WEST TIMOR

HIGHLIGHTS
1 Boti
2 None
3 Tamkesi

SIGHTS
4 Oepuah
5 Tapenpah

ACTIVITIES
6 Cendana Dive
7 Dive Kupang Dive
8 Goa Kristal
see 8 Goa Uihani

SLEEPING
9 Dena Hotel
10 Lavalon Hostel
11 Sotis Hotel

EATING
12 Bekhaus
13 Depot Se'i Babi Aroma
14 Kelapa Restaurant & Sky Lounge
15 Pasar Malam Seafood
see 9 RM Sari Bundo II
16 Rumah Makan Depot Remaja
see 12 Sisterhood Coffee & Eatery
17 Subasuka Paradise

SHOPPING
18 Edon Sasando Musik
see 9 Galeri Alekot
19 Ina Ndao
20 Kain Tenun Tradisional
see 20 Maubesi Market
21 Pak Haji Noer
22 Tempat Pembuatan Sasando

TRANSPORT
23 Terminal Oebobo
24 Timor Tour & Travel

serenading you, you can choose to take lessons at **Edon Sasando Musik** on the outskirts of Kupang, if you're feeling inspired. *Sasando* virtuoso Aby Edon claims that if you have a modicum of musical talent, he'll have you coaxing out a tune within a couple of hours. Not content with playing the instrument, he also designs and builds his own, from the traditional acoustic *(from 4,000,000Rp)* to electric *(8,000,000Rp)* to hybrid *(10,000,000Rp)*, just in case you'd like to take one home with you.

TOP TIP

Local guides are essential for visiting traditional villages, where Bahasa Indonesia isn't widely spoken. They can explain local traditions and customs.

A SPIN AROUND KUPANG

Explore Kupang's top sights on this easy driving tour.

START	END	LENGTH
Pasar Oeba	Pantai Tablolong	54km; 8hr

Despite Kupang's scruffy waterfront, heavy traffic and lack of endearing architecture, there is a certain chaotic charm to West Timor's capital. England's Captain Bligh had a similar epiphany when he spent 47 days here after the emasculating mutiny on the HMS *Bounty* in 1789. Start the morning by absorbing the clamour and pungency of the 1 **Pasar Oeba** produce market and the adjacent fish market. Head east along the coast, then cut south to the fantastic 2 **Museum Nusa Tenggara Timur**, a wonderful introduction to local history and cultural heritage. Amid displays of ceramics and kris (traditional daggers), you'll find ritual masks, elaborate wood carvings and superb examples of ikat. Displays on the **Pasola festival** (p325), traditional music and natural history add context. Proceed to the rambling 3 **Pasar Inpres** to browse fresh produce and buy a *ti'i langga* (*lontar*-leaf hat with a centre plume) from Rote. Head north, then follow the coastal road to the west, past the well-signposted 4 **Monkey Cave**, with macaques hanging around outside. Proceed past the port to 5 **Goa Kristal** (p315) (Crystal Cave), where locals swim in turquoise water and partake in photoshoots. Nearby, 6 **Goa Uilebahan** is another cave with an aquamarine pool and interesting rock formations. Duck inland to frolic at the 7 **Air Terjun Oenesu** before finishing with the sunset at the white-sand 8 **Pantai Tablolong**, 25km southwest of Kupang.

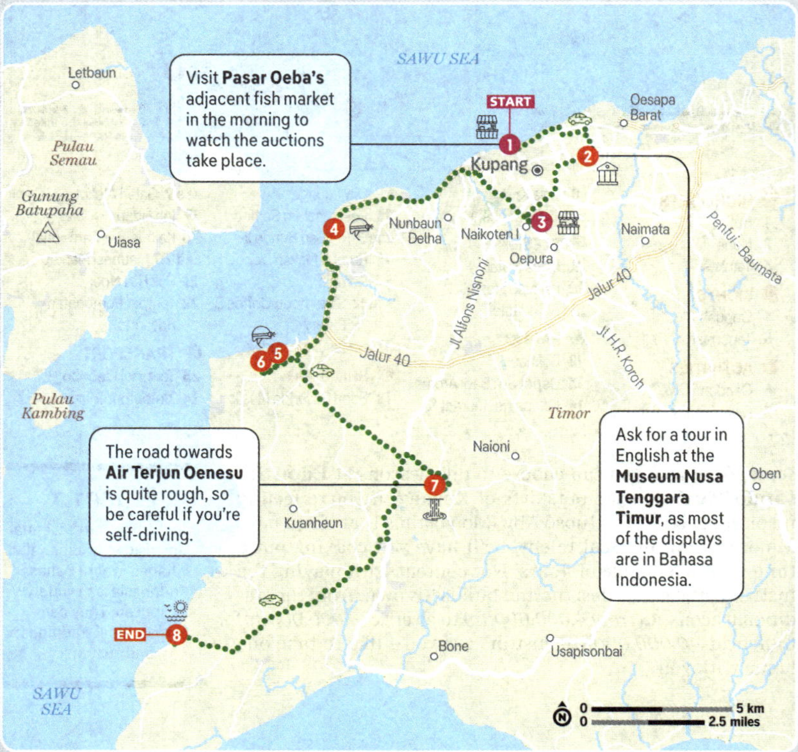

Visit **Pasar Oeba's** adjacent fish market in the morning to watch the auctions take place.

The road towards **Air Terjun Oenesu** is quite rough, so be careful if you're self-driving.

Ask for a tour in English at the **Museum Nusa Tenggara Timur**, as most of the displays are in Bahasa Indonesia.

Hang Out with (Former) Headhunters

Visit a traditional village

Near the market town of Niki-Niki, a gravel road runs for 1km past corn, pumpkin and bean fields to the village of **None**, one of the area's most compelling attractions. You'll stop by one of the *ume bubu* (beehive-shaped huts) at the roadside to greet the village chief. In some ways, this appears to be a typical Dawan village, its cramped and smoky *ume bubu* without windows and its 1m-high doorways sitting alongside modern concrete houses. At the end of the road, you reach the ceremonial grounds that end abruptly in the vine-covered sheer cliff that made the village easy to defend from enemies. It's so peaceful here that it's hard to believe they were hunting heads just two generations ago – the last conflict was in 1944.

If you have a local guide with you, they'll point out the *lopo* (village meeting place) and explain that None has a proud population of 56 families who have lived here for 10 generations and who still adhere to traditional practices.

At the cliff's edge, you'll find a 300-year-old banyan tree and totem pole where shamans once met with warriors before they left on headhunting expeditions. Nearby is a stone platform where enemy heads were once displayed. Proceed to the *ote naus*, an awning beneath which guns and spears were stored. It's here that elders consulted chicken eggs and a wooden staff before predicting if the warriors would prevail. If there was a speck of blood in the egg, a sign of poor fortune, they'd delay their attack. The village women may break out their looms as you're leaving, with weaving demonstrations upon request (a 50,000Rp donation is appropriate) and a decent selection of ikat cloth for sale.

WEST TIMOR'S FORMER HEADHUNTERS

The village of None is home to the animist Dawan people who have lived here for at least 250 years. Set atop a high promontory, its strategic location came in handy for fighting off attackers during a time when tribal wars were rife.

Headhunting among the men of the village was commonplace in this area, a way of intimidating and asserting power over other tribes. Although it's now a thing of the past, there's still a strong sense of pride among the residents of None that the village has never been conquered by rival tribes.

Drop in on Highland Royalty

Not just cats may look at a king

Some 50km northeast of Kefa, accessible via a two-hour drive along a periodically rough road and across windswept ridges, **Tamkesi** is one of West Timor's most isolated and best-preserved villages. Balancing on a jagged rock path, you pass through a keyhole between jutting limestone cliffs to find yourself in the middle of it all. There are two entrances: one is reserved for royalty but often used by travellers; the correct entrance has a sign reading 'Eno Fatnai Naimnune' on a stone platform, from which it's a short uphill walk along a cobblestone pathway under a canopy of trees.

EATING IN SOE & KEFAMENANU: OUR PICKS

RM Sari Bundo II: A typical Padang (West Sumatran cuisine) place in Soe where you can choose various sides to go with your rice. *8am-10pm* $

Bekhaus: A bakery cafe in Kefa with hot and iced coffees and teas, plus snacks like fries and chicken wings. *hours vary* $

Rumah Makan Depot Remaja: Succulent *se'i babi* (Rotinese smoked pork) and *jantung pisang* (banana-flower salad) are standouts at this spot in Soe. *10am-10pm* $$

Sisterhood Coffee & Eatery: City cafe in Kefa that serves bona fide espresso coffees, katsu sandwiches and fried rice. *11am-11pm Mon-Sat, from 1pm Sun* $$

BEST IKAT SHOPPING

West Timor is renowned for its ikat, whether sarongs decorated with complex geometric patterns or antique *kelim* (tapestries). Quality varies, as do the dyes and yarn: pricier pieces use local cotton; others use imports from China.

Maubesi Market: Sells quality ikat that a keen eye may spot.

Kain Tenun Tradisional: Stocks some truly excellent pieces that take a year to make.

Galeri Alekot: Options for all budgets; in Soe.

Ina Ndao: Sources ikat, as well as patterned espadrilles, shirts and ties; in Kupang.

Pak Haji Noer: A Kupang-based ikat expert who stocks collectors' pieces from across Nusa Tenggara, including antiques woven using ancient techniques no longer practised.

MIRZA RIFADA PRAMODYA/SHUTTERSTOCK

Goa Kristal

The house of the *raja* (king) overlooks the village, with the east and west pillars representing the male and female, respectively. Clamber up the stone steps to meet the turbaned king and his family, where you'll offer betel nut (buy it in Manufui, the last village off the main road before turning off for Tamkesi) and make a donation *(per person 50,000Rp)*. After the obligatory respectful chewing, you can take pictures of the low-slung beehive huts built into the bedrock and connected by red-clay paths that ramble to the edge of a precipice. Just don't take pictures of the conical hut where the village's sacred objects are stored, lest bad luck befall you. The same goes if you drop something; don't pick it up immediately and instead alert local villagers, who will first pray to the ancestors for forgiveness.

You can't miss the soaring, craggy limestone cliff. At least once every seven years, the king and the village elders climb the face of **Tapenpah**, sans rope, with a goat, rooster, branches of betel nut, bamboo, coconut, sugar cane and cotton. Depending on the size of the offering, this is done in multiples of seven. Other members of the community also ascend in multiples of seven. They slaughter the goat (but not the rooster), chew betel nut and only come down once everything has been eaten. This **Natamamausa** ritual is performed to give thanks for a good harvest, or to stop (or start) the rain.

EATING IN KUPANG & AROUND: OUR PICKS

Depot Se'i Babi Aroma: Contemporary Kupang chain specialising in *se'i babi*, *sate babi* (pork satay) and other porky bites. *9am-8.30pm* $

Pasar Malam Seafood: Come evening, head for this lamplit seafood market for *ikan* (fish), *cumi* (squid), *kepiting* (crab) and *udang* (prawns). *5pm-midnight* $

Subasuka Paradise: Seafood restaurant right by the sea with a huge menu and Indonesian noodles and rice dishes. *10am-10pm* $$

Kelapa Restaurant & Sky Lounge: Seaview restaurant serving steaks and Indonesian dishes, plus a swimming pool and live music. *8.30am-11pm* $$

If you want to climb the other notable rock face, **Oepuah**, enlist the help of a young villager, but only attempt it if you're a keen scrambler. The view over the village from the top, not to mention the 360-degree views, is invigorating. Tip your adventurous leader 20,000Rp.

Very little Bahasa Indonesia is spoken here, so a guide is essential. The overall mood is warm and welcoming.

MORE IKAT

To learn more about the history, techniques and meaning behind Indonesia's famed woven cloth, ikat, turn to page 300.

Kupang's Underwater World

Indonesia's only freshwater cave diving

While West Timor's dive sites cannot compete with Alor, its lack of currents do make them beginner-friendly. Kupang is also the only place in Indonesia to offer freshwater cave dives, in **Goa Kristal** and **Goa Uihani**, both with up to 50m visibility, limestone tunnels, narrow swim-throughs and stalactite formations. With its fossilized, shell-encrusted walls, a 75m-long channel, a submerged chamber and an air chamber, Goa Kristal is the easier dive of the two. Goa Uihani – a 500m-long sinkhole with three air chambers – is best suited to experienced cave divers, due to difficult access and narrow tunnels. Kupang's dive operators are **Dive Kupang** *(divekupangdive.com; freshwater cave dive 2,000,000Rp)* and **Cendana Dive** *(WhatsApp +62 821 4750 4428; dives from 2,000,000Rp)*.

Visit the Last King in West Timor

Explore the traditional village of Boti

A two-hour ride into the mountains from Soe via an undulating, unpaved road is the traditional village of **Boti**. Here, Ama Namah Benu, the charismatic *kepala suku* (chief), often referred to as the 'last king in West Timor', maintains the strict laws of *adat*.

Bring a guide conversant with local *adat* and the Dawan language spoken in the village. On arrival, you'll be led to the king's house, where you will offer betel nut as a gift. You'll then enjoy sweet coffee with steamed cassava cakes, served by the king's sister.

Day-trippers are expected to contribute a donation *(50,000Rp)*; staying overnight (or longer) in the simple thatched guesthouse allows you to delve deeper into the life of a village that has resisted Christianisation, whose 300 or so inhabitants still follow ancient animist rituals, and whose king has only recently allowed just one child from each family to attend primary and middle school (but not high school, to avoid the clash between mainstream education and ancestral lore). Boti's autonomy is partially due to Dutch colonial powers failing to find the village in times past.

Boti children are named after elements in their natural surroundings. The men grow their hair from an early age – similar to Rastafarians, they view it as their connection to nature. Conversely, when a woman is pregnant, she shaves

TIMOR-LESTE VISA RUN

Crossing the border to Timor-Leste is no longer complicated. It's cheapest to cross at Napan, 20km north of Kefamenanu; or Atapupu, which costs just 60,000Rp by *ojek* from Atambua.

You can also make the 12-hour, one-way journey to Dili, Timor-Leste, for 250,000Rp; arrange 4am pickup with **Timor Tour & Travel** via your lodgings.

Short on time? Catch the 45-minute morning Wings Air flight from Kupang to Atambua, cross the border, and fly back to Kupang.

Europeans from the Schengen Area may visit Timor-Leste visa-free for 30 days. Visitors from other countries are issued a visa on arrival at the border; the fee is US$30 and you must present proof of an onward journey.

WEST TIMOR'S BEST GUIDES

West Timor's traditional villages are a minefield of cultural dos and don'ts. A local guide is essential; some charge 2,000,000Rp per day.

Edwin Lerrick: The irrepressible owner of Kupang's **Lavalon Hostel** (p368) has deep regional knowledge and connections throughout West Timor. *(lavalonbar@gmail.com)*

Ony Meda: A guide with over two decades of experience organising anthropological tours and treks. *(+62 813 3940 4204)*

Willy Kadati: Willy specialises in cultural, botanic and ikat tours of West Timor. *(willdk678@gmail.com)*

Aka Nahak: Enthusiastic, Kefamenanu-based Aka has been touring Timor since 1988. *(timorguide@gmail.com)*

Yabes Olbata: Soe-based guide conversant in the Dawan language, charging 1,200,000Rp per day. *(+62 813 3894 9694)*

LEONARDUS NYOMAN/SHUTTERSTOCK

Boti (p315)

the head of her youngest daughter: a sign for the community to help out where they can. Men and women may marry outside the village, but women will be shunned if they don't bring their husbands back to live with them.

Early in the morning, you'll see the men go off to the fields to grow crops, including bananas, corn, papaya and cash crops of peanuts. The people are notoriously self-reliant, refusing government assistance (even NGO offers of food have caused offence, the implication being that outsiders think they are lazy or poor). The Boti week has nine days, with every ninth day devoted to rest, music and spiritual activities. During the day, you'll be followed around by curious children as you observe women cooking at the outdoor kitchen, going to the river to bring back bamboo 'buckets' full of water, or weaving ikat sarongs. Children as young as six are expected to help out: girls spin thread from locally grown cotton, boys tend animals. Come sundown, the men return and women serve the evening meal in coconut-shell bowls. If you pay 100,000Rp, the men may perform a traditional dance and the women may sing a haunting tune while the king strums his indigenous ukulele.

THE GRAND TOUR OF WEST TIMOR

Drive through West Timor's interiors and around its coastline to take in market towns, villages and beaches.

START	END	LENGTH
Kupang	Kupang	625km; 5 days

Begin in 1 **Kupang**, West Timor's bustling capital. Pause in 2 **Oebelo**, a small salt-mining town 22km from Kupang on the Soe road, to visit the **sasando workshop** (p310), then proceed to the cool, leafy market town of 3 **Soe**, the gateway to fascinating traditional villages. About 17km east of Soe, take the turnoff for 4 **None** (p313), a former headhunting village, before passing through the market town of 5 **Niki-Niki** – market day is Wednesday. Continue through the lush interior to 6 **Kefamenanu**, a visually unimpressive former Portuguese stronghold that's nonetheless a decent overnighter. Just 3.5km from Kefa is 7 **Maslete Village**, with a thatch-roofed *sonaf* (palace), with carvings of mythical birds. About 19km east of Kefa, 8 **Maubesi** is home to the Kefa Regency's best textile market on Thursdays. The Maubesi Art Shop, on the eastern outskirts, has a terrific selection of local ikat. Turn north 11km east to visit 9 **Tamkesi** (p313), a traditional village in a lofty setting, before retracing your steps to just north of Niki-Niki. If it's Thursday, consider making the bone-shaking detour to 10 **Ayotupas** to check out the clamour of the weekly produce market. Just south of Niki-Niki, take the minor road east into the mountains to the animist village of 11 **Boti** (p315). From Boti, descend to the stunning white-sand 12 **Pantai Kolbano**, then return to Kupang, past the dune-backed 13 **Pantai Oetune** and through West Timor's vast rice-growing plains.

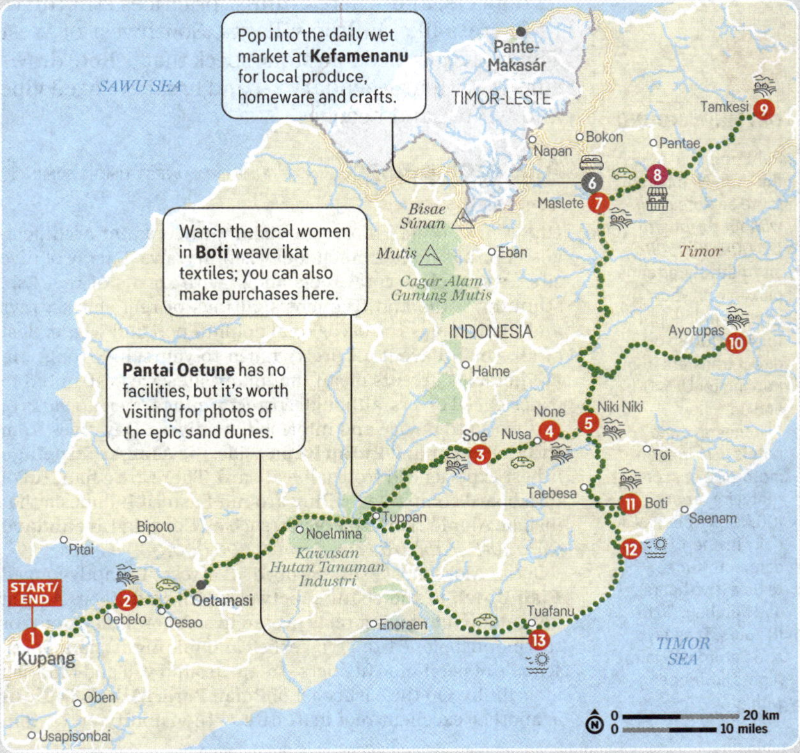

Pop into the daily wet market at **Kefamenanu** for local produce, homeware and crafts.

Watch the local women in **Boti** weave ikat textiles; you can also make purchases here.

Pantai Oetune has no facilities, but it's worth visiting for photos of the epic sand dunes.

Beyond West Timor

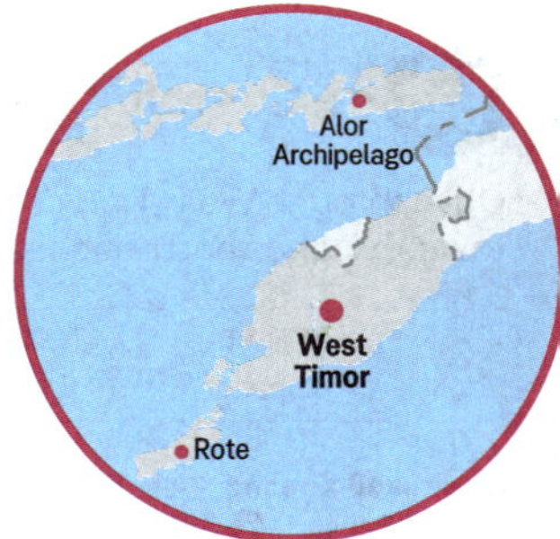

Incomparable underwater worlds, a world-renowned surf break and tiny, seldom-visited islands await, a short plane or ferry hop from Kupang.

Places

If you're a diver, you will have heard of the Alor Archipelago, north of West Timor, and its epic dive sites such as Fish Bowl and Mike's Delight. Odds are, you're heading there right now aboard a liveaboard, all set for underwater exploration, or else staying in a diving lodge on one of its islands. But there's so much more to this tiny, isolated cluster of islands, whose 134 tribes speak 18 languages and 52 dialects, and where animist practices still thrive in fortress-like, hilltop villages. Southwest of West Timor, the parched limestone speck that is Rote draws surfers with its legendary T-Land break, relaxed vibe and white-sand beaches.

GETTING AROUND

Public minibuses ply the Bo'a–Nemberala route on Rote *(with/without surfboard 120,000/70,000Rp)*; alternatively, arrange pickup with your accommodation for 450,000Rp or direct transfers from Kupang for US$100 and up.

Homestays and hotels can arrange motorbike or scooter rental for around 100,000Rp per day. A daily fast ferry (9am) connects Kupang to Bo'a (two hours) and Kalabahi (15 to 18 hours, Tuesday and Saturday). Daily flights link Kupang with Alor.

Alor Archipelago

TIME FROM WEST TIMOR: **50MIN**

Beneath the waves

One of Indonesia's most astonishing underwater archipelagos, Alor has it all: tremendous visibility, a vast array of dive sites, world-class coral reefs abuzz with shoals of reef fish, stunning walls and frequent sightings of reef sharks, rays and turtles, plus the occasional dolphin pod and whale. Best of all, you'll have it all pretty much to yourself. Strong, unpredictable currents mean that many sites are best suited to experienced divers, although correct timings open up parts of this world to novice and intermediate divers. Day dives from **Pulau Pantar** and **Pulau Kepa** aside, the **Alor Archipelago** is best experienced from a liveaboard. There are a handful of liveaboard companies sailing around Eastern Indonesia that include Alor in their itineraries, such as **Coralia Liveaboard** *(coralia-liveaboard.com; from 11,300,000Rp)*.

One of Alor's most exhilarating drift dives is the aptly-named **Fish Bowl**, in the channel between Alor and Kepa. As you float along the sloping reef covered in soft corals, look out for scorpionfish, lone titan triggerfish and midnight snappers as schools of neon-blue fusiliers stream around you and Moorish idols flit by. On the east coast of Pulau Pura, **Mike's Delight** is another excellent reef drift dive with visibility up to 40m and an abundance of hard and soft corals that are alive with parrotfish, damselfish, angelfish and Napoleon wrasse; schools of jacks, passing reef sharks and dolphin pods can be spotted in the deep blue. A stunning slope reef suitable for beginners, combined with a challenging wall dive, **Symphony No 9** off Pulau Pantar offers tremendous coral diversity and density, along with schools of damselfish and basslets, and the opportunity to be suspended beneath the overhang at 15m, scanning the fathomless depths for pelagic life. **Kal's Dream**, a seamount between Pura and Kepa, is also wonderful for passing large pelagics, barracuda, Spanish mackerel, giant trevallies and schooling jacks, with octopus, morays and shrimp hiding in the 12m-deep plateau. Strong currents sweeping over the top of the pinnacle warrant a quick descent.

Rote

TIME FROM WEST TIMOR: **2HR**

Hang ten in Nemberala

Between March and November, the consistent southwest swell brings reliable waves to the white-sand beach of the chilled-out fishing village of **Nemberala** on the west coast of Rote Island, along with a contingent of surfers.

Unlike some other Indonesian surfing hot spots, Nemberala is a friendly place, without locals guarding their favourite surf spots. Breaking at all tides, the main wave here is the legendary **T-Land**, one of Indonesia's longest left-handers, divided into the Peak, the Pyramid and the Mountain (accessible to surfers of different abilities). Nearby is the **Bommie**, a short right-hander reef break, particularly fun at low tide with big swells. If you prefer a heavier, hollow, intense right-hander with few others in the lineup, head for **Sucky Mama's**, 3km north of Nemberala, accessed via a 10-minute boat ride. Another hollow right, **Do'o**, breaks off an uninhabited island a 20-minute boat ride from Nemberala and is perfect for intermediate and expert surfers. Beginners take note: just north of the Nemberala fishing-boat harbour is **Squealers**, a right- and left-hander thus named for the screeches made by novices catching their first wave. About 8km south of Nemberala, **Bo'a** has a spectacular white-sand beach and a mid-tide right-hander with a good tube section, accessed either by paddling out or a 10-minute boat ride. The local surf resorts such as **Manduna Resort** *(mandunaresort.com)* can take you out to other world-class waves that fluctuate according to the wind and tide. Many resorts rent high-quality boards from about 100,000Rp per day.

ARRANGE YOUR ALOR ADVENTURE

Alor Divers: Alor caters exclusively to divers on Pulau Timur's eastern shore. *(alor-divers.com)*

Lazy Turtle Dive Alor: This operation runs daily dives and offers accommodation packages. Book in advance as their six slots fill up quickly. *(lazyturtledive.com)*

Mila Salim: Local guide who arranges cultural excursions across Alor. She runs Kalabahi's first souvenir shop, supporting local craftspeople. *(milasalim619@gmail.com)*

Gabriel Tang: Cultural itineraries of Alor, including visits to traditional houses and dugong trips; Kalabahi-based guide. *(gabriellobangtang@gmail.com)*

Alor Dream Trip: Local guides in Kalabahi who can take you around the islands for snorkelling, wildlife and land-based adventures. *(alordreamtrip.com)*

EATING IN NEMBERALA: OUR PICKS

Blu Oceano: Authentic Italian dishes, homemade bread and pastries, plus desserts, made with ingredients from their garden. *7am-11pm* $$

Luwabafa the Cave: Fresh seafood cooked in a Western Asian fusion style, plus pastas, sandwiches and salads, all under a giant thatched roof. *hours vary* $$

The Pasar: Enjoy excellent coffee, sourdough sandwiches, couscous and feta salads, plus other international dishes at this open-sided, breezy spot. *hours vary* $$

Sagarika: Heritage Indonesian dishes cooked in a stunning open-air kitchen with seats among coconut palms. *8am-9pm* $$

Sumba

TRADITIONAL VILLAGES | FESTIVALS | UNTAMED NATURE

GETTING AROUND

Buses connect Waingapu with Kalala (five hours) and with Tambolaka (five hours) via Waikabubak. Trucks serve Tarimbang, Wanokaka and Kerewe. Most hotels arrange motorbike and scooter rental *(per day 200,000Rp)*. Car rental is around 1,000,000Rp per day including the driver's pay; it's hard to rent a car without a driver.

There are daily flights from Waingapu to Ende (Flores), Denpasar (Bali), Praya (Lombok) and Kupang (West Timor). Ferries run to Ende and Kupang. There are daily flights from Tambolaka to Denpasar, Praya and Kupang, and ferries to Sape in Sumbawa (three weekly, nine hours).

There's something truly enchanting about Sumba. Its intricately woven ikat textiles are displayed in museums worldwide as exemplars of their kind. Its verdant, hilly interior – so unlike Indonesia's northern volcanic isles – is populated by roaming horses and dotted with traditional hilltop villages of tall grass roofs clustered around megalithic tombs. Its Christian villagers still adhere to indigenous *marapu* (spiritual force) practices and animal sacrifice is common. In February and March, warriors on horseback clash en masse while wielding blunt spears during the annual Pasola festival.

Culturally fascinating, Sumba is no slouch when it comes to natural attractions, either. It's encircled by pristine white-sand beaches and pounded by relentless breaks that have been drawing surfers for years, while secret swimming holes, waterfalls and caves beckon further inland. Friendly and low-key, this part of Nusa Tenggara is particularly vulnerable to change. Developers have their eye on Sumba, so go without delay.

A Perfect Day Around Waingapu

Traditional villages, historic sites and a viewpoint

East Sumba's transport hub, **Waingapu**, is a laid-back town with a leafy, dusty centre interspersed with accommodation and small *toko* (stores). It also has a busy produce market, a harbour that becomes redolent with grilled fish after sundown and villages in the middle of it all. From Waingapu, you can launch trips along the north coast and into the interior, seeing traditional villages and archaeological sites all in one day.

Near the **Praikundu Ikat Centre** (p328), 6km south of Waingapu, an awning protects the small archaeological site of **Lambanapu**, whose compact size belies its considerable importance. Extensive archaeological excavations (between 2016 and 2022) have taken place here. It's the burial site of an ancient civilisation of East Sumba's prehistoric people. The

HEINRICH DOMINGGUS DENGI/SHUTTERSTOCK

Lambanapu

physical remains of 45 individuals have been unearthed, along with weaponry, household items and jewellery. The jar burials, no longer practised on Sumba, are thought to date back to the earliest presence of humans in Sumba, and it is hoped that the discovery will shed light on the arrival of Austronesian speakers.

For lunch, head southeast along the coast to grab some hot-and-sour fish soup at the thatched **Amu Dahi** in Melolo village, then proceed to **Praiyawang**, a traditional Sumbanese village near Melolo. It has an imposing lineup of nine stone tombs, the largest being that of the chief of this former kingdom. Shaped like a buffalo, it consists of four 2m stone pillars supporting a monstrous slab (about 5m long and 2.5m wide). Two stone tablets stand atop the main slab, carved with figures. A massive Sumbanese house with concrete pillars faces the tombs, along with a number of *rumah adat* and an uninhabited ceremonial house. Within the tombs, it's permitted to bury siblings, grandchildren and grandparents together, but the deceased can't be buried alongside their parents. Crocodile statues represent the king, turtles are only seen on women's tombs, and the cockatoos and horses symbolise democracy.

On your way back to Waingapu, take the bumpy track to the **Tanau Hills** for exceptional panoramic views of Sumba's unique topography.

Go Chasing Waterfalls

Exploration near Waingapu

A couple of hours' drive (60km) northwest of Waingapu along rough roads, and a further 20-minute trek through savannah or grasslands, depending on the time of year, is **Air Terjun Tanggedu**, arguably Sumba's best waterfall. What awaits will blow you away: two rivers run between time-layered limestone cliffs and converge into waterfall terraces that feed into multiple pools; there are dipping pools nearby.

Continues on p324

MARAPU BELIEFS

The basis of traditional Sumbanese religion is *marapu*, a collective term for Sumba's spiritual forces, including gods, spirits and ancestors.

At death, the deceased join the invisible world of spirits, *praing marapu*, from where they can influence the world of the living. *Marapu mameti* is the collective name for all dead people. The living can appeal to *marapu mameti* for help, especially their own relatives, though the dead can be harmful if irritated.

The *marapu maluri* are the original people placed on Earth by God, and their power is concentrated in certain places or objects, which are often kept safe in the family's thatched loft. Offerings to the spirits involve betel nut and/or animal sacrifice.

TOP TIP

You need a guide to visit traditional villages. Some villages reject visitors if their guide has no contacts within the community. A set donation and signing the visitor book are part of village visits.

SUMBA

HIGHLIGHTS
1 Lambanapu

SIGHTS
2 Air Terjun Tanggedu
3 Air Terjun Wai Marang
4 Praigoli
5 Waigalli
6 Laipopu Waterfall
7 Pantai Dassang
8 Pantai Kalala
9 Pantai Kerewe
10 Pantai Marosi
11 Pantai Nihiwatu
12 Pantai Pahiri
13 Pantai Pero
14 Pantai Rua
15 Pantai Tarimbang
16 Pantai Wainyapu
17 Prailiu
18 Praiyawang
19 Sodana
20 Tanau Hills
21 Waihura

ACTIVITIES
22 Explore Sumba
see 15 Miller's Rights
23 Occy's Left
see 8 Office
see 8 Racetrack
24 Sumba Adventure Tours & Travel
see 24 Tour Sumba
see 22 Yuliana Leda Tara

SLEEPING
25 Maringi Sumba
26 Nihi Sumba
see 17 Praikamarru Guest House
27 Sumba Sunset Surf Camp
see 9 Sumba Surf Camp
28 Wajonata Sumba

EATING
29 Alamayah
30 Amu Dahi
31 Dapur Sumba
see 22 D'Sumba Ate
32 Kedai Sei Babi Karunia
33 Kopi Dari Hati Sumba
34 La Paranda
see 24 Makan Dulu
35 PC Corner
36 Resto Ne'neru Loco
see 22 Soemba Coffee & Resto
37 Talasi Estate at Weetabula
see 31 Warung Gula Garam

ENTERTAINMENT
38 Pasola

SHOPPING
39 Praikundu Ikat Centre

SUMBANESE VILLAGES

Sumbanese villages were traditionally built on hillsides (to see approaching enemies) and consist of either two rows of houses with thatched roofs, or are arranged in a rough circle surrounding the tombs and *kateda* (sacrificial altars) in the centre. Villages typically have several clans living there, and each clan has its own *rumah adat*, where sacred objects are kept and ancestral spirits dwell.

Houses are constructed from bamboo tied together with vines and finished with tall traditional roofs, their bamboo scaffolding covered with dried alang-alang grass. The main struts represent different elements, while the hearth in the centre represents the sun. The underfloor section is for animals; the ground floor is for humans.

Pasola

Continued from p321

Alternatively, get an early start and follow the north coast southeastward in the direction of Kalala to the town of Melolo (where you sometimes see sunbathing crocodiles on the riverbanks), near Praiyawang. Take the smooth, unpeopled road inland for 8km to the parking area overlooking a verdant valley, pay the entrance fee *(50,000Rp)* and descend 15 minutes along some concrete steps, followed by a steep trail, to reach **Air Terjun Wai Marang**, a startlingly blue dipping pool in the middle of the jungle, surrounded by limestone walls and fed by a waterfall.

Wander Wanokaka's Villages & Beaches

Traditional culture and slivers of sand

South of Waikabubak, you'll encounter some of Sumba's most striking scenery, megalithic tombs, pristine beaches and world-class surfing. Taking the main road south, turn off after 8km and follow the narrower paved road west. Passing some Pasola grandstands, with rice-paddy vistas opening up and locals swimming in the river, you'll reach Hapumada, where the road forks. The rougher, partially paved northward fork leads towards the jungly trailhead to **Laipopu Waterfall**. South and downhill from Hapumada is **Waigalli**, a traditional village on a promontory above the sea; further south

EATING IN WAINGAPU: OUR PICKS

Kopi Dari Hati Sumba: A coffee shop with a selection of mains, snacks and dessert, with live music every evening. *hours vary* $

Kedai Sei Babi Karunia: Buy *se'i babi* (Rotinese smoked pork) by weight or opt for other porky dishes. *9am-8pm Mon-Sat* $

PC Corner: Killer views, live music on Saturdays and dishes such as papaya flower with *kangkung* (water spinach) are big draws here. *9am-10pm Mon-Sat* $$

La Paranda: Order chicken, prawns or squid, along with *cah kangkung* (garlicky water spinach) at this breezy restaurant. *10am-10pm Mon-Sat, from 4pm Sun* $$

is the fishing village of **Waihura**, at the western end of the vast, wave-battered, white-sand **Pantai Pahiri**, where the village youth practise bareback horse riding.

A shortcut up a bumpy, unpaved road from Waigalli brings you to **Praigoli**, home to Sumba's most famous megalithic statue – the fleur-de-lis *Lakaruka Jiwa Tada Bita Laka*. If you happen to be in one of the traditional villages while a traditional roof is being fixed, you may come across a roof-fixing ceremony involving a dog sacrifice and the playing of gongs, where all of the village men partake in the fixing while the women cook for everyone in an outdoor kitchen. From Praigoli, take a bumpy, steep shortcut up a particularly scenic road with great views of Pantai Pahiri, passing the turnoff to **Pantai Rua**, a white-sand beach with a resort and some calmer spots for bathing. Further along, you pass the turnoff for the exclusive resort of **Nihi Sumba** (p328) before rejoining the main road towards Kerewe Beach and the Lamboya district. On your right, you'll spy the traditional roofs of the village of **Sodana** atop a steep hill (reachable by rough 4WD track). You may only visit if your guide has contacts in Sodana, as the locals are keen to preserve traditional culture. Shortly after, a turnoff south brings you to the surfing hot spot of **Pantai Kerewe** (p327).

Witness a Ritual Horseback Tournament

Let the battle commence

Pasola (from *pa* meaning 'game' and *sola* meaning 'wooden spear') has to be one of the most extravagant (and bloody) harvest festivals in Asia. Held annually in February and March in West Sumba, it takes the form of a ritual battle between two teams of spear-wielding, ikat-clad horsemen. The bloodier the proceedings, the better the harvest, as the blood is believed to please the spirits. Although the festival is considerably less bloody than it used to be and blunt spears are now used, it's still a dangerous sport. Spectators should be aware of any potential animal welfare issues, including animal sacrifices.

Pasola takes place in Lamboya and Kodi villages in February and in Kodi Bangedo, Lamboya Barat and Wanokaka villages in March. A *rato* (priest) decides the exact timing based on the arrival of a sea worm called *nyale* on nearby coasts, but these days tourism comes first, and eager fans are now given up to a month's warning. Dressed in full ceremonial garb, the *rato* wades into the ocean to examine the worms at dawn; they're usually found on the eighth or ninth day after a full moon.

SUMBA'S MEGALITHIC TOMBS

Megalithic culture on the island of Sumba goes back some 4500 years, and in numerous Sumbanese villages you'll come across megalithic tombs, many of them highly elaborate in appearance. The tombs are rectangular and the grave is covered with a stone plate to resemble an altar or table, with the stone weighing many tonnes.

The erection of these cover stones has traditionally required the sacrifice of buffalo, cows and pigs, with the stones pulled over long distances using tree trunks and lianas to the tune of rhythmic song. Today, trucks are often used to transport the cover stones, but the ceremonies and singing still take place. Once the cover stone is in place, the grave is engraved with scenes from the life of the deceased.

EATING IN WAIKABUBAK & WANOKAKA: OUR PICKS

Resto Ne'neru Loco: Chow down on stir-fried sweet and sour dishes with a side of rice-paddy views. *10am-10pm* $

Soemba Coffee & Resto: Score a proper espresso at this contemporary spot or settle in for a meal of chicken satay or nasi goreng (fried rice). *10am-10pm* $$

D'Sumba Ate: Wood-fired pizzas, seafood, noodles and rice dishes under an open-air, thatched bamboo roof. *noon-10pm* $$

Alamayah: Strong cocktails, coffee and a mix of Aussie and Indonesian dishes in refined surroundings. Open to non-guests through bookings only. *6am-10pm* $$

VISIT VILLAGES NEAR WAIBAKUL & WAIKABUBAK

Those interested in traditional Sumbanese culture will find numerous traditional villages and exceptional stone tombs here. It's best to visit with a guide.

START	END	LENGTH
Waibakul	Manola	70km; 6hr

Starting in 1 **Waibakul**, take the paved road 2.5km south through the ricefields to 2 **Kampung Gallubakul**, home to Sumba's heaviest tomb (70 tonnes), decorated with carvings of the buried king and queen. Allegedly, it took 6000 workers three years to chisel the stone out of a hillside and drag it 3km, using vines and banana-tree rollers. Returning to Waibakul, proceed to tin-roofed 3 **Kampung Pasunga**. Visible from the main road is a particularly impressive tomb with images of a chief and his wife, their hands on their hips, dating from 1926. Take the main Waikabubak road, then turn south up a steep road to 4 **Kampung Bondo Maroto**, a friendly village; overnight stays are possible. Take a different turnoff from the Waikabubak road to 5 **Kampung Praijing**, where you pay a 55,000Rp entry fee. Popular with visitors from Java, it has a lofty viewpoint from which to admire the Instagrammable rows of thatched houses. Proceed to 6 **Waikabubak**, a compact market town. Several traditional villages are walkable from here: 7 **Kampung Tambelar**, just off Jl Sudirman, features impressive *kubur batu* (stone graves). Uphill, beneath a giant ficus tree, 8 **Kampung Tarung** is known for its intricately woven palm-containers; homestays are possible. Some 17km northwest of Waikabubak, a rough road leads to 9 **Kampung Manola**, a village so traditional it eschews electricity; it's populated by elders and children, whose parents live elsewhere.

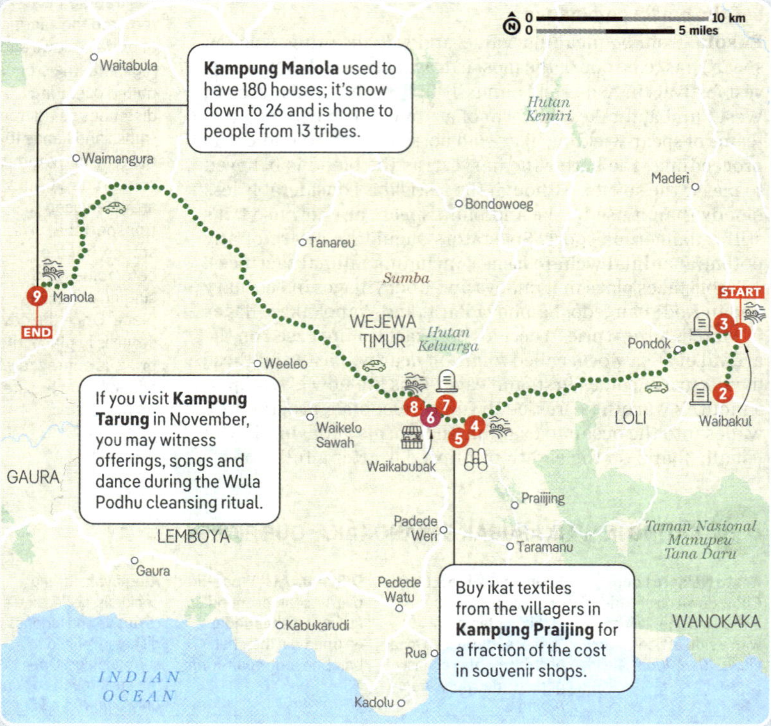

Kampung Manola used to have 180 houses; it's now down to 26 and is home to people from 13 tribes.

If you visit **Kampung Tarung** in November, you may witness offerings, songs and dance during the Wula Podhu cleansing ritual.

Buy ikat textiles from the villagers in **Kampung Praijing** for a fraction of the cost in souvenir shops.

Only in Wanokaka, two days before the main event, opposing 'armies' drawn from coastal and inland villages meet on deserted beaches at night for no-holds-barred, brutal boxing matches called *pajura,* with the combatants' fists bound in thorn-edged palm leaves. Teeth are lost and noses broken, but when dawn breaks, everyone sits on the sand and sings ancestral songs of peace.

The night before the Pasola tournament, participant riders sacrifice chickens to the *rato* in the relevant village, who then consecrates the tournament ground. Early in the morning of the event, spectators gather around the Pasola stadiums, dressed in their best. There's no entrance fee; just get there on time to claim a good vantage point.

Two rows of riders of up to 50 men each, in traditional headgear and their mounts splendidly adorned, charge at each other at breakneck speed, like knights in the Middle Ages. Just when collision feels inevitable and you find yourself holding your breath, they rein in their steeds and hurl the blunt spears at one another. You'll see the most skilled riders not only evade the projectiles with ease but also pluck them out of the air, flinging them back at their opponents. In spite of the violence, the underlying purpose of Pasola battles is peace, with all inter-clan conflicts considered resolved, until the following year.

Catch a Wave in Sumba

Surf's up

The beaches on West Sumba's south coast are on their way to being discovered, and not just by surfers (who've been coming here for years). While the waves in **Pantai Kerewe** are surfable year-round, the best time is March to November, when longboarders come to ride the long, mellow right-hander out front for up to 600m. A 15-minute speedboat ride out to sea, and you have access to a dozen empty left- and right-hander reef breaks for most abilities, including some heavy barrels. North up the coast, **Pantai Pero** has nice lefts and rights on opposite sides of the river mouth, while **Pantai Wainyapu** is good for consistent and clean lefts.

A 30-minute walk from Pantai Kerewe, the white-sand **Pantai Marosi** has a nice beach break, suitable for rookies. At **Pantai Dassang**, a wide sweep of white sand, fronted by a resort, there's more beachside action; drive up to the north end of the beach using a public road unless staying at the resort.

SUMBA'S BEST GUIDES

Erwin Pah: Waingapu-based guide who can arrange caving, rock-climbing and village tours. *(erwinpah9@gmail.com)*

Sumba Adventure Tours & Travel: Pilipus Renggi and his team lead trips into seldom-explored villages, arrange itineraries and more. *(sumbaislandtours.com)*

Yuliana Leda Tara: Expert Tarung-based guide, in demand from anthropologists and filmmakers. Organises West Sumba village tours. *(yuli.sumba@gmail.com)*

Tour Sumba: Hugo and his team of Sumbanese guides offer tour packages across the island, including waterfalls, beaches and villages. *(tour-sumba.com)*

Explore Sumba: Tour company that can arrange day trips, honeymoon packages, tailor-made trips, car rentals and hotel bookings. *(exploresumba.com)*

EATING IN TAMBOLAKA: OUR PICKS

Talasi Estate at Weetabula: Cashew farm with coffee grown and roasted on-site, served with cashew milk. *8am-6pm Mon-Fri, from 9am Sat & Sun* $

Warung Gula Garam: Run by Frenchman Louis, this thatched open-air cafe near the airport plays R&B tunes and serves good wood-fired pizza. *10am-9pm* $$

Makan Dulu: Braised lamb in coconut milk, satay dishes and Sumbanese cassava leaf and rice cream soup are standouts at this breezy restaurant. *11am-9.30pm Mon-Sat* $$

Dapur Sumba: Clean, air-conditioned eatery serving Indonesian and Sumbanese dishes with huge portions. *9am-9pm Mon-Sat, 10am-9.30pm Sun* $$

SUMBANESE IKAT

Displayed in museums around the world as examples of the highest-quality textile, Sumbanese ikat is recognised as the best in Indonesia.

East Sumbanese ikat depicts village scenes, mythological creatures, Pasola tournaments and tribal wars. West Sumbanese ikat does not adhere to the complex ikat-making process and is much simpler, featuring geometric patterns. The most authentic ikat is still made with natural dyes, with each strand of yarn dyed individually before being affixed to the loom. The bark and roots of the mengkudu tree produce red dye; indigo plants produce blue dye; and a mix of indigo and mengkudu produces brown and purple dyes.

The ikat-weaving process is now partially mechanised, which is why vintage ikat pieces fetch collector's prices.

BAYU PAMUNGKAS/SHUTTERSTOCK

Prailiu

The region's legendary, world-class surf spot is **Occy's Left**, which was featured in the film *The Green Iguana* and is off the achingly stunning **Pantai Nihiwatu**. But unless you have deep pockets and are staying at **Nihi Sumba**, it'll remain a dream.

On Pantai Kerewe, the best digs for surfers are **Sumba Sunset Surf Camp** (p368) *(WhatsApp +62 821 4754 6538)*, run by Petu, locally known as 'Raja di Laut' (King of the Sea); he spent eight years working as a lifeguard at Nihi Sumba and can sort out boat transport to the best breaks. Arnaud of **Sumba Surf Camp** *(sumbasurfcamp.com)* is another expert surfer who knows the local breaks; lessons for beginners can be arranged.

Further south along the coast is **Miller's Rights** – a series of rights breaking off **Pantai Tarimbang** and arguably Sumba's most popular wave; the lineup gets busy from May to October.

On Sumba's east coast, the **Office** is a fun wave at the western end of the reef off **Pantai Kalala**, while nearby **Racetrack** is a faster, more intense ride.

Shop for Ikat in East Sumba

Seek out Sumba's best textiles

While in the past, only high-ranking members of Sumbanese society were able to afford ikat, today it's much more common. Near Waingapu, **Prailiu** village has numerous weavers, and prices start from 200,000Rp for small pieces; if you buy direct, the weavers get 100% of the profits. Run by English-speaking Kornelis Ndapakamang, **Praikundu Ikat Centre** *(WhatsApp +62 812 3758 4629; from 1,500,000Rp)* on the outskirts of Waingapu is hung with some of Sumba's most prized ikat, all naturally dyed with detailed motifs. Kornelis is renowned for some of the island's finest pieces, the largest of which go for millions of rupiah. Lengthier ikat workshops are available upon request with the help of **Erwin Pah** (p327).

TAMBOLAKA TO PANTAI KEREWE: THE SLOW WAY

Visit Sumba's villages and natural wonders on this one-day driving tour of the west coast.

START	END	LENGTH
Tambolaka	Pantai Kerewe	127km; 8hr

On the outskirts of 1 **Tambolaka**, the museum 2 **Rumah Budaya Sumba** is an excellent introduction to traditional Sumbanese culture, spiritual beliefs and ikat. Acquaint yourself with coffee- and cashew-nut cultivation at the 3 **Talasi Estate** (p327) before taking the narrow road along Sumba's west coast. An hour's drive brings you to 4 **Weekuri Lagoon**, where the Indian Ocean rages against the cliffs and bursts through blowholes, and where you can swim and snorkel (bring your own gear) in the cerulean waters of the sheltered lagoon. Further south in Karoso village, the road becomes unpaved, acting as a shortcut to the main paved road and the large village of 5 **Bondokodi**, the gateway to Sumba's Kodi district, renowned for its traditional houses.

The best-known traditional house is nearby 6 **Ratenggaro**, situated on a bluff above the mouth of a river, with a breathtaking view and elaborately decorated tombs at the village entrance. However, the aggressive behaviour of its residents is off-putting. Following the bumpy main road, you pass 7 **Paranobaroro**; the house of the Rajah of Kodi features Sumba's tallest (30m) roof. In 8 **Wainyapu** – a **Pasola** (p325) site – take the bridge across the crocodile-infested river and follow the rutted road past turnoffs to traditional waterside villages – Bwanna, Watumalando – then the gorgeous Rita, Katobo and Mambang beaches and a cacao plantation. At 9 **Wetana**, the paved road reappears, leading you a further 29km to 10 **Pantai Kerewe** (p327).

Talasi Estate has a little cafe serving coffee and snacks made with cashews grown on the farm.

Wainyapu is home to around 1400 megaliths, one of the highest concentrations in Sumba.

When the tide goes out at **Pantai Kerewe**, you'll spot the elephant-like Watu Gajah Cecek rock formation.

Nusa Tenggara Islands

Stretching east of Bali and Lombok, Nusa Tenggara comprises over 550 islands. It's dominated by three main ones: Flores, studded with volcanoes, forests and beaches; Sumba, rich in indigenous culture and covered in hills, caves and waterfalls; and West Timor, thronged with traditional villages vying for attention alongside the brash capital. The smaller islands, some inhabited, others not, have their own appeal, from surfable waves and incredible underwater landscapes to the world's largest monitor lizard.

Where to Go if You Love...

Traditional Villages

Boti (p315) A picturesque Dawa village reachable from Timor's Kefamenanu, strictly practising only animist beliefs. Little electricity and traditional dance.

Bena (p297) Bajawa-adjacent Ngada village, with a scenic ridge location, megalithic tombs and ancestral totems.

Tamkesi (p313) Thrillingly located hilltop Dawa village; scale a nearby cliff for tremendous views.

Wae Rebo (p296) Traditional Manggarai village reachable via a scenic hike; stay overnight and hike to a nearby waterfall.

Manola (p326) Take a rough track to this friendly, electricity-free Sumbanese village, populated by elders and children.

Fantastic Waves

Pantai Kerewe (p327) Good surfing year-round in Sumba, with a beach break out front and half a dozen waves easily reachable by boat, including the legendary Occy's Left.

Nemberala (p319) Hit the consistent off-season beach break on Rote's Bo'a; ride the heavy, hollow tube at Suckie Mama's or hit the big T-Land wave.

Pantai Lakey (p304) In Sumbawa, Lakey Peak and Lakey Pipe are within paddling distance; or, ride to Nungas, Cobblestone, Nangadoro and Periscope. Lakey Pipe and Nungas are top kiting destinations from August to October.

Epic Volcanoes

Gunung Inerie (p297) Sweat your way up this spectacularly jagged cone (2245m), starting from Bajawa at 3am to catch the sunrise from the top. Six to eight hours out-and-back.

Kelimutu (p302) Watch the sun's first rays illuminate the three multicoloured lakes from the summit of this volcano – unique in Indonesia – then hike down to Moni through scenic farmland.

Komodo Dragons

Pulau Komodo (p307) The main home of the world's largest monitor lizard; if you're lucky, your guide will spot some handsome specimens near the beach.

Pulau Rinca (p307) Komodo-dragon sightings practically guaranteed, since they often hang out next to the nature museum.

Underwater Landscapes

Komodo National Park (p306) Drift with manta rays at Karang Makassar, encounter reef sharks, turtles, tuna and giant trevally at Castle Rock, and brave the strong currents of the Cauldron to 'fly' over the reef.

Alor Archipelago (p318) Moorish idols, angelfish and fairy basslets await at the Fish Bowl reef, while Kal's Dream means barracuda and shark encounters amid schools of jacks and fusiliers.

Goa Kristal (p315) and **Goa Uihani** (p315) in West Timor are among Indonesia's few freshwater cave dives, with fossil-encrusted walls, mysterious chambers and flooded tunnels to explore.

GEKKO GALLERY/SHUTTERSTOCK

Nemberala (p319)

HOW TO

Choose when to go Hiking and diving are best from April to October (dry season); Komodo dragons are hardest to spot in June and July. Islands are greenest November to March.

Book ahead If visiting traditional villages, contact guides ahead of time. Book liveaboards and diving trips in advance, especially in summer.

Prepare before you go Make sure your innoculations are up to date. Research the dive sites and traditional villages you want to explore.

Budget A guide and car will cost around 1,200,000 to 2,000,000Rp per day, depending on the island and the guide. For liveaboards, budget from US$280 per day.

DIY or Guided Tour?

Flores is easiest to explore with public transport connecting the main towns; it's also easy to rent a car, motorbike or scooter in the main towns and to pootle around on your own, particularly along the Trans-Flores Hwy. Hotels and guesthouses can help arrange local guides if you want to visit traditional villages nearby.

West Timor is logistically trickier: car and scooter rental is possible to arrange in Kupang, but the main places of interest are inland, and you really need to have knowledge of the island's interior, since minor roads are often in poor condition and unlabelled. You must be a very good driver.

In Sumba, cars with drivers are easy to negotiate; few individuals will rent you a car without a driver. Though most hotels can arrange scooter or motorbike rental, and you may see some of the sights off the island's main road independently, minor roads in the interior are often rough and unlabelled.

To visit traditional villages in Flores, West Timor and Sumba, you need to go with a knowledgeable local guide – both to overcome the language barrier (since there are places where Bahasa Indonesia is barely spoken) and to explain the local traditions and customs so that you don't inadvertently break the many unspoken rules.

Kuta

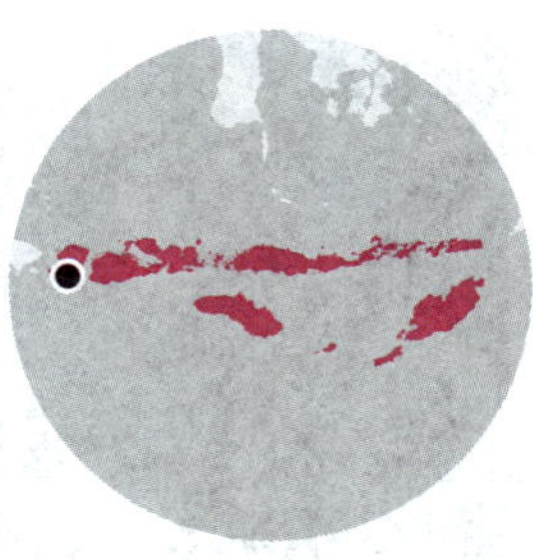

STUNNING BEACHES | FAMOUS SURF | CAFES & SHOPS

GETTING AROUND

Kuta itself is walkable. It takes 15 minutes to stroll the main strip, Jl Raya Kuta. The main streets have footpaths. As the best natural sights are just outside Kuta, it makes sense to rent a car or scooter for the duration of your stay. If you don't drive, you'll have no trouble finding a driver – signs with ride rates for frequented destinations can be found around town, or arranged with most accommodation. The coast makes for a beautiful journey.

TOP TIP

Since Kuta is a popular weekend getaway, accommodation can get booked up on the weekend. If swinging by Friday to Sunday, consider booking in advance if you want the full gamut of places to choose from, especially during July and August.

Fast-growing and increasingly popular, Lombok's Kuta is often confused with Bali's Kuta, despite vast differences. With close proximity to many of Lombok's most acclaimed beaches, Kuta has become a hot spot for surfers and beachgoers. The most fantastic sandy stretches are within just a half-hour's drive of the town's centre. Development has boomed in recent years, from the large-scale Mandalika resort area to the outcrop of trendy restaurants catering to visitors. Regardless of the constant stream of new business, crowds and traffic aren't really a thing here.

You'll see surf shops up and down the town's main streets, with Jl Raya Kuta running from north to south, and Jl Mawun running west to east. While there's no shortage of places to grab a beer on an evening out, the nightlife is far more relaxed here – with most people waking up early to head out for explorations rather than partying the night away.

Get the Lay of the Land

Swims and sunsets

Drive 20 minutes to the east of Kuta to **Tanjung Aan**: a horseshoe-shaped bay that definitely deserves to be your first beach experience in Lombok. Set up shop for the afternoon, grab a coconut and take cooling dips in the sandy-bottomed sea.

When the sun starts to hang low in the sky, hop a few minutes over to **Bukit Merese**: a hill just above Tanjung Aan, locally known for being one of the best places to watch the sunset. Roughly a 15-minute ride from the centre of Kuta, it's a prime spot for views of the south coast in both directions, giving you a taste of what to expect as you plan adventures to more far-flung beaches. You'll have to pay 10,000Rp to enter before you can park and walk to the top of the hill and those 360-degree views. Expect a crowd before sundown, though you'll have plenty of open space to roam.

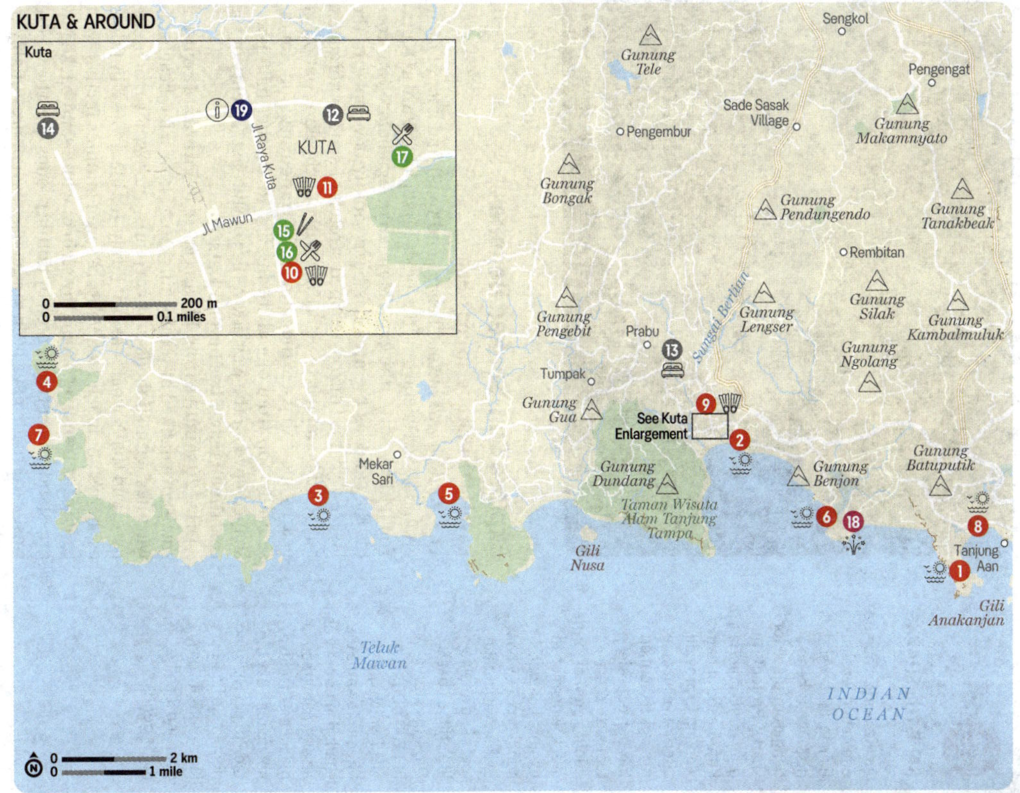

SIGHTS
1 Bukit Merese
2 Pantai Kuta
3 Pantai Lancing
4 Pantai Mawi
5 Pantai Mawun
6 Pantai Seger
7 Pantai Semeti
8 Tanjung Aan

ACTIVITIES
9 Adventure Divers Kuta
10 Blue Marlin Dive Kuta Lombok
11 Scuba Froggy

SLEEPING
12 Lara Homestay
13 Porter Lombok Hotel
14 Sikara Lombok

EATING
15 Jiang Nan
16 Munchies
17 Terra
see 9 Warung Flora

ENTERTAINMENT
18 Bau Nyale Festival

INFORMATION
19 Project Hiu

SAVE THE SHARKS

As the world's number one nation for shark fishing, Indonesia has historically been a dangerous place for sharks. **Project Hiu** *(projecthiu.com)* is a Kuta-based initiative working to provide alternative incomes to shark fishermen through eco-friendly tourism.

Join a crew of former shark fishermen to explore Lombok's south coast by boat, learning about the reefs and marine life off the coast. Day trips start at 1,200,000Rp, all of which goes directly towards the shark-fishing crew as an alternative source of income. If you're not up for a day trip, the Project Hiu shop right in the heart of Kuta has both dive gear and locally made goods.

Explore Sun-Soaked Beaches

Revel in the turquoise coastline

The word *pantai* means 'beach', and you'll find a lot of them around here. For starters, the logical first pick is **Pantai Kuta**. You'll likely notice the giant Mandalika sign before your toes hit the sand, as the area has been rapidly developed in the last few years. This bay-shaped stretch of sand is gorgeous, but you'd be remiss to visit Kuta without checking out other nearby spots that are the pinnacle of tranquility. You can essentially hop from one glittering bay to another half-moon shaped cove all the way down the south coast – plenty of the coastline's magic lies beyond Kuta.

Drive 20 minutes from Kuta's centre to **Pantai Mawun**, a small cove flanked by rolling hills. Apart from a few beachside warungs with sunbeds and coconuts, there's not much else here, and that's what makes it lovely. It's ideal for swimming, as there's not much reef. Venture seven minutes further west to **Pantai Lancing**, a lengthy strip of white sand backed by grasslands, most frequented by doting groups of cattle. These westward roads have been gorgeously paved, presumably in anticipation of more developments, but the area remains rustic and fairly sparse. There are a couple of beach shacks here selling snacks and local dishes.

EATING IN KUTA: OUR PICKS

Munchies: Spacious cafe on the main intersection with all-day breakfasts, lunch and pizzas, plus healthy drinks and wines. *7.30am-11pm* $$

Terra: Fully vegan and gluten-free restaurant with a focus on wellness. The healthy desserts are worth a visit. *8am-10pm* $$

Jiang Nan: Chinese sharing dishes with all the classics like wontons, steamed buns and soup dumplings. Perfect for a casual date night. *1-10pm* $$

Warung Flora: Indonesian favourites right on the main road, including all the *nasi* (rice) and *mie* (noodles) classics, plus soups and curries. *5-10pm* $

HARIADI MAHSYAR/SHUTTERSTOCK

Pantai Mawun

If you're up for a more intrepid adventure, **Pantai Semeti** is a 45-minute drive west of Kuta. Part of the fun is getting there – from the main road, you'll need to then drive down a dirt path with some steep sections and large potholes. It's a rewarding drive through, as the beach is rarely visited and you'll most likely get it all to yourself. There are also some striking volcanic rock formations at one end of the beach that you can climb, which make for epic photos.

Surfing for All Skill Levels

Surf solo or learn from experts

Whether you're a seasoned pro or hopping on a board for the first time, there are plenty of surf spots to accommodate all skill levels. Kuta is a year-round surfing destination, with consistent swell and a variety of different breaks. You'll find it less crowded during the rainy season (roughly from November through March), which can sometimes provide 'cleaner' waves as there's less chop from the wind.

Just 20 minutes' drive from Kuta, the waves at **Pantai Seger** are suitable for all levels, with both lefts and rights. East of Kuta, surf schools such as **Heartbeach Lombok Surf Academy** *(heartbeachlombok.com; sessions from 500,000Rp)* dot the shorelines of **Tanjung Aan** (p332), as well as surfboard rental shacks. A 35-minute drive west of Kuta lies **Pantai Mawi** (not to be confused with Mawun), one of Kuta's most famous surf spots, with strong currents suited for intermediate and advanced surfers. Beware of the semi-treacherous 10-minute ride leading to the beach with its many potholes and loose rocks. The end views are worth it.

For fewer crowds, Are Guling is a 20-minute drive west from the centre of Kuta. This quiet bay offers left- and right-hand breaks that are ideal for intermediate and advanced surfers. You can paddle out from the beach, but be mindful of the currents around the left-hander and the sharp reef at low tide.

BAU NYALE FESTIVAL

Once a year, in February, people flock to the shoreline of **Pantai Seger**, right by the Pertamina Mandalika International Circuit (a racetrack), with a unique quest: capturing *nyale*, a surprisingly colourful species of sea worm. Crowds and ceremonies fill the area as part of the **Bau Nyale Festival** – an age-old tradition that is believed to bring good fortune.

These are regarded as no ordinary worms – the colourful, yarn-like sea creatures are thought to bring prosperity to those who catch them. The exact date depends on the year, but expect crowds if you happen to be in town for the festival. During the other 364 days of the year, Pantai Seger is frequented by swimmers, sunbathers and surfers.

Beyond Kuta

Outside of Kuta lie sleepy fishing towns, empty white-sand beaches, ricefields with mountain views and plenty of traditional Sasak culture.

Places

GETTING AROUND

The main east and west roads along Lombok's southern coast are well paved. When heading westbound, expect steep hills and sharper turns – the area is hilly. Previous riding experience is advised for those who plan to take a scooter.

Northbound towards the mountains, the land is fairly flat. You'll find plenty of amenities along the way, such as minimarts and larger gas stations. Arranging transportation with a driver is generally quick and easy.

It's easy to get into the swing of life in Kuta, but venturing farther along Lombok's southern coast and up north into the foothills of Gunung Rinjani offers wow-worthy scenery and a true escape from it all. West of Kuta, developments dwindle, whereas the twinkling ocean's glow only seems to strengthen. In Lombok's remote southeastern corner, the rugged landscape replete with seaside cliffs remains silent, apart from the occasional small-town hum. Drive an hour and a half north of Kuta to Tetebatu, a charming Sasak village, and you'll be immersed in a verdant landscape of ricefields and farmland. Waterfalls, cultural experiences and fantastic Indonesian food make the decision to visit Tetebatu a no-brainer – this village is worth adding to your list.

Selong Belanak

TIME FROM KUTA: **30MIN**

Surf and swim in clear waters

The picture-perfect bay of **Selong Belanak** is one of the most talked-about beaches on the coast, drawing both locals and visitors to its lengthy, powdery shoreline. Upon arrival, expect to pay around 10,000Rp for parking before a narrow sandy path takes you through a gap in between two beach warungs (food stalls). The view becomes panoramic – an elongated beachfront framed by rolling hills on either side. It's certainly not an empty beach, but there's plenty of room to spread out – especially at low tide. Take a stroll, grab a fresh coconut or go for a surf – it's a popular spot for beginners. You can post up with your own beach towel or opt for a lounge chair in front of one of the warungs, so long as you make a purchase while you sunbathe. Come around 5pm, and you might see the local farmers herding their water buffalo after they've grazed in the nearby fields. It's quite a sight.

RICHARD WHITCOMBE/SHUTTERSTOCK

Selong Belanak

Gerupuk

TIME FROM KUTA: **20MIN**

Surf the breaks near a traditional fishing village

The coastal fishing village of **Gerupuk** is frequented by surfers and overlooks a bay with five different surf breaks that can only be accessed by boat. Simply head to the beach and you'll be met with plenty of locals offering to take you out on their boat. This costs 150,000Rp for three or fewer people, or 50,000Rp per person for more than three people.

The area remains considerably untouched by foreign influence, with just a few fishing boats lining the shore and a handful of small surf shops, homestays and warungs. If arriving from Kuta, you'll pass through the massive Mandalika development's shiny new gate on the way to Gerupuk, though the contrast between the two areas remains stark. Stop by for a quick surf and a roam through the area. Either bring your own board or rent from a nearby surf shop, such as **Rasta Surfshop & Surfschool** *(instagram.com/rasta_surf_shop)* or **Insider Surf** *(insidersurflombok.com)*. Rentals range from 100,000 to 300,000Rp per day, depending on the size of the board.

Tetebatu

TIME FROM KUTA: **1½HR**

Learn about Sasak culture in a beautiful setting

Backed by a postcard-like view of **Gunung Rinjani** (p350), the small village of **Tetebatu** exemplifies traditional Sasak charm. Here, bright-green rice and tobacco fields form most of the landscape, and the air has a lovely lightness to it, thanks to nearby mountain mist and slightly lower temperatures. Several *air terjun* (waterfalls) gushing spring water and flowing over eroded volcanic rock formations are found around the area. **Tetebatu Waterfall** in the heart of town is the most frequently visited.

PACKING FOR DAY TRIPS

Some things can be harder to come by once you leave Kuta, like ATMs and sunscreen. Whether you're packing for an all-day excursion to the **Southwestern Peninsula** (p352) or going to a beach 30 minutes away, packing your day bag accordingly can save some headaches (or rather, heatstroke) down the line.

Most of the further beaches have plenty of small beachside warungs (food stalls), but keeping a water bottle handy, plus some cash and sunscreen, is advantageous. When in smaller towns, cash payments are the norm – that includes getting petrol for your scooter everywhere you go.

THE SASAK TRADITION OF STICK FIGHTING

Stick fighting, a martial art of the Sasak people in Lombok, is a local tradition. Two fighters armed with rattan sticks and a leather shield face off in front of a crowd while traditional music plays. The performance is carried out to ask for rain, as the Sasaks believe that bloodshed from stick fighting results in better rainfall for the season ahead.

Stick fighting happens all over Lombok and also on the Gilis, typically in a centrally located area of the village with enough space for onlookers to view the showdown. The fighting usually starts in July and lasts up until the rain arrives – typically in November or December. Ask your homestay or local guide about stick-fighting events.

MKAZMI/SHUTTERSTOCK

Ekas Beach

Traditional architecture is neighboured by tropical flowers of all shades and the palm-fringed streets have never seen traffic. You'll find homestays and restaurants catering to tourists, but the overwhelming majority of businesses are locally owned – making it a much more authentic experience compared with more completely gentrified areas. Apart from cruising the serene streets of Tetebatu via scooter, the best way to explore the area is by walking tour. Most homestays can connect you with a local guide, often including experiences such as Lombok coffee production, spice markets and the Sasak arts, including weaving and pottery: stop by **Aqila Warung** *(WhatsApp +62 877 5503 0317)* to book locally led tours of the area and cooking classes *(cooking class/tour 150,000/300,000Rp)*. While you're there, enjoy a traditional meal.

You can easily take a day trip out to Tetebatu since it's only a short drive from Kuta, but it's also a great place to wake up in the morning. If you have extra time on your hands, spending a night or two in the area can be a deeply relaxing experience – especially if you're either preparing for or resting up after a mountain trek up Rinjani.

EATING IN TETEBATU: OUR LOCAL PICKS

Warung Monkey Forest: Indonesian plates with a Sasak lens. The curries and vegetable dishes are particularly tasty. Also offers local tours. *7am-10pm* $

Zaeni Warung: Family-run favourite offering Indonesian plates, including rice, noodles, curries and more, along with plenty of fresh juices. *7am-11pm* $

Oktavia Warung: Sasak dishes such as *urap-urap* (vegetables with coconut) and a long list of chicken plates. *7am-10pm* $

Aqila Warung: Delicious Indonesian eats in a restaurant that also offers cooking classes and local tours. *7am-10.30pm* $

Ekas

TIME FROM KUTA: 1¼HR

Unspoiled beach and surf along a tranquil bay

Yet another surfer's paradise on southern Lombok's broad coast, the small seaside village of **Ekas** is contrastingly tiny in comparison with the massive **Awang Bay** on its doorstep. Surfers of all skill levels ride out here year-round for two well-loved waves – **Ekas Outside** and **Ekas Inside**. If you're keen on sticking around for a night or two (or even longer), **Ekas Surf Resort** (p369) *(ekassurfresort.com; surf boat per person 50,000Rp)* has affordably priced rooms and a surf boat to get you out to the breaks.

There's plenty of beautifully mindless lazing under the sun to be had, too. **Ekas Beach** is decorated with fishing boats and tons of open space. Drive just a few minutes south to discover its surrounding area, adorned with spectacular shorelines, some of which are bordered by towering cliffs. **Paradise Beach** and **Pantai Kura Kura** are more remote picks nearby, where you won't hear too much beyond the waves.

Sekaroh

TIME FROM KUTA: 1½HR

Stroll on pink beaches in a remote area

Lombok's southeasternmost corner, **Sekaroh**, might very well be the definition of 'out there'. The coastline here is where it's at, with naturally pink beaches along the northern shores of the region. A quick web search reveals several images with dramatically boosted saturation, but it's true: the sand really *is* a light shade of pink. This phenomenon occurs thanks to the delightful mixture of red reef particles and white sand. You'll find several 'Pink Beach' markers on the map near **Tanjung Sabui**, some of which have irked reviewers expressing ire over discrepancies from the internet's dubious imagery. Expect company and likely an entrance fee of 15,000Rp per scooter, and 20,000Rp per car.

While pink-ish sand can be an enticing lure, there are plenty more lesser-visited beaches along the south shore featuring pristine waters lapping on sand without a single footprint. Rocky outcroppings flank the shores of **Pantai Tanjung Bloam**, next to the gorgeous **Jeeva Beloam Beach Camp** (p369) – a rustic off-grid experience. Further south, **Pantai Antak-Antak**'s staggering cliffs are heavenly. Make your way down to the thin strip of land that's home to **Pantai Lemerang**: this sweeping beach is remote as can be.

While Sekaroh is only 1½ hours from Kuta, don't underestimate the exhaustion that can come with smaller roads in remote areas, especially if you're on a scooter. Plan a day trip.

DIVING & SNORKELLING TIPS

You can slap on some flippers and a mask at any beach that you please, but some of the best marine life experiences are further afield. The lesser-visited **Southwestern Gilis** (p352) – Gili Gede, Gili Asahan and Gili Layar – are fairly sparse when it comes to human activity, yet are teeming with coral and marine life.

From Kuta, it takes about 1½ to two hours to ride up to Tembowong Harbour in Sekotong, where you can organise a private boat for around 400,000Rp. Accommodation offer day-trip packages for snorkelling and diving, but be advised: you'll likely end up paying more than average if your hotel is a fancy one. Shop around a bit.

FOR MORE PINK SAND

If you want to be tickled pink, head to the (pink) sands of Pulau Padar in **Komodo National Park** (p306).

Senggigi

RESORTS | QUIET BEACHES | MOUNTAINOUS BACKDROP

GETTING AROUND

Senggigi is essentially one main road along the coast with short offshoots leading inland and to the beach. The town spans roughly 2.5km from north to south, but the central area is walkable. Some accommodation is closer to Mangsit on the northern end of Senggigi, where the tourist zone begins. The hotels and resorts are fairly spread out, so you may want to rent your own vehicle or save a taxi driver's number for daily outings – unless, of course, you plan to just laze beachside.

TOP TIP

Accommodation is spread out in Senggigi, so check before booking to see you'll be within walking distance of things. Many homestays, hotels and resorts are labelled 'Senggigi', but are actually several kilometres from the town's centre.

Like something out of a 1990s holiday time-capsule, Senggigi rose to fame decades ago as Lombok's premier tourist destination. The scenery is a treat: mountains, doused in junglescape, bordering the deep-blue ocean. This combination is particularly spectacular when viewed from elevated areas on the main road, giving unparalleled views of the entire landscape for vast stretches. Groves of coconut palms provide generous shade close to the water, where people gather for sunset views overlooking Gunung Agung – Bali's mighty volcano – in the distance.

These days, Senggigi is quieter. Longstanding resorts remain on bays up and down the town's coastal stretch, some of which appear empty. There's a low hum of activity, but you're unlikely to encounter anywhere particularly busy. The waters are prime for snorkelling, and you can easily line up a day trip to the Gilis – so if you're looking for a quiet seaside spot, this might be the one for you.

Cruise to Pura Batu Bolong

A serene temple on the water

Not to be confused with the famed Batu Bolong of Canggu, **Pura Batu Bolong** *(by donation)* is a Hindu temple perched on a rocky outcrop looking over the sea. Ornately crafted pagodas and statues stand tall above crashing waves, with small offerings placed around the grounds daily. There's a low hum of activity throughout the day, picking up around sunset when people gather to watch the sky turn hues of sherbet orange and pastel pink. Expect to pay around 5000Rp for parking, plus a donation amount of your choice for entry to the grounds. Come prepared with covered legs, or rent a sarong on arrival *(5000Rp)*. Getting to Pura Batu Bolong takes about three minutes via scooter or car from central Senggigi.

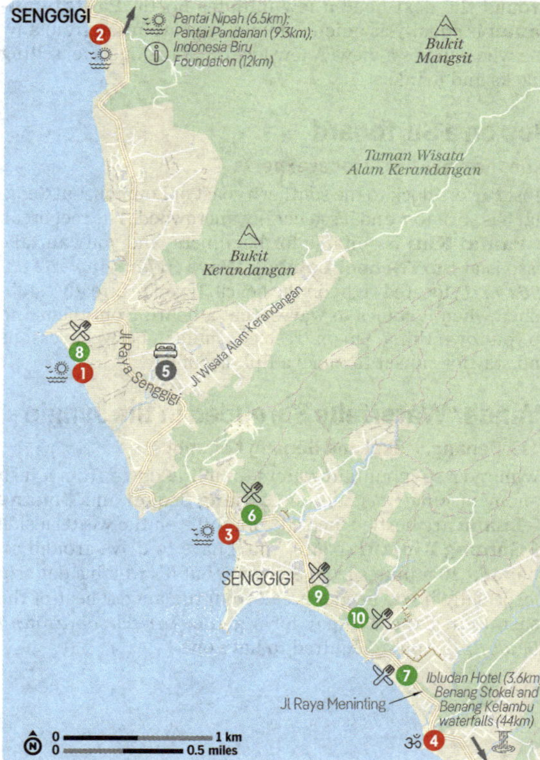

SIGHTS
1 Coconut Beach
2 Pantai Klui
3 Pantai Senggigi
4 Pura Batu Bolong

ACTIVITIES
see 2 Surf School Lombok Wave

SLEEPING
5 Sammy Cottage

EATING
6 Asmara Restaurant & Lounge
7 Begibung Beach & Sunset View Resto
8 Coco Beach Restaurant
9 Pasta Pojok
10 Warung Ijo

Beach-Hop Around the Coast

Soak up Senggigi's laid-back coastline

Walk far enough west anywhere in Senggigi and you'll eventually hit the beach. Consider Jl Raya Senggigi your serpentine route to the surrounding region's best beaches – there's a lot more than what's within the town's limits. For starters, the aptly named **Pantai Senggigi** is the closest beach to the main tourist area, an elongated bay fit for swimming or just hanging out in the shade of a palm tree. Minutes north, **Coconut Beach** is accessible through dusty pathways that weave through a field of sky-high coconut palms. Both locals and tourists gather around the beachside **Coco Beach Restaurant** at sunset, sipping on Bintangs and fresh coconuts. The vibe is family-friendly, and you'll see groups of vacationers young and old kicking back.

For a more secluded experience, a short drive up the coast is a must. **Pantai Nipah** is a 20-minute drive from central Senggigi – a scenic route that'll have you doing double-takes at the wondrous views. This white-sand stretch is bordered by a quintessentially tropical palm-tree forest, and its shores are decorated with more beached fishing boats than tourists.

QUIET WEEKDAYS, BUSY WEEKENDS

Senggigi sees a lot of domestic tourism, especially on the weekends when local families come from other parts of Lombok to hit the beach. While, overall, the area is far less busy than it used to be in years past, there's definitely an uptick in activity on the weekends – typically along the shoreline, right around when the sunset turns the sky a dreamy shade of pastel orange and candy pink.

Regardless of when you go, there won't be nearly as much of a touristy buzz as in Kuta, which has continued to draw more and more attention in the last decade or so.

CORAL RESTORATION

Marine pollution, coral bleaching caused by a warming ocean and overfishing are just some of the threats to Lombok's coral reefs. Based in Pantai Kecinan, a 25-minute drive north from Senggigi, the **Indonesia Biru Foundation** *(indonesiabiru.id)* is an NGO dedicated to protecting Lombok's marine habitats via initiatives including reef restoration and community engagement and education programmes.

Travellers can support its work by joining a reef restoration dive *(from 550,000Rp)* or a snorkelling session to see its ocean-based coral nurseries. The NGO also hosts regular mangrove-planting events and beach cleanups, and volunteering opportunities are available.

Around the next bend a few minutes north, **Pantai Pandanan** is equally as quiet, commanding attention from anyone who catches a view. A few local vendors operate, selling snacks and drinks.

Hop on a Surfboard

Ride the waves with local experts

Most surfers flock to the southern coast of Lombok, but Senggigi has surf, too, and it's generally uncrowded. The reef break at **Pantai Klui** is suitable for beginners, and you can take lessons at **Surf School Lombok Wave** *(WhatsApp +62 831 2962 4531)*, located right on the beach. If you're already established when it comes to waves, rent a board from them and do your own thing. Sip on fresh coconuts in between lessons and stay for sunset to make a full day of it.

Wander Waterfalls Shrouded in the Jungle

Visit Benang Stokel and Benang Kelambu

Swim in crisp mountain waters tumbling down from a lush canopy of jungle vegetation. **Benang Stokel** and **Benang Kelambu** are nestled 'near the foothills on the western side of **Gunung Rinjani** (p350). You'll have to drive around an hour and 20 minutes from Senggigi, but it's worth a day trip – especially if you need a break from the muggy heat of the coastal air. Expect to pay for a guide *(per person around 90,000Rp)* – you're required to have one.

EATING IN SENGGIGI: OUR PICKS

Pasta Pojok: Highly popular spot serving authentic handmade pasta and wood-fired pizza. *11am-10pm* $$

Begibung Beach & Sunset View Resto: Beachside restaurant with Lombok and Indonesian dishes served under thatched umbrellas. *4-10pm* $

Warung Ijo: Simple eatery with Indonesian food, both a la carte and a buffet-style spread with a huge choice of dishes. *8am-10pm* $

Asmara Restaurant & Lounge: Both Indonesian and international cuisine with alfresco tables in a leafy setting right in the centre of town. *4-11pm Mon-Sat* $$

Beyond Senggigi

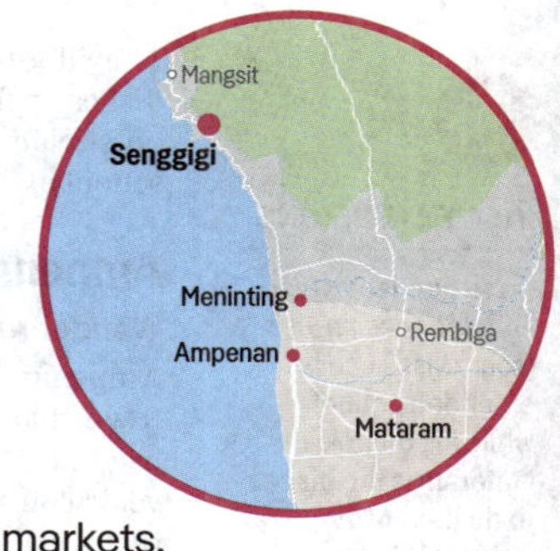

Lombok's urban sprawl is an interesting contrast to its nature, offering traditional markets, historic buildings, street food and cultural experiences.

Lombok's capital city, Mataram, feels like a big town – perhaps because it's the culmination of what was once several villages. Mataram has some unique experiences that provide context to the fabric of Lombok's culture, plus practical city amenities that aren't found in the island's smaller communities. Lively Indonesian markets, fascinating architecture and multidenominational temples with centuries of history make this city rich in heritage. While the population is majorly Sasak Muslim, relics of Hindu culture are found throughout the city. Malls coexist with traditional markets on motorbike-filled avenues.

Ampenan, Mataram and Cakranegara – once villages that blended to form today's Mataram – still differentiate the city's areas. Ampenan borders the sea, and it's a port area with remnants of Dutch colonial-era architecture. Mataram both was and is the government centre, where you'll find administrative buildings and hotels. Cakranegara, the business district, spans the eastern side of the city. It's a commercial area with malls and shops.

Places

GETTING AROUND

Although it's pretty easy to get around the city area, you'll need your own set of wheels. Motorbikes are king here, although there are pavements for covering short distances. The roads are in good condition, and while there can be traffic, the wide lanes of the main avenues assuage the worst of it. Newbie motorbike riders may be intimidated by the broad streets – you should come prepared with riding experience if you're planning to ride anywhere in Indonesia.

Meninting

TIME FROM SENGGIGI: **15MIN**

Join a cooking class with Anggrek Putih Lombok

Food offers an insight into a country's people, culture and history. Whether you're a keen chef or just enjoy tasting new dishes, a cooking class is a fun way to connect with and learn more about the local culture in Lombok. **Anggrek Putih Lombok** *(anggrekputih.com; per person 400,000Rp)* is a family-run cookery school in Meninting, on the outskirts of Mataram. There's an organic garden on-site where most of the ingredients are grown. Friendly and knowledgeable local cooks talk you through the variety of fruit, vegetables and herbs, and you even get to pick fresh ingredients to use in the class (you can choose to join a lunch or dinner session).

VISA EXTENSIONS

If you need to extend your Indonesian visa (some visas can be extended online) while in Lombok, Mataram is the place to do it. **Kantor Imigrasi Mataram**, the immigration office, is located in the heart of Mataram, at the intersection of the main streets of Jl Udayana and Jl Mahoni.

If you entered the country on a 30-day visa on arrival (VOA), you can extend it for another 30 days. From drop-off to pickup, budget five to seven days for the entire process. You'll find it a far less crowded experience compared with Bali's immigration offices. Expect to pay around 500,000Rp for a 30-day extension for your VOA. The phone number is 37-063 2520.

They'll guide you through various Indonesian and Lombok dishes, including curries, satay and vegetarian dishes. There's on-site accommodation, but if you're staying elsewhere, the school also offers free transport to and from class.

Ampenan

TIME FROM SENGGIGI: **20MIN**

Wander Ampenan's historic streets

Ampenan, the western district of Mataram, is an ageing port town that was once used by Dutch colonisers. The port was used heavily for spice trade, and a roam around the area reveals countless weathered buildings with Dutch-style architecture. Today, it's frequented by local foodies and families looking for fresh grilled seafood and other Indonesian plates. Local food vendors post up along the **waterfront** to neighbour established warungs and markets. **Pasar Kebon Roek**, a traditional market, has just about everything when it comes to groceries. From succulent tropical fruit, vegetables, meat and seafood to coffee and sweets – it's a grand selection. You won't find many tourists around here. Pro tip: go first thing in the morning before the heat of the day kicks in.

Mataram

TIME FROM SENGGIGI: **30MIN**

Shop at Mataram's malls and markets

Whether you need warmer clothes to hit the mountains, a rogue item you forgot to pack or you simply want to browse local handicrafts, Mataram is definitely *the* place in Lombok for shopping. **Lombok Epicentrum Mall** *(lombokepicentrum.com)* is the largest of the lot, with four floors of stores, plus a cinema and plenty of food options. A close second goes to **Mataram Mall**, less than 10 minutes east. Clothing, electronics, restaurants and a supermarket can all be found here. As for traditional markets, they're scattered throughout Mataram and vary in size. **Pasar Cakranegara** is one of the more well-known markets, with items ranging from traditional batik fabrics (a classic Indonesian design) to household items and trinkets. These are all authentic souvenirs, compared with more gentrified and touristy areas of Indonesia.

EATING IN MATARAM: LOCAL FOOD

Sukma Rasa Ayam Panggang: Traditional Sasak fare with a menu full of local delights in a comfortable setting outside the busy area. *8am-11pm* $

Sate Rembiga Ibu Sinnaseh: No-frills eatery serving grilled satay, vegetable dishes and other Lombok-style delights. *9am-10pm* $

Rumah Makan Asano: Arguably the best Padang restaurant in town, serving Minang-style rice with various side dishes. *8am-9pm* $

Seafood and Grilled Fish 99: An array of fresh-caught seafood smothered in a variety of different sauces. Arrive hungry. *11am-9.30pm* $

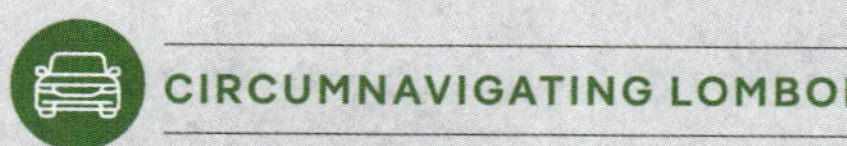

CIRCUMNAVIGATING LOMBOK

Explore Lombok with this driving tour that takes in villages, beaches, highlands and cities.

START	END	LENGTH
Kuta	Kuta	334km; minimum 1 week

Set off from 1 **Kuta** and drive east along the bumpy coastal road, all the way to 2 **Sekaroh** (p339), Lombok's easternmost 'leg'. Here, the peach-hued sands of the pink beaches are a great spot for a break. Head north, driving inland to 3 **Tetebatu** (p337). Take a walk among its rice paddies and rainforest, followed by a swim in the waterfalls. This is a great spot to stay a night or two. Continue north to 4 **Sembalun** (p349), where cooler temperatures, hiking trails and views of **Gunung Rinjani** (p350) await. Spend at least two days here.

Carry on to 5 **Senaru**, where you can swim at **Sendang Gile** (p346) and **Tiu Kelep** (p346) waterfalls. Stay the night, before dropping back down to the west coast where the winding coastal road offers brilliant views at every turn. Around an hour and 20 minutes later, stop at 6 **Pantai Nipah** (p341) for a coconut and a swim. As you drive further south, you'll pass villages and towns that gradually morph into Lombok's urban sprawl. 7 **Senggigi** is worth a stop for its restaurants and souvenir stores, but skip if you're keen for a more local experience. Once you get to the main city area, check out the goods at 8 **Pasar Kebon Roek** market in Ampenan, or drive to 9 **Pasar Cakranegara** for a larger selection of local handicrafts. From here, the hour's drive back to Kuta is easy.

Pull over at **Bayan** to visit **Masjid Kuno Bayan Beleq** (p347), Lombok's oldest mosque dating back to the 14th century.

Pause at **Savana Propok** for magnificent views of the volcano, surrounded by a stunning expanse of grasslands.

Sade is one of Lombok's last remaining traditional villages, with thatched houses and hand-weaving still practised.

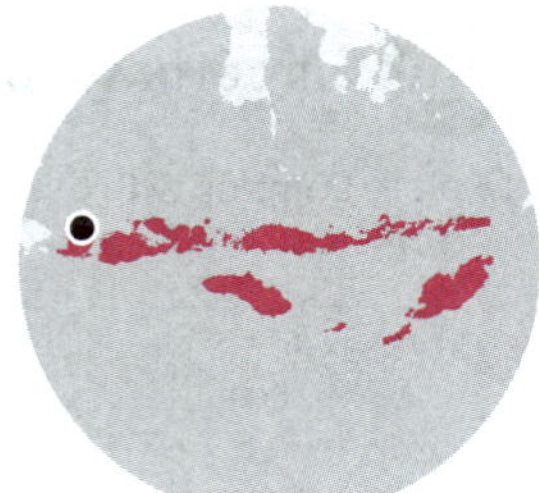

Senaru

RINJANI TREKKING | WATERFALLS | RICE TERRACES

GETTING AROUND

Senaru is a village, so most things are within walking distance. Exploring on foot is common. You can hop on a motorbike and zip around the whole area in a matter of minutes. Some walks to the nature areas around town can take anywhere from 30 minutes to an hour. Either way, the uncrowded streets make it easy to stroll compared with Lombok's busier towns.

TOP TIP

Get to know the locals by staying at a homestay. The hospitality is warm and most family-run accommodation can set you up with information on trekking, local guides and other up-to-date know-how. Many of the surrounding sights don't require a guide, but **Gunung Rinjani** (p350) does.

Senaru is known as the gateway to Gunung Rinjani, Indonesia's second-tallest mountain. While that in itself is a significant enough lure, the small village is also home to misty waterfalls, cultural riches and a labyrinth of lush ricefields. It's far from the buzz, providing a different experience than its coastal counterparts. Although the region faced significant damage following the 2018 earthquake, many homes and businesses have since been rebuilt and cosy homestays, warungs and trekking organisers are once again abundant. A steady stream of trekking enthusiasts continues to fuel tourism in the area, but it remains untouched by mass commercialisation.

Even if you're not fixing for a multiday trek up into some of Indonesia's highest territory, visiting the area is still worthwhile, especially if you're already making a round through the island. The land is lush, and the backdrop couldn't be better, all thanks to the mighty mountainscape that borders the village.

Surrender to Cascading Falls in the Forest

Discover thundering Sendang Gile and Tiu Kelep

Sendang Gile, a waterfall enveloped in a tropical thicket, isn't far off Senaru's main road. This two-tiered fountain has impressive height with cascades roaring down over black volcanic rock and cool waters that are believed to have healing properties. Further down the same trail is the beautiful **Tiu Kelep** with its wide curtain of smaller streams and thundering waters tumbling down the middle. The pools are too shallow for swimming, but the mist of the falls is enough to get you damp. Plus, you'll have to walk across a small river to get there.

The walk from the main road takes around 15 minutes down to Sendang Gile, with stairs most of the way, and an extra 35 minutes to Tiu Kelep. While you'll likely be asked about a tour upon arrival, you can easily walk the trail sans guide. Expect to be followed by a gaggle of local children offering to guide you or carry your belongings – if you don't want to

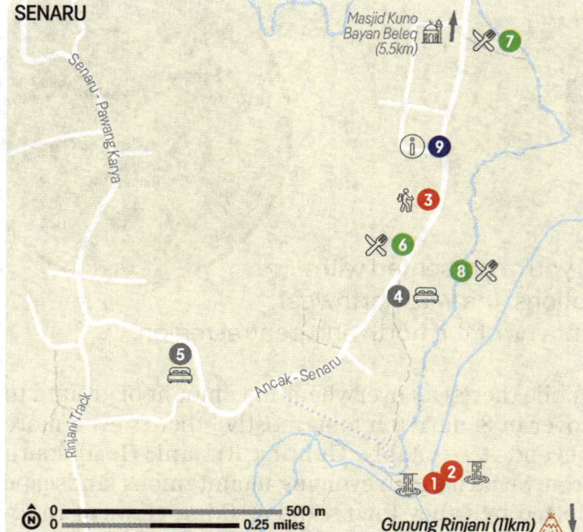

SIGHTS
1 Sendang Gile
2 Tiu Kelep

ACTIVITIES
3 Rudy Trekker

SLEEPING
4 Dragonfly Senaru Lodge
5 Rinjani Lighthouse Cottages

EATING
6 Cafe Rifka
7 Cafe Rinjani Dawn
see 4 Dragonfly Senaru Bar & Resto
8 Rinjani Lodge

INFORMATION
9 Rinjani Women Adventure

pay for their services, politely say 'no thank you' and they'll likely leave you to it. The entrance fee is around 20,000Rp, although some grafters will try to charge foreign tourists five times this price.

A Tour Through Rinjani's Foothills

Stroll the Senaru Panorama Walk

Guided walking tours throughout Senaru and the foothills of **Gunung Rinjani** (p350) offer a deeper insight into the region's flora, fauna and local community traditions, including Sasak cooking and farming. **Rinjani Women Adventure** *(rinjaniwomenadventure.com)* is a local woman-owned and operated trek and tour company that shows travellers around the area. Their **Senaru Panorama Walk** *(per person 450,000Rp)*, led by local women, is a half-day excursion that meanders through small villages and rice terraces. You'll traverse irrigation channels bordered by bamboo groves, ending up at the oh-so gorgeous waterfall nestled in the jungle, **Sendang Gile**. Most, if not all, homestays in the area can also connect you with a local guide for tours around the area.

LOMBOK'S OLDEST MOSQUE

Denda Sukatniwati, trekking guide and founder of **Rinjani Women Adventure**, shares her knowledge.

Bayan is home to the oldest mosque in Lombok, **Masjid Kuno Bayan Beleq**. In the surrounding area, you can learn about culture, religion and traditional life, including the weaving of *sarung tenun* (traditional fabric).

EATING IN SENARU: OUR PICKS

Cafe Rinjani Dawn: Pizzas, burgers, ample vegan options and great coffee, tucked down a little pathway. *7.30am-10pm* $

Cafe Rifka: Family-run spot with fresh, homemade Indonesian and local Lombok dishes, with a wide range of fresh juices. *hours vary* $

Dragonfly Senaru Bar & Resto: Rice, noodles and curries in a friendly little joint, often with live music, and always backed by beautiful views. *9am-10pm* $

Rinjani Lodge: Western and Indonesian dishes with jungle and valley views and free use of pool with purchase of food. *7am-10pm* $$

Beyond Senaru

When leaving Senaru, you're presented with two wildly different options: the wild northwest coast or the vast mountains of the north and central region.

Places

While there's an overwhelming amount of ground to cover in Senaru (on foot, mostly), there's even more beyond it – notably, Gunung Rinjani. Head south from Senaru for an evolving mountainous landscape dotted by valley towns and striking views of Indonesia's second-highest mountain. Serpentine roads loop through the varied terrain, with majestic views at countless turnoffs. Due north of Senaru lies the northwest coast of Lombok, a comparatively untravelled strip. Here, the main road snakes in and out of the ocean's view, passing numerous tranquil small towns. Further west in the Sire peninsula, a small handful of high-end, luxury resorts take up prime beachfront real estate. Apart from the honeymooner vibes, you won't find much else here.

GETTING AROUND

The mountain roads throughout the north and central region of Lombok are wonderfully paved – necessary for some of the steep inclines and sharp switchbacks that come with increasing elevation. If travelling with two people on one motorbike, beware of your collective weight versus the strength of the bike on some of the steep inclines. Motorbikes with lower cubic capacity may struggle when overloaded on intense sections of the route. In contrast, the northwest coast is easy cruising.

Bukit Selong

TIME FROM SENARU: **1HR**

Hike to gorgeous views from a small hill

A vibrant patchwork of varied shades of green makes the view from **Bukit Selong** unique, not to mention utterly photogenic. This viewpoint overlooks a vast stretch of fields, backed by a mountain to the east and the town of Sembalun and **Gunung Rinjani** (p350) to the west. A small parking area leads to an unassuming dirt path, where you'll pay an entry fee of around 10,000Rp before continuing. Less than 10 minutes later, the uphill path leads you to the top. A wooden star-shaped platform beckons photo enthusiasts, but the attraction remains fairly quiet, despite being wildly photogenic. Note that Google Maps might lead you astray. Should you end up at what appears to be a dead end, ask someone to point you in the right direction – it's quite close to the map marker.

Sajang

TIME FROM SENARU: **40MIN**

Swim in Mangku Sakti waterfall

Sajang is a village that most people just drive through on their way to Sembalun. However, it's worth stopping for a few hours to splash about in **Air Terjun Mangku Sakti**. This stunning waterfall is unique compared with Lombok's other waterfalls, thanks to the milky-blue waters that rush through the limestone rapids. Despite this, not many tourists come here, so don't be surprised if you're the only one around. From the main road, you'll have to drive down a dirt road to the parking area, from which a 15-minute walk will lead you to the waterfall. Depending on when you're visiting (high season or a weekend), you'll sometimes find local guides at the main road offering to guide you to the parking area for around 100,000Rp – this is worth paying for an easier experience.

Sembalun Valley

TIME FROM SENARU: **1HR**

A hillside hike to Pergasingan Hill

If Bukit Selong was the appetiser, consider **Pergasingan Hill** the main course. The ascent is often done at sunrise, leading to skyward views of the entire **Sembalun Valley**, plus the entirety of **Gunung Rinjani** (p350) in the distance. It provides an impressive perspective of the landscape and can be done at a fairly steady pace in around two hours, depending on how much time you spend oohing and ahhing at the views on the way. While the soft morning light and mist make for an ethereal sight, it's also lovely at sunset. Entrance to the trailhead costs 50,000Rp. If you arrive before sunrise, expect to pay on your way back down.

SEMBALUN'S SUNNY STRAWBERRIES

Sembalun Valley's mountainous climate is a perfect setting for growing strawberries: something local farmers have leveraged for sweet benefit. The rich volcanic soil and cooler temperatures mean that these juicy berries are all over the place. They're a source of income for the community and a delight for anyone picking up a pack. You'll see farms dotted throughout the sprawling valley.

Contrary to what the Beatles might lead you to imagine, strawberry fields don't actually produce a sea of red colour. The ornate lines of these green plants are organised into rows, with most of the fruit hanging below. Whether you want to pick them yourself at a local farm or sample from a vendor, they're pretty much everywhere.

EATING IN SEMBALUN: OUR PICKS

Kedai Sawah Sembalun: Chow down on Indonesian dishes in this popular open-air cafe in the middle of flower fields and farmland. *8am-9pm* $

Sembalun Clasik Cafe: Simple and straightforward menu with homecooked rice and noodle dishes, and a selection of local coffees. *8am-11.30pm* $

Kebon Kupi Sembalun: Away from the main road, enjoy fried rice, soups, fried snacks, coffee and juice with a side of mountain views. *9am-7pm* $

Mahakala: Sembalun's best restaurant serving tasty Western and Indonesian dishes, plus quality coffee, with amazing views across the valley. *8am-8pm* $$

ROB_TRAVEL/SHUTTERSTOCK

TOP EXPERIENCE

Gunung Rinjani

Measuring up at an impressive 3726m, Indonesia's second-highest mountain is both mighty and revered. The breathtaking Gunung Rinjani is sacred for both the Sasak and Hindu people, and is a frequent pilgrimage sight. The volcano's summit makes for a strenuous hike that isn't for the fainthearted, but the incredible views are among some of Indonesia's most lauded.

DON'T MISS

- Gunung Rinjani National Park
- Danau Segara Anak
- Senaru Crater Rim
- Surya Sakti Waterfall
- Rinjani Hot Springs
- Mountainside camping

Gunung Rinjani National Park

The entirety of Gunung Rinjani National Park spans some 413 sq km, including the greater radius of Gunung Rinjani itself. The volcano's elevation places it in a biogeographical crossroads, where the land differs from what is typical of Southeast Asian terrain, evolving into arid landscape instead. If you're not keen on lacing up your boots and hiking to the summit, the foothills of Gunung Rinjani reveal a distinctly different and mesmerising ecosystem.

PRACTICALITIES

● rinjaninationalpark.com ● per day entrance fee 250,000Rp
● open to climb Apr-Dec

A Sacred & Cherished Landscape

Each year, the Balinese perform ceremonies atop Rinjani to honour the gods and spirits. It's one of three peaks they consider sacred, along with Gunung Bromo in Java and Gunung Agung in Bali. The Sasaks ascend the slopes to pray when the moon is full. Their faith, Wetu Telu, is a melange of Hindu and Islamic beliefs, as well as ancestral worship and animism.

Planning Your Hike

Climbing Gunung Rinjani is not permitted from 1 January to 31 March. While that sounds like a big chunk of time, you don't want to climb it in bad or dangerous weather. If you're planning to hike, make sure your trip isn't during rainy season (mid-November to March). April through November are typically favourable months. Finding a guide is quite easy, as tourism in the area accounts for a large part of the economy – you'll be able to join a trek fairly last-minute. Check out an independent trekking agency such as **Rudy Trekker** *(rudytrekker.com)* or ask a homestay; nearly all of them are well connected with local guides.

The Hike

After departing from either Senaru (p346) or **Sembalun** (p349), trails ascend through rainforest teeming with wildlife. The route is challenging, but frequented by many people, plenty of whom aren't experienced hikers. That said, it's not exactly cruisey – this is a real trek.

The Crater Rim

Once the landscape shifts from lush to arid, the crater rim reveals a panoramic view of the skyline and summit beyond. For less-experienced hikers, it's possible to hike for two days and one night to reach – and finish at – the crater rim.

The Summit

Expect loose rocks, soft ground and a steep gradient on the final gruelling stretch to the summit. The topside views are nothing short of staggering, revealing the crater below and the landscape beyond. This prized peak takes a minimum of three days and two nights to reach, with the first night spent camping along the crater rim. Most hiking groups begin their second day before sunrise. Longer trips of three nights are also available.

Danau Segara Anak

Crescent-shaped and deeply blue, Danau Segara Anak is a volcanic lake west of Gunung Rinjani's attention-commanding massif, just below the crater rim. The word *danau* means 'lake', and *segara anak* is 'child of the sea' – alluding to the lake's similarities to the ocean.

Rinjani Hot Springs

If you decide to do the three-day, two-night hike, you can continue to the summit or head down from the crater rim to experience the natural hot springs beside Danau Segara Anak. It takes two hours to reach these natural pools – an airy downhill hike that floats through low-hanging clouds. The hot thermal waters flowing from **Surya Sakti Waterfall** make for a picturesque scene.

ALTERNATIVE TREKKING ROUTES

The overwhelming majority of treks begin from either Senaru or Sembalun, but you can also start from **Tetebatu** (p337) on the mountain's southern slope. You'll meet far fewer hikers on the way up, and you can reach the summit in a two-day, one-night ascent. If you've flown in, this also cuts travel time to and from your starting point, as Tetebatu is just an hour away from **Lombok International Airport**.

TOP TIPS

- A local guide is required; don't try to hike without one. Read up on Senaru, Sembalun and Tetebatu to decide where you want to start from.
- Research trekking companies thoroughly before booking.
- Spend more time hiking the same distance if you're less experienced.
- Phone service is available in most of the park, but spotty inside the crater.
- Bring much warmer clothes than you think you'll need on a tropical island.
- Don't try to break in brand-new boots.
- Pack swimwear if you fancy a dip in the hot springs.
- There's not a lot of shade. Wear sunscreen like it's your job.

Southwestern Peninsula & the Secret Gilis

SECLUDED ISLANDS | DESERTED BEACHES | LEGENDARY SURF

GETTING AROUND

The main road of the Southwestern Peninsula, Jl Raya Sekotong, runs from Lembar to the westernmost point of Lombok, changing its name to Jl Raya Pelangan and Jl Raya Siung along the way. It's a smooth road, with hills and bends after Lembar. Further west, the road hugs the coast and flattens out. Smaller roads in the area are often dirt and gravel, which can be tricky – especially on the approach to Desert Point. A few bemos run between Lembar and Pelangan.

Rustic and mellow, Lombok's Southwestern Peninsula is full of deserted beaches, world-class surf and undisturbed local life – it's the type of place where passersby smile and wave at each other. The peninsula's one large road meanders along its northern shore, weaving through small villages. This ribbon-like route ascends in a circuitous nature over arid-looking hills, playing peek-a-boo with views of the aqua coastline.

While there is a handful of accommodation, ranging from chilled-out beachside bungalows to upmarket boutique hotels, most of them are offshore on the Southwest Gilis. For a long time, this series of blissfully low-key islands, often dubbed 'the Secret Gilis', was something of a word-of-mouth phenomenon – the type of place you only hear about from locals or backpacking aficionados. However, they're quickly earning a reputation for their gorgeous waters and landscape, and are seeing an increase in visitors, especially among day-trippers from Kuta.

Explore a Tranquil Chain of Islands

Visit Gili Nanggu, Tangkong, Sudak and Kedis

While the Gili Islands have become a much-discussed experience of Southeast Asia's traveller trail, this tiny chain of partially inhabited islands epitomises off-grid at its finest. A bountiful array of marine life, including intricate corals and multihued fish of all sizes, surrounds each island's rim. **Gili Nanggu** – the westernmost island of the bunch, where most tours go – is known for the prime snorkelling spots. The neighbouring islands, **Gili Tangkong** and **Gili Sudak**, are also fantastic places to snorkel. **Gili Kedis** might be the tiniest island to actually make it on a map – it's a whimsical patch of sand emerging from the sea with only a scruff of vegetation. These islands don't offer accommodation, but it's possible to camp overnight. Ask your tour operator for more details as they can provide camping gear and food.

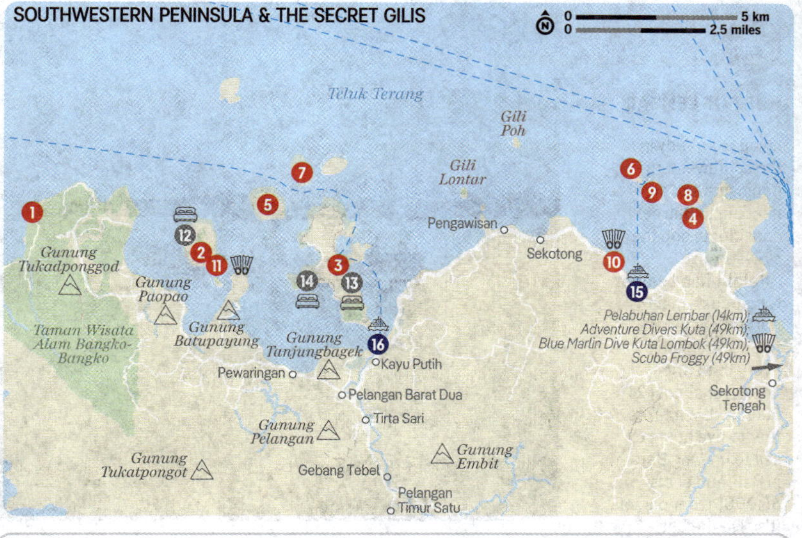

SIGHTS
1 Desert Point
2 Gili Asahan
3 Gili Gede
4 Gili Kedis
5 Gili Layar
6 Gili Nanggu
7 Gili Rengit
8 Gili Sudak
9 Gili Tangkong

ACTIVITIES
10 Blow Bubbles Divers
11 Oceanway

SLEEPING
12 Bleu Mathis Gili Asahan
13 High Dive Gili Gede Resort
14 Yellow Coco Gili Gede

TRANSPORT
see 16 Sekotong Boat Transport & SSBT Tour Agent
15 Tawun Harbour
16 Tembowong Harbour

Many tours leaving from Kuta and labelled 'the Secret Gilis' will take you around Gili Nanggu and its neighbours. If you're looking to venture onward to the Gilis out west (yes, there are even more – Gili Gede and its neighbours) then be sure to mention before booking. If you're already slowly roaming the Southwest Peninsula, you can organise a tour from either **Tembowong Harbour** (close to Gili Gede, Asahan, Layar, and Rengit) or **Tawun Harbour** (close to Gili Nanggu, Tangkong, Sudak and Kedis), where a few tour agencies operate. One of the most highly rated is **Sekotong Boat Transport & SSBT Tour Agent** *(WhatsApp +62 821 4554 6823)* based in Tembowong Harbour, which offers boat charters, snorkelling tours and island-hopping adventures.

There are no public boats or taxi boats in this area, but you'll find several independent boatmen who offer their local expertise in the form of private tours. Getting a ride to any of these islands is typically priced per boat, starting around 400,000Rp. The price will depend on how many people you're with, so booking a boat with a group is your best bet. Should you go it solo, you'll pay more but will have the peace of a boat all to yourself.

TOP TIP

There are some lodgings on the northern coast, but the Southwest Gilis – 10 minutes by boat – have the best beaches and lodgings. You could day trip to the Southwestern Peninsula from Kuta, Senggigi or Mataram, but it's a one-to-two-hour journey there and back.

PORT OF LEMBAR

If you're already in the southwestern peninsula and are heading to Bali next, consider taking the slow ferry.

Pelabuhan Lembar is Lombok's main port for car ferries to Bali, which run every 1½ to three hours, for almost 24 hours a day. It takes four to five hours to sail to Padang Bai in Bali, and costs 65,000Rp per person. It's also the best option if you're hiring a scooter or car and want to take your vehicle with you, costing 169,400Rp per scooter, while cars start from 1,184,100Rp depending on the size.

Tickets are available to purchase on ferizy.com, or at the ticket office at the port.

Snorkel in Paradise

The best of Gili Gede, Asahan, Layar and Rengit

Closer to Lombok's westernmost edge lies another collection of gorgeous isles. **Gili Gede**, the largest of the bunch, is also the most developed. This interestingly shaped island is ringed by dazzling reefs and white-sand beaches, only some of which appear to be touched by human influence. To the west, the beautiful **Gili Asahan** offers an undisturbed getaway with not much to do besides unwind on palm-shaded beaches and explore the colourful reefs around the island. **Gili Layar** and **Gili Rengit** border some of the area's best offshore snorkelling spots, where massive coral formations dominate the ocean's floor. It couldn't get more serene. Again, the best places to organise a snorkelling trip around these islands are at **Tembowong Harbour** (p353) and **Tawun Harbour** (p353), although accommodation on Gili Gede and Gili Asahan will often include a pickup service from the mainland.

Even fewer travellers seem to make it out here, although there's a greater selection of salty beachfront stays and boutique hotels across Gili Gede and Gili Asahan. Gili Layar and Gili Rengit don't offer accommodation. The quintessential beach bungalows at **Yellow Coco Gili Gede** (p369) are the perfect place to unplug and have a rustic digital detox. Those looking for a sumptuous, 'treat yourself' type of experience will find it at **Bleu Mathis Gili Asahan** – where personal plunge pools overlook the serene shoreline. If you're coming to snorkel, gear is typically provided on tours or can be rented from your accommodation. It's definitely the go-to activity around here.

WISSUTA.ON/SHUTTERSTOCK

Gili Gede

Surf Desert Point's Famous Waves

Catch Lombok's most iconic wave

It's as far west as it gets on the Southwestern Peninsula: **Desert Point** is a famous break, albeit a temperamental one. Roughly a 15-minute drive from the fishing village of Bangko Bangko, this landscape is mostly desolate without much around (you know, besides arguably some of the world's best surf, but no big deal). Expect much better conditions during the dry season (from May to September), when offshore winds from the north create longer barrels. Even during this period, it can be an arduous waiting game when conditions suddenly go calm and leave everyone hanging for more.

Desert Point requires an advanced skill level when it comes to surfing and navigation. Getting here is a bit of a mission, but that's part of what makes it so special. While the main road along the coast (Jl Raya Siung) is in pretty good condition, once you turn off left at the fork in the road leading away from Bangko Bangko, it transforms into more of a treacherous dusty gravel path that can have even the most experienced motorbike drivers wincing over surprise potholes for 3km. So prepare for a proper road trip. There is only a handful of simple accommodation here and no surf schools or rental shops, so make sure to bring your own gear.

THE PENINSULA'S BEST SNORKELLING & SCUBA DIVING OPERATORS

Many Kuta-based scuba and snorkelling trips head over to the Southwest Peninsula, as well as operators closer to the Secret Gilis.

Scuba Froggy: Dive courses, plus daily dive and snorkelling trips. *(scubafroggy.com)*

Blue Marlin Dive Kuta Lombok: Dive classes and day trips to reefs. *(bluemarlindive.com)*

Adventure Divers Lombok: Dive and snorkelling excursions, plus PADI courses. *(adventure-divers-lombok.com)*

The High Dive Gili Gede Resort and PADI Scuba Dive Centre: Beachfront villas on Gili Gede, combined with a dive centre. *(thehighdive indonesia.com)*

Blow Bubbles Divers South Gilis: Dive centre close to the Southwestern Gilis. *(blowbubbles divers.com)*

Oceanway: Dive centre on Gili Asahan, with courses and accommodation. *(oceanwaydive.com)*

Gili Trawangan

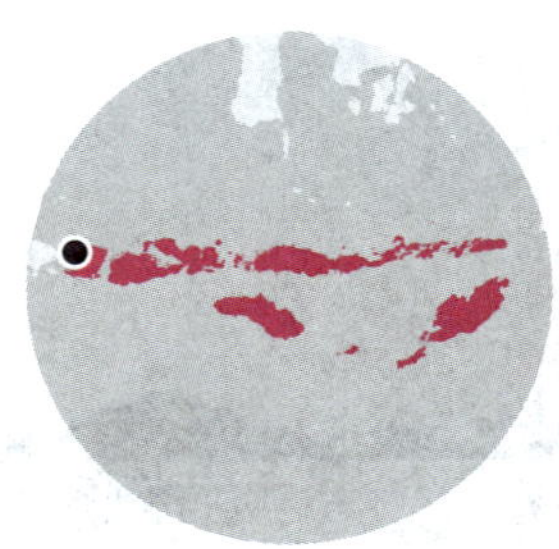

SUN & SAND | WILD PARTIES | GREAT DIVING

GETTING AROUND

Motorised vehicles are banned in the Gilis. Explore on foot or rent a bicycle – the entire island is walkable and mostly flat, apart from a modest hill to the southwest. The *cidomo* operate like taxis, but we can't recommend them due to concerns over how the horses are treated. Nowadays, local organisations such as Horses of Gili *(horsesofgili.com)* provide supplies and support to the horses through veterinary care and education, but there's still a ways to go.

TOP TIP

Ramadan, the Muslim fasting month, varies each year, moving back by ten days a year (February to March in 2027). This brings a quieter Gili T, with music being turned off early at bars and restaurants. You won't find any big parties during this time.

Arriving at Gili Trawangan's port, you might wonder what you've let yourself in for, with crowds of people waiting to get on the boat you just got off. The main strip has a unique pace: bicyclists and *cidomo* (horse-drawn carts) share a dusty lane with meandering pedestrians. The first few minutes on Gili Trawangan might feel less than tranquil, but venture beyond the beachfront bars and hotels to reach an easygoing, beautiful coastline. Affectionately called 'Gili T', this island exudes friendliness and couldn't be more laid-back if it tried. Coastal views of Lombok's rugged shoreline and Bali's towering Gunung Agung in the distance are simply a chef's kiss.

If you're looking for a great party, you'll find it here. But it's also easy to escape the noise. Roam the crisscrossed pathways of the island's centre over to the west coast, where serene sands remain between looming developments. Inland, the call to prayer echoes five times a day.

Join in the Famous Party Scene

Hit the nightlife 'til sunrise

Whether you throw back a questionable volume of Bintangs with your toes in the sand or join a full-on pub crawl, Gili T's nightlife accommodates. Known for getting rowdy, Trawangan's social scene ranges from beachfront shacks to fancy resort bars and worn-in backpacker staples. Partying is an all-night affair here, with things starting to get busy at around 11pm and lasting all the way to 5am.

Casa Vintage *(instagram.com/casavintagebeach)*, a beachside bar and restaurant that gets buzzy, is popular for sunset libations. **Lava Bar** *(instagram.com/lavabargilit)* always draws a crowd with cheap drinks and Friday bingo. Midweek festivities are a staple at **Tír na nÓg** *(tirnanogbar.com)*, an Irish sports bar with a particular knack for throwing Wednesday

SIGHTS
1 Gili Trawangan Beach
2 Gili Trawangan Sunset Beach

ACTIVITIES
3 Blue Marlin Dive
4 Compass Divers
5 DPM Diving Gili Trawangan
6 Glenn Nusa Wreck
7 Manta Dive
8 Shark Point
9 Trawangan Stingray Divers

SLEEPING
10 Pearl of Trawangan
11 PinkCoco Gili Trawangan
12 Radika House

EATING
13 Banyan Tree
14 Casa Vintage
see 7 Coffee & Thyme
15 Jali Kitchen
16 La Cala Beach Club
17 My House
18 Taste Cafe & Restaurant
19 The Shack Restaurant & Bar
20 Warung Jaman Now

DRINKING & NIGHTLIFE
see 13 Lava Bar
see 7 Sama Sama
21 Tír na nÓg
22 Window Sports Bar

INFORMATION
see 20 Gili Eco Trust

bangers. Reggae music colours the scene at **Sama Sama** *(instagram.com/ samasamareggaebar)*, a two-storey reggae bar full of both locals and travellers nearly every night of the week – especially Saturdays.

Most of these nightlife spots are located with a few minutes from each other along the island's southeast coast where the harbour is, so it's easy to hop (or stumble) from one spot to another. There are also several beach bars along the west coast such as **Window Sports Bar** *(instagram.com/windowsportsbar)* which offer a more relaxed night out.

ILLEGAL SUBSTANCES

On notoriously rowdy Gili Trawangan, you'll spot some beachside cafes openly advertising the sale of magic mushrooms, and it's not uncommon to get offers of drugs while walking on the street. This is despite Indonesia's strong anti-drug stance.

It's worth keeping in mind that Indonesia has extremely strict laws against illicit substances, and intoxication and/or possession is punishable by lengthy imprisonment, or worse. While the island has earned a party reputation over the years, as a country, Indonesia is firmly anti-drugs, and it's important to remember this to avoid trouble.

Discover the Quieter Side of Gili T

Quiet snorkelling

Primo spots to swim and snorkel are found in droves throughout the island's quieter areas: the south, north and entire west coast. Seeing as the shoreline spans the entire perimeter, picking a specific beach isn't entirely necessary – but **Gili Trawangan Sunset Beach** lives up to its name, with sundowner views and lots of open space. Keep heading north for **Gili Trawangan Beach**, a long stretch of quiet sand with much less activity than the busy eastern coast. That said, you're not going to have a hard time finding a good place to swim around here. There aren't any public bathrooms, but you'll find little shops along the beaches selling snacks and drinks, and you're never too far from a cafe or restaurant. Do check the tides; swimming at high tide is better when the rocky coral formations are submerged.

EATING ON GILI T: OUR PICKS

The chocolate mousse is highly rated

Taste Cafe & Restaurant: Fresh dishes with plenty of seafood options, ideal for light lunches on the beach. *7.30am-9.30pm* $$

My House: Authentic Italian cuisine in a courtyard garden setting. *noon-9.30pm* $$

Coffee & Thyme: Sandwiches, pastas, salads and homemade cakes, plus fruit juice and coffee. *7am-9pm* $

The Shack Restaurant & Bar: A mix of Western and Indonesian dishes, from breakfast to all-day snacks and mains. *7.30am-10pm* $$

Jali Kitchen: Asian-fusion cuisine with Indonesian-, Thai- and Vietnamese-influenced plates, all served in a leafy setting. *noon-10pm* $$

Warung Jaman Now: Indonesian fare, plus burgers, pasta and smoothie bowls, dished up in chilled-out surroundings. *8am-11pm* $

Banyan Tree: Small bites, soups, sandwiches and heartier mains, plus a full menu of coffee, juices and health drinks. On the beach. *7am-8pm* $$

La Cala Beach Club: BBQ meat and seafood, salads, sandwiches and a long cocktail list, with seats right on the sand. *8.30am-11pm* $$

DANIEL WILHELM NILSSON/SHUTTERSTOCK

Scuba diving, Gili Trawangan

Scuba Dive the Gilis

Discover a wealth of marine life

Roughly 25 different dive sites are located in the Gilis' greater Marine Protected Area. Tiny creatures – pygmy seahorses, mantis shrimp, pipefish – flutter about the corals. There are also plenty of large species, including whitetip and blacktip sharks.

Dive sites are found all over the Gili map. **Shark Point** lies west of Gili T, living up to its moniker, with sharks and turtles gliding around. **Turtle Heaven** is another aptly named, turtle-filled site on the east side of Meno. **Manta Point** (also referred to as Sunset Reef) is just south of Gili T, with mantas and plenty of smaller fish flitting between the corals. Experienced divers can venture down 45m to the **Japanese Wreck**, a Japanese patrol boat that sunk off the southern coast of Gili Air.

You're spoilt for choice when it comes to dive centres and schools in the Gilis, especially on Gili T where dive centres are found all along the east coast – take your time reading reviews and comparing prices before committing to one. It's also worth popping in and getting a feel for the place and the people. One of the best-known dive schools is **Blue Marlin Dive** *(bluemarlindive.com; PADI Open Water course 6,400,000Rp).*

GILI T'S BEST DIVING SCHOOLS

Blue Marlin Dive: The Gili T branch of a popular diving school. They're in Senggigi and Kuta, too. *(bluemarlindive.com)*

DPM Diving Gili Trawangan: Scuba courses and day trips for beginners and advanced divers, located steps from the east shore. *(dpmdiving.com)*

Manta Dive: Dive centre and resort combo with training facilities on both Gili T and Gili Air. *(manta-dive.com)*

Compass Divers: Dive courses and accommodation, with private and hostel dorm rooms, just steps from Gili T's ferry port. *(compassdiving.com)*

Trawangan Stingray Divers: Courses ranging from beginner to divemaster in the northeast corner of the island. *(trawanganstingraydivers.com)*

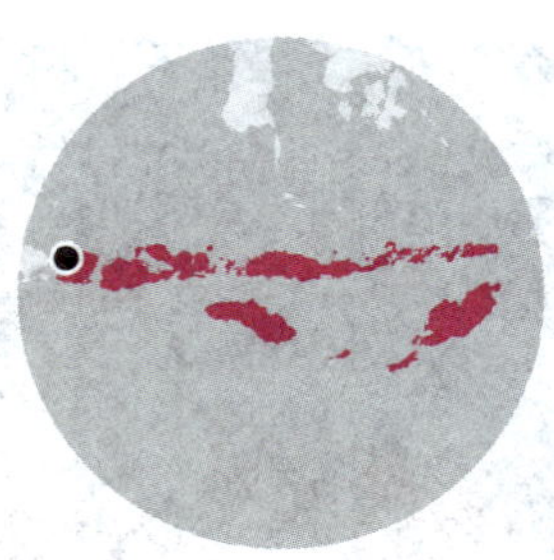

Gili Meno

PEACE & QUIET | SASAK CULTURE | SNORKELLING SPOTS

GETTING AROUND

Walking and cycling are the ways to get around Gili Meno. You might see a rogue electric scooter – but they're silent. It's an arduous workout to ride a bicycle around the island's sandy outer edge. If you try, be prepared for an upper body workout as you walk your bike in an uncomfortably high volume of sand. It's better to walk the coast and save cycling for the inland area.

TOP TIP

If you're heading from Trawangan to accommodation on Meno's west coast (the opposite side of the island's public **port**), organise a private ride right to the shore. Ask some of the boatmen near the port if they'll take you, ideally with another stray traveller or two to split the cost. A private boat costs around 300,000Rp – fairly economical, and highly convenient for a group.

Stunningly calm and undisturbed, little Gili Meno is by far the most chill of the trio. If you're after a true escape, you'll find it here. This tiny oval-shaped island is also the most traditional of the three Gilis, where the lovely hum of local Sasak life continues on without as much tourist-catered development. Meno has all the same natural delights as the others: alabaster sand in all directions and translucent water that glows aqua under the sun's strong rays. The small port lies on the eastern coast, where a handful of low-key accommodation and places to grab a bite dot the sand. On the west coast, a few glitzy stays change up the vibe, luring honeymooners and luxury-lovers to revel in stylish solitude. Inland, coconut groves shade traditional Sasak homes. There's a big old saltwater lake adorned with mangroves, too – and you might just have its boardwalk all to yourself.

Snorkel Around the Gilis

Underwater sculptures and intricate corals

Most snorkelling excursions sample different spots across all three Gilis. You have two options: join a snorkelling trip or rent the gear on your own. Snorkelling can be enjoyed from any Gili beach, but some of the best spots are off the northern and western coasts of Meno, where colourful tropical fish dart in and around the reef. Off Meno's west coast lies **Nest**: an underwater sculpture made famous on social media by photography-loving visitors on their snorkel sojourns. Sculpted from environmental-grade concrete, 48 human figures stand in a circle and are slowly becoming a part of the oceanscape. You'll find tour boats hovering around the area throughout the day, mostly full of people from Gili T and Gili Air. Pro tip: you can DIY and swim right up to it from **Bask** (p369) on Meno's shore in just a few minutes. Be aware that this spot can get very busy – visit first thing in the morning or right before sunset to avoid the crowds.

GILI MENO

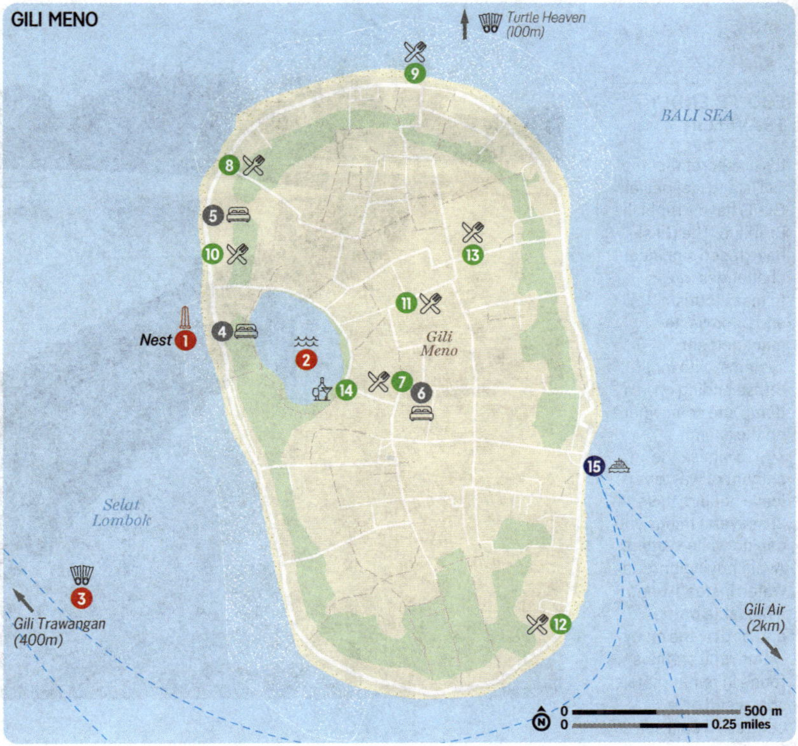

HIGHLIGHTS
1 Nest

SIGHTS
2 Danau Gili Meno

ACTIVITIES
3 Bounty Wreck

SLEEPING
4 Bask
5 Mahamaya
6 Rabbit Tree

EATING
7 Backyard Island Cafe
8 Bubbles Bar & Restaurant
9 Easy Warung & Bar
10 Malfina Beach Bar & Resto
11 Tip of the Tongue Warung
12 Umar Resto
13 Warung Licung Bamboo

DRINKING & NIGHTLIFE
14 Brother Hood

TRANSPORT
15 Public Boat Landing

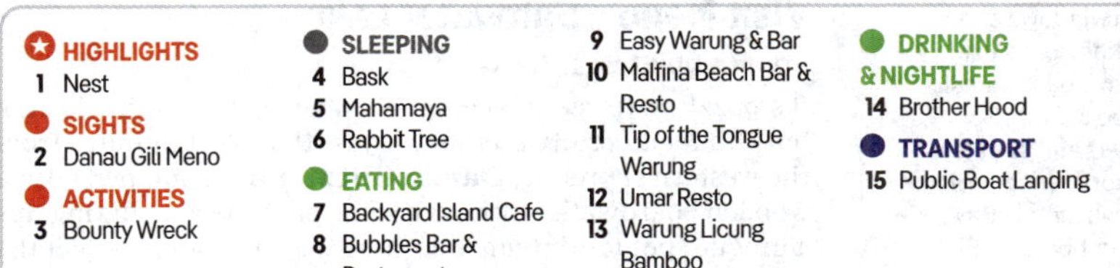

Renting a snorkel set (a mask with snorkel plus fins) costs around 50,000Rp at most accommodation. Corals in shallow waters have seen better days, sadly, due to bleaching. Thankfully, regeneration efforts have been strong and continue to make hopeful progress with BioRock technology – and there's still plenty of coral to see. The cost of snorkelling boat trips depends on how long you go for. Some excursions only last two hours, while others can be a full-day affair. Expect to pay around 200,000Rp to join a group tour, and upwards of 700,000Rp for a private boat. On all three islands, you'll find little stalls around the harbour advertising snorkel trips, making it easy to compare prices. Some also offer glass-bottom boat trips, which are a fun alternative if you don't fancy getting in the water.

ECO-FRIENDLY TRAVELLING

It's no secret that the Gili Islands (especially Gili T) have a rubbish problem. The Gilis have faced significant challenges due to mass tourism and poor waste-management systems, with most refuse ending up in a dump site somewhere on the island.

To minimise the amount of waste you leave behind, there are several things you can do while visiting. Avoid buying bottled water. Instead, bring a reusable bottle and pop by the many water-refill stations found in restaurants, shops and dive centres – you'll see them advertised in windows and shopfronts, usually asking for a small fee of 5000Rp per refill. It's also worth bringing your own metal straw, toothbrush and hairbrush or comb, as many hotels still provide single-use plastic toiletries and straws.

Visit Meno's Saltwater Lake

Roam a quiet boardwalk

It's puzzling to see such a big old lake on such a tiny island, but Gili Meno's saltwater lake is just that. Just minutes from the western shoreline, **Danau Gili Meno** is equipped with a wooden boardwalk – although some parts need updating. It's a unique spot for the sunset, where the still waters reflect the sherbet-coloured sky with a thin strip of vegetation forming the horizon. It's the type of place where you'll likely go 'Huh, that's interesting', before carrying on with your day. A quick stop to check it out is worthwhile, but by no means should you budget a significant amount of time to visit it.

EATING BEACHSIDE ON GILI MENO: OUR PICKS

Malfina Beach Bar & Resto: Fabulously located beach bar on the west coast, with a mix of Western and Indonesian food. *8am-10pm* $

Umar Resto: Simple, homemade Western and Indonesian dishes with tables, beanbags and loungers on the sand. *8am-9pm* $

Bubbles Bar & Restaurant: Good for both vegetarians and meat eaters, with beanbags to lounge on, lovingly shaded by beach umbrellas. *7.30am-9pm* $$

Bask (p369): The ultimate fancy experience with artfully crafted plates and thoughtful details in a sleek, minimalistic setting. *7am-10pm* $$

AKTURER/SHUTTERSTOCK

Wooden boardwalk, Danau Gili Meno

Near the entrance to the lake's boardwalk, the super friendly **Brother Hood** bar welcomes visitors warmly. It's more than a watering hole – this community hub organises rubbish collections for a greener Gili Meno and also hosts donation-based workshops centred around art and upcycling. The best way to learn what's currently going on is to simply stop by and say hello. So come for the lake, but stay for the inevitable good vibes and post-sunset reggae jam-sesh next door.

GILI ECO TRUST

Although the underwater scenery remains awe-inspiring to this day, destructive fishing practices, coupled with an intense El Niño season back in the late 90s, have caused significant damage to the reefs of the Gilis, even more evident in shallow dive sites above 18m.

Gili Eco Trust *(giliecotrust.com)*, a Trawangan-based NGO, was founded back in 2002 to protect the surrounding reefs from illegal and damaging fishing. Some businesses on Gili T might ask if you're interested in making a reef donation for 50,000Rp, which goes directly to reef restoration and protective patrolling. The organisation has made significant contributions to and progress in eco-preservation across the Gilis since its inception.

EATING ON GILI MENO: INDONESIAN FOOD

Backyard Island Cafe: Simple place for pizza, seafood and grilled dishes, as well as curries and Indonesian classics. *noon-11pm* $$

Tip of the Tongue Warung: Local dishes and lots of fresh seafood, in a quiet spot in the centre of the island. *6.30am-10pm* $

Warung Licung Bamboo: Huge selection of local dishes, including plenty of vegetarian options. *10am-10pm* $

Easy Warung & Bar: Waterside warung with prime sunset views, plus grilled fish and fruity cocktails. *10am-10pm* $

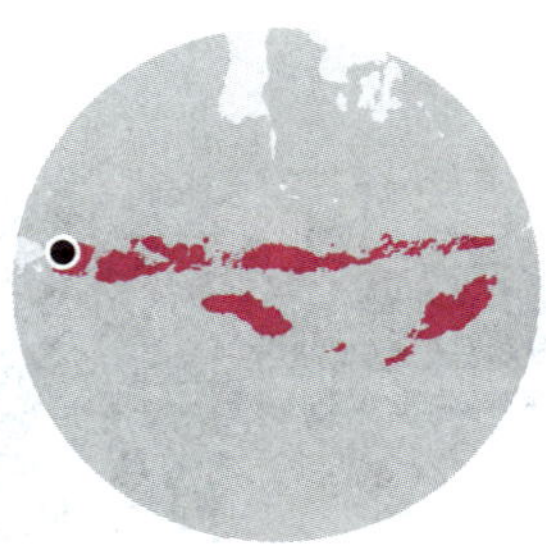

Gili Air

LAID-BACK VIBES | POWDERY BEACHES | DIVING & SNORKELLING

GETTING AROUND

You can walk from the top to the bottom of Gili Air in 20 minutes – strolling is easy here. Mostly paved main streets connect to smaller sandy offshoots, which comprise most of the north. Gili Air has the best conditions of all three islands for cycling, but you'll still find some beachside sections that are too sandy for riding. Gili Air is only about a 15 minute ride from Bangsal Port on Lombok. Take the public boat or negotiate a private ride from one of the portside companies.

TOP TIP

Lock your bike whenever it's not in sight. Rather than fastening the lock around a stationary object every time, you can simply loop it around the wheel so it renders the bike immobile until you're ready to roll again. This goes for all three of the Gili Islands.

Mellow yet upbeat Gili Air is the best of both worlds. Fusing a bit of Trawangan's social energy with Meno's pleasant lull, the island's perimeter is full of bright and inviting beach bars, longstanding dive centres and a range of accommodation, from simple and homey to barefoot luxury. It's hard to pick favourites when it comes to beaches in the Gilis, but the overall vibe and scenery of Gili Air's shoreline is something special. Hushed in some corners and animated in others, you can recharge in peace but engage in tropical merriment whenever the mood arrives.

The heart of Gili Air has paved streets, unlike its neighbouring islands. While the central area is lined with tourist-catered shops and a sprinkling of Western-looking restaurants, a short walk off the main path reveals quiet palm-tree groves dotted with Sasak architecture, grazing livestock and children playing games, often with their *ibu* (mothers) working nearby.

Wander the Cheerful Streets of Gili Air

Charming shops and inviting warungs

After stepping off the boat at Gili Air's southward-facing **port**, jovial streets entice. There's a bit of a buzz along Jl Mojo, a lane leading to the island's centre. You'll find everything from tour agencies to gelato shops, stores filled with handmade trinkets and a smattering of little cafes serving both Indonesian and Western cuisine. Here, warungs with savorous Indonesian buffets border Aussie-style breakfast joints and Italian restos. Take as long as you like wandering down the street – a good 45 minute stroll will allow plenty of time to shop and drink.

Steps from the port, **Il Gelato Damonte** *(instagram.com/ilgelatodamonte)* beckons with fresh waffle cones and countless sweet flavors (there's also a branch on the west coast). **Warung Parida**'s buffet-style Indonesian food is always ready, serving generous portions for as low as 25,000Rp per plate. **JUJU Zero Waste Store & Vegan Cafe** *(instagram.com/juju.zerowaste)* has a little gift shop with handmade

ACTIVITIES
1 3W Dive Center
2 Flowers & Fire Yoga
3 Frog Fish Point
4 Gili Air Wall
5 H2O Yoga
6 Han's Reef
7 Lovely Spa
8 Next Level Scuba

SLEEPING
9 Akasia Villas
10 Gili Lumbung Bungalows and Bar
11 Island View Bar & Bungalow
12 Manta Dive Resort
13 PinkCoco Gili Air
14 Puri Air Beach Resort
15 Sayang Mama Inn
16 The Koho Air Hotel

EATING
17 Barefoot Blondie
18 Il Gelato Damonte
19 Juju Zero Waste Store & Vegan Cafe
20 Pachamama Cafe & Cantina
21 Papaya Restaurant & Beach Club
22 Warung Parida
23 Warung Sunny

DRINKING & NIGHTLIFE
24 Chili Bar & Segar
25 Ugem Bar

SHOPPING
26 Coco Loca
27 Mojo Boutique
see 27 Sunkissed

TRANSPORT
28 Public Boat Landing

goods, plus a menu of fresh juices, smoothies and healthy eats. For more retail therapy, **Mojo Boutique**, **Sunkissed** *(instagram.com/sunkissed.boutiques)* and **Coco Loca** *(instagram.com/cocoloca_gili)* sell island-essential clothing such as tropical shirts, swimwear and accessories like hats and sunglasses. If you're not in the market for clothing, these shops also stock a great selection of gifts and local, Lombok-made products such as handwoven baskets, textiles and toiletries made from natural ingredients, all of which make for lovely souvenirs.

SHIPWRECKS AROUND THE GILIS

A small trio of once-bouyant ships are scattered around the Gili Islands, all with different stories.

The **Japanese Wreck** (p359) lies at a depth of 45m underwater, between Gili Air and Lombok, and dates back to the 1940s. Theories as to why the wreck sunk are murky – some say it was abandoned, others assert it was struck by a torpedo.

Bounty Wreck – the result of a storm 15 years ago – is off Meno's southwest coast.

The last of the lot, the **Glenn Nusa Wreck**, was actually intentional: this former tugboat was cleaned and sunk in 2016 to form an artifical reef and a new dive site.

HAE-KYUNG JEONG/SHUTTERSTOCK

Swings in the water, Gili Air

Kick Back on Gorgeous Beaches

Gili Air's beach hangouts

Like the rest of the Gilis, Gili Air is gifted with a ring of white-sand beach met by azure waters. It's arguably some of the archipelago's best shoreline, both for its condition and the lovely establishments that line the shore. The sunset views from the north coast are a point of local pride, and there's no shortage of beanbags shaded by fringed umbrellas to post up under. The east coast, lined with eateries and dive shops, is popular during the day – later on, everyone heads north and west as the sky descends into a swirly canvas of soft pink and deep orange.

On the eastern coast, **Ugem Bar** *(instagram.com/ugembar)* and neighbouring **Chili Bar & Segar** *(instagram.com/chilibar_giliair)* draw a loyal customer base with their bamboo loungers and cabanas on the sand. A handful of cheerful beach cafes surround **Puri Air Beach Resort** *(puriairbeachresort.com)* on the north coast, all with lovely views of the neighbouring islands. Further west, you can find swings in the water at both **Gili Lumbung** *(instagram.com/gili.lumbung_giliair)* and **Island View Bar & Bungalow** *(WhatsApp +62 878 6588 0103)*. Expect a queue for the Instagrammable swings at sunset.

In the Gilis, swimwear is fully accepted on the beach and at the pool, but anywhere else is disrespectful. Throw on a cover-up if you're leaving the shoreline.

EATING ON GILI AIR: OUR PICKS

Warung Sunny: Indonesian classics for both veggie and meat eaters and freshly grilled seafood. Also offers cooking classes. *10am-10pm* $

Barefoot Blondie: Western-style brunches and snacks, plus excellent coffees and baked treats, right by the harbour. *7.30am-5pm* $$

Papaya Restaurant & Beach Club: Popular spot for barbecue and cocktails on the west coast, particularly busy at sunset. *10.30am-11pm* $$

Pachamama Cafe & Cantina: Healthy plant-based dishes, plus guilt-free desserts, smoothies and coffee. *11am-10pm* $$

Dive & Snorkel Gili Air's Coast

Enviable waters and excellent spots

Snorkelling (and scuba diving) conditions are blissful around Gili Air, with coral reefs just off the eastern shore. **Han's Reef** is home to sea turtles and magnificent corals. Slightly north, there's **Frog Fish Point**, where sea critters such as ghost pipefish and scorpion fish flutter about. The **Gili Air Wall** lies southwest, with a solid drop-off that extends about 30m deep. If you're swimming out with snorkel gear from the shore, don't be surprised if you swim back to a different spot; the current causes some drift which is potentially hazardous for weaker swimmers. You should be aware of the tides and the changes these bring.

You can also join a boat trip around the Gilis with a local provider such as **Manta Dive**, **3W Dive Center** *(3wdivegili.com; fun dive 600,000Rp)* or **Next Level Scuba** *(next-level-scuba.com; fun dive 600,000Rp)* – all on Air's east coast. They offer various courses but if you're already qualified, you can also do fun dives around the islands. The price for fun dives includes all equipment rental and guides, and the more fun dives you do, the cheaper it is per dive.

Slow Down with Yoga & Wellness

Unwind, stretch and relax

We don't realise how much noise there is in our lives until we find ourselves somewhere totally tranquil, away from the fast-paced rhythm of everyday life. Gili Air is the ideal place to take a break and slow down, listening to the waves lapping the shore and the sea breeze rustling through the trees. And what better surroundings to ground yourself with some yoga and self-care? There's a real sense of relaxation on Gili Air, evident from the number of yoga studios and spas on the island.

Get into a chill groove at **Flowers & Fire Yoga Garden** *(flowersandfire.yoga)*, a treehouse yoga studio shrouded in verdant foliage near Gili Air's heart. They also have a healthy cafe and cosy accommodation. A few minutes north, **H2O Yoga and Meditation Center** *(h2oyogaandmeditation.com; yoga class 150,000Rp)* offers vinyasa flow, traditional hatha and various yin classes in a spacious shala.

Spa-seekers can find plenty of small spas throughout the island, with a one-hour massage ranging from 150,000Rp to over 300,000Rp at fancier spots. **PinkCoco Gili Air's** spa *(instagram.com/pinkhotels)* is in a colourful setting fit for pampering, with floral decor and a long list of treatments. Further north, **Lovely Spa** *(WhatsApp +62 878 1669 2236)* offers Balinese massage for great value in a simple, open-air setting.

ISLAND-HOPPING

Many people choose to visit all three islands, spending a night or two on each one. Day trips are also possible, but you'll want to limit a trip to just one other island in a day to allow time to sightsee.

The best option is the public speedboats that run between the islands, usually hourly between 9am and 4pm – these cost 85,000Rp per person. For more flexibility, organise a private speedboat which typically costs 300,000Rp. They take up to ten people, so this often works out cheaper if you're with a large group.

The best way to organise an island hopping-trip is to visit the various boat companies at the harbour on each island. The currents in between the islands are notoriously strong, so don't attempt to swim between them.

Places We Love to Stay

$ Budget $$ Midrange $$$ Top End

Flores

MAP p294

Arnolds Family Homestay $ This Bajawa homestay is clean, comfortable and comes with homecooked meals. Arnold can help with information and arranging tours and transportation.

Bintang by Tobias Lodge $ Owner Tobias is a fount of local information for Moni. Simple tiled rooms come with hot water, and the cafe serves a Western/Indonesian mashup.

Blasius Monta Homestay $ Wae Rebo–expert Blasius runs this friendly 15-room spot, right by the trailhead. If the phone signal is patchy, text him *(WhatsApp +62 813 3935 0775)*.

Mama's Homestay Ruteng $$ One of the nicer accommodation in Ruteng with bright, spacious rooms and a peaceful garden. Owners Faldi and Nina are knowledgeable on the local area.

Seaesta Komodo Hostel $$ All-round crowd-pleaser with cheery blue-and-white rooms, seriously comfy dorms, a full social calendar and a rooftop bar catering to backpackers and divers.

Kelimutu Crater Lakes Ecolodge $$$ Nestled by the riverside east of town in Moni are 21 rooms and villas, with solar power, outdoor sitting areas and a restaurant.

Sumbawa

Lakey Peak Haven $$ Hilltop Bali-style 'haven' with two-storey surf shacks overlooking a chequered pool deck and distant breaks. Reserve in advance.

Lakey Peak B&B $$ Friendly, family-run place featuring spacious rooms with terraces, en-suite bathrooms and air-con. There's a huge rooftop with views of the Nungas surf break.

West Timor

MAP p311

Lavalon Hostel $ A dorm and two air-con doubles, run by living Nusa Tenggara encyclopedia and former Indonesian film star Edwin Lerrick in Kepang.

Dena Hotel $ Unremarkable yet clean rooms in Soe with air-con and wi-fi, across the road from the market. Soe's best digs.

Sotis Hotel $$ This Kupang waterfront mid-rise features stylish rooms with pops of colour, two pools, a spa, a decent restaurant and bar.

Alor

La P'tite Kepa $$ This French-owned, solar-powered dive resort consists of 11 bungalows with sea and island views, outdoor bathrooms and memorable meals.

Rote

Mulia Bungalows Nemberala Beach $$ Air-con bungalows just steps away from Pantai Nemberala. Outdoor bathrooms.

Villa Santai $$$ Waterfront villa with spacious bungalows surrounded by tropical gardens, plus a beachfront bar, swimming pool and fresh meals.

Sumba

MAP p322

Wajonata Sumba $ This secluded resort 2km east of Kalala Beach consists of basic bamboo huts with porches looking out onto the garden and beach.

Sumba Sunset Surf Camp $$ Four traditional bungalows with mosquito nets, set up to accommodate couples, friends or families.

Praikamarru Guest House $$ Sumbanese-style thatched cottages on the outskirts of Waingapu. Simple but clean and comfortable rooms. Owner Eddy is full of local knowledge.

Maringi Sumba $$$ Beautifully designed bamboo pavilions with oval glass doors and outdoor bathrooms, powered by solar energy. In Tambolaka.

Kuta

MAP p333

Lara Homestay $ Family-run homestay just off the main stretch. Bright and airy en-suite rooms, some with balconies.

Sikara Lombok $$ Modern rooms overlooking a spacious garden and pool deck, just off Kuta's main street.

Porter Lombok Hotel $$ Hillside boutique hotel. Has spacious rooms, a restaurant with a varied menu and a yoga shala.

Selong Belanak

Singon Lombok Homestay $ Updated, modern rooms and mountain views, slightly inland from Selong Belanak beach.

Tropik Resort $$ A range of wooden bungalows and modern one-to-three-bedroom villas; there's a huge pool and lush garden.

Gerupuk

Anto Guesthouse $ The simple, clean rooms here have air-con and private bathrooms, just a few steps from the beach.

Dome Lombok $$ Nine uniquely designed dome-shaped structures in a lush setting. Healthy cuisine and hilltop views.

Tetebatu

WinaWani Bungalow $ Cosy wooden cottages overlooking rice terraces and gardens. Offers walking tours and cooking classes.

Les Rizieres $$ Charming decor, views of Gunung Rinjani and a ricefield as a backyard at this homestay and cafe.

Ekas & Sekaroh

Ekas Surf Resort $$ Chilled-out surf accommodation: surf camps, kitesurfing and snorkelling for enthusiasts of all levels.

Jeeva Beloam Beach Camp $$$ Series of A-frame bungalows in a secluded and rustic setting, right on a private beach.

Senggigi MAP p341

Sammy Cottage $ This friendly guesthouse has private rooms (breakfast included), in close proximity to Coconut Beach.

Ibludan Hotel $$ Eco-friendly rooms in a tropical garden setting with a pool, close to Senggigi's main area.

Mataram

Dewi Sri Guesthouse $ Dorms and private rooms close to the heart of Mataram. Plenty of shared common space and a pool.

Prime Park Hotel $$ Upscale yet laid-back hotel featuring a rooftop pool with city and mountain views, close to Mataram's centre.

Senaru MAP p346

Dragonfly Senaru Lodge $ Volcano views, simple rooms and homecooked meals in a guesthouse right by Senaru's waterfalls.

Rinjani Lighthouse Cottages $$ Eco-friendly guesthouse right in front of Gunung Rinjani National Park. In-house coffee shop and bungalows set in a garden.

Sembalun Valley

Sembalun Kita Cottages $ Cosy rooms in a beautiful garden. Has mountain views and is set back from the main road.

Bukit Tiga Lima Boutique Hotel $$ A-frame cabins right on the main road leading into the village of Sembalun, surrounded by mountain views.

Bobocabin Gunung Rinjani $$ Modern and minimalist tiny cabins with views of Gunung Rinjani and Pergasingan Hill.

Southwestern Peninsula MAP p353

Yellow Coco Gili Gede $ Easygoing and unpretentious cabins with mosquito nets, on the beach facing mainland Lombok.

High Dive Gili Gede Resort $$ Beachfront resort offering scuba diving and other water-sport activities, plus tours of the surrounding islands.

Gili Trawangan MAP p357

Radika House $ Simple but spacious rooms with friendly vibes, close to the action yet still quiet.

Pearl of Trawangan $$ Ocean-view rooms and cottages with bamboo roofs, right on the southeast coast.

PinkCoco $$$ Stylish adults-only hotel by the beach, living up to its namesake with rose-coloured decor in 27 all-pink rooms.

Gili Meno MAP p361

Rabbit Tree $ Whimsically designed hostel quite literally in the island's middle, with unique furnishings.

Mahamaya Gili Meno $$ Resort with beachfront villas, one- and two-bedroom suites, and family rooms that mix modern with traditional.

Bask $$$ The definition of splurge and modern luxury, providing arguably the most 'treat yourself' resort experience around.

Gili Air MAP p365

Sayang Mama Inn $ Beautifully designed rooms with verandas, in a quiet spot just a two-minute walk to the beach.

The Koho Air Hotel $$ Charming boutique hotel just steps from the port, with an eco-friendly focus.

Akasia Villas $$$ Serene and spacious villas on a quiet road, plus hanging swings and floating breakfasts.

For places to stay in Maluku, see p415

PURWANTO NUGROHO/SHUTTERSTOCK

Above: Diving, Pulau Ternate (p374); Right: Pulau Dodola (p386)

Researched by
Marco Ferrarese

Maluku

DIVING, VOLCANO HIKES & OCEAN JOURNEYS

Coral reefs, jungle-clad volcanoes and sandy beaches fronting cerulean seas set the stage for off-the-beaten-path adventures in one of Indonesia's least-visited regions.

Today, you might never guess that the idyllic islands of Maluku were once the world's only source of nutmeg, cloves and mace, and played a crucial role in global geopolitics and economics. But between the 16th and 18th centuries, the fight for control of the Spice Islands (then known as the Moluccas) spurred European colonialism across Southeast Asia and, through a series of wrong turns and one auspicious land swap, also shaped the modern world.

SABINE_LJ/SHUTTERSTOCK

Once the spice monopoly was broken, Maluku returned to gentle obscurity for two centuries until WWII, when the Japanese established bases and airfields on Morotai and other islands. Vestiges of the battles between the US and Australian Allied forces and the Empire of Japan include sunken plane wrecks, jungle bunkers and rusted ammo. In 1950, Ambon, Buru and Seram became the centre of the short-lived Southern Malukan independence movement, though it was extinguished within a few months by the Indonesian military. Between 1999 and 2002, episodes of sectarian violence between Christians and Muslims caused many of Maluku's islands to cascade into an all-out civil war.

Memories of historic tensions may be why the region today has gone in the other direction: it's now a little-visited tropical paradise with a welcoming mix of cultures. Inter-island transport, however, is frustratingly inconvenient. Patience and flexibility are required to reach the pristine reefs, stroll the empty stretches of powdery white sand and climb the perfectly formed volcanoes.

THE MAIN AREAS

PULAU TERNATE
North Maluku's volcanic gateway. **p374**

PULAU HALMAHERA
Volcano climbs, island escapes and WWII history. **p382**

PULAU AMBON
Jagged coastlines, wild nature and city life. **p388**

BANDA ISLANDS
Forts, colonial history and coral reefs. **p400**

KEI ISLANDS
Cerulean beaches at Indonesia's easternmost end. **p409**

Find Your Way

Wedged between Sulawesi and the island of New Guinea, Maluku comprises scores of islands. The main gateways, Ternate in the north and Ambon in the centre, have cities with flight connections to Jakarta and other parts of Indonesia.

Pulau Ternate, p374
Practically all volcano, this former sultanate has black-sand beaches, legend-shrouded lakes, fine snorkelling and delicious Malukan food.

Pulau Ambon, p388
The city has enough stuff to keep you busy for days, but hit the coastal road to feel the magic of Ambon's wilderness.

Banda Islands, p400
The former heart of the colonial spice trade beguiles with outstanding reefs, friendly fishing villages and a cone-shaped volcano.

Kei Islands, p409
A remote eastern archipelago with some of Indonesia's most beautiful beaches and a budding tourism scene.

BOAT
Regular speedboat services run to neighbouring islands. For longer journeys (such as Ambon to Banda Islands), book passage on a Pelni ferry.

MOTORBIKE
As in other parts of Indonesia, you'll find the easiest way of getting around is by *ojek* (motorbike taxi). You can also hire your own scooter for DIY exploring.

BANGOLAND/SHUTTERSTOCK

Benteng Belgica (p403)

Plan Your Time

You need time and favourable ferry schedules to explore Maluku in depth. With a minimum of one week, pick one or two groups of islands and fly there from either Ambon or Ternate.

One Week in Central Maluku

- Settle in **Ambon** (p388) for a few days, enjoying city comforts and beautiful nature like **Taeno Waterfall** (p396) and **Lubang Buaya Morella** (p393). Take an overnight Pelni, fast ferry or flight to the Banda Islands to summit **Gunung Api** (p408), snorkel at **Run** (p407) or dive at fortress-clad **Ai** (p404).

Two Weeks in North & Central Maluku

- Spend two days exploring the beaches, lakes and forts of **Ternate** (p374). Catch a boat to Halmahera and cruise to Tobelo for access to fuming **Dukono** (p387) and snorkelling on **Meti** (p384) or **Morotai** (p386). Fly to **Ambon** (p388) via Ternate and from there to the **Kei Islands** (p409) for lazy days on stunning beaches.

SEASONAL HIGHLIGHTS

MARCH TO MAY

Relatively few visitors means good deals. Expect sunny weather and parades for Ternate's **Legu Gam Festival** (p377).

JUNE TO AUGUST

It's raining in Ambon, the Bandas and other southern Maluku islands. In Ternate, the **Kora-Kora Festival** (p377) celebrates boat racing.

SEPTEMBER TO NOVEMBER

Standout festivals, such as **Meti Kei** (p411) in Kei Kecil and the **Spice Island Festival** in Banda Neira.

DECEMBER TO FEBRUARY

Sunny skies and clear, calm seas that are excellent for diving and other aquatic activities.

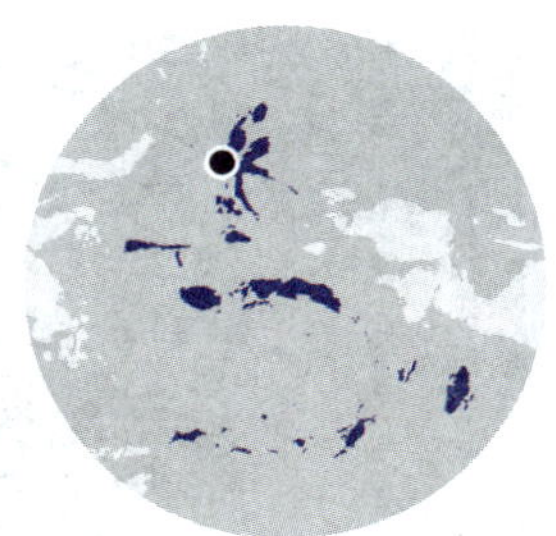

Pulau Ternate

SNORKELLING | FORTS | BLACK-SAND BEACHES

TOP TIP

Almost all accommodation on Pulau Ternate can be found in Kota Ternate. There's a good mix of boutique and midrange hotels here, as well as homestays, which provide a more immersive glimpse of life on the islands. Expect higher prices than in western parts of Indonesia.

The dramatic volcanic cone of Gunung Api Gamalama (1721m) dominates Pulau Ternate, the stunning island gateway to North Maluku. Settlements are sprinkled around its lower coastal slopes, with villages on the east coast coalescing into the region's biggest town, Kota Ternate.

Kota Ternate is a busy place of steep, labyrinthine lanes hanging for dear life on the volcano's flanks, plus little cafes frequented by a youthful crowd that stays out late. Attractions extend well beyond the city limits, where the quieter island backdrop is swathed in jungle and scenic black-sand shorelines await.

Stunning 16th-century forts recall the early wealth of Ternate and its neighbour, Tidore, which revolved around cloves – once highly valued in Europe as a food preservative and a cure for everything from toothaches to sexual dysfunction. Tiny Ternate is also where 19th-century scientist-explorer Alfred Russel Wallace penned the letter that helped Charles Darwin complete his landmark theory of natural selection.

GETTING AROUND

Babullah Airport is 6km from central Ternate, with direct Sriwijaya and Wings flights to Jakarta, Makassar and Manado – the latter is useful for onward connections to Bali. Use InDrive or Grab ride-hailing apps. For better chances of finding a ride, offer the driver an additional 10,000Rp to enter the airport toll road, otherwise walk 500m to the main road and call from there. If you're travelling light, you can also go by *ojek*. Once in Kota Ternate, it's easy to flag down *ojeks (10,000 to 20,000Rp)*.

Ferry passengers disembark at the **Ahmad Yani Port** on the island's southeastern coast. *Angkot* and bemos (minibuses) connect Kota Ternate's **bemo terminal** in front of the fish market to outlying villages, but none go all the way around the island. Travelling by *ojek*, hired scooter or car is the best way to get around.

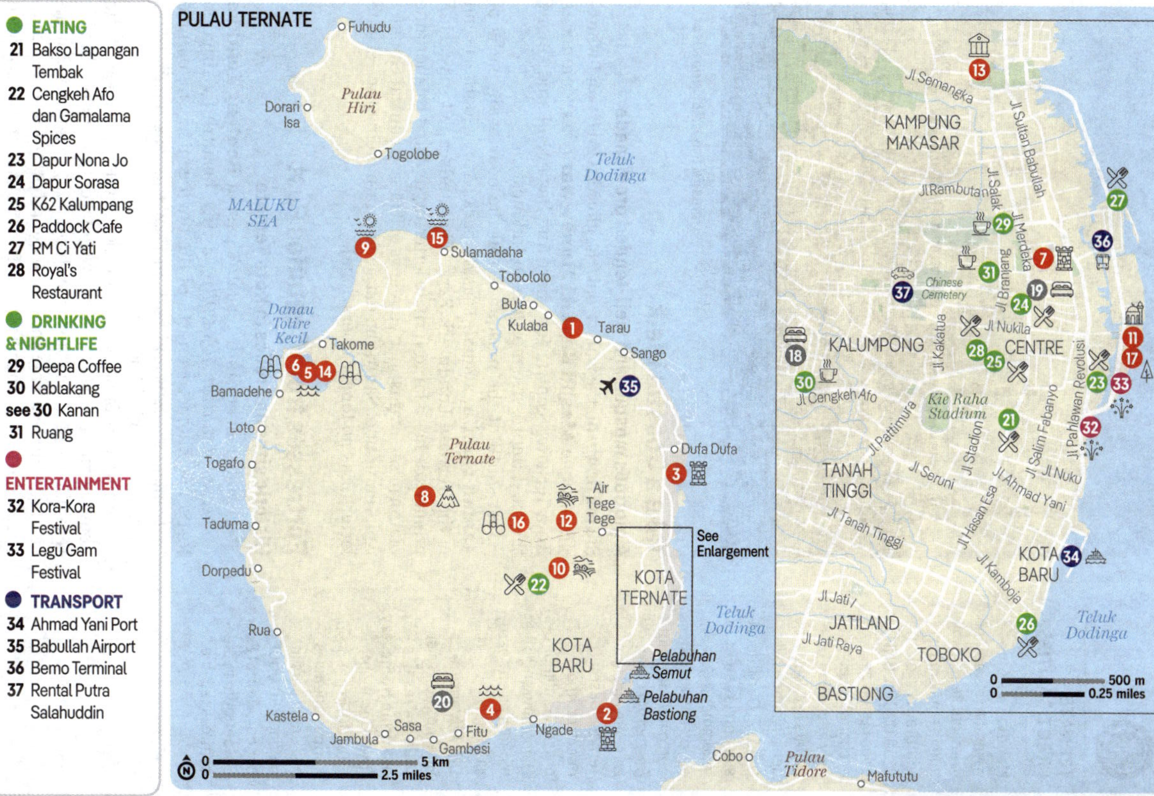

SIGHTS

1 Batu Angus
2 Benteng Kalamata
3 Benteng Tolukko
4 Danau Ngade
5 Danau Tolire Besar
6 Danau Tolire Besar main viewpoint
7 Fort Oranje
8 Gunung Api Gamalama
9 Jikomalamo
10 Marikurubu
11 Masjid Raya Al Munawwar
12 Moya
13 Museum Kedaton Kesultanan Ternate
14 Pulo Tareba Takome
15 Sulamadaha
16 Taman Love
17 Taman Nukila

ACTIVITIES

see 9 La Conna Dive Centre

SLEEPING

18 Kurnia Homestay
19 Muara Hotel
20 Villa Ma'rasai

EATING

21 Bakso Lapangan Tembak
22 Cengkeh Afo dan Gamalama Spices
23 Dapur Nona Jo
24 Dapur Sorasa
25 K62 Kalumpang
26 Paddock Cafe
27 RM Ci Yati
28 Royal's Restaurant

DRINKING & NIGHTLIFE

29 Deepa Coffee
30 Kablakang
see 30 Kanan
31 Ruang

ENTERTAINMENT

32 Kora-Kora Festival
33 Legu Gam Festival

TRANSPORT

34 Ahmad Yani Port
35 Babullah Airport
36 Bemo Terminal
37 Rental Putra Salahuddin

TERNATE PRACTICALITIES

Money: There are several ATMs around town, but keep in mind that the maximum withdrawal is often 1,250,000Rp. BNI does currency exchange, likely only accepting US dollars in crisp, large-denomination bills.

Guides: Guesthouses and hotels can recommend guides, or you can reach out to Kelana Malut *(instagram.com/kelanamalut)*, a Ternate-based operator who organises climbs of Gamalama and other mountains on nearby islands.

DIY Adventures: Hire motorbikes at **Villa Ma'rasai** (p415) or **Kurnia Homestay** (p415) for about 150,000Rp per day. Various agencies hire small cars at around 250,000Rp per day. **Rental Putra Salahuddin** in the centre is reliable.

ARMAND JOSO/SHUTTERSTOCK

Masjid Raya Al Munawwar

Take a Coastal Walk

A glorious mosque and well-tended promenade

Sitting pretty on the waterfront, the glorious green-and-white-tile mosque **Masjid Raya Al Munawwar** *(free)* dominates Kota Ternate's central foreshore and has been listed among the most impressive mosques in Indonesia.

Just south of the mosque, stroll the boardwalk paths of **Taman Nukila**, a small seaside park. At its southern end is the Ternate Landmark Park. The landscaped sea-facing promenade has a large Ternate lettering sign and a panoramic platform set against perfect views of Tidore's conical Gunung Api Keimatubo. Sadly, the magic fountain facing the Ternate lettering is no longer operational.

Fortresses from Centuries Past

Historic sites and relics in Kota Ternate

Start your journey into Ternate's past at **Benteng Tolukko** *(expected donation 10,000Rp)*, a tiny, beautifully situated fort a few kilometres north of the town centre. Surrounded by tropical gardens and built in 1522, this was the first Portuguese stronghold on Ternate.

The fort is infamous for a quirky detail: when seen from above, its narrow shape with two adjacent towers on the side resembles a phallus – it was built this way to adapt to the area's immediate topography. Tolukko is better preserved than the island's two other *benteng* (forts); stroll on the cramped battlements for panoramic views of Tidore and Halmahera.

The next key landmark to the south is **Museum Kedaton Kesultanan Ternate** *(museumternate.org; free; donations to guides welcome)*. Built in 1813 and restored in a semi-colonial style, this former sultan's palace contains historic weaponry and memorabilia from the reigns of past rulers, whose lineage dates back to 1257. After a recent struggle over succession, a new sultan, Hidayatullah Sjah, was installed in 2022. It's closed on Mondays.

Around 1km northwest of the **Masjid Raya Al Munawwar**, the sprawling Dutch-built **Fort Oranje** *(Benteng Oranye; free)* dates from the early 17th century. The complex has lawns where Ternateans come for peaceful strolls while kids play soccer or practise martial arts. There are a few rusted cannons here, and you can walk a section of the bastion while imagining the Dutch governor inspecting his troops. Two small exhibition spaces cover local history (signage in Indonesian only). The fort is also used as a community art and event space.

Another 4km south, the 1540 **Benteng Kalamata** *(Benteng Kayu Merah; by donation)* is dramatically situated on the waterfront, staring down Ternate's old foe, Tidore. Wander the unusual angular geometry of its outer walls while enjoying the views.

Catch a Traditional Festival

Parades, dancing and lots of food

Two festivals showcase Ternate's traditional culture. The **Legu Gam Festival**, usually held for a couple of days between late March and mid-April, is a great time to see parades of dancers in traditional costumes and the reenactment of ancient Moluccan rituals. Later in June, the **Kora-Kora Festival** celebrates the island's marine heritage. **Taman Nukila** fills up with art, dancers and stalls laden with traditional foods, while the Kora-Kora boats race offshore.

Walk Through the Leftovers of a Volcanic Eruption

Black rocks and sea views at Batu Angus

Follow the island road north out of town and you'll reach **Batu Angus** shortly after passing the airport (10km from the centre). Here, black volcanic rock in striking shapes covers the landscape, with vibrant shoots of greenery emerging from the earth. The setting is the result of **Gamalama's** (p379) powerful eruptions in 1737. Wide, well-maintained lanes snake through the sprawling site, which is best visited using your own vehicle. Pack some snacks and rest under one of the many gazebos en route; the small lookout tower has a worthy vantage point over the lava-filled expanse and the black-sand coast.

SMALL ISLAND, BIG ART SCENE

Zandry Aldrin, local musician and community director, talks about his island's most rocking spots. *@zandryaldrin*

In October, the alternative rock festival Rocktober held at Fort Oranje attracts 3000 people nightly and showcases the best Ternate bands.

The fort is always open for different art and community happenings, with ongoing initiatives and classes throughout the year, such as graphic design, traditional music and even water purification. There's also a fully equipped music studio for local bands to practise.

Don't miss the cafe **Kablakang** (p378) for fortnightly music shows organized by the Kong Collective *(facebook.com/kong.collective)* and Dari Timur Bersuara *(instragram.com/daritimurbersuara)*.

y the delicious corn perkedel

EATING IN KOTA TERNATE: TREAT YOURSELF

Dapur Nona Jo: A local favourite for hearty Maluku tuna cuts with rice and sambal. Pass the tunnel-like entrance and sit in the cosy upstairs section. *10am-11pm* $$

Royal's Restaurant: Upscale by Ternate standards, has much-lauded, wide-ranging Chinese-Indonesian dishes and standout seafood. *10am-11pm* $$

Paddock Cafe: Linger over rice bowls, noodle soups and Vietnamese coffee with live music at this sleek, three-storey place with great rooftop views. *3pm-midnight* $$

Cengkeh Afo dan Gamalama Spices: Ancient cooking concept up on Gamalama's slopes. Bookings are essential *(WhatsApp +62 813 4010 0140)*. *10am-10pm* $$$

A CURSED LAKE

Danau Tolire Besar may be beautiful, but its mythological origins are more than a little creepy.

Locals fervently believe that the lake was formed after an incestuous father impregnated his daughter. Cast out of their village, the pair attempted to flee. But because they had invoked the ire of the gods, the village's homes sank into the earth, water came flooding in and all the residents turned into crocodiles.

The big lake (Danau Tolire Besar) is where the father once stood, while the smaller lake (Danau Tolire Kecil) formed where the daughter fell. Don't laugh it off: the lake harbours plenty of crocodiles. In 2023, a crocodile pulled a boy into the water who allegedly cursed as he went down the crater to fish.

Chill Out on a Black-Sand Beach

Catch some rays at Sulamadaha

Near the island's north end, **Sulamadaha** is a slender black-sand beach with heavy swells and, sadly, ruined coral. Come during the week and it's deserted; on weekends it's packed with visitors and food stalls selling grilled seafood.

Snorkel around a Stilted Settlement

Take the plunge at Jikomalamo

Several kilometres past Sulamadaha, a lane runs north to the secluded stilted houses of **Jikomalamo**, a tiny bay with a wide sandy cove that's popular for swimming and snorkelling thanks to its amazingly clear water. Access is via the many stilted restaurants, perfect for the compulsory bite and down-time between excursions. **La Conna Dive Centre** *(instagram.com/laconnadive.official; WhatsApp +62 813 2005 0307; from 1,768,000Rp for three dives, three-person minimum)* rents snorkelling gear and offers diving.

Stand above a Magical Lake

Enjoy the views at Danau Tolire Besar

Beyond the village of Takome in the northern part of Ternate, a paved lane climbs to the rim of the jade-green crater lake **Danau Tolire Besar**.

You can enjoy the view along the crater rim from two viewpoints – one on the northwestern side of the lake, facing the Gamalama volcano, and a second one on the eastern side at the conservation area and campsite **Pulo Tareba Takome** *(instagram.com/pulotareba_takome; entry 5000Rp, camping without/with your own tent 65000/35000Rp)*. The conservation area is home to the Simaru bird, as well as 22 endemic species. The second viewpoint has a simple driftwood cafe, low chairs, a fire pit for chilly evenings and a wooden platform from where you can see the lake profiled dramatically against the sea – an amazing sight at sunrise.

ARTSY CAFES IN TERNATE: OUR PICKS

Live music gigs every fortnight.

Kanan: Charming cafe with wooden furniture, alt-rock music crackling from vintage speakers and a crowd of young locals. Smoking is permitted. *7am-midnight*

Kablakang: Irresistibly bohemian garden cafe with a few tables set under corrugated iron awnings by a barrage of palm trees. *8am-11.30pm Tue-Sun*

Ruang: Central little cafe set inside a one-storey house, with portraits of the sultan and art hanging on the exposed bricks walls. Decent coffee. *10am-midnight*

Deepa Coffee: Set beyond the entrance of a nasi goreng stall, this cafe is a favourite with the local youth and has barista coffee and unvarnished walls. *10am-midnight*

Money-Worthy Views

Admire the verdant scenery of Danau Ngade

Danau Ngade is a pleasant, spring-fed bowl lake surrounded by forest. Take the steep lane to the west of the lagoon to see it from above; there are great panoramas across the straits to the conical islands of Tidore and **Maitara** (p381), as featured on Indonesia's 1000Rp notes. The lake is about 6km southwest of Kota Ternate.

Climb a Rugged Volcano

Get up close and personal with Gamalama

Ternate's iconic peak, **Gunung Api Gamalama** (1715m), makes for a challenging one-day climb, but the views are magnificent so long as the clouds cooperate. Before heading out, make sure it's safe to climb and possibly ask your accommodation for a local guide – Kelana Malut *(instagram.com/kelanamalut)* runs trips for 350,000Rp per person. Remember, this is an active volcano and the most recent eruption was in 2018. There are two trails to the summit: the track from **Marikurubu** (275m) and, north of there, the more interesting and easier path from **Moya** (347m), which skirts former plantations, fragrant with clove, cinnamon and nutmeg plants. Allow three or four hours to make the steady ascent up to a small camping area where the two trails converge. From here, it's another 45 minutes along loose rocks to the summit. Go early for the best views before the clouds arrive, and don't attempt the climb in the rain.

A less demanding alternative that still gets you halfway up the mountain – possibly offering better chances for unobstructed views – is **Taman Love**, a popular local hiking spot and camping area equipped with an Insta-friendly viewing platform shaped like a heart. It's a one- to two-hour hike from the end of the Moya road where cars must stop.

STRUGGLES WITH EUROPE

The first Portuguese settlers arrived in Ternate in 1511. Tidore responded by inviting the Spaniards. Both islands found their hospitality rapidly exhausted as the Europeans tried to corner the spice market and covert the islanders to Christianity.

When Ternate's Muslim population rebelled in 1570, Sultan Hairun (Khairun) was executed and his head staked on a pike. The besieged Portuguese held out in their citadel until 1575 when the new sultan turned it into his palace.

The Spaniards, and later the Dutch, made themselves equally unpopular. They played Ternate off against Tidore and fought for control of an elusive clove monopoly. Although the Dutch eventually prevailed, the sultanates survived, remaining well-respected institutions to this day.

EATING IN KOTA TERNATE: CENTRAL PICKS

RM Ci Yati: In the market (Pasar Gamalama), this is a great spot to try *popeda*, a sticky sago-flour glue, with various accompaniments. *10am-11pm* $

K62 Kalumpang: Smart two-storey cafe and restaurant serving reliable Indonesian staples and a few pan-Asian and Western dishes. *10am-midnight* $$

Bakso Lapangan Tembak: Popular brick-and-tile eatery specialising in *bakso* (meatballs), which can be fried or added to a clear soup. *10am-10pm* $

Dapur Sorasa: One block south of Fort Oranje, Sorasa is an inviting spot to enjoy a wide-ranging menu of seafood, chicken and duck dishes. *10am-11pm* $$

Beyond Pulau Ternate

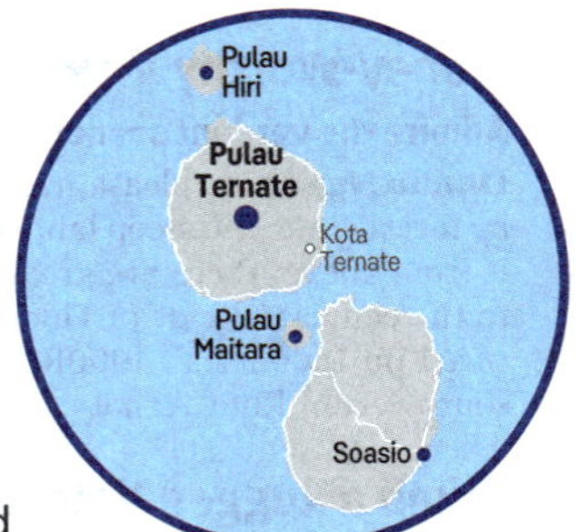

Take a speedboat to Tidore, a peaceful island with historic ruins, pretty beaches and a towering volcano.

Places

GETTING AROUND

Boats depart every 30 minutes or so from **Pelabuhan Bastiong** in Ternate to the town of Rum *(20,000Rp)* on Tidore's northwest shore or Pulau Maitara. From Rum, frequent bemos run to Soasio and Goto using the south-coast road.

If you want to circle the island and make stops along the way, your best bet is to hire an *ojek* for the day *(around 150,000Rp)*. Short *ojek* hops in Goto and Soasio cost around 10,000Rp.

Boats to **Pulau Hiri** *(10,000Rp)* leave from a little **port** about 500m from Sulamadaha beach until around 5 or 6pm, departing when full.

A short hop from Ternate, the island of Tidore is less populous, less commercial and less frenetic than its similarly sized sibling and historical rival. The sultanate, which endured from 1109 until the Sukarno era, was re-established in 1999. Today, the 37th sultan presides over a sublime volcanic island dotted with brightly painted wooden homes bordered by flower gardens, shaded by mango trees and coconut palms, and scented by sheets of drying cloves and nutmeg. There are also fragmented vestiges of the past here, including several forts dating back to the 17th century. Two other islands are within easy reach and make for equally idyllic getaways after exploring Tidore's villages and beaches.

Soasio

TIME FROM TERNATE: **1HR**

Remnants of a colonial past

Drowsy **Soasio** feels more like an overgrown village than an island capital. It has fewer shops than the nearby port town of Goto, but it does have a monopoly on Tidore's cultural and historical sights. Soasio is also where you'll find the best spread of accommodation on the island should you decide to stay the night.

A few kilometres south of the centre, the grey stone walls of **Benteng Tahula** *(free)* rise up like some lost fragment of medieval Europe. A legacy of Spain's short-lived presence in Tidore, this early 17th-century fort is well preserved, with orderly market gardens within and spectacular views to Halmahera from the battlements. It's a steep climb up some 120-odd steps to the top.

No less spectacular, **Benteng Torre** *(free)* is another colonial relic, this one left by the Portuguese. After obtaining permission from Sultan Gapi Baguna (the sixteenth sultan of Tidore), Sancho de Vasconcelos erected the fortress in the 1580s. Curiously, this permission came on the heels of the Portuguese expulsion from Ternate by Sultan Baabullah Khairun in 1570 for killing Sultan Khairun. Broken lava flows, vivid tropical foliage and commanding views of the southern approaches to the island make this a worthy, picturesque traipse up the hill from the centre of Soasio.

Pulau Maitara

TIME FROM TERNATE: **20MIN**

Panoramas, snorkelling and mangroves

A mere 20-minute speedboat hop from Ternate, **Pulau Maitara** is ideally located for its fine views of Gamalama rising to the north and Mt Kie Matubu soaring over Tidore to the east. The clear waters around the island have some coral and offer decent snorkelling. Or you can just relax by the waterfront at **Pantai Maitara**, where you'll find oversized letters spelling 'Maitara Island' framed against the seaside. From there, hop on an *ojek* and head 1.5km south to **Posi Posi Ngusu Lenge**, a two-hectare expanse of preserved mangrove forest with a short boardwalk trail.

Pulau Hiri

TIME FROM TERNATE: **20MIN**

Cloves, beaches and sharks

The volcanic cone of the 600m-high, three-peaked Mount Hiri beckons from this islet just off Ternate's Sulamadaha beach. It was the last step in the sultan's family's escape during WWII. Learn about clove cultivation in the foothills, where grassroot family business **Pala Gura Mariolaha** (*WhatsApp +62 821 9382 9261*) produces *minyak cengkeh* (clove oil) and welcomes visitors. A spice steam sauna is in the plans.

You'll need wheels or an *ojek* to reach **Baru Ma Adu** *(instagram.com/destinasi_wisata_hiri_tomajiko;5000rp)*, a campsite with three idyllic palm-fringed locations perched above an ocean-slanting cliff; it's in Tomajiko village. Contact Wawan Ilyas (*WhatsApp +62 852 9828 6372*) to book a spot: tents for two cost 80,000Rp and hammocks just 5000Rp. Nearby, along the coast, is **Gurabala (Batu Lubang)**, a stone arch.

Before leaving, make a pit stop at **Hiri Homestay** near the port, famous for promoting a questionable feeding for black tip reef sharks – it's best to rent their snorkelling gear (*50,000Rp*) and chase them yourself. Owner Kadir also organises a reasonable round-island exploration tour from Ternate, including lunch, for 150,000Rp.

SPEAKING TIDOREAN & TERNATEAN

Though separated by just 2km of water at the narrowest points, the islands of Tidore and Ternate maintain their own separate identities. Each island has its own language – part of the North Halmahera umbrella, which itself is of West Papuan origin.

Ternate, however, claims its language is the most significant since it was spoken by the sultanate of Ternate and became the lingua franca during the spice trade.

Curiously, a record of the Ternate language dates back to the 15th century, when it was originally written using the Jawi alphabet, making it one of the region's only languages with a pre-European literary tradition.

Pulau Halmahera

CORAL-FRINGED BEACHES | VOLCANOES | WILDLIFE

TOP TIP

If you don't speak fluent Bahasa Indonesia, get an English-speaking guide for all travel here. Be aware that outside of Tobelo, Jailolo, Sofifi and, to a lesser extent, Maba and Buli in eastern Halmahera, only basic village homestays are available.

Maluku's biggest island encompasses four mountainous peninsulas, several volcanic cones and dozens of offshore islands. As it's sparsely populated and hard to get around, Halmahera's potential for diving, bird-watching and beach roaming remains almost entirely untapped.

Not even promoting Sofifi as the provincial capital of Maluku has stimulated tourism on Halmahera. While the island's north is reasonably developed and parts of the east have seen some mining investment, much of the south remains off the beaten track, with roads ending past the town of Mafa. Eastern Halmahera's interior, with its national park and rare bird species, is rarely visited.

Halmahera was formed when two islands collided around one million years ago, but its geological past doesn't feel so remote, particularly when climbing one of its fabled volcanoes, where you can see how the sputtering eruptions continue to reshape the landscape. Intrepid travellers with plenty of time have some fascinating possibilities for exploration.

GETTING AROUND

The most popular way to access the island is by speedboat from Ternate's **Pelabuhan Semut**; boats leave when full. For the northwestern coast, head for Jailolo *(one hour)*. For Tobelo, Galela and the east, first cross to Sofifi *(40 minutes)* or Sidangoli *(30 minutes)*.

Upon arrival, drivers offer shared Kijang taxi transport to Tobelo *(around 200,000Rp per person)*. There's no other public transportation – the alternative is bringing a motorcycle on one of the four daily ferries leaving from Ternate's **Pelabuhan Bastiong** (p380) to Sofifi (however, most rental agencies will not allow inter-island crossing). Infrequent bemos move between villages in northern Halmahera, while *ojeks* and *bentor* (motorcycle rickshaws) can be found in the towns.

HIGHLIGHTS

1 Gunung Dukono

SIGHTS

2 Aketajawe-Lolobata National Park
3 Army Dock Beach
4 Gunung Gamkonora
5 Gunung Ibu
6 Mamuya
7 Meti
see 3 Monumen Trikora
see 3 Museum Perang Dunia II & Trikora
8 Museum Rakyat
9 Nakota waterfall
10 Pantai Kupa Kupa
11 Pantai Luari
12 Pantai Marimbati
13 Pulau Dodola
14 Susupu
15 Teruo Nakamura statue

ACTIVITIES

16 KPA Lentera Alam

SLEEPING

17 Ake Jawi Resort
see 3 Hotel Molokai Morotai
see 10 Kupa Kupa Beach Cottages
18 Meraksi Flower
see 7 Meti Cottage
see 3 Penginapan Mutiara Inn
see 18 Sleepwell

EATING

see 18 Cafe Love Story
see 18 Kokiroba Mangi
see 3 Mutiara Coffee & Eat Cafe
see 3 Rumah Makan Prima Rasa

TRANSPORT

see 16 Tobelo Ferry Port
see 18 Tobelo Speedboat Terminal

WAR COMES TO NORTH MALUKU

During WWII, Japan viewed Halmahera and the surrounding islands as essential in its quest for dominance across Southeast Asia. In 1942, the Japanese established Kao Bay as a naval base, creating nine different airstrips on the island.

By 1944, US Allies saw the region as pivotal in liberating the Philippines. Knowing Halmahera was heavily defended, US and Australian troops set up operations on nearby Morotai, capturing its minor Japanese base during the fighting that raged intermittently until the end of the war. Among the Japanese defenders who retreated to Morotai's mountain hinterland was the famous Private Nakamura, who did not discover that the war was over until 1973.

AULIA_ULYA/SHUTTERSTOCK

Gunung Gamkonora

Relax on Sandy Shores

Beach-hopping and village views

Around 13km north of Tobelo, **Pantai Luari** *(free)* is a shaded white-sand beach fronting a horseshoe-shaped bay. The water is calm enough for swimming, and there's decent snorkelling and diving off the cape. Owing to its unusual location, Luari is a fine spot to see both the sunset and the sunrise, and there are vendors selling snacks.

Some 15km south of Tobelo, **Pantai Kupa Kupa** *(free)* is a partially shaded white-sand beach that's empty during the week and draws locals on weekends. It's a pleasant spot for swimming and there's reasonable snorkelling just offshore. There's an oil terminal at the far southern end of the beach, but walk north and there are plenty of photogenic views. There are well-located bungalows here, too.

For a more remote taste of Halmahera, set your sights on **Pantai Marimbati**. A pleasant 12km *ojek* excursion (30 minutes) from Jailolo takes you to this long black-sand beach. En route, the road passes through a mix of Christian and Muslim villages, where you'll see many thatched *rumah adat* (traditional houses). Reached by an entirely different road via Akelamo, **Susupu** (aka Sahu) is a picturesque volcano-backed village north of Pantai Marimbati, and separated by a narrow waterway.

Snorkel by World War II Ruins

Explore Meti island

A short hop from Halmahera's northeast coast, **Meti** is a small forest-covered island that makes an excellent base for exploring the region thanks to the eco-friendly **Meti Cottage** (p415). Around 400 families, largely Christian, live on the island. There are several WWII ruins, including Japanese bunkers, a bomb crater and the remains of a Japanese plane submerged in 25m of water just off the island. There's good snorkelling here – keep an eye out for the well-camouflaged walking shark.

Spot Endemic Species in the Tropical Forest

Bird-watching in Aketajawe-Lolobata National Park

Stretching across some 167,000 hectares in the centre of Halmahera, **Aketajawe-Lolobata National Park** *(facebook.com/aketajawe.lolobata; WhatsApp +62 853 4225 8008; 150,000Rp)* is a mix of lowland and montane rainforest with an impressive level of biodiversity. It's home to 53 species of mammals, including the ornate cuscus, which is endemic to the island. The bird-watching is superb with more than 200 recorded species. Most birders here have their hearts set on spotting the standardwing bird of paradise. The park is also home to the 2000-odd semi-nomadic Togutil people.

There are various access points into the park. Among the easiest to reach is via the **Ake Jawi resort** in the village of Binagara, located about a two-hour drive east of Sofifi. From there, you can hire local guides to take you to a standardwing lek a few kilometres from the village.

Climb an Active Volcano

Test your limits on Gunung Gamkonora

Your safest bet for a volcano adventure on Pulau Halmahera is the island's highest summit, **Gunung Gamkonora** (1571m), which last erupted in 2007. The 8km hike (nine hours round trip) starts just above sea level at a volcanology post near Desa Gamsungi. It goes through coconut, nutmeg and clove plantations before entering the jungle, leading to a spectacular U-shaped valley hemmed by towering walls on each side. The 1330m-high viewpoint at the valley's northern end offers views of a lake backed by Gamkonora's occasionally fuming craters. The mountain's summit lies beyond two more knolls, from where you can see amazing 360-degree panoramas stretching from Halmahera's northern volcanoes to Gamalama and Gunung Api Kiematubo on Ternate and Tidore. It's 42km north of Jailolo.

Gunung Ibu (1325m), meanwhile, is a dangerously active summit on the northeast side of Halmahera. In 2024, it was deemed to be off limits to hikers after an eruption damaged the access trail from Desa Duono village, and in January 2025 residents were evacuated after Ibu spewed 4km of ash plumes in the sky.

MORE VOLCANO CLIMBS

In Maluku, it's also possible to summit the almost perfect cone of **Gunung Api** (p408) in the Banda Islands and **Gamalama** (p379), the verdant volcano that makes up the best part of Ternate island.

GUIDES FOR HALMAHERA'S ACTIVE VOLCANOES

Even though access is not strictly controlled, only foolhardy individuals would climb an active volcano alone. Local guides help you navigate labyrinthine lava flows and stay safe. Fees start at 700,000Rp per group for Gunung Dukono.

In low-activity times, thrill seekers and adventure photographers can contact English-speaking guide Alexius Djangu (*WhatsApp +62 821 8830 3077; alex_djangu@yahoo.com*) for all-inclusive trips from Jailolo to Gunung Ibu (*3,000,000Rp per person with meals and porter).* Guests camp in the primary rainforest at a 2km distance from the bubbling crater and move again at 4am to get as close as possible.

Guides are also compulsory for Gunung Gamkonora: ask Alexius Djangu or Ternate-based operators like Kelana Malut *(instagram.com/kelanamalut)*.

MOROTAI FERRY PRACTICALITIES

A Morotai-bound ferry *(45,000Rp)* leaves Tobelo Port at 9am from Monday to Saturday, taking about three hours. Speedboats *(155,000Rp)* leave throughout the day when full from a small **speedboat terminal** in the city.

For Pulau Dodola, public ferries *(60,000Rp round trip)* depart Daruba Ferry Terminal from Saturday to Monday at 11am, arriving at 1pm, and return to Daruba at 3pm. Or you can charter a speedboat *(1,200,000Rp)*.

To leave Morotai, convenient boats with bunk beds *(220,000Rp)* and private berths *(620,000Rp)* make the overnight journey to Ternate's **Ahmad Yani Port** (p374) every day except Tuesday and Sunday.

A weekly service to Bitung, near Manado in Sulawesi, leaves on Thursdays between 1 and 3pm, taking a day and a half.

Visit World War II Sites

Unique history on Morotai

Even though it's been touted as one of Indonesia's upcoming '10 New Balis' since 2016, blissful **Morotai** still doesn't see much traffic. But Maluku's sizeable northernmost island, just off the northern tip of Halmahera, was once a hive of WWII activity. On 15 September 1944, US and Australian troops led by General MacArthur landed on **Army Dock Beach** – now Morotai's most accessible, lined with gazebos and little restaurants – meeting little resistance from the 500 Japanese soldiers left to guard the island.

Near the main town of Daruba, the large **Museum Perang Dunia II & Trikora** remains closed, with only a few tanks parked out front. Across the large central square by the sea, a **memorial statue** celebrates the Trikora, founded in 1961 to free West Papua from the Dutch.

Further away, Morotai's historical heritage is best preserved at **Museum Rakyat** *(donations welcome; WhatsApp +62 853 4070 0517)*, lovingly managed by Mr Muhlis Eso. The collection of dug-up, rusted wartime ammo, weapons, oxygen masks and more includes several highlights, such as a hand-cranked air-raid siren and a still-functioning American Willys MB jeep equipped with a machine gun. It's also known as the Museum Swadaya Perang Dunia Kedua di Morotai.

Finally, there's a photographic memorial to the iconic Teruo Nakamura, a Japanese soldier who remained in Morotai until 1974, 29 years after the war ended. His **statue** can also be found on a roundabout leading to Nakamura village, from where a long paved road leads to the swimmable **Nakota waterfall**.

Swim in Underwater Paradise

Day trip to Pulau Dodola

A 30-minute speedboat ride southwest of Morotai, white-sand **Pulau Dodola** is popular with domestic tourists. Two islands, Dodola Besar and Kecil, which are around 500m apart, join at low tide. Dodola is great for weekend trips when cheap public boats are available. A few rustic government cottages help those who want to stay, but consider that there's nothing here but sand and crystal-clear water.

EATING IN TOBELO AND MOROTAI: OUR PICKS

Kokiroba Mangi: Funky container-style cafes and warungs selling Indonesian and Western food, next to the local government office's gardens. *10am-10pm* $$

Cafe Love Story: Tucked above a sundry store, this cafe has artsy murals along its stairway and a hall to wait for Morotai passages. *1pm-1am* $

Rumah Makan Prima Rasa: A beloved Morotai warung specialising in chicken dishes and fried fish. Beware of their spicy sambal. *10am-9pm* $

Mutiara Coffee & Eat Cafe: A cosy outdoor area strewn with potted plants and tables, serving coffee, cakes and a few mains. *10am-11.30pm* $$

TOP EXPERIENCE

Gunung Dukono

Fancy standing before a roaring volcano watching plumes of ash spewing from deep within? Gunung Dukono (1229m) is one of Indonesia's most active, having erupted almost continuously since 1933. This hike of a lifetime takes you across an otherworldly landscape of ancient lava flows and volcanic sand plains to peer inside the dangerously active, smoke-belching crater.

SABINE_LJ/SHUTTERSTOCK

Choosing a Trail

The original trail begins at **Mamuya** village, where the volcanology office can give you names of suggested guides. At the time of research, it was safer to use a better-maintained second trail from Roku village. **KPA Lentera Alam** in Popilo village, 7km north of Tobelo and in the vicinity of the **ferry port**, organises trips. Contact guides Owin *(instagram.com/owin_hiking; WhatsApp +62 822 3160 7004)* and Sam *(WhatsApp +62 853 9406 0497)*, keeping in mind that little English is spoken.

Getting to the Crater

Save hours of walking by taking a three-wheeler pickup *(700,000Rp round-trip for seven people)* or *ojek (100,000Rp round-trip per person)* through durian plantations to **Parkiran 2**, from where it's a 7.5km hike to the crater via five *Pos* (stops). Figure five hours.

Overnight Camping

It's far better to overnight *(700,000Rp guide fee per group)* as the active crater puts on a fireworks display while you sleep just 2km away – it sounds like the roar of a jet plane. Pos 5 is a five-minute walk from a barebones campsite with no toilets. In the morning, if the weather's clear and not too windy, brave the crater climb and enjoy stunning views of **Gunung Gogodom** (1111m), **Gunung Bale-Bale** (925m) and the islands off Tobelo.

TOP TIPS

- Check the wind and the direction of smoke plumes to avoid falling ash.
- Wear a helmet near the crater and use a selfie stick to photograph its insides more safely.
- Never climb when the volcano is not rumbling – silence means that sudden eruptions may throw scorching, deadly rocks your way.

PRACTICALITIES

- free
- guide compulsory

Pulau Ambon

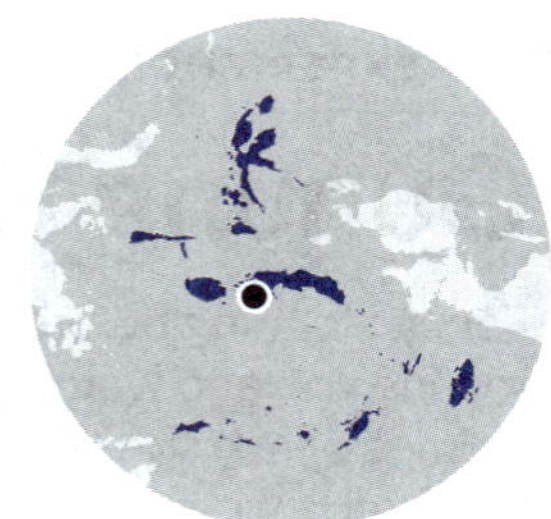

CITY LIFE | SCUBA DIVING | GREAT OUTDOORS

> **TOP TIP**
>
> If you're planning to visit north Maluku from Ambon on Mondays and Fridays, Trigana Air flies to Ternate with a stop at Sanana on Sulabes island for about 1,500,000Rp. The catch is you can't buy tickets online: go to the **Trigana Air office** in Ambon or contact them by WhatsApp at *+62 852 4475 7625*. Tickets sell out quickly.

Maluku's most prominent and populous island is lush, gently mountainous and indented with two great hoops of bay. The sprawling capital, Kota Ambon, is not much of a charmer. But the coastal villages and jagged shoreline west and north of the airport make Ambon so much more than just another transport hub. Take your time: the bay is known for excellent muck-diving, while the southern coast has clear waters and intact coral. Leitimur, the more developed south, is joined to the northern Leihitu area by an isthmus at Passo and the iconic **Jembatan Merah Putih** bridge.

Ambon had a complicated past with the Portuguese and Dutch vying for control during the colonial period, followed by a Japanese takeover in WWII and a controversial massacre of POWs. It was also the hotbed of the bloody Maluku Sectarian Conflict between Christians and Muslims, which ravaged the region between 1999 and 2002. Today, economic growth and tourism have reignited pride in the island's cultural heritage.

GETTING AROUND

Pattimura International Airport is a 30-minute drive (20km) to Kota Ambon. The official taxi rate is 170,000Rp (negotiable to 150,000Rp), or exit the airport's fenced area and hop the red *angkot* line to central **Pasar Mardika** for 20,000Rp. From here, the green *angkot* has stops at **Pelabuhan Yos Soedarso**, where Pelni ferries arrive and depart. All other boats depart from Tulehu on the northeast coast. About 200m east of Pasar Mardika along Jl Pantai Mardika is **Terminal Tulehu**, with *angkot* and bemos headed to **Tulehu port**, Waai, Liang, Morella and the northern coast of Leihitu. One-way fares are between 20,000 and 30,000Rp. *Ojeks* are readily available, as are taxis – book via Grab, Gojek or InDrive. Hire a motorbike from **Wisma Grace Hotel** (p415) *(150,000Rp per day)*; **Ambonise Rental** *(rentalmotorambon.blogspot.co.id; WhatsApp +62 821-3459-4700)* has bikes and cars *(130,000Rp per day)*.

Underwater Adventure

Diving and snorkelling off Ambon

Ambon's wide urban **bay** – as deep as 500m in some places – has an abundance of underwater life that makes it a celebrated **muck-diving location**. There are up to 30 dive sites within the bay alone, plus many more around the coast and the three Tiga Islands off Asilulu village on Ambon's northwestern corner.

Highlights elsewhere around the island include coral-crusted volcanic pinnacles off Mahia, Hukurila's blue hole, a huge underwater arch at **Pintu Kota** and the *Duke of Sparta* shipwreck, allegedly sunk by the CIA in 1958. During action-packed drift dives between the Tiga Islands, you'll meet bumphead parrotfish, Napoleons, dogtooth tuna, vast schools of fusiliers, dolphins, sharks and turtles. You can also glimpse the big stuff at **Tanjung Sial Timur** (Bad Corner), where strong currents attract pelagic fish off Seram's southern tip.

As special as those sites can be, it's the muck that draws the crowds for oddities such as the psychedelic frogfish, 15 varieties of rhinopia, manta shrimp, zebra crabs, banded pipefish, pygmy squid and seahorses. Come between October and April: most local dive outfits close between May and September due to rough seas and poor visibility.

AMBON'S DIVE OPERATORS

Only a few diving centers are open on Ambon, mostly in Laha.

Spice Island Divers and Resort: Located in Laha on Ambon Bay, this boutique outfit will introduce you to Ambon's Twilight Zone, which is full of unique critters like the Ambon frogfish. The resort, with seafront villas and a restaurant, makes a great base.

Blue Rose Divers: Another Laha operation specialising in all creatures small and smaller. There's top-notch muck-diving plus opportunities to visit some healthy coral spots. You can spend the night at its simple four-room guesthouse.

Ambon Dive Center: Located in Sawattelu on the north coast, this small outfit offers abundant muck-diving, but it doesn't have lodging. *instagram.com/ambondivecenter*

Relics of the Past

Culture and history in Kota Ambon

Take a break from the beaches and dive sites to check out some of the city's intriguing historical sights. Ten minutes south of Kota Ambon, the modest **Museum Siwalima** *(siwalima.atspace.com; entry 3000Rp, guided English tour 50,000Rp)* is set in sloping landscaped gardens adorned with Japanese and Dutch cannons and a scowling statue of **Pattimura**, with *parang* (machete) aloft. The collection is dedicated to Malukan material culture, including fish traps, stone tools, model longboats, brass jewellery and an elongated tifa drum crafted from bamboo and ancient bone. Traditional Indonesian wedding costumes from across the archipelago are exhibited in the topmost gallery.

Known to locals as the Australian Cemetery, the neatly manicured **Commonwealth War Cemetery** *(cwgc.org/visit-us; free)* was designed by a British landscape architect in honour of Allied servicemen killed in Maluku and Sulawesi in WWII. It's built on the site of a former POW camp, adding to its poignancy.

Continues on p394

AMBON RESTAURANTS WITH A VIEW: OUR PICKS

View: Near Patung Christina Martha Tiahahu, the View has cold beer and other temptations on a lovely outdoor terrace with a sweeping panorama. *10am-10pm* $$

Bayview Restaurant: Tuck into Western comfort fare or Indonesian classics, or sip a Guinness on the photogenic 7th-floor deck of the City Hotel. *8am-11pm* $$

Red Brick Cafe & Resto: Mellow family favourite with fine views, burgers, kung pao chicken, laksa noodle soup and beer. *10am-11pm* $$

Oui Sky Pool & Bar: On the 9th floor of the Golden Palace Hotel. Enjoy great town and harbor views from the bar or the pool. *9am-10pm* $$

PULAU AMBON

Pulau Seram
Teluk Ambon
Jl Pantai Mardika
Military Zone (No Access)
Sungai Tomu
Jl Rijali
Jl Yos Sudarso
Jl Pala
Jl AY Patty
Jl AM Sangaji
Jl Sultan Babullah
Jl Pattimura
Jl Jan Paays
Jl Ahmad Yani
Jl Diponegoro
Jl Dr Latumenten
0 1 km
0 0.5 miles
Kaitetu
Hila
Saith
Negri Lima
Ureng
Asilulu
Lai
Larike
Wakasihu
Tapi
Allang
Liliboi
Hatu
Laha
Tawiri
Teluk Ambon
Eri
Latuhalat

HIGHLIGHTS
1 Taeno Waterfall

SIGHTS
2 Ambon Bay
3 Benteng Amsterdam
4 Commonwealth War Cemetery
5 Danau Wae Ela
see 3 Gereja Tua Immanuel
6 Jembatan Merah Putih
7 Maluku Governor Office
see 3 Masjid Wapaue
8 Museum Siwalima
9 Namalatu Beach
10 Pantai Pintu Kota
11 Pantai Wae Rahung
12 Pattimura Park
13 Patung Christina Martha Tiahahu
14 Puncak Elshadday Anjel's Siwang
15 Santai Beach
16 Sopapei Beach
17 World Peace Gong

ACTIVITIES
18 Ambon Dive Center
19 Blue Rose Divers
20 Puncak Gunung Salahutu
21 Rumah Pohon Waai
22 Sagu Negeri Rutong
23 Spice Island Divers & Resort

SLEEPING
24 Swiss-Belhotel
25 The City Hotel
26 Wisma Grace

EATING

see 25 Bayview Restaurant
27 Imperial
28 Mie Ikan dan Ayam Khas Namlea
29 Neo Coffee & Bistro
30 Rasa Gurih
31 Red Brick Cafe & Resto
see 30 Sari Gurih
32 Sarinda
33 View

DRINKING & NIGHTLIFE

34 Kopi Tradisi Joas
35 Oui Sky Pool & Bar
see 34 Sibu-Sibu

SHOPPING

36 Pasar Mardika

TRANSPORT

37 Ambonise Rental
38 Pattimura Airport
39 Pelabuhan Yos Soedarso Ambon
40 Terminal Tulehu
41 Trigana Air Office
42 Tulehu Port

MOTORCYCLE TOUR

The Ambon Motorcycle Loop

Ambon has plenty of interesting stops scattered around the island, which make for a whirlwind day tour or a more relaxed two-day loop. Begin in Leihitu, the northern part of the island. You'll trace the sandy northeastern shores before circling back around through mangrove-draped coast and beautiful, jagged cliffs to the northwest. From here, turn south and drive back to the bridge, then cross to the jungle-clad hilltops of central Leitimur.

1 Natsepa Beach

Begin at this long beach *(entry 5000Rp, plus 5000Rp per motorbike)* facing Leitimur's viridian southeastern edges. There are tables, rental tubes and often Christian groups playing guitars on the beach.

The Drive: Pass Tulehu port and reach Waai via the mangrove-draped coastal backroad.

2 Waai Village

This quiet village has a **sacred eel pond** beyond the creek where local women do their laundry. You need to buy eggs from the local sundry shop to feed the eels – a family living near the pond manages this for a donation of around 100,000Rp – or they won't come out of their hiding holes. If you have time, make an inland diversion to the **Waai waterfall**.

RADITYA PUTRA TITAPASANEA/SHUTTERSTOCK

Natsepa Beach

The Drive: As you leave Waai, you'll pass the interesting **Damai Church**, topped by three towers. Cut inland to reach the beaches around Liang and Hunimua port, where ferries leave for Seram island.

3 Liang

Pantai Hunimua *(5000Rp plus 5000Rp for parking)* and **Pantai Liang** are connected and good for sunbathing and swimming. A few hundred metres west is Liang, hugging cerulean **Pantai Alfath**.

The Drive: From Liang, the road deteriorates as you traverse the 13.2km of beautiful switchbacks across coastal knolls to Morella. Of note is **Halassy Beach** (5000Rp), a steep tumble down the road, with gazebos and a wooden deck over a speckle of transparent sea. There's a restaurant and some rooms to spend the night.

4 Lubang Buaya Morella

Lubang Buaya Morella is a popular spot for snorkelling *(3000Rp, plus drinks or food)* and has a well-conserved reef cascading down an impressive underwater canyon. You can hire a *prahu* (outrigger canoe) for a paddle around the area. There's coral and plenty of colourful aquatic life if you swim around the bend (north) after you enter the water. It's busy on weekends.

The Drive: Ride back a lengthy 15km across central Leihitu, cross the iconic Jembatan Merah-Putih and continue 16km west along Leitimur's northern coast, passing through Kota Ambon and then Amahusu Beach. Stay focused as you ascend the steep and winding road to Bukit Paralayang, near the southern tip of the island.

5 Bukit Paralayang

The popular viewpoint **Bukit Paralayang** *(5000Rp, plus 5000Rp for parking)*, in the southern hills of Ambon, opens at 5am for sunrise and closes after sunset at 7pm. Walk west of the little coffee shop to find paths leading to uncrowded viewpoints over the forest-fringed southern coast.

AMBON'S SECRET SPOTS

Sonny Ay, a tour guide and co-owner of Wisma Grace, suggests some of his favorite little-known spots around Ambon island. *@wismagrace*

Rumah Pohon Waai: One of the best spots to see beautiful mountain scenery; experience glamping in Ambon's hills and swim in the stunning Waai waterfall.

Sopapei Beach: I like visiting when the tide is low; it's the best time to see how long and pristine this beach is.

Sagu Negeri Rutong: An interesting cooking experience in Rutong that tells the story of how sago is made from scratch

Puncak Elshadday Anjel's Siwang: If you want to see one of the best views from the top of Ambon Island, this is the place to go.

RIANA AMBARSARI/SHUTTERSTOCK

Benteng Amsterdam

Continued from p389

A symbol of Kota Ambon, the **World Peace Gong** *(5000Rp)* was placed here in 2009 in hopes of repairing the rifts that began during the Ambon Conflict of 1999. Right in front is **Pattimura Park**, featuring a statue of the national Ambonese martyr, a symbol of Indonesia's independence, who led a rebellion against the Dutch in 1817 and was executed. The southern side of the park features a large *padang* (square) fringed by the imposing **Maluku Governor Office** on its eastern side and some mural art.

About 2km east along Jl Tukabessy and then Jl Rijali is where the uphill climb to the top of a hill fringed by gardens begins. This is where the **Patung Christina Martha Tiahahu** pays homage to another great Moluccan freedom fighter. Wielding a spear, Indonesia's national heroine overlooks the city beneath her. It's a great place to watch the sunset.

The Es Pisang Ijo is sweet-tooth bliss!

EATING IN AMBON: OUR PICKS

Sari Gurih: Fronted by a sizzling grill, this multilevel space has first-rate seafood and a picture menu to help you decide. *9am-10pm* $$

Rasa Gurih: The *ikan bakar* (grilled fish), perfectly roasted and smothered in chilli by the coal-stoking chef, is fall-off-the-bone fresh. *9am-10pm* $$

Imperial: Shrimp, fish, squid: the seafood is all outstanding, and there are good Chinese dishes if you want a break from Indonesian fare. *10am-10.30pm Mon-Sat* $$

Mie Ikan dan Ayam Khas Namlea: A hair salon that doubles as a noodle joint – the Manado-style *mie cakalang* with shredded fish is delicious. *10.30am-7pm* $

Snorkel off Scenic Beaches

Coastal beauty in southern Leitimur

Latuhalat, Leitimur's southern tip, straddles a low pass culminating in **Santai** and **Namalatu**, a pair of well-shaded beaches popular with locals at weekends. Neither offers great swimming, but divers and snorkellers will find plenty of reef action offshore. You can walk between the two beaches in 15 minutes. It's much more tranquil than busy Kota Ambon, but you're still only a 40-minute bemo ride from the city.

Relics from the Past

Architectural intrigue in Hila and Kaitetu

A trio of sights lie close together near the north-central shores of Leihitu. In Hila, the **Benteng Amsterdam** *(entry by donation)* is a whitewashed fort that was first laid out in 1637. Though some of the exterior walls have been rebuilt with concrete, the inner tower, with its brick floors and thick walls, is fluttering with resident swallows and has fine views over the sea, particularly from the top floor (watch your step on the steep stairs).

A short walk south of the fort is the **Gereja Tua Immanuel**, a tiny thatch-roof church that's gone through various incarnations over the centuries. It began life as the Catholic Santo Jacobus under the auspices of the Portuguese, who built a church here in the early 16th century. Around 100 years later, the Dutch took it over and expanded it, reworking it again in 1780 when it became a Protestant church and took the name Immanuel. Note the small choir loft where musicians would play.

A few blocks away lies the pretty wood and thatch-roofed mosque **Masjid Wapaue**, originally built in 1414 on nearby Gunung Wawane. It was moved in 1614 to the village of Tehala (6km away) and transferred again in 1664 to its present site. It's the oldest mosque on Pulau Ambon still in use and one of the few of its kind still standing in Indonesia. Today, 12 different men (the Tukang Dua Belas) from three villages serve as master carpenters and work on the mosque's meticulous upkeep. Various panels in English explain its history and innovative building techniques. Non-Muslims can visit outside prayer times.

AMBON'S GREAT OUTDOORS

Chrisz Tahapary, a local teacher with a passion for outdoor adventure, recommends places to camp in Ambon. *@chrisztahapary*

Danau Wae Ela, near Desa Negeri Lima on the northwestern coast of Ambon, is a wild lake full of bird life. I like to get in my inflatable kayak and watch them fly across the lake.

Pantai Wae Rahung is a secluded southern beach near Hukurila, perfect for camping in good weather.

Pantai Pintu Kota (p389) has a rock shaped as a tunnel door by the sea. I go rappelling there, and the diving is also very good.

Puncak Gunung Salahutu is 1083m tall and quite a hard climb. People generally camp at the top to wait for the clouds to clear; you can see as far as Seram and Haruku islands.

y the Rarobang coffee with ginger, milk and kenari leaf.

AMBON'S CAFES & BAKERIES: OUR PICKS

Sibu-Sibu: Stars deck the walls of this ever-popular coffee shop and bar, which plays live Malukan music while serving snacks. *7.30-11pm Mon-Sat* $

Kopi Tradisi Joas: Ambon's intellectuals gather at this old-school institution over rich mocha-style 'secret-recipe' coffees. *8am-8pm Mon-Sat* $

Sarinda: With its outside terrace seating and central location, Sarinda is a good place to start the day with pastries and decent coffee. *8am-10pm* $

Neo Coffee & Bistro: Sink into a banquette at one of Ambon's most elegant cafes, which serves drinks plus Indonesian fare. *9am-11.30pm Mon-Sat* $$

TOP EXPERIENCE

Taeno Waterfall

When Kota Ambon's traffic gets to be too much, leave the city behind and refresh yourself at this spectacular natural spot. Forty-metre-high Taeno Waterfall is one of the tallest and grandest in Maluku, and it's only a 20-minute drive from central Leihitu. The twin falls slosh at the bottom of a steep creek, where wide pools await swimmers.

ANDRI TRI PUTRA/SHUTTERSTOCK

TOP TIPS

- Combine your visit as a stop on a longer itinerary to northern or western Leihitu.
- Climbing back up is a slog. Plan to spend time at bottom, and bring a portable chair, a book and even a stove to fire up some coffee.
- Avoid visiting during or after rain.

PRACTICALITIES

- entry 5000Rp

Getting There

Taeno Waterfall, also called Telaga Pange after the name of the nearby village 1.2km to its south, is just 6km north of Jembatan Merah Putih, right outside the northern urban sprawl of Teluk Ambon. Catching a rideshare from the city is convenient; otherwise, the well-paved road is suitable for self-driving on rental scooters and cars.

Descending to the Falls

After the checkpost on the main road where the entry fee is collected, a concrete path leads visitors down the hill. It can be quite slippery, especially after rain, so pay attention. About 500m down from the ticket booth, the path turns into very steep staircases – take it slow. Rest assured that going back up is tough. If you don't feel up to the challenge, you may want to reconsider this trip.

Enjoy a Dip

Look on your right at the bottom of the creek to see the twin waterfalls. The cascading waters empty into a couple of ponds hemmed by rocks – it's possible to swim here safely. A little path helps you to get closer for the best views.

CRUISING LEIHITU'S WESTERN COAST

Strike out on Ambon's wildest coast, discovering historic villages and breathtaking rock formations.

START	END	LENGTH
Puncak Love Allang	Batu Lubang	20.2km; 2hr to 3hr

Drive 13km west of Pattimura Airport and stop at 1 **Puncak Love Allang** *(3000Rp)*, a mast-shaped viewpoint over a wave-swept bay. Keep following the coastal road to Allang village to see the traditional 2 **Baleo Latu Suli Siwa Hina Allane** house, built in 1877. Look for the crocodile carvings on the roof beams and a 1740 Dutch bell. Descend to 3 **Tanjung Allang**, another beautiful viewpoint over a wave-battered cliff.

It's 7km west to 4 **Huluwa Beach**, where a staircase leads to a tiny strip of land sheltered by tall fig trees and a large boulder. On the right, via a rock passage, there's a safe spot to swim. Driving past Wakasihu village, look for 5 **Pulau Batusuanggi**, a monolith jutting out of the sea, and stop at 6 **Morea Larike Eels Conservation**, where freshwater eels gather in quiet pools behind the village. Buy a bag of fish *(20,000Rp)* and feed the eels, or let a guide do the work for a tip.

The two impressive crags of 7 **Batu Layar** come next, right by the roadside. Stop for a contemplative drink at the streetside warung. End at 8 **Batu Lubang**, an impressive cave by the stony shore, reached by walking off the road – friendly locals will help find the way. Inside, the cave opens into a small forested area, which is a cool camping spot.

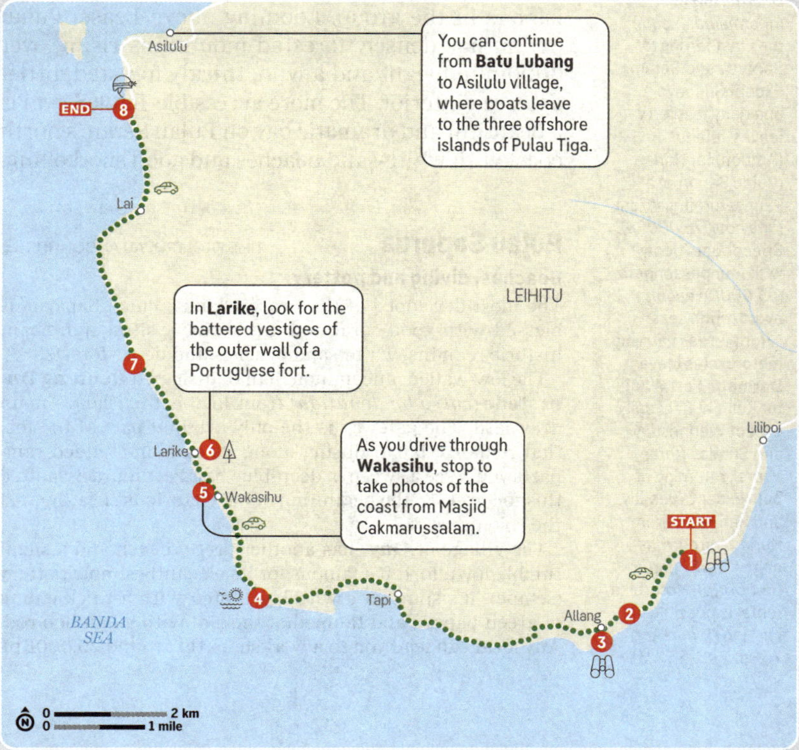

You can continue from **Batu Lubang** to Asilulu village, where boats leave to the three offshore islands of Pulau Tiga.

In **Larike**, look for the battered vestiges of the outer wall of a Portuguese fort.

As you drive through **Wakasihu**, stop to take photos of the coast from Masjid Cakmarussalam.

Asilulu
END 8
Lai
7
LEIHITU
Larike 6
5 Wakasihu
4
Tapi
Allang
2
3
START 1
Liliboi
BANDA SEA
0 2 km
0 1 mile

Beyond Pulau Ambon

The little-visited islands near Ambon make for rewarding adventures both on land and in the sea.

Places

GETTING AROUND

Dharma Indah *(dharmaindah.com)* runs fast ferries to Saparua and Seram. Except Sundays, one daily fast ferry leaves Tulehu (Ambon) for Haria (Pulau Saparua) at 9am, returning at 7am *(one hour, 75,000Rp)*. Speedboats depart with four passengers *(85,000Rp each)*; avoid rough seas.

Roro ferries carrying motorcycles leave **Dermaga Feri Waai** for Kulur at 8am daily except Wednesday and Sunday *(three hours)*, returning at 3pm except Tuesday and Saturday. From Haria, shared vans go to Kota Saparua *(15,000Rp)*. Motorbike rental is possible via Mr Vino *(WhatsApp +62 822 4873 5923)*.

Just east of Ambon, the Lease Islands (pronounced 'leh-AH-say') consist of three easily accessible yet delightfully laid-back isles with a scattering of old-world villages, lovely bays and the odd great-value beach retreat plunked right along the seaside. Several crumbling Dutch forts attest to the islands' one-time strategic importance. There's decent diving and snorkelling amid vibrantly healthy reef systems off Pulau Molana and Nusa Laut, two of the smaller islands in the group. Looming above Lease, Pulau Seram has densely forested mountains rising over 3000m in height and a wild, thickly forested, little-accessed interior. The more accessible Teluk Sawai is a beautiful and dramatic bay on Pulau Seram's north coast with white-sand beaches and good snorkelling.

Pulau Saparua

TIME FROM PULAU AMBON: **1HR**

Beaches, diving and pottery

The most developed of the Lease Islands, Pulau Saparua is blessed with good coral and muck-diving sites, significant historic remains, white-sand beaches and dense forests.

The low-walled, uncommon diamond-shaped **Benteng Duurstede** *(entry by donation)* from 1676 is the island's main drawcard. The gateway is the only original part of the fort that remains, but traipsing along its cannon-studded ramparts you'll see a sweep of deep-blue bay. Pattimura assaulted this fort in 1817, the beginning of his victorious siege against the colonisers.

The village of **Ouw** has another pretty beach and a small tumbledown fort; it's famous for its elegantly simple pottery (sempe). It's spun on a wheel, sculpted with a thick chunk of green papaya and tamped at the rim with a bamboo rod. Any local can lead you to a workshop (tip around 20,000Rp).

Kulur's offbeat northwestern shore

Whether you're traversing this small island via your own scooter or hugging an *ojek* driver, it's worth travelling to the lesser-visited northwestern coast near Kulur. A small paved path leads off the road to **Goa Puteri Tujuh** *(Seven Princesses Cave; free)*, a limestone hollow filled with seven pools of incredibly transparent water. It's perfect for a refreshing dip, although it's not very well maintained. A 1.7km ride from here is the wide and sandy **Pantai Kulur**, a beach with clear water and dramatic views of Seram's southern coast. Sadly, most of the coral is broken.

Pulau Seram

TIME FROM PULAU AMBON: **2½HR**

Stunning northern bays

Seram's most scenic highlight is **Teluk Sawai**, a beautiful wide bay backed by soaring cliffs and rugged, forested peaks. It's accessed via the village of **Saleman**, famed for cliffs that are home to flocks of bat-like Lusiala birds. From Saleman, boats go around the headland to the dramatic limestone cliffs by the stilt-house village of Sawai, passing by **Pantai Ora**, a beautiful bay with stunning azure waters.

Boat or kayak trips from either village *(half-/full day 500,000/1,000,000Rp)* head to offshore coral gardens, often including stops at the **Keramba Heart** – a giant heart-shaped *keramba* (fish trap), popular with drone photographers – and **Air Belanda** (Dutch Water), a beach with a cold spring flowing from the mountains into the ocean. You'll feel the temperature difference as you swim.

Adventures in Manusela National Park

Established in 1997, the remote **Manusela National Park** *(instagram.com/btn_manusela; WhatsApp +62 811 4791 000; 150,000Rp per day, plus 20,000Rp for hiking)* occupies a large chunk of central Seram and attracts bird-watchers searching for rare parrots. Home to four villages and a number of minority peoples, the park is mountainous and covered in thick jungle.

At the time of research, the reserve's highlight – the hardcore five- to seven-day trans-Manusela trek to Maluku's highest peak, **Gunung Binaiya** (3027m) – was closed following the death of a Javanese hiker in May 2025. Contact the park to ask for the latest. The area is also home to the 424m-deep **Gua Hatusaka**, the deepest cave in Indonesia. It's only open to spelunkers with a permit.

VISITING SERAM

Darma Indah's fast ferries depart from Tulehu to Amahai (Seram) at 9am and 6pm. They return at 8am and 4pm daily, except Sundays when they only run at 3pm. Roro ferries for vehicles also leave for Seram throughout the day from the small **Hunimua port**, 3km east of Liang village. They arrive at the smaller **Waipirit port**, a three-hour drive from Amahai.

Once on Seram, accommodation in **Saleman village** or **Pantai Ora** can help organise onward transport from Amahai (*about 300,000Rp one-way in a shared taxi, or 800,000Rp if chartering a car*). Staying in Pantai Ora is expensive. Cheaper guesthouses in Saleman organise half-day tours to Pantai Ora for about 350,000Rp per boat. Exploring more can set you back about 1,000,000Rp per boat per day.

Banda Islands

SNORKELLING & DIVING | HISTORY | ISLAND LIFE

TOP TIP

If you're flying, several well-connected locals can help get the hard-to-book seats on SAM Air. Contact Reza at **Nutmeg Tree Dive** (p404) and Abba at **Cilu Bintang Estate** (p415). For the latest on ferry schedules, check **Dive Blue Motion**'s website *(dive-bluemotion.com/getting-here)*.

Combining natural beauty, a warm heart and a palpable, fascinating history, this remote cluster of 10 picturesque islands isn't just Maluku's top travel destination, it's one of the most atmospheric locations in Indonesia. Impressive undersea drop-offs are filled with multicoloured coral gardens, which makes for superlative snorkelling and diving. The central islands – Pulau Neira and Pulau Banda Besar (the great nutmeg island) – curl in picturesque crescents around a pocket-sized tropical version of Mt Fuji (Gunung Api). You can climb, village-hop, hike and snorkel for days on end.

Outlying Hatta, Ai and Nailaka have undeveloped beaches, while Run, a gnarled limestone island sprouting nutmeg and cloves, is a gorgeous historical footnote. Getting to the islands takes time, but with a fast-boat service from Ambon (in the dry season) and reliable Pelni services, the Bandas are becoming more accessible. So get here now, before everyone else does.

GETTING AROUND

Pelni ships sail several times weekly between Ambon and **Banda Neira Port**. The overnight crossing takes 14 hours on the cleaner *Kapal Pangrango*, or eight hours by day on the *Kapal Labobar* or *Sangiang*. Check schedules at pelni.co.id or via the app about a month ahead. A faster option is the Dharma Indah service *(dharmaindah.com; 700,000Rp)*, which departs Ambon's **Tulehu Port** (p388) Fridays at 9am and returns Sundays at 9am. The four-hour crossing is quicker but prone to cancellations in wetter months. Flights cut travel time to one hour: SAM Air *(about 500,000Rp)* flies twice weekly between Ambon and Banda Neira, though delays are common and tickets can't be booked online.

On Pulau Neira, most places are walkable. Boats to other islands leave from Banda Neira Port near the market. Charters are affordable: around 1,500,000Rp for a full-day island hop for up to 10 people, or 700,000 to 1,000,000Rp to Banda Besar, Pulau Pisang or Pulau Karaka.

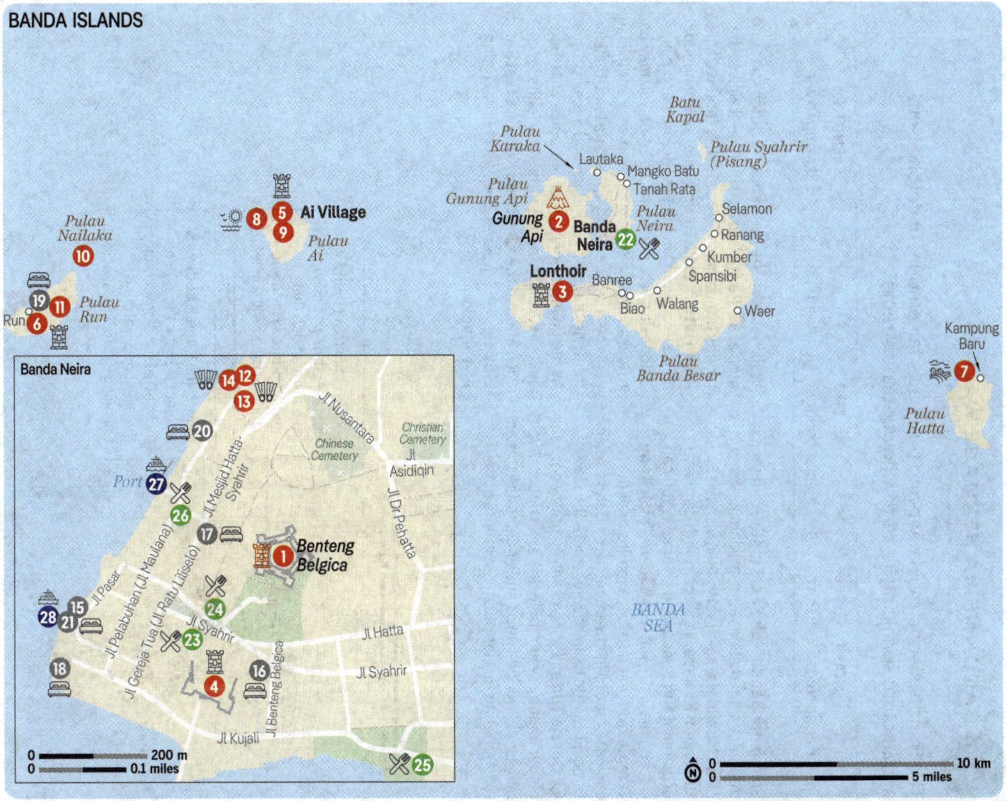

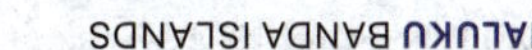

BANDA ISLANDS

HIGHLIGHTS
1 Benteng Belgica
2 Gunung Api

SIGHTS
3 Benteng Hollandia
4 Benteng Nassau
5 Benteng Revenge
see 3 Blood Stone
6 English Fort
see 5 Gereja Betlehem
7 Kampung Lama
see 3 Kelly Plantation
see 3 Lonthoir
8 Pantai Sebila
see 3 Pohon Sejuta Umat
9 Pulau Ai
10 Pulau Nailaka
11 Pulau Run
see 3 Sumur Pusaka Negeri
see 10 Swan Fort

ACTIVITIES
12 Dive Bluemotion
13 Naira Dive
14 Nutmeg Tree Dive

SLEEPING
15 Bintang Laut
16 Cilu Bintang Estate
17 Delfika
18 Delfika Guesthouse 2
see 5 Green Coconut
19 Guesthouse Nailaka
20 Hotel Maulana
21 Vita Guesthouse

EATING
22 Cafe Terapung
see 16 Cilu Bintang Estate
see 17 Delfika Cafe
23 Kedai Paparipi
24 Nutmeg Cafe
25 Serenade
26 Spice Island Cafe

TRANSPORT
27 Banda Neira Port
28 Small Jetty to Gunung Api

Pulau Nailaka
Run
Pulau Run
Ai Village
Pulau Ai
Pulau Karaka
Lautaka
Mangko Batu
Tanah Rata
Batu Kapal
Pulau Syahrir (Pisang)
Pulau Gunung Api
Gunung Api
Banda Neira
Pulau Neira
Selamon
Ranang
Kumber
Spansibi
Lonthoir
Banree
Biao
Walang
Waer
Pulau Banda Besar
Kampung Baru
Pulau Hatta
BANDA SEA
0 10 km
0 5 miles

Banda Neira
Port
Jl Nusantara
Christian Cemetery
Chinese Cemetery
Jl Asidiqin
Jl Dr Pehatta
Jl Mesjid Hatta-Syahrir
Benteng Belgica
Jl Pasar
Jl Pelabuhan (Jl Maulana)
Jl Gereja Tua (Jl Ratu Liliseto)
Jl Syahrir
Jl Hatta
Jl Syahrir
Jl Benteng Belgica
Jl Kujali
0 200 m
0 0.1 miles

BANDA NEIRA HERITAGE WALK

The Banda Islands' main town and port has a fair amount of colonial-era architecture sprinkling its narrow flower-filled streets.

START	END	LENGTH
Banda Neira Pelni Port	Masjid Agung Al-Mujahidin	1.2km; up to 2hr

Start at 1 **Banda Neira Port** (p400) and traipse through the market past the striking minarets of 2 **Mesjid Hatta-Sjahrir**, then visit the 3 **Rumah Budaya**, a museum with displays of colonial and Bandanese artefacts. You can just see the 300-year-old 4 **Sun Thien Kong Temple** from the outside, a reminder of the ancient Chinese involvement in the Banda spice trade. Enter the main square, where the 1852 5 **Gereja Tua** still showcases its pretty portico of four chubby columns. Inside are a decorative bell-clock, wooden pews and ancient flagstones, remembering former Dutch governors of the island.

Walk between the two imposing Dutch forts and stop at 6 **Parigi Rante**, a memorial well to the bloody Banda Massacre of 1621. A short walk away is 7 **Hatta's Exile House**, where Mohammed Hatta lived from 1936 to 1942 before becoming Indonesia's vice president. To enter, you may have to join an organised tour. A short walk south is the neglected yet imposing 8 **Istana Mini**, built in the style of the Bogor Palace and once occupied by the governor-general of the Dutch East Indies. Just east up the road, Banda's two faiths face each other at the 9 **Gereja Katolik Stasi Santa Lidya** and the green-roofed 10 **Masjid Agung Al-Mujahidin**.

Locals claim that **Mesjid Hatta-Sjahrir** was converted from the mansion that accommodated Hatta and Sjahrir on their arrival in 1936.

Among the **Rumah Budaya's** artefacts, check the *kapsete* (helmet) of the warrior dance that went underground following the 1621 massacre.

Besides photos, a typewriter and clothes at **Hatta's Exile House**, there's a schoolhouse that inspired an entire generation of anti-colonial youth.

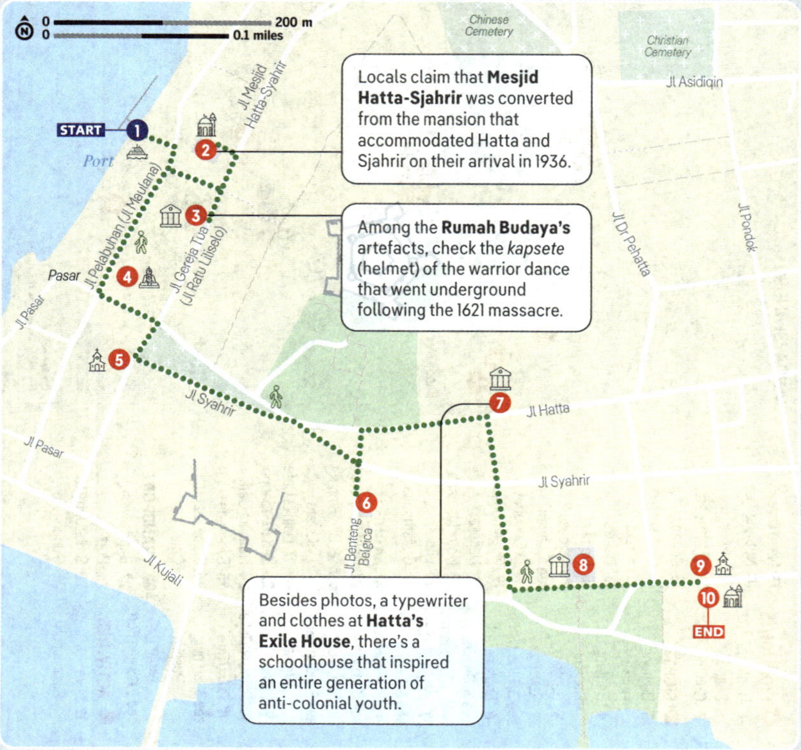

Visit the Fortresses of Banda Neira

A lesson in colonial history

A classic star fort and UNESCO nominee, **Benteng Belgica** *(10,000Rp donation)* was built on the hill above Benteng Nassau in 1611, when it became apparent the lower bastion was an inadequate defence. The five massive, sharp-pointed bastions were crafted to deflect the cannon fire of a potential English naval bombardment. In 1796, it caused quite a scandal in Holland after the Brits managed to seize the fort (albeit briefly) without firing a shot. To reach the upper ramparts, take the second arch on the left from the central courtyard. Be sure to look for the old jail, where locals were imprisoned if they dared sell their spices to the English.

Tucked into tropical foliage nearby, the quietly crumbling **Benteng Nassau** was built in 1609 against the wishes of the *orang kaya* (local leaders) on foundations abandoned by the Portuguese 80 years earlier. In 1621, the fortress played a role in the horrific Banda Massacre, in which Jan Pieterszoon Coen, the new governor general of the VOC (Dutch East India Company), ordered the virtual genocide of the local population. More than 2800 Bandanese were slaughtered. Of the survivors, 1700 were subsequently enslaved, with only a few hundred escaping to the Kei Islands.

Explore Banda Besar

Plantation strolls, views and more history

The largest island of the group, hilly **Banda Besar** is a great day trip and offers the chance to wander through the **Kelly Plantation**, where centuries-old, buttressed kenari trees tower protectively over a nutmeg grove. Banda Besar is also home to the Van den Broeke Plantation run by Pongky Van den Broeke, the last *perkenier* (nutmeg planter). Prongky represents the 13th generation of a Dutch colonial family, who have been involved in nutmeg cultivation since the 17th century.

One of Banda's best views is from the **Pohon Sejuta Umat** viewpoint *(1000Rp)*, reached on a 15-minute climb from the village of **Lonthoir**. There are two trees here with exposed roots that have become a popular Instagram frame for Indonesian tourists. It's in front of the chunky, overgrown ruins of **Benteng Hollandia**. Built in 1624, this was once one of the biggest Dutch fortresses in the East Indies until it was shattered by a devastating 1743 earthquake.

THE BEST OF THE BANDA ISLANDS

Lukman A Ang, chief of Banda Neira's Chinese Association and owner of the **Bintang Laut guesthouse**, recommends his favorite islands. *@story_bandaneira*

To me, **Pulau Ai** has everything one can find in the Bandas – welcoming locals, nutmeg plantations, beautiful sea and healthy underwater life. Pulau Run may be better known because of the history of the swap with Manhattan, but Ai has the most beautiful sunsets – especially on its western side.

I'd pick **Banda Besar** for history and authentic village life. If you have the time to get off the beaten track, Waer village is lively and another good sunset spot.

For beaches, diving and marine life, **Hatta** is tops in the Bandas.

EATING IN BANDA NEIRA: OUR PICKS

Cilu Bintang Estate: The outstanding nightly buffet features grilled fish, locally spiced soups, plus curries, fritters, salads and more. *7.30am-10pm* $$

Delfika Cafe: Come to this verdant courtyard setting for grilled fish, fried eggplant, noodles, rice and Western fare (spaghetti, milkshakes). *7.30am-11pm* $$

Hotel Maulana (p404): Overlooking the seaside, Maulana is an unrivalled spot for sunset drinks or a leisurely meal of Indonesian or international dishes. *8am-10pm* $$

Cafe Terapung: Hidden on the southeastern side of town, this spot has delicious, spice-scented *ikan bakar* with ample servings of vegetables and rice. *8am-10pm* $$

BEST BANDA DIVE OPERATORS

Dive Bluemotion: A professionally run German-Indonesian outfit with well-maintained gear, two boats and fair prices. As with other operators, it's closed from June to August.

Nutmeg Tree Dive: Attached to the recommended guesthouse of the same name, they offer a range of all-inclusive dive and accommodation packages, and can take you to more than 40 dive sites.

Hotel Maulana: Earns positive reviews for its well-run diving excursions. It has a good mix of waterfront accommodation options and a decent restaurant.

Naira Dive: Naira Dive offers plenty of variety, with multiday packages available.

Back in the village, walk to **Sumur Pusaka Negeri**, a sacred well hidden during Dutch colonial times as it was the island's sole source of water for cleansing before Islamic prayers. It sits at the bottom of a forested hill draped with the tombs of an atmospheric Muslim cemetery outside of which rises the **Blood Stone** monument, which reports the three points of agreement between the Dutch and the locals that stated the former could trade spices and own land, but not interfere in local matters of beliefs and religion.

Snorkelling & Seaside Stays

Beaches and coral on Hatta

A stunning flying-saucer-shaped island of jungle-swathed limestone trimmed with white sand, **Pulau Hatta**, once known as Rozengain, has no nutmeg. Its only historic relevance was a comical episode where the eccentric Captain Courthope raised a Union Jack just to enrage the Dutch.

These days, Hatta is one of the most popular destinations in the Banda Islands, thanks to its crystal-clear waters and reefs rich in marine life. Just off the fine beach at **Kampung Lama**, where the island's accommodation is clustered, is a natural underwater 'bridge' that creates a beautiful blue hole over part of Hatta's stunning vertical drop-off. Forests of delicate soft coral alongside huge table and fern corals, clouds of reef fish and superb visibility make this Banda's top snorkelling spot. Leatherback turtles, reef sharks, trigger fish and an impressive roll-call of species are all here. There's an ever-growing number of homestays on Hatta, stationed in a line on the beach at Kampung Lama.

Fish & Forts

Coral reefs and colonial fortifications on Ai

The island of **Ai**, about an hour's boat ride from Banda Neira, is justly famed for its remarkably accessible and brilliantly pristine coral drop-offs just a flipper-flap away from the shoreline. There's a lot to see directly in front of the village, especially in October when groups of Napoleon fish appear along with migrating dolphins and whales. Sea life is likewise impressive off **Pantai Sebila**, the island's best beach (a 15-minute walk west of the village), where an exceptionally stark wall, crusted with coral and laced with sea anemones, juts straight down.

Ai's other main attraction is the four-pointed star fortress that sits in the centre of the village, its walls still intact. The fort has been known as **Benteng Revenge** ever since the Dutch slaughtered the locals for siding with the British in the early 17th-century battle for control of the spice trade. Clambering up through the fort, you can find several well-preserved cannons lying on the ground, with the VOC symbol of the Dutch East Indies Company still clearly legible. Near the fort, you can take

MALUKAN FORTS

On Ternate island, **Benteng Tolukko** (p376) and **Fort Oranje** (p377) are among the region's best preserved colonial edifices. Hop over to Tidore to catch the views from Spanish-built **Benteng Tahula** (p380). Tiny Saparua has **Benteng Duurstede** (p398), where national hero Pattimura fought the colonisers.

SAIL & SNORKEL AROUND BANDA NEIRA

Chartering a boat is quite affordable. Explore the smaller islands around Pulau Neira, where you can swim and snorkel to your heart's content.

START	END	LENGTH
Banda Neira Port	Banda Neira Port	6km; half-day

Sail around Banda Neira to **1 Pulau Shyarir** (aka Pulau Pisang), a small banana-shaped island off the northern tip of Banda Besar. The main western beach has a long, idyllic stretch of sand dotted with large boulders. Walk via the concrete steps at the beach's northern end over the headland to **2 Tanjong Seram**, Pulau Shyarir's northernmost cape. You can sit on a bench and enjoy views of shallow turquoise waters, with Banda Neira backed by Gunung Api in the background. A peculiar flat-top islet and dive site, **3 Batu Kapal**, rises near the end of the cape.

Get back on the boat and sail west to **4 Pulau Karaka**, a small inhabited chunk of forest-covered limestone off the northern shore of Gunung Api. A small metallic lighthouse stands on top of a rock on its eastern side. Stop at Pulau Karaka's southwestern tip, where an exposed area of black, cube-like volcanic stones tumble into the shallows with good snorkelling. From here, it's a few minutes' ride to the excellent **5 Lava Flows** snorkelling site, an underwater canyon right beneath the cone of Gunung Api. Continue circumnavigating Gunung Api's coast anticlockwise, sailing past beautiful rock formations and caves, of which **6 Gua Kelawar**, a large limestone hollow where you can jump in aquamarine waters, is another popular swimming spot.

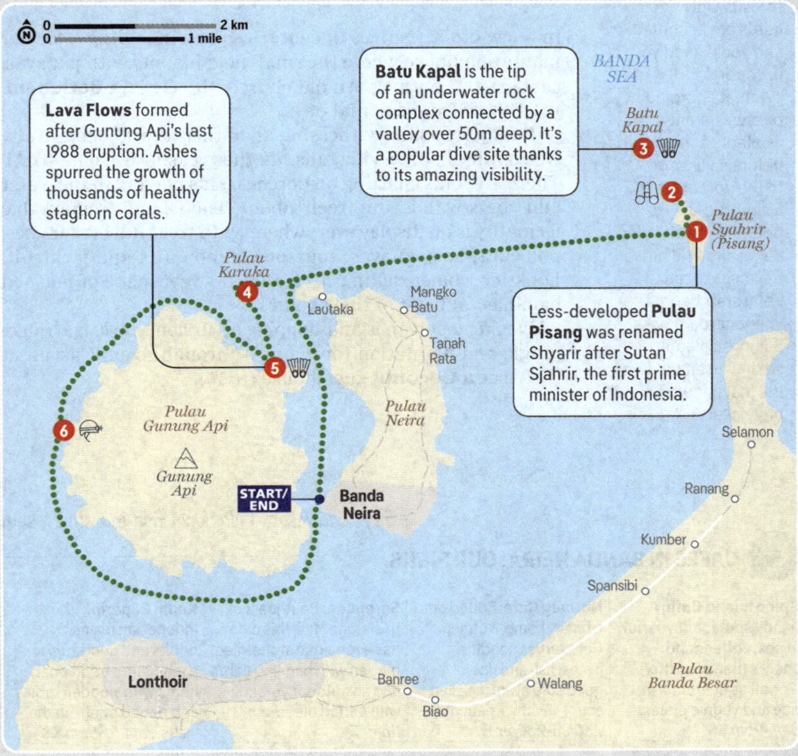

Lava Flows formed after Gunung Api's last 1988 eruption. Ashes spurred the growth of thousands of healthy staghorn corals.

Batu Kapal is the tip of an underwater rock complex connected by a valley over 50m deep. It's a popular dive site thanks to its amazing visibility.

Less-developed **Pulau Pisang** was renamed Shyarir after Sutan Sjahrir, the first prime minister of Indonesia.

PURCHASING PELNI TICKETS

Before purchasing Pelni boat tickets, you first need to find a reliable schedule, as it changes month to month. Register for an account on the Pelni app as the website doesn't always function.

You can reserve tickets, but must pay in person – at an Indomaret, for example. Alternatively, go to a Pelni office (in Ambon, it's located near **Pattimura Park** (p394)). Only debit cards are accepted, and you'll need your passport.

Actual boarding passes are only available a few hours before sailing: go to the port at least a couple of hours before the scheduled departure and brave the mess to get Pelni staff to print your boarding pass. Sailings sell out, so don't wait until the last minute to buy tickets.

in a few other vestiges of centuries past, including a former plantation house where the small field blooms with papayas, cassava and nutmeg. An old church, the **Gereja Betlehem**, is left over from colonial days.

Highlights aside, witnessing an authentic and delightfully welcoming fishing village is another reason to come to Ai. There are folks chatting on porches, kids playing in the water and goats wandering freely about. The island's remarkable fecundity is on display everywhere, with trees full of mangoes, pomegranates, guavas, soursops, jambu airs and jackfruit. Look for women selling *utri* (a fried sweet made of mashed bananas) in front of their homes.

If you're not on an island-hopping excursion, you can arrange jungle and plantation tours on Ai through Ayem Nasrun at the **Green Coconut** guesthouse (p415).

CAFES IN BANDA NEIRA: OUR PICKS

Try Ikan Asam Pala, local fish in nutmeg soup

Spice Island Cafe: A handy spot for flavourful juices, coffees and snacks (banana fritters) as well as heartier fish, rice and veggie plates. *8am-9pm* $$

Nutmeg Cafe: Bolted onto a family home, Nutmeg Cafe serves noodles, juices, fish and rice, a good *soto ayam* (chicken soup) and thick pancakes. *7.30am-9.30pm* $

Serenade: Southeast of the Istana Mini, this cafe has a romantic stone-tiled garden with hanging lights and an outdoor veranda with period tiles. *5pm-11pm* $$

Kedai Paparipi: Indonesian mains, tidbits and good *kopi* in a renovated traditional home with wooden tables and period prints on the walls. *7am-9.30pm* $$

PAUL HARDING 00/SHUTTERSTOCK

Pulau Nailaka

TRADING PULAU RUN FOR NEW YORK

After the Dutch ravaged Ai in 1616, English forces retreated to their trading post on Run. Increasingly besieged, the same eccentric Captain Courthope who taunted the Dutch on Hatta (formerly Rozengain) put honour above survival in a preposterously futile last stand, refusing even the most reasonable offers to leave.

Somehow British sovereignty was maintained, even after the Dutch atrocities in 1621, when all of Run's nutmeg trees were systematically destroyed. The Dutch eventually took Run, so in 1674 the English agreed to swap it for an island in North America. The island was Manhattan. Not a bad deal, as it turned out.

The Islet That Shaped America

Adventures on Run and Nailaka

Pulau Run, for all its historical gravitas, is no more than a remote chunk of limestone swathed in jungle and surrounded by deep blue sea. The village is an appealing network of steps and concrete paths backed by vine-draped limestone cliffs, with attractive views between the tamarind trees from the top end of Jl Eldorado.

A daytime stroll here takes in the beauty of village life: children in school uniforms clambering up fruit trees, freshly harvested mace drying on doorsteps and the call to prayer sounding above the roosters roaming village gardens. Run's main attraction is diving the coral wall that lies 70m to 150m off the island's northwestern coast (accessible by boat); it's known as Depan Kampung ('In Front of the Village'). Visibility is magnificent.

Looming over the island is the old **English Fort** (once held by Captain Courthope) that perpetuated the Spice Wars and resulted in the famous trade of Run for Manhattan. From the pier, walk to the main lower path, turn right and follow the stairs up, up and up to the rough track leading to the overgrown ruins. Off the northern tip of Run are the powdery white sands of **Pulau Nailaka**, an islet so small you can explore it in 10 minutes, drinking in dazzlingly photogenic views of Gunung Api. Tucked into the interior are piles of coral rocks in a rough perimeter, which once made up the small **Swan Fort**, built by the English.

TOP EXPERIENCE

Gunung Api

Set in the centre of the archipelago like a watchful giant, the Gunung Api volcano rises above the island for which it is named, offering awe-inspiring views from its 656m-high summit. Written about for centuries as a key location for the colonial spice trade, Gunung Api's last major eruption was in 1988, but minor fumarole activity is still ongoing.

JAVARMAN/SHUTTERSTOCK

TOP TIPS

- Get an early start as there isn't much shade. Don't climb if it's wet.
- Bring hiking poles or a sturdy walking stick as the descent is definitely hazardous.
- There are no facilities on the mountain: bring all the food and water you need for the entire day.

PRACTICALITIES

● free ● boat transfer 10,000Rp each way, per person

Reaching the Trailhead

There's only one clear hiking path on the eastern side of Banda Api island, right across from a **small jetty** near **Delfika Guesthouse 2**. It takes less than five minutes to cross from Banda Neira. Boatmen will drop you off at the beginning of the trail.

Hiking Up

Fit hikers can reach the top in about two hours, with another two hours for the descent. Guides *(from 200,000Rp, including boat transport to the island)* are not necessary but can be arranged through any hotel. The unrelenting slope is arduous, with slippery tree roots and precarious rocks, and the descent is even more dangerous given the loose scree. Once you reach the upper flanks, the forest recedes and the views are breathtaking. Near the crater, wisps of smoke waft out of crevices, and parts of the ground feel hot.

Sunrise Hikes

Sunrise from Gunung Api's summit is glorious, but you need to have perfect weather and start as early as 3am. Take a guide if you decide to climb in the dark as they can also organise better rates for boat transport at night.

Kei Islands

BEACHES | TRADITIONAL VILLAGES | SNORKELLING

Hidden away in Maluku's far southeastern corner, closer to Darwin (Australia) than Jakarta, the Kei Islands are home to some of Indonesia's most spectacular beaches. Picture kilometres of powdery white sands lapped by limpid cerulean seas, which appear to be as flat as a swimming pool on calm days. Hard to reach and little known, the archipelago's comely shorelines are largely the domain of village fisherfolk and their children, who are often delighted to share their remote slice of paradise with visitors from far-flung parts of the world. Other attractions among these 112 islands are coral reefs, forested villages, sparkling waterfalls and caves where myths still abound.

Kei culture is fascinating and distinct, with three castes, holy trees, bride prices paid in *lela* (antique table cannons) and a strong belief in *sasi* (a prohibition spell). Little English is spoken on the islands, but locals are overwhelmingly friendly.

TOP TIP

Be sure to pack some provisions before making the trip to the Kei Islands. Dining options are extremely limited here. The towns of Tual and Langgur have a few simple warungs, but elsewhere restaurants are nonexistent, so you'll be eating your own meals wherever you stay.

GETTING AROUND

Kei Kecil has the Kei Islands' only airport, **Karel Sadsuitubun Langgur**, served by daily one-hour Wings Air flights from Ambon. Taxis (150,000Rp) and *ojeks* reach the airport in 30 minutes from Langgur, just south of town. The islands are also accessible by sea. Pelni's Kapal Labobar sails from Banda Neira *(13 hours)*, the only overland way to reach Tual from the Bandas without backtracking to Ambon by air. There's also a much longer Pelni route from Kaimana in southwestern Papua via Dobo in the Aru Islands. Pelni ships dock at **Tual port** on Kei Kecil, across the bridge from Langgur on neighbouring Pulau Dullah.

Public bemos between Langgur, Ohoililir and Ohoidertawun are infrequent, so renting a scooter *(from 100,000Rp per day)* is best. A daily speedboat links Kei Kecil and Kei Besar, leaving Elat around 1pm or 2pm for **Watdek Ferry Terminal** *(1¼ hours)* and returning at 9am.

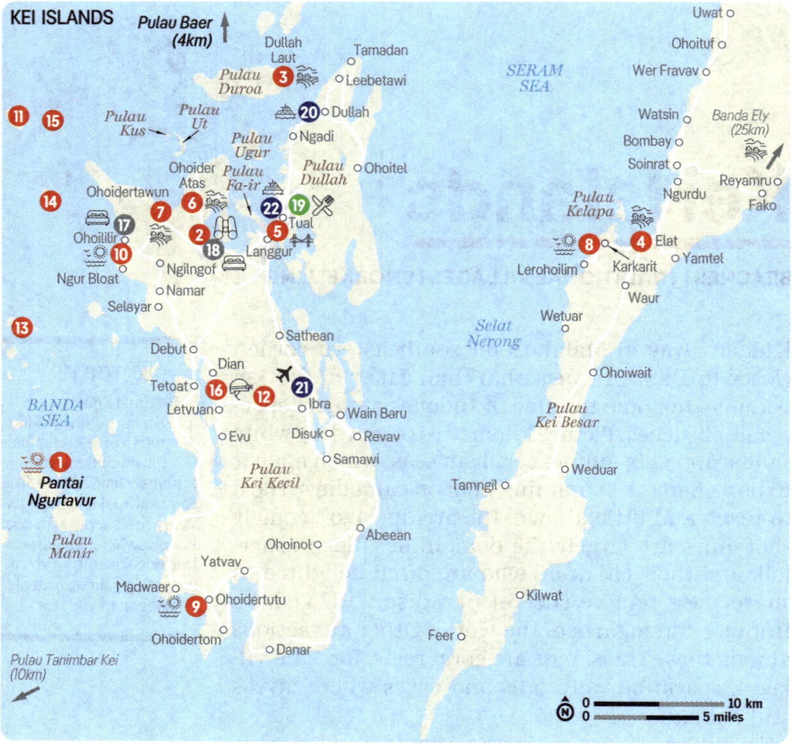

KEI ISLANDS

HIGHLIGHTS
1 Pantai Ngurtavur

SIGHTS
2 Bukit Masbait trailhead
3 Dullah Laut
4 Elat
5 Jembatan Usdek
see 5 Kampung Pelangi
6 Ohoider Atas
7 Ohoidertawun
8 Pantai Daftel
9 Pantai Ohoidertutu
10 Pasir Panjang
11 Pulau Er
12 Pulau Kei Kecil
13 Pulau Nai
14 Pulau Ngaf
15 Pulau Ngodan

ACTIVITIES
16 Goa Hawang

SLEEPING
17 Coaster Cottages
see 7 Savana Cottages
see 10 Tria Maria Cottage
see 7 Tumbuh Oasis
18 VidFauw Oasis Villa

EATING
19 Coffee Kanda Cafe
see 18 Forganza Cafe
see 5 Kopi Dari Hati
see 10 Ten Cafe

ENTERTAINMENT
see 10 Meti Kei Festival

TRANSPORT
20 Dullah Port
21 Karel Sadsuitubun Langgur Airport
22 Tual Port
see 5 Watdek Ferry Terminal

Plunge into Gin-Clear Waters

Beaches and snorkelling on Pulau Kei Kecil

Kecil is home to many of the best beaches in the island group. The most famous tourist draw is **Pasir Panjang** with its 3km of highly photogenic white sand that's so powdery it feels like flour, fringed with swaying coconut palms. Despite its beauty, the beach is often quiet, except on local holidays and weekends when karaoke outfits crank up the volume near the access points: Ngur Bloat (south) and Ohoililir (north).

Like many beaches on Kei Kecil, the water at Pasir Panjang is shallow, and at low tide, the water recedes a long way. Snorkellers will find more joy at the reefs off the nearby islands of **Pulau Ngaf**, **Pulau Er** and **Pulau Ngodan**. Guesthouses can arrange charter boats *(1,000,000Rp per day)*, but bring your own gear. You may also see local fishermen build a *bagan* (fishing platform) by the shore – these large wooden structures are then hauled out to sea and used for overnight fishing.

Slow Down in Ohoidertawun

A waterfront, caves and petroglyphs

The charming village of **Ohoidertawun** sits by a lovely bay that, at low tide, becomes a vast, white-sand tidal flat where craftspeople sit in the palm shade carving canoes. A holy tree on the waterfront beside **Savana Cottages** is believed to enforce peace and bind relationships. A footpath and stairway lead north to **Ohoider Atas** village. At low tide, you can splash across the sand flats past small caves cut in the limestone cliffs (some contain human bones). After around 25 minutes, you'll begin to notice the mysterious red-and-orange petroglyphs painted on the cliff faces.

There are several guesthouses in the village, which are also the best places to organise snorkelling trips to the nearby coral-rich reefs of **Pulau Ngaf**, **Pulau Er** and **Pulau Ngodan**. Motorbikes can also be hired for 150,000Rp per day.

Celebrate the Tides

Join the Meti Kei festival

Held every October, the **Meti Kei festival** revolves around a natural phenomenon where the tide recedes far off Kei Kecil for a few weeks each year – sometimes up to 5km or more offshore. The locals celebrate on Pasir Panjang and other beaches by fishing, using spears or traditional 'nets' made of coconut palm leaves to sweep in the fish. There's also traditional dancing, live music and a parade.

KEI KECIL'S HUBS

Connected by the covered **Jembatan Usdek**, which crosses the two central islands of Kei Kecil and Kei Dullah, the twin towns of Tual (to the north) and Langgur (to the south) are the Kei Islands' commercial centre and transport gateway.

Tual has the main **port** (p409). On the southern bank of the bridge on Tual's side is **Kampung Pelangi** – an urban beautification project of sea-facing homes painted in a rainbow palette. Although fading, it still offers interesting insight into Tual's jumble of cultures, including the descendants of Arabs who migrated from the Middle East 250 years ago.

Strung along broad avenues across the bridge, Langgur offers the best accommodation options for a range of budgets, though most visitors wisely head straight for the beaches.

EATING & DRINKING IN KEI KECIL: OUR PICKS

Ten Cafe: Overwater restaurant with beautiful views at the southern end of Pasir Panjang. Indonesian mains like nasi goreng and grilled chicken. *noon-9pm* $$

Forganza Cafe: *Ikan bakar*, vegetables and chicken served in overwater decks between Langgur and Pantai Pasir Panjang. Perfect for sunset dinners. *9am-10pm* $$

Coffee Kanda Cafe: In Tual, this coffee shop has a large outdoor area and stage. They also serve delicious *roti bakar* (grilled bread), dim sum and tidbits. *10am-midnight* $$

Kopi Dari Hati: Lively outdoor area filled with wooden tables and tall chairs. Sip Americanos, cappuccinos and hot chocolate and frappes. *10am-1am* $$

SUPERNATURAL SASI

Maluku has many hidden undercurrents of magical beliefs and traditions. One belief that's still widely practised is *sasi*, a kind of prohibition spell used to protect property and prevent trespassing. The only physical barrier is a janur palm frond, but few would dare to break a *sasi* for fear of the unknown effects.

For countless generations, *sasi* have prevented the theft of coconuts and ensured that fish aren't caught during the breeding season.

However, in 2003 some cunning Kei Islanders put a *sasi* on the Tual–Langgur bridge. The boatmen then made hay by transporting islanders who refused to risk travelling on the bewitched bridge. It remained unused until authorities finally raised cash for a *sasi*-removal ceremony.

Visit Traditional Pulau Tanimbar Kei

Beaches and villages

Further off Kei Kecil are other outlying islands with lovely beaches and turquoise waters, the most intriguing of which is **Pulau Tanimbar Kei**, southwest of **Ohoidertutu** (p414). The island is famed for its traditional village, powdery sand and magnificent snorkelling. There's no tourist infrastructure, but the locals are friendly and welcoming. The public boat from Tual is unreliable, often making the trip only once a week, so trips are hard to plan unless you're willing to shell out up to 2,000,000Rp to charter a boat.

Walk on a Sandbar

Tidal magic at Pantai Ngurtavur

The most popular Instagram destination in the Kei Islands for domestic tourists, **Pantai Ngurtavur** is a stunning and slender strip of sand – supposedly the longest sandbar in Indonesia – emerging out of the Banda Sea just off Pulau Waha at low tide. It's only accessible by charter boat from the port of Debut on Kei Kecil's west coast. The journey takes about 1½ hours.

Remember, the beach is only visible at low tide, so arrange your trip accordingly. Locals on Pulau Waha ask for a conservation fee of 200,000Rp per boat, so be prepared to pay up when you arrive.

Get Off the Beaten Path in Pulau Kei Besar

Remote villages and dramatic coast

Scenic Kei Besar is a long ridge of steep forested hills edged with remote traditional villages and a few white-sand beaches (better for taking photos than for swimming). Roads are very poor – no more than dirt trails in places – and outside of a handful of places in the main village of **Elat**, there are no guesthouses or restaurants. Expect intense curiosity from locals and take your best *kamus* (dictionary) as nobody speaks English.

Southwest of Elat, a lane through palm fronds and bougainvillea leads 6km to **Pantai Daftel**, a shallow, slender white-sand beach that stretches for 1.8km, all the way to the village of Lerohoilim.

Fine *ojek* excursions from Elat include picturesque Yamtel village (4km east), Waur (4km south) and the charming west-coast villages of Ngurdu (3km), Soinrat (4km), Bombay (7km) and Watsin (8km), all with bay views, stone stairways and rocky terraces.

The east coast of Kei Besar has attractive tidal rock pools but no beaches. Villages are comparatively isolated, steeped in superstitious traditions, and locals tend to speak the local Kei language rather than Bahasa Indonesia. **Banda Ely** in the extreme northeast is a settlement that Bandanese refugees founded after fleeing Dutch atrocities.

TOP EXPERIENCE

Pulau Baer

Thanks to its seclusion and breathtaking expanse of turquoise waters, this inhabited island is one of the Keis' most coveted spots for a half-day trip. Often compared to a mini-version of Papua's Raja Ampat, Pulau Baer (also spelt 'Bair') offers a mix of open bays, soaring karst formations and smaller canals where snorkelling is the only way to explore.

ARIE ADONIA/SHUTTERSTOCK

Getting There

Dullah Port in the village of Dullah Darat, 10km north of Tual, is the departure point for Kei Kecil's outlying islands, the northwesternmost of which is Baer. The boat journey takes about an hour. Boatmen ask around 800,000Rp (maximum 10 people) for a half-day trip, and include a couple of other snorkelling stops en route. Accommodation in Ohoililir and Ohoidertawun usually offer the same tour for a slightly higher price.

Bring a Mask & Fins

Boats can navigate the main bay and the larger passages – a canal with two sheer rock walls has become a photographic 'rite of passage' for most Indonesian travellers – but to really enjoy Pulau Baer you have to get into the water. Bring a swimsuit and a snorkelling mask.

Views from the Sky

The best views are aerial, and drone footage here is particularly stunning. The alternative is to climb out over the sharp limestone rocks to take pictures, as the panoramic wooden walkway that the government built in 2016 has now collapsed, and we were told there are no funds to fix it.

TOP TIPS

- Only make the trip on a sunny day or you'll risk missing the area's stunning colours.
- Never step on the rocks barefoot. Water shoes are a must.
- Good days are hot and sunny throughout the journey – don't forget your reef-safe sunscreen.

PRACTICALITIES

- boat charter from 600,000 to 900,000Rp

BEST SNORKELLING SPOTS NEAR KEI KECIL

Ronald Reyaan, local tour guide, former Trash Hero Kei leader and manager of **Vidfauw Oasis Villa**, lists his favourite places to snorkel. *@baronda_ pulaukeitrip*

The only dive centre on Kei Kecil closed during COVID-19, so all we have now is snorkelling.

In front of **Dullah Laut**, Pulau Adranan's main village, are large patches of staghorn coral that are healthy and a delight to snorkel above.

Between **Pulau Ngodan** (p411) and **Pulau Er** (p411) is a lesser-known sandbank with healthy corals.

Shaped like a T-Rex, **Pulau Nai** has great snorkelling right above the 'dino's head' and along the island's northern shore. Most people go here after visiting **Ngurtavur** (p412) sandbank.

HALE WISTANTAMA/SHUTTERSTOCK

Goa Hawang

Explore Southern Kei Kecil

Caves, springs and beaches

Despite its relative proximity to Langgur, you may be surprised by just how remote the far south of Kei Kecil feels. The only way here is by *ojek* or rented motorbike, but if you make the journey you'll find caves, freshwater springs and stunning beaches, as well as villages that few foreigners ever visit. Folks will be joyfully surprised at your presence.

Off the road to Letvuan, the **Goa Hawang** *(10,000Rp)* are striking limestone grottoes with luminous blue water that makes for a memorable swim – though you'll also be sharing the space with resident bats and big spiders. On weekends, the caves can get crowded with locals.

Down at the island's cape is a magnificent, forlorn sweep of powdery white sand known as **Pantai Ohoidertutu**.

Find Jesus on a Hilltop

Hike up to Bukit Masbait

An offbeat trail in the village of Kelanit, south of Ohidertawun, leads to Kei Kecil's highest point, the 300m **Bukit Masbait** *(free)*. Come here for fine views over Pulau Fair and Langgur town, especially at sunrise. It's a quick 15-minute hike up the hill through the arch at the end of Kelanit's paved road. Go via a square with the statue of Jesus carrying the cross.

Places We Love to Stay

$ Budget $$ Midrange $$$ Top End

Pulau Ternate

MAP p375

Kurnia Homestay $ Run by charming Aty, who speaks great English, the Kurnia is a pleasant homestay in a quiet neighbourhood 1km from the town centre.

Muara Hotel $$ Above the Muara shopping mall, rooms here are big and bright. The best have balconies with great views over Fort Oranje towards the sea.

Villa Ma'rasai $$$ Set amid greenery 7km from the centre, this atmospheric place has striking rooms with tropical views; it's a great base for arranging tours.

Pulau Halmahera

MAP p383

Meraksi Flower $ Tobelo's best homestay option has squeaky clean accommodation and a friendly owner who speaks not a word of English.

Sleepwell $$ A range of clean rooms with hot water, TVs, air-con and breakfast. It's in the centre of Tobelo.

Kupa Kupa Beach Cottages $$ A delightfully laid-back spot in Tobelo's southern reaches. Has well-kept bungalows surrounded by a lush garden and a beach out front.

Meti Cottage $$ This rustic, sustainably run resort on Meti Island has simple waterfront lodging, outstanding tours and delicious meals (steak, fresh fish, octopus, lobster).

Pulau Morotai

MAP p383

Hotel Molokai Morotai $$ Midrange hotel with spacious rooms right by the ferry port to Tobelo. Has its own little beach.

Penginapan Mutiara Inn $$ The house behind the cafe of the same name offers 14 clean rooms with large comfortable beds.

Pulau Ambon

MAP p390

Wisma Grace $ A delightful Kota Ambon guesthouse with a kind-hearted English-speaking host happy to share a wealth of island knowledge.

The City Hotel $$ Stands out from the midrange crowd thanks to the solicitous staff, rooftop restaurant and distinctive design – stripped pine and artwork.

Swiss-Belhotel $$$ Kota Ambon's plushest hotel has sizeable, comfortable rooms and the efficient staff speak English well. There's a gym, restaurant and spa.

Pulau Saparua

Penginapan Perdana - Lease Indah $ Two ageing yet well-run budget hotels in one. The basic but large rooms come with air-con and mandi bathrooms and are set around a leafy courtyard.

Penginapan M & J $$ Homestay with clean, large rooms and light breakfast included. It's set in a quiet area on the northern end of Saparua Town.

Banda Islands

MAP p401

Vita Guesthouse $ One of several budget-friendly options in the market area, Vita has a great bayside location with simple rooms around a waterfront palm garden.

Guesthouse Nailaka $ On Pulau Run, Mr Burhan and family offer a warm welcome (and some English). Four en-suite rooms, one with air-con.

Delfika $$ Pleasant rooms set around an attractive plant-filled courtyard restaurant. A second location puts you by the waterfront.

Hotel Maulana (p404) **$$** The big draw at this old classic is the prime waterfront location, with great views from the terrace restaurant.

Green Coconut $$ This Pulau Ai place has basic rooms in an appealing seafront location in the village. The owner speaks a little English.

Cilu Bintang Estate $$$ Banda Neira's finest hotel is in an immaculate Dutch-colonial reproduction and has stylish rooms, a great restaurant and on-site tours.

Kei Islands

MAP p410

Coaster Cottages $ Budget rooms at the far northern end of Pasir Panjang, set in beachside bungalows shrouded by tropical vegetation. You'll need transport if staying here.

VidFauw Oasis Villa $$ Perfect long-term rental with three rooms, two with shared toilet, in a secluded house with a fully equipped kitchen and a wooden deck. By the sea between Langgur and Ohoidertawun.

Tria Maria Cottage $$ Right on the beach, these three cheerfully painted bungalows make a magnificent base on Kei Kecil's Pasir Panjang.

Tumbuh Oasis $$$ This Dutch-Indonesian Ohoidertawun beachfront hotel has four well-appointed boutique rooms inside dark wooden cottages, plus a Western breakfast and loungers by the beach.

Researched by
Anthony Ham

Papua

REMOTE, WILD & STEEPED IN TRADITION

Even a country as full of adventure as Indonesia has its final frontier. Here it is: Papua, half of the world's second-biggest island, New Guinea.

With reefs that hold 75% of the world's hard corals, forests that contain half of Indonesia's plant and animal species, and diverse indigenous communities who speak more than 400 distinct languages, Papua is nothing if not extraordinary. It may be the youngest part of Indonesia, but its strong tribal traditions span thousands of years; this is a place where some people still hunt their food with bows and arrows. It's also a sometimes trackless wilderness where roads are so scarce that you usually have to take to the air to travel between towns. And more than any other part of Indonesia, this province can feel like a different country – which is what many Papuans, who are Melanesian and ethnically distinct from other Indonesians, would prefer it to be.

Travel here is neither cheap nor easy. Yet those who come are awed by the charm of Papua's peoples, the resilience of its cultures and the grandeur of its landscapes, which include the highest peaks in Oceania. The fairy-tale seascapes of Raja Ampat are the province's biggest lure – in fact, they're the only place most foreigners ever see. The hope is that the growing buzz here will one day extend eastward to the rest of Papua, where equally world-class dive sites with whale sharks, untouched jungles with birds of paradise, and remote highland villages with terraced gardens and stilted homes await the willing and intrepid.

DUDAREV MIKHAIL/SHUTTERSTOCK

THE MAIN AREAS

RAJA AMPAT
The Amazon of the oceans. p420

JAYAPURA & SENTANI
Indonesia's fastest-growing city. p434

PULAU BIAK
Dive into WWII history. p440

THE BALIEM VALLEY
Hike the remote Papuan highlands. p444

WASUR NATIONAL PARK
Big birds and rare wallabies. p455

For places to stay in Papua, see p458

JAFARSODIK/SHUTTERSTOCK

Left: Diver with golden jellyfish, Misool (p428), Raja Ampat; Above: Raja Ampat (p420)

Find Your Way

Papua spans half of the world's second-largest island, New Guinea, and shares an 824km land border with PNG. It's vast, heavily forested, mountainous and has virtually no roads connecting its disparate cities – for now!

PLANE

The best way to get around is by plane. All cities have airports with connections to either Jayapura or Sorong. Lion Air is the main operator, and its flights are rescheduled with infuriating frequency. Small missionary air services go where noone else does.

FERRY

The cheapest way to get around is aboard the Pelni liners that link cities along the same coastline two or three times each month. Be warned: these ferries are incredibly slow and often populated with shady characters.

Raja Ampat, p420
Dive some of the world's finest reefs, then chill on white-sand beaches or search steamy jungles for birds of paradise.

The Baliem Valley, p444
Traditional Papuan culture thrives in these remote highlands, which are best explored on multiday village-to-village treks.

Wasur National Park, p455
Wallabies and cassowaries roam this park's lowland forests, which are like a slice of the Aussie bush in eastern Indonesia.

SIMONE TOMAZELA/SHUTTERSTOCK

Divers with whale sharks, Taman Nasional Teluk Cenderawasih (p433), Nabire

Plan Your Time

Navigating Papua is complicated and few attempt to see it all in one go. A wiser idea is to pick key areas based on passions such as diving, birding, hiking or art.

A Two-Week Stay

- Hit the highlights and comprehend Papua's wild extremes. Spend your first night in **Sorong** (p430) and the next six in **Raja Ampat** (p420), where you'll dive, daydream and laze on empty beaches. Head back to Sorong for the onward flight to Wamena (via Jayapura) in the remote highlands. Cap off the trip with a four-day hike through the **Baliem Valley** (p450).

With a Bit More Time

- Avid divers might tack on side adventures from Sorong, such as swimming with whale sharks in **Triton Bay** (p432) or **Taman Nasional Teluk Cenderawasih** (p433). Wildlife enthusiasts may want to detour to the **Pegunungan Arfak** (p431) or **Wasur National Park** (p455). Adventurous trekkers could visit traditional **Papuan villages** (p453).

SEASONAL HIGHLIGHTS

JANUARY TO MARCH
These are the best months for diving and snorkelling around Raja Ampat.

MAY TO JUNE
The dry season starts to crank up all across the island, with the biggest impact in the interior. Birding begins in June.

JULY TO SEPTEMBER
The heart of the dry season. The later the better for hikers, as roads will be passable and the ground solid.

OCTOBER TO DECEMBER
Surfers flock to surging waves in Biak and Manokwari on the north coast.

Raja Ampat

SUPERB LANDSCAPES | UNRIVALLED REEFS | CASTAWAY BEACHES

GETTING AROUND

To reach Raja Ampat, you must first endure Sorong, which has direct flights from Jakarta and Bali. Ferries depart from Sorong's Pelabuhan Rakyat for Waisai (on Waigeo) at 9am and 2pm daily, returning at the exact same times from Waisai. The journey takes two hours with both economy seats and a frigid VIP lounge. Online booking isn't available; just show up. Alternatively, **Susi Air** *(susiair.com)* flies small planes between Sorong and Waisai's Marinda Airport. Those travelling to other islands typically arrange onward transfers from Waisai.

The secret's out. With its sublime scenery of steep, jungle-covered islands, white-sand beaches, hidden lagoons, spooky caves, weird mushroom-shaped islets, dancing birds and pellucid turquoise waters, Raja Ampat (Four Kings) is one of the most beautiful island chains in the world. A decade ago, its 1500-plus isles were so far-flung – and riddled with logistical hurdles – that only diehard divers made the effort. Now, while many hurdles remain, travellers increasingly stop by to see what all the buzz is about.

Conservationists consider Papua's Bird's Head Peninsula to be a global epicentre of marine life, and Raja Ampat – dubbed a 'species factory' – harbours the greatest diversity of all. This includes more than 1400 reef-fish species and more than 600 hard corals. Think of it like the Amazon of the earth's oceans. Responsible tourism plays a big part in protecting this globally important treasure by providing sustainable income sources and funding conservation initiatives.

Dancing in Paradise

Birding on Waigeo and Gam

Raja Ampat is a corner of the earth that has become a byword for biodiversity abundance, and not everyone comes here to dive. After all, Raja Ampat was well-known among birders long before the mainstream diving community discovered its many charms.

Chances are, if you're not sailing off on a liveaboard or zipping over to a high-end dive resort, your trip to Raja Ampat will begin on **Waigeo**, at the ferry dock in **Waisai**, the capital of the Raja Ampat Regency and home to a little over 8000 people. The town itself is no attraction, yet even those planning to spend the bulk of their trip elsewhere often enjoy a night or two at one of the many resorts and homestays that line the road out to the quaint village of **Saporkren**, a base for spotting both the red and Wilson's birds of paradise.

MIHIRJOSHI/SHUTTERSTOCK

Wilson's bird of paradise, Waigeo

One of the big advantages of coming here is that Waigeo offers the most accessible bird-watching in Raja Ampat and is the only place – other than Batanta – where you can find both species. Visitors typically depart their lodgings around 4.30am for a viewing area behind the diminutive **Marinda Airport**. All told, it's less than 3km round trip from the parking area to the two blinds: a lower one for the ground-mating Wilson's and an elevated platform for the tree-mating red. To have the birds all to yourself, you can hike about 6km from Saporkren to a separate, less-developed series of viewing blinds high in the hills. You'll need to get up super early, of course, if you go the DIY route; ask your resort or homestay for advice on where to go.

Birds of paradise are very much creatures of habit and tend to return to the same spots each morning, all but guaranteeing sightings. For those accustomed to watching wildlife, you'll know how rare that is!

The scene that awaits is one of nature's great sights. Expect red males to shake their lavish tail feathers and wiggle their booties up and down the bare branches of their favourite trees. Male Wilson's will busy themselves tidying up a forest clearing before dramatically puffing out their chests. Of course, all of this behaviour is to court the far-less-colourful females, who are rarely impressed enough to seal the deal. While you wait in the blinds, sweating in the muggy morning air, you may also see (or hear) hornbills, sulphur-crested cockatoos and yellow-billed kingfishers, all of whose morning calls echo across the jungle.

Many visitors combine bird-watching with a cooling dip in **Kali Biru**, a radiant, cyan-blue river about an hour northeast of Waisai.

It's also possible to see the red bird of paradise on **Gam**, near the villages of **Sawinggrai** and **Yenwaoupnor**, as well as tens of thousands of (very large!) fruit bats flying at sunset over **Pulau Mioskon**, just off the coast. Village guides are readily available on both Gam and Waigeo; ask at your homestay.

Continues on p429

RAJA AMPAT HOMESTAYS

Stay Raja Ampat is a social enterprise with an information centre at the Waisai pier and manages area homestays. Most 'homestays' are simple palm-thatch bungalows close to or over the sea. Several now have private bathrooms, but many just have a shared *mandi* (ladle bath). In general, they're cheap, run by Papuan families and include three fish-based meals a day. The most popular homestay islands, Kri and Arborek, have had issues with trash and rats (do your research!). Stay Raja Ampat's website *(stayrajaampat.com)* is superb for booking and trip planning; the Stay Raja Ampat Travellers' Forum on Facebook is *the* place to find fellow travellers interested in sharing inter-island boat costs.

TOP TIP

All visitors need a **Raja Ampat Marine Park Entry Permit** *(700,000Rp)* that funds environmental protections and patrols. An additional **Raja Ampat Visitor Entry Ticket** *(300,000Rp)* funds tourism infrastructure. Fees can be paid on arrival in Waisai. Visit kkprajaampat.com or stayrajaampat.com for the latest details.

RAJA AMPAT
Wayag
1
NORTH MALUKU
Pulau Kawe
Kabare
Pulau Gebe
Pulau Waigeo
Waisilip
HALMAHERA SEA
4
Teluk Kabui
31
Pulau Gag
24
Pulau Gam
21
Pulau Kri
8
18
Pulau Mansuar
See Enlargement
Dampier Strait
Pulau Wai
22
23
Marandanweser
3
Pulau Batanta
Sagewin Strait
Samate
Pulau Salawati
11
Pulau Kofiau
Boo Islands
Wejim
Waigama
Pulau Misool
10
27
Harapan Jaya
Lilinta
26
MALUKU

HIGHLIGHTS

1 Wayag

SIGHTS

2 Arborek
3 Batanta
4 Kali Biru
5 Kri
6 Mansuar
7 Pasir Timbul
8 Piaynemo
9 Pulau Mioskon
10 Pulau Misool
11 Salawati
12 Saporkren
13 Sawinggrai
see 8 Telaga Bintang
14 Waisai
15 Yenwaoupnor

ACTIVITIES

16 Blue Magic
see 7 Cape Kri
17 Manta Sandy
18 Melissa's Garden
19 Mike's Point
20 Passage

SLEEPING

21 Avinsea Homestay
22 Batanta Diving Homestay
23 Biryei Homestay
24 Cove Eco Resort
see 5 Daroyen Village
25 Hamueco Dive Resort
see 2 Kalabia Homestay
26 Misool Resort
27 Nut Tonton Homestay
28 PapuArts Alter-Native Stay
29 Raja Ampat Biodiversity
30 Raja Ampat Eco Lodge
31 Raja4Divers
32 Sandy Guesthouse
see 7 Sorido Bay Resort
see 5 Turtle Homestay

TRANSPORT

33 Marinda Airport

Raja Ampat Liveaboards

Get up close to serene manta rays and giant clams, gape at schools of barracuda, fusiliers or parrotfish, peer at tiny pygmy seahorses (pictured below left) or multicoloured nudibranchs, and, with luck, encounter wobbegong and epaulette (walking) sharks. The reefs of Raja Ampat have hundreds of brilliantly coloured soft and hard corals, and the marine topography varies from vertical walls and pinnacles to reef flats and underwater ridges. The easiest way to see it all is on a liveaboard.

The Best Boats for...

World-Class Divers

Seven Seas *(thesevenseas.net)* This high-end Bali-based company runs a lovely 40m Buginese schooner holding up to 16 guests in plush staterooms with en-suite bathrooms. Trips typically combine Raja Ampat with Triton Bay.

Dewi Nusantara *(dewi-nusantara.com)* A traditional three-masted wooden schooner takes 18 passengers in spacious staterooms on extended journeys that may venture to Triton Bay or the Banda Islands.

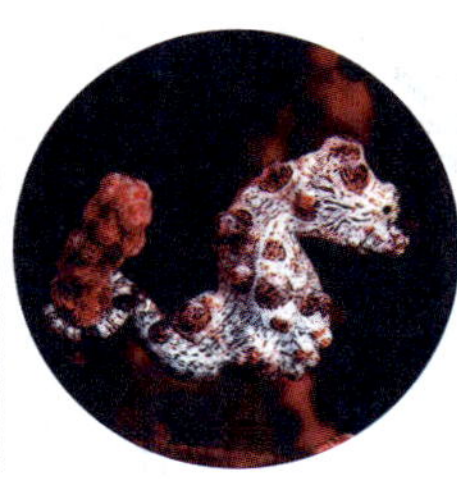

CONNECT IMAGES - CURATED/SHUTTERSTOCK

Big Blue Indonesia *(bigblueindonesia.com)* Relatively new operator run by a group of international dive instructors. Ships only carry eight passengers and the weeklong itineraries are relatively affordable.

Aspiring Marine Biologists

Barefoot Conservation *(barefootconservation.org)* Paying volunteers board marine-conservation expeditions on the 30m wooden pinisi *Ratu Laut* (pictured opposite), which has hot showers and air-con cabins. Barefoot also runs land-based programs on Arborek.

Budgeteers

Raja Ampat Adventures *(rajaampatadventures.com)* This popular locally run liveaboard starts at US$1195 for a week of sailing and is possibly the cheapest option around.

Epica Prides itself on opening up Raja Ampat to all budgets, with six basic twin cabins and two shared bathrooms with freshwater showers. Groups are generally kept to a four-diver maximum per guide and split by experience.

Kira Kira This budget-friendly two-masted schooner holds a maximum of eight passengers and runs on solar energy, making it supremely quiet.

Luxury Travellers

Pindito *(pindito.com)* A leading liveaboard with six double cabins and two twins on a boat decked out with all the comforts. Itineraries almost always include Misool.

Damai II *(dive-damai.com/damai-ii)* This gorgeous 40m vessel offers its 12 guests all the comforts, including satellite wi-fi, plus a spa and camera room.

Gaia Love *(divegaia.com)* While this spacious luxury yacht lacks character, there's no denying the sky-high comforts, including a 'creative space' for camera equipment and lavish meals.

Non-divers

Seatrek Sailing Adventures *(seatrekbali.com)* On these wide-ranging educational outings, you might search for birds of paradise, hike into dense rainforests, snorkel remote reefs or travel in the footsteps of Alfred Russel Wallace (p429).

Calico Jack *(calicojackcharters.com)* Offers a snorkelling cruise for non-divers aboard a lovely wooden pinisi. Other adventures include bird-watching, hiking, kayaking and stand-up paddleboarding.

Ratu Laut

HOW TO

Who should dive Although there are exceptions, Raja Ampat is more set (and more appropriate) for advanced divers. There are *some* dives and courses available for relative novices.

Be aware Most dives are drift dives with strong, nutrient-rich currents that may also hamper visibility. Take caution near mangrove forests, which are hunting grounds for saltwater crocodiles.

When to dive You can dive year-round, although the usually smooth seas can get rough from July to September. Heavier rains hit from May to September.

Further reading Serious divers should purchase *Diving Indonesia's Bird's Head Seascape*, which is an invaluable resource for Raja Ampat as well as Teluk Cenderawasih and Triton Bay.

Liveaboards Versus Dive Resorts

For many visitors, the ultimate Raja Ampat experience is cruising around on a Bugis-style schooner specially kitted out for world-class dives. More than 60 Indonesian- and foreign-owned liveaboards do regular one- to two-week cruises, usually starting and ending in Sorong. Some itineraries combine Raja Ampat with Teluk Cenderawasih or Triton Bay, and most boats carry between eight and 16 passengers. There really is no better way to see the archipelago's breadth. That said, trips aren't cheap and some people argue that they give little back to the Papuan communities visited along the way. Do your research: shoddy liveaboards have gone up in flames in recent years.

Dive resorts, meanwhile, generally offer all-inclusive packages of a week or more and focus on spots within about a 10km radius of the resort. They can be much cheaper and far more comfortable, with luxurious overwater bungalows, three exquisite meals a day and a stronger Papuan identity. Valid insurance and dive cards are required at all reputable places.

Many homestays on Arborek, Kri and Gam also offer diving, but the guides can be short on professional training and the equipment is sometimes subpar. If you do dive with a homestay, ask to see its certification.

SIMON SHIN KWANGSIG/SHUTTERSTOCK

Divers near barrel sponges (p428)

TOP EXPERIENCE

Raja Ampat Diving

Stay in bungalows out over the water and dive some of the most prolific coral reefs on the planet. No, you're not in the Maldives, but the wonderful world of Raja Ampat, a world-class diving destination and astonishing fount of biodiversity. More than 75% of the planet's total species of hard coral are found in this remarkable place. Dive right in.

DON'T MISS

- Kri
- Mansuar
- Manta Sandy
- Arborek
- Piaynemo
- Wayag
- Misool

Get Your Bearings

Ironically, most visitors don't actually spend the majority of their time on any of Raja Ampat's Four Kings (Waigeo, Batanta, Salawati and Misool). Instead, a string of smaller, roadless islands in the Dampier Strait holds the largest concentrations of homestays, the best dive sites and many of the most sought-after attractions. Boating around this area can be a trip highlight.

PRACTICALITIES

- stayrajaampat.com
- kkprajaampat.com

Arborek, Kri and Mansuar are among the most central of Raja Ampat's northern islands, making them good launchpads for onward journeys or stops on boat trips departing from Waigeo.

Kri & Mansuar

Kri, due south of Gam, is backpacker central. It's small and manageable, covered in rolling forest and ringed by beaches and cheap homestays, as well as more upmarket dive resorts. Most are on the flatter north shore. A top snorkel site here is **Cape Kri**, while the offshore sandbar **Pasir Timbul** is an Eden for Instagrammers. Neighbouring **Mansuar** is more rugged with few flat areas, a ridge of limestone and several Robinson Crusoe beaches. There's great coral and nice snorkelling on both islands, including at the pier at Mansuar's Sauwandarek Village, though fish feeding and litter can occasionally sully the otherwise pristine waters. Keep in mind that currents can be strong, as in much of Raja Ampat.

One of our favourite dive sites is nearby, at the famous **Manta Sandy**, where small wrasses clean huge manta rays with 5m wingspans. It's between Mansuar and Arborek.

Arborek

Pancake-flat **Arborek** to the west is a rather built-up cay ringed in homestays. It can be a good base for budgeteers, but isn't a place you'd go out of your way to visit, except maybe to get closer to Papuan culture. Islanders sell crafts (such as *noken* tree bark bags) and often paint their bodies to stage traditional dances for visiting liveaboards.

Scenic Lookouts

Boat trippers often combine snorkelling with a visit to Raja Ampat's biggest attraction, **Piaynemo**, a scenic lookout with dreamy views over the Fam Islands, which poke out of calm, turquoise waters like bushy mushrooms. The hike up is a relative breeze thanks to stairs and several viewing platforms. There are food stalls at the pier below. Here, as elsewhere, avoid the illegally hunted lobster and coconut crabs. Nearby is a second, slightly more challenging rock scramble for views of a star-shaped lagoon, **Telaga Bintang**.

Many visitors mistake Piaynemo for the stock image of Raja Ampat used in promotions. It's actually the similar, though much larger, **Wayag**, about 30km northwest of Waigeo. Due to Wayag's remote location, it's mostly liveaboards that visit here. For those who do make it, the 760m climb up Pindito, its highest peak, is truly mesmerising.

CASH IS KING

Many homestays, dive operators and boat captains in Raja Ampat only accept cash. Very few take credit cards; the only ATMs are in Waisai (or Sorong). Bring more cash than you think you'll need for ferries, inter-island boat transfers, accommodation, the park permit, the environmental fee, and attractions and tours.

TOP TIPS

- Don't tell them we told you, but some places that only take cash *may* accept a transfer through **Wise** *(wise.com)* if you're stuck.
- Year-round diving is possible, although seas can get choppy from July to September (the Raja Ampat/Sorong area gets its heavier rain from May to October).
- Raja Ampat is better suited to advanced divers; it's not exactly a learn-to-dive hot spot.
- There's a decompression chamber in Waisai, but the quality of the facility is unreliable; the nearest decent chamber is in Biak, which opened in 2023.

SPEEDBOAT RENTAL

Renting speedboats to traverse Raja Ampat isn't cheap. In general, expect to pay 700,000Rp to 1,000,000Rp (one way) for trips from Wasai to Kri, Mansuar and Arborek, or about 2,000,000Rp per person for a full day trip (with several stops) to Piaynemo and back, inclusive of the many entrance fees at attractions along the way. Visiting Wayag from Waisai can cost between 15,000,000Rp and 20,000,000Rp per boat for up to about 10 people.

Misool

Misool is a 150km boat journey southwest of Sorong and, as such, lives in a world of its own. Its southeastern coastline, strewn with jagged karst formations, is one of Raja Ampat's wildest and most wondrous corners. The island itself is home to many stunning natural attractions, including vast caves, bird-filled jungles and carpets of undersea corals. There's also a popular lagoon that's shaped like a heart and two saltwater lakes where you can swim with thousands of (stingless) golden jellyfish. One of the best ways to experience Misool's highlights is on a multiday homestay-to-homestay kayaking trip with **Millekul Adventures**.

Misool is home to the luxurious **Misool Resort** (p458), Raja Ampat's leading dive centre and biggest conservation champion. Its charitable foundation single-handedly preserves and patrols 1220 sq km of ocean known as the Misool Marine Reserve, which offers supreme snorkelling and diving opportunities.

The small islands off Misool's southeastern corner have stunning coral. The pristine reefs attract pygmy seahorses, epaulette sharks, manta rays and a vast range of schooling fish. Liveaboards visit the region, but the easiest way to dive around Misool is to stay on the island.

Other Top Dive Sites

Off Pulau Kerupiar, **Mike's Point** is an advanced dive site with strong down currents. The site was mistaken for a Japanese ship during WWII and subsequently bombed. While the damage is still visible above the water, the undersea life has flourished down below. There's lots of hard and soft coral and big schools of sweetlips, jacks and barracuda. There's also a famous overhang and a gorgonian fan garden. Beware of dangerous currents.

Elsewhere, the **Passage** is a series of sites along a 20m-wide saltwater river between Waigeo and Gam – it's heaven for those in search of nudibranchs, sponges and tunicates ('sea squirts'). Sharks, archerfish, turtles, rays and schools of bumphead parrotfish are seen here, too, but beware of the crocodiles!

Melissa's Garden is a top site in the Fam Islands with calm waters, stunning coral and masses of fish.

And finally, expect tasseled wobbegong sharks, schools of barracuda and jacks, massive manta rays and plenty of corals and smaller creatures such as pygmy seahorses at **Blue Magic**, a submerged seamount. It's only for advanced divers and is a real favourite among experienced local dive professionals.

LAUREN SURYANATA/SHUTTERSTOCK

Blue-spotted tree monitor

Continued from p421

For more professional guides, serious birders might consider Charles Roring of Wildlife Papua (p432) or Eko Lesomar of Discover Papua Birding (p442), both of whom have a deep knowledge of local fauna. Most other tour operators offer tours here, including birding specialist Papua Expeditions (p449).

Fall off the Map on Batanta & Salawati

The sea less travelled

Batanta is the smallest of the 'Four Kings' (the name given to the four largest islands). It's densely forested with thundering waterfalls and some of the best – though, it must be said, least accessible – birding in the archipelago, including birds of paradise and cassowaries. This is the only place in the world to spot the endangered blue-spotted tree monitor and is one of the last refuges of the Waigeo spotted cuscus. Its seagrass beds also offer prime habitat for dugongs, which have been scared off elsewhere. Despite all this, surprisingly few day-trippers come to Batanta. There are a handful of homestays and resorts (with excellent house reefs) ideal for those who want to get away from it all. Most are located in the string of tiny islets that dot Batanta's northern coastline. We hope it stays this way and doesn't get swept up in the current hype surrounding the other islands.

If you thought Batanta was quiet, **Salawati**, to the south, is positively soporific. Very few travellers make it out this way, and though many liveaboards sail past, there are no resorts or homestays and it's the least visited of the 'Four Kings'. If you do make it this far, you'll discover a world filled with dense sago forests, rural villages and several WWII sites, including Japanese bunkers and some undersea wrecks.

ALFRED RUSSEL WALLACE

Few people realise that there were actually two men who co-conceived the theory of evolution through natural selection. Charles Darwin and the Galápagos Islands are familiar names, but Alfred Russel Wallace and the isles he studied (including Raja Ampat) have been mostly forgotten to time. The English naturalist became obsessed with birds of paradise and spent months near Yenbeser village (where there's a replica of his small hut), using them to inform his work. He also identified what's known as the Wallace Line, which separates the Indonesian archipelago in two. Animals to the west have Asian origin, while those to the east are Australasian. Wallace's book, *The Malay Archipelago*, is one of the region's most fascinating travelogues.

Beyond Raja Ampat

Two humming cities provide access to West Papua's wilder wonders, including frenzied coral reefs and montane forests brimming with birds.

Places

GETTING AROUND

Sorong is the region's main airport, with incoming flights from Jakarta and onward connections to Kaimana and Manokwari. From Manokwari you can reach Nabire. Airport taxis to each respective town can be expensive, starting at 120,000Rp in Sorong and 150,000Rp in Manokwari. Beyond airport gates there are public *taksi* for about 10,000Rp. In both towns, *ojek* (motorbike taxi) riders with yellow helmets can get you around for between 10,000Rp and 20,000Rp per trip. Sorong is also served by ride-hailing app Grab.

Beyond Raja Ampat, the greater province of West Papua is made up mostly of two large peninsulas – the Bird's Head (also known as Vogelkop or Kepala Burung) and the more southerly Bomberai Peninsula – as well as several hundred offshore islands. This is part of one of Asia's most underrated wildlife-watching destinations, with highlights including scoping out birds of paradise, diving little-visited reefs and swimming with serene whale sharks. Sorong and Manokwari are well-connected urban bases from which to launch your explorations. The former is an obligatory stop on the way to Raja Ampat, while the latter is a hub for surfing, birding and religious tourism. Elsewhere, secluded bays, virgin forests and traditional Papuan towns lure only the adventurous.

Sorong

TIME FROM RAJA AMPAT: **2HR**

Prep for Raja Ampat

Sorong sits at the northwestern tip of the **Bird's Head Peninsula** and is Papua's second-largest city. It's a busy port, a base for oil and logging operations in the region and an air hub for West Papua, but few travellers hang around longer than it takes to get on a boat to the Raja Ampat Islands.

While you wait, you might visit the **Vihara Buddha Jayanti** (Pagoda Sapta Ratna), a Buddhist temple built by the local Chinese community. It offers sweeping views over Sorong, drawing crowds at sunset. Alternatively, early risers enjoy the sunrise frenzy at **Pasar Jembatan Puri**, a fish market that's busy from about 5am to 7.30am.

The two best places to stock up on supplies are the **SAGA** and **MEGA** supermarkets, which lie at either end of town.

Manokwari

TIME FROM SORONG: **1HR**

Churches, beaches and a table mountain

Capital of Papua Barat (West Papua) province, Manokwari sits on Teluk Cenderawasih, near the northeastern corner of the

Bird's Head Peninsula. It's a rather sluggish place that merits a visit mainly for the natural attractions in the surrounding area, notably the Pegunungan Arfak and northern beaches.

Local Christians visit the offshore island of **Pulau Mansinam**, where two German missionaries settled in 1855 and became the first to evangelise in Papua. The picturesque, rainforest-covered island is home to a small village looked over by a wannabe Rio de Janeiro statue of Christ. There's also a pleasant beach along its western and southern shore with plenty of shady picnic areas and good snorkelling. Outrigger boats sail here from a pier in **Kwawi**, 2.5km southeast of central Manokwari. Take an *ojek* at Mansinam pier to reach the beaches.

For a livelier beach with restaurants and water sports, head to **Pantai Pasir Putih**, 5km southeast of Manokwari. Or, for a nice nature stroll without leaving the city, you can hike up **Taman Gunung Meja**. This protected park on 'table mountain' holds a small Japanese WWII memorial and has nice birdlife.

Surf's up

There's been a strong push in recent years to turn Manokwari into Papua's premier **surf destination**, and there's good reason for it – there are at least 10 great breaks within a 30-minute drive of the town centre. A newly paved road connects most of them along the northern coast, from **Pantai Amban** to **Pantai Bakaro**, where the open Pacific pounds against sand banks and reefs from October to April. You'll rarely share the waves with anyone else, unless you show up in November during the World Surf League's Manokwari Pro. The Dutch-run surf lodge **Amban Beach House** (p458) is your best source for surf intel.

Pegunungan Arfak

TIME FROM SORONG: 1HR + 1HR

A birders' paradise

The thickly forested Pegunungan Arfak, rising to more than 2900m south of Manokwari, is a region of beautiful tropical scenery, exotic wildlife (especially birds) and a mostly indigenous Papuan population of Hatam, Moley, Meyakh and Sough, who once occupied traditional 'thousand-leg' stilt houses. The first Papuan revolt – and one of the biggest – against Indonesian rule happened here from 1965 to 1968.

ALCOHOL IN PAPUA

If your dream beach vacation involves piña coladas, Papua probably isn't for you. Alcohol is banned in many parts of the region, while in others it's extremely hard to find (and extremely expensive once you do find it). In some places, such as Sorong, Biak or Jayapura, you can find drinks in nicer hotels, but don't expect beer – and certainly not wine – in supermarkets or restaurants beyond Sorong. International travellers can bring 2.25L of alcohol per person into Indonesia, or purchase 1L from duty free on arrival. Before heading to Raja Ampat, you might also want to stock up on beer at SAGA in Sorong – even a cold Bintang is hard to come by on the islands.

EATING IN SORONG: OUR PICKS

Layar Gading: Seafront dining at its finest with a good breeze, epic sunsets and well-priced noodle and rice dishes to complement the pricier fish feasts. *11am-10pm* $

Janji Jiwa: Slick air-conditioned coffee chain by the airport has locally sourced coffee and sells cheap *nasi jeruk* dishes. *9am-10pm Mon-Sat, noon-10pm Sun* $

Pizzeria Terrazza di Sorong: Fluffy, cheesy pizzas, served in an oasis-like terrace, as well as pasta, burgers, salads and cold Bintang! *1-9.30pm Tue-Sun* $$

Gallery Fusion: The evening buffet at the Vega Hotel is so sprawling and packed with grilled-to-order seafood that it's easily the best deal in town. *6-10pm* $$

THE BIRD'S HEAD SEASCAPE

The Bird's Head Seascape lies at the heart of the Coral Triangle and comprises more than 225,000 sq km of West Papuan waters, from Teluk Cenderawasih to Triton Bay. Much of it is included in a network of 26 marine protected areas (MPAs), which span 52,300 sq km of coral-rich waters and hold at least 200 documented dive sites. A consortium of international NGOs, including the Nature Conservancy, WWF and Conservation International, has worked here since 2004 developing strong relationships with local and national governments, universities and coastal communities to ensure the seascape's long-term protection. Conservation International's website (birdshead seascape.com) lists resources where you can learn about local marine tourism.

The best-known bird-watching base is the **Mokwam** region, a collection of four small villages – Syobri, Kwau, Mokwam and Mingre (the nicest) – all perched a few kilometres apart down a side road about 50km from Manokwari. To find the endemic birds (including the superb bird of paradise, the magnificent bird of paradise, black sicklebill and western parotia), you'll need a guide. The best time to visit is from May to October.

Trips are not cheap as they require 4WD transport, local accommodation and food, as well as an assortment of village fees ranging from guides to hides, firewood and community contributions – all of which are subject to wild fluctuations. **Hans Mandacan** *(0821 9946 9312)* is an excellent local guide with intimate knowledge of the forest and his own basic mountainside retreat, the **Papuan Lorikeet Guesthouse**. Another experienced guide is **Zeth Wonggor** (0852 5405 3754), who has worked with, among others, Sir David Attenborough. Manokwari-based **Travel Papua** (p449) also runs trips here.

Tambrauw

TIME FROM SORONG: **3HR**

Experience untamed nature

Between Sorong and Manokwari lies the little-explored Tambrauw Regency, which is brimming with natural splendour and adventure. Its tree-shrouded mountains are home to several birds of paradise species, while offshore islands are ringed in coral, with secluded white-sand shorelines that are favoured by nesting leatherback, olive ridley and green turtles. Fledgling ecotourism projects come and go here. Your best source for travel intel is Charles Roring of **Wildlife Papua** *(wildlifepapua.com)*, a pioneer in opening the region up to tourism. Many of his trips are based out of the serene **Sansapore Pacific Park Beach Resort** on the beach in Sausapor, three hours by 4WD from Sorong.

Triton Bay

TIME FROM SORONG: **1HR** + **2HR**

The next Raja Ampat?

Some in the diving community whisper that the undersea ecosystems of Triton Bay (Teluk Triton) might be even more impressive than those of Raja Ampat. While that's still up for debate, the wealth of marine life at Triton Bay is extraordinary (though the visibility can, at times, be as little as 5m). Among the many highlights found in the region's 30-plus dive sites are pygmy seahorses, Nursalim flasher wrasse, Triton Bay walking sharks, wobbegong sharks, big pods of dolphins,

EATING IN MANOKWARI: OUR PICKS

Tabea Social House: Good coffee, cheap rice bowls, exceptional cleanliness and a quirky international aesthetic make this a solid budget option. *10am-10pm* $

Billy Cafe: Easily Papua's kitschiest restaurant, serving its seafood inside a kooky aquarium. *8am-10.30pm* $$

Café Laut: Mansinam Beach Resort's popular seafront restaurant charms in the evening with rope lights, frequent live music and excellent *ikan bakar*. *8am-10pm* $$

Inggandi Beach Restaurant: Manokwari's top waterfront dining destination, with a mix of seafood and Chinese dishes. *11am-10pm* $$

SERGEUWPHOTO/SHUTTERSTOCK

Whale shark, Triton Bay

sweetlips, surgeonfish and arguably the most spectacular soft corals – and micro habitats – in the world. If that wasn't enough, there's also the big daddy of them all, whale sharks, which are attracted to the fishing *bagang* (fishing platform).

Occasional liveaboards divert from Raja Ampat to head this way. Otherwise, there's really only one true dive resort: the pioneering **Triton Bay Divers**. It's set on Aiduma Island with eight elegant wooden cottages on a beautiful white-sand beach. The all-inclusive weeklong model includes 15 dives. Access to Triton Bay is via the airport in Kaimana, followed by a two-hour boat transfer. Peak season runs from October to April.

Nabire

TIME FROM SORONG: **2HR**

Swim with whale sharks

When fishermen off the east coast of the Bird's Head Peninsula set out wooden platforms to lure fish in the 1990s, some unexpectedly large ones started showing up: whale sharks! In 2002, this special habitat became **Taman Nasional Teluk Cenderawasih**, Indonesia's largest marine park at a whopping 14,535 sq km. Since then, some 160 different whale sharks have been spotted.

Close encounters with these harmless giants are almost guaranteed any day, though waves can make the seas rougher for humans from October to March. The best place to see them is near Kwatisore village, about 1½ hours by boat from the city of Nabire. The castaway-cool **Kali Lemon Dive Resort** is the closest lodging to the *bagang* where the whale sharks hang out. Many liveaboards come this way, too.

DIVE CHECKLIST

Before choosing a dive operation in Papua, check that it meets the following recommended requirements.

Proper certification: The shop employs certified divemasters and/or instructors.

State of the equipment: The condition of the equipment and storage facility meets your standards.

Boat safety: The boats are in good condition and not overloaded on dive trips.

Emergency preparedness: The dive shop has oxygen and first-aid kits, along with staff trained in responding to emergencies.

Dive insurance: The dive shop either requires or strongly recommends that individuals carry dive insurance.

Attentiveness: The dive shop responds promptly and professionally to questions.

Jayapura & Sentani

LAKE VIEWS | HARBOURSIDE DINING | PAPUAN ARTS

GETTING AROUND

Jayapura's airport is the hub of Papuan aviation, with flights to and from Sorong, Wamena, Merauke, Nabire, Manokwari, Makassar, Biak and Jakarta. Internal travel in Papua inevitably means flying in and out of here. Official airport taxis from Sentani to Jayapura's centre (24km) cost 250,000Rp, though you can often pay half that using a local ride-hailing app such as Grab or Gojek. Count on the journey taking at least an hour.

TOP TIP

The published rate for hotels in Jayapura and Sentani (as well as elsewhere in Papua) can be up to double what you find on local booking platforms such as Traveloka or Tiket.com. It's rarely cost-effective to book directly with the property or at a check-in desk on arrival.

Jayapura is the largest city on the island of New Guinea and the fastest-growing urban area in Indonesia. Yes, the city centre is hot and swarming with incessant traffic, but there's no denying the appeal of its setting, perched beautifully between steep, forested hills overlooking the sea. The Dutch established the first settlement here in 1910, naming it Hollandia. Following the Indonesian takeover in 1963, it was rebranded as Jayapura (Victory City). The provincial capital now sprawls for 20km along the Teluk Imbi, incorporating the formerly separate towns of Argapura, Hamadi, Entrop, Abepura and Waena. Some 30km to the west is the booming airport town of Sentani. It sits between the forested Pegunungan Cycloop range and serene Danau Sentani, which hosts a lovely festival in June and features island fishing villages accessible by boat. With nice hotels and restaurants, and much less traffic, many travellers prefer to base themselves here.

Immerse Yourself in Papuan Tribal Art

Visit Museum Loka Budaya

Papua's astonishing cultural diversity deserves a showpiece museum that marks the rites and showcases the physical touchstones of that diversity. It *almost* happens at the **Museum Loka Budaya** *(25,000Rp)*. For some it's an opportunity missed. For others – and we count ourselves among this school of thought – it's a promising B+ start, but it could do better. Notably, the labelling could be better and sections of the museum also sometimes close without warning or explanation.

There's nothing wrong with the collection, however, which is world-class, a fact owed to an accident (both literal and figurative) of history. Many of the pieces held by the museum were selected by Michael Rockefeller and his team in the 1950s for exhibition at New York City's Metropolitan Museum of Art. The works ultimately remained in Papua, however, as Rockefeller disappeared in 1961 after his canoe capsized offshore in the Asmat region. It's believed he either drowned or was eaten by cannibals.

JAYAPURA & SENTANI

SIGHTS
- **1** Abar
- **2** Babrongko
- **3** Bukit Tungku Wiri
- **4** Museum Loka Budaya
- **5** Pantai Base G
- **6** Pulau Asei
- **7** Situs Megalitik Tutari
- **8** Tugu MacArthur

ACTIVITIES
- **9** Papua Explorer

SLEEPING
- **10** ASTON Jayapura Hotel
- **11** FOX Hotel Jayapura
- **12** Horex Hotel Sentani
- **13** Hotel Jasmine
- **14** Suni Garden Lake Hotel & Resort
- **see 12** Unique Hotel

EATING
- **15** Blue Café
- **see 12** Bubur Mandala
- **16** Haven Café
- **17** Resto & Cafe Rumah Laut
- **see 16** Resto Rumah Gunung
- **18** Yougwa Restaurant

DRINKING & NIGHTLIFE
- **19** Hangover Resto & Lounge
- **20** Pit's Corner

ENTERTAINMENT
- **21** Festival Danau Sentani

SHOPPING
- **22** Pasar Hamadi

INFORMATION
- **23** Polda
- **24** Polresta

TRADITIONAL PAPUAN CULTURE

Indonesia is a cultural mosaic, but Papua takes it to new levels. It's home to 200-plus indigenous peoples, including approximately 280 different languages, as well as migrants to the region from all over Indonesia. The latter dominate in the cities and make up about half of Papua's population. Indigenous Papuan culture is much more apparent in the villages than the towns. It has changed greatly under the influence of Christian missionaries and the Indonesian government. Tribal warfare, headhunting and cannibalism, practised by some tribes well into the second half of the 20th century, have all but disappeared. But reverence for ancestors and pride in cultural traditions such as dances, dress and woodcarving persist.

ARIAPRITA/SHUTTERSTOCK

Pantai Base G

The museum belongs to Cenderawasih University, at once a hotbed of Papuan nationalism and an institution dedicated to celebrating and documenting Papuan culture. There are many highlights here, among them the best collection of Asmat carvings and 'devil-dance' costumes outside Agats. The museum also contains fine crafts – including giant war shields and evocative masks – from across Papua, as well as an archive of intriguing historical photos.

The museum's small art store has luggage-friendly souvenirs (you'll find similar items at craft stores on Jl Perikanan, just north of **Pasar Hamadi**). The museum is next to the large Auditorium Universitas Cenderawasih, on the main road in Jayapura's Abepura district.

Learn about Local Foods

Go to market and learn to cook

Those with a passion for food should get in touch with Welly Manufandu of **Papua Travel Guide** *(papua-travelguide.com)*. She can teach you everything you need to know about, for example, a traditional Papuan pit roast, which contains sago, cassava and sweet potatoes. For something a little more hands-on, take her day-long tour, which includes a trip to the local market to shop for lunch ingredients. It's a priceless crash course in Papuan food traditions. She's pretty savvy about what you can and can't find back home, and can suggest replacements. Following the market, you'll go to a family home to cook the meal. It's a great day and Welly is a fabulous host.

Beach Bases & War Monuments

Dive into Greater Jayapura's WWII history

The area around Jayapura is one of Asia's least-known theatres of war. It was here, in 1944, that 80,000 Allied troops landed to dislodge the Japanese in the **Battle of Hollandia**, which was the largest amphibious operation of WWII in the southwestern Pacific. Named with startling candour as Operation Reckless, the landings at Tanahmerah Bay and Humboldt Bay took place after US codebreakers deciphered Japanese communications that revealed that Hollandia was only lightly defended. With Allied (mostly US) soldiers outnumbering Japanese fighters by nearly four to one, and supported by US and Australian bombers, the operation was a stunning success, and the Japanese were driven from their foothold in the east of the island, never to return.

The US administrative HQ was located at an idyllic beach just north of Jayapura; it's now known as **Pantai Base G**. Today, more than 80 years later, little remains of the US presence. Instead, you'll find a nearly 3km-long crescent of sand lined with wooden picnic platforms tucked beneath palms. Most days here, it's easy to imagine that the battle, which claimed nearly 4000 lives, never happened. And aside from its historical significance, it's the best beach that's easily accessible from Jayapura (via the 'Base G' *taksi*) and is usually empty, except on Sundays, when the locals come in droves. Beware of the many rocks in the water.

Closer to Sentani is **Tugu MacArthur**, a monument to General Douglas MacArthur with breathtaking views of Danau Sentani. This was where he set up his headquarters after US forces took Jayapura (then called Hollandia) in April 1944. Today, the site is occupied by a small memorial and a room with displays on the American and Japanese participation in the fighting.

Get to Know Danau Sentani

Explore a tropical lake

You'll get a bird's-eye view of 96.5-sq-km Danau Sentani, snaking its way between picturesque green hills, as you fly in or out of Sentani. On the ground, it's worth taking a day to explore the area, either through a local tour operator or by hiring a private taxi for the day.

This stunning lake has 19 islands and numerous fishing villages of wooden stilt houses along its shores. Many specialise in Papuan crafts, and each has its own specialty, including **Babrongko** (for woodcarvings), **Abar** (for ceramics) and **Pulau Asei** (for bark paintings). Visiting the latter, which is an island, involves a fun and cheap **boat trip** *(10,000Rp)* away from the shore at Kalkote, 11km east of Sentani.

HANDS-ON PAPUAN EXPERIENCES

Welly Manufandu, owner of Papua Travel Guide, shares her favourite hands-on experiences. *papuatravelguide.com*

Bark painting in Sentani

Discover how to do traditional bark painting with an art lesson on Pulau Asei. You'll learn the meaning behind the iconography as you paint your own piece.

Coffee in Lanny Jaya

Trek through the highland coffee plantations of local brand Tiyom in Lanny Jaya, two hours from Wamena. Then return to learn about roasting and taste some fresh-brewed arabica beans.

Drum carving on Biak

On Biak, where my family comes from, you can book a lesson to learn how to carve traditional island symbols onto a *tifa* drum, which is used in the local *wor* dance.

EATING & DRINKING IN JAYAPURA: OUR PICKS

Pit's Corner: Premier coffee house and barista training school in a hip modern building. A long list of coffee drinks and well-priced Indonesian food. *8am-10pm* $

Resto & Café Rumah Laut: This enchanting upmarket gem, on stilts over the water, is where locals come when they want to impress. *9am-10pm* $$

Blue Café: Prime waterfront views, frequent live music and solid grilled-fish dishes make for a great evening by the harbour. *10am-9pm* $

Hangover Resto & Lounge: If you're craving burgers or burritos or something stronger than a Bintang, this boisterous seafront resto-bar ticks most boxes. *11am-2am* $$

PAPUA TRAVEL ALERT

Swaths of the Papuan interior are sometimes off limits to tourists because of the Organisasi Papua Merdeka (Free Papua Organisation; OPM), which Indonesia labels as a terrorist group. OPM stages occasional protests demanding Papua's independence, and they turned violent in 2019 and 2023 in Jayapura and Wamena respectively. OPM also has an armed wing that's feared for its attention-grabbing actions, including the kidnapping and killing of a New Zealand pilot in a remote highlands region in 2024. When applying for a *surat jalan* (travel permit), police will generally inform you of off-limits areas, mostly in the highlands. It's a good idea to check the latest news before planning a trip into the Papuan interior.

On the lakeshore about 6km west of Sentani, just past the village church in Doyo Lama, you'll see the entrance to **Situs Megalitik Tutari**, a mysterious hillside archaeological site composed of various arrangements of rocks and stones, as well as dozens of rock paintings of fish, turtles, crocodiles and lizards. The carvings are in six different fenced-in areas, all reached along a 1.5km concrete path up and into the forest.

Neighbouring **Bukit Tungku Wiri** is a free hilltop walkway dotted in covered gazebos, and receives far more visitors. Follow the rainbow-painted stairs up to a plaza with a giant cross before continuing on a 2km paved path along a grassy ridgeline above the lake. Do as the locals do and time your visit for an hour before sunset for cooler weather and stirring views.

The best time to visit the lake is in mid-June during the **Festival Danau Sentani**, which features spectacular traditional dances and chanting as well as elaborate boat parades, live music, craft fairs and more. Started in 2008 and staged in Kalkote, it grows bigger and better every year.

EATING & DRINKING IN SENTANI: OUR PICKS

Haven Café: Fresh juice, strong coffee, plus salads, pizzas and well-prepared local dishes on a serene terrace filled with tropical plants. *11am-8.30pm Wed-Mon* $

Resto Rumah Gunung: There's a giant menu of seafood and vegetarian dishes at this fine restaurant with striking Papuan wood carvings. *9am-9pm* $

Bubur Mandala: This squeaky clean restaurant and coffee house does excellent chicken and noodle dishes, plus its signature *bubur* (sago porridge). *7am-9.30pm* $

Yougwa Restaurant: Enjoy the breezy wooden terraces set over a lake 13km east of town. Try the *ikan gabus* (snakehead fish). *10am-6.30pm Mon-Sat, 11am-5pm Sun* $$

WIRESTOCK CREATORS/SHUTTERSTOCK

Bukit Tungku Wiri

Get Your Papua Travel Permit

Secure your *surat jalan*

It's not often that we label something as practical as getting a permit as an experience, but getting your *surat jalan* (travel permit) is a quintessential Papuan travel experience.

Indeed, for many travellers, the main reason to stop in Jayapura is to obtain this important piece of paper. At the time of research, exactly where a *surat jalan* was required seemed to depend on who you asked. You definitely won't need one in any major city (Sorong, Jayapura, Manokwari) or the islands of Raja Ampat. You shouldn't need one for Biak or Wasur, either. You *will* want to get one for any trip into the highlands (Yali, Korowai, Baliem Valley) or remote areas down south such as Asmat.

The *surat jalan* is obtained from the **polresta** *(9am-3pm Mon-Fri)* or **polda** *(facebook.com/poldapapuaofficial; open 24hr)* in Jayapura. You should present a list of every place you intend to visit, with the exception being places that are considered to be in West Papua. Be sure to bring your passport, two passport photos (with a *red* background - local photo kiosks can get you sorted) and photocopies of your passport's personal details page and your Indonesian visa.

The procedure normally takes a few hours and no payment should be requested. Note that tour guides can often do all of this for you in advance. The duration of the permit depends on how long you request and the expiry date of your visa. Make several photocopies of the permit, as well as your passport, in case you have to hand it over.

CROSSING INTO PAPUA NEW GUINEA

There's just one land border crossing between Papua and Papua New Guinea that's open to foreigners, and you'll find it 60km east of Jayapura at Skouw (figure on a 90-minute drive). Keep in mind that this border occasionally closes, usually due to political tensions. The PNG consulate in Jayapura can issue 60-day tourist visas, but the application process takes up to five business days. It's best to stop by at least a week in advance to ask for the latest visa requirements, which may include a letter stating your travel plans, proof of funds, photocopies of your passport, two passport-sized photos and a confirmed onward air ticket. For details, check the PNG immigration website (ica.gov.pg).

Pulau Biak

ABUNDANT CORALS | EMPTY BEACHES | WWII MEMORIALS

GETTING AROUND

Flights arrive in Biak from Jayapura, Manokwari and Jakarta (via Makassar), as well as the neighbouring island of Yapen. ASDP Indonesia Ferry and Pelni have liners heading east to Jayapura and west to Sorong (and beyond) weekly and biweekly respectively. Public *taksi* reach most places of interest around the island, with yellow ones circling Kota Biak and blue ones venturing to the villages north and east of the town. Services often wind down in the afternoon. Chartering a car or taking a trip with PT Ekowisata Papua Tours & Travel (p442) is easiest.

Biak ranks among Asia's most underrated and least-known island destinations. One of Papua's biggest offshore islands, Biak is a humble beauty, a relaxed and friendly place with great diving and wild empty beaches. Hardly anyone comes here, and what tourism infrastructure there is dates back to a mini-boom in the 1980s. This serene outpost was the site of major WWII battles between the USA and Japan, leaving it littered with rusty war relics both on land and below the sea, adding much historical interest to the stirring natural beauty at every turn. There are striking emerald-green rivers, flamboyant birds and thriving walls of coral offshore and in the adjacent Padaido Islands, which for many are the real attraction. The main town is Kota Biak, which is clean, orderly and your only logical base. Elsewhere, there are small rural villages centred around big, bold churches.

Explore Biak's WWII History

Bombs, beaches and the south coast

Biak saw fierce fighting during WWII, with about 11,000 Japanese and nearly 500 Americans reported killed in the Battle of Biak (1944). There are several historic sites worth visiting, including the Japanese Cave **Goa Jepang** *(50,000Rp)*, 4km northeast of Kota Biak. It was used as a base and hideout by thousands of Japanese soldiers, 3000 of whom died when US forces bombed a hole in the cave roof, dropped petrol drums into it and then bombarded it from above. Take the staircase that leads down into the main cave, where you can clearly see the hole made by the bombing with tendrils and tree roots hanging eerily down through the gaping orifice. Unlike many WWII sites that consist of decontextualised relics, this one hauntingly evokes the era.

There's also a small museum here with old war relics, including grenades and artillery shells, as well as the rusty carcasses of American army jeeps and a Japanese 'Zero' fighter plane.

Heading away toward Bosnik (a village 18km east of Kota Biak known for its bustling **morning market** on Tuesdays,

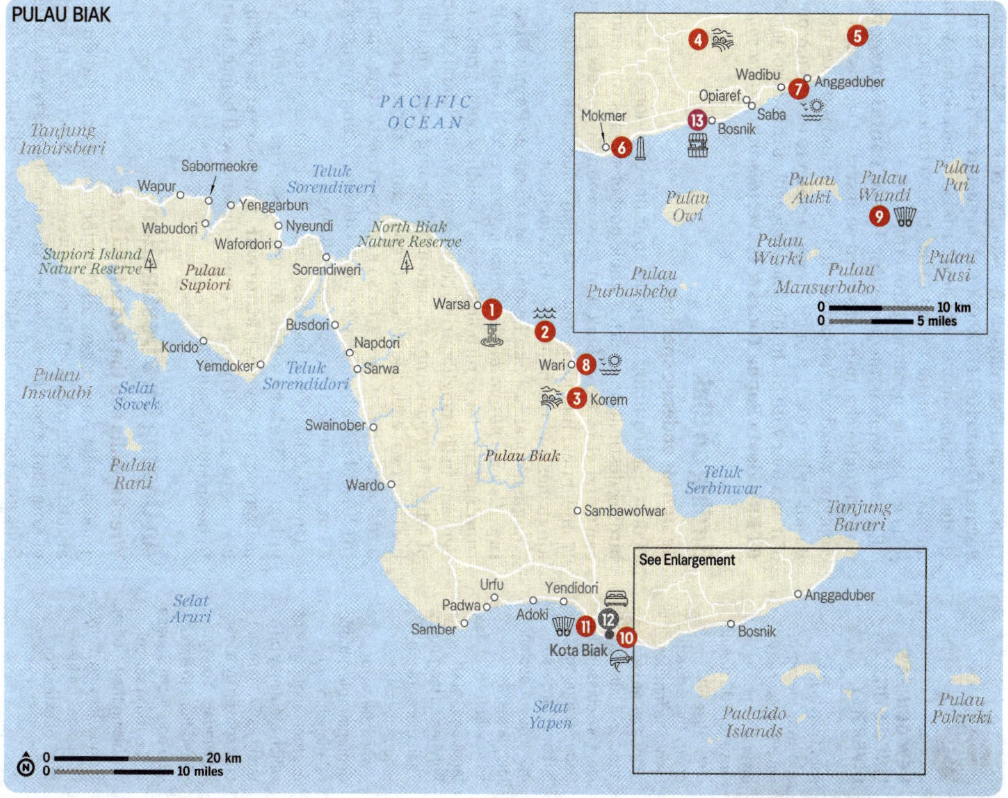

SIGHTS
1 Air Terjun Wafsarak
2 Batu Pica
3 Korem
4 Makmakerbo
5 Mnurwar
6 Monumen Perang Dunia Ke II
7 Pantai Anggopi
8 Pantai Wari

ACTIVITIES
9 Biak Padaido Divers
see 11 Catalina Wreck
10 Goa Jepang
11 Nirmala Beach Diving Center

SLEEPING
see 10 Asana Biak Papua
see 11 Nirmala Biak Beach Hotel
12 Padaido Hotel

EATING
see 12 Depot Afifah
see 12 House of Supernova
see 12 Restaurant 99
see 12 Warung Makan Barokah

SHOPPING
13 Pasar Bosnik

NEW GUINEA'S LINGUISTIC DIVERSITY

New Guinea is far and away the world's most linguistically diverse region, with close to 1000 distinct languages and nearly three dozen language families (Papua alone has about 428 languages). Most are classified as Papuan languages, but there are also many Austronesian languages, as well as Admiralty Islands languages and Polynesian languages. Then there are the language isolates – which have no demonstrable genetic relationship with another language – of which there may be as many as 37. Many are only spoken by a few individuals. Younger generations in Papua, who only learn Bahasa Indonesia in school, are losing their mother tongue, leaving many languages on the brink of extinction.

TOP TIP

Carry some extra cash in small denominations when going to the beach. There will always be someone waiting to charge a nominal fee, be it for entry, parking, the use of covered gazebos or some combination of all three. This is normal and expected of local visitors, too.

Thursdays and Saturdays) is the swooping concrete **Monumen Perang Dunia Ke II** *(100,000Rp)*, an austere and slightly neglected Japanese monument and burial ground adorned with mementos. If you don't want to pay the overpriced entry fee, you can see the monument from the road.

East of Bosnik is the appealing beach, **Pantai Anggopi**, which is quite charming. It's lined with small gazebos and is empty on weekdays. You can reach the beach and war sites near Bosnik by blue *taksi*, though it's much easier to make a day out of it on a tour with the highly knowledgeable Benny Lesomar of **PT Ekowisata Papua Tours & Travel** *(discoverpapua.com)*.

Birding on Biak

Search for endemic species

Biak is fast acquiring a reputation as one of Indonesia's best birding destinations, with a whole host of species you simply can't find elsewhere. Biak and its surrounding islets boast 17 endemics, including the strikingly blue Biak paradise-kingfisher and the multihued Biak lorikeet.

English-speaking Eko Lesomar of **Discover Papua Birding** *(discoverpapua-birding.com)* is your resident bird guide, running trips for ornithologists and wildlife photographers here and in the neighbouring Numfor and Yapen islands, both of which have an embarrassment of birding riches, including their own endemic species (Yapen claims three species of birds of paradise!). He can also arrange trips to Raja Ampat (p420) and elsewhere. Prices vary, with everything from short excursions up to two-week expeditions.

On Biak, he often focuses on interior forests near the village of **Makmakerbo** for native species, as well as a mangrove estuary near **Mnurwar**, which attracts visiting herons, egrets and ospreys. Expect to wake well before dawn to be on site for sunrise.

An Unsung Dive Destination

Wrecks, walls and the Padaido Islands

Though Raja Ampat gets all the glory, some intrepid divers argue that the corals off Biak are even more spectacular. East of Kota Biak, there are several excellent wall dives near Marau, Saba and Wadibu, which are also good snorkelling spots, as is Anggaduber. The star dive, however, is down to the **Catalina Wreck**. This amphibious American aircraft used to fight the Japanese is now a lovely refuge for sea creatures, between 20m and 30m below the surface. In place of the bombs and torpedoes it once carried, it now comes equipped naturally with corals, as well as multitudes of angelfish, squirrelfish and bumphead parrotfish. **Nirmala Beach Diving Center** *(nirmaladiveresortbiak.com; 3-day dive package per person 5,000,000Rp, snorkelling per person from 500,000Rp)*, located just onshore of the wreck, is the island's premier dive outfit, run by an experienced Indonesian-American couple.

For many visitors, the Padaido Islands are a trip highlight. These 36 paradisiacal outcrops (just 13 of which are inhabited) boast crystal-clear waters and white-sand beaches that back up to virgin jungle. Erick Farwas from **Biak Padaido Divers** (*biakpadaidodivers@yahoo.co.id; 2-tank dive 900,000-3,000,000Rp, full equipment rental 300,000Rp, full-day snorkelling trip 1,500,000Rp*) runs a guesthouse on Pulau Wundi and offers dives across the archipelago.

Top sites include a cavern dive off Pulau Wundi, the wreck of a Philippine fishing vessel off Pulau Rasi and a wall dive off Pulau Mansurbabo, which gets huge schools of barracuda. Day-tripping snorkellers may want to focus on Pulau Owi and Pulau Rurbas Kecil, which are closer to Kota Biak (and thus quicker and cheaper to visit).

You'll see the greatest number of fish from February to October. Choppy seas can complicate travel (and visibility) November to January.

Biak's Remote North

Splashing in rivers, waterfalls and beaches

If you really want to get a visual on Papua's largely unknown potential as an off-the-beaten-track beach paradise, head to Biak's little-visited north coast, just an hour from Kota Biak by car or *taksi*. This unspoiled region is home to Biak's nicest beaches, waterfalls and riverine villages.

The cross-island road hits the Pacific at **Korem**, where the shimmering, emerald-green Kali Korem winds through dense forest to the sea. The original town of Korem was destroyed by a tsunami in the 1996 Biak earthquake; look for a small memorial on the road out to the wide, driftwood-strewn beach.

To swim, it's better to head just west to **Pantai Wari**, a sweeping crescent of sand at the end of a deep horseshoe bay. This serene beach has shaded picnic areas and two rustic cabins that you can rent for an evening. Continuing west is a string of scenic and largely empty beaches, many of which have waves you can often surf between November and February. **Batu Pica** is a shallow, ocean-fed pool where locals sell coconut water. Local tip: skip the artificial swimming area and head just beyond to the natural rock pools, which lie on an elevated perch above the crashing waves that fill them.

Among the many waterfalls found in this part of Biak, **Air Terjun Wafsarak** is the most accessible, lying just steps from the coast road. It's a popular spot among local kids, who climb on tree roots to the top of the falls and jump into the deep pool below. For tours to this region, contact Benny Lesomar at PT Ekowisata Papua Tours & Travel.

THE MISSING ROCKEFELLER

The disappearance of Michael Rockefeller in 1961 brought Dutch New Guinea to the top of global headlines over a period of several months. The wild child of US vice president Nelson Rockefeller (and the great-grandson of oil scion John D Rockefeller) developed an obsession with Papuan tribal art, which he collected for display back in New York. It ultimately led to his disappearance and presumed death on an expedition to Asmat gone terribly wrong. Whether he drowned offshore or was cannibalised by the Asmat people has been the source of much debate. The 2014 book *Savage Harvest* by Carl Hoffman is a fascinating read that claims to solve the decades-old mystery once and for all.

EATING & DRINKING IN BIAK: OUR PICKS

House of Supernova: Crowd-pleaser with coffee, cocktails and karaoke, as well as Indonesian and Western dishes. *9am-midnight Mon-Sat, from 5pm Sun* $

Warung Makan Barokah: This simple, wildly popular roadside place serves barbecued fish and chicken slathered in a tangy secret sauce. *4pm-midnight* $

Depot Afifah: No-nonsense local cooking a few steps from the fish market. Fresh-grilled Papuan fish served with three homemade chilli sauces. Bliss! *8am-10pm* $

Restaurant 99: This brightly lit Chinese restaurant with a funky terrace is in the heart of town and does stellar seafood. *8am-9.30pm* $$

The Baliem Valley

REMOTE VILLAGES | PAPUAN CULTURE | MOUNTAIN TREKKING

TOP TIP

Foreigners landing in Wamena will need to head directly to the *polresta* (police station) to get a stamp on their original *surat jalan* (p439). Be sure to also bring a copy of your *surat jalan* travel permit; and passport photo page. The procedure should only take a few minutes and there should be no fee.

The legendary Baliem Valley is the most accessible destination in Papua's interior. It's also a gateway to another world. The Dani people who live here had almost no contact with the outside word until the mid-20th century, when change came at a rapid rate as Dutch explorers, American anthropologists, German missionaries and Indonesian migrants arrived in waves. Dani life has changed enormously as a consequence. And yet, the valley and its surrounding highlands remain an area where tradition reigns supreme. Trekking here transports you to a world filled with experiences to be savoured.

The valley's portal is Wamena, a sprawling, mainstream Indonesian creation. The tallest structure is a 50m-high cross, while the top attractions are bustling markets. But travellers spend little time in Wamena, with the charm of the highlands lying in the mountains beyond, which are dotted with tidy Dani villages, some of which display their mummified ancestors.

Where Is Your Gourd?

Exploring Wamena's traditional markets and shops

If Wamena is where Indonesia comes to the Baliem Valley – most businesses in town are owned by non-Papuans – the

GETTING AROUND

Despite its relative isolation, Wamena is well connected to Jayapura via several daily flights. Onward journeys to small highland airstrips are typically purchased on the spot through missionary airlines such as AMA or MAF. Overcrowded bemos (minibuses) head out along the main roads from Wamena, departing from scattered terminals adjacent to the markets of Jibama, Sinakma and Misi; most run until about 3pm and leave when full. Fares depend on the distance. For trips within town, *ojek* (motorbike taxis) and becak (bicycle-rickshaws) charge between 10,000Rp and 25,000Rp. You can charter a vehicle for out-of-town trips to the trailhead in Sogokmo (from 600,000Rp) or Jiwika (from 800,000Rp).

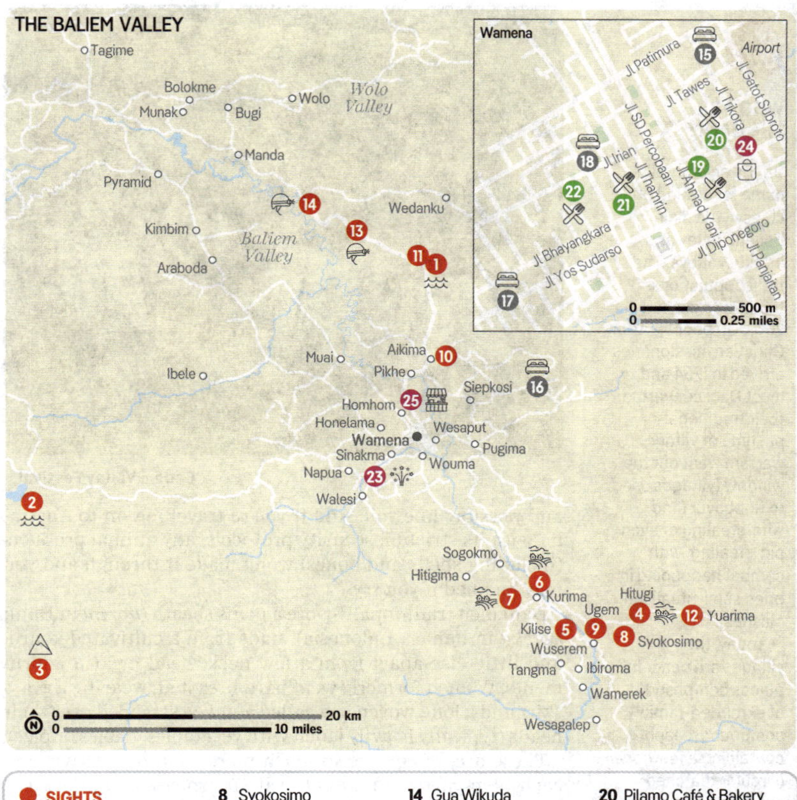

SIGHTS
1 Air Garam
2 Danau Habbema
3 Gunung Trikora
4 Hitugi
5 Kilise
see 10 Pasir Putih Wamena
6 Seima
7 Sogokmo Atas
8 Syokosimo
9 Ugem
10 Werapak Elosak Mummy
11 Wimontok Mabel Mummy
12 Yuarima

ACTIVITIES
13 Gua Kotilola
14 Gua Wikuda

SLEEPING
15 Baliem Pilamo Hotel
16 Baliem Valley Resort
17 Pintu Biru Hostel
18 Putri Dani Hotel

EATING
19 An Meke Coffee Roastery & Art Studio
20 Pilamo Café & Bakery
21 Rumah Makan Fakhira
22 Schop

ENTERTAINMENT
23 Baliem Valley Festival

SHOPPING
24 Koteka Art Shop
25 Pasar Jibama

markets are where rural Papua takes over the city. A morning spent in the city's markets is easily the best thing you can do in Wamena.

The Dani are experts in the art of **body adornment**. Handicrafts found across the Baliem Valley include necklaces, pectorals, armbands and nose piercings made from pig tusks, cowrie shells, bones, carved stone or feathers. Many of the assorted head decorations are made of cassowary or bird-of-paradise feathers and should be avoided. Not only is it pushing these creatures closer to extinction, but trade in such items is illegal and airport customs will confiscate them

WHO ARE THE DANI?

Dani is an umbrella name for around 30 clans in the main Baliem Valley and its side valleys. The total population is thought to exceed 200,000 people. After Christian missionaries arrived in 1954 and most Dani converted, their traditional pastime of village warfare went out the window (villages used to fight over land, wife-stealing or even pig-stealing, with combat happening in brief, semi-ritualised clashes).

Today, the villages are peaceful places composed of extended-family compounds, each containing a few *honai* (circular thatched huts). Many Dani are polygamous, with men having several wives. Families gather together over an open flame each evening in a standalone grass-floored kitchen, with nearly every meal featuring plain, steamed sweet potatoes or stewed sweet-potato leaves.

TANYA KEISHA/SHUTTERSTOCK

Baliem Valley Festival

and possibly fine you. And if you're travelling on to Australia with its strict biosecurity protocols, any animal products (including shells and bones) won't make it through and you may be fined if you try.

Dani men traditionally wore a penis sheath (*horim* in Dani; *koteka* in Bahasa Indonesia) made from a cultivated gourd, and little else apart from a few neck, head or arm adornments. Women formerly went bare-breasted, wearing a grass skirt and a long woven bag called a *noken* strapped over their heads (typically heavily laden with vegetables, babies or pigs).

These are, of course, so much more than decorative, and each item carries great cultural and spiritual significance. *Koteka* are still worn for ceremonies, while *noken*, made from shredded tree bark rolled into thread, remain widely used, particularly in rural villages. It's in the markets that you'll come across many of these items for sale, and maybe even a few traditionally clothed Dani. Don't just stare and take pictures, try and strike up a conversation. There's usually someone around who can help translate.

Most markets in town are quite small, but **Pasar Jibama**, about 2km north of Wamena, is a terrific place to shop for traditional crafts and immerse yourself in local life. In neat rows beneath open-sided shelters, colourful piles of fruits and vegetables – such as taro, wax gourds, pandanus and sweet passion fruit – share display space with slippery river fish and pens filled with pigs. Although quite orderly by the standards of city markets, it's a sensory overload and a place where shouts get louder and tropical smells get stronger the longer the day goes on.

The traditional artefact and craft section is quite small, but there's still plenty to choose from. A few stalls do sell *koteka* penis gourds In the same area, look for stalls selling traditional medicine. And a final word of warning: pickpockets operate throughout the market, but they're especially drawn to wherever tourists gather.

Pasar Misi, in the south of Wamena, is a similar deal with perhaps more stalls out in the open, but otherwise the same mix of local produce, fresh fish and meat, and a few traditional stalls.

More artefacts from the Baliem Valley – as well as Asmat, Korowai and PNG – can be found at a collection of shops along Jl Trikora. The best of the bunch is **Koteka Art Shop**, which has Asmat woodcarvings, Sentani bark paintings, PNG masks and, of course, *koteka*, the most popular souvenir around. Prices vary according to the size, materials and your negotiating skills.

Go Hog Wild!

The traditional pig feast

Kumugima and Obia, just north of Wamena, are among the villages where traditional **Dani pig feasts** and colourful **warrior dances** based on ritual warfare are sometimes staged for tourists. They should be requested a day or two in advance. Normally held for weddings, funerals and other important occasions, pig feasts are massive events that involve the participation of an entire community.

The meal begins with a big bonfire to heat the cooking stones. When piping hot, they're placed into an earthen hole, which is lined with leaves and branches. Vegetables such as sweet potatoes, taro and wax gourds go in first, followed by another layer of leaves and stones. This creates a steamy bed for the pig, which is ceremonially sacrificed and splayed on top. The giant mound is sealed shut with a carpet of grass for one hour. When smoke billows into a thick cloud, the feast is ready.

You'll enjoy a much more authentic experience if you're able to attend a traditional local wedding, but, failing that, this is a worthwhile alternative. Be aware, of course, that this is not for the faint-hearted – a live pig will be killed in front of you.

Most Papuan tour companies can make the necessary arrangements, or ask your hotel to see if there's one already taking place.

BALIEM VALLEY FESTIVAL

This three-day festival, held during the second week of August, features pig feasts, pig racing, spear throwing and Dani music on instruments such as the *pikon* (a kind of mouth harp). The highlight is mock tribal fighting where village men dress up in full regalia and reenact old-time battles and their accompanying rituals.

Nearby tribes such as the Yali and Lani participate, too (the Lani stage a similar festival in November). Hotels book up well in advance for these dates. The spectacle can be interesting, though it feels a bit voyeuristic and even exploitative at times, with tourists chasing after performers for photographs. Visiting the Dani in their villages is a far more authentic and rewarding experience.

EATING & DRINKING IN WAMENA: OUR PICKS

Pilamo Café & Bakery: A long menu of Indonesian classics, plus pool tables, karaoke and a bakery. *8am-11pm Tue-Sat, 5pm-midnight Sun, noon-11am Mon* $

Rumah Makan Fakhira: Come for the best *ayam bakar* (grilled chicken) in town, or, of all things, Turkish kebabs. *8am-9pm Mon-Sat* $

An Meke Coffee Roastery & Art Studio: An Meke does great coffee, Indonesian snacks and light meals. Art too. *1-7pm Mon-Sat* $

Schop: Wamena's flashiest restaurant, with a faux Japanese garden, and coffee, noodles and nasi goreng. Occasional live music. *9.30am-9pm Mon-Sat, 5-9pm Sun* $$

MISSIONARY AIRLINES

The only way to reach many towns in the Papuan interior is via missionary-run airlines such as **AMA** *(Associated Mission Aviation; amapapua.com)* and **MAF** *(Missionary Aviation Fellowship; maf.org)*. They both fly small propeller planes to highland airstrips. While their focus is not tourism, they will occasionally carry travellers when seats become available. Some, such as AMA, will also allow you to charter flights. Common destinations with airstrips handy to trekkers include Angguruk, Pronggoli, Kosarek and Walerek.

Another option for remote airstrips is **Susi Air** *(susiair.com)*, which has the widest flight network in Papua and prides itself on 'reaching the unreachable'. Its planes are also available for charter flights.

Go in Search of Old Mummies

Visit the local ancestors

The northeastern Baliem Valley is great day-tripping terrain, with scenic hiking, many caves and traditional villages where the Dani preserve the corpses of notable ancestors with smoke in order to retain some of their power.

The supposedly 300-year-old **Werapak Elosak mummy** in Aikima, 8km from Wamena, is the easiest to reach. But the most celebrated – and best preserved – is **Wimontok Mabel mummy**, kept at the tiny settlement of Sumpaima, 300m north of Jiwika (look for the black 'Mummy' sign about 17km from Wamena). Just before entering the village, you'll find a small military checkpoint, where you must show your *surat jalan*.

Wimontok Mable was a powerful 18th-century chief. You can view his blackened corpse for 220,000Rp, though you can try bargaining that down a bit. Many women in this community are missing the tips of their fingers, which they've battered and amputated with rocks as an act of grieving, typically following the death of a close relative. Several older men still wear *koteka*, and women will often change into traditional clothes and bring out handicrafts when visitors arrive. Here, as elsewhere, it's important to ask permission before taking photos. Expect to pay 10,000Rp per shot.

The women of Sumpaima also act as **guides** *(200,000Rp)* for the one-hour hike up a steep path to **Air Garam**, a group of saltwater wells. There, they'll demonstrate how they soak sections of banana trunks in the water before drying and burning them to use the resulting ashes as salt.

Explore the Caves & Sand Dunes of Northeast Bailem

Experience Baliem's natural wonders

Heading north from Jiwika, the road is flanked by imposing rocky hills where you'll find **Gua Kotilola** and **Gua Wikuda**, two of the area's myriad caverns. The latter is more impressive and said to be several kilometres long, though you're only allowed to access the first 100m, which has a few stalagmites and stalactites. Ask for the lights to be turned on!

The other natural attraction worth visiting is **Pasir Putih Wamena**, a stretch of white sand dunes near Aikima that mark the remnants of a dried-up lake. The area is one of the most popular spots near Wamena for a half-day hike.

CHRIS PIASON/SHUTTERSTOCK

Wimontok Mabel mummy, Sumpaima

A Lake in the Clouds

Exploring the northwestern Baliem Valley

The western side of the Baliem Valley is less scenic than the eastern. The best reason to travel here is **Danau Habbema**, a lovely lake 45km west of Wamena. It sits amid grasslands at about 3320m in altitude, with dramatic snowcapped mountains in view – Gunung Trikora (4750m) rises to the south. The surrounding alpine ecosystem of dwarf cypresses and rhododendrons is a big draw for nature lovers.

A chartered car with driver will cost about 2,500,000Rp from Wamena. The drive is about 1½ hours each way on a mostly paved road, passing a military checkpoint 7km outside Wamena at Napua; have your *surat jalan* ready. Alternatively, you can drive there and trek back for three days through cloud forests along the Kali Ibele, hiring a guide in Wamena to coordinate logistics. The usual route, starting from the lake, is via Yobogima (a forest clearing) and then through a spectacular gorge to Daela village and on to Pilia and Ibele.

Check the current political situation before setting off. At the time of research, the lake was occasionally off limits to foreigners due to OPM activity (p438).

BEST PAPUAN TRAVEL AGENCIES

Papua Explorer: German-run outfit specialising in high-end adventure trips to Carstensz Pyramid, Asmat and similarly remote locales. *(papua-explorer.com)*

Papua Expeditions: Big on birding, this multilingual Sorong-based outfit is great for West Papua destinations plus Wasur. *(bird-watching-papua-adventure-travel.com)*

Travel Papua: In Manokwari, with custom ecotourism trips to Nabire, Arfak, Korowai, Raja Ampat and more. *(travelpapua.com)*

Papua Jaya Tours: Based in Jayapura, Antoni Sitepu is well versed in the ways of the Baliem Valley, Korowai and Yali. *(papuajayatours.com)*

Papua Travel Guide: Welly Manufandu, the only female Papuan guide, runs backpacker trips around Baliem Valley, Asmat, Korowai and Sentani (her home base). *(papua-travelguide.com)*

Honai **(circular thatched huts)**

TOP EXPERIENCE

Hiking the Southern Baliem Valley

South of Wamena, the Baliem Valley narrows and the Kali Baliem (Baliem River) becomes a ferocious torrent. For hikers, this southern stretch is the most popular and most scenic destination. Over the course of four days, you'll climb narrow rainforest trails, cross rivers on wobbly hanging footbridges and traverse hillsides where the only sounds are birds, wind and the water far below.

DON'T MISS

- Sogokmo Atas
- Kilise
- Sleeping in a *honai*
- Hanging bridge at Yuarima
- Terraced fields
- Syokosimo
- Seima

What to Expect

There's no official trekking route here, nor are there signposts. Think of it more as a labyrinth of local paths linking disparate villages. While it's possible to hike the Baliem Valley on your own, you'd need to have a good grasp of Bahasa Indonesia to negotiate sleeping arrangements, understand local customs and access traditional grass-floored kitchens, not to mention find your way on the faint, splintering trails. It would be very easy to get very lost if trekking alone. In other words: get a guide!

As you go, you'll share sweet potatoes and shake many hands in customary greeting with the Dani. Many villages have some kind of homestay, be it a *honai* (circular thatched hut), church hall or teacher's home. Prices are generally fixed at 150,000Rp per person, with an additional 50,000Rp for firewood and 50,000Rp to use the grass-floored kitchens.

Day One

A standard four-day, three-night trek begins at **Sogokmo Atas**, 15km southeast of Wamena, near the Kali Yetni, a small tributary of the Baliem, which spills down wooded hills. Cross the wooden bridge over the stream and climb to Yilino, the first traditional village, with a scattering of *honai* (circular thatched huts) . You'll climb 10km from here to a big white church at the entrance to **Kilise**, a tidy village of stone walls and lush gardens with a privileged view over the Baliem Valley. Stay in the homestay here run by the local pastor, where you'll sleep in a *honai* surrounded by fruit trees.

Day Two

This is a demanding 17km trek, but it begins with a gentle descent to the Kali Baliem. Here you'll find the first of many scary hanging bridges to come; always check each one carefully. There's a long woodsy climb from here following the Kali Mugi into the easterly Mugi Valley. The taxing uphill slog ends in the town of **Hitugi**, where you head downhill into a valley covered with wiry trees. Cross the hanging bridge back over the Mugi at **Yuarima** and sleep at the caretaker's house next to the church.

Day Three

Begin on the valley floor, hiking through a muggy, fern-filled forest along a thin, slippery path. Don't rush: hikers have died slipping from muddy trails into the river below. After about an hour, you'll rise through terraced fields of sweet potato to a sweeping Mugi Valley viewpoint in the quaint *honai*-dotted village of **Syokosimo**. It's a steep, winding and sometimes slippery plummet from here back to the Mugi, which you'll cross on another hanging bridge before ascending on the far side to **Ugem**, returning to the Baliem Valley after 13km of trekking. Sleep in the bare church hall.

Day Four

A relative breeze with just 12km of mostly downhill walking. The wide-open views of the Baliem Valley as you descend to the village of **Seima** are truly breathtaking. Looking west, you'll be able to see where you started trekking several days ago as you wind through terraced farmland. After crossing the frothy, angry Baliem on a final hanging bridge, you'll rise up to the tarmac road at Sogokmo, where you can catch transport back to Wamena.

WHAT'S INCLUDED?

For exploring Baliem and beyond, always keep a careful eye on what's included in any trekking expedition (typically all ground transport, meals, homestays, guiding fees and side activities, as well as porters or cooks). Get the details in writing! It's common to pay the majority of the fee upfront; many guides don't have money in the bank to front costs on their own.

TOP TIPS

- BYO sleeping bags and travel pillows if you've concerns about hygiene and comfort.
- Beyond your standard hiking clothes, remember a sweatshirt or fleece, sun hat and rain jacket.
- Useful gear includes: trekking poles, torch, portable power bank (there's little electricity here), filtered water bottle (you'll be refilling from streams) and a good book (evenings are long).
- Bring your own food from Wamena.
- Expect to pay between 250,000Rp and 750,000Rp per day for a guide.

Beyond The Baliem Valley

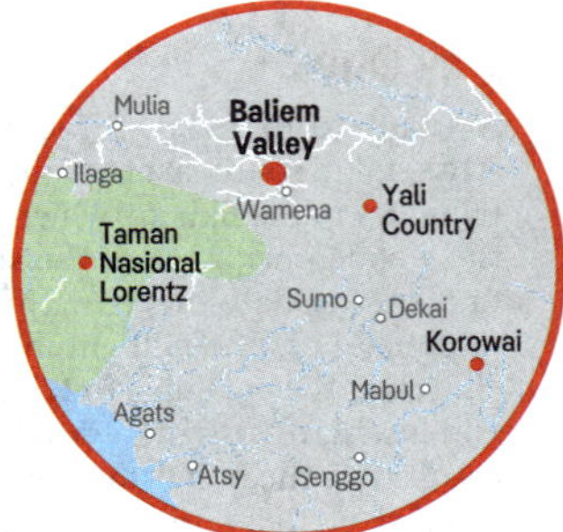

Welcome to the wilderness, where wobbly wooden treehouses, frothing rivers and craggy peaks cradling rare equatorial glaciers beckon trekkers into the mountainous hinterland.

Places

GETTING AROUND

Reaching these areas often means chartering small planes to remote airstrips and/or travelling vast distances up wild rivers. You will absolutely need a guide for Korowai and the peaks of Taman Nasional Lorentz. Guides are strongly recommended for Yali country, too. Whether you find a Wamena-based guide or book a specialised tour with a Papua travel company (p449), expect prices to be in the thousands of dollars. As always, the larger your group size, the cheaper it becomes per person.

The Papuan highlands beyond the Baliem Valley rank among the most remote places on earth. And that, of course, is precisely the allure for those who make the considerable effort to visit. Daring mountaineers go crazy thinking about the challenges – both physical and logistical – of attempting Carstensz Pyramid (Puncak Jaya), Oceania's highest peak. Meanwhile, the muggy jungles that are home to the Yali and Korowai attract those as eager for intense tropical hikes as they are for powerful cultural immersion. To visit this area is to leave all modern conveniences behind. These are, after all, lands of raw natural wonder and time-honoured traditions. Travel here isn't quick or cheap, but for the willing and able it can be a priceless experience.

Taman Nasional Lorentz

TIME FROM THE BALIEM VALLEY: **FROM 1½HR**

Oceania's highest peaks

Papua is home to Oceania's tallest summits, including the granddaddy of them all – 4884m **Carstensz Pyramid** (Puncak Jaya) – as well as the nearby **Sumantri** (4870m) and **Gunung Trikora** (4750m). Remarkably, given its near-equatorial location, Carstensz Pyramid has several rapidly retreating glaciers on its slopes. The Sudirman Range is the highest point on earth between the Himalayas and the Andes, and its peaks are frequently dusted in snow, which is quite the sight when you're sweating in the steaming jungle and looking up.

Climbing Gunung Trikora is possible from Danau Habbema (p449; 45km west of Wamena), but requires several nights of camping at high, cold altitudes, along with a stash of permits and the services of a recognised Indonesian tour company.

As always in Papua's remote highlands, security is often an issue due to political instability and violence. This is why

Carstensz Pyramid

Carstensz Pyramid is the least climbed of the world's famed Seven Summits (the highest peaks on each continent). When the situation deteriorates, the only safe way to reach the summit is to take a helicopter to the Yellow Valley base camp from Timika, bypassing the troubled regions normally navigated on foot. Beyond that, a high level of fitness, lots of preparation and solid mountaineering skills are required.

Summit Carstensz *(summitcarstensz.com)* is a reliable Timika-based specialist that's been organising expeditions since the 1990s.

TIMIKA & THE GRASBERG MINE

Timika is a fast-growing city that sees few travellers beyond those headed to Carstensz Pyramid. Its existence is largely tied to the Grasberg Mine, which has the world's largest recoverable lodes of gold and copper. The mine is co-owned by Freeport-McMoRan, Rio Tinto and the Indonesian government, whose police and army form part of the security force. Grasberg makes billions of dollars in annual profits, yet very little of it reaches the local Papuan population. This has been a regular source of friction since the 1970s, when the first violent clashes took place. Installations and workers were frequent targets of OPM-attributed attacks in the early 2020s. The reaction from the Indonesian government has usually been swift and heavy handed.

Yali Country

TIME FROM THE BALIEM VALLEY: **2 DAYS**

The lesser-trekked highlands and traditional Yali culture

Over the Baliem Valley's eastern walls lies the stunningly situated home of the **Yali people**. Only contacted in the 1960s the Yali are one of the more traditional highland peoples. Although many villagers have taken to shorts and T-shirts, older men may still be seen in 'skirts' of rattan hoops, with penis gourds protruding from underneath. Missionaries provide much of the infrastructure, such as schools and transport. But traditions remain strong among the Yali, and if you were looking for immersion into one of the last and most remote hunter-gatherer forest societies on earth, Yali is the kind of place you'll want to mount an expedition.

Yali country is a great destination for adventurous trekkers with time to explore. The most popular trek runs from Sogokmo to Ugem in the Baliem Valley (p451) up the Mugi Valley, over a 3500m pass near Gunung Elit with at least one night (often two) camping, then down to Abiyangge, Piliam and Pronggoli in Yali country. There are long, steep ascents, and the upper reaches over Gunung Elit involve climbing up and down several rustic wooden ladders (check they're

HARVESTING SAGO

Perhaps the most impressive endeavour of the Korowai (other than treehouse building) is sago harvesting. This laborious process begins with clan members chopping down a large palm tree with a stone axe, then splitting open the core and beating it to a pulp with stone tools while entertaining each other with traditional songs. Next, they use river water to send the material through a natural filtration system constructed entirely of palm-tree parts, which separates a nutritious starch that can feed a family for weeks. The task takes the better part of a day and is often undertaken mainly by women.

operational before setting off). It takes another one or two days from Pronggoli to **Angguruk**, the biggest Yali village, which has a large market.

We *strongly* recommend that you visit the region as part of a guided tour organised by a reputable tour operator. They'll help you negotiate logistics, advise you on the security situation and provide invaluable language interpreting and explanations about the various practices you'll encounter. Travel Papua (p449) runs an 11-day Yali Valley Tour.

If you do end up going it alone, village stays are basic and cost 150,000Rp per person per night. Angguruk is the most developed village and has a good guesthouse. Other villages put travellers up in *honai* (circular thatched huts), schoolhouses and other suitable structures. From Angguruk, you can hike back or wait for a seat on a missionary airline departing from the small airstrip. Either way, it's highly recommended to hire a guide in Wamena, who can also arrange a porter to carry food and supplies.

Korowai

TIME FROM THE BALIEM VALLEY: **45MIN** + **8HR**

Disappear into another world

Southeast of Wamena, amid a maze of rivers flowing south from the highlands, live the Korowai people, semi-nomads and architects of towering treehouses that historically protected them from animals, enemies, floods, mosquitoes and evil spirits. The Korowai weren't contacted by missionaries until the late 1970s, and though many have since settled in villages of ground-level homes, a few still live their traditional way of life.

Many Papua-based companies and guides offer trips to the area, starting in the Indonesian-built settlement of **Mabul**, eight hours upriver from the airport in Dekai. An organised tour of about 10 days is, for all intents and purposes, the only feasible way of visiting. Depending on group size, you're looking at between US$1500 and US$2000 per person, with just over half your time in Korowai territory. Papua Explorer (p449) has a range of tours through Korowai country.

Cultural immersion here goes as deep as you want it to go, and bold travellers are welcomed to climb into the highest treehouses and pitch tents inside them. (Note that at least one visitor has died falling from a precarious ladder, as have many locals). Most villages also offer lower treehouse options and huts on stilts. Expect lots of hiking through the hot, humid jungle. Crafts, including prized dog-tooth necklaces, giant carved shields and stone tools, should be on sale along the way, while villagers will typically demonstrate traditional activities such as fish poisoning, trap building and sago harvesting. Don't forget to try the wiggly sago worms! Although these grubs are often eaten raw, women also roast them over an open fire.

Wasur National Park

BIRDS OF PARADISE | FOREST HIKES | WALLABIES

The 4130-sq-km Wasur National Park will fascinate anyone with an interest in birds and marsupials. Part of the Trans-Fly biome straddling the Indonesia–PNG border, it's more similar in appearance to Far North Queensland than it is to Raja Ampat. Here, instead of a rolling tropical jungle, you'll find low-lying savannah, swamps, dry forests and slow-moving rivers that inundate much of the land during the wet season. This little slice of the Australian bush marooned in eastern Indonesia even houses wallabies and tree kangaroos, though illegal hunting means numbers are falling. Few foreigners make it here. Those who do are mostly birders in search of colourful kookaburras, prehistoric-looking cassowaries and fanciful birds of paradise. Wasur is also known for its giant termite mounds, which rise like earthen sculptures up to 5m in height. The park lies just 20km east of the provincial capital Merauke, making it less remote than it might initially seem.

Kangaroo, Wasur National Park (p456)

TIRTA SUJATA/SHUTTERSTOCK

GETTING AROUND

All trips to Wasur begin in Merauke, which receives flights from Jayapura and Jakarta (with a stopover in Makassar). Those with extra time and patience can arrive via biweekly Pelni ferries from Sorong via Agats. Once in Merauke, hire a car or *ojek* (motorbike taxi) to take you to the park, paying a minimum of 1,000,000Rp for the day. You can hire cars with drivers on your own at the airport, but securing a guide in advance is crucial for spotting wildlife and arranging park accommodation. Tours are more expensive but simplify things to no end.

TOP TIP

Wasur experiences a strong annual monsoon season, when most tracks become impassable. Make sure to time your visit for the later part of the dry season (mid-July to November), when there are fewer mosquitoes and more chances of spotting wildlife while hiking atop solid ground.

Kangaroos, Wallabies & Birds of Paradise

Watching wildlife in Wasur

Imagine hiking through the bush, when suddenly, you see a wallaby. It's only after a few moments that it registers: you're in Indonesia, not Australia. Few people realise that wallabies and tree kangaroos live beyond Australia's shores, and the chance of seeing them in Indonesia is reason enough to make the effort to reach Wasur.

But let's start with the birds. Wasur National Park has 114 species of birds, a remarkable 74 of which are endemic. And none of Wasur's bird species are more sought-after than the birds of paradise. The greater, king and red bird of paradise all live here, and can, of course, be seen performing elaborate courtship dances each morning at favoured grounds such as **Agrindo**, 90km north of Merauke, and **Kokoyam**, 90km east of Merauke. No less wowing are the crowned pigeons, mound-building scrubfowl and large flightless cassowaries. The cassowaries in particular are quite the prize, but never get too close to one if you're on foot.

Then there are the kangaroos and wallabies, which join nocturnal marsupials such as cuscuses and sugar gliders. The two main wallaby species are the agile wallaby (also present across the water in Australia) and the Papuan forest wallaby. A handful of Papua's endemic tree kangaroo species are found in the park as well.

Wasur's southern part is best for wildlife spotting as it has more open grasslands and coastal areas. Prime spots include **Rawa Biru**, an indigenous village 45km east of Merauke, where you can sleep in local houses for 150,000Rp per person. From Rawa Biru, it's a two- to three-hour walk to Prem, which has a small savannah surrounded by water. There's a good chance of seeing wallabies and waterbirds here.

There's an information centre at the park entrance, where you pay a 150,000Rp per-day park fee. Inside, there are three basic government-run shelters in which you can sleep, with advance notice, for 200,000Rp. The closest one is just a few kilometres past the park entrance at **Biras**, where there are also picnic facilities and a 'representative forest' – actually a large wildlife enclosure with cassowaries.

Dusty workaday Merauke is your staging ground for any visit. Jl Raya Mandala is Merauke's main street, home to most hotels, restaurants and shops, while **Pantai Lampu Satu** is a lively beach where residents gather to watch the sun plunge into the ocean.

Bony Kondahon *(bonykondahon70@gmail.com)* is an excellent English-speaking local guide who can help arrange tours. He charges about 750,000Rp per day for guiding and cooking and can set up overnight stays in tents or park shelters.

DIY: THE ASMAT REGION

The Asmat region to the northwest of Merauke is a massive, remote, low-lying area of muddy, snaking rivers, mangrove forests and tidal swamps, where many villages are built entirely on stilts.

The Asmat people, formerly feared for their headhunting and cannibalism, are now mostly celebrated for their woodcarvings, which are among the most prized of Papuan arts. Works are best viewed at the **Museum Kebudayaan dan Kemajuan Asmat** *(asmatmuseum.org)* or the **Asmat Queen Art Shop**, both in the regional capital of Agats.

Asmat is a fascinating area to explore, but requires time, money and patience. Most visitors boat along the jungle-lined rivers to different villages, buying artefacts and watching traditional performances. Papua Explorer (p449) offer tours here.

Places We Love to Stay

$ Budget $$ Midrange $$$ Top End

Raja Ampat

MAP p422

Batanta

Batanta Diving Homestay $ Great food, engaged hosts, clean rooms and an amazing house reef with dugongs and manta rays. A favourite on remote Batanta.

Biryei Homestay $ One of the few homestays at this price point with en-suite bathrooms, this Batanta hideaway is as great for birding as it is snorkelling.

Arborek

Kalabia Homestay $ The mattresses could be comfier, but this homestay on Arborek's north shore is otherwise well liked, with sturdy overwater bungalows and sweeping views.

Waigeo

Sandy Guesthouse $$ Husna, the owner of this basic guesthouse in Waisai, works for the tourism board and can set up all kinds of unique Waigeo experiences. Rooms lack the romance of sleeping over the water.

PapuArts Alter-Native Stay $$ Yes, there are the obligatory overwater bungalows, but what really makes this Waigeo midranger stand out is the exquisite food, exceptional cleanliness and surprise sunset treats.

Hamueco Dive Resort $$ While 'resort' is a stretch, these overwater en-suite bungalows with air-con are well priced and serene, despite being a 15-minute drive from Waisai.

Raja Ampat Eco Lodge $$$ This secluded, sustainably minded Waigeo lodge runs bird-watching trips, has hookah diving and paddleboarding, and makes delicious food sourced from an on-site permaculture garden.

Kri

Turtle Homestay $$ Tidy private bungalows on Kri's quieter southern shore with proper beds, en-suite bathrooms and access to an excellent house reef.

Daroyen Village $$ These overwater bungalows on Kri are well liked, with hammocks on the balconies.

Sorido Bay Resort $$$ Luxurious beachfront bungalows filled with Papuan art. The owners practically pioneered diving here and place a strong focus on conservation.

Gam

Avinsea Homestay $ This hideaway with overwater bungalows on Gam's Tanjung Putus gets rave reviews for food, location and its hosts' attentiveness.

Raja Ampat Biodiversity $$$ Excellent value for money at this upmarket beachfront resort on Gam, which caters equally to divers and those wanting to snorkel, kayak or go birding.

Raja4Divers $$$ This classy dive resort, whose rooms enchant with fine Papuan art, lies on a palm-fringed beach on Pulau Pef off western Gam.

Misool

Nut Tonton Homestay $$ One of the few homestays off Misool's stunning southeastern coastline. Its overwater bungalows are on a limestone island and have air-con and evening electricity.

Misool Resort $$$ This private island dive resort is the standard bearer for luxury, with speedboat transfers, farm-fresh meals, aromatherapy massages and dreamy overwater or beach-facing villas.

Yeben

Cove Eco Resort $$$ On a private island not far from Piaynemo, Cove is a nicely priced resort with a variety of five- to 14-night packages catering to either divers or snorkel adventurers.

Sorong & Manokwari

Favehotel $$ Rooms here are about the same quality as other airport hotels, but half the price and with more colour and flair.

Mansinam Beach Hotel $$ The best deal in town, with pricier (though still quite affordable) 3rd-floor rooms offering views over Pulau Mansinam. Standard lower-level rooms are less appealing.

Amban Beach House $$ This surf lodge on Pantai Amban, run by Travel Papua (p449), is the area's most serene accommodation. Three tasteful rooms with air-con and cold showers.

Jayapura

MAP p435

Hotel Jasmine $ The hallways are a bit wonky and the rooms slightly tired, but Jasmine nevertheless has an appealing old-school charm and a convenient city-centre location.

FOX Hotel Jayapura $$ Sure, it has spotless rooms, great service and a rooftop bar, but FOX stands out most for its fun, flashy, creative design.

ASTON Jayapura Hotel $$ This polished hotel from a local chain ticks all the right boxes, with a solid gym, pool, spa and international restaurant.

Sentani

MAP p435

Unique Hotel $ For convenience and price, this cheery but basic option on the airport road is perfectly adequate. Has air-con rooms and cold showers.

Horex Hotel Sentani $$ Affordable business hotel that's walking distance from the airport, with large and immaculate rooms, comfy king beds and 24-hour room service.

Suni Garden Lake Hotel & Resort $$ The rooms aren't perfect, but the manicured grounds sure are charming at this well-priced upmarket retreat set around a giant pool.

Biak

MAP p441

Padaido Hotel $$ A hidden delight down an unassuming alley. Five cheery and affordable marine-themed rooms overlooking a pretty harbour.

Asana Biak Papua $$ Brimming with history, yet showing its age, this sprawling oceanfront property shines brightest with its rich Papuan decor and sunset-aligned infinity pool.

Nirmala Biak Beach Hotel $$ Exceptionally clean rooms and four spacious cottages perch above the sea at this dive-focused hotel, which doubles as a yacht club.

Wamena & the Baliem Valley

MAP p445

Pintu Biru Hostel $ This rare Papuan hostel is exactly what onward hikers crave: knowledgeable English-speaking hosts, good breakfasts (especially the coffee) and a cheery vibe.

Putri Dani Hotel $$ Most rooms at this small, family-run inn surround a tranquil Japanese garden. It's at the cheaper end of Wamena's overpriced hotel scene.

Baliem Pilamo Hotel $$ Room quality varies widely by price point, but this remains the hotel of choice for most travellers, with some Papuan personality and leafy grounds.

Baliem Valley Resort $$$ This stunning German-run hotel occupies a gorgeous hillside position outside Wamena. Superb cottages and one of the best collections of Papuan art on the island.

Merauke

MAP p456

Marina Hotel $ If budget is your main concern, this central no-frills option is the best deal in town. Rooms are acceptable and clean and have cold showers.

Swiss-Belhotel $$ Merauke's most stylish option, with all the business-class frills. The bar, restaurant, water pressure and wi-fi don't always reach the same heights, however.

Sorido Bay Resort, Raja Ampat

For places to stay in Sumatra, see p534

HIDJIRI AZIM/SHUTTERSTOCK

Above: Gunung Kerinci (p497); Right: Sumatran orangutan, Gunung Leuser National Park (p466)

THE MAIN AREAS

GUNUNG LEUSER NATIONAL PARK
Unforgettable sightings of Sumatran orangutans. p466

PADANG
Riverside city with a rich culinary tradition. p482

BANDA ACEH
Tsunami relics, surfing and diving. p500

Researched by
Mark Eveleigh

Sumatra

RAINFORESTS & WILDLIFE, ISLANDS AND VOLCANOES

World-class waves, magical undersea worlds, rainforests and dramatic volcanoes: welcome to Sumatra, Indonesia's largest island and one that challenges and delights.

Sumatra was beholden to the whims and demands of the Sriwijaya, the Dutch, the English and the Japanese, before Indonesia took its own bull by the horns following independence in 1945. It's not been an easy ride, as Sumatra's location on the so-called Ring of Fire has resulted in multiple catastrophic earthquakes, tsunamis and volcanic eruptions.

In many places local travellers outnumber international visitors by the hundreds and you're likely to be embraced (metaphorically) as a novelty...and (literally) as a prop for countless selfies. Indonesians are discovering what Westerners have known for decades: Sumatra is stunning and it rewards those who take the time to explore. There's still plenty to be uncovered on the island: waves that were glanced over in the past are being whispered about again, as Pulau Nias, Krui and the Mentawai Islands become more popular. National parks and protected wilderness areas require time to access but invariably delight travellers with the tenacity to plunge a little deeper into the equatorial jungles.

The people of Sumatra are as varied as the landscapes: from Muslims in Aceh to Christians in Danau Toba and from the matrilineal Minangkabau of West Sumatra to barkcloth-clad Mentawai shamans. All are united by a sense of hospitality towards visitors and by a respect and love for the wild and wondrous region they call home.

BETHANY CAITLYN/SHUTTERSTOCK

PULAU NIAS
Great waves and intriguing feudal cultures. p508

BENGKULU
Colonial history and lots of beaches. p516

PALEMBANG
South Sumatra metropolis with unforgettable markets. p522

Gunung Leuser National Park, p466

One of the world's greatest wildlife experiences and a hot spot for jungle adventures. The best place to see Sumatra's red apes in their natural habitat.

Banda Aceh, p500

Much maligned for its strict sharia laws, Aceh is unexpectedly welcoming, with spectacular marine habitats and one of the world's richest coffee cultures.

Pulau Nias, p508

Home to legendary waves, intriguing feudal cultures and magnificent traditional villages that remain largely overlooked by travellers.

PRIVATE CAR

A private car is the most convenient way to get around. It can be surprisingly affordable if you buddy up with other travellers. The ride-hailing app Grab is indispensable for shorter journeys, and also offers day-rates. Hotels and homestays can usually recommend reliable drivers.

Padang, p482

The historic riverside city that's home to *masakan Padang* cuisine is much more than just a starting point for jungle expeditions and 'surfaris' among the Mentawai Islands.

PUBLIC TRANSPORT

Overnight buses can save on hotel prices but be prepared; they're usually frigidly cold, blaring with Indonesian techno and thick with cigarette smoke (all factors that fend off driver sleepiness). Rail travel can be more appealing and is sometimes incredibly cheap (as little as €2 to travel nine hours).

PLANE

Swapping a 10-hour bus journey for a 40-min flight (often for less than €25) can bring far-flung destinations into reach. Lion Air has a reputation for delays and Susi Air flights can be complicated to book (tip a Grab driver or rider to help).

Bengkulu, p516

One of Indonesia's most appealing cities with dramatic colonial and independence-era history, endless beaches and surrounding forests.

Find Your Way

Sumatra is absolutely huge: it's the sixth-largest island in the world. You'll either have months to explore (and you'll scratch the surface) or you can focus on getting to know the highlights of one particular area well.

Plan Your Time

Travel takes time here: often the roads are terrible and the ferries are late...or don't depart at all. Decide on your absolute priority experience, then arrange the rest of your trip around it.

JOHN SEATON CALLAHAN/GETTY IMAGES

Surfing, Lagundri Bay (p508)

Five Days of Fun

- Arrive in **Medan** (p472) and head directly to a riverside homestay in lovely **Bukit Lawang** (p466). Spend the evening at a restaurant and get acquainted with delicious Sumatran cuisine, then climb out of bed at dawn to start your jungle hike. Overnight among the orangutans at a jungle camp and wake to the whooping call of gibbons. Return to town via the Sungai Bohorok (Bohorok River) on a raft of **inner tubes** (p468).

- Move on to Berastagi for a good night's sleep before a sunrise hike up **Gunung Sibayak** (p474). Head south, breaking the journey at the **Sipiso-Piso Waterfall** (p480), before reaching Samosir Island on **Danau Toba** (p476).

- Spend the morning exploring **Batak cultural sights** (p477) before catching the ferry and driving back to Medan, where you can relax at your riverside accommodation before the next day's flight.

Seasonal Highlights

Surf season is April to October and hiking is year-round. Travel to Sumatra's islands after October can be challenging, thanks to wilder weather.

MARCH

Ramadan (usually from February into March) can be a complicated time to travel, especially in Aceh and the Minangkabau areas, where eateries tend to close during the daylight hours.

MAY

Dry season kicks in, making this an ideal time for jungle trips. Thinner vegetation makes it an optimal season for spotting wildlife and birds. River travel can get tougher, however, and involve dragging canoes across rapids.

JUNE

The Krui Pro and Nias Pro surfing events lure hotshot surfers from around the world. It makes for an unforgettable spectator sport, but some surfers complain of crowded breaks.

A Fortnight of Adventure

- Head first to **Pualu Nias** (p508) to visit the fascinating fortress villages (Hiliamaetaniha is the friendliest and most appealing) with their daredevil traditional stone-jumpers. Test your own nerve at **Lagundri Bay** (p508) on one of the world's legendary surfing waves.

- Fly to **Banda Aceh** (p500), via a connection in Medan, for a few days snorkelling the pristine reefs of **Pulau Weh** (p504). From the mainland, at Banda Aceh, you can catch an overnight bus to the lovely lakeside town of **Takengon** (p507), the Gayo coffee heartland.

- Next stop is **Ketambe** (p470) to experience a 'wilder' and more adventurous **Gunung Leuser National Park** (p466) jungle trip among the orangutans and, with a lot more luck, tigers and elephants. Fly out from **Medan** (p472).

A Month-Long Island Odyssey

- From **Padang** (p482) head to **Kerinci Seblat National Park** (p497) for a camping trip at **Danau Gunung Tujuh** (p496). Move coastwards again for a jungle expedition of a different sort on **Pulau Siberut** (p488), where you can spend a few days living in one of the tribal communities.

- Take an overnight bus across the mountains to the historic city of **Bengkulu** (p516) before flying along the coast – 40 minutes in a single-prop Cessna – to **Krui** (p531) for a week of surfing and/or exploring one of Indonesia's most gorgeous coastlines.

- Make the scenic drive to **Bandar Lampung** (p529) where you can explore Chinatown and the colourful fish market before taking the nine-hour train ride – an unbelievable value at less than €2 – up to **Palembang** (p522) for your flight back home via Jakarta.

AUGUST

This is high season so pre-book accommodation and treks. While prices can be higher, bear in mind that this can also be a great time for solo travellers to join existing tours at reduced costs.

OCTOBER

Fruit season is a highlight of the calendar for humans and orangutans alike. Local people converge on Bukit Lawang to watch the apes... and also to consume the famous highland durians.

NOVEMBER

The start of the rainy season is also the peak month for rafflesia blooming – although the world's biggest bloom occurs pretty much year-round. Accommodation is still widely available.

DECEMBER

Banda Aceh's local beaches are good for surfing, while nearby Pulau Weh is ideal for diving year-round.

Gunung Leuser National Park

JUNGLE TREKKING | WILDLIFE SPOTTING | RIVER TUBING

GETTING AROUND

Bukit Lawang and Ketambe are homestay heavy. Bukit Lawang's popular places are on either side of the river, but vehicles other than motorbikes can't access most riverside accommodation. Instead, you're dropped off at the edge of town at the carpark, where you'll probably meet what Bukit Lawang villagers refer to as 'hunter guides'. The town has its share of excellent guides...but these opportunists are probably the least reliable. Instead book recommended accommodation (and perhaps your trek) in advance – in which case the homestay will usually send a member of staff to escort you.

Gunung Leuser National Park spans 2.6 million hectares of lowland rainforests, peat swamps, montane and coastal forests, and alpine meadows in North Sumatra and Aceh. This is the only place in the world where you can see Sumatran orangutans, rhinoceroses, tigers and forest elephants in the wild.

Spend a day or two at the lovely riverside town of Bukit Lawang – the gateway to the park – and you're almost guaranteed to have excellent sightings of Sumatra's great red ape. Ketambe (in Aceh) is harder to reach but offers wilder and less crowded trekking. Hikers who take the challenge of a guided hike between Bukit Lawang and Ketambe may encounter elephants (and, very occasionally, even tigers).

Leuser, Kerinci Seblat National Park and Bukit Barisan Selatan National Park (the three parks that make up the UNESCO Tropical Rainforest Heritage of Sumatra site) are all under threat from oil-palm plantations and poaching.

Go Hiking in Bukit Lawang

Search for orangutans in the rainforest

The forests around Bukit Lawang are home to the densest population of wild Sumatran orangutans on the planet. While there's no such thing as guaranteed sightings, experienced guides are almost certain to be able to locate at least one or two within a relatively short distance of the park entrance. The feeding platforms that were part of the rehabilitation programme here have long since been removed, but the great red apes (who can live to about 40 years old) have a long memory and are familiar with the fruiting trees near the town.

Seeing an orangutan in the wild is truly awe-inspiring, whether it's an intimidatingly powerful alpha male, with cheek flanges like rusty satellite dishes, or a nursing mother with a cute baby. Since orangutan offspring stay with their mothers for up to eight years, it's relatively common to see these famously 'solitary' apes in pairs.

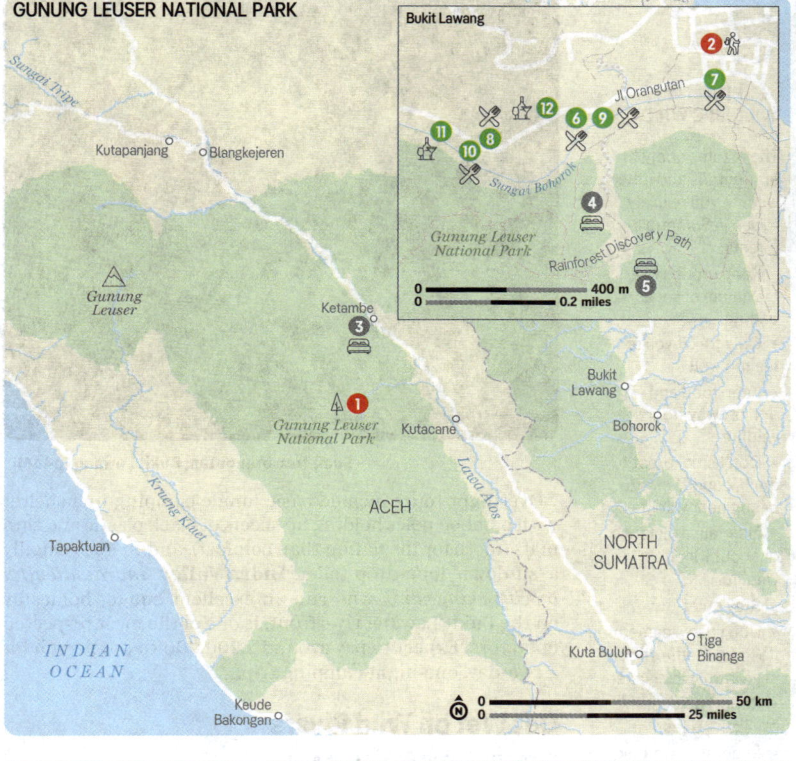

SIGHTS
1 Gunung Leuser National Park

ACTIVITIES
2 Bukit Lawang

SLEEPING
3 Friendship Guesthouse
4 Indra Valley Inn
5 On the Rocks
see 3 Thousand Hills Guest House

EATING
6 Eriono Guesthouse & Restaurant
7 My Resto
8 Nature Soul
9 Waterstone
10 Wild River Cafe

DRINKING & NIGHTLIFE
11 Indra Valley Homestay and Resto
see 9 Jack's Bar
12 Kayana Pool Bar

The name Bukit Lawang translates, with just a touch of poetic license, as 'Gateway to the Hills'. While you can do a half-day hike with a high chance of spotting an orangutan, aim to spend at least one night camping for a more fulfilling jungle experience. A two- or three-day hike not only gives you a real taste of jungle travel (with the attendant leeches, giant ants and mosquitoes) but also offers a potential encounter with species that are rarely seen close to the village. Pig-tailed macaques are the more decorous cousins of the thieving long-tailed macaques in Bukit Lawang village, and the shy Thomas leaf monkeys are adorable with their white cheek tufts and jet-black mohawk hairdos.

TOP TIP

Choose (or ask for) a hike away from the most popular jungle trails. Your presence in virgin forest with a local guide offers another set of 'patrolling' eyes and contributes to the conservation of the area.

KEEPING WILDLIFE WILD

These rules apply to orangutans and other wildlife you're likely to see in Sumatra's forests.

- Keep groups to a maximum of seven people.
- Only trek if you're feeling well.
- Keep food and drinks away from wildlife.
- Don't smoke, eat, drink, cough, sneeze or spit near wildlife
- Maintain a distance of about 10m from wildlife.
- Stay quiet.
- Don't use a camera flash or a selfie stick in an intrusive manner.
- Report guides who break the rules.
- Recognise warning signs: orangutans make kissing sounds and drop branches (and sometimes poop) when stressed or angry.

SOAPSPHOTOGRAPHY/SHUTTERSTOCK

Sumatran orangutan, Bukit Lawang (p466)

Overnight tours include basic jungle camping in a shelter with bamboo poles holding up sheets of black plastic and thin mats (more for insulation than comfort), and there is usually a 'sit down' long-drop toilet. **Indra Valley** *(indravalleyinn bukitlawang.com)*, who run an excellent budget homestay on the Bukit Lawang riverfront, is one of the most respected operators. Expect to pay around 2,200,000Rp per person for a two-day, one-night camping trip.

Get Wet on Wild Rivers

River tubing in Bukit Lawang

Bukit Lawang's jungle treks can usually be combined with a wild tubing trip down the fast-flowing **Sungai Bohorok** (Bohorok River) as a fast-track back through the forest to your accommodation. It's hardly Zambezi-style whitewater rafting, but it's sure to inspire a few whoops and squeals as you splash through the rapids.

Many lodges and homestays offer tubing as a stand-alone experience, too: budget 400,000Rp per person for around three hours of fun, as you drift downstream from Bukit Lawang to the town of Bohorok. You'll return by bus (no trekking

EATING IN BUKIT LAWANG: OUR PICKS

Nature Soul: Great coffee and cinnamon rolls might draw you in, but it's the delicious egg *rendang* that's likely to keep you coming back. *8am-10pm* $$

Waterstone: Get a table overlooking the river and watch spear-fishermen hunt by headlamp while you tuck into excellent vegetarian curry. *8am-10pm* $$

My Resto: This friendly warung has an extensive menu. The chicken curry and potato *rendang* are favourites, along with the selection of medicinal teas. *9.30am-10pm* $

Wild River Cafe: Don't miss the varied *sambal* (sauces) at this popular riverside cafe. A wide selection of dishes, plus great fresh juices. *6.30am-10pm* $

involved) and, for a supplement, you can include an additional riverbank picnic. It's an experience that's highly popular with domestic tourists (especially from Medan) and at weekends this section of the river can often be quite noisy and crowded.

Better still, combine the rafting with a two- or three-day jungle trek. Regardless of who you book with, these treks often end at the campsite near the beautiful little waterfall known as **Batu Miring** (Sloping Rock). A cool dip and a hammering shoulder-massage under the falls is an ideal way to celebrate the end of a few days of backpacking!

Rafting these upper reaches of the river offers an opportunity to see exciting wildlife: otters are surprisingly common, there are huge monitor lizards, and long-tailed macaques are often seen swimming confidently across the fast-flowing river. The 40-minute tubing trip back down to Bukit Lawang is a wonderful way to experience the forest-covered chasms.

WHAT TO EXPECT ON A JUNGLE HIKE

All hikers in Bukit Lawang need a guide, and the package price includes park fees. The village can get busy at weekends and in holiday season, so pre-book your accommodation and trek. A three-day, two-night trek tends to cost around 3,100,000Rp per person, but solo travellers can usually join existing tours to reduce costs. It might seem expensive...until you see the logistics and labour involved in getting food and supplies into the jungle – up to three inflatable tubes have to be carried for two hours on a porter's back. The trail is often extremely hilly and, given the hot and humid jungle climate, is suited to hikers with a reasonably high level of fitness.

Hone Your Jungle Culinary Skills

Bukit Lawang cooking classes

Traditional home-cooking in Sumatra begins with foraging for the freshest ingredients and the most potent spices and herbs at the local market. A morning or afternoon spent cooking in a family home is far more than a mere culinary experience, it's an opportunity to see how the majority of Bukit Lawang's residents live.

The forest ecosystem is protected and firewood is less freely available these days, so most meals are prepared on gas – with the obvious exception of barbecued fish. You might help prepare whatever happens to be the family meal of the day, or you could make a special request: for example *ayam rendang* (chicken slow-cooked in spicy coconut paste) or, for a vegan option, *nangka* (jackfruit) *rendang*. The best things in life can't be rushed and you'll learn about the combination of at least a half-dozen local spices – cinnamon, cardamom, star anise, lemongrass, kaffir lime leaf, bay leaf – that are combined to create the perfect slow-cooked *rendang*. Dodi Heriyanta at **Bukit Lawang Jungle Trekking** *(bukitlawang-jungletrekking.com)* works hard to improve the standard of life in the local community and can arrange classes in a family home for 560,000Rp (maximum five guests).

DRINKING IN BUKIT LAWANG: OUR PICKS

Jack's Bar: Choose from Bukit Lawang's best cocktail menu (try the 'majito') in a timber jungle-bar that could be straight out of a Tarzan movie. *10am-late* $$

Indra Valley Homestay and Resto: Laid-back riverside vibe in a family-run bar. Take your beer to the back to relax on the riverside balcony. *7am-10pm* $

Eriono Guesthouse & Restaurant: A riverside spot that advertises 'bloody cold beer'. Wonderful for snacks like the delicious spring rolls. *8am-10pm* $

Kayana Pool Bar: An appealing bar with a big garden, pool tables, reggae music (often live) and an extensive menu of the most potent cocktails west of Bali. *10am-late* $$

LOCAL LAWS & CUSTOMS

Ketambe is officially in conservative Aceh, so it's important to respect local cultural practices. Women and men usually bathe in rivers fully clothed - you won't see women in bathing suits. Aceh is well known for its marijuana, and generations have used it as a food seasoning, medicine and recreational drug. It's said it was brought to the jungles by Dutch colonists and it was popular until being outlawed in the 1970s. It is illegal throughout Indonesia (and considered a type-1 narcotic), and that law is heavily enforced under Aceh's sharia law. Still, it may be offered on jungle treks, so if you're only there for the nature, it's wisest to be blunt and let guides know you're not interested in drugs.

See a Wilder Side of Gunung Leuser

Jungle hiking in Ketambe

To get further off the beaten track either head for Simolap or, if you like your orangutans combined with lianas the thickness of your chest, fig trees that you can scarcely see the top of and giant rafflesia flowers, cross the Aceh border for a jungle trek around **Ketambe town**. Reaching Ketambe is something of a mission, but a trip out here - about six hours from Medan - rewards tenacity with a wilder and more exclusive jungle experience than you will usually get from more accessible Bukit Lawang.

The orangutans here are entirely wild (there has never been feeding in this area) so sightings are less certain. Nevertheless, most day hikes into the jungle are rewarded with sightings of at least a couple of orangutans. Opt for two or three nights camping in the jungle and sightings often go up into double figures. While it's never good to get too close to wild animals (especially such powerful ones), you might be surprised to realise how unfazed the great red apes are by human presence. In this area, ecotourism plays a huge part in conserving the forests so your visit is likely to bring an environmental benefit to this more remote section of the park.

Tigers, rhinos, tapirs and elephants are also present in this area but chances of sightings are slim unless you're willing to devote at least a week to camping in the jungle. Macaques, gibbons and the extremely cute Thomas leaf monkeys, in contrast, are fairly common sightings. The majestic rhinoceros hornbills are frequent sightings that thrill birders - you'll hear the distinctive locomotive 'chug-chug' sound of the air pockets under their wings before you see them.

FELINEUS/SHUTTERSTOCK

Sumatran tiger, Gunung Leuser National Park

Where you stay in Ketambe usually dictates who you do a jungle trek with as homestays often have their own guides. Park entrance fees cost 150,000Rp per day. One highly experienced guide is Ishak, who like many Indonesians goes by only one name and is known to his friends simply as Is. He's worked frequently with researchers and combines scientific knowledge with local jungle wisdom...and more than his share of fascinating anecdotes. He can lead guided day treks or take you for a week in the jungle. Contact him on WhatsApp *(+62 822 9501 5407)* and budget around 600,000Rp per person per day, for a minimum of two people.

Harvest a Jungle Orchard

Visit a Ketambe *kebun*

When fruit is hard to come by in the jungle, it's not unusual for the orangutans to visit the *kebun* (orchards) on the steep hillsides above Ketambe. And who could blame them? The cultivated cacao, durian, mangosteen, passion fruit, mango, snake fruit and, of course, bananas must seem irresistible. Fortunately, the farmers here tolerate the orangutans – resorting to harmless deterrents such as black-and-white painted motorbike tyres draped around the trees like huge snakes.

Jungle guide Ishak, also known as Is, leads guests for a half-day visit to his family's plantation, where they learn about fruit, betel nut, patchouli oil and rubber production. You can taste wild ginger and candlenut and find out why locals prefer their smaller, tastier wild coffee beans to the cultivated robusta. Figure on 300,000Rp per person, for a minimum of two. Lunch in the *kebun* provided.

DID YOU KNOW?

Ishak, better known as Is, is a Ketambe-based jungle guide. *WhatsApp +62 822 9501 5407*

It's a well-known survival tactic for humans to get water from lianas, but on the high slopes elephants access water in just the same way.

It's amazing to watch orangutans using leaves as umbrellas or self-medicating from mineral-rich river banks.

Tapir only seem to appear when you're completely lost!

The wild buffalo are known locally as *noang* – some people believe that they kill tigers with their poisonous horns.

You have to spend a lot of time in the jungle before you see a tiger...and they always seem to turn up when you least expect it.

Beyond Gunung Leuser National Park

Complete with jungles, volcanoes, unique cultures and Danau Toba (the world's biggest crater lake), this region is Sumatra's biggest drawcard for international travellers.

GETTING AROUND

Private cars are often the best way to travel, but Medan hotels can advise on buses. Most visitors arrive on Danau Toba's Samosir Island via the ferry from Parapat (the last leaves at 6pm), which drops you at the nearest jetty to your accommodation. To get from Bukit Lawang to either Danau Toba or Berastagi, you'll either need to find a private car or go by bus via Medan. A fun way to get around Medan is with the Maxride app, which uses only newly introduced three-wheeled *bajaj* 'tuk-tuks'.

Luckily for travellers who have limited time, some of Sumatra's highlights are located fairly close (in Indonesian terms) to Medan: one of the island's main entry points and its biggest city. While many travellers skip Medan, it's worth taking the time to become acquainted with its unexpectedly cosmopolitan character and colonial history. But with so much adventure awaiting in the interior, it's hardly surprising that most visitors are anxious to get to places like the spectacularly beautiful Danau Toba, soaring volcanoes around Berastagi and all the plummeting waterfalls, irresistible hikes and fascinating cultural sights. Beware in particular of the enthralling Batak Highlands, centred on relaxing Samosir Island, as the region might lure you into an extended stay – it's famously hard to leave!

Medan

TIME FROM BUKIT LAWANG: **2 TO 3HR**

Witness the beauty and brutality of colonial Medan

The heart of Medan's colonial quarter lies along Jl Ahmad Yani. Walking north from Jl Palang Merah to Lapangan Merdeka (Independence Sq), you'll notice some spectacular buildings from the Dutch era, including Bank Indonesia (dating from 1907), Balai Kota (the town hall) and the main post office (built in 1911).

Medan's history also had a dark side, however, with indentured labourers suffering under a system that bordered upon slavery. Across the region, virgin forest was cleared to make way for tobacco, rubber and (more recently) palm-oil plantations, a problem that continues today.

A fountain in Medan in honour of Nienhuys, the founder of tobacco plantation the Deli Company, was unveiled in 1913 and demolished in 1958. Interesting side note: the former home of

Wooden sculpture, State Museum of North Sumatra

Nienhuys in the Netherlands now houses the headquarters of the NIOD Institute for War, Holocaust and Genocide Studies.

There's more information on this defining period in the **State Museum of North Sumatra** *(10,000Rp)*, along with a collection that includes ancient stone sculptures, Batak wooden carvings, coffins from Pulau Nias and relics of Dutch and Japanese occupation. The museum is closed on Mondays.

Author Dirk Aedsge Buiskool *(WhatsApp +62 811 600 0358)*, owner of Tri Jaya Tour & Travel, has been researching and writing about Medan's fascinating history for decades (p474). He leads historic tours of the city and region from his base at the lovely Hotel Deli River (p534) in a beautiful riverside spot on the edge of the city.

Walk with the Medan Hash House Harriettes

Wherever you come across **Hash House Harrier** meetings in Southeast Asia they usually tend to be expat dominated. Medan Hash House Harriers, however, is way more interesting thanks to being almost entirely Indonesian. In contrast to the strictly male-only Hash House Harriers (which meets on Mondays), the Harriettes welcome visitors regardless of their chosen pronouns. They meet every Thursday evening to 'run' (it's actually a sedate walk) and to socialise (drink beer).

VISA ISSUES FLYING INTO MEDAN

Travellers who have flown into Medan from other Indonesian islands via Malaysia may not realise that their visa was cancelled the moment they exited Indonesia. If this happens to you, you'll need to purchase another single-entry Indonesian visa on arrival (at the time of writing it was 500,000Rp cash, with a surcharge if paying by card). This can be both frustrating and expensive, especially if you've gone to great lengths to renew your visa in advance while in Bali, for example. It can often work out that a quick 'visa-run' – even a same-day in-and-out trip – to Malaysia serves as a hassle-free way to get a brand-new visa on arrival before the 30-day visa expires.

EATING IN MEDAN: BEST VEGETARIAN

Socrates Vegan: Enjoy feasting on spicy meals that feature many variations of *terong* (eggplant). *10am-8pm Wed-Mon* $

Medan Vegetarian: A family-run Padang-style place with vegetarian options and a changing menu. The coconut curries are highly recommended. *7am-7.30pm* $

Senorita Coffee: A great place to sip coffee or taro latte while snacking on fried cassava, sweet potato and vegan samosa rolls. *11.30am-8.30pm* $

VOI Vegan: Excellent vegan noodles and 'meat' – styled as steak, deer and duck. The vegan pizzas are excellent, with bases made with red spinach and beet. *11.30am-8.30pm* $

MEDAN'S MULTICULTURAL MAKEUP

Dirk Aedsge Buiskool is the owner of Hotel Deli River (p534) and the author of *Shaping Medan: The Role and Impact of Prominent Chinese, 1890–1942.*

Medan went from a small village in 1870 to a booming plantation town. The people who arrived here all came from afar: European planters mainly from the Netherlands and many workers from Java and China, because the area was only sparsely populated and the local workforce was small. The Medan area produced the best tobacco in the world, even better than Cuba. You can still see the remnants of that wealth in the colonial architecture. Today, the city is known for its cultural diversity, with communities of Chinese, Javanese, Batak and Minangkabau.

Hash House Harriers like to refer to themselves as 'a drinking club with a running problem'. This venerable group, which has been going since 1975, is made up almost entirely from members of Medan's Chinese, Indian and Batak communities. They are happy to welcome drop-in visitors and, since many members have a good command of English, they provide unexpected insight to this famously cosmopolitan city while at the same time offering a chance to get some exercise – and drink beer.

The venue changes each week and you'll see a side to the city or surrounding countryside that you might never have come across otherwise. And it's all in the company of friendly, informative (and in the end, quite tipsy) guides. Arrange your own transport and contact Kim (Stoler) through WhatsApp to find out where the next meeting point is *(+62 811 608 7650)*. You'll pay 80,000Rp for a meal and beers.

Berastagi

TIME FROM BUKIT LAWANG: **5HR**

Summit Gunung Sibayak

At 2212m, Gunung Sibayak is the high point (literally and figuratively) of North Sumatra. There's an inescapable jolt of adrenaline to be had from the whiff of sulphur-scented air, emanating from an active crater lake. It's possible to climb Gunung Sibayak without a guide, but don't attempt it alone

MEDAN'S BEST INTERNATIONAL RESTAURANTS: OUR PICKS

Cahaya Baru: A simple restaurant that has a great range of Indian food from across the subcontinent. The vegetarian curries are favourites. *10.30am-9pm Tue-Sun* $

Lebanon Restaurant: This Middle Eastern restaurant in Cambridge City Square Mall is famous for its biryani (mutton, chicken or prawn) and fish curry. *10am-10pm* $$

Jurung Jumbo Seafood Restaurant: Offering fusion dishes, this upscale establishment is popular with Medan's Chinese gourmands. *11am-3pm & 6-10pm* $$$

Fountain Resto: A Chinese-owned restaurant that features an eclectic menu with everything from beef lasagna to strawberry waffles and ice cream. *10am-9.30pm* $$

PANYAHATANSIREGAR/SHUTTERSTOCK

Gunung Sibayak

and only go during the day. Foreigners have gone missing and perished on the mountain in the past; there's a memorial to them near the car park.

Going with a guide is a safer and more impressive experience, and they'll be able to help you summit in time for sunrise. Nachelle Homestay (p534) offers **guided hikes** *(from 600,000Rp, including transport and snacks)*, dependent on the weather. You'll save money if you can gather a few people to share the cost, so ask around the homestay. The adventure starts at 4am, with a short drive up to the parking area and **registration office** *(entry 20,000Rp)*. Watch your step because the clay track can be slippery after rain and the rattan forests are viciously spiky – watch your head and hands too! You emerge from the treeline onto a moonscape dotted with sulphur-coloured vents, swirling with acrid steam.

The hike is about 6km out-and-back from the car park. The peak has a 'Top of Mt Sibayak 2212' sign and – if the weather is clear – a breathtaking view of neighbouring Gunung Sinabung.

Soak in Sibayak's hot springs

You don't need to have climbed Gunung Sibayak to reward yourself with a soak in the nearby hot springs – though most travellers experience them as a relaxing finish to an organised sunrise hike.

Continues on p480

HIKING VOLCANOES: SAFETY FIRST

Even if a volcano is quiet, like Gunung Sibayak was at the time of writing, this can change in an instant – especially when there are active hydrothermal systems. Apart from the danger of eruption, it's important to remember that the volcanic environment is in itself hostile. The gases emitted from fumaroles are toxic, and on Gunung Sibayak there are many noisy vents belching steam. Sulphur dioxide can damage your lungs and throat, and if hydrogen sulphide is also being emitted, it can be deadly. Local guides tend to take guests up close to check out the fumaroles with their brilliant sulphur-yellow rings, but be aware of the risks and don't get carried away by bravado.

EATING IN BERASTAGI: OUR PICKS

Waroeng FB: Friendly staff and an eclectic clientele. Try the *nasi bakar* (rice cooked with spices in a banana leaf) with chicken and mushroom. *10am-10pm* $

RM Cia You: The kwetiau fried noodles are recommended, but make sure you leave space for the *mochi daifuku* (Japanese glutinous rice cakes). *7am-9pm* $

Cafe J Vayona: A charmingly decorated restaurant. Try the 'superhot' *ifume goreng* (fried spicy noodles) if you dare. *7am-9pm* $

I'baz Coffee: Berastagi's best bet for great coffee and Western meals (pizza, quesadillas) as well as local staples in a modern industrial venue. *11am-11pm* $

ORANG_LOKAL/SHUTTERSTOCK

TOP EXPERIENCE

Danau Toba

Danau Toba (Lake Toba), which has possibly seen more tourism over the past 30 years than anywhere in Sumatra, remains a bucket-list destination. Around 74,000 years ago, the Toba supervolcano exploded in what's considered the largest eruption in human history, leaving the world's biggest crater lake and picturesque Samosir Island (the fourth-largest freshwater island). But it's the rich Batak culture that's the region's most appealing aspect.

DON'T MISS

- Hiking highlights
- Batak museums
- Swimming spots
- Touring by becak
- Batak 'matchmaking' festival
- Highland road to Aek Natonang Lake

Hike from Tuk Tuk Village

At 900m above sea level, **Samosir Island** is idyllic hiking terrain. It's at its loveliest shortly after dawn when the golden highland sunshine is glinting on the forested hills and paddy terraces. A particularly beautiful loop hike from Tuk Tuk (covering roughly 6km to 7km, depending on where you're staying) takes you through the magma domes west of Tuk Tuk peninsula and over a woodland ridge to farmland where you'll see teak, mango and the six Cs that are at the focus of local agriculture: candlenut, cacao, coffee, cloves, corn and cassava.

The loop is signposted 'Walking Trek', but the trail is narrow and winding so it's best to get advice about the route in advance or hire a local guide. Annette Horschmann, who runs **Tabo Cottages Tours** *(tabocottages.com)*, has spent

ROCKY SIAHAJA/SHUTTERSTOCK

Ferry on Danau Toba

three decades hiking around Samosir Island. She's mapped out some of the loveliest hiking routes here, totalling more than 30km. Guided hikes start at 800,000Rp for a three-hour tour for two people.

A highlight of the Tuk Tuk magma domes route is a short detour (just 100m) that will take you to the lesser-known stone chairs and animist carvings in Sipilakka village and, later in the walk, the sprawling meadows (known to locals as Bukit Beta) where you'll see large herds of grazing water buffalo. They're docile, but it's wise to keep your distance, especially if they have calves.

Batak Museums

Batak culture is incredibly complex. The only effective way to get a real insight is to hire a knowledgeable local guide who can explain the intricacies of the traditional religion. If you prefer to explore under your own steam, hire a scooter (Samosir's well-maintained roads are relatively peaceful) and visit the two main Batak museums, along with the famous **Batu Kursi Raja Siallagan** (Stone Chairs of King Siallagan).

Museum Huta Bolon Simanindo *(20,000Rp)*, a 21km ride along the shoreline north of Tuk Tuk, is a well-preserved group of traditional houses with intricate wooden carvings. The museum has fascinating collections of artefacts, including tools, musical instruments, weapons, textiles and even games. While information cards in these displays are unfortunately only in Bahasa Indonesia, the main information boards around the complex have been translated into English. Up until the pandemic the museum offered regular traditional dance performances, and there are hopes that they will resume in the future. The museum is open 8am to 4pm.

TUK TUK FOR FOODIES

Ganda Mangara Tua Tamba (better known as Rio) runs cooking classes at his Alyssa Restaurant (p480). Tuk Tuk is one of Sumatra's culinary highlights, and he recommends the following dishes.

Naniura is best described as Batak ceviche: it's raw fish marinated for several hours in lime, andaliman pepper and candlenut.

Babi panggang karo, known locally as 'BPK', is grilled pork served in a spicy sauce.

Saksang is minced pork stewed in blood and coconut milk.

Arsik is an entire fish, usually carp, stewed with turmeric, torch ginger and, everyone's favourite, andaliman pepper.

MAGICAL DANAU TOBA

It may seem like not much has changed on Samosir Island since the era of the hippies. There are still plenty of menus listing mushrooms, and when the price tag is around 300,000Rp for a serving, you can be sure they're not the common grocery-store variety. Restaurant signs along Tuk Tuk's main street also openly advertise magic mushrooms. Be forewarned, however, that they are definitely illegal.

The **Tomok Batak Museum** *(5000Rp)* is smaller, but the main exhibition – a particularly statuesque *rumah bolon* (Batak house) – is packed with even more fascinating traditional equipment and regalia. While the staff are not particularly informative, there are tags in English on some pieces in the collection. It's open 8am to 5pm.

Ganda Mangara Tua Tamba *(WhatsApp +62 813 6138 5020)*, better known as Rio, is a recommended guide who can clue you in on Batak beliefs.

Swimming in Danau Toba

It would be a pity to visit the caldera of a supervolcano – in this case a caldera that's 100km long, 30km wide and more than half a kilometre at its deepest – and not go for at least a token dip. Danau Toba's cool, crystalline waters are irresistible on a hot afternoon and you're never far from an idyllic swimming spot. Many of Tuk Tuk's waterfront resorts and homestays offer access to good, weed-free swimming. **Pantai Batuhoda** *(20,000Rp)*, at Samosir's northernmost tip, is the island's most famous beach and has snack stalls (try the fresh-pressed sugar-cane juice), sunbeds and the obligatory selfie spots. It's open from 9.30am to 6pm. For something more subdued and romantic, head just a kilometre south to **Pasir Aek Natio**, where there's a lovely Batak house and a little cafe with a lawn. It's a little piece of lakeside paradise.

KHLONGWANGCHAO/SHUTTERSTOCK

Tomok Batak Museum

Tour Samosir by Becak or Cycle

A great way to see the highlights of Danau Toba is to travel by becak (motorcycle-rickshaw). A short becak ride to somewhere like the Batak Museum in Tomok will cost around 50,000Rp. Romlan Guesthouse (p534) organises tours from 200,000Rp (taking in the King's Tomb and Stone Chairs) to 650,000Rp (a day trip taking in most of Samosir's highlights). The price is for a full becak, so up to four people can share the cost.

The cycling's also good here, and a guided bike ride from Romlan to the King's Tomb, a coffee plantation and a traditional Batak village costs 600,000Rp for two. For something with more downhill free-wheeling, have Tabo Cottages (p534) drop bikes at the Tanjungan viewpoint, from where you can ride 16km back to Tuk Tuk, including 9km of downhill. It's 650,000Rp, including bike hire and transport.

The Gondang Naposo Festival

Danau Toba has been getting back to its Batak roots with the multiday Gondang Naposo Festival, which involves an ancient courtship event involving the traditional Batak dance known as *tortor.*

Historically, this event was arranged by parents in remote villages; the young women and men would meet during the dancing...and it would all end in marriage! Today it's seen more as a way to celebrate Batak culture, although a few youngsters may still swap WhatsApp numbers and exchange selfies. The traditional attire for the ceremony is eye-catching: the bare-chested men are clad in blue sarongs, with a *ulos ragi hidup* (sash) draped around one shoulder. The women are dressed in red and blue with white sashes and red headwear. The dances build steadily to the beat of *gondang* (drums) and the trill of *sarune* (flutes). The trance-like movements, coordinated at first, becomes frenetic until, in the end, no one seems to know the steps and the dancing dissolves in hilarity.

Though tricky to plan since it's only held sporadically, it's a fun event to watch and something that shouldn't be missed if your trip happens to coincide.

Take the High Road to Aek Natonang Lake

Located near the northern shore of little Aek Natonang Lake, the bizarrely named Thompson Island is perhaps unique for being an island in a freshwater lake that is itself on an island... in a larger freshwater lake...on another island.

If that's not an intriguing enough reason to visit, then the gorgeously sweeping mountain road that winds 16km up from Tomok on the Danau Toba shore certainly is. Be aware that at the time of writing, the road had been partially destroyed by a landslide and a timber bridge was serving as a replacement. It was navigable on two wheels but not four. There were hopes that the road would reopen completely before the end of 2025. But even under normal circumstances the road is best tackled on two wheels; if you're not a competent rider then hire a becak (with a particularly good engine) to make the climb.

UNPACKING THE BATAK HOUSE

Batak houses were built with three levels, with buffaloes, chickens and pigs residing on the ground level. Steps lead to a small door – you have to duck to enter, showing respect to the house and the inhabitants (both the living and the spirits). The house's upper level is for the spirits, as well as storage and drying vegetables.

TOP TIPS

- Private ferries from Parapat run from 9am to 9pm, but can be erratic. Try to arrive early and be patient. Local guide Michael Sirait *(WhatsApp +62 812 6227 0473)*, who owns a cafe by the ferry dock in Parapat, always has up-to-date info.
- Tuk Tuk (which gets its name from the mortar used to pound betel nut) hangs like a ripe papaya off the trunk of Samosir Island. With Sumatra's best collection of cafes, bars and restaurants, it is the ideal base from which to explore.
- Book accommodation in advance to avoid hustlers and touts.

TRADITIONAL TEXTILES OF THE BATAKS

Ulo are traditional hand-woven Batak textiles that are commonly presented as ceremonial gifts for events such as births, deaths and marriages. Depending on the quality of the weaving, a Batak connoisseur can instantly gauge the wearer's status. The job of weaving *ulo* was traditionally given to women; it takes several months to complete one. Traditional *ulo* are still made in the three villages of Tongging, Paropo and Silalahi on Danau Toba's northwestern shore. Pop into the sheds where they're made today and you'll see women (and these days also men) operating the complicated upright wooden looms. The original back-strap looms can be seen in traditional villages like Huta Bolon – they use their weight to create tension while seated.

HIGHCLASSPHOTO/SHUTTERSTOCK

Air Terjun Sipiso-Piso

Continued from p475

Sibayak's many springs usually consist of concrete pathways separating open-air blue-tiled pools of different sizes, each containing hot spring water of varying temperatures. Women and men (the former fully clothed, the latter in shorts and T-shirts) spend hours taking dips. **Mitra Sibayak** *(15,000Rp)* is recommended and has a range of pools and excellent views of the mountains, as well as the Sibayak geyser. There are plenty of little warung (food stalls) to get food, and some hot springs have small cafes so you can easily spend all day soaking, relaxing and feasting.

Sipiso-Piso Waterfall

TIME FROM BUKIT LAWANG: **4HR**

Get misty under a highland cascade

From the clifftop car park, where there's a row of warung and souvenir sellers (plus someone collecting the 7500Rp entry fee), **Air Terjun Sipiso-Piso** looks impressive enough, but walk down the steps to the bottom and you'll be rewarded by an invigorating (and drenching) experience. The water emerges from an underground river and pours out of a cave to tumble some 120m down to what is almost a little patch of highland

EATING IN DANAU TOBA: OUR PICKS

Alyssa Restaurant: While there are signs advertising pizza, it's Rio's barbecued fish, pork and lobster that's the real crowd pleaser. *8am-11.30pm* $

Today's Cafe: This cute little cafe has over 100 meals on offer and good local information if you need it. Not fast food, but worth the wait. *8am-10pm* $

Jenny's Restaurant: This restaurant has become legendary and can get busy even in low season. Try charcoal-grilled lake fish with chips and salad. *8am-10pm* $

Maruba: Enjoy the lake view with your freshwater lobster or *ikan naniura* (raw fish marinated in Batak spices and candlenut). *9am-10pm* $

cloud forest, complete with more than its fair share of mosquitoes. Even if you're relatively fit, allow about an hour to do the entire walk – there are 1216 stone steps in the return trip between the clifftop and the base of the falls. It can be a serious cardio workout for the elderly and extremely challenging for anyone with mobility issues. It's well worth the effort, though, and the cool spray at the foot of the falls is a refreshing reward of sorts for all the sweating you'll do on the way back up. The car park is only 300m from the main road, so most organised tours and private drivers stop here during the three-hour drive between Berastagi and Danau Toba.

Pematangsiantar

TIME FROM BUKIT LAWANG: **5HR**

Take a ride on a vintage BSA becak

Pematangsiantar is a convenient stop on the road between Medan and Danau Toba, and home to a historic attraction of an unexpected sort. Vehicle buffs and petrol-heads are invariably astonished to find a fleet of vintage British-made BSA motorbikes here serving as becak (motorcycle-rickshaws). You'll usually find a few around the edge of Taman Bunga park. Haggle a price (around 150,000Rp per hour is generous) and you can explore the old town in what might be Indonesia's most unlikely form of public transport. Ask nicely and some owners might even give you a chance to ride one.

Relics of the celebrated Birmingham Small Arms company (which ceased production in 1973), these venerable 350cc becak – along with a few rarer 500cc – are found only in central Pematangsiantar. Two decades ago the fleet numbered more than 200, but only around 50 remain in running order. The most common models are c1954, but there are a few dating back to 1941 that have been in the same family for three generations. Phased out over the years by an invasion of Japanese Hondas, the last of these beloved bikes continue to function – frequently still starting with a single kick – 70 years after they rolled out of the factory.

In 2016 a monument was unveiled on the eastern corner of Taman Bunga to this 'Icon of Pematangsiantar'. It represents a BSA becak, sculpted perfectly in stone, steel and concrete. The faithful old BSA riders will tell you with a wry smile that the monument (which will almost certainly outlive the last BSA) was Japanese built.

SUMATRA'S UNIQUE URBAN TRANSPORT

Getting around Sumatran cities is often hot, dusty and noisy...but it's never boring! The variety of urban transport is mind-boggling. The most dramatic examples are the vintage BSA becak in Pematangsiantar and the classic Vespas that putter around Padang Sidempuan (p495). Medan recently imported a fleet of Indian tuk-tuks (known here as *bajaj*), which can be booked through the Maxride ride-hailing app. In many villages, *bentor* (motorised pedicabs) designed to seat two passengers often serve as miniature school buses carrying 12 or more. In the southern cities of Palembang and Bandar Lampung you'll still see fleets of cycle-trishaws; in Bukittinggi the last of the *dokar* (horse-drawn carriages) still carry shoppers to and from the morning market.

DRINKING IN DANAU TOBA: BEST NIGHTLIFE

Tabo Cottages (p534): Sit out beside the lakeside lawns with a delicious mango sherry and enjoy the relaxed vibe of this lovely resort. *8am-10pm*

Rumba Restaurant: Perhaps Tuk Tuk's most popular high-street restaurant, home to the extremely potent Long Island Toba arak cocktail. *8am-midnight*

Roy's Pub: Roy's rocks with live music on Friday and Saturday nights. The adjacent coffee shop also serves good gin and tonic on the terrace in the evening. *7am-midnight*

Willem's Resto Café & Bar: An immense industrial-style hangout (or hanger) with regular live bands. Wine and a variety of imported spirits. *10am-11pm*

Padang

CUISINE | ARCHITECTURE | BEACH ESCAPES

GETTING AROUND

There's a convenient train from Padang's Minangkabau Airport to the Pulau Aie railway station (near the river), but unfortunately it only runs after the day's first flights. If you're travelling with a lot of baggage (eg a surfboard), your best bet is to arrange a pickup with your accommodation or tour operator.

The typically useful Grab and Gojek ride-hailing apps have been supplanted in Padang by the cheaper but less reliable Maxim. Download the app; it's the best way to get around town and out to the hotels around Pantai Air Manis.

Padang's highlight is its food, which is found across Indonesia for good reasons: it's affordable, instantly available and delicious. But Padang has so much more to offer. Colonial-era buildings are being revitalised along the river, the city's low-rise landscape is easy to navigate and Chinatown is irresistibly enticing. Padang changed dramatically in the 1990s when the Mentawai Islands became a surfing hot spot, though it was the treks to the tribes on Pulau Siberut that originally lured travellers. An earthquake in 2009 caused widespread devastation and the area continues to experience significant tremors as it sits astride one of the planet's most powerful seismic zones. Today, Padang is the gateway town for thousands of surfers bound for the Mentawai waves and dozens of liveaboard boats are moored along the river, loaded with surfboards and ready to set off. At more than €2500 for an average 10-day 'surfari', the industry has become an economic powerhouse.

Dine Padang Style

Get to know the local cuisine

Sit down in a Padang-style restaurant and within moments an array of dishes will be unloaded onto your table. The arrangement is that you only pay for what you eat (or touch), but the beauty is that even if you want to sample everything, it's unlikely to break the bank. Just leave the food you're not interested in and you won't be charged for it. *Rendang* (beef coconut curry) is the most iconic dish in *masakan Padang* (Padang cuisine), but other recognisable dishes include boiled eggs (usually in sauce or curry), omelet, *ayam goreng* (fried chicken) and *ayam bakar* (charcoal-grilled chicken, usually marinated in coconut sauce). The whole thing can be a bit full-on for a solo traveller – especially with all the plates lined

SIGHTS
1 Museum Adityawarman

SLEEPING
2 Bat & Arrow

EATING
3 Kopigo Pondok
4 Markez Soul Food & Coffee
5 Padang Old Town Resto Gallery
6 Padangsche Spaarbank
7 Restoran Selamat
8 Rumah Makan Pak Gole
9 Safari Garden
10 Waroeng Gaul
11 Waroenk Om Ping

DRINKING & NIGHTLIFE
see 2 Bat & Arrow
12 PW Cafe & Resto
13 Teebox

SHOPPING
14 Pasar Raya

TRANSPORT
15 Mentawai Fast

up in front of you – as it's unusual to do anything on your own in Indonesia. If you find yourself in this situation, just point out a few things from the display cabinets. Most people choose a meat or fish dish, something with egg – perhaps spicy *telur balado* (boiled eggs covered in red chilli sauce) – and a vegetable dish. Vegetarians usually go for tempeh or *tahu* (tofu). Restaurants are invariably Muslim-run, so you won't find alcohol here, but your meal can usually be paired with refreshing *es jeruk* (sweet orange juice).

TOP TIP

Take time to get acquainted with *masakan Padang* (Padang cuisine) and you'll find that it'll serve you well in any city in Indonesia. You're sure to find a few reliable staples on any menu wherever you see a 'RM Padang' sign.

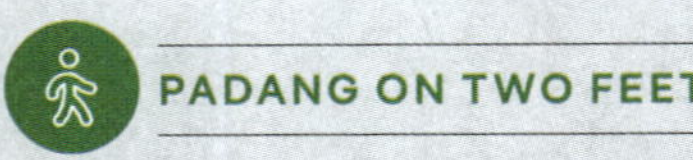

PADANG ON TWO FEET

Explore the architectural heritage of old Padang, once West Sumatra's most important trading hub.

START	END	LENGTH
Siti Nurbaya Bridge	RM Pak Gole	2km; 1½hr

Begin at the foot of Padang's iconic 1 **Siti Nurbaya Bridge** and head upriver along Jl Batang Arau. 2 **Geo Wehry & Co** was built in 1920 as a warehouse for one of the largest import-export companies in the Dutch East Indies; other grand colonial-era buildings on this street include the 3 **Mandiri building**, built in 1930 for the Dutch bank NIEM, and 4 **Spaarbank**, built in the early 1900s by a Padang-based Freemason group.

Turn left into Jl Klenteng to enter the enchanting old Chinese quarter – reminiscent of Penang's famous Georgetown (before gentrification) – and walk left down Jl Klenteng II to see clan houses and community centres such as 5 **Himpunan Keluarga Tan**, 6 **Hok Teng Tong** and 7 **Perhimpunan Keluarga Tjoa Kwa**. Retrace your steps to stop in at the mesmerising 8 **See Hin Kiong** temple then, 50m up the street, enter the colourful market 9 **Pasar Tanah Kongsi**. Pause for a snack as you wind between stalls then head towards the river on Jl Niaga and turn left onto Jl Ps Batipuh, where you'll find 10 **Masjid Muhammadan**, which was established in 1723 and is probably Padang's oldest mosque. Note the stained glass above the doors.

Continue rubbernecking the gorgeous old buildings along Jl Ps Batipuh and end your walk with a meal at 11 **Rumah Makan Pak Gole** (p487), serving delicious *rendang* since 1951.

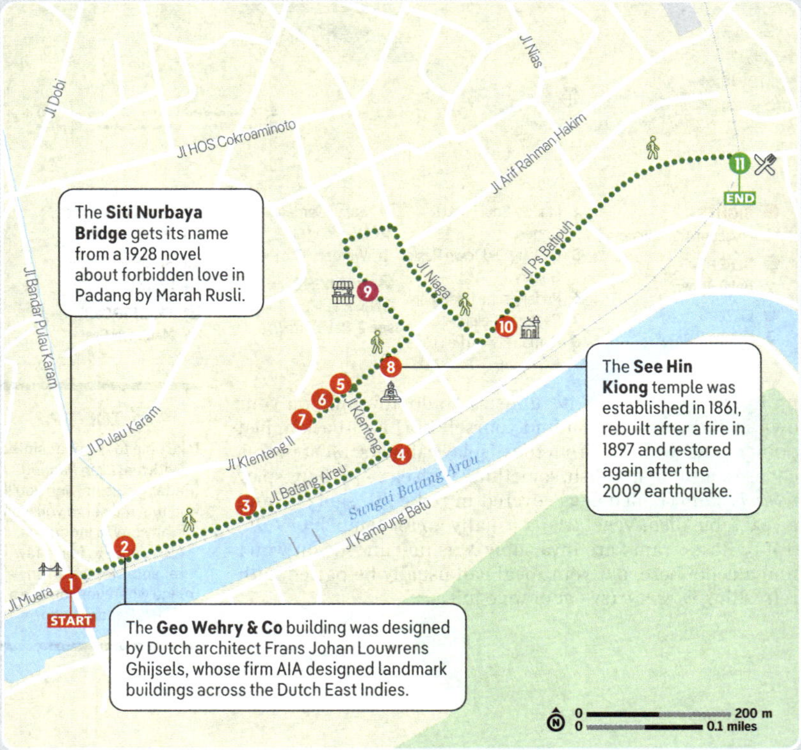

The **Siti Nurbaya Bridge** gets its name from a 1928 novel about forbidden love in Padang by Marah Rusli.

The **See Hin Kiong** temple was established in 1861, rebuilt after a fire in 1897 and restored again after the 2009 earthquake.

The **Geo Wehry & Co** building was designed by Dutch architect Frans Johan Louwrens Ghijsels, whose firm AIA designed landmark buildings across the Dutch East Indies.

Insights into the Proud Minangkabau People

Visit the Museum Adityawarman

The **Museum Adityawarman** *(5000Rp)* is one of the best-value cultural experiences on the entire island. Its enchanting gardens with their ponds and fountains are so romantic that signs have been erected to dissuade courting couples. The building itself is styled on a lovely timber Minangkabau palace, its iconic sweeping roof representing buffalo horns. Inside are exhibits, with explanations in English, that explain the origins of these roofs, as well as of the Minangkabau people themselves. The museum can get a little hot and stuffy, but go downstairs to the air-conditioned basement area, which houses some of the most precious historical artefacts in the collection. Across the patio behind the palace is a separate building with fascinating exhibits dedicated entirely to the history and traditions of *rendang* cooking. It's open from 10am to 4pm.

Get Lost In Pasar Raya, Padang's Huge Market

The centre of the shopping universe

All Sumatran cities have a large market, but Padang's Pasar Raya sprawls across several city blocks. There are sections dedicated to every trade imaginable, from gold dealers and tailors to opticians and butchers. The colourful fruit and vegetable market, mostly centred on Jl Sandang Pangan, is perhaps the most fascinating for visitors to the tropics, but the nearby butcher's section with endless crates of live chickens might not be everyone's scene. The sections of the market where garbage and offcuts are collected can get quite ripe as the afternoon sun begins to heat up – as will the area with durian stalls. Rather than just wandering aimlessly, try to find a reason to support a local business by spending a few dollars. Perhaps buy some snake fruit or *jajan* (cakes), or cool off with a deliciously refreshing glass of sugar-cane juice. It's a great excuse to interact with a vendor and to get a real sense of what an economic powerhouse such backstreet markets can be. If you want to see citizens going about their daily lives, Pasar Raya is a must-visit. It's open from 7am to 6.30pm.

MINANGKABAU WOMEN RULE

The Minangkabau people are believed to have migrated from Indochina to what is now West Sumatra about 4000 years ago. Unusually, society here developed along matrilineal lines. According to Minangkabau *adat* (traditional laws and regulations), property and wealth are passed down through the female line; the eldest living female is the family matriarch. The most important male in the household is the mother's eldest brother, who replaces the father in taking responsibility for the children's education, upbringing and marriage prospects. Consensus is at the core of the ruling philosophy, and the division of power between the sexes is regarded as complementary – 'as the skin and the nail act together to form the fingertip', according to a local expression.

INTERNATIONAL RESTAURANTS IN PADANG: OUR PICKS

Safari Garden: A favourite with surfers who come for the fusion cuisine and beer. Don't miss the *rendang* pizzas. *10am-10pm Mon-Fri, to 11pm Sat & Sun* $$

Padang Old Town Resto Gallery: A riverside spot with a pleasant patio and an air-con interior; enjoy an extensive menu of Thai dishes. *11am-10pm* $

Kopigo Pondok: The best place for an early pre-ferry start, with great coffee and continental and American breakfasts in a beautiful vintage building. *6am-2am* $$

Markez Soul Food & Coffee: A Chinatown institution serving everything from fish and chips to *steak au poivre*. *11.30am-10pm Sun-Thu, to 11pm Fri & Sat* $

THE LEGEND OF SWEET WATER BEACH

Pantai Air Manis (Sweet Water Beach) has an intriguing stone that's shaped like a man in what could be a yoga pose. It was created by two artists in 1980 as a representation of a local folktale that warns against the dangers of acting in an unfilial, selfish manner. The story tells of Malin Kundang, an ungrateful son who went to sea and made a fortune. When he came back home, he looked down on his mother and ignored her. Predictably enough, his next adventure ended in tragedy.

Unfortunately, the water is not so sweet these days and surfing is no longer recommended due to pollution.

Visit West Sumatra's Great Mosque

Climb the minaret for Padang views

Completed as recently as 2019, this might not be the most historic mosque in Sumatra, but the **Masjid Raya Sumatera Barat** (which can accommodate up to 20,000 worshippers) is one of the most beautifully designed in the country. Masjid Raya Syekh Ahmad Khatib Al-Minangkabawi Sumatera Barat – to use its full name – is unmistakably Minangkabau in style. It was designed to withstand earthquakes and to serve as a refuge in case of a tsunami.

Non-Muslim visitors are welcome outside of prayer times. Women can borrow a robe and a caretaker will be happy to show you inside (tips are appreciated). The interior is cooled by a giant fan and by pools at the back of the prayer hall.

Padang's 2009 earthquake resulted in some budget-trimming, so that today there's only a single elegant minaret, rather than one at each corner of the complex. A security guard will, for a small tip, be happy to unlock the padlocked doors and light your way up the 240 steps to the viewing platform. This is the best view in the city.

NIGHTLIFE IN PADANG: OUR PICKS

Bat & Arrow: Padang's most popular surfer's hub, with accommodation upstairs. Come here for the live music, a round of beers or to play pool. *10am-late*

PW Cafe & Resto: A fun hangout with occasional live music, DJs and a menu that makes for light reading (beers include 'Bali Hay' and 'Heyneken'). *8pm-2am*

Padangsche Spaarbank: A beautifully restored colonial-era building with a riverside garden. Great for tapas and sundowners. *10am-10pm*

Teebox: Known for its karaoke and cocktails (a heady mix), this mega entertainment plaza is tacky and fun enough to inspire a late night. *6pm-3am Mon-Sat*

DAVE SAU/SHUTTERSTOCK

Pasar Raya (p485)

Sample Padang's Most Famous Dish

See how beef *rendang* is made

If it's not hot enough for you in central Padang's sunbaked streets, head to **Rumah Makan Pak Gole** near the railway tracks at the edge of Chinatown. This is where Pak Gole's family has been preparing the city's best beef *rendang* for 75 years: look for the sweltering kitchens (more like a smoke-blackened barn) behind the warung.

The chefs light wood fires under the great steel cauldrons at 5am, so that the beef can cook slowly in the spicy coconut sauce for more than five hours – it's ready just in time for lunch. After lunch a new batch is made for the evening meal. The chefs (who will certainly be grateful for a small 'refreshments' tip) will be happy to pass you the extra-large wooden paddle so you can have a stir yourself...but it won't be long before you recall that old cliche about staying out of the kitchen if you can't stand the heat!

HOW TO ORDER MASAKAN PADANG

Even for locals, the immense variety of food on display in a *masakan Padang* eatery can be bewildering. A good command of Bahasa Indonesia only helps a little, since some dishes have regional, colloquial or even Dutch names. Here are some standards that you'll find in most places.

- **Perkedel kentang** Fried potato cakes, a bit like hash browns.
- **Kangkung** Water spinach, usually cooked with red onions and garlic.
- **Gulai nangka** Jackfruit curry; note the shredded jackfruit looks a lot like meat.
- **Telur balado** Boiled eggs baked in spicy chilli sauce.
- **Es jeruk** *Padang* restaurants are always alcohol-free; this refreshing drink is basically fresh, sweetened orange juice.

LOCAL RESTAURANTS IN PADANG: OUR PICKS

Waroeng Gaul: One of Padang's busiest dining spots attracts a young local crowd with its excellent Javanese duck. Arrive early. *8am-10.30pm* $

Rumah Makan Pak Gole: A family-run business preparing slow-cooked beef *rendang* since 1973. Wander out the back to see the bubbling cauldrons. *7am-8pm* $

Restoran Selamat: A simple eatery near the Pasar Raya market that's one of the most popular in the city for *masakan Padang*. *10am-4pm* $

Waroenk Om Ping: A great Chinatown lunch stop that's also popular for its selection of fresh juices and signature *kopmil* (coffee and chocolate milk). *10am-11pm* $

Beyond Padang

West Sumatra is a particularly fascinating and welcoming place to launch a Sumatran sojourn, and has convenient flights to and from Jakarta.

Places

Padang is the logical starting point for countless West Sumatra adventures, from the surf- and culture-rich Mentawai Islands to the vibrant Minangkabau style of Bukittinggi, one of Indonesia's most appealing cities. Some spots, such as Harau Valley and Danau Maninjau, have seen an increase in domestic tourism – not always for the best, given the excesses of the 'selfie' boom – but Padang offers surprisingly easy access to pristine jungle wilderness. Pulau Siberut and Kerinci Seblat National Park are a day trip away while the jungles around Rimba are almost on the city's doorstep. You might choose to attend duck and bull races (separately) or hunt the majestically huge and stinky rafflesia flower. If you're heading north, pause to sample an environmentally friendly *kopi luwak* (civet coffee) before heading onwards across the equator.

Mentawais

Experience tribal life on Pulau Siberut

Before the Mentawai Islands hit surfing headlines in the 1990s, it was the tribal culture that brought travellers to this archipelago of about 70 islands. Board the ferry from Padang to **Siberut** (Mentawai's main island) and among the heap of boardbags you'll still see a few backpacks that look like they're more geared for jungle travel. It's a shame that more

GETTING AROUND

The slow ferry to Pulau Siberut has erratic departures but tends to sail twice a week, taking 11 to 12 hours for the crossing. Most travellers opt for the fast ferry (Mentawai Fast takes just four hours) that leaves on Tuesday, Thursday and Saturday, although it's also dependent on weather conditions. While Grab is the ride-hailing app of choice for northern Sumatra, Maxim dominates Padang, and offers both cars and motorbikes. Surfers flying into Padang usually prefer Garuda airlines, which doesn't charge extra for surfboards.

visitors don't head to Pulau Siberut's interior, since village stays are an important part of the economy for under-represented communities and play a part in keeping tribal traditions and culture alive. And for adventurers, the experience is an incredibly exciting one.

In a region where even the most isolated tribesmen are most likely to sport shorts and T-shirts, it's a rare experience to visit a community where men (shamans at least) still dress in bark loincloths on an everyday basis.

Getting to the communities (by ferry, pickup truck, dugout canoe and on foot) is just the beginning of the adventure. You sleep on a thin mattress on the floor of a timber *uma* (traditional thatched house), eat sitting cross-legged on the floor, wash in the river and 'do your business' (as the guides say) under the trees. Naturally, you're always accompanied by an interpreter who can explain the complexities of tribal life, but travellers are invariably amazed at how quickly they're made to feel they're part of the family, despite the lack of a common language.

Once you're with the tribe there's usually no fixed itinerary – you'll simply do whatever the activity of the day happens to be. You might go into the jungle to harvest *tamra* (the giant sago grubs that are ingeniously 'farmed' by the tribes), or search for a suitable *baiko* tree to prepare *kabit* (barkcloth). You could go fishing with the women – wading waist-deep in palm leaf skirts, which are worn as camouflage to confuse the river shrimp! You might also learn to fire the traditional bows and arrows (still the hunting weapon of choice) and learn how the poison for the arrows is made. For many visitors a highlight of the experience is the chance to pick up a unique souvenir in the form of a *titi* (traditional hand-tapped Mentawai tattoo) with ink made from ash and sugar-cane juice.

There are no smartphones or internet here, so the surprisingly late evenings are more likely to revolve around traditional singing and dancing to the beat of a monkey-skin drum. **Mentawai Tribe** *(mentawaitribe.com)* has excellent multilingual guides from the tribal communities and Christina, their ace chef, can provide what is likely to be the most sumptuous jungle meals you'll ever have.

Surfing the Mentawais

The Mentawai Islands are a perpetual 'pipe dream' for surfers worldwide thanks to the glassy perfect waves. It's sometimes onshore but, with a swell that sweeps right across the Indian Ocean, it's never flat.

Expect a combination of mellow waves alongside powerful barrelling ones, all within a short boat ride or sometimes even within walking distance. **Pulau Siberut** is best known for its status as a UN Biosphere Reserve, while **Pulau Sipora** is a pickup point for resorts in the popular Playground area. Katiet, on Pulau Sipora's southern tip, has Lance's Left and Lance's Right. **Pulau Pagai Utara** (North Pagai) is getting more attention these days, with a few resorts opening on its west coast near the consistent Macaronis break. A new airport on Pulau Sipora opened in 2023 and Susi Air now flies in from Padang.

TRAVELLING IN THE MENTAWAIS

Few surfers encounter logistical problems when travelling around 'the Ments', as the islands are colloquially known. If you're travelling on a liveaboard boat or paying package prices at a surf camp, your problems will be dealt with for you. But for travellers heading into the interior, it's a whole other story: the four-hour (minimum) ferry trip is just the start. Be prepared for an hour or two rattling along a swampy road in the back of a pickup (expect to help push), then another hour or so in a dugout canoe powered by a lawn-mower engine (expect to help pull). You'll spend at least an hour hiking through jungle, often with water, mud and leeches up to your knees.

PACKING FOR THE JUNGLE

Pack as lightly as possible and prepare for real adventure. Use dry bags (cheap at the Eiger travel store in Padang) or double-bag everything. The Siberut jungle is unusually swampy and muddy and many operators supply Wellington boots (check in advance). If so, don't bother to carry hiking boots or trainers. Flip-flops are useful around the village, but sport sandals are best in the rivers. Take natural soap, ample insect repellent, sunscreen and a hat. A head torch is vital and a sarong can double as a towel and sheet. Mattresses, pillows and mosquito nets are supplied. Bring a swimsuit or bathe in your underwear. Take a water-filter bottle and a travel hammock...and consider donating the latter to the *uma* (traditional thatched house).

Surfers who want to get further off the radar opt for a surf charter (p498), while those staying at surf camps usually book a package that includes airport transfers, accommodation in Padang, ferries and local boat shuttles to the breaks. This does away with a lot of hassle, but it's expensive and not necessarily appealing to independent travellers. Low-budget alternatives involve catching the ferry to south Siberut, staying at a budget homestay in Peipei village and asking around for a boat to take you out to the surf breaks around the Bengbeng and Ebay area. There are also homestays near the celebrated Lance's Right at Tua Pejat (southern Sipora). Costs can add up quite fast, but with a little determination you'll find yourself surfing the same waves as someone paying a premium to stay at a chic surf camp.

Bukittinggi

TIME FROM PADANG: **2½HR**

Explore Bukittinggi's Fort de Kock

A visit to the hilltop fortress known as **Benteng de Kock** *(50,000Rp)* comes with a moral dilemma. The entry fee would appear to be great value since it also covers entrance to the Kinantan Zoo. While the conditions in which the animals are incarcerated are less than ideal, it has to be said that the zoo has made improvements in animal welfare over the last decade. It is also making headway in educating the public about Sumatra's natural riches.

Unfortunately, there's no option to pay only for access to the shady hilltop that is site of the 19th-century Dutch fort. On weekends and public holidays, the parks and ruins are great for meeting local people, as entire families come out to picnic in the picturesque vintage gazebos that line the hillside. Even if you do decide to skip the zoo, be sure to walk across the soaring 90m-long **Limpapeh Bridge** (only accessible from within the fort), which offers incredible views across the old city. Walk just a little beyond the far end – just after the sadly tethered elephants – and you'll have a chance to visit the Rumah Adat Baanjuang, an immense timber Minang-style building. Fort de Kock is open 8am to 6pm, from Saturday to Thursday.

Wander the Japanese wartime tunnels

The World War II Japanese tunnels – known locally as **Lubang Jepang** *(25,000Rp)* – are probably the most startling of Bukittinggi's many historical sites. Beyond the ticket turnstiles are spectacular views across Sianok Canyon, which defines Bukittinggi's western boundary. Be aware that the viewpoint comes with the obligatory troop of marauding macaques.

But while local guides might describe Sianok as the Sumatran Grand Canyon, it's the Japanese tunnels that really steal the show. You descend 141 stone steps (with multicoloured LED lights hindering what little night-vision you might have had) to a haunting warren of tunnels that allegedly run for 1.4km in total. Even on busy days, there's enough space to slip away and wander in solitude – with only the resident

BUKITTINGGI ON TWO FEET

Take a stroll through the old centre of Bukittinggi and you'll come across atmospheric old buildings, busy market stalls and historical landmarks.

START	END	LENGTH
Benteng de Kock	Rumah Kelahiran Bung Hatta	1.6km; 1hr

Begin at the entrance of 1 **Benteng de Kock**, a 19th-century Dutch fortress whose leafy grounds are a popular recreational space. Walk away from the entrance and descend the stairs on your left along 2 **Gang Kampung Jawa Lamo**, past old, photogenic wooden homes. Turn left onto Jl Teuku Umar and gaze up at the picturesque 3 **Jembatan Limpapeh** pedestrian bridge, high overhead. Cross the road into 4 **Janjang Pasanggrahan**, a colourful lane the Dutch-Indonesian government created in 1908 to connect Bukittinggi's markets. It's now decorated with contemporary murals.

At the top of the stairs turn right onto Jl Cindua Mato, where you'll find Pasar Atas (the new 'upper market'). Continue to the 5 **Jam Gadang** clocktower, a much-loved Bukittinggi landmark and a great spot to rest. Over the road you'll see 6 **Istana Bung Hatta**, the home of Indonesia's first vice-president. Walk to the northeast corner of the clocktower square to descend Jl Lereng, flanked by market stalls. Eventually you'll cross a footbridge to reach busy 7 **Pasar Bawah** ('lower market'), where stalls spill onto the surrounding alleys. Turn left up Jl Syech Arrasuli until you reach a busy junction. On the opposite side of this junction you'll see 8 **Rumah Kelahiran Bung Hatta** (p493), the birthplace of independence hero Bung Hatta and the final stop on your walking tour.

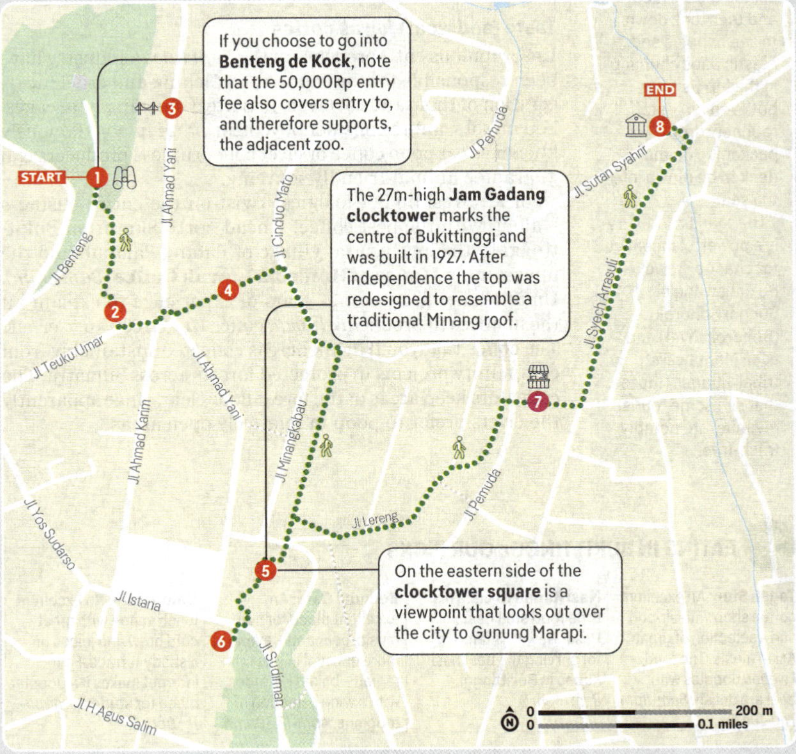

If you choose to go into **Benteng de Kock**, note that the 50,000Rp entry fee also covers entry to, and therefore supports, the adjacent zoo.

The 27m-high **Jam Gadang clocktower** marks the centre of Bukittinggi and was built in 1927. After independence the top was redesigned to resemble a traditional Minang roof.

On the eastern side of the **clocktower square** is a viewpoint that looks out over the city to Gunung Marapi.

SUMATRA'S PLASTIC PROBLEM

Many of Sumatra's tourist attractions are swamped with rubbish. The tourism boom has been great for the economy, but local 'paket' tourists consistently leave polystyrene lunch packaging and plastic Aqua bottles strewn across Instagram-famous beauty spots. Sumatra's litter problem affects land and water: it can be a shock to watch dolphins leaping and flying fish skipping across the surface and then look down to see nappies and plastic bags churning in the ferry's wake... but even ferry staff routinely drop packaging on the deck to be blown into the sea.

The tourism industry is a powerful incentive for change, however. Bukit Lawang's Sungai Bohorok (Bohorok River) and even Mentawai's tribal villages (those that see some tourist revenue) are notably trash-free.

CHAKRA GSTOCK/SHUTTERSTOCK

Lubang Jepang (p490)

bats for company – among the spooky ammunition rooms, barracks, prison, kitchen and the so-called ambush room, which was presumably once booby-trapped. The site is open from 7am to 6pm.

Taste (and wear) *luwak* coffee

Unscrupulous entrepreneurs in the *kopi luwak* industry have been responsible for the capture, trafficking and cruel incarceration of thousands of civets in battery-farming wire cages. You might want to consider boycotting *kopi luwak* (famously known as cat poop coffee or civet coffee) unless producers can guarantee animal-friendly sourcing.

For a refreshingly ecological twist on the entire business – along with the best coffee! – head north 8km from Bukittinggi to the lovely rural village of Batang Palupuh and the unassuming **House of Rafflesia Luwak Coffee** *(8am-8pm)*. Umul Khairi draws on 15 years of experience to explain all the nuances in producing *luwak* coffee from free-range civets. The coffee that you'll drink here is collected sustainably from community projects in protected forests across Sumatra. The collectors keep areas of the forest floor clear, since apparently the civets prefer to poop in relatively open areas.

EATING IN BUKITTINGGI: OUR PICKS

Tageh Step: An excellent coffee shop with air-con and a selection of great Asian meals. The fried *kwetiau* noodles with beef are delish. *8am-11pm Thu-Tue* $

Nasi Kapau Ni Lis: This little food stall near Pasar Bawah is famous for serving the best *nasi Kapau* in Bukittinggi. *8am-6pm* $

Bedudal Cafe: An excellent place for live music, beer and – even more unusual in this region – baked potatoes with a wide selection of toppings. *4pm-12.30am* $

Naluri Cafe: An excellent lunch venue with great cold brew and juices on a shady terrace. Fast internet makes it a popular place for students. *noon-11.50pm* $

The beans are roasted over hard cinnamon wood for the boosted heat intensity as well as added flavour. You can order your coffee served either Italian moka style or local style. Whichever you opt for, try it with a pod of locally grown vanilla.

Before you go, take the opportunity to see if cat poop coffee makes you look younger (in addition to its countless other health benefits). Ibu Umul will scrub your face with the damp coffee grounds, and you can keep on sipping your coffee until it's time to reveal your blemish-free civet-poop-exfoliated face.

One kilogram of coffee beans will set you back 2,500,000Rp, but a cuppa is amazing value at just 30,000Rp – and the face-scrub experience is free. The coffee shop is also a hangout for guides who can take you to find flowering rafflesia (the world's biggest bloom) in the nearby **Batang Palupuh Nature Reserve**.

Walk the line at the equator monument

Drive 50km north from Bukittinggi town (about 90 minutes) and you'll reach the Earth's equator, marked by an immense 15m-diameter globe beside the Trans-Sumatra Highway's northbound lane. It's doubtful that you'll want to make the four-hour drive from Padang merely just to visit the **Monumen Equator** in Bonjol town, unless you're drawn to the admittedly quirky and unique novelty of having one foot in each hemisphere. If that's the case, bear in mind that the actual equator lies about 130m south of the monument. Either way, the monument makes for an irresistible stopping point for anyone road-tripping between Bukittinggi and, say, Danau Toba.

Bonjol was a stronghold during the Padri War (1821–37), a conflict between the Minangkabau Muslims and the local chieftains, who were assisted by the Dutch. Also at the equator complex is the impressive little **Museum Tuanku Imam Bonjol** *(5000Rp)*, which houses weapons, relics and religious artefacts from the period. The museum is open from 8am to 6pm, from Thursday to Tuesday.

The birthplace of Bung Hatta

Rumah Kelahiran Bung Hatta (the birthplace of independence hero Bung Hatta) is a colonial-era timber home that now houses a small museum. Unless you're particularly fascinated by the key figures in Indonesia's independence struggle, you might not find the Hatta family memorabilia particularly appealing. It's worth visiting this gorgeous building, however, to get an insight into how upper-class Indonesians lived during the colonial era. Bung Hatta's bicycle and the family *dokar* (horse carriage) are still parked in the backyard. Remove your shoes on the way into the house; there are wooden clogs in the yard so that you can check out the kitchen area, which is still equipped with utensils and has changed little since the independence hero lived here.

THE DISTINCTIVE FLAVOURS OF NASI KAPAU

Nasi Kapau is similar to the *masakan Padang* buffet style of eating except that the wide varieties of dishes are usually accompanied by the fragrant *Kapau* rice. Particularly adventurous gourmands might enjoy regional specialities that are rarely found outside Bukittinggi. Cow offal, in particular, is central to *nasi Kapau* with tripe, spleen, brains, lung, tendons and skin being favourites. Western tastes might gravitate more to *dendeng balado* (spiced crispy beef) or *kalio*, a moister regional version of *rendang*. While this is a meat-heavy cuisine, vegetarians won't be disappointed as delicious cassava, eggplant and *nangka* (jackfruit) are all common at *nasi Kapau* establishments.

THE PAGARUYUNG KINGDOM

In the 14th century the Padang area was part of the mighty Pagaruyung kingdom, which stretched through central Sumatra and into much of the region beyond. In the 1370s the kings even sent envoys as far as China, but their rule effectively ended in 1663 with the arrival of the Dutch. Remaining evidence of the Pagaruyung kingdom can be seen at the Grand Palace outside Bukittinggi, though the magnificent wooden construction burnt down in 2007 and has since been rebuilt. It's equally impressive within, with soaring pillars and walls covered in brightly coloured ceremonial banners. There's a museum inside (no English captions) and three levels with views of the surrounding village and countryside.

Harau Valley

TIME FROM BUKITTINGGI: **1HR**

Duck and bull races

The rapidly developing tourist attractions of Harau Valley now include a 'mini Europe' where you can take your selfie with a scale model Stonehenge or the Eiffel Tower in the background. On a more traditional front, meanwhile, is **duck racing**, which takes place at various locations on many afternoons during the June through October racing season. Most guides and homestays in Bukittinggi should be able to tell you exactly when and where.

It's a light-hearted community activity watched by Minangkabau inhabitants of all ages, so even if you're not a dedicated duck fancier it's a great way to hang out with the locals. The event starts with the serious business of the number draw, after which both the duck's bill and the owner's chest are printed with matching numbers. When the flag drops, ducks take to the air and fly to the finish line. If it's a neck-and-neck (or bill-and-bill) photo-finish the winner is identified by phone-camera footage. The duck is then reunited with its owner so that prizes can be awarded.

For something equally authentic, visit the buffalo-racing course in Tanah Datar Regency (just south of Bukittinggi). Traditionally held in the rice paddies to celebrate the harvest, **Pacu Jawi** ('bull races') are now held for tourists every Saturday at different paddy fields. A pair of bulls run on a muddy rice-paddy track that can be up to 250m long, while a jockey stands behind them, 'waterskiing' on a wooden plough while holding the bulls by their tails. Injuries are quite common for the jockeys and, while the bulls are not whipped, their tails are sometimes bitten to make them run faster. Hotels and homestays can usually advise where the next race will be and there are often day-long tours, typically costing around 1,000,000Rp, that include various other sights.

Danau Maninjau

TIME FROM PADANG: **3HR**

The view across Danau Maninjau

Danau Maninjau is a lake that was formed by a volcanic explosion some 52,000 years ago. The waterfront is famously accessed from a crazily winding rollercoaster descent that includes 44 switchbacks, so it takes at least an hour to get to the shore from Bukittinggi. Each hairpin is numbered, with several featuring warung (look in particular for No 27 and No 37), where you can snack and enjoy the view. Once you make it to the waterfront, the 50km drive or ride to circumnavigate the lake is 'plain sailing'. There are a few cycle-rental spots in Maninjau village, but in general the bikes have seen better days and a scooter is likely the better option.

You might be surprised to see a lot of trucks heading up the hill, transporting huge plastic containers of live fish. Fish farming boomed in the late 1990s, and its rapid increase has raised questions about the environmental impact on the lake.

You don't have to tackle the 44 hairpin turns to see the best of Danau Maninjau, since the best view is from **Puncak Lawang**, the peak high above Lawang village. This too is a

WANOEL AZMI/SHUTTERSTOCK

Vespa scooter, Padang Sidempuan

lovely hour-long ride from Bukittinggi through dense forest and pristine paddies. Lawang village has some spectacular examples of traditional Minangkabau homes, along with what might be the world's most deliciously sweet sugar-cane. Be sure to stop by the roadside at one of the *es tebu* (cane juice) stalls.

The Puncak Lawang hilltop features a cafe and gardens with swings and zip-lines. It's a beautiful spot when it's not busy and the hillside does indeed offer the most gorgeous view of Danau Maninjau.

Padang Sidempuan

TIME FROM PADANG: **9HR**

Take a ride on a Vespa becak

In the 1960s, the highland town of Padang Sidempuan received an influx of Italian-built Vespa scooters. More than half a century later, 200 or so are still serving as public transport in the form of becak fitted with sidecars. If you're passing through Padang Sidempuan – on a road trip between Danau Toba and Bukittinggi, for example – and have even a mild appreciation for retro design, take the opportunity to stop for a quick jaunt on one of these puttering veteran scooters. An hour-long tour of the town will normally cost you about 100,000Rp. Feel free to split the cost since, although the sidecars look like single-seaters, they often carry three and even four people home from the markets.

Most models here tend to date back to the mid-1970s, but you'll even see a few classic gems dating back to the 1960s. A few are clearly doted upon and have stayed in the same family. Others have been 'preloved' many times over. The majority have seen better days and the ones that are too battered to serve as passenger transport often continue to run for decades as cargo transport with simple platforms bolted on the side. Whatever their condition, these vehicles remain prized possessions.

LEGEND OF THE BUFFALO

Buffaloes are a huge part of Minangkabau culture and history. In fact, it's said that the word *kerbau* (buffalo) is likely the origin of the tribe's name. Folklore has it that the threat of attack by a Javanese king led the forefathers of the Minangkabau to propose a bullfight instead of a battle. The Javanese chose their biggest and meanest bull, but the clever West Sumatrans simply attached sharp spurs to a half-starved calf. As soon as it spotted the bull it dashed forward and, in a desperate attempt to find milk, disembowelled the gigantic bovine. Many say that Minangkabau means 'the winning buffalo', although there are those who claim that it means 'river buffalo'.

THE ELUSIVE ORANG PENDEK

The enigmatic *orang pendek* (literally, 'short person') has been talked about in the Kerinci forests for generations. Eyewitnesses describe the creature as being about 1m tall, more ape than human, but walking upright on the ground. Folktales say that its feet face backwards so it can't be tracked in the forest, but some farmers who claim to have seen it frequently will often shrug and say that there's nothing mystical about it: it's just another animal, they'll tell you...like the tiger only more common.

The creature's elusive habits have made it a mythological celebrity – a sort of Sumatran yeti – but some naturalists have hypothesised that it could be a sub-species of black orangutan that somehow survived when Mt Toba exploded 74,000 years ago.

RICO YULIYANTO/SHUTTERSTOCK

Gunung Kerinci

Rimba Ecolodge

TIME FROM PADANG: **1½HR**

A jungle escape on the outskirts of Padang

Despite being on the mainland and less than 5km from Padang's city centre, just reaching **Rimba Ecolodge** *(rimba-ecoproject.com)* is quite an adventure. First, you have to take a taxi from Padang to the village of Bungus, 40 minutes to the south, where you board a **small boat** *(500,000Rp for up to four people)*. The coastline is so craggy and convoluted that the boat takes a further 50 minutes to reach Rimba's jungle paradise.

The property itself, founded by a French-Indonesian couple, is delightfully off-the-grid in an enchantingly Robinson Crusoe sort of way so that it's almost impossible to imagine that the city lies just beyond the jungle-clad slopes.

The sweeping arc of white sand that fronts the lodge has wonderful snorkelling and the hilly backdrop is an ideal place for hiking, either guided or alone (staff can give instructions so that it's impossible to get lost). If you don't think this is true wilderness, get Reno Putra, the Indonesian owner, to tell you about the time a tiger came down the hill and ate his dog!

Danau Gunung Tujuh

TIME FROM PADANG: **6HR**

Go hiking and camping at a crater lake

At 2003m, Danau Gunung Tujuh (Seven Mountains Lake) is Southeast Asia's highest crater lake. It's a place of almost mystical beauty.

It takes about three to four hours to hike up to the lake. Once there, you may be able to pay a fisherman (there's only one who lives there on a semi-permanent basis) to paddle you the 4km across the impressively big lake. The jungle is remote enough to have spectacular wildlife and you have a good chance of seeing tapir or tiger tracks, though both are so elusive that it's extremely unlikely you'll be blessed with actual sightings. Sitting around a campfire listening to tales of tiger encounters or waking to the whoop of gibbons are experiences that you're unlikely to ever forget. You'll need a reliable and experienced guide: **Wild Sumatra** *(wildsumatra.com)* charges 4,800,000Rp per person for a two-day camping trip, including transport from Padang.

Birders from around the world flock here for sightings of various hornbills, Schneider's pitta and the crested wood partridge. Keep an eye out in the lower forest for pitcher plants, some species of which are found nowhere else.

Gunung Kerinci

TIME FROM PADANG: **6HR**

Climb Southeast Asia's tallest volcano

There's no doubt that the hike to the summit of **Gunung Kerinci** (3805m) is a highlight of any Sumatran adventure. It's a real privilege to watch sunrise from the peak of eastern Indonesia's highest peak.

Most hikes up Gunung Kerinci begin with a six-hour drive from Padang and a night at Kersik Tuo. From there it's just over 4km to the **Kerinci Seblat National Park** entrance at Pintu Rimba, where the trailhead begins at 1755m above sea level.

The volcano is usually tackled over two days, with tents pitched at a base camp about 800m short of the summit – close enough for a 4am wake-up call and an hour-long predawn hike to reach the peak by sunrise. It's not easy: the path is steep and eroded and, once above the treeline, the scree is extremely slippery. Sometimes it feels as if you take three steps up only to slide back two. Apart from being the country's highest volcano, Kerinci is also the highest Indonesian peak outside of New Guinea island.

After summiting you'll head back down to the base camp for breakfast, then take another five hours or so to get back to Pintu Rimba. It's illegal and foolhardy to hike Gunung Kerinci without a guide. This is a serious expedition that needs proper preparation: you'll need full camping gear, a warm sleeping bag, waterproof clothes and a head torch (all of which can be hired in Kersik Tuo if needed). Nights are freezing so don't fall into the trap of expecting a tropical climate, and don't attempt the climb in wet weather.

Most organised packages include transport from Kersik Tuo, entry fees and permits, porters to carry and assemble your tents and somebody to cook meals. **Wild Sumatra** *(wildsumatra.com)* can arrange a four-day trip including transport to and from Padang for 4,600,000Rp (based on one person). As usual, always confirm exactly what's included in the cost when you book and remember that you'll cut costs by sharing.

DON'T MENTION THE TIGER!

In many parts of Sumatra it's considered extremely bad luck to mention tigers while you're actually in the jungle. Instead of talking about the *harimau* ('tiger' in Bahasa Indonesia) people from jungle communities are more likely to call them by another name, most often *nenek* (grandmother) or sometimes simply 'the Boss'. It's perfectly fine to speak about the *harimau* once you are safely back in the village, but in the forest it's considered polite, for obvious reasons, to use terms of utmost respect. You might hear the word *macan* too – although it technically means leopard, in Sumatra it's often used to mean tiger.

Surf Charters in Sumatra

In the 1990s, surfers (mostly Australians) started exploring Sumatra's best breaks by boat, hiring local fisherfolk to take them around. The reasons were many: there was no tourism infrastructure on the islands and flights to the island were erratic or non-existent. Despite new airports, greater infrastructure and the fact that few undiscovered breaks remain, hopping on a charter boat for 10 to 12 days is an irresistible option for surfers from all over the world.

Who to Choose if You Like...

Small Groups

Carpe Diem 1 *(olasnavigator.com; US$2455 for an 11-day charter)* Regularly explores some of Sumatra's remotest surf spots. Run by experienced surfers who place utmost importance on safety and uncrowded waves.

The Asia *(asiasurfcharterssumatra.com; US$2695 for a 10-day charter)* Purpose-built vessel for long-range surf exploration. Equipped with snorkelling and fishing gear and two speedboats.

Orca Laut *(orcalautsurf.com; US$2465 for an 11-day charter)* Eight berths in three cabins; includes unlimited use of two tenders for surfing and fishing, plus onboard Starlink internet.

Traditional Vessels

Maki Boat *(makiboat.com; US$3445 for an 11-day charter)* A beautiful Sulawesi-built traditional schooner with air-con and in-depth knowledge of Mentawai's most famous breaks.

Nusa Dewata *(nusadewata.com; US$1355 per day, up to seven guests)* A sleek 21m timber sloop built in Nusa Lembongan. Owners recommend a pickup from any Mentawai camp.

Budget-Friendly Options

Saraina *(sarainasurfcharters.com; US$2040 for a seven-day charter)* This 20m motor-cruiser hosts six to nine guests and is one of the most affordable charters; shorter trips possible.

Wild Cat Surf Charters *(wildcatsurfcharters.com; US$1900 for an 11-day charter)* A fast catamaran for exploring all parts of the Mentawais. Perhaps the cheapest option, sleeping 10 in eight single beds and two queens.

Wave Hunter *(wavehuntermentawai.com; US$2750 for an 11-day charter)* Explore Mentawais, Telo or Banyak Islands in comfort at a great price. Air-con cabins and two speedboats.

Luxury Charters

MV Addiction *(addictionsurfing.com; enquire for prices)* A fast and stable 24m high-speed catamaran that only takes full groups (max eight) for pure, uncrowded, high-end surf adventures.

Sibon Jaya *(siboncharters.com; US$4190 for an all-inclusive 12-day charter)* Explore Mentawai, Telo and Enggano in comfort in a gorgeous 21m aluminium catamaran with four private suites and one large cabin.

Pulse Surf Charters *(pulsesurfcharters.com; US$3870 for an all-inclusive 12-day charter)* A custom-designed high-speed aluminium catamaran that's also equipped for exploring the Banyak archipelago.

Seriti *(prayacharters.com; US$3230 for an 11-day charter)* One of the most popular Banyak and Mentawai tours, including use of two auxiliary boats, full air-con, four meals a day, daily video analysis and...free beer.

WIRESTOCK CREATORS/SHUTTERSTOCK

Surfers, Sumatra

HOW TO

When to go Surfing season runs from March until November, with prices only reduced (if at all) in November and the first months of the year.

Book ahead Subscribe to the email lists of your desired surf-charter company so you know when trips have been released for reservations. They book out fast.

Before you go Buy travel insurance with emergency evacuation, as it's rarely included. Let those at home know if you're going to be out of contact.

Budget The rate per person varies between around US$170 and US$350 per day; make sure you're happy with the inclusions. Extra beer often needs to be organised before departure.

Private Charter or Existing Group?

Private charters are ideal if you can get a group of surfing friends together. Choose your friends wisely, though – you're about to spend a substantial amount of time enclosed in a relatively small space. Find out the living space allocation of the vessel you're considering and try to resist the temptation to max-out the group size: sleeping quarters on cheaper charters are usually dorm-style and compact, so comfort can be hugely boosted if you have a smaller group. Consider the surfing abilities of your group, too; Sumatra's best reefs are ideally suited to intermediate to advanced surfers and beginners sometimes struggle to find less challenging conditions.

Joining an existing tour is a potentially great way to make new friends – but it can be intense and, initially at least, you'll be spending lots of time with strangers. Bigger boats have the benefit of separate living areas and even berths so you don't have to share a dorm. The group might differ in interests or the time they want to spend in the waves, so it's best if two tenders are available so that passengers can engage in a range of activities or divide and conquer for simultaneous 'surf raids' on two spots. Most operators can get your surfboards to the boat and all will arrange overnight accommodation before you board. This removes a lot of hassle and is recommended.

Banda Aceh

UNIQUE RELIGION | GREAT COFFEE | DISASTER RECOVERY

GETTING AROUND

Some sights are grouped together near the Tsunami Museum, which you can explore on foot. For sights that are further away, Grab or Gojek ride-hailing apps are ideal. For airport or ferry transfers or tours, a private driver is best. Tsunami-survivor Pak Saiful *(WhatsApp +62 852 6018 0318)* has a reliable car, a good command of English and a wealth of information, as well as dramatic tales of that horrific event. There's no public transport to Lhok Nga's beaches, but homestays and hotels can always arrange transport, and you can rent a motorbike with a surfboard rack upon arrival.

The city of Banda Aceh, at the northern tip of the main island of Sumatra, is an example of the resilience of the Sumatran islanders. Islam is said to have entered Indonesia though Aceh in the 12th century and has certainly maintained powerful roots in Banda Aceh. Faith only got stronger after the 2004 tsunami, as mosques stood solidly while everything around them was swept away by the 30m wave. Their survival was seen as a sign of the divine. Over time, homes, markets and public buildings were rebuilt and today Banda Aceh often surprises people as a vibrant and hospitable city with an irresistible cafe culture (Gayo coffee grows in its surrounding hills) and an eye-opening collection of tsunami-related sights. Nevertheless, Banda Aceh is mostly popular as the gateway to surf spots and beaches, as well as the diving and snorkelling bliss of Pulau Weh, a short hop away by fast ferry.

Banda Aceh's Tsunami Legacy

Tsunami monuments and museums

Of the estimated 230,000 people who died during the devastating 2004 tsunami, over 160,000 were from Aceh. Needless to say, the people of Banda Aceh will never forget that day, and there are several powerful reminders that serve to bring the scale of the devastation into poignant focus for visitors.

The **Museum Tsunami Aceh** *(museumtsunami.acehprov.go.id; 20,000Rp)* is the best first stop to learn about the tsunami and the recovery efforts that extended for years. You enter this beautifully designed building through a dark tunnel with dripping 30m-high walls – designed to bring to mind what the wave must have looked like when it hit. In effect, it's the harrowing photo displays that evoke the devastation – and the beginning of the cleanup – most powerfully. A 10-minute video is a stark reminder of how quickly an event can change

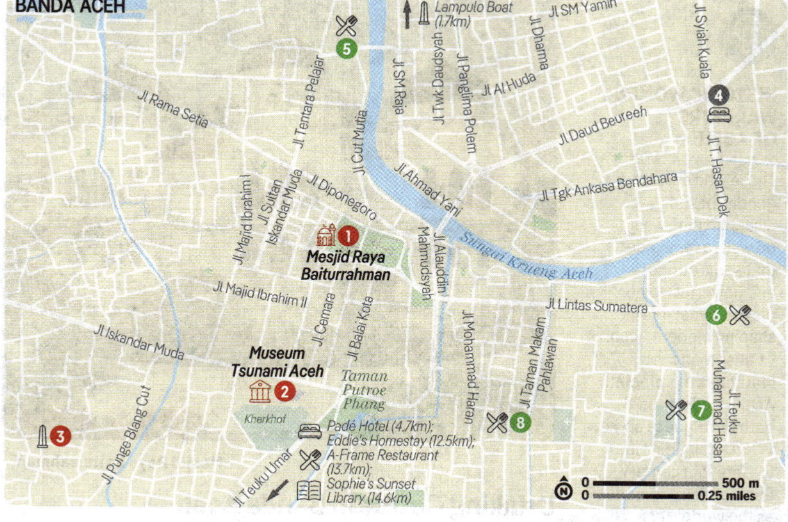

HIGHLIGHTS
1 Mesjid Raya Baiturrahman
2 Museum Tsunami Aceh

SIGHTS
3 Museum PLTD Apung

SLEEPING
4 Lala Hostel

EATING
5 Ata Kopi
6 Dhapu Kupi
7 Kupi Nanggroe 24 Jam
8 Warkop Zakir

everything; it's similarly heartrending to stand in the circular chamber surrounded by the names of victims. The museum is open from 9am to 11.30am and 2pm to 3.30pm.

The wave was powerful enough to carry a 2500-tonne power-generating vessel 5km inland. The PLTD Apung ship, having wiped out every building in its path, still rests today among a cluster of smashed buildings and now serves as the **Museum PLTD Apung** *(7000Rp)*. It's surrounded by several monuments, including a clock with the exact time and date of the initial earthquake incorporated into a replica wave. It's open from 9am to noon, 2pm to 3.30pm and 4pm to 5pm.

Another boat, known locally as **Lampulo Boat** *(desalampulo.com; also signposted as 'Boat Di Atas Rumah' – the boat on the house)*, was left high and dry, propped up on a roof 1km from the river where it was moored. There's a faded photo exhibition here too – some images are particularly graphic – showing the death and destruction. Admission is free but the donation box should not be overlooked. As is the case with Museum PLTD Apung, a series of raised walkways offer a view of the Lampulo Boat in its surreal location.

While the city looks vibrant and perhaps even fully 're-covered', many locals who survived the tsunami lost family members and emotional scars remain. Broach the topic with sensitivity and you'll find that many Acehnese have astounding tales of survival – and heartbreaking stories of loss – to share.

TOP TIP

Aceh often makes headlines for its penchant for sharia-style punishment. Come with an open mind and you'll find that the Acehnese are among Indonesia's most hospitable people. Be aware that beyond the usual tourist trail, couples sharing rooms might be asked by hotel staff to show a copy of a wedding certificate.

HISTORIC WOMEN WARRIORS OF ACEH

Those who enforce gender-based discrimination would do well to remember that some strong and powerful women played a vital role in shaping modern Aceh.

Laksamana Malahayati protected Aceh's coast from both Portuguese and VOC Dutch fleets in the late 16th century. She's often regarded as the world's first female admiral.

Sultanah Nahrasiyah, queen of Aceh until 1428, was said to be a wise and compassionate ruler who oversaw the rise of Islam in her kingdom.

Cut Nyak Dhien, whose portrait is on the 10,000Rp banknote, was an Acehnese resistance heroine who fought with great strategic skill against the Dutch.

Suke Kawai Istana was a women-only corp of elite troops who protected the sultanate palace in the 17th century.

MUHAMMAD IQBAL/SHUTTERSTOCK

Mesjid Raya Baiturrahman

Drinking Coffee in Banda Aceh

Robusta served with a flourish

Expensive arabica coffee is grown in the nearby Gayo Highlands, but in Banda Aceh baristas prepare their robusta coffee with a level of flair that would challenge the most flamboyant Greenwich Village coffee maker. Your *kopi tarik* ('pulled coffee') is created through an arm-waving process that filters the coffee multiple times through what looks like a large sock. The coffee is sweet (unless you choose otherwise) and perfectly aerated when it lands in your glass after about 30 seconds of this athletic blending.

With alcohol banned and its history of exceptional coffee, Aceh lives its cafe lifestyle to the full. These local cafes – often more like alcohol-free beer halls – are usually the only places where friends and courting couples can socialise.

A Book Lover's Beachfront Bohemian Dream

Visit Sophie's Sunset Library

Anyone who loves books, memorabilia and sunsets on the beach (and even more books) will enjoy the little patch of paradise, that lies at the northern end of Babah Kuala Beach, just 20 minutes from the city centre. Sophie, the owner of

EATING IN BANDA ACEH: OUR PICKS

Ata Kopi: A gigantic Aceh-style coffee hall. Specialises in sweet, strong *kopi tarik* ('pulled coffee'), filtered through what appears to be an old sock. *24hr* $

Warkop Zakir: One of Banda Aceh's most popular hangouts. Try the *soto Medan* (Medan soup) or *martabak* (a flaky pastry pie). *6am-midnight* $

Kupi Nanggroe 24 Jam: Another great coffee shop, with excellent drinks and food stalls. On Friday afternoons clerics from surrounding mosques preach here. *24hr* $

Dhapu Kupi: A rare example of a smaller boutique cafe, rather than the typical Banda Aceh coffee hall. Popular enough to draw a crowd at all hours. *24hr* $

Sophie's Sunset Library *(instagram.com/sophies_sunset_library)*, is 10 years old and this enchanting library was founded by her parents, Raihan and Dendi (a historian and an ex-Reuters cameraman). The lovely old house is full of memorabilia, vintage furniture and, of course, hundreds of great books (in Bahasa Indonesia, English and Dutch). You can borrow a book, order from the menu – try Raihan's excellent *roti canai* or homemade lemon juice – and chill in the garden. Most visitors are lured by a love of books, and many find Instagrammable photos amid the vintage backdrops. Some visitors even rent a **tent on the lawn** *(250,000Rp per night; up to four people)*. There are occasional poetry readings and the family, all skilled musicians and singers, put on performances.

Whatever brings you here, bear in mind that this is primarily a community project that was founded to give local kids and adults access to literature. Make a donation, leave a book or order from the menu – try to leave more than you take. It's open from 9am to 9pm, Tuesday to Sunday.

A Mosque's Survival Story

Proof of divine intervention?

The fact that Banda Aceh's main mosque, the majestic monochrome **Mesjid Raya Baiturrahman**, has been left untouched by both earthquake and wave is seen as a direct intervention by the divine. The mosque dates from the 12th century, but sections were added by the Dutch in 1879 and 1936, then by the Indonesian government in 1957. After the 2004 tsunami it famously needed little more than a cleanup.

To visit, you need to remove your shoes and to cover up (you can borrow appropriate clothing, including headscarves for women, from the office in the underground car park). Non-Muslims cannot enter the prayer hall, but those who visit on a Friday afternoon will see thousands praying outside under the space-age retractable sunshades. It's open from 4.30am to 10pm.

Experience Sunsets, Surfing & Seafood

Embrace Banda's beach life

The neighbouring beaches of Lhok Nga and Babah Kuala are Banda Aceh's version of a surfer's paradise. **Lhok Nga** stretches 2.5km south from the Krueng Raba rivermouth, and hotshot surfers are drawn to the beach-break known as Cement Factory. The huge factory that gave the break its name is a monstrous eyesore at the southern end of the beach, but **Babah Kuala** (curving prettily from the northern bank of the Krueng Raba) is cleaner and infinitely more picturesque. The waves here are surfable right through the tides, and the months from October to April are typically blessed by offshore winds. The left-hander (near the river) can be fast and hollow but the right and the famous peak known simply as A Frame are suitable for intermediate surfers...unless the waves get over head high. You can rent boards from A-Frame Restaurant and motorbikes with board-racks are available for hire from Eddie's Homestay (p534).

THE SILENCE OF SHARIA

In 2015 Aceh became the only province in Indonesia to implement sharia law. If you're wondering why it's quieter than your average city, it could be because karaoke – that never-ending Indonesian soundtrack – is banned. More seriously, people have been caned for homosexuality, a 'morality offence' in Aceh but not illegal elsewhere in Indonesia. Drinking alcohol is illegal for both Muslims and non-Muslims, and punishment following a sharia-court process is public caning. Foreigners get caught up in the laws, but technically non-Muslims can choose to be punished under sharia law or Indonesia's criminal code. In some traditional areas there are strict rules against unmarried tourists sharing hotels rooms – a copy of a wedding certificate might be demanded by hotel staff.

Beyond Banda Aceh

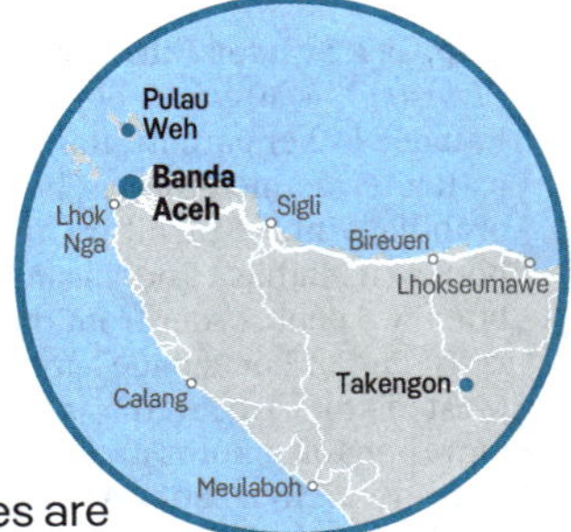

Pulau Weh's clear waters and pristine beaches are the stuff that desert-island dreams are made of, while Takengon's Danau Lut Tawar offers a refreshing taste of highland life.

Places

While Aceh has its share of surfing beaches, Pulau Weh, near Indonesia's northernmost tip, has world-class diving and snorkelling. Dramatic marine life, vibrant coral gardens, wrecks and even underwater volcanoes have put it on the bucket list of any scuba enthusiast. The two main areas that appeal to travellers are the little beachfront village of Gapang (with several dive centres and great cafes) and Iboih (3.5km to the north), which has more of a chilled forest-bungalow vibe.

Both figuratively and geographically, Pulau Weh is the cherry on top for visitors to Sumatra. If you're heading south from here, consider taking the high road to lovely Takengon and the scenic mountain lake known as Danau Lut Tawar.

GETTING AROUND

The fast ferry from Banda Aceh to Pulau Weh costs 100,000Rp and leaves Sumatra's mainland three times a day, taking 40 minutes. The slow ferries (35,000Rp) leave at around the same times but – taking 1½ hours – offer a more relaxing introduction to slow island life. Once there, you'll need to catch a becak (motorcycle-rickshaw; 150,000Rp) or private taxi (200,000Rp) for the 40-minute drive to Gapang or Iboih. It's easy to rent a motorbike (around 100,000Rp) to get around.

Pulau Weh

TIME FROM BANDA ACEH: 1½HR

Dive in Pulau Weh's stunning waters

With more than 20 recognised dive sites, including a WWII wreck and an underwater volcano, it's not surprising that Pulau Weh is a bucket-list destination for any keen underwater explorer. Dive centres are mostly centred around Iboih and Gapang. **Monster Diving** *(monsterdiving.com)* operates from Gapang, as does long-established **Lumba Lumba Diving Centre** *(lumbalumba.com)*. There's someone to advise at the Lumba Lumba reception desk from 8am to 8pm every day. Expect to pay around 350,000Rp for a fun dive; talk the plans through beforehand so you know what's included and what dive sites will be most appealing given your interests, skill level and the prevailing diving conditions.

There's wildlife galore where the Andaman Sea meets the Indian Ocean. **Batee Tokong** (Central Rock) has a deep sloping wall covered in gorgonian sea fans. **The Canyon**, a spot that sees parrotfish, barracuda and occasionally visiting whale sharks, has a spectacular double pinnacle. For experienced divers, **Arus Balee's** sweeping currents make it a favourite

22AUGUST/SHUTTERSTOCK

Diving, Batee Tokong, Pulau Weh

site for drift dives, and there's even a 130m German steamship, the *Sophie Rickmers*, which was deliberately sunk by her crew in WWII. **Shark Plateau** is a world-class dive spot and early morning dives are best for encountering sharks.

Snorkel above the bubbles

Snorkelling through warm bubbles emanating from the heart of an underwater volcano is one of the most surreal experiences that Indonesia has to offer. There are several places in the archipelago where you can do this, but few that are as intense as the submarine plateau of underwater vents that lies just offshore, 2km southeast of **Gapang**. In places, the entire seabed is stained yellow with sulphur and appears to be boiling as bubbles rise like floating diamonds. When the wind is onshore the smell of sulphur is noticeable even from the coastal road.

Day-long snorkelling tours cost around 1,350,000Rp for two people. The vents are only about 20m offshore (and only about 5m deep at low tide) so, if you're travelling on a budget, just hire snorkelling gear, rent a scooter and park near the rocky beach. Iboih has countless rental shops where you can get mask, snorkel and fins for around 50,000Rp per day; a scooter will set you back 100,000Rp. Beware of currents and remember that it's never advisable to dive alone.

GET YOUR BEARINGS

Pulau Weh is known by a few names. People in Banda Aceh ask if you're heading to Sabang, which is actually the capital of the island that's usually called Weh (or sometimes We). The ferry arrives in Balohan, on the southeast coast. Sabang and Sumur Tiga Beach (a popular spot for hotels) are further north, with Gapang and Iboih located about 40 minutes away, through forest to the northwest. You don't go through the capital to get to either of the latter. Kilometre 0 is 7km northwest of Iboih, past a smattering of small resorts, warungs (food stalls) and a few obligatory souvenir stalls. Roads are winding and steep, but with manageable traffic it's a good place to explore by rented scooter.

EATING IN PULAU WEH: OUR PICKS

Pachamama Indah: This appealing bakery on the Gapang strip has outstanding sweet pies, cookies and homemade ice cream. *8am-8pm Tue-Sun* $

Mama Mia's Restaurant: A friendly beachfront resort with delicious home-cooked Acehnese and Sumatran specialities, plus good pizzas. *8am-10pm* $

Molina's Cafe: Go for the excellent curry but leave space for the outstanding coffee, waffles and selection of fruit-flavoured ice cream. *10am-9pm Fri-Wed* $

Dee Dee's Kitchen: A friendly family-run restaurant where Dee Dee cooks freshly made meals, including great curries and barbecued fish. *8am-10pm* $

A LITTLE VOLCANO'S BIG HISTORY

Pulau Weh is what remains of a partially collapsed volcano that was filled by the sea from the northeast. At 617m, the volcanic peak is the highest point on the island. And it's active: hot springs and fumaroles (vents releasing volcanic gas and vapours) are found both on land and under the water. Apart from a booming tourism industry, Pulau Weh might seem like an economic backwater, but during the Dutch era Sabang was a major coal and water depot for steamships exiting the Strait of Malacca and heading into the Indian Ocean. For a short period of time in the 1970s, the whole island was a duty-free port.

BANG HARLEN/SHUTTERSTOCK

Goa Putri Pukes, Takengon

Marine life is less abundant than at other nearby sites, so perhaps combine a snorkelling trip here with another spot where you'll have more colourful sightings.

Stand on top of Indonesia

Pulau Weh's northern tip (a 15-minute rollercoaster ride from Iboih) is famous as Indonesia's **Kilometer Nol** (Kilometre Zero). A huge monument – evocatively wind-smashed and dilapidated – marks the spot. Among the souvenirs are some appealing warungs selling Acehnese *rujak* (a spicy fruit snack); there's also a fairly aggressive troop of macaques. It's a prime selfie spot for weekend visitors from Banda Aceh.

Walk just a little further beyond the monument for a more poignant experience. Don't worry – the macaques seem to avoid this area since there are no food stalls. A boardwalk leads down a series of 96 steps through the forest to the rocky coastline. It's almost as if the pounding Andaman Sea was determined to bite off this last chunk of Indonesian territory, leaving the boardwalk in a twisted wreck just a few metres short of the shoreline. Despite the soaring monument, Pulau Weh is not actually the Indonesia's northernmost point: the tiny naval outpost of Pulau Rondo lies about 20km to the north.

Pulau Rubiah's mysterious history

Pulau Rubiah, just 10 minutes in a wooden motorboat from the concrete jetty at Iboih beach, makes for an enjoyable half-day visit. It has some good eateries on pleasant stilted platforms and you can hire snorkelling equipment (50,000Rp for a mask, snorkel, fins...and, should you wish, an inflatable vest).

It can be crowded – especially at weekends – but just take a short walk over the hill to the eastern side of the island (barely 250m) and you'll find a hidden bay where you're almost guaranteed to be able to snorkel in solitude. There was a little warung here, but for the past five years this side of the island has remained almost entirely deserted.

For such a tiny island (less than 1.5km long), Pulau Rubiah has a surprisingly rich history. The 246-year-old tomb of Siti Rubiah (the wife of a Muslim cleric) stands among the warungs. On the hill above you'll find a ruined Dutch hospital that was once a quarantine centre for pilgrims returning from Hajj, back when leprosy was a feared disease. If it seems strange that the grand whitewashed buildings are entirely overlooked, bear in mind that this site is widely said to be haunted. The stories all seem to revolve around Dutch ghosts, with never the hint of a phantom leper.

A return boat transfer to Pulau Rubiah costs 150,000Rp (for two people); transfers run from 8am to 6pm.

Takengon

TIME FROM BANDA ACEH: **6HR**

Ride a motorbike through the Gayo Highlands

Despite having little in the way of spectacular sights, Takengon (1200m above sea level) is an unexpectedly cool town in every sense of the word. Visitors tend to bypass Aceh's Gayo Highlands during their 600km overland journey between Banda Aceh and Bukit Lawang. But spend time exploring the lovely lake or meeting locals in Takengon's appealing coffee shops and you could end up wondering why this picturesque 'Land above the Clouds' isn't on everybody's Sumatran wishlist.

It's hard to escape coffee culture in the Gayo Highlands, but you're in the heart of one of the world's most celebrated arabica cultivating regions – why would you want to? Hire a motorbike through **Visit Gayo Travel** *(instagram.com/visitgayo.travel; around 120,000Rp)* and take a circular ride around Danau Lut Tawar to see what's at the root of this caffeine obsession. Among the rearing hillside of pines, acres of rice paddies and hamlets shaded with majestic mango trees, only rarely are you out of sight of the polished greenery of coffee bushes.

The most famous site on Danau Lut Tawar's north shore is **Goa Putri Pukes**, a subterranean cavern with a rock formation resembling a princess (Putri Pukes) who, legend has it, turned to stone rather than be carried away from her family. You might be surprised to see village dogs (a rare sight in any strictly Muslim region), but they're used to protect crops from herds of wild pigs. The pigs are hunted only rarely and the meat is invariably transported over the state boundary.

Allow at least two hours to complete the 50km loop around the lake; you'll want to enjoy the mind-blowing viewpoints and grab a coffee along the way.

ARABICA COFFEE: ACEH'S BLACK GOLD

The Dutch might have brought coffee to the East Indies (to Java, actually, in 1696), but some say that the Acehnese were the ones who perfected it. Gayo arabica is among the world's most celebrated gourmet coffee beans, and Takengon takes coffee appreciation to new levels with its flavoured coffees and super-cool vintage coffee shops.

Sanger (potent coffee served with condensed milk and sugar) is the traditional drink, but you'll find plenty of other drinks to sample – especially among the cold brews. If you want to sip truly unforgettable coffee while seated under the shade of a coffee plantation, head 6km southwest of Takengon to **Galeri Kopi Indonesia**.

Pulau Nias

LEGENDARY SURF | RICH CULTURE | WILD COASTLINE

GETTING AROUND

Ferries to Pulau Nias from Singkil and Sibolga can be erratic and are frequently cancelled due to the whims of the Indian Ocean. Most visitors – in particular, surfers drawn by those same whims – tend to avoid these complications with a direct flight from Medan to Gunungsitoli, Nias' capital. From the airport it's a three-hour drive to Sorake Bay on good, almost empty roads. There's no public transport so book a car through your accommodation or be prepared to haggle at the airport. Expect to pay around 600,000Rp each way.

TOP TIP

Be aware that the nearest ATMs to Sorake are in the town of Teluk Dalam, 25 minutes away. It's easiest to bring cash with you.

Almost the entire west coast of Sumatra is a surfer's dream. And in fact, it's nothing short of amazing that the area's incredible natural wealth and cultural bounty doesn't lure more visitors. Nias, in particular, is home to some of the most intriguing traditional feudal communities and warrior traditions on our planet. Fortunately, the days of headhunting are over and Nias' centuries-old villages are extremely welcoming places to visit. The vast majority of visitors, surfers and explorers all tend to base themselves in Lagundri Bay (Teluk Sorake), where a wide range of homestays and surf camps overlook the legendary surf break – a freight-train right-hander that barrels far across the bay. Even if you're not into surfing, this area, which has some good cafes and a laid-back beach vibe, is an ideal place to rent a scooter and explore the ancient villages, jungle-clad hills and deserted beaches that lie nearby.

Pulau Nias' Legendary Wave

Take up the challenge at Lagundri Bay

Surfers have been drawn to Lagundri Bay on Nias' southwestern tip for decades. Also known as Teluk Sorake or Sorake Bay, its history is the stuff of campfire tales, with prominent themes of headhunting, sorcery and human sacrifice. This isn't ancient history either; the first Australian surfers to ride Lagundri's waves, as recently as 1975, claimed to have been stalked by a rogue shaman bent on collecting a human head.

Surfing has become the main tourist drawcard and is something of an obsession on Nias – sadly, relatively few surfers seem to be aware of the area's spectacular cultural wealth. The immensely powerful earthquake that struck here in 2005 actually improved the already near-perfect wave, making it more powerful, faster and hollower. Lagundri's famous right-hander is best between June and October, when it's regarded as one of the world's best waves. Although swells tend to be smaller between November and March, and the

● **SIGHTS**
1 Bawomataluo
2 Hiliamaetaniha
3 Lagundri Bay
4 Lahusafao
5 Moale Beach
6 Rockstar Point
7 Zöma Beach

● **SLEEPING**
see 3 Hash & Family Surf Camp
8 Salty Dog Hostel
9 Sozinhos Surf Lodge

● **EATING**
see 3 BEO's Pub
see 3 Casa Bebas
see 3 Raffiel Cafe and Pizza

winds less favourable, you can still get some good days with less crowded lineups.

Whatever the season, Lagundri Bay is not a place you'd want to learn how to surf – it's just not a beginner's wave. You can, however, hone your skills on less powerful waves at **Rockstar Point** (a 25km drive up the east coast) or at the beach break at Lagundri, which is also a good swimming beach.

Discover Secret Beaches

Explore the west coast

Surfers are now combing the west coast of Pulau Nias in search of empty waves, a result of Lagundri Bay's consistent (and sometimes overwhelming) popularity. Much of the west coast is still a DIY adventure; some surfers stay in losmen (basic accommodation) around the village of Afulu and hire local boats to take them up and down the coast. Even if you're not looking for empty waves, consider an idyllic country road trip to **Zöma Beach**, a deserted, palm-shaded strip of sand an hour west of Sorake. It's famous for its spectacular sunsets, but given the state of the road, we wouldn't advise making the ride home in darkness. **Moale Beach** – 20 minutes further up the west coast – is another irresistibly wild spot for an afternoon of beach bumming and sunbathing. Bring water as both beaches are completely wild and there's nowhere to buy provisions.

Visit Traditional Villages

Centuries-old hamlets in Hiliamaetaniha and Lahusafao

For hundreds of years, the Nias islanders built elaborate villages around a cobblestone main street. One of the oldest

CUCKOO FOR COCONUTS

On exiting the surf break you might be surprised to see young entrepreneurs dashing knee-deep over the jagged reef to meet you with a fresh coconut. And it shouldn't come as a surprise that seafood and coconuts are delicious staples on this tropical island. Look out for *hambae nititi* (crab meat cooked in coconut milk) or *silio guro* (minced shrimp baked in a banana leaf with grated coconut). For something different, try *babae* (sautéed pork with mung beans and grated coconut). And for a healthy dessert, finish with *gowi nihandro*, mashed cassava with – you guessed it – grated coconut.

SUMATRA'S SURFING COMMUNITY

Ella McCaffray is a pro surfer and the winner of the 2024 Nias Pro surf competition. *@ellamccaffray*

Lagundri Bay creates some of the most powerful and perfectly shaped right barrels on the planet. I've returned to experience this incredible wave several times since I first surfed here in 2022. It's been amazing to see all the generations surfing together, united by a love for this wave. This beautiful little surf community is part of what I feel makes Nias such a special place. As a female travelling solo, I feel very safe in this part of Indonesia. Besides a few new restaurants, not much has changed in the four years I've been visiting. I hope it never changes too much.

ADIL ARMAYA/SHUTTERSTOCK

***Omo sebua*, Bawomataluo**

surviving communities – with buildings that date back three centuries – is **Hiliamaetaniha**. Despite its relative accessibility (just 1km inland from Sorake Bay), few outsiders ever visit this fascinating community with its double row of ship-like wooden houses. As in most of these ancient settlements, access is via a steep set of steps – park your motorbike at the foot of the stairway.

The first view of the double row of statuesque timber houses is nothing short of breathtaking. There could even be something intimidating about these 'warlike' hamlets if it weren't for the friendliness with which the inhabitants greet visitors. There's no charge to enter, but buying a drink or snack at one of the general stores will help to break the ice. You'll soon find that people are keen to practise their English, and even keener still to allow you to practise a few phrases of Bahasa Nias.

The easiest way to reach these communities is on a rented scooter, as the access is always steep and you can get a little closer by using the motorbike parking areas at the edge of the village.

Another charming village, **Lahusafao**, is a lovely 40-minute drive from Sorake Bay up into the highlands, though be aware that the road is narrow, potholed and better suited to scooters than to cars. The timber *omo hada* houses with their steep roofs are constructed without nails, and so fared better than

EATING IN SORAKE: OUR PICKS

Hash & Family Surf Camp (p535): Sorake's most generous home-cooked meals, like fish barbecued on coconut husks, are served at this surf camp. *7am-9pm* $

Casa Bebas: Lisa from Florence prides herself on her coffee, banana bread and focaccia...and fantastic Javanese *jamu* pick-me-up drinks. *7am-3pm* $$

Raffiel Cafe and Pizza: This excellent beachfront bar, complete with pool table, serves what are probably the best wood-fired pizzas on Nias. *7am-10pm* $

BEO's Pub: Start your day with BEO's big breakfast then catch the sunset later on while tucking into Baja fish tacos and a cold Bintang. *8am-10pm* $

the rigid concrete buildings that bore the brunt of the damage during the 2005 earthquake.

The villagers are proud of their beautiful hamlets and there's always a lot to see and photograph, so it's easy to spend an hour or more visiting each place. With a little luck, a villager will invite you to see the interior of one of these spectacular buildings.

The Warrior Athletes of Nias

Stone jumping at Bawomataluo

Bawomataluo (Sun Hill) is the most famous of the traditional villages on Pulau Nias. It was built between 1830 and 1840 and – while slightly more touristy than the others in the area – it is renowned as the setting for *lompat batu* (stone jumping). Stone jumping was once a form of training for warriors; the jumpers had to leap over a high stone wall, some of which are over 2m tall. These days the motivation is chiefly financial (ie being paid by tourists), but the local stone jumpers are still seen as heroes in their community. Bawomataluo's jumping stone is in the wide stone courtyard, right near the *omo sebua* – known to local guides as the king's house. This building is thought to be the oldest and largest traditional house on the island. For a small donation you can look around its timber-beamed interior and admire the drum that signals the beginning and end of meetings, as well as the original wooden carvings and rows of pig jawbones that commemorate ceremonies. Outside is the king's stone throne, next to a large stone phallus and stone tables where the deceased were once left to decay. To arrange a stone-jumping exhibition either ask in the village or arrange it through your homestay. The cost for a single jump starts at 150,000Rp. It might seem expensive for a display that only lasts a few seconds, but bear in mind that considerable risk is involved. If you're sceptical, the villagers will happily allow you to try it out for yourself.

Keep Your Cool During a War Dance

Meet Bawomataluo's warriors

The traditional feudal village of Bawomataluo is known for its warriors' dramatic dances. Even today, it's a performance that often instills fear in the hearts of bystanders. The frenzy, costumes, weapons (spears, swords and shields) and almost trance-like vibe can be intensely intimidating. What you'll see is a reenactment of past battles and fighting techniques, with men – often the elders – wearing their full tribal war regalia as they psych themselves up for what could have been, in the time of their fathers, mortal combat. The war dances are still held to welcome officials and celebrate holidays and regional events. Either arrange your visit with these events in mind or pitch in with others to pay for a performance. Ask at your guesthouse or directly in the village.

WARFARE ON PULAU NIAS

Traditionally, Nias' communities were presided over by a *kepala desa* (village chief), who headed a council of elders. Beneath the aristocratic upper caste were the common people, and below them were the enslaved people, who were often traded between villages. Until the first years of the 19th century, Pulau Nias' only regular connection with the outside world was through the slave trade. Sometimes villages would band together to form federations, who subsequently fought each other when enmities shifted. Prior to the Dutch conquest and the arrival of missionaries, inter-village warfare was fast and furious, spurred on by the desire for either revenge or slaves. Human heads were needed for burial rites, wedding dowries and the construction of new villages.

Beyond Pulau Nias

Pulau Nias is an ideal launch pad for some of Sumatra's estimated 419 outlying islands.

Pulau Nias is an ideal starting point for explorations into the mysterious tangle of the Banyak Islands (literally, 'Many Islands') or the lesser known Telo Islands. While the Hinako Islands are easily accessible from Nias, it's likely that, wherever else you travel in this area, you're likely to spend a lot of time waiting for – and riding on – boats.

It's an eight-hour ferry ride from Gunungsitoli (Nias' capital) to the mainland port of Singkil, which is the main access point for the Banyak Islands and Pulau Simeulue. Singkil also has a unique adventure appeal all its own thanks to a wetland wilderness that's home to spectacular wildlife, including orangutans who are frequently courageous enough to wade among the monstrous 5m-long crocodiles.

GETTING AROUND

Due to time restraints (and the fact that most visitors are encumbered with surfboards), travellers in Nias tend to fly in from Medan. Boats leave from various ports for the Banyak Islands, Telo Islands and the little Hinako archipelago (less than 10km off Nias' west coast). If you choose to fly back to Medan, you could fly, for example, to Pulau Simeulue or drive eight hours to the ferry port of Singkil to reach the Banyaks (p498).

Singkil

TIME FROM NIAS: **8HR**

Take a boat cruise in the Rawa Singkil Wildlife Reserve

Fish are not a natural part of the orangutan diet, but these intelligent apes are nothing if not versatile. In the **Rawa Singkil Wildlife Reserve** *(entry 300,000Rp, usually included in the tour price)* they've learned to wade into the water – braving the area's voracious crocodiles – to raid fish traps.

Unlike typical orangutan habitats, Rawa Singkil is a wetland reserve that's only accessible by boat. Be sure to check with your guide in advance since the waterways can get so choked up with plants that at times they are almost impenetrable. It can be quite an adventure to find yourself hauling the motorboat – *African Queen* style – through an almost solid wall of greenery.

Under more favourable conditions, seated comfortably on a mat in a motorised wooden sampan, it's a more relaxing alternative to the hilly trekking conditions that you find in both Bukit Lawang and Ketambe. The first sign that you've arrived in orangutan country is usually the shadowy clumps of nests high in the canopy. Orangutans can't actually swim, but they will occasionally wade into water that is chest-deep, and seeing one of the great red apes in such a situation is a once-in-a-lifetime sighting.

Other primates you're likely to spot include Thomas leaf monkeys, long-tailed macaques, pig-tailed macaques, gibbons and possibly siamang. Remember to bring binoculars because you will see a good variety of waterbirds, too. There are smaller freshwater crocodiles in this area (to see the 6m monsters you'll need to explore the coastal waterways around Kuala Alas). Contact **Sumatra Tour Travel** *(WhatsApp +62 822 9410 7162)* to book a boat tour into the Rawa Singkil Wildlife Reserve. Figure on 800,000Rp per person for a tour. A ranger station opened at the entrance to the reserve in early 2024.

Search for giant crocodiles

Travellers usually pass straight through Singkil in their rush to catch transport to the Banyak Islands or Pulau Nias. However, this sprawling town is on the doorstep to one of Sumatra's most environmentally important areas. The *kuala* (estuary) of the **Sungai Alas** (Alas River), which separates Singkil from Rawa Singkil Wildlife Reserve, is home to freshwater, estuarine and saltwater crocodiles.

Once you've climbed into the boat, your adventure takes you through the briny estuary and a tangled landscape of mangroves. Low tide and sunny weather are optimum conditions for croc spotting, since this is when the giant reptiles tend to haul themselves out to sunbathe. While fish form the main part of the crocs' diets, they're highly opportunistic killers – frequently grabbing bush pigs, deer, monkeys, livestock and pets. Unfortunately, inhabitants of the stilted riverside village of Teluk Rumbia (mostly fisherfolk) report that in recent years the crocodiles seem to have become more aggressive and are often seen close to their homes.

It used to be a local tradition that wedding parties would venture into the channels to collect mussels for their nuptial feast, but lately the crocs have become too aggressive. In February 2025 a woman who was checking fish traps was killed when she was dragged out of her boat by a 5m croc.

You're likely to see several specimens in the narrow channels of nipa and sago palms and your boat driver will probably cut the engine to let the vessel drift, giving you time to marvel at their size before they slip soundlessly into the water. You can book swamp tours and arrange ongoing transportation through the area with **Sumatra Tour Travel** *(WhatsApp +62 822 9410 7162).*

SWAMP SURVIVAL

The north bank of the Sungai Singkil (Singkil River) is protected as the Rawa Singkil Wildlife Reserve. This area, which connects with the Gunung Leuser National Park ecosystem, is home to an estimated 1500 Sumatran orangutans (10% of the wild population). It's also a habitat for critically endangered Sumatran tigers, rhinos and elephants. However, deforestation in the reserve increased dramatically following COVID-19, with new canals being built to drain the peat wetlands and ready them for illegal oil-palm plantations. A ranger station was established in early 2024, but as this area is off the tourist radar, its plight gains little international attention. Bear in mind that your presence here, along with your tourist dollars, could be a powerful force for improvement.

North Sumatra Islands

Many travellers find it difficult to access the tangle of hundreds of islands that lie off Sumatra's west coast. Unless you have a good command of Bahasa Indonesia, it's easiest (and most cost-effective) to plan a trip through a surf camp or homestay. If you're determined to explore under your own steam, then look for locations that are easier to access. Either way, here are a few highlights to help you choose the perfect escape.

Where to Go if You Like...

Surfing Uncrowded Breaks

The **Hinako Islands** – one of surfing's unsung frontiers – lie off Nias' west coast. More exposed than Pulau Nias itself, these islands see bigger and even more consistent waves. With a left-hander at Asu and a strong right-hander at nearby Bawa, good surf is almost guaranteed.

Pulau Asu, one of eight small islands in the Hinako archipelago, has neither roads nor electricity, but it does have good **accommodation** *(sozinhossurflodge.com)* and empty lineups. You can organise a speedboat for the 30-minute trip from Sirombu on Nias' west coast to the Hinako Islands.

The **Telo Islands** lie two hours south of Teluk Dalam on Nias. There are 20 or so breaks here, including some that are good for novices and plenty for more experienced surfers.

Snorkelling Pristine Reefs

You might assume that Sumatra's wave-smashed west coast would have little in the way of prime snorkelling and diving locations. However, this stretch of more than 500km of remote (usually uninhabited) islands offers unlimited appeal for submarine explorers.

Sikandang Island, for example (one of the Banyak Islands), has almost 6km of continuous beaches and calm, turquoise lagoons and bays that make for perfect snorkelling.

Nina's Bungalows *(banyak-island-bungalow.com)* is another appealing and affordable Banyak snorkelling destination.

Even surfing islands usually have a sheltered, leeward coast; the eastern shore of **Telo Island**, for example, is a prime snorkelling area even when the swell is hammering the west coast.

Jungle Treks & Nature

Simeulue Island, 115km offshore of Sumatra, encompasses 1838 sq km of land (including outlying islands) and offers great scope for trekking. Transportation costs mean that the island has been spared the oil-palm plantations that have plagued so much of Sumatra's main island. You'll find wild beaches here, which are rarely marred by even a single footprint. There are also forested hillsides filled with birdlife and tumbling jungle waterfalls that beckon for a cooling swim.

Wildlife fanatics head to **Pulau Bangkaru** in the Banyak Islands, where you can volunteer to help support the celebrated turtle conservation project. Green turtles gather on Bangkaru, and you can witness the laying (and hatching) of eggs at any time. Gigantic leatherback turtles weighing up to 500kg come to nest between November and March.

Sikandang Island

HOW TO

Cut costs In general, the bigger main islands are typically cheaper since you can rely on public ferry services and most areas are accessible via rented motorbike.

Quiet season While low season (from November to February) can be a cost-effective time to travel, bear in mind that resorts and homestays that focus on surfers may be closed.

Transport charges When you book with a homestay or surf camp, be sure to enquire what boat transfers are included and whether or not there are complimentary excursions.

***Jam karet* – 'rubber time'** Boat schedules change depending on the weather and sometimes, it seems, on whims. Public boats may leave late, early or not at all. It pays to go with the flow.

The Cost of Paradise

The Banyak Islands are served three times a week by ferry from Singkil town. The archipelago's name means 'many islands' and, with an official count of 71 of them, there is unlimited potential for island-hopping, so long as you have ample time, patience and funds.

If you're on a budget, Pulau Simeulue (north of the Banyak Islands) can be a good option since the 12-hour night ferry from the mainland costs just 80,000Rp (500,000Rp if you upgrade to an air-con cabin) and you can then explore with a hired motorbike.

With more money to spend, you might be surprised to learn that a ritzy resort on a private island can be surprisingly affordable when compared with other parts of the world. **Diamond Island Eco Resort** *(diamondislandecoresort.com)* in the Banyaks is a favourite with surfers and has access to a range of jungle and wildlife-oriented activities. Pulau Sifauruasi, a private island in the Telos archipelago, is home to luxury **Resort Latitude Zero** *(resortlatitudezero.com)*, which has easy access to almost 20 great surf breaks. The Tua Pijet area (sometimes written 'Tuapejat') of North Sipora Island is gaining a reputation among surfers as 'the new Bali' for its range of hostels and homestays. As such, it's an ideal base from which to explore under your own steam.

Bengkulu

COLONIAL HISTORY | BEACHES | WORLD'S BIGGEST FLOWER

GETTING AROUND

Isolated Bengkulu still feels like a remote frontier town, but this city rewards anyone who has the determination to get here. There are regular overnight buses from Padang (22 to 24 hours) and Palembang (12 hours). With a population of just over 300,000, Bengkulu is a pleasant place to walk around and is well served by taxis and motorbikes through the Maxim ride-hailing app. Grab and Gojek are less common here.

It was in 1818, after Fort Marlborough had just celebrated its hundredth birthday, that Thomas Stamford Raffles of Singapore fame came to take charge of old 'Bencoolen' – the city now known as Bengkulu. A hotbed of malaria, Bencoolen was considered to be one of the worst postings in the British Empire, but after a few years under Raffles' supervision the cash crops of pepper, nutmeg, sugar cane and coffee were all being harvested.

Bengkulu has a dramatically chequered history that stretched through Dutch colonisation and Japanese occupation, and it also played a pivotal part in the struggle for independence. If the city is famous for one thing nationally, it's the fact that the first Indonesian flag was stitched here – you can still see the sewing machine!

Bengkulu is not just for history buffs, however: this charming city also has appealing beaches, great coffee culture and, on the jungle-clad slopes of the Barisan Mountains, clustered pods of the world's biggest flower, *Rafflesia arnoldi*.

Visit a Historic Sumatran Fortress

Explore Fort Marlborough's multicultural history

The whitewashed bulwarks of **Fort Marlborough** *(20,000Rp)*, Bengkulu's most notable historical site, have an unexpectedly cosmopolitan history. The British erected it in 1713 using an Indian labour force, none of whom reportedly returned home.

After the English left, the even more aggressive Dutch won few friends; their enforced economic policy of growing spices instead of rice meant mass starvation for the locals. Later, the Japanese had a brief albeit terrifying stranglehold here. In the last years of Dutch dominion, the colonial forces infamously interrogated Indonesia's President Sukarno in a Fort Marlborough cell. That cell (Ruang Interogasi Sukarno) – along with armories, ammunition stores and garrisons – now

TOP TIP

There are three flights per week to/from Krui in tiny single-propeller Cessna Grand Caravans. A flight along the West Sumatran coastline in one of these airplanes might be one of Sumatra's best-value experiences. Although prices fluctuate, a ticket typically costs just 450,000Rp.

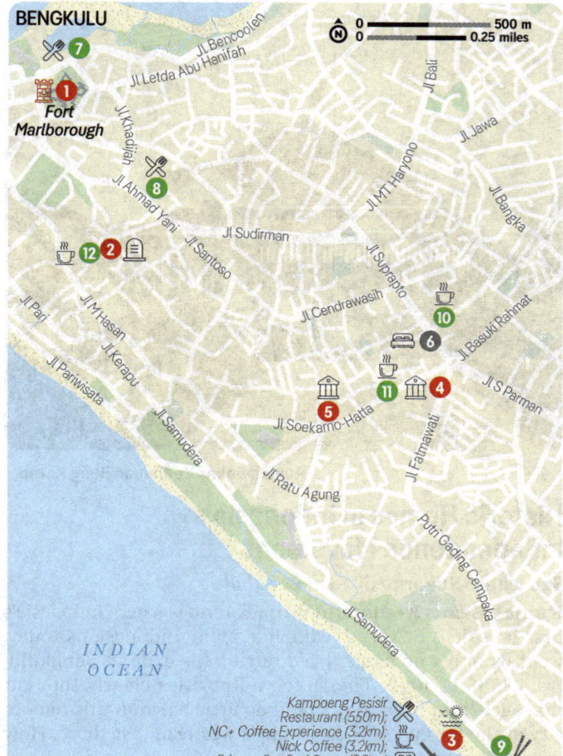

HIGHLIGHTS
1 Fort Marlborough

SIGHTS
2 British Cemetery
3 Pantai Panjang
4 Rumah Ibu Fatmawati Soekarno
5 Soekarno House Museum

SLEEPING
6 Sinar Sport Hotel

EATING
7 Rafflesia Beach Club
8 Rumah Makan Sederhana
9 Ta Wan

DRINKING & NIGHTLIFE
10 Bandrek Agus Barata
11 Caffeine
12 Tjahta Hati

houses an interesting museum. Unfortunately, only the titles have been translated into English.

Reproductions of poignant letters that British colonisers sent home are also on display, and many of them paint a vivid picture of how life must have been for this small garrison at the mercy of tropical diseases. For an even more vivid picture, take a 10-minute walk south of the fort to the **British Cemetery** (Makam Inggris), where whitewashed tombs and mowed lawns testify to the demise of some of the region's first Western settlers.

Heavy iron cannons still face out to the Indian Ocean, and from Fort Marlborough's northern bastion you can look across to Zokat Beach, a favourite with local surfers. The view from the western bastion, more appealing still, looks down Jl Panjaitan into what might be Indonesia's most picturesque and timeless Kampong Cina (Chinatown). The fort is open from 8am to 4pm daily.

THOMAS STAMFORD RAFFLES IN BENGKULU

Thomas Stamford Raffles was the lieutenant-governor of Bengkulu (then commonly known as Bencoolen) from 1818 until 1823. During that period, he buried four of his children in the city. The world's biggest flower bears his name, but Raffles is also famously credited with the clever designs of the shophouses of Singapore with their regulation 'five-foot-way' arcades (*kaki-lima* in Bahasa Indonesia). It may well have been in Bengkulu's Chinatown where he first came to appreciate the rows of multicoloured shophouses that were fronted by covered walkways offering shelter from rain and sun. It was a logical design that the Chinese may have imported from their Hokkien homelands long before Raffles arrived.

JAMOTRET/SHUTTERSTOCK

Rumah Bekas Kediaman Bung Karno

Historic Homes in Indonesia's Independence Movement

See where Sukarno lived in Bengkulu

Rumah Bekas Kediaman Bung Karno is where Indonesia's first president Sukarno (who, like many Indonesians today, went by only one name) lived during his exile in Bengkulu, from 1938 to 1942. The Dutch authorities clearly thought that such 'rabble-rousers' could do little harm in this remote city at the far end of their colony's westernmost shore. How wrong they were.

Today, the lovely old timber house is the **Soekarno House Museum** *(20,000Rp)*, though unfortunately most of its furnishings were removed in recent years, and it is now little more than an empty shell, with information boards and old photos. An idiosyncratic hint of the mindset of the country's founding father can be seen in the one remaining bookcase in Sukarno's office, where there are original copies of the books he read during exile.

Just a 10-minute stroll along Jl Soekarno Hatt and Jl Fatmawati brings you to a smaller timber house known as **Rumah Ibu Fatmawati Soekarno** *(5000Rp)*. This is where 20-year-old Fatmawati lived when Sukarno chose her to be his third wife. This house is a more interesting visit since it retains its original furnishings – the most notable being the Singer sewing machine with which Fatmawati famously stitched the first Indonesian flag. The caretaker of the house, Pak Marwan, who was a small child when he first met Fatmawati, is a great source of information and anecdotes.

Just 150m away is one of the Indonesia's most striking monuments: a majestically oversized **bronze sculpture** of the city's most celebrated daughter, seated at her sewing machine while the traffic on Bundaran Fatmawati circulates around.

Both homes are open from 8am to 4pm.

Shooting the Curl in Bengkulu

The local surf scene

Pantai Panjang (Long Beach) runs for 7km up the entire coastline of the city, and Bengkulu has many empty waves. Most surf spots are beach breaks, including the favoured A-frame break in front of the police station that, in a powerful head-high swell, is sometimes likened to the celebrated Puerto Escondido (Mexican Pipeline). There are also some perfectly peeling pointbreaks – secret spots perfect for longboarding that should remain nameless, but which locals say will often break cleanly for over 500m. The surf scene here is still in its infancy and while local surfers are welcoming, you're unlikely to find rental boards. In comparison with the logistical headaches involved in reaching the islands, surfing Bengkulu and the surrounding coastline is a cinch. **Pringgading Surf Camp** *(instagram.com/pringgadingsurfcamp)*, just 300m from Pantai Panjang and with a quiver of surfboards that guests can use, is the ideal base (p535). You can also rent a motorbike or arrange a driver if you want to explore further afield.

Pulau Enggano's Monster Waves

Surf the Indonesian Waimea

Is Pulau Enggano Sumatra's last 'undiscovered' big wave? It doesn't have much in the way of accommodation, and surfing charters find it difficult and expensive to reach, but the international surfing community still whispers in awe about the mighty waves that break here. It's said that Australian surf pioneer Martin Daly discovered Pulau Enggano's waves before those in the Mentawai Islands. Back in 1970s, a photo circulated of Australian pro surfer Tom Carroll surfing a monster wave '...somewhere'. Tom later confirmed that that 'somewhere' was Pulau Enggano.

Half a century after that photo was taken, Pulau Enggano's waves remain pretty much undiscovered. It only got 24-hour electricity in 2023 and the erratic ferry from Bengkulu takes 12 hours to sail the 160km to the island. There's an airport now, with twice-a-week flights from Bengkulu, but the flights, as with the boats, are all notoriously weather dependent. It all adds to the mystique.

WHERE LOCALS WORK OUT

Pantai Panjang's waterfront promenade runs alongside the white-sand beach for around 7km. In the evening, seafood stalls come to life at the northern end, but the mornings are for the active. Beginning at sunrise, the beach attracts lots of serious joggers (and not-so-serious walkers). Over the last couple of years the southern section has been cleared of illegally built shacks and warungs, and as a result it now feels increasingly wild as you walk south. It's said that until about a decade ago there were even dangerously aggressive wild elephants in the marshes at the southernmost tip. However, the beach is considered dangerous for swimming because of the currents. Warning signs are up and the police are often vigilant.

EATING IN BENGKULU: OUR PICKS

Rumah Makan Sederhana: Bengkulu's most famous *masakan Padang* (buffet style) eatery is popular and a great place to meet locals. *9am-9.30pm* $

Rafflesia Beach Club: It might come as a surprise to find a Bali-style beach club nearly under the shadow of the old fort. *10am-midnight* $$

Kampoeng Pesisir Restaurant: In a prime location along Pantai Panjang is Bengkulu's best-known spot for fresh-caught grilled fish. *9.30am-10pm* $$

Ta Wan: Bengkulu is proud of its Chinese culinary heritage and many locals head to this location in Bencoolen Mall for a great meal. *10am-10pm* $$

FIVE SUMATRAN COFFEE BEANS

Nichel Saputra was a finalist in the Indonesia Youth Barista Championship 2024. *@nichelsaputra*

Bengkulu Hyperwash: A high-clarity washed coffee from Mantesa Family. Clean, floral and tea-like.

Gayo Avatara: This Acehnese gem from Hendra Maulizar won the Coffee of Excellence award

Aceh Bener: A modern expression of Aceh's heritage from Bener Meriah. Comforting, clean and subtly complex.

Kerinci Anaerobic Natural: From the volcanic soils of Mt Kerinci, this anaerobic natural offers jammy fruit, winey depth and a long fermented finish.

Semendo: Produced by Finca Ali using Hermetic Sealed Natural processing, this South Sumatran lot bursts with fruity intensity and purple notes.

Get a Caffeinated Buzz

Appreciate coffee in Bengkulu

NC+ Coffee Experience is 19-year-old Nichel Saputra's homage to the unique flavour and boldness of Sumatran coffee. It's a journey that sweeps across the country and into the realm of several award-winning international coffee producers. Known to his friends as Nick, Saputra's own coffee appreciation started at age 12, when his parents opened a coffee shop. These days his barista space has the feel of a mad scientist's laboratory. Located on the 2nd floor of the family's surf camp, Nick's enthusiasm shines through as his guests – for as little as 50,000Rp – witness for themselves the astounding difference that the thickness of the lip on a cup, or even a cup's colour, brings to the flavour. And in case you're wondering, a narrow-lipped cup makes coffee taste bolder and more acidic, while coffee from a pink cup is said to taste 20% sweeter than the same brew served in a white cup!

ATMOSPHERIC BENGKULU CAFES: OUR PICKS

Caffeine: Well-known for its proper coffee and wide range of desserts – a cosy cafe for sweet treats. *8am-8pm Thu-Tue*

Nick Coffee: Located in the Pringgading area, this spot is ideal for a laid-back lunch near the beach. *10am-9pm Mon-Fri, to midnight Sat, 10.30am-11pm Sun*

Tjahta Hati: A quiet place for reading or chatting, and popular for discussions of Bengkulu's heritage and literature. *4-11pm Tue-Sun*

Bandrek Agus Barata: This pavement stall is one of the best places to try *bandrek* (a gingery, peppery hot drink, thickened with yolk from a duck egg). *7pm-midnight*

AKUNRINO/SHUTTERSTOCK

Rafflesia blossom, Bukit Barisan hills

WHY I LOVE BENGKULU CITY

Mark Eveleigh, Lonely Planet writer

After several visits, I'm increasingly astounded that Bengkulu is so often overlooked by travellers. The small, easily navigated city has historic charm and Chinatown is a real delight to stroll around. My perfect Bengkulu day might start with a sunrise walk along Pantai Panjang before a longboarding session on the perfectly peeling left-hand wave in front of the fort. I'd have lunch in Chinatown and probably linger for some lazy people-watching from a pavement coffee shop. The beach is the best place for sundown, after which I'd head to the night market (Kuliner Malam on Jl KZ Abidin II) for spicy nasi goreng and a cup of hot, gingery *bandrek*, thickened with duck egg.

You'll try coffee from Nick's family plantation, which, at an elevation of 1200m to 1400m above sea level, is the highest in Bengkulu area. Also look out for the 'ozonic natural espresso' in which berries cleansed with ozone gas are fermented for exactly 144 hours to create an even bolder Sumatran arabica 'with a slate-clean aftertaste'.

The coffee experience changes depending on the time of day. Go in the afternoon and you might even get a chance to sample Nick's litchi milk tea or litchi affogato, in which, as he points out, flavoured ice cream is used to complement espresso, rather than the other way around. Allow at least an hour to get the most out of this experience, and book a day in advance *(WhatsApp +62 851 6291 1244)*.

Track Down the World's Biggest Blossom

Searching for rafflesia

The **Bukit Barisan hills** are one of the best places in the world to find specimens of rafflesia. Since there's no flowering season for the gigantic spotted red blooms – which can reach a diameter of up to 1m – it sometimes takes quite a bit of tenacity to track them down in the jungle. Bengkulu-based driver Alpin Suhendra *(WhatsApp +62 821 8237 4398)* can usually advise whether or not there are accessible blooms from the road. He offers a guided day trip to see the plants for 1,000,000Rp for up to three people. Trips include a visit to a waterfall, a cuppa at a tea plantation and sunset in the mountains.

Palembang

RIVER PANORAMAS | IRRESISTIBLE CUISINE | FASCINATING CULTURE

GETTING AROUND

With regular daily flights from Jakarta, Palembang is a highly convenient (if underused) access point for Sumatran adventures. The city has a reliable public transport system, with a huge fleet of *angkot* (minibuses) and a modern overhead light-rail transit (LRT) system. Most visitors will find that the Grab or Gojek ride-hailing apps are the fastest (and still affordable) way to explore. Small *ketek* motorboats are available for puttering to waterfront areas, while a faster *spidbot* can be chartered (from about 50,000Rp for a short journey) to zip you further along the river.

With its location on the sweeping Sungai Musi (Musi River), perennially busy with bustling timber cargo boats, Sumatra's second-biggest city (population 1.7 million) has the irresistible edgy feel of a jungle-frontier trading post. A rich history that dates back over a thousand years – long before the days of the mighty Sriwijaya Empire – and a vibrant modern cultural life make Palembang a great starting point for trips through southern Sumatra. Wherever you stay in the city, you'll be sure to find your attention returning to the waterfront and the iconic Jembatan Ampera bridge, which spans the Musi.

Often overlooked by travellers, Palembang is arguably Sumatra's most appealing major city. Many of the intriguing markets and excellent cafes and restaurants sell the traditional delicacy *pempek* (cassava flour dumplings), of which the locals are justifiably proud.

Sultanate Heritage

History, culture and tradition

As befits an ancient sultan's palace, the first thing to do upon entering the **Sultan Mahmud Badaruddin II Museum** *(20,000Rp)* is take off your shoes. Rebuilt in 1825 after the Dutch destroyed the building, this gorgeous stone-and-timber palace saw many incarnations before opening as a museum. It served as the Japanese headquarters during World War II and as a command post of the Sriwijaya Military Command during the War of Independence. More recently it became one of Sumatra's most informative and well-maintained museums – an improvement, it must be said, on the Balaputradewa Museum (p525; which outranks it as the official museum for South Sumatra).

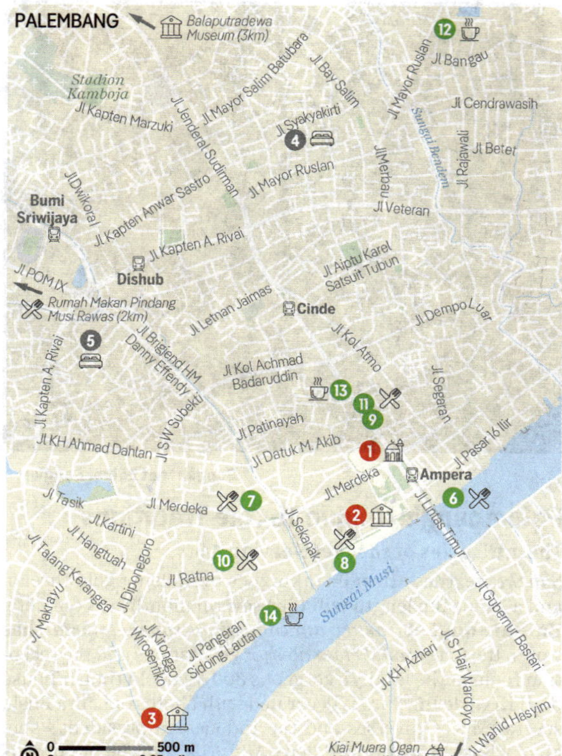

SIGHTS
1 Sultan Mahmud Badaruddin I Jayo Wikramo Mosque
2 Sultan Mahmud Badaruddin II Museum
3 Zainal Songket

SLEEPING
4 Hotel Domino
5 The Zuri Palembang

EATING
6 Mbok War
7 Pempek Aan
see 4 Pempek Lince
8 River Side Restaurant
9 Rumah Makan Katayo Minang
10 Saudade
11 Smile Cafe & Resto

DRINKING & NIGHTLIFE
12 Luthier Coffee
see 6 Musi Icon
13 Serenatakopi
14 Tujuan Kopi

The displays are well laid out with informative noticeboards, and each one includes a QR code that links to an in-depth audio explanation in English. If you really want to get a thorough grounding in local history, culture and traditions, you could spend at least two hours wandering through the various rooms of this two-storey building listening to the explanations. You'll learn about the sultanate itself, of course, and the trade routes and various wars that made Palembang so incredibly important in the Middle Ages. The layers of information in this museum are far deeper and more far-reaching than trade and war; displays covering everything from Wayang Palembang puppetry to the intricacies of circumcision paraphernalia. Life, death and marriage are a focus and there's an entire room devoted to wedding ceremonies. The museum is open Tuesdays to Sundays from 8am to 4pm.

TOP TIP

Palembang is one of the few cities where becak (pedicabs) are still common. Along with the traditional bicycle variety, you'll also commonly see a motorised version, often known in Indonesia as *bentor* (literally becak-motor). They are most often found in the poorer backstreet quarters and market areas.

THE MIGHT OF THE SRIWIJAYA EMPIRE

Palembang was already a great trading city, dominating the Strait of Malacca, when the Sriwijaya Empire began to expand sometime in the 7th century. Throughout the next 600 years, the Buddhist kings of Sriwijaya extended their mercantile and religious influence throughout the Malay Archipelago and China, even going so far as to found monasteries in southeastern India. Around 1000 CE the Chola maritime powers from India began to whittle away at Sriwijaya dominions in Java, and in 1025 the Cholas plundered Palembang itself, capturing the king. By the end of the 12th century, when the Javanese Majapahit rulers had risen to eminence, Sriwijaya had been reduced to a relatively minor kingdom.

BAGUS UPC/SHUTTERSTOCK

Songkets **at Zainal Songket**

Palembang's Unique Textile Traditions

The intricacies of *songket* weaving

Songket textiles are painstakingly woven using gold thread, and a single 2m length will take several months to complete. **Zainal Songket** *(instagram.com/zainalsongketofficial)* has woven the finest *songket* textiles for generations and the reception room at the family's gorgeous 300-year-old timber house on Jl Ki Gede Ing Suro is decorated with photos of Laura Bush, several Miss Universes and the Indonesian president's son, all of whom have shopped here. At the back of the building is a fascinating museum devoted to the textiles, with an additional collection of antique household implements. The shop and museum are open from 9am to 9pm; there's no charge, but donations are welcomed.

The intricacies of *songket* production are mind-boggling, and specific motifs (eg *songket nago besaung*, the fighting dragon *songket*) were traditionally reserved for royalty. If you're generous with your tip, the staff might invite you to see the room where the magical weaving is actually undertaken. During busy periods as many as 10 women sit at the backstrap looms in the low-ceilinged room under the building. If you want to splash out on a once-in-a-lifetime souvenir, a top-quality *songket* will cost you about US$900.

EATING IN PALEMBANG: OUR PICKS

River Side Restaurant: A popular waterfront restaurant for fresh fish and tapas-style tasting plates. Be sure to sample the prawn *lumpia*. *noon-10pm* $$

Mbok War: This converted cargo boat is one of Palembang's most iconic lunch spots. It's a Padang-style buffet – point at what looks most appetising. *8.30am-4pm* $

Smile Cafe & Resto: A convenient location just north of Jembatan Ampera, this eatery has a good range of international staples, from ekado rolls to beef wraps. *9am-10pm* $$

Saudade: Apart from the super-strong magic coffee, there's nothing Portuguese about this little cafe. The toast with *kaya* (coconut jam) makes for a perfect breakfast. *8am-10pm* $

Learn about South Sumatra's Early History

From crafts to hunter-gathers

The **Balaputradewa Museum** *(Museum Negeri Sumatera Selatan; 15,000Rp)* is a sprawling complex of seven big exhibition halls. If you have a specific interest in crafts (perhaps that ever-present weaving tradition!) or other aspects of local culture, the exhibits here will keep you occupied.

If your interests are a little more prosaic, we'd suggest starting in the room dedicated to the archaeological excavations in Gua Harimau (the Tiger Cave), which is about 150km southwest of Palembang. This exhibit provides insight into the hunter-gatherer lifestyle of early human inhabitants, who lived in this region between 3000 and 14,000 years ago and belonged to both the Austronesian and Austromelanesoid races. There are also rooms dedicated to the 300 years of Dutch colonisation and to the (much shorter, but no less harrowing) Japanese occupation. Before you leave, be sure to walk through the gardens to the northern edge of the complex where you'll find the majestic Rumah Limas, a traditional 'pyramid' house of the sort that was once central to Palembang culture. The museum is open Tuesday to Sunday from 8.30am to 3.30pm.

Dig into Palembang's Famous Snacks

Sample *pempek* with (or without) Super OMG spicy sauce

You won't be in Palembang long before somebody asks what you think of *pempek*. The people of Palembang are inordinately proud of the huge variety of these cassava-flour dumplings. You'll see *pempek* on menus and restaurant signs everywhere, but if you're in any doubt about the level of obsession, just head to Sentral Kampung Pempek where the entire lower half of Jl Mujahidin is dedicated to nothing but *pempek* stalls and restaurants. Varieties to look out for are *adaan* (fried), *lenjer* and *keriting* (two varieties of boiled *pempek*) and *pipi krizpi* (little offcut slivers of deliciously chewy fried cassava dough). The delicious *kapal selam* variety (literally, 'sunken ship') consists of a whole egg cooked inside a package of cassava dough. **Pempek Lince** *(pempeklince.com)* is the city's most famous establishment – *kapal selam* is made with duck egg rather than chicken, and all the varieties are accompanied with a homemade spicy sauce, graded from slightly spicy up to Super OMG.

DURIAN CITY

If Palembang wasn't already so obsessed with *pempek* (cassava-flour dumplings), it would probably be known as Indonesia's capital of durian. The famously smelly king of fruits – those prehistoric-looking spiky green cannonballs – are found all over the city. During the height of the season (typically September to December) visitors and traders flock to market areas where the air becomes permeated with the hot latrine-like scent. Stall-holders typically banish durian vendors to remoter sections of the market. At Pasar Kuto you'll find them downwind, two blocks to the west! Not only eaten as a fruit, durian is also a popular ingredient in a variety of *pempek* and is even fermented to make an unexpectedly delicious sauce, known as *tempoyak*.

PALEMBANG'S BEST CAFES: OUR PICKS

Tujuan Kopi: Palembang's favourite hipster hangout in a Dutch era warehouse. Great coffee – try *es kopi keju* (iced cheese coffee)! *8am-11pm*

Musi Icon: A converted cargo boat serving good food and excellent coffee, including an extremely potent and delicious Vietnamese drip. *9am-midnight*

Serenatakopi: A cool coffee shop with rooftop views down the frantically bustling Jl Jenderal Sudirman. Try the Next Level Cookies. *8am-11pm*

Luthier Coffee: Speciality coffees served by an Indonesian barista champion. The Natalie mocktail is aromatic coffee with a hint of grapefruit and lime candy. *7am-10pm*

DAILY LIFE ON THE GREAT SUNGAI MUSI

The 525km-long Sungai Musi is Sumatra's biggest river and the sixth longest in Indonesia, and it drains an area about twice the size of Belgium. Even in Palembang City (80km upriver from the ocean) it carries roughly 30 times the volume of water that passes down the Thames in London. Even today, the Sungai Musi is central to the local economy. You'll see colourfully painted timber cargo boats *(tongkang)* loading cargo to be taken as far away as Muara Rawas (about 320km upriver), beyond which the Musi is no longer navigable to large vessels. Smaller *ketek* motorboats putter across the river, shuttling cargo to waterfront communities, while nifty little *spidbots* hurry shoppers between the city's waterfront markets.

Visit South Sumatra's Palatial Mosque

Where the sultans once prayed

South Sumatra's oldest mosque is an architectural gem. Originally built by Sultan Mahmud Badaruddin I in 1738, the prayer hall is truly majestic with European lamps, gorgeous carvings and gigantic ironwood pillars (said to be sunk 10m underground). The **Sultan Mahmud Badaruddin I Jayo Wikramo Mosque** once backed directly onto the river and the sultans would answer the prayer-call by mooring their ceremonial boats to the mosque steps. Today it has a maximum capacity of 17,000 worshippers.

If you leave your shoes at the front steps, you're more than welcome to wander around the grounds and exterior of the mosque, although worshippers prefer that non-believers observe the prayer hall only from the doorway. If you ask at the security gate, Pak Iqbal (who has a smattering of English) will be happy to show you around the exterior and explain some of the unique aspects of the mosque's design. There's no charge but donations are appreciated. There are certainly some quirky architectural influences at work here – not least the 1748 minaret, which might be described as a pagoda. A much taller and more Arabic-influenced minaret was added in 1975.

Skip across the Sungai Musi by Spidbot

Take a ride to the Kiai Muara Ogan Mosque

Located in the Kertapati quarter on the southern bank of the Sungai Musi, the **Kiai Muara Ogan Mosque** lacks the grandeur of Sultan Mahmud's creation. But it's said to be Palembang's second-oldest surviving mosque (1890) and has a faded charm all its own. As is typical of a South Sumatran mosque of this era, the roof and minaret are noticeably Chinese in style.

The most exciting thing about a visit here is that it's best reached via *spidbot* from Terminal Kapal Kecil (the small boat terminal) on the Musi's north bank, just downriver from Jembatan Ampera. The zipping voyage – cutting between gargantuan coal barges at speeds of around 40km/h– is an adrenaline rush.

Be prepared to haggle with boatmen, but you should be able to negotiate a *pergi pulang* (round-trip journey), including 20 minutes of waiting time, for around 100,000Rp. It's enough time since you can only peer into the prayer hall from the courtyard, where the quarter's soccer-crazed boys are likely to be having a kick-around.

WHERE TO EAT *PEMPEK* IN PALEMBANG: OUR PICKS

Pempek Lince: This family-run business is the place to try the regional culinary treasure at its finest. *8am-6pm Mon-Sat, 8am-noon Sun* $

Rumah Makan Katayo Minang: A simple *masakan Padang* establishment north of the river. Known for excellent *rendang* and *pempek*. *24hr* $

Pempek Aan: One of dozens of *pempek* stalls that stretch 100m up Jl Mujahidin. It's popular for the *kapal selam* (sunken ship) *pempek*. *7.30am-10pm* $

Rumah Makan Pindang Musi Rawas: Locals bring guests here to impress them with *pempek* and the house speciality *pindang patin* (spicy fish soup). *9am-9pm* $$

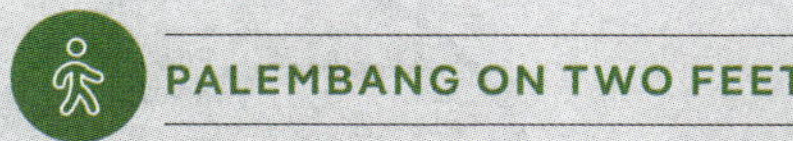

PALEMBANG ON TWO FEET

A wander on both banks of the Sungai Musi passes some of Palembang's most exciting markets and bustling backstreet quarters.

START	END	LENGTH
Kampong Kapitan	Pasar Kuto	4km; 1½hr

Begin near the southern end of the Ampara Bridge at 1 **Kampong Kapitan**, where you'll find a crumbling mansion constructed four centuries ago as the family home for a Chinese *kapitan* (captain). From here you could head north along the riverbank, but we'd recommend cutting south through the narrow alleys onto Jl KH Azhari and the 2 **Pasar Buah 7 Ulu** fruit market. You'll see the tower that serves as the pedestrian access onto Palembang's iconic 3 **Jembatan Ampera** bridge. Descend to the northern riverbank using the other tower and detour west for 300m to see 4 **Benteng Kuto Besak**.

Walk back under the bridge and along the covered boardwalk in the 5 **Terminal Kapal Kecil** where dozens of zippy motorboats wait to shuttle passengers. Cut through the huge five-storey 6 **Pasar 16 Ilir market** and walk two blocks north to 7 **Palembang Bird Market**. Not only famous for its songbirds, you'll also find everything from Siamese fighting fish to pet iguanas. Disturbingly, there are sometimes even baby macaques here. Follow Jl Sayangan back towards the river, detouring into the little Lorong RK Lama to check out the colourful 8 **Tantrayana Zhen Fozong temple**. From here you could consider hiring a pedicab (about 15,000Rp) for the 1.5km stretch to your final destination: the 9 **Pasar Kuto market**.

The **Pasar Kuto market** is an authentic backstreet market – steamy, noisy and highly aromatic. For something even more aromatic check out the durian section one block west!

Tongkang (vibrantly painted timber boats) load their cargo at the docks in front of **Pasar 16 Ilir market**.

Benteng Kuto Besak still serves as a military installation almost 250 years after it was built.

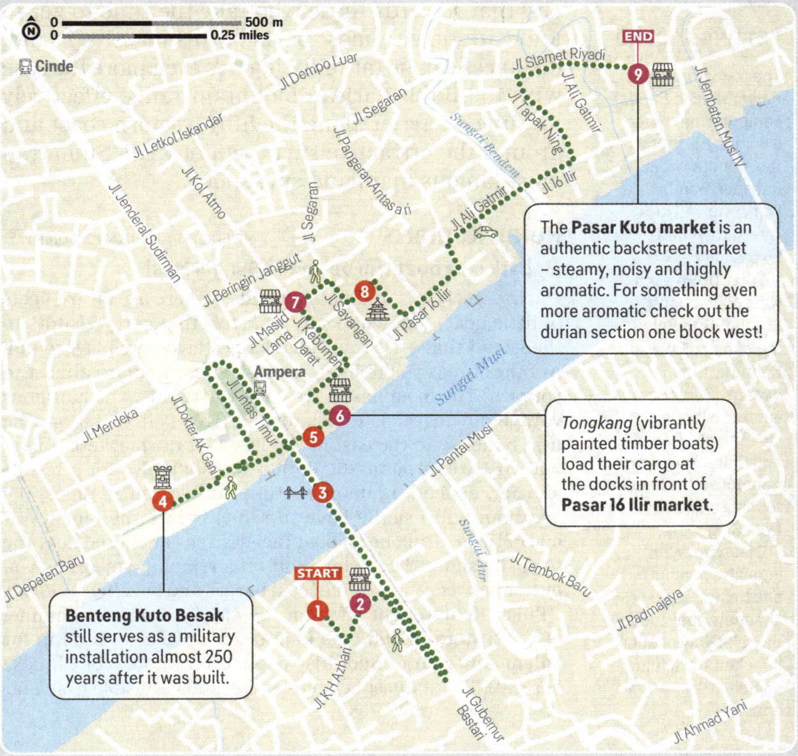

Beyond Palembang

As Sumatra's second-largest city, Palembang is the ideal base from which to discover the relatively unexplored south.

Places

GETTING AROUND

The train from Palembang to Bandar Lampung makes for a unique trip, but the mountain road between Bandar Lampung and Krui is best travelled by private car (1,200,000Rp each way). Palembang has flights to Pulau Bangka and Pulau Belitung. But in general, Sumatra's eastern islands (specifically Batam and Bintan) are more popular with domestic tourists and visitors from Singapore or Malaysia. With intensive mining and busy shipping channels, they lack the relatively pristine beaches you'll find on Sumatra's western coast.

Come to South Sumatra to travel down Sumatra's longest river (the Sungai Musi) on a traditional timber boat or to take a ride on what might be the world's cheapest railway journey – an incredible value at only 32,000Rp for a nine-hour ride to Bandar Lampung. While Bandar Lampung is famous primarily as a port city connecting Sumatra with Java (less than 30km away across the Sunda Strait), this is a city that rewards those who take the time to get to know it. As with most parts of this massive island, distances can be intimidating. It's even more the case with the Bukit Barisan mountain range effectively forming a barrier along the hilly western coast and around the attractive surf town of Krui, Sumatra's most famous mainland surf spot.

Pulau Kemaro

TIME FROM PALEMBANG: **30MIN** 

Embark on a boat trip down the Sungai Musi

During weekends and public holidays there are entire fleets of little boats, known locally as *ketek*, that carry visitors to the island that serves as Palembang's favourite playground. At other times you're likely to have Pulau Kemaro almost to yourself. The most hassle-free way to organise the half-hour voyage downriver is to ask at the River Police Station (the first building to the east of the Pasar 16 Ilir market). A boat will cost you around 200,000Rp to 350,000Rp for a return journey, depending upon waiting time. At quiet times, the boatman will usually have to refuel before the journey at one of the floating houseboat fuel-stations anchored near the opposite shore. Then you're off on a relaxing voyage as you putter between gargantuan coal barges and buzzing *spidbots*.

Pulao Kemaro, cut off from the city by a narrow channel of the **Sungai Musi**, has long been a place of worship for Palembang's large Buddhist population (mostly of Chinese descent). The statuesque nine-level pagoda is visible from afar

SONY HERDIANA/SHUTTERSTOCK

Sungai Musi, Pulau Kemaro

and at weekends you'll see worshippers lighting gigantic candles (some over 2m tall) and burning incense in the famous **Klenteng Hok Tjing Bio** temple.

Walk to the eastern edge of the temple complex, beyond the cluster of warung and coconut vendors, and you'll see an ancient fig tree. This is the famous Pohon Cinta (Love Tree): legend has it that couples who carved their names in its bark would live happily ever after. The tradition became so prolific – and visitor numbers so high at weekends – that the tree had to be protected by a fence.

On the island's southern shore is a timber boardwalk stretching for almost 1km through the stilted **Kampong Air** (Water Village) where you'll find a fish restaurant called Resto Apung Sesera and several small antique shops supposedly selling treasures that were retrieved from the historic Sungai Musi.

Bandar Lampung

TIME FROM PALEMBANG: **9HR**

Take a South Sumatran railway journey

The 9¾-hour train journey between Palembang and Bandar Lampung (near Sumatra's southernmost tip) is just 32,000Rp – less than the price of a cup of coffee and possibly the best-value railway journey on the planet.

THE LEGEND OF PULAU KEMARO

Legend has it that Siti Fatimah, a Palembang princess, married a Chinese trader called Tan Bun An. After the wedding they sailed to China, where the groom's parents gave them a gift of seven large jars. The couple promised not to open the jars until they returned to Palembang but, arriving near Pulau Kemaro, Tan Bun An could no longer wait. His disappointment on discovering that the contents were merely salted mustard seeds was such that he threw the jars overboard. As he threw the last jar it smashed against the deck, revealing the treasure that was hidden beneath the seeds. Tan Bun An and Siti Fatimah leapt overboard to try to retrieve the other six jars and were never seen again.

EATING IN BANDAR LAMPUNG: OUR PICKS

Puti Minang Sumur Batu: If you've just arrived from Java, this is a good bet for your first *masakan Padang* as it's clean, affordable and reliably delicious. *24hr* $

Kenangan Kopi-Ruko Chandra : An international Chinatown cafe with Spanish lattes and fresh-baked *pain au chocolat*. *7am-9pm* $

WaHaHa Seafood: Locals flock to this industrial-style warehouse eatery, less than 200m from the fishing harbour, for fresh fish (some of it live). *10.30am-9pm* $$

Sukacita Veggie: A ready-made fast meal – buffet style – featuring vegetarian and vegan specialities. Don't miss the *nangka* (jackfruit) *rendang*. *7am-5pm* $

THE DEATH RAILWAY

On 24 May 1944, Japanese soldiers began enforced labour on a railway that would ultimately cut right across Central Sumatra, connecting the Strait of Malacca with the Indian Ocean at Padang. They used 6600 prisoners (mainly Dutch Indo-Europeans) as labourers, along with about 1000 British POWs and 300 prisoners from the USA, Australia and New Zealand. Alongside them were an undisclosed number of *rōmusha*, conscripted labourers who were mostly Sumatran peasants. Through a cruel twist of fate, the railway was finally completed on the same day that Japan surrendered. Records show that an estimated 20,000 Indonesian labourers died during the railway's construction, alongside 703 POWs.

AYUTIAR/SHUTTERSTOCK

Pasar Ikan Tradisional Gudang Lelang, Bandar Lampung

The 389km journey begins in Palembang's Stasiun Kertapati (departing daily at 8.30am) and ends at Bandar Lampung's Tanjung Karang station (at 6.15pm). In the other direction, the departure is also at 8.30am, but the 18-stop northbound journey is inexplicably 25 minutes faster and thus has a scheduled arrival in Palembang at 5.50pm.

Needless to say, at this price this is hardly a luxury journey. Seats are firm (to say the least) and locked in a very upright position, but the carriages are clean and well maintained. This historic route was inaugurated by the Nederlandsch-Indische Staatsspoorwegen (Dutch East-Indian State Railways Company) in 1927, more to serve plantations and the mining industry than for public transport. The mines are still in evidence, but most of the plantations – in those days largely *karet* (rubber) – have been superseded by *sawit* (oil palms). Apart from marvelling at the degradation caused by endless rows of oil palms, the journey is primarily a wonderful way to meet local people and to get to know your travelling companions.

Be aware though that this great-value journey is super popular and, especially during holiday season, tickets (available over the counter at the stations or through kai.id) often sell out days ahead. Book in advance.

Sumatra's most colourful fish market

At the southern end of Jl Ikan Bawal (Chinatown's main thoroughfare), is **Pasar Ikan Tradisional Gudang Lelang**, one of Sumatra's most vibrant fish markets. Foreign visitors are rare here and if you take time to mingle rather than just snap photos, it can be a great place to interact with Bandar Lampung townsfolk. It's wise to wear closed shoes or sports sandals since the floor is puddled with fish oil and squid ink.

Turn left just before the pier that marks the southern end of the market, and you'll see a small warung serving sweet black coffee on the boardwalk next to the vibrantly painted boats. The array of fish and seafood species is startling: there are various types of rays, barracudas and, more disturbingly, baby hammerheads. Unusually, this is an afternoon market and is open from 1pm to midnight.

Local history lessons at the Museum Lampung

Lampung Provincial Museum *(5000Rp)* is the ideal place to immerse yourself in the cultural wealth of Southern Sumatra. Unusually, most exhibits are clearly signposted in both English and Bahasa Indonesia. You'll see historical artefacts dating from prehistoric times through the colonial era: learn about the meanings of traditional motifs in the weaving industry, or peruse the exhibits featuring local flora and fauna (including some off-putting taxidermic displays). Look out for the array of musical instruments, tools and weapons from various eras in Bandar Lampung's history. A series of miniature models of traditional homes is slightly overshadowed by the full-sized replicas outside, in front of the main building. The museum is open from 8am to 2pm, Tuesday through Sunday.

Krui

TIME FROM BANDAR LAMPUNG: **6HR**

Explore an unsung surfers' paradise

The coastline around the town of Krui must be one of the world's most idyllic surf hangouts. Sure, there are wilder wave-pounded coastlines in Indonesia, with rollers to challenge even the most intrepid big-wave charger. But for most surfers, the Krui coastline is hard to beat. The town itself offers little appeal, but the beaches, points and reefs that stretch for more than 50km to the south offer waves to suit all abilities, from absolute novices up to lip-smashing hotshots. Just as importantly, there's all the infrastructure needed to keep travelling surfers content for months at a time: good cafes (with beer and billiard tables), countless pleasant homestays, a few chic resorts, plus affordable **scooter rentals** *(about 65,000Rp per day)*. There are a couple of small surf shops for rentals and surf wax...plus the all-important ding-repair shacks.

The ideal base is **Tanjung Setia** (30 minutes south of Krui town), home to the highly consistent left-hand point break known as Ujung Bocur, plus countless other accessible spots such as Mandiri Beach, the Peak, Krui Left and Krui Right. Indonesia – especially Bali – is often challenging for travellers unused to motorbikes but, while caution is still recommended, Tanjung Setia's sleepy country lane is as good a place to boost your confidence as any. Rental bikes are invariably fitted with

GETTING TO KRUI

While it's possible to reach Krui by plane (or bus) from Bengkulu in the north, most visitors – especially surfers – come via Java and Bandar Lampung. The ferry from Java is convenient since it's only about two or three hours by road from Jakarta to Merak (the port on Java's west coast), but it's even quicker and more convenient to take one of the regular flights (several daily) from Jakarta's domestic terminal to Bandar Lampung's Radin Inten II Airport. From Bandar Lampung, it typically takes between six to seven hours in a private car to get to Krui. Call Esti *(WhatsApp +62 853 6739 1090)*. The drive through part of Bukit Barisan Selatan National Park is an interesting one. Tigers and elephants live here and are occasionally seen on the road!

EATING IN KRUI: OUR PICKS

Lani's Resto: Tanjung Setia's premier surf hangout, this is the place for wave-chargers' tall stories, beer, billiards and Sumatra's best pizzas. *noon-10pm* $$

Leafy's Cafe: A great breakfast and lunch venue, offering quality coffee, a hearty full English breakfast and a variety of curries. *8am-8pm* $

Yoi Beach House: Surfer soul food to start the day (shakes, smoothie bowls and coffee), and a cocktail menu to toast Krui's famous sunsets. *8am-10pm* $$

Ninety Five: Snacks, rice bowls and burgers in a laid-back space, just down the road from Sumatra's most consistent left-hand point break. *2.30-11pm Tue-Sun* $

SOUTH SUMATRA'S PROTECTED AREAS

Bukit Barisan Selatan National Park is one of only three habitats (the others being Kerinci Seblat and Gunung Leuser) that are estimated to hold more than 30 Sumatran tigers each. This is the minimum considered viable to support a feasible population. At the time of research (mid-2025) Bukit Barisan Selatan was off-limits to tourists after a spate of tiger attacks on humans.

Way Kambas National Park (abutting Sumatra's southeastern coast) is home to the celebrated **Sumatran Rhino Sanctuary** *(rhinos.org)*. The park is also known for its forest elephants, but there have been complaints of riding and restrictive shackling among elephants there. **Safari Waykambas** *(safariwaykambas.com)* can arrange visits to the park.

board racks, so set out northwards from here, avoiding the main road as much as possible, and you'll find a coastline that is still adorned with coconut palms, where herds of buffalo shuffle lazily along the beach. Further north, beyond Krui, you'll find Jenny's (right hander), Honeysmacks Peak and Jimmy's (left hander). The list goes on, with countless other rarely surfed (and frequently unnamed) spots to choose from.

If you didn't arrive with a board, just ask around in Tanjung Setia or, if you want something of higher quality, rent from **Lefty's** *(250,000Rp)* in Krui or from **Hello Mister** (a little cheaper and also in Krui).

Horse riding on Pantai Mandiri

Pantai Mandiri's arc of white sand stretches unbroken for more than 12km and is perfectly suited for horse riding. The beach is largely deserted most of the time, with just a few low-key resorts and warung with stilted *pondok* (huts) for diners. The only distraction is likely to be a small herd of lazy buffalo grazing under the shade of the palms or wallowing in the river-mouth shallows. You can spend an hour riding at a sedate walk along the sand, or embark on an adrenaline-popping canter through the shallows with an experienced guide. No actual riding experience is necessary. Visit **La Surf Krui Bungalow** *(instagram.com/lasurf_krui)* or call Nunuk to book *(WhatsApp +64 896 8341 1070)*. Rides are 300,000Rp per person.

Waterfalls and wildlife in the Krui jungle

The 15-minute drive to **Bendungan Way Biha** (Way Biha Dam) from the surfer hangout of Tanjung Setia is the start of an adventure. You'll be entering a swathe of uninhabited jungle that forms a barrier roughly 70km long down the Krui coastline. From the dam, a motorboat takes you upriver for about 50 minutes, until the Sungai Way Biha (Way Biha River) becomes too narrow to be navigable. From here you're faced with about an hour's walk to **Air Terjun U-Putri** (U-Putri Waterfall), which drops picturesquely over a series of three ledges. At about 8m it might not be the highest waterfall in Sumatra (that would be Ponot Waterfall in North Sumatra) or the most spectacular (arguably Sipiso-Piso; p480) but it is an unimaginably idyllic spot, with a perfect bathing pool at the base.

Adam at **Jungle Surf** *(WhatsApp +62 853 6739 1090)* can arrange a full-day jungle experience here for 250,000Rp, including a picnic lunch at the waterfall and a return to the motorboat via inner tube (rather than walking back). This pristine jungle wilderness area is connected with Bukit Barisan Selatan National Park and is a haven for some of the last Sumatran rhinos – of which only 40 or so remain in the wild.

In 2024, the *Jakarta Post* reported that two men were killed and another badly injured in tiger attacks about 20km east of Air Terjun U-Putri. While it's extremely unlikely you'll see any tigers, Siamang gibbons are often seen at the waterfall, and from time to time visitors are even blessed with sightings of orangutans.

BANDAR LAMPUNG ON TWO FEET

Experience the temples, monuments and tangled alleys of Bandar Lampung's traditional Chinese quarter, either on foot or in a vintage pedicab.

START	END	LENGTH
Tugu Pagoda	Krakatau Monument	5.5km; 2hr

Start at the newly built ❶ **Tugu Pagoda** (Pagoda Monument) and walk south down Jl Ikan Hiu (Shark St). Turn left into ❷ **Jalan Tongkol**, which is lined entirely with food stalls. At the main junction continue southwards to the waterfront fish market ❸ **Pasar Ikan Tradisional Gudang Lelang** (p530), where you can see the fleet of brightly coloured fishing boats. From the port follow Jl Ikan Mas (Gold Fish St) until you wind up at the spectacular facade of ❹ **Thay Hin Bio Temple**. Weaving southwards you come to the monumental 84-year-old ❺ **Bodhisattva Temple** on Jl Ikan Kembung (Bloatfish St!).

From here, Jl Ikan Paus (Whale St) starts off as a wide thoroughfare where swallows swoop and dive among the three-storey ❻ **Bird Nest Towers**, where nests are harvested to make Chinese soup and 'medicinal' tea. The street steadily narrows as it runs 600m north, giving you the feeling that you're about to be swallowed by the Biblical leviathan. Finally it becomes so narrow that you can touch the walls on either side with outstretched arms. Just as you begin to think you should turn back, a flight of stone steps leads you onto busy Jl WR Supratman. ❼ **Krakatau Monument**, commemorating the horrific explosion of 1883, is just 250m to the east in Taman Dipangga (Dipangga Park).

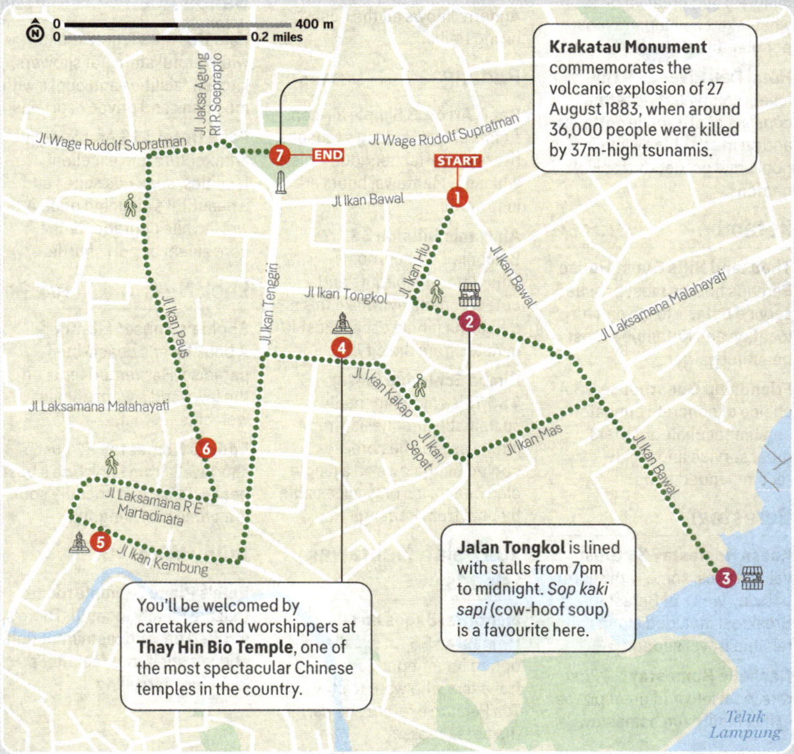

Krakatau Monument commemorates the volcanic explosion of 27 August 1883, when around 36,000 people were killed by 37m-high tsunamis.

Jalan Tongkol is lined with stalls from 7pm to midnight. *Sop kaki sapi* (cow-hoof soup) is a favourite here.

You'll be welcomed by caretakers and worshippers at **Thay Hin Bio Temple**, one of the most spectacular Chinese temples in the country.

Places We Love to Stay

$ Budget $$ Midrange $$$ Top End

Bukit Lawang

MAP p467

Indra Valley Inn $ A riverside location and helpful staff make this a great bet, not only for accommodation but for jungle trekking trips.

On the Rocks $$ On the southern bank of the river, away from Bukit Lawang's main tourist strip. Chalets have verandas and sunken bathrooms.

Medan

Batik Hotel Medan $$ Conveniently located for access to the airport (45 minutes) and great value for what might be Medan's most popular three-star hotel.

Hotel Deli River $$$ This lovely colonial-style retreat consists of attractive cottages and an irresistible swimming pool amid gorgeous tropical gardens.

Ketambe

MAP p467

Thousand Hills Guest House $ Perhaps not the most polished service but worth staying for location and Ketambe's most beautiful garden.

Friendship Guesthouse $$ A choice of concrete bungalows and timber chalets. Offers great service and highly recommended tours.

Berastagi

Kaesa Homestay $$ Great-value rooms, some with shared balcony views of Berastagi. Breakfast included along with reliable travel support.

Nachelle Homestay $$ First-rate local info and great pizzas in this family-run homestay. The rooms are super clean and comfortable.

Danau Toba

Leokap Homestay $ Great value at this lakeside property, which has spacious rooms with private verandas. The staff are extremely helpful and rent motorbikes.

Romlan Guesthouse $$ Cheaper rooms are available, but try to reserve one of the two gorgeous Batak houses for an only slightly higher rate.

Tabo Cottages $$$ This sprawling lakeside place makes for a wonderfully relaxed stay. Annette knows all the best hiking trails.

Padang

MAP p483

Bat & Arrow $ Simple air-con rooms above Padang's raucous riverside surfer hangout. Noisy when the Mentawai boats are in town.

Air Manis Hillside $$ Balconied timber rooms complete with birdlife and cute leaf monkeys make this a delightful jungle escape just 10 minutes from the city.

Rimba Ecolodge (p496) $$$ This environmentally sustainable Indonesian-run jungle escape has breeze-cooled bungalows on a jungle-clad beach. It's only accessible by boat from Padang.

Tua Pejat, Mentawai Islands

Mentawai Bagus Local Homestay $$ An excellent option for independent travellers who want to stay in Tua Pejat to explore and surf the best breaks.

Crow's Nest $$ Located on Jati Beach, this guesthouse has terrific views and a laid-back beach vibe.

Bukittinggi

Hello Guesthouse $ Unbeatable city-centre location at this bright and spotless guesthouse. Owner Ling can advise on onward travel.

Villa Copenhagen $$ Arrive as a guest, leave as a friend – this super-hospitable guesthouse is memorable for rooftop breakfasts overlooking urban rice paddies.

Banda Aceh

MAP p501

Lala Hostel $ A great hostel with helpful staff, hot showers, kitchen facilities and bunks with mod cons and privacy curtains.

Padé Hotel $$$ Arabic-style architecture and excellent facilities, spacious suites and a beautiful swimming pool. A worthwhile upgrade for the convenient airport shuttle.

Lhok Nga

MAP p501

Sophie's Sunset Library $ A book lover's beach-bum paradise. Has rented tents on the lawn and a warm family welcome.

Eddie's Homestay $$ Just a short walk from Lhok Nga's best beach, this super-friendly spot is a prime surf hangout.

Pulau Weh

Pele's Place $ Simple rooms that are ideally located. There's a stilted bar and restaurant right above a sheltered reef that's ideal for snorkelling.

Lumba Lumba $$ Cool, spacious dive-centre bungalows with great views and easy access to lovely Gapang beach.

Pulau Nias

MAP p509

Salty Dog Hostel $ Cheap, simple, relaxed and welcoming, this hostel features wood-fired pizzas and a cool little bar. It's 25 minutes from Sorake.

Hash & Family Surf Camp $$ Prime location with grandstand views of the legendary Lagundri Bay wave. Hash offers a warm welcome and arranges introductions to the traditional villages.

Sozinhos Surf Lodge $$$ A dream surf camp with just two fully-serviced bungalows next to a wonderful barrelling Pulau Asu (Hinako Islands) left-hander.

Banyak Islands

MB Camp Singkil $$ The spacious rooms here have huge balconies and shared bathrooms overlooking a river – and crocodiles are often in view! An ideal launchpad for Banyak trips.

Diamond Island Eco Resort $$$ On a private island in the southern Banyaks, this surf camp features luxurious oceanfront bungalows and a range of jungle activities.

Bengkulu

MAP p517

Pringgading Surf Camp $$ A stylish hangout with great rooms, a shady courtyard and tempting plunge pool. Nick also serves Sumatra's best coffee!

Sinar Sport Hotel $$ A modern hotel across the road from the food market, with decor that will appeal to any sports fan.

Palembang

MAP p523

Hotel Domino $ Palembang's best-value modern hotel. The best lunch in the city is served at the neighbouring Pempek Lince.

The Zuri Palembang $$$ Popular luxury hotel at an unbeatable price. This city-centre property features Sumatra's best rooftop infinity pool.

Bandar Lampung

Yunna Hotel $ A reliable business-style hotel that's excellent value. The clean, well-equipped rooms are conveniently located for Chinatown's unforgettable eateries.

Amaris Hotel $$ Bright, spacious rooms in a modern property that's strategically located between the old city and the port.

Krui

Jungle Surf $ You'll never want to leave this super-friendly homestay. It's just a minute's walk from Krui's best surfing wave.

Lani's $$ Tanjung Setia's most popular surfer hangout, thanks to its great rooms, outstanding service and even better pizzas.

Amy's Place $$$ American Amy is a Krui pioneer and her place features lovely chalets and a view over a blissfully uncrowded surf break.

TATAN DANIEL/SHUTTERSTOCK

Tabo Cottages, Danau Toba

Researched by
Anthony Ham

Kalimantan

ORANGUTANS, RAINFORESTS & RIVERS

Kalimantan is a rugged paradise: home to iconic wildlife, little-seen national parks, Indonesia's longest rivers, vast swathes of jungle, hidden mountains and remote beaches.

Kalimantan is Indonesia's wilderness; this is where you go to get off the tourist trail. It occupies almost three-quarters of the island of Borneo, and much of it is remote rainforest that's mostly accessed, if at all, by winding waterways. The reward for intrepid visitors is a huge diversity of flora and fauna, some unique to Borneo, including the noble orangutan – Asia's only great ape.

Travellers with time can attempt the epic Cross-Borneo Trek, one of the world's great adventure-travel routes. But there are many other opportunities for less-strenuous rainforest exploration and wildlife spotting in some of Indonesia's least-visited national parks. In some places, river journeys lead to the villages of the indigenous Dayak people, whose longhouses are still scattered across the interior.

There's a frontier feel to Kalimantan. Divided into five provinces, the region is relatively undeveloped in comparison to many other parts of Indonesia. Most visitors fly in solely for speedy orangutan tours, and Western travellers remain a novelty. Offshore are the idyllic islands of the Derawan Archipelago and some of the finest diving and snorkelling in all of Indonesia.

Big changes are on the horizon, however. East Kalimantan has been chosen as the location for Indonesia's new capital, while the rapacious exploitation of the region's abundant natural resources continues to pose environmental challenges. For now, though, Kalimantan still calls adventurers.

BRAMANYURO/SHUTTERSTOCK

THE MAIN AREAS

WEST KALIMANTAN
Dayak and Chinese culture, colonial heritage. p542

CENTRAL KALIMANTAN
Orangutans and national parks. p554

SOUTH KALIMANTAN
Floating markets, trekking and rafting. p560

EAST KALIMANTAN
Epic river journeys, diving and beaches. p567

For places to stay in Kalimantan, see p584

BANG RICCI/SHUTTERSTOCK

Left: Gawai Dayak (p543); Above: Whale shark near Pulau Derawan (p578)

Find Your Way

Kalimantan's five provinces cover an immense area and transport is generally more expensive than elsewhere in Indonesia. Roads link major cities and towns, as do regional flights, but many places are only accessible by boat.

West Kalimantan, p542

A hub of Dayak and Chinese culture, West Kalimantan is also home to Indonesia's longest river, remote national parks and even a few beaches.

Central Kalimantan, p554

The orangutans of Tanjung Puting National Park are the biggest draw in Kalimantan and can be seen via a storybook river journey.

East Kalimantan, p567

Cruise the mighty Sungai Mahakam into the heart of Borneo, or dive and snorkel with manta rays in the Derawan Archipelago.

South Kalimantan, p560

Lively Banjarmasin has photogenic floating markets, while the mountain village of Loksado tempts with splendid hiking and rafting options.

BUS, CAR & TAXI

Kalimantan's roads are mostly mediocre two-lane highways and journey times are long. Buses are increasingly being superseded by minivans and shared taxis. Hiring a car and driver is relatively inexpensive by Western standards. Use Grab and Gojek – the local rideshares – to get around cities.

PLANE

A number of airlines – Wings Air, Lion Air, Batik Air, Super Air Jet and Citilink – connect Kalimantan's cities and link the region with the rest of Indonesia. Flights have become more expensive but are often the only alternative to lengthy road journeys.

BOAT

A variety of vessels ply Kalimantan's rivers and link the mainland to the islands. They range from large ferries and deluxe houseboats to cramped speedboats *(spids)* and canoe-like craft with engines. Don't expect too much in terms of comfort.

Plan Your Time

Observing orangutans is an unmissable experience, but diving or snorkelling in the Derawan Archipelago is almost as wondrous. With more time, head upriver into the jungle for a taste of wild Borneo.

LILI AINI/SHUTTERSTOCK

Pulau Sangalaki (p580), East Kalimantan

If You Only Do One Thing

- Make tracks for **Tanjung Puting National Park** (p556) in Central Kalimantan, where houseboats await to sail you through the rainforest to meet some of the park's orangutans. You're certain to see plenty of other primates, including proboscis and macaque monkeys and gibbons, as well as hornbills, multicoloured kingfishers and maybe the odd crocodile.

- **Take a night hike** (p558) to encounter the snakes and spiders who share the jungle. Relaxing on the deck of your houseboat as darkness falls and then being roused in the early morning by the jungle waking up is almost as memorable an experience as the wildlife spotting. Plan on three days, two nights.

Seasonal Highlights

June to August is high season in Kalimantan. Orangutans become harder to spot in the rainy season that runs from November to February.

JANUARY

Chinese New Year takes place in January or February. Singkawang's large ethnic Chinese community stages a unique and extravagant celebration and it's a fab time to be in town.

FEBRUARY

Ramadan often falls around this time and spills over into March until 2027. Many shops and restaurants close and hotels are booked out.

APRIL

Shoulder season means fewer visitors, while hungry orangutans are out and about and the visibility is fine for diving. It's a much underrated time for visiting.

A Week to Travel Around

● Begin in the buzzing riverine city of **Banjarmasin** (p560) in South Kalimantan, where houses on stilts and mosques line the waterways. Make an early start and journey by long-tail boat to Banjarmasin's fun floating markets just as dawn breaks. You're likely to be one of just a handful of visitors.

● Visit the pretty riverside village of **Loksado** (p564) in the foothills of the Meratus Mountains, where you can trek to waterfalls and remote Dayak villages, or take to the river on a bamboo raft.

● Visit the diamond diggers, then drive to Palangka Raya for an overnight in **Sebangau National Park** (p554). Continue on to **Tanjung Puting National Park** (p556).

More Than a Week

● Swap the jungle for the white-sand beaches of the **Derawan Archipelago** (p578), off the coast of East Kalimantan. Base yourself on **Maratua Atoll** (p579), a tropical paradise in the Celebes Sea, where turtles swim off the beaches and manta rays and reef sharks circle the nearby islands, whose colourful reefs are some of the most spectacular in Indonesia.

● Alternatively, head west by boat from **Samarinda** (p574) along the **Sungai Mahakam** (p570) on a multiday river journey that will take you to Dayak villages and stilted settlements over lakes, while proboscis monkeys watch from the riverbanks and hornbills fly overhead.

MAY

Pontianak in West Kalimantan is a great place to experience **Gawai Dayak** (p543), the Dayak Harvest Festival. Outlying villages party for days and attending a festival here is unforgettable.

AUGUST

Banjarmasin in South Kalimantan marks Indonesia's **Independence Day** on 17 August. Traditional boat races are staged along the Sungai Martapura.

SEPTEMBER

Head to Tenggarong in East Kalimantan for the **Erau International Folk & Art Festival** (p571), which showcases local cultures and customs.

NOVEMBER

The onset of the rainy season and abundant fruit means that orangutans and other wildlife become more elusive. Although you could get lucky, rain can spoil your trip and humidity is high even when it's not raining.

West Kalimantan

NATIONAL PARKS | DAYAK CULTURE | CHINESE HERITAGE

GETTING AROUND

West Kalimantan's capital Pontianak is the main transport hub, with flights to Putussibau and elsewhere in Kalimantan and Indonesia. Daily buses connect Pontianak to Putussibau and Pangkalan Bun, as well as Kuching in Malaysia, but journey times are long. For Singkawang, it's easiest to travel by shared taxi. Two daily speedboats run from Pontianak to Sukadana. There's very little public transport in cities and towns. Use the Grab or Gojek apps to find motorcycle taxis or cars in Pontianak and Singkawang. Elsewhere, ask your hotel to hook you up with a driver.

West Kalimantan is little visited even by Kalimantan standards. Travellers who do make it here will find Indonesia's longest river, the Sungai Kapuas, winding its way across the province, as well as remote national parks up on the border with Malaysia. Further south on the coast, sleepy Sukadana is the gateway to the seldom-seen Gunung Palung National Park, where wild orangutans roam.

This is also the Dayak heartland. The riverine capital Pontianak sits right on the equator and hosts the memorable Dayak Harvest Festival every May. The north of the province is also a fine place to explore Dayak culture, with traditional longhouses around Putussibau still in use and easy to access. West Kalimantan is also home to large ethnic Chinese communities. Singkawang in particular is a hub of Chinese culture, with many temples and restaurants, as well as being one of the only places in Kalimantan where visitors will find Dutch colonial buildings.

Pontianak: A City of Many Cultures

Equatorial riverside life

Pontianak likes to boast that it's an equatorial city, but there's far more to West Kalimantan's capital than geography. Split in half by the wide Sungai Kapuas, Pontianak is one of Kalimantan's thrilling cultural mosaics. Almost one-third of the population are ethnic Chinese, while there is also a significant Dayak community living alongside Malays and other immigrants from across Indonesia. This diversity is an essential part of Pontianak's appeal, as reflected in every aspect of its daily life, from culinary options to festivals, architecture and even places of worship.

To get a formal primer on all this diversity, stop by the **Museum Provinsi Kalimantan Barat** *(10,000Rp)* for an informative introduction to everything from religion to language and other cultural touchstones. For something a little more dynamic, plan to be in town in May for the exuberant

Dayak Harvest Festival, which is the most public cultural celebration of all.

Pontianak's architecture also tells a fascinating story. This was once an independent sultanate, and its oldest and most atmospheric quarter is **Kampung Beting**, a riverside district of stilted houses on the eastern side of the Sungai Kapuas. On your exploration of the neighbourhood, check out the faded glory of **Istana Kadriah** *(admission by donation)*, the former palace of the sultan, and **Mesjid Abdurrahman**, a handsome all-wooden mosque named after the first sultan that dates back to 1821. To get to Kampung Beting, catch a canoe taxi across the river from just south of the **Central Market**, itself a fascinating mix of produce, crafts and faces from across the region. It's worth setting aside time for.

Around 3km north of Kampung Beting on the same side of the river is **Tugu Khatulistiwa**, a monument marking the site of the equator. Thanks to continental drift, if you've made it this far, you can make it a little further – walk just 117m north of the monument if you want to stand with a foot in each hemisphere. To reach the site from Kampung Beting, take an *opelet* (minibus) for 3km northwest on Jl Khatulistiwa.

Party Like a Dayak

Celebrate Dayak Harvest Festival

Every May Pontianak hosts the biggest Dayak celebration in Kalimantan, when local people gather for **Gawai Dayak**, the Dayak Harvest Festival ('Gawai' means 'festival'). It's a massive party that brings together representatives of the more than 200 different ethnic groups indigenous to Kalimantan and Borneo, who are collectively known as the Dayaks.

Today, most of Kalimantan's three million or so Dayaks are Christian or Muslim, but Gawai Dayak acts as a reminder of the old animist religions that once held sway on Borneo. The festival's official purpose is for the Dayaks to give thanks to their traditional gods for the rice harvest, but it's just as significant as a powerful tool of cultural expression and celebration of Dayak identity.

Gawai Dayak is normally staged in late May in Pontianak with **Rumah Radakng**, a massive Dayak longhouse west of the city centre, as the main venue. For the tens of thousands of spectators it's the dancing that is the principal draw, with the different delegations parading in elaborate traditional costume and then staging a Dayak dance-off as they compete with each other in performing dances, some of which

Continues on p546

GETTING TO MALAYSIA FROM PONTIANAK

Two daily buses depart in the morning for the nine-hour journey from Pontianak to Kuching in Malaysia via the Entikong–Tebedu border crossing, 245km northeast of Pontianak. This is the main border crossing between West Kalimantan and the Malaysian state of Sarawak. Buy tickets for the bus at the Damri office in Pontianak on Jl Pahlawan.

The crossing is open from 7am to 4pm on the Indonesian side and 8am to 5pm on the Malaysian side (Sarawak is one hour ahead of West Kalimantan) and is usually hassle-free. Visitors from the US, Canada, Australia and most European countries get a three-month visa on arrival. Buses and planes link Kuching with the rest of Malaysia.

EATING IN PONTIANAK: OUR PICKS

Warung Kopi Asiang: Pontianak's famous coffee house is run by local legend Mr Asiang. Always crowded, its outdoor stools are fun in the morning. *5am-6pm* $

Mie Tiaw Apollo: Apollo has been serving tasty noodles and rice dishes since 1968. It's constantly busy. *1.30pm-midnight* $

Chai Kue Siam A-Hin: Longstanding spot for dumplings (steamed or fried) and other Chinese-style dishes. Plenty of veggie options. *10am-10pm Wed-Mon* $$

Abang Kepiting: Seafood emporium with plenty of marine life – crabs, lobster, prawns, squid and fish – on display. *10am-10pm Mon-Sat, noon-10pm Sun* $$$

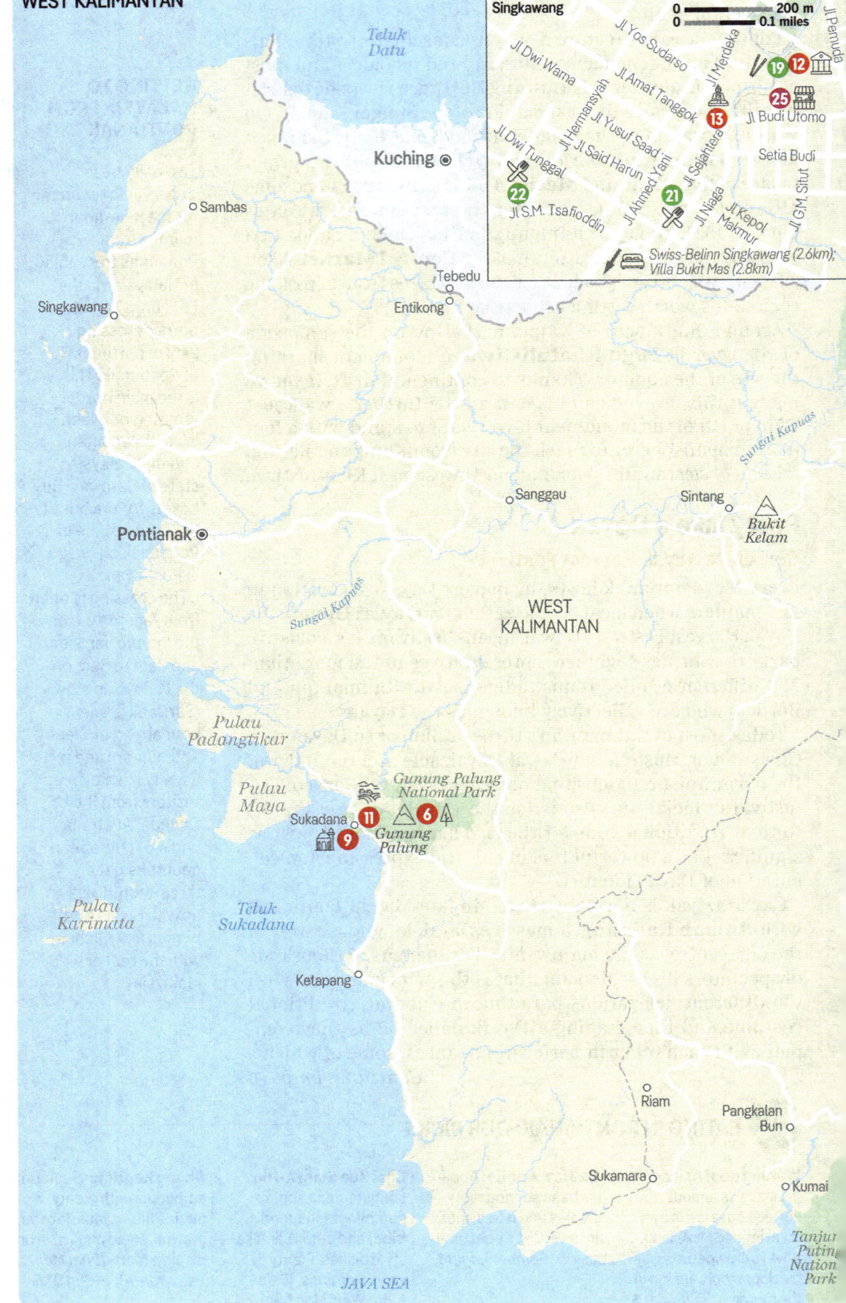
WEST KALIMANTAN
Singkawang
0
200 m
0
0.1 miles
Jl Yos Sudarso
Jl Pemuda
Jl Dwi Warna
Jl Merdeka
Jl Amat Tanggok
Jl Budi Utomo
Jl Hermansyah
Jl Yusuf Saad
Jl Sejahtera
Setia Budi
Jl Dwi Tunggal
Jl Said Harun
Jl Ahmed Yani
Jl G.M. Situt
Jl S.M. Tsafioddin
Jl Niaga
Jl Kepol Makmur
Swiss-Belinn Singkawang (2.6km); Villa Bukit Mas (2.8km)
Teluk Datu
Kuching
Sambas
Tebedu
Entikong
Singkawang
Sungai Kapuas
Sanggau
Sintang
Bukit Kelam
Pontianak
Sungai Kapuas
WEST KALIMANTAN
Pulau Padangtikar
Gunung Palung National Park
Pulau Maya
Sukadana
Gunung Palung
Pulau Karimata
Teluk Sukadana
Ketapang
Riam
Pangkalan Bun
Sukamara
Kumai
Tanjung Puting National Park
JAVA SEA

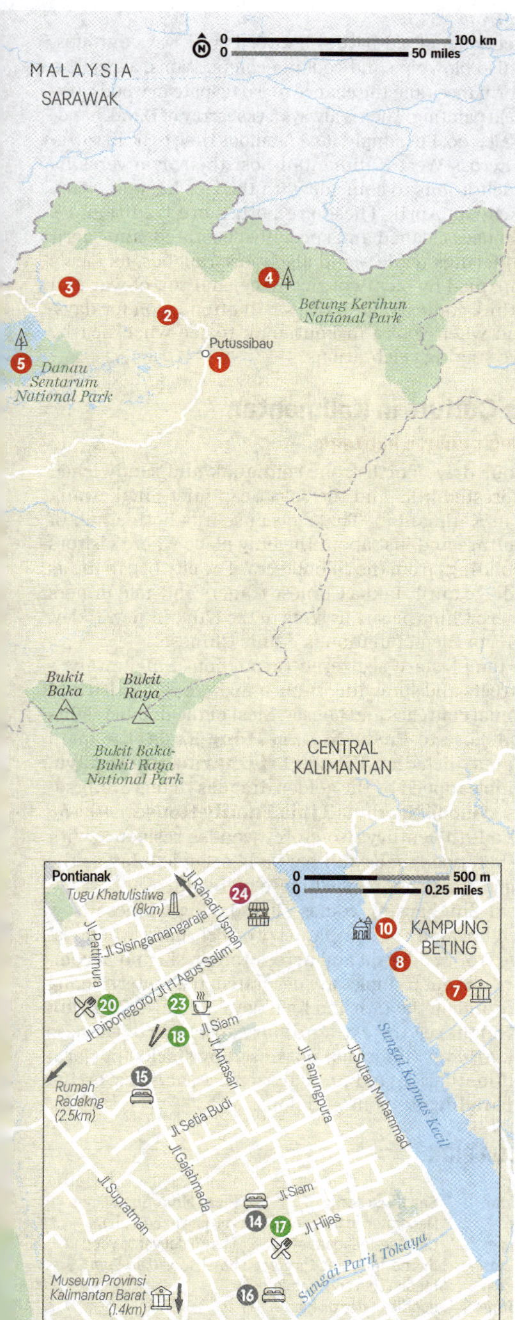

SIGHTS
1 Ariung Mandalam
2 Betang Banua Tengah
3 Betang Sadap
see 1 Betang Sauwes Tunggan
4 Betung Kerihun National Park
5 Danau Sentarum National Park
6 Gunung Palung National Park
7 Istana Kadriah
8 Kampung Beting
9 Masjid Agung Oesman Al-Khair
see 1 Melapi I
10 Mesjid Abdurrahman
see 9 Pantai Pulau Datok
11 Sedahan
12 Tjhia Family House
13 Vihara Tri Dharma Bumi Raya

ACTIVITIES
see 9 ASRI
see 1 Kompakh Adventure

SLEEPING
14 Aston Pontianak
see 1 Hotel Grand Banana Putussibau
15 Hotel Green Leaf
see 1 Hotel Multi 88
16 Hotel Neo Gaja Mada
see 9 Mahkota Kayong Hotel
see 9 Penginapan Family

EATING
17 Abang Kepiting
18 Chai Kue Siam A-Hin
19 Choi Pan Tho Ce
see 1 Fanhaus
see 1 Imecca House Cafe & Resto
20 Mie Tiaw Apollo
21 Pizza Mom
22 Restoran Vegetarian Maitreya
see 9 Rumah Makan Citra Minang
see 1 Rumah Makan Dua Putri
see 9 Rumah Makan Pondok Bakau
see 9 Rumah Makan Simpang Tugu
see 25 San Kheu Jong

DRINKING & NIGHTLIFE
see 9 Container Café
see 1 Income Cafe
23 Warung Kopi Asiang

SHOPPING
24 Central Market
25 Pasar Malam Hong Kong

INFORMATION
see 9 Gunung Palung National Park Office

BEST KALIMANTAN TOURS

Borneo Eco Adventure: Can arrange all things Kalimantan, from orangutan and national park tours to the Cross-Borneo Trek. *(borneo-ecoadventure.com)*

De'Gigant Tours: Specialises in Sungai Mahakam and wildlife-spotting trips, plus tours across Kalimantan. *(borneotourgigant.com)*

Kompakh Adventure: Can get you to remote West Kalimantan longhouses and national parks. *(instagram.com/kompakh)*

Liesa Tanjung Puting: Has a fleet of houseboats; the best option for budget orangutan tours in Tanjung Puting NP. *(liesatanjungputing.com)*

Wow Borneo: Upmarket river-cruise operator in Central Kalimantan with comfortable boats. *(wowborneo.com)*

Continued from p543

are re-enactments of old battles between rival Dayak groups. There are also blowpipe and cooking competitions, as well as music performances and the chance to participate in wood carving and shield painting. There's always a vast array of Dayak handicrafts on sale, too. Put simply, it's a fabulous time to be in town.

Villages across West Kalimantan host their own versions of these celebrations to coincide with the rice harvest; some start as early as April. These are both more traditional – with longhouses cleaned and specially decorated, and sacrifices and offerings made – and also more raucous, as meals are accompanied by plenty of rice wine, and tug-of-war and arm-wrestling contests. Festivities will often go on for days. Ask around when you're in Pontianak to see when nearby villages are staging celebrations.

Chinese Culture in Kalimantan

Singkawang's unique heritage

A three-hour drive north from Pontianak and sandwiched between forested hills and the Java Sea, quiet Singkawang is unique in Kalimantan. That's because it is both a hub of Chinese culture and just about the only place where visitors will find buildings from the colonial era. The city began life as a Dayak village until Hakka Chinese traders and gold miners from southern China began arriving in the 17th century. Today, around 40% of the population is ethnic Chinese.

Chinese temples are scattered throughout Singkawang's low-rise streets and sprawling suburbs, where you'll also find Dutch colonial churches and houses. Most of the notable sights are located close to **Pasar Malam Hong Kong**, the main shopping area, including **Vihara Tri Dharma Bumi Raya**, an 1878 temple topped by the golden dragons that are Singkawang's city symbol. Nearby is **Tjhia Family House** *(entry by donation)*, a 19th-century two-storey wooden residence with expansive verandas that's still partially occupied. It was the former home of a prominent Chinese merchant.

Somnolent Singkawang comes alive during Chinese New Year, which normally falls in January or February, when visitors arrive from Malaysia and across Indonesia and accommodation books out. Temples are decorated, red lanterns hang everywhere and on the 15th and final day, known as **Cap Goh Meh**, you might see the extraordinary spectacle of Chinese and Dayak *tatungs* (holy men possessed by spirits) perform acts of self-mutilation and animal sacrifice while cavorting amid the parading dragons and lions.

EATING IN SINGKAWANG: OUR PICKS

Choi Pan Tho Ce: There are now two branches of this local hot spot around town; it's famed for delicious and delicate all-veg dumplings. *8am-6pm* $

Restoran Vegetarian Maitreya: Offering Chinese-style veggie dishes in a simple setting, it's best and busiest at lunchtime. *7am-7.30pm* $

San Kheu Jong: Decorated in traditional Chinese-teahouse style, this no-frills place is great for dim sum and standard noodle or rice dishes. *7am-midnight* $$

Pizza Mom: Sometimes you just need a pizza. They'll deliver to your hotel, too. *10am-9pm* $$

EXPLORE SINGKAWANG'S CHINESE & COLONIAL HERITAGE

Stroll Singkawang's most atmospheric neighbourhood for insight into the city's history.

START	END	LENGTH
St Francis of Assisi Church	Choi Pan Tho Ce	2km; 3hr

Start early to beat the heat, beginning at ❶ **St Francis of Assisi Church** on Jl Ahmed Yani. Head north on Jl Ahmed Yani, before turning right on Jl Said Harun. Walk east to ❷ **Tugu Naga Emas**, a photogenic golden dragon wrapped around a black pillar. Backtrack 50m, turn right on Jl Sejahtera and walk north through Singkawang's traditional shopping district, where the streets are lined with shop houses, some with balconies and wooden window shutters. At the top of Jl Sejahtera is ❸ **Vihara Tri Dharma Bumi Raya**, the city's most historic Chinese temple. From the temple head north on Jl Merdeka, where you'll see the green-and-white minarets of ❹ **Masjid Raya Singkawang**, the city's main mosque, on your left. Continue north on Jl Merdeka and on the right you'll find ❺ **Taman Burung**, a small riverside park. Next to the park is the former ❻ **Dutch Administrator's House**, a dilapidated 1920 white wooden bungalow with a red-tiled roof. Directly opposite the house is another red-roofed ❼ **colonial-era home** from 1902, now used as a local government office. Return to Vihara Tri Dharma Bumi Raya and head east on Jl Budi Utomo to ❽ **Tjhia Family House**, Singkawang's oldest residential building, before ending your tour with a dumpling lunch at the next-door branch of ❾ **Choi Pan Tho Ce**.

Vihara Tri Dharma Bumi Raya is one of almost 1000 Chinese temples in the city.

The golden dragon wrapped around **Tugu Naga Emas** is the symbol of Singkawang.

The **St Francis of Assisi Church** was built in 1905 in Dutch colonial style.

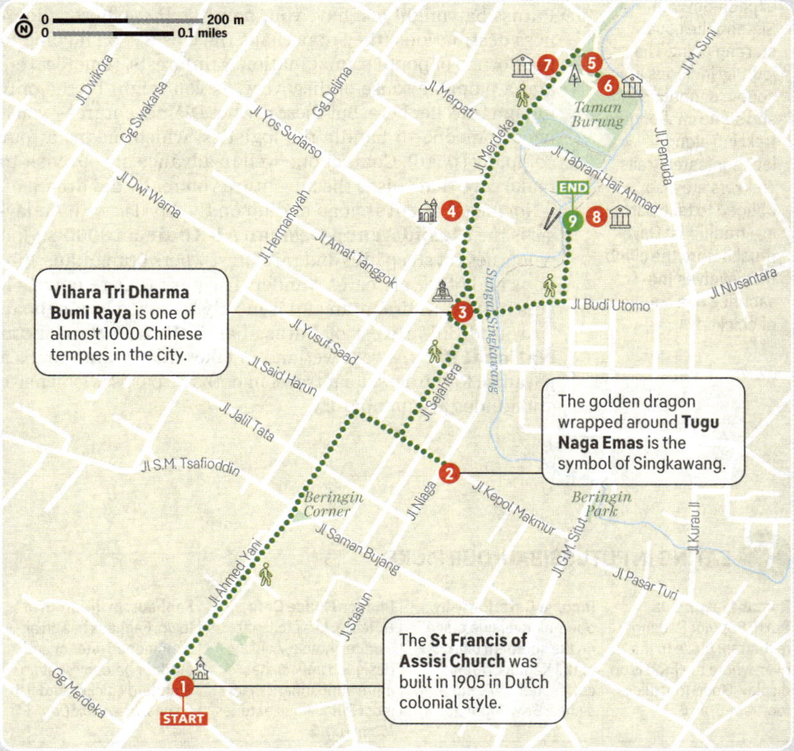

KALIMANTAN'S HIGHEST PEAK

Kalimantan isn't just rainforest. There are a lot of mountains here as well, with the highest of them being **Bukit Raya** (2278m), which sits almost on the border of West and Central Kalimantan in the **Bukit Baka–Bukit Raya National Park**. Local Dayak consider the mountain a sacred place and, perhaps as a consequence, the fees to climb it are steep, too. It's a minimum nine-day expedition, with Sintang the usual starting point. The journey includes a couple of boat rides and some challenging trekking along leech-infested trails. Trekkers are also obliged to take part in a traditional Dayak ritual before the climb that involves the sacrifice of a couple of chickens.

NGURAH PRADNYANA/SHUTTERSTOCK

Betung Kerihun National Park

Two Remote National Parks

Visit Betung Kerihun and Danau Sentarum

If you're looking for adventure, two national parks around Putussibau might just have your name on them. Both wilderness destinations, they're perhaps the closest you'll come to the Borneo of popular imagination: rainforests, remote rivers and a palpable sense of discovery, as you might be the only foreign traveller here. But these are not DIY adventures – you'll need someone to handle the logistics, which means a tour company (p546). Contact one well in advance of your visit to make sure that this is the adventure you really did dream of.

Northeast of Putussibau and up on the border with Malaysia is the **Masjid Agung Oesman Al-Khair**, an 8000-sq-km wilderness of steep hills and rainforest where orangutans, gibbons and other primates wander. The park is as remote as it gets in West Kalimantan and is mostly accessed by longboat.

Around 60km west of Putussibau is **Danau Sentarum National Park**, a vast wetland of lakes and swamp that's a paradise for birders. Boat travel in both the parks is expensive and guides are mandatory.

EATING IN PUTUSSIBAU: OUR PICKS

Rumah Makan Dua Putri: Popular Padang restaurant close to the river, where the food is on display. Good fruit juices, too. *9am-8pm* $

Income Cafe: Partially open-air riverside place on the southern bank of the Kapuas, offering coffee, tea and simple dishes. *8am-10pm* $

Imecca House Cafe & Resto: In a pleasant wooden house, quirkily designed Imecca has more atmosphere than most Putussibau eateries. *10am-9pm* $

Fanhaus: In the north of town, Fanhaus has an air-conditioned interior and outdoor balcony seating. Standard chicken and fish dishes. *10am-10.30pm* $

Sukadana: Where Borneo Meets Bali

Beaches and Hindu temples

Sleepy Sukadana was once only known as the gateway to the nearby Gunung Palung National Park (p552), and it certainly is that. And it's true that there's not a whole to see or do apart from launch an expedition into the park. And yet the town has a distinctive character and a languid seaside charm, thanks to its picturesque setting on a sweet slice of West Kalimantan's coast. Occupying a fold of curving coastline behind which rainforested hills roll away into the distance, Sukadana has superb sunsets, an attractive beach and a nearby village that's a unique blend of Balinese and Kalimantan culture. All of this makes it a worthy destination in its own right.

Getting here is part of the adventure. Speedboats make the scenic five-hour run from Pontianak via the delta of the Sungai Kapuas, passing along a tributary and finally across a stretch of the Java Sea. Visible from miles away is Sukadana's huge mosque, the all-white seafront **Masjid Agung Oesman Al-Khair**, a gift from one of Indonesia's richest men.

Around 3km south of town is **Pantai Pulau Datok**, one of Kalimantan's more attractive mainland beaches. Shaded by casuarina trees, with jungle at either end, it's fine for swimming and is mostly empty during the week.

Ask at your accommodation for a motorcycle taxi or car to head to **Sedahan**, a pretty village surrounded by rice paddies that nestles at the foot of Gunung Palung. It's 10km northeast of Sukadana. Sedahan has a unique feel thanks to the migrants from Bali who settled here. Hindu temples are scattered around and people wear traditional Balinese dress. There are hiking trails and waterfalls close to the village. Simple homestays can be arranged in advance by contacting Yayat at the ASRI office (p552) in Sukadana.

NATIONAL PARK COSTS

Kalimantan's eight national parks are some of the most remote, pristine and little-visited in Indonesia. Accessing them, though, doesn't come cheap. Entry fees are 150,000/250,000Rp per day during the week/weekend and guides with food are at least 300,000Rp a day. Getting to the parks can be pricey and transport inside them, often by boat, is also expensive. Add in accommodation, and the cost of visiting a national park really adds up (at least by Indonesian standards), especially for solo travellers. Make sure you pick your park carefully and look for other travellers to share the cost of a guide. Visiting as part of a tour is sometimes the cheapest option.

EATING IN SUKADANA: OUR PICKS

Rumah Makan Pondok Bakau: Seafood restaurant perched on a wooden platform above the mangroves. Try the spicy sour fish soup. *9am-9pm* $

Rumah Makan Simpang Tugu: By the durian monument in the centre of town, serving Indonesian standards with shaded outdoor seating. *9am-9.30pm* $

Rumah Makan Citra Minang: Solid Padang restaurant with tasty meat and fish dishes and lots of veggie options. *9am-9pm* $

Container Café: A hot spot for Sukadana's youth, offering coffee, tea, juice and basic rice and noodle dishes. *10am-10pm Mon-Thu, 3pm-midnight Sat* $

PACIFIC IMAGICA/ALAMY

Dayak longhouse, Putussibau

TOP EXPERIENCE

Putussibau's Longhouses

Way up in the north of West Kalimantan is Putussibau, a riverine market town that's an ideal base for exploring some of the best-preserved traditional Dayak longhouses in Borneo. Putussibau's longhouses also combine well with trips to two remote national parks and connects easily to Tanjung Lokan, the start or end of the epic Cross-Borneo Trek (p576).

DON'T MISS

- Betang Sauwes Tunggan
- Ariung Mandalam
- Melapi 1
- Betang Banua Tengah
- Betang Sadap

Dayak Culture

The Dayaks are the indigenous people of Borneo. They have a population of over 4.5 million and consist of more than 200 different ethnic groups who speak 170 languages and dialects. Traditionally, the Dayaks were animist forest dwellers who lived in longhouses – one-storey buildings large enough to house a village – and were known for headhunting, deadly blowpipes, extensive tattoos and stretched earlobes. These days, most Dayaks are Christian or Muslim and they all have

PRACTICALITIES

● a few weekly flights connect Putussibau with Pontianak, although they're prone to cancellation ● two daily buses make the 14-hour journey from Pontianak

mobile phones. But despite the impact of the modern world, Dayak tribal identity persists and some Dayaks still live and hunt in the most remote pockets of Borneo. This is especially true in West Kalimantan, where around one-third of the population is Dayak.

The town of Putussibau is cut in half by the Sungai Kapuas. The main part of town occupies the northern bank of the river and was once the haunt of Dayak headhunters before it became a colonial outpost at the end of the 19th century. Today, it's the last settlement of any size on the Sungai Kapuas, and is still mostly populated by various Dayak groups.

Longhouses near Putussibau

Most people come to Putussibau for the superb *betang* (traditional longhouses) dotted around the surrounding area. These are some of the largest traditional structures that are still in use in Kalimantan, and some house 30 or more families. The longhouses vary dramatically; a few of them are historic structures elevated on ironwood pillars, while others resemble old military barracks with rusting corrugated iron roofs.

The closest longhouses to Putussibau are **Betang Sauwes Tunggan**, which is 7km southeast of town and home to 30 families, and the authentic and welcoming **Ariung Mandalam**, which is 8km east of Putussibau and close to the village of Nanga Sambus. Also nearby is **Melapi 1**, the first of five longhouses along the Kapuas upstream of Putussibau. It's a 10km boat ride southeast from town.

Other Longhouses

Further afield are historic **Betang Banua Tengah**, an 1864 longhouse around 50km northwest of Putussibau, and **Betang Sadap**, 93km northwest of Putussibau, which has a reputation as being one of the most friendly longhouse communities.

Longhouse Etiquette

Most *betang* welcome visitors and overnight stays are possible, but it's always a good idea to give advance notice of visits, especially for the more distant longhouses or if you want to arrange accommodation or see a dance performance. Always ask permission before entering the longhouse or taking photos. You'll normally be introduced to the local headman or a visitor liaison, who will insist that you join them for tea or coffee, the modern equivalent of a welcoming ceremony. Unless you speak some Bahasa Indonesia, your trip will be much easier and more informative in the company of a guide or translator. **Kompakh Adventure** *(tel 0813 5260 1248)*, a local ecotourism initiative in Putussibau, can arrange guides and transport.

THE SUNGAI KAPUAS

The Sungai Kapuas (Kapuas River) is Indonesia's longest waterway. It originates in the foothills of the Muller Mountains in the heart of Borneo and snakes 1143km west to Pontianak before emptying into the Java Sea. Its upper reaches are home to vibrant Dayak communities as well as the lakes and wetlands of Danau Sentarum National Park (p548).

TOP TIPS

- Unlike the Sungai Mahakam in East Kalimantan, no official passenger boats ply the Kapuas.
- Travellers will need to negotiate a ride on the cargo boats that make the seven-day journey upriver from Pontianak to Putussibau. Expect many stops along the way.
- Boats depart from just north of Pontianak's Central Market.
- You can break the bus journey from Pontianak by overnighting in the riverside town of Sintang, from where it's also possible to access Danau Sentarum National Park.

ASRI

Conservation organisation **ASRI** *(Alam Sehat Lestari; alamsehatlestari.org)* runs a unique programme that has been startlingly successful in combating illegal logging in Gunung Palung National Park. ASRI operates a medical clinic in Sukadana where communities who opt to conserve the forest and report illegal logging receive discounted health care. It's the only medical clinic in the world where patients can pay by bartering seedlings, handicrafts and even compost. Since ASRI began in 2007 there's been an 89% reduction in illegal logging in the park.

ASRI welcomes suitably qualified volunteers for six-week stays. English-speaking Yayat, who works in the ASRI office, can also arrange homestays in Sedahan. Contact him on WhatsApp at +62 895 3563 02026.

Visit Gunung Palung National Park

Orangutans and primary rainforest

The 900-sq-km Gunung Palung National Park is one the premier rainforest-trekking destinations in Kalimantan – and Indonesia, for that matter – thanks to its superb landscapes and wildlife diversity. With a population of around 2500 orangutans, this is one of the few places in the world where visitors have a good chance of seeing these majestic apes in the wild. But there's plenty of other fauna, too. Acrobatic gibbons, proboscis monkeys, sun bears, forest deer, clouded leopards, crocodiles and a huge variety of bird species all call the park home.

Equally diverse is the flora, with the park encompassing eight different habitats including mangrove, swamp forest and mountain rainforest. Having suffered from illegal logging and mismanagement in the past, the park has rebounded in recent years. It has some of the last great pockets of primary rainforest in Borneo; there are old-growth trees here that are so large that four people can't reach around them.

DAUS85/SHUTTERSTOCK

Butterflies, Gunung Palung National Park

GEORG MULLER

The Muller Mountains take their name from Georg Muller, a German-born soldier and explorer who was the first Westerner to cross the mountain range. Muller served in the Royal Netherlands East Indies Army, which posted him to Borneo in 1818. Based in what is now West Kalimantan, Muller undertook several expeditions to map the region. The 55-year-old Muller crossed the mountains in 1825 while exploring the upper reaches of the Sungai Kapuas, but was subsequently ambushed by local Dayaks who beheaded him. Some 70 years later, the Dutch explorer Anton Nieuwenhuis became the first European to cross Borneo from Pontianak to Samarinda, naming the mountains in Muller's honour.

Visitors walk the same (sometimes) steep trails as the orangutans, through thick forest and past rushing streams and waterfalls. Count on around five hours a day of walking. There's also the option of travelling by boat into the heart of the park. With many areas closed for research, most people find a night or two here is enough. There's basic accommodation in the park or you can arrange a homestay in the village of Sedahan (p549), which is a motorbike ride away from the park entrance.

While a number of operators offer expensive tours, this is one national park in Kalimantan that's cheaper to access as an independent traveller. To do so, it's essential to contact the **park office** *(tel 0898 1331 800)* in Sukadana in advance to arrange a guide and transport and to get your permits. Don't roll up expecting to get into the park the same day.

SUNGAI MAHAKAM JOURNEYS

You don't have to be attempting the Cross-Borneo Trek to visit the towns and villages along the river Sungai Mahakam (p570). Travelling up and down the Mahakam from Samarinda is an adventure in itself.

Central Kalimantan

ORANGUTANS | RIVER CRUISES | CITY LIFE

GETTING AROUND

Pangkalan Bun is the transport hub for Tanjung Puting National Park, with regular daily flights to elsewhere in Kalimantan (sometimes via Jakarta or Surabaya) and the rest of Indonesia. There's also an airport at Palangka Raya. Kumai, a 30-minute drive southeast of Pangkalan Bun, is the port where boats depart for Tanjung Puting National Park. Buses connect Pangkalan Bun with Pontianak, Palangka Raya and Banjarmasin. Buy tickets at the bus company offices. Use the Grab or Gojek apps to find motorcycle taxis or cars. Hotels can also arrange transport.

This is Kalimantan's most visited province, purely because it's home to the orangutans of Tanjung Puting National Park, which is reached via a memorable multiday journey on a houseboat. There's a near certainty of seeing orangutans and other wildlife in the park (outside of the rainy season, from November to February) and so the vast majority of people who want to see the apes do so here. That's despite the fact that the world's largest population of wild orangutans, over 6000, can be found in the less popular Sebangau National Park in the south of the province. Sebangau can be reached from the city-that-wanted-to-be capital, Palangka Raya.

Around 80% of Central Kalimantan is forest, mangroves and swamps. It's the largest province in Indonesia, about 1½ times the size of Java, so road journeys are long. This is also Dayak territory and almost half of Central Kalimantan's population is indigenous to Borneo.

Wildlife Spotting at Sebangau National Park

Swamps, wildlife and boat trips

Occupying over 5600 sq km of Central Kalimantan, Sebangau National Park is little visited, despite being home to the world's largest population of wild orangutans – over 6000. Like many Indonesian national parks, Sebangau has a chequered history and was devastated by both legal and illegal logging in the 1980s and 1990s. Now, only around 15% of the park is fully forested. Thousands of gibbons also live here alongside endangered bird species, including rare storks.

There are two main areas to explore in the park. Your best chance of seeing orangutans is at **Punggu Alas**, but it's harder to get to. It's reached via a 3½-hour drive from Palangka Raya to the boat jetty, followed by one hour or more in a motorised canoe. The second option is **Sungai Koran**. First you drive half-an-hour from Palangka Raya to the village of Kereng Bangkirai. From the boat jetty it's another hour past

pandanus-lined riverbanks in a motorised canoe to Sungai Koran station. Sightings are patchy.

The park is virtually all peat-swamp forest, which makes hiking difficult as your feet will plunge through the trail – a boat is better. Transport can be arranged, along with a guide, at the national-park post in Bangkirai. Borneo Eco Adventure (p546) and Wow Borneo (p546) offers cruises here, too. There is one basic guesthouse at Punggu Alas, but Palangka Raya, Central Kalimantan's capital, is just up the road.

HIGHLIGHTS
1 Tanjung Puting National Park

SIGHTS
2 Orangutan Island
3 Sebangau National Park

ACTIVITIES
4 Liesa Tanjung Puting
5 Wow Borneo

SLEEPING
6 Arsela Hotel
see 5 Bukit Raya Guesthouse
see 2 Ecovillage
7 Flora Homestay
see 4 Majid Hotel
see 6 Mercure Pangkalan Bun
see 7 Rimba Lodge
see 2 Rungan Sari
see 5 Swiss-Belhotel Danum

EATING
see 5 Felicita
see 5 Kampung Lauk
see 5 Rumah Tjilik Riwut

SHOPPING
see 5 Toko Hai Tuah

Visit Orangutan Island

See rehabilitated orangutans from the water

Part of the Borneo Orangutan Survival Foundation, **Orangutan Island** *(Kaja Island; orangutan.or.id)*, is an 11-hectare rehabilitation site for rescued orangutans north of Palangka Raya. To get here, drive for one hour (38km) north of Palangka Raya to the boat jetty at the village of Sei Gohong, from where it's 500m by boat. You can't go ashore, but there's a good chance of seeing the orangutans as you circle the island. Both Borneo Eco Adventure (p546) and Wow Borneo (p546) offer tours here. Expect to pay 500,000Rp per person for a half-day tour from Palangka Raya.

TOP TIP

June to August is the peak time in Tanjung Puting National Park, with as many as 50 or even 60 boats cruising the waterways in search of orangutans. But the best time to see the apes is in March and April, when there are few tourists.

EATING & DRINKING IN PALANGKA RAYA: OUR PICKS

Rumah Tjilik Riwut: Local Dayak dishes (fish in coconut milk with rattan shoots) served in a pleasant garden restaurant and art gallery. *noon-9pm Mon-Sat* $$

Kampung Lauk: A hot spot for locals, who come for the grilled fish, good-value set meals and live music. It's across the river from the city centre. *9am-9pm* $$

Felicita: A rare Western restaurant in Kalimantan worth recommending. Pizza, pasta, salads and fine cakes in a semi-outdoor setting. *9am-10.30pm Tue-Sun* $$

Toko Hai Tuah: There are no real bars in Palangka Raya, but this perpetually busy liquor store offers thirsty travellers a wide selection of foreign alcohol. *noon-3am*

AL CARRERA/SHUTTERSTOCK ©

Orangutan

TOP EXPERIENCE

Tanjung Puting National Park

Tanjung Puting National Park is the most popular tourist destination in Kalimantan as visitors are nearly guaranteed to encounter magnificent orangutans as well as other primates. The journey to see them – up winding waterways through the jungle – gives this adventure world-class appeal. Children, in particular, love the combination of apes and boats, but this experience delights people of all ages.

DON'T MISS

- *Klotok* (houseboat) travel
- Pondok Tanggui
- Camp Leakey
- Tanjung Harapan
- Night trekking
- Pondok Ambung

Sekonyer Village

Most people book three-day, two-night tours of the park. Every morning *klotok* boats depart the river port of Kumai, a short drive from Pangkalan Bun, and head down the Sungai Kumai before turning into the Sungai Sekonyer and entering the park. On board your *klotok* will be your guide (mandatory), and a cook and boat crew. At this point the Sungai Sekonyer is a muddy brown colour, thanks to the runoff from nearby palm-sugar plantations, and is lined with thick mangroves whose ferns reach out over the river.

PRACTICALITIES

● park entry per boat/person 100,000/250,000Rp, incl in package tours ● open 24hr

PAUL HARDING 00/SHUTTERSTOCKV

Klotok **(covered, open-sided houseboat), Sungai Sekonyer**

Sekonyer Village, on the left bank of the river and technically not inside the park (which is on the right bank), is the first settlement you'll reach. A wooden orangutan sculpture on the boat dock greets visitors. It's an unremarkable place, home to park rangers and people working on the palm-oil plantations. Flora Homestay (p584) by the boat dock offers basic but expensive riverside rooms.

Tanjung Harapan

Upriver from Sekonyer Village is Tanjung Harapan, the first orangutan feeding station. It's a 700m walk through the forest from the boat dock. The apes come here at around 3pm in the afternoon, and, like the apes at all the feeding stations, are mostly semi-wild orangutans who have been rehabilitated and released in Tanjung Puting after being in captivity. The feeding station here is a wooden platform loaded with fruit and buckets of soy milk, separated from visitors by a rope.

Before long you'll see the surrounding trees shaking as the apes approach, although a few orangutans crash through the foliage at ground level and just wander nonchalantly through the crowds to the platform. It's common to see mothers with an infant clinging to them, as well as the local alpha male occupying the centre of the platform. Some apes take an interest in the people observing them; others turn their backs as they suck on mangoes and bananas. Either way, the photo opportunities are excellent. Boats often dock overnight at Tanjung Harapan; they tie up before darkness descends and the jungle falls quiet.

KLOTOK TRAVEL

Travelling up the Sungai Sekonyer by *klotok* – a covered, open-sided houseboat – is one of the pleasures of a visit here. Boats can be small, with space on deck for a couple of mattresses, a table and a viewing area, or lavish, with air-con cabins and hot showers. Expect excellent meals, a guide adept at spotting wildlife and peaceful nights spent listening to forest sounds.

WILD OR SEMI-WILD?

Some visitors are disappointed that the orangutans at the feeding stations in Tanjung Puting National Park are so habituated to humans; indeed, they are classified as semi-wild. Although the park does have wild orangutans (which are shy and only seen fleetingly), as the park says, 'these orangutans return to Camp Leakey *not* because they lack foraging skills, but because there is simply not enough tropical rainforest and wild fruit to sustain them.'

ASIA'S GREAT APE

Four great ape species belong to the *Hominidae* family: orangutans, chimpanzees, gorillas and humans. Orangutans ('forest human' in Malay) share 97% of our DNA, and an old Dayak legend has it that our auburn-haired cousins were originally humans who climbed into the trees and abandoned speaking to escape having to work.

Night Trekking

On either your first or second evening here, you'll be given the option of night trekking with a park ranger. The one- to two-hour treks are normally held at Pondok Ambung, Pondok Tanggui or Tanjung Harapan. Wearing a head-torch (head-lamp), this opportunity to view nocturnal wildlife is a truly illuminating experience. You're almost certain to encounter Borneo pit vipers hanging from the branches of trees, while on the forest surface many tarantulas emerge from their burrows and giant forest ants crawl around. There's also the possibility of seeing pythons. If you're truly fortunate, you may spot tarsiers: tiny, shy primates with enormous eyes who feed on insects and spiders.

Riverside Wildlife

As you head upriver, more and more wildlife becomes visible. Endemic black hornbills fly overhead, stock-billed kingfishers perch on riverside branches and crocodiles can be glimpsed in the river. One of the most prized species for birders is the storm stork that flies overhead or lands on the highest treetops.

Although there are no guarantees, you might also see wild orangutans feeding in the foliage, especially in the morning. It's always a thrilling sight, but these wholly wild orangutans are much shyer than their semi-wild forest companions, and often flee if the boat gets too close.

Proboscis monkeys are another of Tanjung Puting's great prizes – watch for family groups with a dominant male

ZARUBA ONDREJ/SHUTTERSTOCK

White-bearded Borneo gibbon

alongside the river. Other possible sightings include long-tailed and pig-tailed macaques, the white-bearded Borneo gibbon and maroon leaf monkeys.

Pondok Tanggui

Pondok Tanggui is the second orangutan feeding station and, for us, it's the best one because visitors can get really close to the apes – the feeding platform is just 10m away. Feeding starts at 9am, with the platform reached via a 1km walk through the forest. Bring drinking water as it gets hot here, and arrive by 8.30am in high season to secure a front-row position.

The orangutans approach from all directions, either descending from trees or by walking up the same trail that tourists use. The apes often stay after the fruit and milk is gone, and will climb a nearby tree to watch the visitors or hang out, meaning there's plenty of time to observe them. Feedings at Pondok Tanggui are also often enlivened by marauding packs of long-tail macaque monkeys, who like to raid the platform and make off with as much fruit as possible, much to the annoyance of the orangutans.

Pondok Ambung

A research station co-run by the Orangutan Foundation International NGO, Pondok Ambung uses remote infrared cameras to monitor the park's nocturnal wildlife. Elusive tarsiers and clouded leopards have been seen here, and this is the prime spot for night treks to search for spiders, snakes, insects and strange glowing mushrooms. Plenty of primates hang out in the area, too, as do sun bears.

Camp Leakey

As your *klotok* heads toward Camp Leakey, the final stop on your tour, the Sungai Sekonyer narrows dramatically, the water colour changes to its natural inky black and the jungle closes in. Keep an eye out for wild orangutans here.

Camp Leakey is the original research station in Tanjung Puting and the location of the third orangutan feeding station. Named in honour of the late paleoanthropologist Louis Leakey, whose assistants included famed primatologists Drs Jane Goodall, Dian Fossey and Biruté Galdikas, who established Camp Leakey in 1971. The camp is a collection of wooden buildings, with the feeding platform located a 1km walk from the boat dock.

Feeding time is 2pm and this station often attracts white-bearded gibbons, who sit in the trees above the platform ready to swing down and grab fruit before the orangutans arrive. The gibbons are spectacularly quick through the trees, moving much faster than other primates. There are usually also macaques squatting on the boat dock watching the *klotoks* arrive.

After visiting Camp Leakey, boats turn around – not an easy manoeuvre when the river is so narrow and jammed with other *klotoks* – and head downriver to anchor for the night.

A MOTHER'S LOVE

Orangutans are the largest living arboreal animals on Earth, and the bond between a mother and her young is among the strongest in the animal kingdom, with children staying with their mothers for seven years as they learn how to survive in the rainforest.

TOP TIPS

- The ideal length of a tour is three days and two nights. Two-day tours are also possible, but that means skipping one of the feeding stations.
- Expect all-inclusive costs to start at 10,000,000/13,000,000Rp for a single/double on a three-day tour.
- Count on paying a minimum tip of 100,000Rp per crew member after a three-day tour.
- If you're pressed for time it's possible to hire a speedboat (4,500,000Rp) in Kumai to head to and from Camp Leakey in one day.
- Don't wear flip-flops (thongs) in the jungle; there are fire ants and leeches around.

South Kalimantan

FLOATING MARKETS | TREKKING | RAFTING

GETTING AROUND

Banjarmasin has South Kalimantan's main airport, with connections to elsewhere in Kalimantan and Indonesia. The airport is 30km southeast of the city centre: a taxi costs around 155,000Rp. Banjarmasin's vast new bus terminal is 17km southeast of the city centre. Two daily buses make the five-hour trip to Loksado at 8am and 9am. There are also daily morning buses at 10am to Palangka Raya, Pangkalan Bun, Balikpapan and Samarinda, but journey times are long. Use the Grab or Gojek apps to find motorcycle taxis or cars in Banjarmasin. In Loksado, hotels can arrange transport.

South Kalimantan offers the chance to explore buzzing Banjarmasin, Kalimantan's liveliest big city. Banjarmasin's photogenic floating markets are its most enduring attraction, but numerous other sights also lie within reach. Visitors can tour the largest diamond fields in Indonesia, or, in complete contrast, trek and raft around tranquil Loksado, an attractive village in the Meratus Mountains. Here, the nearby waterfalls and cool mountain air are a refreshing counterpoint to the lowland jungles. And just outside Banjarmasin is the opportunity to take a river cruise to look for proboscis monkeys and see traditional boatbuilders at work.

The smallest of Kalimantan's five provinces, South Kalimantan is the homeland of the Banjar (or Banjarese) people, a Bornean ethnic group with their own language and cuisine. Try *soto Banjar*, a delicious soup of shredded chicken and noodles flavoured with cinnamon. Around three-quarters of the population is Banjarese; visitors will find Dayak villages up in the mountains.

Get a Taste for Banjari Architecture

Mosques and traditional homes

If you've got a half-day to spare in Banjarmasin, get out and explore the city's surviving Banjari architecture.

Start with **Pulau Kembang**, an island with a boardwalk and lots of macaque monkeys. Nearby is **Masjid Sultan Suriansyah**, a beautiful 1746 wooden mosque built on the site of the first Islamic place of worship in Borneo.

Other riverside sights worth checking out include **Mesjid Raya Sabilal Muhtadin**, a large flat-domed mosque in the centre of Banjarmasin. It looks like something out of a science-fiction movie, especially when floodlit at night. A cake market – **Pasar Wadai** – sets up outside the mosque during Ramadan.

SIGHTS
1 Cempaka Diamond Fields
2 Masjid Agung Al Karomah
3 Merdeka Bridge
4 Mesjid Raya Sabilal Muhtadin
5 Museum Lambung Mangkurat
see 5 Penggosokkan Intan
6 Pulau Alalak
7 Pulau Bakut
see 7 Pulau Curiak
see 2 Rumah Adat Banjar
8 Rumah Anno
9 Soetji Nurani Temple

ACTIVITIES
10 Borneo Eco Adventure
11 River Tubing
12 Tailah

SLEEPING
13 Hotel Victoria River View
14 Kalsel Park
see 11 Mountain Meratus Resort
see 11 Penginapan Pesona Meratus
15 Summer B&B
16 Swiss-Belhotel Borneo Banjarmasin

EATING
see 5 Depot Rudy H
see 5 Garuda
see 5 Kampung Kecil
see 5 Kampung Lauk
17 Rumah Makan Cinto Raso
18 Saraba Nyaman
19 Warung Novi

SHOPPING
see 2 Pasar Martapura

Almost directly opposite the mosque on the other side of the river is **Rumah Anno**, a handsome 1925 traditional wooden Banjari house that's sometimes open to the public. Walk back to **Merdeka Bridge** and you'll see **Soetji Nurani Temple**, a red-walled 1898 Chinese temple that sits in what used to be the heart of Banjarmasin's Chinatown, until the area was redeveloped in recent years. The temple is open to visitors during the day.

TOP TIP

Banjarmasin is spread out and the traffic is a perennial tangle. Allow plenty of time to get to the airport and bus terminal. Try to avoid Loksado on weekends and public holidays, when hotels are booked out by local tourists.

TOP EXPERIENCE

Banjarmasin's Floating Markets

Banjarmasin sprawls for miles on either side of the Sungai Martapura – and it's the river and its canals that define the city. Stilted wooden houses, mosques, shops and restaurants line the waterways here, an atmospheric reminder of traditional Banjarmasin riverside life. Visiting a daily floating market, like Pasar Terapung Lok Baintan, is the best way to experience this watery world.

AFFANDI RAHMAN HALIM/SHUTTERSTOCK

Vendors

TOP TIPS

- Bring a jacket – it's chilly in the morning.
- The market is best between 6am and 7am; it ends by 8.30am.
- To get a coveted overhead picture, looking down onto the boats, you'll need to go ashore and walk across the bridge and take pictures from there.

PRACTICALITIES

- tours leave the city at 5am
- it takes 75 minutes to reach the markets on the northeastern outskirts of Banjarmasin

Pasar Terapung Lok Baintan

To visit Pasar Terapung Lok Baintan, expect to meet your guide at 5am. As you set off down the Sungai Martapura, lights from riverside homes cast eerie reflections on the water; early risers stretch on their decks while the predawn call to prayer rings out from neighbourhood mosques.

By the time dawn breaks, your boat will be surrounded by mostly women vendors paddling skiffs loaded with fresh produce, clothing and crafts, while customers from local shops and restaurants circle around looking for the best deals. Pineapples, lychees, rambutans, coconuts, bananas, jackfruit, pumpkins, dried fish and all manner of vegetables are on offer, and the boats and bartering make for a supremely photogenic sight and sensory treat. Grab a coffee and a Kalimantan doughnut from a floating cafe and practise your Bahasa Indonesia with the friendly market ladies who enjoy a chat and a smile.

There's another daily floating market, **Pasar Terapung Kuin**, west of the city centre, though it's more touristy. On Sundays a small floating market sets up to the side of the Merdeka Bridge in the centre of Banjarmasin.

Take a Half-Day Boat Tour

See monkeys and boats

All Banjarmasin guides can arrange a four-hour boat trip to two of our favourite local attractions. Adrift in the river right in the heart of Banjarmasin, **Pulau Alalak** is home to a handful of boatbuilding workshops, where traditional craftsmen still fashion wooden boats and canoes as they have done for centuries. The northern end of the island is connected to the mainland by a bridge, but going by boat with a guide is easier and more atmospheric.

Further upstream, **Pulau Curiak** and the larger **Pulau Bakut** are two islands that are reliable spots to see the proboscis monkey (or large-nosed monkey), one of Kalimantan's most sought-after species. Boats circle the islands, and there's a good chance of seeing these unusual-looking creatures.

Expect to pay around 500,000Rp for the boat and another 500,000Rp for the guide.

Discover Indonesia's Biggest Diamond Fields

Watch miners pan for precious stones

The **Cempaka Diamond Fields**, known locally as Desa Pumpung, are one of the most historic and strangest sights in Kalimantan. Diamonds have been mined here for 600 years and, despite the fact that these are the largest diamond fields in Indonesia, traditional mining methods are still employed. The landscape is strewn with craters where miners have dug down to find sediment-laden water, which is then pumped uphill via hoses and sieved in ramshackle wooden contraptions, before being emptied into a pit in which a miner sits waist-deep panning the water for treasure.

This is mining that's more reminiscent of the 1849 California gold rush than the 21st century. The 1000-odd miners work in small groups, with many from families that have been doing the job for generations; some of the fields are fringed with ornate houses belonging to miners who made it rich. They're a friendly bunch and are normally happy to explain their work to visitors. Most of the diamonds they find are small, between 0.5 and 1 carats, but agate and amethyst are also frequently found, along with gold. The mines are about 40km southeast of Banjarmasin and are closed on Fridays. You'll need a guide if you want to speak to the miners.

BANJAR PEOPLE

Around 4.1 million people in Indonesia identify as Banjar. The vast majority live in South Kalimantan, with smaller communities in Central and East Kalimantan. Originally an Austronesian people, the Banjarese rose to prominence in the 16th century with the founding of the Sultanate of Banjar in what is now South Kalimantan. The sultanate grew rich producing and trading pepper, but was abolished by the Dutch colonial authorities in the mid-19th century after a brief war. Today, many Banjarese have intermarried with Dayak or Javanese people, but the Banjar language continues to be widely spoken, while Banjar cuisine – especially its soups and cakes – has spread beyond Kalimantan to become a staple of Indonesia's food scene.

EATING IN BANJARMASIN: OUR PICKS

Soto Banjar Bang Amat: The most famous place to try *soto Banjar* is at this ramshackle riverside joint. *7.30am-4.30pm Sat-Wed, to 3.30pm Thu* $

Warung Novi: There's nothing fancy here, but the *soto Banjar* is in the running for the best in town. *9am-10pm* $

Rumah Makan Cinto Raso: Deservedly popular Padang place in the centre of Banjarmasin, where the food is on display. *8am-10pm* $

Saraba Nyaman: This floating restaurant on the river is another excellent place for seafood and other Banjari dishes. *9am-8.30pm* $$

DIGGING FOR DIAMONDS

Supian Suri, a miner, talks about mining for diamonds and other precious stones in the Cempaka Diamond Fields.

I was born in Cempaka and have been mining since I left school. My father and grandfather were also miners, so it seems like normal work to me. It can be dangerous if there's a landslide; one of our group was killed a few years ago. But I don't worry. We always pray before we start digging at a new site. I trust in Allah.

I make good money but, of course, it depends on what we find. The diamonds are small, but we find agate every day, although that's not so valuable. We also find gold frequently and we can sell that for 700,000Rp a gram.

The Road to the Diamond Fields

Make stops along the way

Travelling to the mines takes you past **Rumah Adat Banjar** *(entry by donation)*, a stunning traditional Banjari home, just across from the river in **Teluk Selong Ulu**. Built in 1811, it's one of the best preserved examples anywhere in South Kalimantan with its airy main room, soaring ceilings and intricate wood carvings. Descendants of the original owners still live in the house.

A few kilometres up the road, in the busy trading town of **Martapura** and just south of the grand **Masjid Agung Al Karomah** mosque, is the sprawling market **Pasar Martapura**. The sedate shops that trade in diamonds, other gems and jewellery occupy the southern end of the market, while the more traditional vendors sprawl over a number of blocks: you'll see fish, fruit and other fresh produce, plus household goods and a handful of souvenir stalls. Martapura is also known as a centre for Islamic teaching.

The nearest city to the mines is **Banjarbaru**, 35km southeast of Banjarmasin, the capital of South Kalimantan. While you're here, step into **Museum Lambung Mangkurat** *(muslam.kalselprov.go.id; 5000Rp; closed Monday)* on Jl Ahmed Yani, Banjarbaru's main street. It's a worthwhile stop thanks to some above-average displays on Banjar culture and history. Nearby, too, is **Penggosokkan Intan** *(free)*, a local government centre where visitors can see diamonds and other precious stones being tested for purity and cut and polished. You can make a purchase, though there's little pressure to buy.

Mountain Life in Loksado

Trekking and rafting at altitude

Pretty Loksado makes a great upland retreat from the South Kalimantan plains. Nestled at the end of the road in the foothills of the Meratus Mountains, this part-Dayak settlement is as close to an earthly Elysium as visitors will find in Kalimantan. The final section of the five-hour drive from Banjarmasin is up a winding and rising road through forested hills cut through with streams and hidden waterfalls. Loksado itself is a small village, its sloping main street tracking the Sungai Amandit as it curves through the countryside, and the cool mountain air here is a real relief after the heat and humidity of the lowlands.

This is trekking and rafting country, with numerous trails to follow and rivers to tube or float downstream on a bamboo raft. Hikes around Loksado are especially worthwhile because they offer wildlife-spotting opportunities – expect to see macaque monkeys, pythons, iguanas, eagles and owls. You'll also have the chance to visit Dayak villages, where you can sleep in the local longhouse and clamber across rickety suspension bridges. There are numerous waterfalls and, if you trek far enough, pristine primary forest and some serious mountain peaks.

MUSLIM HANAFI/SHUTTERSTOCK

Sunrise near Loksado

The walking here ranges from moderate to billy-goating up the side of steep slopes. One multiday option is to summit 1901m **Gunung Besar** (the tallest peak in the Meratus Mountains), a three- to four-day trek. Guides are essential: they can be hired locally for 400,000Rp or in Banjarmasin (p560).

For the local tourists who come to Loksado in increasing numbers, the main reason is the chance to play in and on the **Sungai Amandit** (Amandit River). **Tubing** the river is one popular option, but being poled downstream on a bamboo raft by a Dayak boatman is the main attraction. Depending on water levels, the experience can be relaxing or spirited as you perch on a raft made of bamboo poles lashed together, while the boatman navigates through the rocks. The forest is all around and you'll certainly hear plenty of wildlife, even if you don't see it. All accommodation in Loksado can organise rafting or tubing trips. Expect to pay 300,000Rp for a two- to three-hour rafting trip that ends with visitors returning to Loksado by motorcycle taxi.

A couple of daily morning buses travel from Banjarmasin to Loksado, or a taxi will cost 800,000Rp. Loksado gets busy on weekends and public holidays, but there's an ever-growing choice of mostly riverside places to stay at, with the pick of the accommodation in the south of the village. There are a few simple restaurants and shops, but most close by 8pm.

MERATUS MOUNTAINS

The Meratus Mountains loom above Loksado, with the highest peak, Gunung Besar, being one of the few mountains in Kalimantan that actually offers a view from its summit. The mountain range cuts South Kalimantan in two and is home to remote villages populated by the semi-nomadic Meratus Dayak, rare birds and even a few orangutans. However, the mountains have suffered environmental damage from extensive logging and the clearing of land for agriculture. Visitors will spot piles of timber by the side of the road and deforested hills on the final part of the journey to Loksado. Nevertheless, the most distant stretches of the mountains are still covered in primary forest, now an increasingly rare sight in Kalimantan.

EATING IN BANJARBARU: OUR PICKS

Kampung Lauk: This friendly, open-sided restaurant has wonderful fish dishes (the Lasin was spectacular) and large servings. *10am-10pm* $

Garuda: If Kampung Lauk is full, nearby Garuda takes up the slack with tasty Banjari food and decent seafood. *8am-5pm Mon-Sat* $

Kampung Kecil: This Banjarbaru outpost of the popular Indonesian chain is a good fallback when you want something quick and local. *10am-10pm* $

Depot Rudy H: If you can't find something on the menu here, there's no hope: there's seafood, Indonesian, Chinese, Banjari and more. *10am-10pm* $

BEST CENTRAL & SOUTH KALIMANTAN GUIDES

Jenie Subaru: Organises trips in Tanjung Puting and Sebangau National Parks. *(WhatsApp +62 857 6422 0991; jeniesubaru@gmail.com)*

Joe Yas: Banjarmasin guide; arranges excursions across Central, South and East Kalimantan. *(WhatsApp +62 812 5182 8311)*

Yadi: Banjarmasin guide with extensive city experience and across Kalimantan. *(WhatsApp +62 813 5193 6200)*

Syadhian: This engaging and experienced guide is the owner of Borneo Eco Adventure. *(+62 821 1009 4658; info@borneo-ecoadventure.com)*

Tailah: Can take you to floating markets in Banjarmasin or on treks around Loksado. *(WhatsApp +62 858 2103 5791)*

IMAN SATRIA/SHUTTERSTOCK

Swamp cowboy, Kandangan

Watch Swamp Cowboys at Work

Where the buffalo roam

Visiting Loksado can be combined with a trip to the swamp cowboys of the vast wetlands north of nearby Kandangan. This is one of Kalimantan's most unusual and photogenic adventures: watching swamp cowboys herding water buffalo from canoes rather than horses.

The flat floodplains and lowland swamp north of **Kandangan** make traditional farming all but impossible. Instead, the region is home to a huge wetland ranch, where herds of water buffalo are corralled in elevated pens by night and let out to swim to their waterlogged grazing areas during the day. The swamp cowboys use their canoes to herd the paddling buffalo to pasture or to their favourite mud holes, before leading them back to their corrals around dusk. It's an amazing sight and best seen in the early morning or late afternoon.

To get to the wetlands, take a taxi to the riverside town of **Negara**, 30km northeast of Kandangan along an elevated road lined with stilted villages. From Negara, charter a boat (250,000Rp) at the dock near the main market for the one-hour journey to the buffalo herds. You can also access the wetlands from the town of Amuntai, 55km north of Kandangan.

There are basic guesthouses in Negara; better hotels can be found in Amuntai and Kandangan.

East Kalimantan

RIVER JOURNEYS | IDYLLIC ISLANDS | BOOMING CITIES

East Kalimantan is the place to come to live out those exotic dreams of heading into the heart of Borneo or diving with manta rays and whale sharks off the sublime tropical islands of the Derawan Archipelago. Remote as it is, though, East Kalimantan is also home to Balikpapan and Samarinda, two of Kalimantan's biggest and most vibrant cities, offering travellers the chance to reconnect after long journeys.

With hundreds of rivers bisecting its rainforests, inland East Kalimantan can really only be explored by boat. The multiday voyage up the Sungai Mahakam (Mahakam River) from Samarinda is one of Borneo's great adventures, taking travellers deep into the island via tiny towns, lakes and wildlife-rich jungle. The truly hardy can carry on and attempt the Cross-Borneo Trek. In contrast, the Derawan Archipelago offers some of the best diving and snorkelling in Indonesia, as well as gleaming white-sand beaches that are remarkably empty.

GETTING AROUND

East Kalimantan is vast and remote, so pack some patience when it comes to moving around. Although the major cities of Balikpapan and Samarinda have well-connected airports, boats are the principal form of transport in much of East Kalimantan. A variety of vessels connect Samarinda with inland Borneo via multiday river journeys, while speedboats from Berau provide access to the islands of the Derawan Archipelago. Buses link Balikpapan and Samarinda, but elsewhere shared taxis have mostly superseded public transport. Travelling by road here is generally slow.

Explore Booming Balikpapan

Postindustrial beaches and markets

Balikpapan is unlike anywhere else in Kalimantan: it's a thriving seaport thanks to flourishing offshore oil and gas production. Sit on the yellow sand of **Kemala Beach**, one of a number of reasonable city beaches here, and you'll see tankers moored out in the Makassar Strait and oil rigs in the far distance. It's hardly a wilderness experience of the kind you might have dreamed of in Borneo, but it does have the power to hold visitors in its thrall, in postindustrial fascination and a world away from any appreciation of pristine beauty.

Balikpapan once had a sizeable population of foreign workers. There are far fewer now, but the city still retains a vaguely cosmopolitan vibe, especially in comparison to Kalimantan's other cities. There are even a few bars and Western-style restaurants. Jl Jenderal Sudirman is the main drag, where hotels, banks, malls, cafes and restaurants cluster.

Continues on p574

EAST KALIMANTAN
MALAYSIA
SARAWAK
Kayan Mentarang National Park
Sungai Kayan
Sungai Kayan
NORTH KALIMANTAN
Betung Kerihun National Park
Sungai Mahakam
Tiong Ohang
EAST KALIMANTAN
Kutai National Park
Sungai Balayan
Tenggarong
Samarinda
CENTRAL KALIMANTAN
Balikpapan
Panajam
Tanahgrogot
SOUTH KALIMANTAN
Balikpapan
Pasar Kebun Sayur (5km)
Jl Martadinata
Jl P Tendean
Jl Ahmad Yani
Jl Tanjung Pura
Jl Suparjan
Jl Pranoto
Open House (1.6km)
Kemala Beach (1km)
Jl Sudirman
Selat Makassar
0 400 m
0 0.2 miles

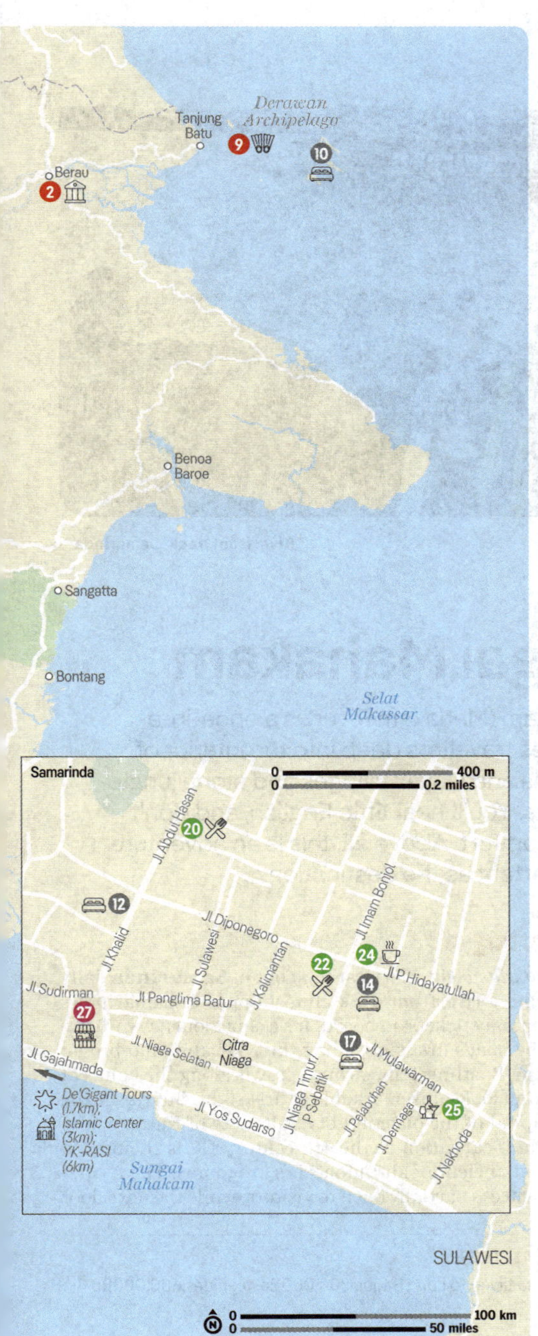

SIGHTS
1 Catholic Church
2 Keraton Sambaliung
3 Kutai National Park
4 KWPLH Sun Bear Conservation Center
5 Mancong Longhouse
6 Mulawarman Museum
see 2 Museum Batiwakkal
7 Samboja Lestari
8 Sungai Wain Protection Forest

ACTIVITIES
see 10 Maratua Paradise Resort
see 10 Nabucco Island Resort
9 Scuba Junkie Sangalaki
see 9 Tasik Divers

SLEEPING
10 Borneo Cottage Maratua
see 9 Derawan Fisheries Cottage
see 6 Grand Elty Singgasana Hotel
11 Hotel Gran Senyiur
12 Hotel Grand Kartika
13 Hotel Monita
see 2 Hotel Palmy
14 Kost Guesthouse
15 Louu Taman Jamrud
see 10 Maratua Guesthouse
16 Maryam Guesthouse 2
17 Mercure Samarinda
see 10 Nouri Cottages
18 Novotel Balikpapan
19 Penginapan Abadi
see 10 Penginapan Ananda
see 9 Reza Cottages
see 2 Rumah Kedaung

EATING
20 Ayam Goreng Banjar
21 Ocean's Resto
22 Rumah Makan Amado
23 Warung Soto Kuin Abduh

DRINKING & NIGHTLIFE
24 Kedai Kofi
25 Muse
26 RPM Cafe

ENTERTAINMENT
see 6 Erau International Folk & Art Festival

SHOPPING
27 Pasar Pagi

MR.ARDI/SHUTTERSTOCK

Riverfront dock, Samarinda

TOP EXPERIENCE

Up the Sungai Mahakam

Travelling the Sungai Mahakam (Mahakam River) is a once-in-a-lifetime experience that takes travellers deep into the interior of Borneo via tiny riverine towns and Dayak villages and along jungle-lined, wildlife-rich waterways. You'll hear little English, and don't expect much in the way of comfort. Above all, this is an adventure where the journey is as important as the destination.

DON'T MISS

- Tenggarong
- Kota Bangun
- Lake District
- Muara Muntai
- Melak
- Tering
- Long Bagun

Tenggarong

Two *kapal biasa* (river ferries) chug out of **Samarinda** daily at 7am from a riverfront dock almost opposite Samarinda's bus station. Buy tickets on board. It's a short journey to Tenggarong, the boat's first stop, along the wide and mud-brown **Mahakam**. Bustling Tenggarong sprawls along the banks of the river and looks unremarkable at first sight. But this is the former capital of the once-mighty Sultanate of Kutai, whose first Hindu incarnation in the 4th century CE is thought to be the most ancient of all Indonesia's kingdoms. The former sultan's palace is partially open to visitors, while the next-door

PRACTICALITIES

● *kapal biasa* ticket to Long Bagun 200,000Rp ● guides 600,000Rp per day

MR. DONNI/SHUTTERSTOCK

Erau International Folk & Art Festival

Mulawarman Museum *(20,000Rp)* chronicles the culture and history of the Kutai kingdom and has some impressive Yuan and Ming dynasty ceramics. Try to be in Tenggarong for the **Erau International Folk & Art Festival**. Normally held in August or September, this annual celebration of local cultures draws a big crowd, with events held at the palace and around town. Tenggarong's handful of hotels books out at this time.

Kota Bangun

A few hours upriver from Tenggarong is Kota Bangun. The journey along the **Lower Mahakam** to this point is the least interesting stretch for scenery, and the river is always busy with giant barges hauling coal to the coast from the mines upriver. Some people choose to travel this section by bus or car, picking up boats in Kota Bangun. It's a sound idea, as Kota Bangun is where travellers leave behind big towns and enter a world of sleepy riverine settlements.

Kota Bangun drowses in the afternoon sun, its low-rise wooden houses dominated by the riverfront mosque. There are a couple of simple guesthouses and a few restaurants, all of which close by 9pm. Foreigners will attract a lot of attention.

If you do come here by *kapal biasa*, it's worth getting off and travelling on by *ces* – wooden canoe-like vessels with lawnmower-like engines and a tarp for a roof. After Kota Bangun there are endless wildlife-rich tributaries leading to intriguing villages that you won't see from the big ferries.

For onward travel, Kota Bangun is where travellers leave behind big towns and enter a world of sleepy riverine settlements. Local boatmen hang out at a jetty on the riverfront. Negotiate a day-long ride to take you to the next town, Muara Muntai, via the lakes and wetlands of the Mahakam's Lake District. Expect to pay around 1,500,000Rp per day for a *ces*.

THE LAST SUNGAI MAHAKAM DOLPHINS

Fewer than 70 river dolphins swim the Sungai Mahakam. Mahakam dolphins are a critically endangered subspecies of the Irrawaddy dolphins, found in Southeast Asia's other major rivers. These grey-blue, snub-nosed dolphins face threats from fishing nets, boat engines and an increasingly polluted river with coal-mine and palm-oil-plantation runoff. Samarinda-based NGO **YK-RASI** *(ykrasi.org)* works to protect these enchanting creatures.

TOP TIPS

- Guides aren't essential for the journey. However, they will make your life much easier if you don't speak any Bahasa Indonesia.
- There are ATMs in Muara Muntai and Melak, but don't rely on them – bring plenty of cash.
- Speedboats heading upriver or downriver normally depart between 8am and 9am. Buy tickets the day before.
- *Kapal biasa* dock and depart at all hours. Don't expect them to be on time.
- Samarinda-based **De'Gigant Tours** (p546) *(borneotourgigant.com)* offers multiday tours of the Mahakam in comfortable *klotok* houseboats.

MODIK OR MAULIR?

One phrase you'll be sure to hear on the Mahakam is *'Modik or maulir?'* The first word is a mashup of *mau udik* (want upriver) and colloquially means to head back to the place of your origin (millions of Indonesians *modik* during the Idul Fitri holiday). *Maulir* comes from *mau hilir* (want downriver), a bittersweet direction.

Lake District

Swapping the *kapal biasa* to clamber aboard a low-slung *ces* brings you closer to nature almost immediately. If you speak some Bahasa Indonesia, the boatmen can also act as guides. They're quick to spot hornbills or monkeys, and will take you to the places you're most likely to encounter them. Soon after leaving Kota Bangun, the village of Muara Pela appears on the left of the river, with lakes and wetlands visible in the far distance. This is the prime place for spotting the Mahakam's dwindling population of river dolphins, and boatmen will circle in search of them. After that, your *ces* will bounce across the big expanse of **Danau Semayang** (Lake Semayang).

On the other side of the lake is Melintang, an entirely stilted settlement perched over the water and connected to the mainland by a precarious bamboo bridge. From here, boatmen turn into narrow tributaries of the Mahakam, where the forest reaches over the water, passing small villages on the way into Muara Muntai.

Muara Muntai

The streets of this riverside town are connected by a network of valuable ironwood boardwalks, down which motorbikes clack constantly. A heavily Muslim town, Muara Muntai has a couple of guesthouses and restaurants and makes a fine base for exploring **Danau Jempang** (Lake Jempang), the largest of the three wetlands in the Lake District, and the surrounding Dayak villages.

Danau Jempang is a bird-watcher's paradise: look out for kingfishers, hornbills and storks. But as your *ces* heads out of

PAUL HARDING 00/SHUTTERSTOCK

Mancong Longhouse

Muara Muntai towards the lake, it is proboscis monkeys who occupy the trees. You'll almost certainly see the big-nosed, long-tailed primates gambolling along the riverbank and occasionally swimming in the river. Across the lake is Tanjung Isay, a small Dayak village with a historic longhouse: **Louu Taman Jamrud**. It's guarded by carved totems and it's possible to stay here. Also nearby, in Mancong Village, is the exquisitely restored 1930s **Mancong Longhouse**. If water levels permit, you can get to Mancong by boat, otherwise hop on a motorbike in Tanjung Isay for the 10km ride.

Melak

The four-hour journey by *ces* from Muara Muntai to Melak sees boats weaving around vast clumps of water hyacinth on Danau Jempang, before turning down a winding channel lined with giant banyan trees. The proboscis monkeys are often just metres away here, along with macaques and monitor lizards, while forest birds fly overhead and the insects in the jungle chatter incessantly. Boats rejoin the Mahakam at **Muara Pahu**, a collection of stilted villages, before heading into Melak.

There are Dayak villages and the odd longhouse around Melak, the largest town on the Mahakam after Tenggarong. The thirsty will also find a couple of liquor stores here. If you want to avoid taking the much slower *kapal biasa*, two daily *spids* – speedboats – leave Melak for Samarinda around 9am, hammering down the river in a spine-compressing six hours.

Tering

Deep in gold-mining country, Tering is really two villages divided by the Mahakam. Tering Baru is a Malay settlement where *kapal biasa* dock. Much more interesting is the Dayak community of **Tering Lama** on the north bank of the river. Hop a *ces* across the river to see Tering Lama's magnificent **Catholic church**, an all-wood structure with a bell tower suspended from towering pillars and carved totems outside the entrance.

Tering, an hour's drive from Melak, is sometimes the final stop for *kapal biasa*, depending on water levels. If the *kapal* can't move on, you can catch a morning *spid* here for the four-hour journey to Long Bagun.

Long Bagun

Travellers who make it to Long Bagun can congratulate themselves: this is the final stop for *kapal biasa*. There's only one more settlement upriver and that's the village of **Tiong Ohang**, a six-hour ride in a *spid*, from where Cross-Borneo trekkers march off into the Muller Mountains (p576). Long Bagun is a small but interesting majority-Dayak village with an attractive longhouse. If water levels are right, *kapal biasa* dock 3km south of the village at Ujoh Bilang. Otherwise *spids* make the journey downriver to Tering.

BOATS OF THE MAHAKAM

Kapal biasa The workhorses of the Sungai Mahakam, these double-decker ferries make multiday journeys from Samarinda to Long Bagun. The open lower deck is for short-distance travellers, cargo, fuel and motorbikes. Long-distance passengers travel on the enclosed upper deck.

Spid These powerful speedboatsthat skim along the Mahakam at speeds of 40 knots per hour. *Spids* are noisy and cramped, especially for tall or large people.

Ces Pronounced 'chess', these are the Indonesian version of the long-tail boats found across Southeast Asia. They're perfect for exploring narrow jungle waterways and for wildlife spotting.

INDONESIA'S MOST LIVEABLE CITY

Balikpapan has consistently been voted as Indonesia's most liveable city in local polls over the last decade. But while the city's seaside setting is pleasant, it's the oil and gas in the sea that's the real reason Balikpapan is booming. Oil was first discovered off Balikpapan in the 1890s, transforming what was then a sleepy fishing village populated by Bugis migrants from Sulawesi into one of Borneo's key economic hubs. During WWII the Australians and Japanese fought for control of the oil refinery here. Today, Balikpapan's oil and gas industry is still the most profitable sector of Kalimantan's economy, and migrants from across Indonesia continue to flock here looking for work.

Continued from p567

Pasar Kebun Sayur, a market 5km north of the city centre, is also worth a browse for handicrafts, souvenirs and traditional Dayak remedies. Use the Grab or Gojek apps to find motorcycle taxis and cars.

Discover Balikpapan's Conservation Side

Visit three conservation projects

Balikpapan is also about strange juxtapositions – it's a complicated, modern Borneo that you find here. Just down the road from the oil-and-gas-filled horizon are a couple of worthwhile conservation projects that you can visit on a day trip. Chief among them is **Samboja Lestari** *(orangutan.or.id; adult/child 500,000/250,000Rp)*, 45km north of Balikpapan, which houses orangutans and sun bears.

South of here is the **KWPLH Sun Bear Conservation Center** *(beruangmadu.org; entry by donation)*, where visitors can observe the resident sun bears. Also close to Balikpapan is the **Sungai Wain Protection Forest** *(entry incl guide 100,000Rp)*, which is home to 90-odd orangutans.

Samarinda, East Kalimantan's Riverside Capital

Gateway to inland Borneo

Samarinda, the capital of East Kalimantan, sits at the end of the mighty Sungai Mahakam. Its strategic location is the principal reason to visit, as Samarinda is the starting point for epic journeys upriver into the heart of Borneo, including the epic Crosss-Borneo Trek. The city's **Islamic Center** is the largest mosque in Kalimantan. It looks splendid when lit up at night – visitors can climb an adjacent observation tower for awesome river views. But there's little else to see apart from the busy main market, **Pasar Pagi**.

Most travellers use their time here to prepare for the multiday journey along the Sungai Mahakam, which slices sprawling Samarinda in half as it winds through the city.

Visit Kutai National Park

An underrated park for orangutans

If you're not heading inland, and even if you are, Samarinda also acts as a gateway to Kutai National Park, which is a five-hour drive north of town, via Sangatta. All but abandoned in

EATING & DRINKING IN BALIKPAPAN: OUR PICKS

Warung Soto Kuin Abduh: Always-busy spot for South Kalimantan specialty *soto Banjar*, a cinnamon-flavoured chicken and noodle soup. *11am-10pm* $

Open House: Atmospheric hilltop restaurant with semi-open-air spaces. Serves Dayak, Indonesian and Western dishes. *noon-10pm Mon-Fri, from 11am Sat & Sun* $$

Ocean's Resto: Popular waterfront restaurant in Balikpapan's nightlife zone. The seafood is pricey, but there are also Western options. *10am-10pm* $$$

RPM Cafe: Amenable bar with cold beer and nightly live music. There are a few other bars and karaoke joints nearby. *4pm-1am*

Sun bear, KWPLH Sun Bear Conservation Center

the 1990s, Kutai has bounced back and 2000 wild orangutans are now estimated to live here, as well as proboscis monkeys, gibbons, langurs, clouded leopards, large monitor lizards and numerous species of orchids.

Samarinda-based guides and guides assigned at the park HQ can take visitors down the numerous forest trails and most people will get to see wildlife here. It's also possible to go deeper into the park by boat.

See Historic Berau

Journey to islands and caves

Berau (aka Tanjung Redeb) was once the centre of a sultanate that ruled the surrounding area for 300-odd years, and this river port on the Sungai Berau in the north of East Kalimantan remains an important trading hub. The writer Joseph Conrad spent time here during the 1880s as a sailor, and his first novel *Almayer's Folly* is set in a fictionalised version of Berau.

These days Berau is best known to travellers as a transit town, thanks to its airport, which spares visitors the 15-hour road journey from Samarinda, and the daily speedboats to the dreamy islands of the Derawan Archipelago. But the **Museum Batiwakkal** *(entry by donation)*, on the site of the original sultan's palace, offers a reasonable summary of the history of

Continues on p578

JUNGLE TREKKING

Rustam, a Samarinda-based guide, talks about the Cross-Borneo Trek.

The jungle is my life. I've done the Cross-Borneo Trek 46 times. I always travel with Dayak people as porters. The Dayak are different now; they all have cell phones. But phones don't work in the deep jungle and the Dayak are still great hunters, so we always have fresh fish or meat to eat.

The deep jungle hasn't really changed. But you need to go into the Muller Mountains to find primary forest. It's mainly secondary forest along the Sungai Mahakam.

The Muller Mountains are always the hardest part of the trek. But travelling the river rapids is more dangerous, especially in the rainy season. Many locals have died and even a few foreigners.

EATING & DRINKING IN SAMARINDA: OUR PICKS

Ayam Goreng Banjar: Locals rave about the crispy-skinned chicken and spicy sambal at this Banjari restaurant near the riverfront. *9am-9pm* $

Rumah Makan Amado: Another popular Banjari restaurant serving super *soto Banjar* and chicken satay. *8am-10pm* $

Kedai Kofi: Friendly old-school coffee shop located in one of Samarinda's now rare wooden houses. Sources its beans from Sulawesi. *10am-midnight*

Muse: An eight-floor entertainment complex featuring a nightclub, karaoke and a rooftop pub and restaurant with a decent selection of beers. *6pm-3am*

RED IVORY/SHUTTERSTOCK

Hornbill

TOP EXPERIENCE

The Cross-Borneo Trek

One of the world's great adventure-travel routes, the Cross-Borneo Trek offers seriously intrepid travellers the chance to traverse the world's third-largest island from east to west (or vice versa), via remote rivers and a challenging weeklong hike through jungle-clad mountains. This is a serious undertaking and is not to be attempted lightly.

DON'T MISS

- Boat travel on the Sungai Mahakam
- Forest and river wildlife
- Tiong Ohang
- Forest trekking in the Muller Mountains
- Arriving in Tanjung Lokan
- Boat ride to Putussibau

The Route

The route connects **Pontianak** in West Kalimantan with **Samarinda** in East Kalimantan via the Muller Mountains, which rear up in the centre of Borneo and are the source of the headwaters for the island's two longest rivers: the Kapuas and the Mahakam. The Kapuas runs through West Kalimantan to Pontianak, while the Mahakam snakes its way to Samarinda on the east coast. So by travelling up one river, hiking over the Muller Mountains and then journeying down the other river, it's possible to cross Borneo.

Debate rages over which direction to do the trek in. The consensus seems to be that starting in Samarinda (p574) and travelling east to west is logistically easier, while travelling west to east from Pontianak (p542) is less taxing physically. But whichever way you go, you have to cross the Muller Mountains, by far the hardest part of the journey.

There are significant potential hazards along the way, from deadly rapids to brutal trekking through dense rainforest, while the nearest help or hospital is days away. But few people can say that they have crossed Borneo on foot. Like climbing Mt Everest, you do the trek for the personal achievement and the lifelong memories it will leave you with.

Upriver

Most trekkers start in Samarinda, on the banks of the Sungai Mahakam. From here, you can travel upriver by a succession of boats, both big and small, via lakes and wetlands and tiny riverine towns where you will be the only foreigner. This is the best part of the journey for wildlife spotting: you're almost certain to see proboscis monkeys swinging through the trees by the side of the river, as well as hornbills and multi-coloured kingfishers.

The final part of the multiday upriver journey is by speedboat through fierce rapids to **Tiong Ohang**, a village in the foothills of the Muller Mountains, from where you journey another two hours to the trailhead for the trek. It's possible to find guides and porters in Tiong Ohang, but we strongly advise that you make your arrangements in advance with a reputable tour operator.

Crossing the Mountains

Once in the **Muller Mountains**, you face trekking through thick rainforest for five to six hours a day. This isn't like walking a trail in a national park. Instead, you'll need to forge your own path, hacking through leech-infested jungle with a machete following barely discernible trails: this is where your guide earns his money. There are numerous creeks to wade across (some chest-high), steep inclines to scale and lots of bugs. At night, campsites are a clearing covered with a tarpaulin and cooking is done over an open fire. Some superfit trekkers able to hike for a taxing eight hours a day make it across the mountains in five days. Seven days is more likely, but you should budget for 10 days.

Downriver

Trekkers emerge from the mountains at the village of **Tanjung Lokan** on the banks of the Sungai Kapuas. From here it's an exhilarating seven-hour boat ride downriver to **Putussibau**, plunging through gorges and numerous sets of rapids. No scheduled passenger vessels make the long journey from Putussibau down the Kapuas to Pontianak (although it is possible to negotiate a ride on a cargo boat), so almost everyone either flies or catches the bus instead.

GUIDES

We recommend two East Kalimantan guides, each of whom speaks English and has extensive experience of this major expedition: **Abdullah** *(WhatsApp +62 821 5772 0171)* specialises in multiday trips along the Sungai Mahakam and beyond from Samarinda, while Samarinda-based **Rustam** *(WhatsApp +62 812 585 4915)* is also a highly recommended Cross-Borneo Trek and East Kalimantan expert.

TOP TIPS

- It normally takes at least 17 days to complete the journey and it costs around US$4000 for two people; some guides won't take a solo traveller.
- A number of Kalimantan tour operators can arrange guides, porters and transport. You shouldn't attempt the trek unless you are fit, determined and have some previous experience of jungle trekking.
- You could try and make all the arrangements for the Cross-Borneo Trek by yourself, but it will take days just to get everything sorted, and you really should speak Bahasa to ensure there are no misunderstandings. It's much easier to go with a guide or tour company.

BEST FOR ORANGUTANS

M Syadhian is a guide and the owner of Borneo Eco Adventure (p546).

I've visited all of the national parks in Kalimantan and in my opinion the best place to see orangutans is at Tanjung Puting National Park (p556). There's nowhere else where you can get this close to wild orangutans. And you can also see wild orangutans from the boat, as well as other species. But there are some people who don't like the experience, because the feeding stations don't feel so wild. If you want to see really wild orangutans, I like Kutai National Park (p574), in East Kalimantan. This park is quite small, so there's a really good chance of seeing orangutans.

BANG RICCI/SHUTTERSTOCK

Whale shark, Pulau Derawan

Continued from p578

the sultanate. It's also possible to visit **Keraton Sambaliung** *(free)*, the surviving 200-year-old royal palace, which sits almost opposite the museum on the other side of the river. At night, seafood restaurants open up along Jl Pangeran Antasar.

Another reason to come to Berau is to access the jagged limestone karst formations and forest around **Merabu**, a Dayak village that's a five- to six-hour drive south of Berau along some rough roads. You won't see much wildlife, although animals are all around. Instead, the main draw here are caves, especially **Goa Beloyot**, a cliff-side cavern full of stencilled handprints that are thousands of years old. The cave is reached via a half-day hike. You can also make the taxing two-hour trek to **Puncak Ketepu**, a viewpoint from where the entire panorama of karst formations unfolds before you. All accommodation in Merabu is homestays and visitors must pay a compulsory donation to the village: introduce yourself to the village headman when you arrive.

Borneo's Tropical Islands

Diving Pulau Derawan

Paradise is a much-overused cliché when it comes to sun-kissed tropical islands, but there are places where it's absolutely true. The 31 islands of the **Derawan Archipelago** is one such place.

Isolated in the Celebes Sea off the East Kalimantan coast, these mostly uninhabited islands are surrounded by colourful reefs and turquoise water that laps at white-sand beaches fringed by palm and casuarina trees. The archipelago forms part of the **Coral Triangle**, one of the richest and most diverse marine environments on earth, and the diving and snorkelling here is simply world-class.

Tiny **Pulau Derawan** (Derawan Island) is just one of two islands that is inhabited and is the one closest to the mainland.

It's now a popular destination for local tourists and Chinese divers. To cope with the influx, the original fishing village has expanded overwater, with wooden boardwalks lined with stilted guesthouses running out to sea, allowing visitors to snorkel directly beneath their accommodation. Sea turtles are a common sight here.

Pulau Derawan is the base for a number of dive operators. The top dive sites are around 70 to 80 minutes away by speedboat. Manta rays, barracuda, whale and thresher sharks can all be seen. The March to October dry season is the best time for diving. Note that this isn't really a destination for novice divers: currents are strong and some sites are only for those who are at least advanced open-water divers. A fun one-day, two-dive trip will cost around 2,000,000Rp.

While Pulau Derawan isn't as remote or idyllic as Maratua Atoll, the other inhabited island in the archipelago, it's cheaper to stay here. There are many accommodation options, but only a handful of simple restaurants in the village, which can be walked from end to end in 15 minutes. There are daily boats to Pulau Derawan from the port of Tanjung Betu, 110km east of Berau, but boats heading from Berau to Maratua Atoll normally stop here as well. Bring cash.

Swim with Manta Rays

Dive and snorkel Maratua Atoll

Maratua Atoll is a horseshoe-shaped slice of tropical heaven. Ringed by mostly empty white-sand beaches, with a jungle interior populated by macaque monkeys and monitor lizards, this is the biggest island in the Derawan Archipelago and sits close to the premier dive spots in the area. Water visibility is generally better here than off Pulau Derawan – 15m to 25m – and the sea is so rich in marine life that if you swim 20m offshore you're almost certain to encounter sea turtles paddling placidly past. An hour away by boat is legendary Manta Point, where many manta rays congregate, while other nearby dive spots are home to a variety of sharks, schools of barracuda, unique stingless jellyfish, multicoloured hard and soft corals, and tons of reef fish.

The island was once the haunt of sea gypsies and many of the 3000-odd population are descended from them. Maratua's two main settlements are the villages of **Teluk Harapan**, where most speedboats arrive and depart, and **Payung-Payung**, in the south of the island close to the rustic airport. Both villages have a few simple restaurants, guesthouses and homestays.

Scattered up and down the coast are an ever-growing number of all-inclusive resorts, some decidedly upmarket. Maratua isn't really a budget destination and, if you're not diving, you'll need to hire a boat for 1,500,000Rp a day to hit the simply sublime snorkelling spots offshore. All resorts can arrange this, but Arief at Borneo Cottage Maratua and Rivi at Nouri Cottages (p585), both just south of Teluk Harapan, can organise a boatman and rent you a mask and fins if you're staying in the village.

BEST DERAWAN DIVE OPERATORS

Borneo Cottage Maratua: Affable Arief has been diving off Maratua Atoll for 20 years and speaks English. Snorkelling, too. *(borneocottagemaratua.com)*

Maratua Paradise Resort: Longstanding dive shop here overlooks a gleaming white-sand beach on Maratua Atoll. *(maratua.com)*

Nabucco Island Resort: Professional outfit on Maratua Atoll that gets consistently good feedback. SSI and PADI courses. *(nabuccos-resorts-indonesien.com)*

Scuba Junkie Sangalaki: Efficient operator based on Pulau Derawan; runs a variety of multiday dive packages. *(sangalakidiveresort.com)*

Tasik Divers: Located on Pulau Derawan's best beach in the north of the island. Two modern dive boats and lots of experience. *(derawandivelodge.com)*

SWIFT KNOWLEDGE

East Kalimantan has its own soundtrack: a high-pitched chirping that never seems to stop. The deafening cacophony of bird calls is pumped out from rooftop megaphones and is aimed at coaxing colonies of swiftlets into building nests using their saliva in the tall, tower-like concrete structures they inhabit all over the province.

The nests are the key ingredient in bird's-nest soup, a high-protein delicacy that's supposed to boost the immune system and is popular in China and Southeast Asia. You'll see and hear swiftlet colonies all over Kalimantan, but they're especially prevalent in the towns and villages along the Sungai Mahakam.

Your first stop should be **Pulau Kakaban**, 30 minutes southwest of Maratua. A 10-minute walk along a boardwalk brings visitors to a forest-fringed inland lake that's home to four bizarre species of jellyfish that have lost their stinging capabilities after generations of existing in an environment free of predators. There are thousands of these jellyfish in the lake, ranging in size from tiny to relatively large. To avoid harming them, don't snorkel with fins. And certainly don't follow the example of some thoughtless tourists who hold the jellyfish in their hands for photo opportunities – killing or injuring a living creature is never worth a photo.

Further southwest is small **Pulau Sangalaki**, which is surrounded by superb reefs and white-sand beaches where sea turtles lay and hatch their eggs and where baby turtles take their first steps. Indeed, Sangalaki is reckoned to be the prime nesting location for green turtles in Southeast Asia. Boats can only access these beaches at high tide; otherwise you'll be wading ashore. There's a 150,000Rp fee to visit Sangalaki, but it's free to snorkel the reefs here and snorkel you should – it's an amazing experience. The coral is super-vibrant

SONY HERDIANA/SHUTTERSTOCK

Baby turtles, Pulau Sangalaki

and attracts a huge variety of reef fish, while the water is normally crystal clear.

Best of all, though, is awesome **Manta Point** off Sangalaki's west coast, one of the few places in the world where divers and snorkellers are likely to encounter manta rays all year round. The shallow water here means there's plenty of plankton for the rays and often their fins are visible as boats approach. Once in the water the gentle giants are all around you and it's a remarkable sight as they circle with their vast mouths agape.

Getting to Maratua takes some effort. There's a weekly flight on Saturday from Tarakan in North Kalimantan, which then travels onto Berau, but it's a small propeller plane and seats sell out fast. Otherwise, a couple of daily speedboats depart Berau at 11am for the three-hour run to Maratua, normally via Pulau Derawan. The boats return to Berau at 9am from Teluk Harapan's jetty. There's also a weekly speedboat to Tarakan at 8am on Sunday, departing from Payung-Payung. You could also charter a speedboat; count on around 3,000,000Rp to/from Berau.

NUSANTARA: INDONESIA'S NEW CAPITAL

Palangka Raya was once groomed to take over from Jakarta as Indonesia's capital, hence its unusually wide boulevards. While that never happened, Kalimantan has once again been tapped to be the site of the country's future capital. After decades of complaints about Indonesia being too Java-centric, and with Jakarta literally sinking under the weight of its overstretched infrastructure, a new capital called Nusantara is being built in East Kalimantan. At an estimated cost of US$34 billion, Nusantara will sit more or less in the geographical middle of the Indonesian archipelago. The 2560-sq-km city will be constructed in five phases, with work expected to be completed by 2045.

Beyond East Kalimantan

The north of Kalimantan is real frontier land: home to some of the most pristine and unexplored rainforest on Borneo.

Places

North Kalimantan is the newest of Kalimantan's five provinces, carved out of northern East Kalimantan in 2012. It's one of the least-populated and least-seen regions in Indonesia. Few foreigners make it here. Those that do are mostly heading to the neighbouring Malaysian state of Sabah via the border crossing beyond Tarakan, the only city of any size in North Kalimantan.

Determined travellers with plenty of time can head to Kayan Mentarang National Park, a massive expanse of rainforest near the frontier with Malaysia. The park is home to a lot of wildlife and is so remote that new species are still being discovered here. It's also possible to access the islands of the Derawan Archipelago from Tarakan.

Kayan Mentarang National Park

TIME FROM EAST KALIMANTAN (BALIKPAPAN): **1¾HR** 

Explore remote rainforest

Covering a vast area of around 13,600 sq km, Kayan Mentarang National Park sits opposite the Malaysian state of Sarawak and occupies a big chunk of North Kalimantan. Its isolation means that the park contains the largest unbroken stretch of rainforest left in Borneo, and there's a huge diversity of wildlife roaming it, including clouded leopards, rare pangolins, tarsiers, slow lorises and a variety of monkeys, gibbons, wild cats and bears. There are also Dayak communities in and around the park.

This is truly a place of wonder, and like all journeys of discovery, the hard work of getting here will likely reward you many times over.

But, yes, visiting all of that wilderness doesn't come easy, and getting here in the first place can also be a challenge. The closest airport is outside Long Bawan, a village to the north of Kayan Mentarang National Park. Otherwise, it's a two-day journey by road and river from Tarakan. It's also possible to access the southeast of the park via Long Punjungan, which

GETTING AROUND

Tarakan's airport has connections to Balikpapan and Maratua Atoll. There's also a Saturday morning speedboat from Tarakan to Maratua via Pulau Derawan. Long Bawan is the nearest airport to Kayan Mentarang National Park and has a daily flight to Balikpapan. There are direct ferries between Tarakan and Tawau in Malaysia.

Slow loris

can be reached by a long boat ride from Tanjung Selor in the south of North Kalimantan. Once you reach the park, at the very least you will need a guide – tourism infrastructure is almost non-existent, trails are poorly marked if at all, and you'll need to be entirely self-sufficient. There are also places that are only accessible by boat.

In short, unless you speak Bahasa and have lots of time to negotiate the logistics, we strongly recommend that you make arrangements through a tour operator. For example, both De'Gigant Tours (p546) and Borneo Eco Adventure (p546) organise trips here and are reliable and professional.

There were formerly a number of ecotourism projects inside the national park, but most are now inactive; homestays in Dayak villages are still possible.

Tarakan

TIME FROM EAST KALIMANTAN (BALIKPAPAN): 1¼HR

Get to know North Kalimantan's only city

Tarakan is North Kalimantan's only city and contains around one-third of the province's population – the rest of its inhabitants are thinly spread out across the province. Located on Pulau Tarakan, just off the coast of Kalimantan, Tarakan is an unremarkable place, but its airport and boat links, as well as a reasonable spread of hotels, make it the logical base for anyone intent on exploring North Kalimantan. Most travellers pass through en route to the border further north with Malaysia, or come here for the weekly speedboat to the Derawan Archipelago.

It's also an opportunity to visit a provincial Kalimantan city, far removed from any tourist hype, that's just quietly going about its business.

Accommodation, restaurants and banks cluster in the centre of town around the **Grand Tarakan Mall**, about 3km north of the port. The airport is 3.5km north of the city centre.

GETTING TO MALAYSIA FROM TARAKAN

There are ferry and speedboat services between Tarakan and Nunukan (both in Indonesia) and Tawau (Sabah). If you miss the direct Tarakan–Tawau ferry service, there are normally five or six daily ferries from Tarakan's port 100km north to Nunukan, where a daily 9am boat makes the 90-minute journey to Tawau. Immigration on the Indonesian side is inside the Nunukan international ferry terminal. It's possible to change Indonesian rupiah for Malaysian ringgit here. Once in Tawau, visitors from the US, Canada, Australia and most European countries get a three-month visa on arrival. From Tawau there are onward air and bus connections with the rest of Sabah, including the capital Kota Kinabalu.

Places We Love to Stay

$ Budget $$ Midrange $$$ Top End

Pontianak MAP p544

Hotel Green Leaf $ Acceptable budget option. The cheapest rooms are windowless and small, but they have air-con and the location is fine.

Hotel Neo Gaja Mada $$ Hip midrange choice with clean, modern, comfortable and compact rooms in the centre of town. The rooftop bar and restaurant has nightly live music.

Aston Pontianak $$$ Pontianak's poshest hotel has a pool and gym, as well as restaurants and a bar. Rooms are big and well maintained.

Singkawang MAP p544

Swiss-Belinn Singkawang $$ Singkawang's top choice, with big modern rooms and efficient service. It's attached to the Singkawang Grand Mall.

Villa Bukit Mas $$ Away from the city centre in a quiet hillside location, with big but nondescript rooms. The staff are friendly.

Putussibau MAP p544

Hotel Multi 88 $ Low-rise place in the north of town. The air-con and fan rooms are clean but bathrooms are basic.

Hotel Grand Banana Putussibau $$ Newish hotel that is Putussibau's best, with a rooftop restaurant and rooms that are modern and comfortable, if plain.

Sukadana MAP p544

Penginapan Family $ The top budget choice. Big rooms have air-con, cold-water *mandi* (baths) and squat toilets. Transport can be arranged.

Mahkota Kayong Hotel $$ Seafront hotel with faded rooms, some with balconies offering fine sunset views. There's a restaurant that sells expensive beer.

Tanjung Puting National Park MAP p555

Majid Hotel $ The best budget option in Kumai, just metres from where *klotok* (houseboats) depart. If you've booked a tour with Liesa Tanjung Puting (p546), you stay here free.

Flora Homestay $$ Right by the river in Sekonyer Village, Flora has three simple wood cabins that offer a truly immersive Borneo experience. Pak Bana is eager to please, and tours can be arranged here.

Arsela Hotel $$ Pleasant Pangkalan Bun hotel with faux traditional architecture, spacious, modern rooms and English-speaking staff. Also has a cafe and restaurant.

Rimba Lodge $$$ One of only two accommodation options inside the park. The wooden cabins are rustic for the price, but you're riverside and wildlife is all around.

Mercure Pangkalan Bun $$$ Pangkalan Bun's best full-service hotel close to the centre of town. Rooms are stylish, service attentive and the facilities (restaurant, swimming pool) are top-notch.

Palangka Raya MAP p555

Bukit Raya Guesthouse $$ Set around a tree-filled garden, this is one of Kalimantan's most relaxing guesthouses. Trips to Sebangau National Park can be arranged here.

Rungan Sari $$ The closest hotel to Orangutan Island northwest of Palangka Raya, the Rungan Sari has simple bungalow-style rooms that are fine for a night.

Ecovillage $$ Also close to Orangutan Island, this place is set back off the road and has decent rooms that make a good base for the excursion to the island.

Swiss-Belhotel Danum $$$ A little out of the way (it's 5km northwest of the centre), but it's Palangka Raya's best; ask for a pool-view room.

Banjarmasin MAP p561

Summer B&B $ Banjarmasin's most distinctive digs, with a 1980s retro theme and a mix of budget and midrange rooms that are simple but spacious.

Hotel Victoria River View $$ Riverside and central: handy for an early morning boat pickup for the floating markets. The cheapest rooms are windowless.

Kalsel Park $$ High on a ridge in Tahura Sultan Adam, 56km southeast of Banjarmasin, the new-in-2025 Kalsel Park has smallish cabins and larger glamping tents, all with air-con and superb sunset views.

Swiss-Belhotel Borneo Banjarmasin $$$ It's starting to look its age, but this riverside hotel has a pool and restaurant and is still the best top-end city-centre option.

Loksado

MAP p561

Penginapan Pesona Meratus **$$** The pick of the village cheapies with spacious, fan-cooled rooms and Western toilets. Prices here are almost budget.

Mountain Meratus Resort **$$** Loksado's top option, with big wooden rooms, semi-open-air bathrooms, wi-fi and a serene location by the river. Treks can be arranged.

Balikpapan

MAP p568

Maryam Guesthouse 2 **$** Rooms here are windowless but clean, with OK beds, and are better than other Balikpapan budget digs.

Hotel Gran Senyiur **$$** This characterful hotel has large wood-floored rooms and attractive old-school furniture. The rooftop Sky Bar offers tremendous city and sea views.

Novotel Balikpapan **$$$** A swish, central option with comfortable rooms. There's a pool and gym, and some English is spoken.

Samarinda

MAP p569

Kost Guesthouse **$** Cheerful cheapie with compact but clean rooms that share tolerable showers and toilets. Motorbikes can be rented here.

Hotel Grand Kartika **$$** Modern place with decent beds close to the riverfront and restaurants. The cafe serves the cheapest beer in town.

Mercure Samarinda **$$$** Samarinda's newest and most comfortable hotel offers the best service in town and has a rooftop bar and restaurant with tremendous river views.

Sungai Mahakam

MAP p568

Penginapan Abadi **$** Friendly family guesthouse in Muara Muntai with compact rooms and shared bathrooms. Helpful owner Nisa can arrange a boat to Melak.

Hotel Monita **$** The rooms are tired at this Melak hotel, but there's hot water – a rarity in these parts – and wi-fi. Owner Emi speaks English well.

Grand Elty Singgasana Hotel **$$** Tenggarong's top option has a pool, but rooms are plain for the price. It's up a hill overlooking town.

Berau

MAP p568

Rumah Kedaung **$$** Berau's most bucolic accommodation is this collection of wooden cabins with small balconies set in a leafy garden. It's 4km from the city centre.

Hotel Palmy **$$** Modern midrange option just back from the riverfront and 1km from the dock for speedboats to the Derawan Archipelago.

Pulau Derawan

MAP p568

Derawan Fisheries Cottage **$$** Comfortable wooden cabins perched above the sea on a jetty on the south side of the island.

Reza Cottages **$$** Compact overwater bungalows with hot water and air-con. A good spot for snorkelling and turtle watching.

Maratua Atoll

MAP p568

Penginapan Ananda **$** This family guesthouse has spotless rooms with Western toilets. It's the best of Teluk Harapan's budget choices.

Nouri Cottages **$$** The beachside wooden cabins here book out fast. It's just south of Teluk Harapan. Owner Rivi speaks English.

Maratua Guesthouse **$$$** Large and well set-up wooden rooms perched above a nice beach. Helpful owners Junaid and Anna speak English.

Tarakan

Hotel D'CaLia **$$** Solid Tarakan midranger has reasonable rooms with safety boxes and is equidistant from the port and the airport.

Swiss-Belhotel Tarakan **$$$** This smart option has a bar and restaurant. You may even hear some English spoken here.

NIZAR KAUZAR/SHUTTERSTOCK

Mahkota Kayong Hotel, Sukadana

For places to stay in Sulawesi, see p638

PATRICK GOGEISSL/SHUTTERSTOCK

Above: Rammang Rammang (p599); Right: Whale shark, Gorontalo (p627)

Researched by
Paul Harding

Sulawesi

DIVE INTO INDONESIA'S MYSTERY ISLAND

From highlands to the reef, mountain-dwelling Torajans to the seafaring Bugis, Sulawesi offers more than a hint of mystique and adventure.

The convoluted island of Sulawesi offers plenty of surprises. Many travellers are drawn by the highland culture of Tana Toraja, the gloriously isolated Togean Islands or the diving around Bunaken or Bira, but fewer know of the ancient megaliths of Bada Valley, the volcanic craters of the Minahasa Highlands, the karst landscape of Rammang Rammang or the near-deserted islands around Pulau Selayar.

Just as this splay-limbed tropical island was formed by the complex and sometimes violent mashup of tectonic plates, its fascinating social fabric has brought together diverse ethnic groups, religions and ecosystems. Flanked by teeming waters and reefs, Sulawesi's interior is mountainous and cloaked in dense jungle, where rare species such as nocturnal tarsiers and flamboyant maleo birds survive – as do proud cultures, long isolated by barely penetrable topography.

Meet the Torajan highlanders, with their elaborate funeral ceremonies and curious architecture; the Minahasans in the north, offering spicy dishes of anything from pork *sate* to bat kebab; and the lowland and coastal Bugis, Indonesia's most successful and feared seafarers. Minorities such as Bajau sea nomads have also played an integral role in the island's history and can be visited in stilt villages around the Togeans and Banggai.

The Dutch took over the lucrative spice-route trade in the 17th century, establishing their fort in Makassar (Ujung Pandang), and held the island until Japanese occupation in 1942. Sulawesi became part of the Indonesian republic in 1950.

PAUL HARDING/LONELY PLANET

THE MAIN AREAS

MAKASSAR
Waterfront mosques at the coastal capital. p590

BIRA PENINSULA
Beaches and diving down south. p600

TANA TORAJA
Traditional highland culture and people. p608

TOGEAN ISLANDS
Remote island paradise. p621

MANADO & PULAU BUNAKEN
Northern diving and adventure. p629

Find Your Way

South and Central Sulawesi are reasonably well served by road, but distances can be long and transport slow. Islands such as the Togeans and Bunaken are accessible by boat. Makassar and Manado are the main flight hubs.

Tana Toraja, p608

Traditional highland culture, mountain views and frequent funeral ceremonies a luxury bus ride from Makassar.

Manado & Pulau Bunaken, p629

North Sulawesi's best urban nightlife in the regional capital; scuba diving and island adventures offshore.

PLANE

Daily flights between Makassar and Manado are convenient for exploring north and south separately. Otherwise, connections aren't great. There are useful airports in Palu, Gorontalo and Luwuk, but most connections are routed through Makassar. Susi Air serves minor routes.

BUS & TAXI

Luxury air-con buses connect Makassar with Tana Toraja and Bira. Elsewhere it's local buses, long-distance bemo (minibus) or chartered taxi. Shared taxis have replaced buses entirely on some routes; while quicker and more expensive, they aren't necessarily more comfortable.

Makassar, p590

Steamy coastal capital with a fine waterfront mosque, harbour and modern shopping malls.

PAUL HARDING/LONELY PLANET

Pulau Bunaken (p629)

Plan Your Time

Sulawesi is spread out, so you'll need to plan ahead and preferably break your trip into chunks – at least north and south. The two ends are conveniently connected by air from Makassar to Manado.

Pressed for Time

- If time is short, spend a day or two in **Makassar** (p590) with a visit to **Rammang Rammang** (p599), then board a luxury overnight bus to the cool highland region of **Tana Toraja** (p608). From a base in **Rantepao** (p609), spend three days exploring the hill villages and burial caves by motorbike, car or on foot; you'll almost certainly see a local funeral ceremony.

A Week or More

- Tropical islands, beaches and diving are a big draw. In the south, head to **Bira** (p600) and the islands around **Pulau Selayar** (p605), where the seasonal diving is superb. For anyone making the long cross-island trip, you can stop with relief in the remote **Togean Islands** (p621). In the north, **Pulau Bunaken** (p629) is the place for underwater exploration.

SEASONAL HIGHLIGHTS

APRIL TO OCTOBER

Humidity starts to drop; peak season for **scuba diving**, **hiking** and **festivals**.

JUNE TO AUGUST

Funeral ceremonies in Tana Toraja. August sees the **Toraja Coffee Festival** (p617).

NOVEMBER TO MARCH

The wet season is also low season for tourism, though it's the best time for **muck diving** in the Lembeh Strait.

CHRISTMAS

Chistmas is celebrated in Christian-majority regions, especially in North Sulawesi and Tana Toraja.

Makassar

ARCHITECTURE | SEAFOOD | MALLS

TOP TIP

Makassar's highlights are along the Pantai Losari waterfront promenade. One block inland is Jl Somba OPU, the local shopping street. The best shopping malls are south of the centre while the harbour, airport and Maros region are north. Until 1999 the official name of Makassar was Ujung Pandang; both names are still used.

Makassar is a proud and historic regional capital promoting itself as the 'Centre Point of Indonesia', both geographically and culturally. The Centre Point globe monument and dazzling 99-dome triflesque mosque showcase the city's contemporary architecture, giving the waterfront a dynamic visual appeal and contrasting with the remaining bits of Dutch architecture, most notably Fort Rotterdam.

One of Indonesia's primary ports, Makassar feels more gritty and working class than modern and urbane, with a polyglot population of Makassarese, Bugis and Chinese residents. There are few major sights here, but a day or two exploring the waterfront, *pinisi* (Makassar or Bugis schooner) boat harbour, renowned fish restaurants and contrasting modern shopping malls is a worthy urban introduction to your Sulawesi travels.

Mosques & Museums

Modern Islam and colonial past

Makassar has a beguiling mix of Dutch architecture and contemporary mosques, as well as a new wave of design emphasising Sulawesian cultural heritage, such as Torajan houses and *pinisi* boats.

GETTING AROUND

Most travellers arrive in Makassar by air; a prepaid taxi from the airport to the centre costs around 100,000Rp and takes only 30 minutes via the near-empty toll road. Luxury buses for Tana Toraja arrive and depart from the respective bus-company lots east of the centre. Blue *pete-pete* (minivans) still service destinations around town (5000Rp), while red ones go further afield (from 10,000Rp).

Bluebird Taxis are reliable and comfortable but ride-hailing apps Grab and Gojek (cars and motorbikes) work well and are cheaper than taxis. For short trips around town, motorcycle becaks *(bentor)* hang around outside hotels and tourists spots – you can try bargaining, but most short trips start at around 10,000Rp. Tuk-tuk-style Maxicabs also operate around town (at the time of writing the app was only available for Android).

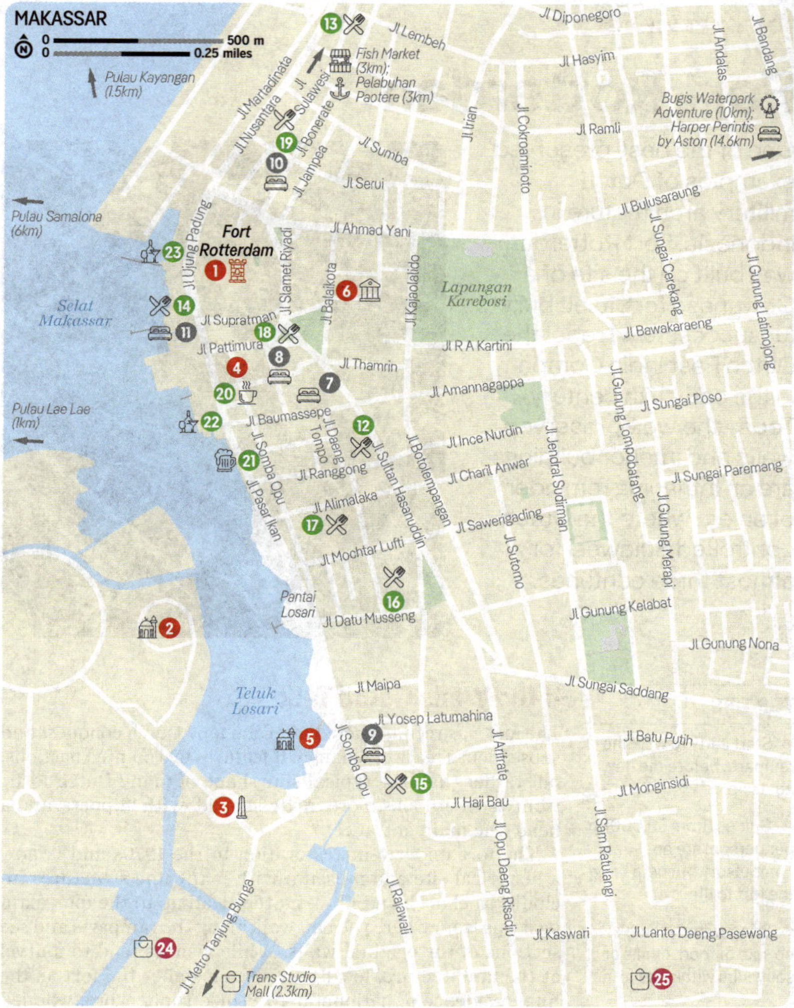

MAKASSAR

0 — 500 m
0 — 0.25 miles

Jl Diponegoro
Jl Lembeh
Fish Market (3km); Pelabuhan Paotere (3km)
Jl Hasyim
Jl Andalas
Jl Bandang
Pulau Kayangan (1.5km)
Jl Martadinata
Jl Nusantara
Jl Sulawesi
Jl Bonerate
Jl Jampea
Jl Sumba
Jl Irian
Jl Cokroaminoto
Jl Ramli
Bugis Waterpark Adventure (10km); Harper Perintis by Aston (14.6km)
Jl Serui
Jl Bulusaraung
Pulau Samalona (6km)
Jl Ujung Padung
Fort Rotterdam
Jl Ahmad Yani
Jl Slamet Riyadi
Jl Balaikota
Jl Kajaolalido
Lapangan Karebosi
Jl Sungai Cerekang
Jl Gunung Latimojong
Selat Makassar
Jl Supratman
Jl Pattimura
Jl R A Kartini
Jl Bawakaraeng
Jl Thamrin
Jl Amannagappa
Jl Sungai Poso
Jl Gunung Lompobatang
Pulau Lae Lae (1km)
Jl Baumassepe
Jl Daeng Tompo
Jl Somba Opu
Jl Sultan Hasanuddin
Jl Botolempangan
Jl Ince Nurdin
Jl Jendral Sudirman
Jl Ranggong
Jl Chairil Anwar
Jl Sungai Paremang
Jl Pasar Ikan
Jl Alimalaka
Jl Gunung Merapi
Jl Sawerigading
Jl Mochtar Lufti
Jl Sutomo
Pantai Losari
Jl Datu Musseng
Jl Gunung Kelabat
Jl Gunung Nona
Jl Maipa
Jl Sungai Saddang
Teluk Losari
Jl Yosep Latumahina
Jl Batu Putih
Jl Arifrate
Jl Monginsidi
Jl Haji Bau
Jl Opu Daeng Risadju
Jl Sam Ratulangi
Jl Rajawali
Jl Metro Tanjung Bunga
Jl Kaswari
Jl Lanto Daeng Pasewang
Trans Studio Mall (2.3km)

HIGHLIGHTS
1 Fort Rotterdam

SIGHTS
2 Asmaul Husnah 99 Kubah
3 Centre Point of Indonesia
4 Jl Somba OPU
5 Masjid Amirul Mukminin
see 1 Museum Negeri La Galigo
6 Museum of Makassar

SLEEPING
7 Aston Makassar
8 D'Prima Pattimurra
9 Ge JacMart
10 Legenda Beril Hostel
11 Swiss-Belhotel Makassar

EATING
12 Bistropolis
13 Coto Nusantara
14 Fish Warungs
15 La Piccola Italy
16 Lae Lae
17 RM Nelayan
18 RM Sulawesi Baru
19 Rumah Makan Pate'ne

DRINKING & NIGHTLIFE
20 Jokka
21 New Kafe Kareba
22 Pier 52
23 Popsa District

SHOPPING
24 Phinisi Point Mall
25 Ratu Indah Mall

TOP EXPERIENCE

Fort Rotterdam

One of the best-preserved examples of Dutch military architecture in Indonesia, Fort Rotterdam was built on the site of a Gowanese fort, itself built to (unsuccessfully) repel the Dutch East India Company in the early 17th century. Today the well-preserved walls and interior buildings are an intriguing reminder of an era where the Dutch controlled Sulawesi for almost three centuries.

PAUL HARDING/LONELY PLANET

TOP TIPS

- Start early to walk the ramparts before the day heats up.
- Guides (from 50,000Rp per person) are not compulsory but help bring the fort to life.
- Bring water – there's no sale of food, drinks or souvenirs within the fort.

PRACTICALITIES

● entry by donation; sign the guest book and leave a tip ● 7.30am-6.30pm

If the Walls Could Talk

The fort was reconstructed after the 1667 Dutch conquest and subsequent Treaty of Bolanga. It features five pointed bastions, but rather than the typical star shape of many Dutch forts, from above it looks more turtle-shaped, with 'flippers' and a head (the main entrance).

The fort underwent restoration in the 1970s and is now a historical site and museum with many fine structures including a church and library. Steps lead up to the four main bastions from where you can walk along the ramparts and see sections of the original walls. While visitors tend to marvel at the architecture, local tourists remember the fort as the final residence of national hero Prince Diponegoro, who led the Java rebellion against Dutch occupation. He was imprisoned here for 25 years until his death in 1855.

Museum Negeri La Galigo

Spread across two buildings, **Museum Negeri La Galigo** *(10,000Rp)* is a large airy space with an assortment of exhibits, including a site plan of the fort, models of *pinisi*, Palaeolithic artefacts, Tana Toraja rice bowls, musical instruments and traditional costumes. It's a modest collection but worth the admission and 30 minutes' exploration.

On the reclaimed waterfront opposite Pantai Losari, the stunning bright-orange-and-white **Asmaul Husnah 99 Kubah** (99-domed mosque), completed in 2019, stands like a beacon, visible from everywhere along the waterfront. Reach it by passing the dramatic 'Centre Point of Indonesia' globe sculpture and a cable bridge shaped like a *tongkonan* (traditional Torajan house). Non-Muslims are welcome inside – and it really is a breathtaking cavernous space – but footwear must be removed and women should wear a headscarf.

Prior to the construction of Asmaul Husnah, the small but stylish twin-domed **Masjid Amirul Mukminin** (aka the 'floating mosque') was the main place of worship along the waterfront. It's still popular with locals and is photogenic after sunset when it's illuminated.

There's a good museum at Fort Rotterdam, while the more modest **Museum of Makassar** *(free),* in another Dutch building, covers aspects of city history in old photographs, costumes and art. Very little is explained in English, but volunteer guides will offer to show you around free of charge. The museum is open 9am to 3.30pm Monday to Friday.

COTO MAKASSAR

South Sulawesi's signature dish is *coto Makassar*, a rich broth of beef and offal, spiced up with pepper, cumin and lemongrass. The city's most famous *coto* (pronounced *choto*) eatery is Coto Nusantara, opposite the port area on Jl Nusantara about 1km north of Fort Rotterdam – the walls are decorated with photos of celebrity Indonesian patrons. *Coto* is traditionally considered a breakfast or lunch meal, so serious *coto* restaurants don't stay open late. The soup is prepared in a large vat with chopped-up beef and organs and served in a small bowl along with a plate of *ketupat* (rice steamed in palm leaves). A variation on the dish is *konro*, which uses ribs instead of beef.

Harbour Life

Bugis boats and fish market

Pelabuhan Paotere *(10,000Rp),* 4km north of the city centre, is a large working port where Bugis sailing and cargo ships berth. The boats are not as traditional these days but still photogenic, and the local port workers are accustomed to tourists wandering around with cameras. The nearby **fish market** is also atmospheric and very pungent early in the morning, when giant tuna and every sea creature imaginable are traded, some destined for Makassar restaurant tables but most exported. It becomes impossibly crowded by mid-morning.

Any motorcycle *bentor* will take you there and back for around 50,000Rp, including waiting time (which works out cheaper than two Grab taxis), or you can take a blue bemo to the corner of Jl Cakalang and Yos Sudarso, from where the harbour is a 1km walk.

EATING IN MAKASSAR: OUR PICKS

Coto Nusantara: Sample the rich local beef soup *coto Makassar* at this city-wide famous hole-in-the-wall restaurant north of Fort Rotterdam. *7am-6pm* $

La Piccola Italy: Most locals agree this cute little restaurant, with authentic pizza, pasta and chequered tablecloths, is the best Italian in town. *10am-11pm* $$

RM Sulawesi Baru: *Ayam goreng* and *ikan bakar* – fried chicken and grilled fish – are the specialities at this popular local. *10am-10pm* $

There are two more branches in town.

Bistropolis: Stylish air-conditioned bistro serving international standards, including steak and pizza, as well as gelato and espresso coffee. *10am-11pm* $$

CITY SLEEPS IN STYLE

Makassar has a broad range of accommodation and plenty of cheapies but it stands out in Sulawesi for the affordable deals available at its top-end hotels. On booking websites you can find some great deals (less than 500,000Rp for a double) on rooms at places like the Aston, Swiss-Belhotel, Hyatt and Melia. To put it in perspective, you can sleep cheaper in a four-star place here than in some basic beach bungalows in Bira and the Togean Islands. Benefits include lavish buffet breakfasts (sometimes at extra cost), swimming pool, gym, spa, rooftop bar and five-star service. These hotels also have some of Makassar's finest restaurants. So go on, splurge a little! For recommendations see p638.

All That Glitters

Browse Makassar's golden shopping street

Jl Somba OPU is Makassar's vintage shopping strip, known primarily for its gold, silver and jewellery shops. This is no Dubai, but it's interesting to browse the open-fronted shops dripping with bracelets, necklaces, souvenirs sold by smartly dressed staff. Another local product on display at the *toko* (shops) here is *minyak tawon* (wasp oil), a herbal oil produced exclusively in Makassar for more than a century. It's used on everything from massage to insect bites and skin complaints. Of the many ingredients (including cloves and eucalyptus oil), there are no wasps – it's just the marketing logo. The premium product has a white cap, the cheaper one a red cap.

Islands Ahoy

Take a boat trip

There are several islands off the coast of Makassar that local boat captains will be eager to take you out to. None could be considered idyllic but they're popular with locals and can offer a break from the city.

The best is **Pulau Samalona**, with white sands, waters clear enough for snorkelling and just enough distance from Makassar to shed pollution. Warungs (food stalls) sell cold drinks and basic meals. A boat ride here costs 450,000Rp (return) for up to six people and takes about half an hour.

Tiny **Pulau Kayangan**, a 10-minute ride from Makassar's harbourfront, has nothing more than a small beach and a derelict ghost resort. Locals still come out here on weekends, as it's a short trip, but it's strictly for novelty value.

Pulau Lae Lae is the inhabited island directly across from the harbour, with a tight warren of concrete alleys and village homes on one side and a stretch of coarse sand on the other.

Boats for the islands leave from two small harbours: one opposite Fort Rotterdam and one further south down a lane near Makassar Golden Hotel (look for signs to 'Dermaga', though the touts will find you anyway).

EATING IN MAKASSAR: BEST FOR SEAFOOD

Rumah Makan Pate'ne: Super-fresh Makassarese fish and Indonesian classics with authentic flavours and budget prices. *8am-10pm* $

RM Nelayan: Barbecue aromas waft from this fresh-fish grill restaurant, where *ikan* (fish) is served with a selection of six condiments. *10am-10pm* $$

Lae Lae: Renowned seafood restaurant serving no-frills grilled fish, cooked on a street-side barbecue and served with rice and vegetables. *10am-midnight* $$

Fish Warungs: Local fish warungs (food stalls) serving cheap *ikan bakar* (grilled fish) alfresco style on the foreshore opposite Fort Rotterdam. *5-10pm* $

PAUL HARDING/LONELY PLANET

Pinisi (Makassar schooner)

Family Thrills & Chills

Chill out in monster malls

Makassar's modern air-conditioned shopping malls make for a relieving escape from the city's oppressive heat, and offer a surprising range of family activities, from cinemas to roller rinks, arcade games, food courts and ice-cream parlours. Top of the pile for family fun is **Trans Studio Mall** *(trans entertainment.com)*, open 10am to 10pm – a giant indoor theme park and shopping mall that features the refrigerated **Trans Snow World** with manufactured snow playgrounds, mini Skidoos and even chairlifts. Tickets start at 180,000Rp.

Nearby, and just south of the CPI monument, smaller **Phinisi Point Mall** *(phinisipoint.com)*, open 8am to 11pm, is another house of family fun, with an eight-screen cinema, free children's playground, bowling alley and roller-skating rink.

Ratu Indah Mall *(malratuindah.id)*, open 8am to 10pm, is more about boutique shopping than entertainment, but it still offers a cinema complex and a kids' playground.

An alternative to indoor entertainment, **Bugis Waterpark Adventure** *(bugiswaterpark.id)* has giant water slides and multiple pools and water playgrounds. It's open 9am to 6pm Saturday to Thursday, and is around 12km east of the waterfront (about an hour by taxi).

DODO'S TOP TIPS

Dodo Mursalim, legendary local tour guide, shares tips on Rammang Rammang and his home city, Makassar. *WhatsApp +62 812 412 9913, @dodomursalim*

Since I have been guiding tourists for more than 30 years, Rammang Rammang has become the most popular trip from Makassar. The river trip is very special and peaceful. Be sure to start your trip from Pier 1 and make stops along the way to Berua village.

In Makassar, everyone should visit Fort Rotterdam, the traditional boat harbour and the mosques on our waterfront. A good place for a cheap fish lunch is Pate'ne in the Chinatown area. Some of my favourite restaurants are RM Nelayan, Ratu Gurih Seafood Market and Seafood Losari.

DRINKING IN MAKASSAR: OUR PICKS

Jokka: This main-street coffee shop uses locally sourced and ground beans for lattes and frappes. The adjacent souvenir shop sells Torajan coffee. *9am-11pm*

Popsa District: This open-sided food court facing the harbour has sea breezes and a youthful crowd; there's often live music in the evening. *10am-midnight*

Pier 52: The alfresco deck at Makassar Golden Hotel serves reasonably priced beer all day, with Indonesian food and views of the 99-dome mosque. *7am-11pm*

New Kafe Kareba: This evening-only alfresco bar opposite Pantai Losari is the place to hang out with a cold Bintang and nightly live music. *4pm-1am*

MAKASSAR WATERFRONT WALK

Makassar sprawls a long way inland from the coast, but most places of interest can be found on or near the waterfront.

START	END	LENGTH
Fort Rotterdam	Asmaul Husnah 99 Kubah	3km; 1hr

Start at ❶ **Fort Rotterdam** (p592), Makassar's grand, well-preserved colonial fort and museum, where you can walk the fort walls and take a guided tour. Cross the road past the fish warungs (food stalls) and walk south to the waterfront proper. The ❷ **Pantai Losari** promenade starts just south of the Makassar Golden Hotel – there's no beach here anymore but boats dock on the waterfront, and there are fine views across to the mosque. Tables and food-and-drink stalls set up here from around 5pm, and locals begin to crowd in for sunset selfies and street-food snacks – the whole strip is packed most evenings, especially on weekends when there's a carnival atmosphere. Look out for various sculptures and monuments dedicated to local culture (a sailing ship, Torajan house etc) and famous people such as Gandhi and Nelson Mandela.

At the southern end of the promenade is ❸ **Masjid Amirul Mukminin** (p593) – the small 'floating mosque' is reflected in the water. Continue around the waterfront, past models of Torajan houses and the globe monument ❹ **Centre Point of Indonesia** in the middle of a large roundabout. Crossing the cable bridge here brings you to the redeveloped western waterfront and the highly photogenic landmark ❺ **Asmaul Husnah 99 Kubah** (p593), the 99-domed mosque that looks like a giant trifle.

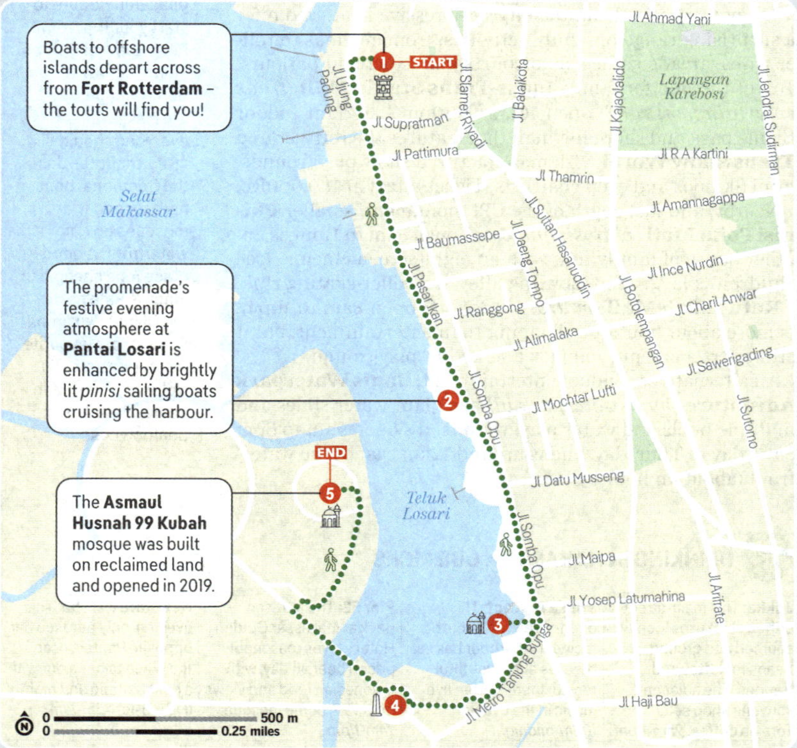

Boats to offshore islands depart across from **Fort Rotterdam** – the touts will find you!

The promenade's festive evening atmosphere at **Pantai Losari** is enhanced by brightly lit *pinisi* sailing boats cruising the harbour.

The **Asmaul Husnah 99 Kubah** mosque was built on reclaimed land and opened in 2019.

Beyond Makassar

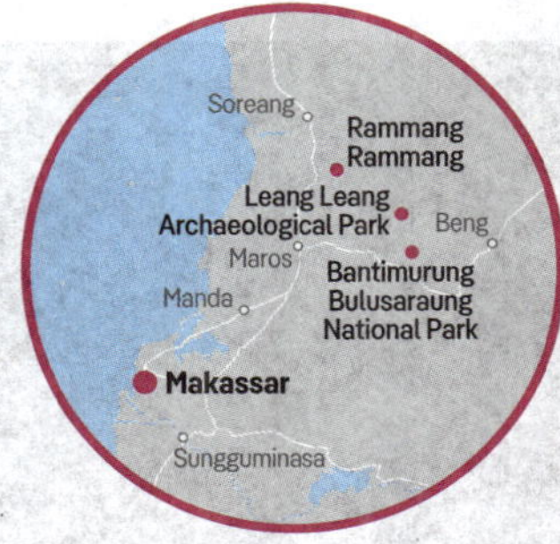

There are some areas of outstanding natural beauty a short drive out of the Makassar urban sprawl.

The Maros district north of Makassar is said to contain some of the world's largest karst fields, where soft limestone and porous marble riddle the landscape with caves, sinkholes and weird and wonderful surface formations. The region was mined extensively for limestone and marble until the early 2000s when local environmental pressure resulted in the creation of a protected geo-park and tourism area.

The most popular trip and a highlight of the region is Rammang Rammang, a scenic valley of villages, palm groves and a meandering river tributary surrounded by imposing karst mountains. Nearby caves and waterfalls can easily be visited on a day trip to Rammang Rammang – hire a driver/guide in Makassar and make the most of it.

Leang Leang Archaeological Park (p598)

ADNING/SHUTTERSTOCK

Places

GETTING AROUND

Most people hire a car and driver/guide for a full day in Rammang Rammang for around 600,000Rp from Makassar. For a little extra you can include stops at Leang Leang and Bantimurung. Solo travellers may be able to hire an *ojek* or motorcycle becak for around 300,000Rp. Otherwise *pete-pete* (minivans) run regularly to Maros from where you can change to Salenrang village. There's a new Rammang Rammang train station but the originating station is located inconveniently well north of Makassar.

EKA UTAMA/SHUTTERSTOCK

Bantimurung Falls, Bantimurung Bulusaraung National Park

Leang Leang Archaeological Park

TIME FROM MAKASSAR: **1HR**

Ancient cave paintings

The caves of the **Leang Leang Archaeological Park** *(20,000Rp)* are noted for their ancient paintings and handprints. Recent studies of nearby caves have dated the art at over 40,000 years old, making them the oldest pictographs in the world. There are 60 or so known caves in the Maros district, riddled into the soft limestone karst. The main handprint paintings are in a signposted cave reached via some steps.

Get to Leang Leang by taxi or tour, best combined with a day trip to Rammang Rammang.

Bantimurung Bulusaraung National Park

TIME FROM MAKASSAR: **1HR**

Waterfalls and butterflies

Bantimurung Bulusaraung National Park *(255,000Rp)*, is home to **Bantimurung Falls**, set amid lushly vegetated limestone cliffs. At least 250 species of butterflies have been recorded here but at ground level it's often crowded with day-trippers, especially on weekends. Many foreign travellers are put off by the high nationalpark entry fee, but it's a scenic spot to spend a couple of hours and can easily be combined with a day trip to Leang Leang and Rammang Rammang.

TOP EXPERIENCE

Rammang Rammang

Like a watercolour painting come to life, the valley of Rammang Rammang is a scenic canvas of looming karst mountains, palm-fringed jungle and emerald-green fields that makes a photogenic day trip from the city. The highlight is the evergreen gondola-style boat trip by river through the jungle – don't miss it.

PAUL HARDING/LONELY PLANET

Boating Through the Hills

The adventure begins at Dermaga 1 dock near the village of Salenrang, where you can hire a boat with driver (from 200,000Rp for up to four people). Stops along the river include **Taman Batu Kampung Latu**, where for a tip a local farmer will guide you through a labyrinth of rock formations. If visiting in the late afternoon, ask your guide or boat driver about the **bat caves**. Around sunset, thousands of bats pour out from caves in the cliffs to start their nightly feeding, only to run the gauntlet of eagles looking for a feed of their own.

Berua Village

At the farming-turned-ecotourism village of **Berua** *(10,0000Rp)*, enclosed in a bowl of spectacular karst hills, a 3km-loop boardwalk trail takes you to a number of impressive viewpoints and signposted *gua* (caves; the best is Crystal Cave). The ponds here were once fish farms but tourism has become more lucrative than farming, so the practice is all but abandoned. Rice is still grown in season when the fields turn lush green. The village has two simple friendly homestays, or you can stay at Rammang Rammang Eco Lodge (p638), halfway along the river.

TOP TIPS

- Although you don't need a guide, arranging a car and driver/guide in Makassar will avoid the hassle of transport.
- If time is short, start at Dermaga 2, opposite the Rammang Rammang Eco Lodge.
- Look out for new electric-powered boats, which are both quieter and more ecofriendly.

PRACTICALITIES

- rammangrammang.com

Bira Peninsula

BEACHES | DIVING | ISLAND CULTURE

GETTING AROUND

There is no public transport to speak of in Bira, though some locals will provide *ojek* service. Warung Bamboo and several guesthouses rent motorbikes. You can easily walk between Bira and Bara beaches at low tide, otherwise it's a 2km trek along the road running above the beach.

There are direct minibuses and shared taxis to/from Makassar (five to six hours). Returning from Bira to Makassar they leave in the morning; book via your lodging the day before.

TOP TIP

Access to Bira and Bara costs 20,000/55,000Rp per local/foreigner levied once at the tollbooth when you first enter. If you're on foot or motorbike the booth attendants won't stop you, presuming you've already paid, but it's a levy that goes towards upkeep of beaches, so pay it once and keep your receipt.

Bira is a fishing village at the southernmost point of mainland Sulawesi with a string of sandy beaches and some of the best scuba diving and snorkelling in the region. There's plenty to do here: take a short boat ride to nearby Liukang Loe island to see locals making the famous Bira silk sarongs, watch skilled craftspeople building huge *pinisi* boats right on the beach, and savour the sunrise *and* sunset from the dramatic windswept lookout jutting into the Flores Sea.

Bira has a typically laid-back end-of-the-road beach vibe, though it gets crowded with Makassarese escaping the city on weekends. There's a good range of beachfront accommodation, mainly along neighbouring Pantai Bara, and several professional dive outfits ready to take you out to Pulau Kambing and beyond. It's also the ferry point for boats to Pulau Selayar and long-haul Pelni ships to Flores.

The Beaches of Bira

Picture-perfect *pantai*

Pantai Bira, the main village beach, is a decent crescent of white sand lined with souvenir stalls and basic warungs. The large number of outrigger boats, water-sports operators and conservative locals crowding the shoreline means it's not a great place for swimming or sunbathing. Much better is **Pantai Bara**, a prettier stretch fringed by low cliffs, palm trees and beachfront and cliffside resorts that manage to blend in with the vibe and are popular with travellers. You can walk here in 30 minutes from Bira along the beach when the tide is out, or drive along the back road behind the cliffs to access the resorts.

On the other side of town, past the ferry harbour, **Pantai Panrang Luhu** is another long, coconut-fringed affair with a string of accommodation places that are popular with weekenders from Makassar. *Pinisi* shipbuilders operate beneath the cliffs at the northern end.

SIGHTS

1 Jembatan Kaca
2 Kaluku
3 Panorama Titik Nol
4 Pantai Bara
5 Pantai Bira
6 Pantai Panrang Luhu

ACTIVITIES

7 Blue Planet Dive Resort
8 Cape Bira
see 11 Gaia One Boutique Diving
9 South Sulawesi Divers

SLEEPING

10 Bara Coco
11 Cosmos Bungalows
12 Nusa Bira Indah
see 11 Tevana House Reef

EATING

13 Akasha Beach Club
see 10 Bara Coco
see 11 Cosmos Cafe
14 D'Perahu Resto
15 RM Claudya
see 11 Seascapes
see 11 Tevana Vida Kitchen
16 Warung Bamboo

TRANSPORT

see 16 Warung Bamboo

BEST OF BIRA

Nur Anjas, Selayar-born, Bira-based guide and guesthouse owner, shares his tips and experiences for the Bira Peninsula. *WhatsApp +62 822 5009 1987; @anjasbira*

I came to live in Bira from Selayar in 1999 and have been guiding visitors in the area ever since. My advice for travellers is to experience snorkelling and diving at Kambing Island and Liukang Loe where you can watch locals making the Bira sarong. I also like to guide visitors to the cliff views at Titik Nol and the *pinisi* boatbuilders at Tanah Beru. A unique experience north of Bira is visiting the Kajang indigenous tribe in traditional Tana Toa village, kept far from modernity, where the villagers all wear black clothing.

Beach Boatbuilders

See *pinisi* take shape

Boatbuilders use age-old techniques to craft traditional ironwood *pinisi* ships right on the beach at **Kaluku** (also called Pantai Pinisi, or 'Shipbuilders Beach'), about 2km north of Bira village, and at **Pantai Tanah Beru** (a much larger operation), 14km from Bira on the road to Bulukumba. You'll see wooden boats of various sizes in varying stages of completion, supported by timber scaffolding and ready to be hauled out to sea by hand-winch when completed. The only real concession to modernity is the use of power tools, but you'll still see plenty of handsawing and hammering. *Pinisi* were traditionally two-mast sailing vessels built and sailed for trade or warfare by the seafaring Bugis people, but these days most of the boats are outfitted as motorised liveaboards for the dive industry or other tourism ventures such as luxury sailing trips.

Island Day Trip

Swim and snorkel at Liukang Loe

Only a 15-minute speedboat ride from Bira, the small island of Pulau Liukang Loe has two fishing villages and rewarding, uncrowded snorkelling on the shallow reef that stretches for around 1km off the northern coast to Shark Point. Spend an hour or two wandering the sandy laneways of Ta'Buntuleng village (where boats dock) and you'll likely see locals weaving heavy colourful cloth on traditional handlooms beneath their raised houses. Although little English is spoken, the experts are happy to demonstrate their weaving technique; they produce cotton shawls and sarongs along with the coveted silk Bira sarong, worn by men on special occasions (such as weddings) and valued at up to 1,500,000Rp. Depending on the design, a quality sarong can take up to a month to produce.

Although the island is an easy day trip, there are a couple of homestays on Liukang Loe where you can really chill out and find some peace. The best is **Ocean Holiday**, run by village head Jafar, with comfortable rooms fronting the beach at the eastern end of the village. Another option is **Wisma Ramli**.

Snorkelling day trips to Pulau Liukang Loe cost around 500,000Rp by speedboat from Pantai Bira; most guesthouses and hotels can arrange trips. If you just want to visit the island you should be able to negotiate a return crossing on a local boat with an hour or two of waiting time for 350,000Rp. Equipment (mask and fins) can be rented for about 50,000Rp per day from kiosks on Pantai Bira or directly from the boat captain.

Friday is delicious Indian buffet night

EATING IN BIRA: OUR PICKS

Tevana Vida Kitchen: Malaysian vegetarian food is the speciality at this intimate boutique hotel and restaurant. *7am-10pm* $$

Akasha Beach Club: Asian and Western flavours meet at Akasha's stylish clifftop restaurant; pizza, pasta and noodles along with seafood buffet spreads. *7am-10pm* $$

Seascapes: One of the fine cliff-side guesthouse restaurants overlooking Pantai Bara with Indonesian and international offerings. *8am-8pm* $$

D'Perahu Resto: At Anda Beach Hotel, this quirky well-regarded restaurant is shaped like a traditional boat, with a deck overlooking Pantai Bira. *10am-10pm* $$

PAUL HARDING/LONELY PLANET

Boatbuilders, Kaluku Beach

Dive with Sharks

Pulau Kambing and beyond

Renowned as one of the 'sharkiest' diving locations in Indonesia, Bira offers some spectacular scuba diving when conditions are right and it's remote enough that there are rarely large groups of divers. The islands off Bira lie at the tip of southern Sulawesi where oceanic currents converge, bringing upswells of cool water from the depths and lots of pelagic life.

The seas can be rough off Pantai Bira and it's not always possible to reach islands such as **Pulau Kambing** ('Goat Island'), around 7km south, which harbours the most popular dive sites. But there are more sheltered sites closer to shore, where you can spot macro life, including nudibranchs, seahorses and prolific reef fish.

On Kambing's eastern side, the **Great Wall of Goat** has a remarkable vertical wall teeming with reef life. Sharks (including hammerheads and threshers) and rays (mantas and devils) are typically encountered. **Cape Bira** is an impressive site off the extreme tip of the mainland with a lovely swim-through; whitetip sharks, shrimps and pipefish are common. **Fish Market** is for experienced divers, where an underwater seamount teems with sea life, including huge groupers, jacks and Napoleon wrasse.

ECO-DIVE OUTFITS

Gaia One Boutique Diving: Based at Tevana House Reef, this boutique and eco-minded outfit is involved in reef preservation and coral-planting projects, as well as cleaning the beach with its EcoBira initiative. *(tevanahousereef.com/gaiaonediving)*

Blue Planet Dive Resort: There are a couple of bungalows and dorms at this recommended outfit; Blue Planet is involved in reef preservation and data-collection projects under the IndoOcean Project. *(blueplanetdiveresort.com)*

South Sulawesi Divers: A well-managed dive centre started by Elvis, a serious German diver who has long been operating in the region. Based out of Mangga Lodge. *(south-sulawesi-diver.com)*

EATING IN BIRA: OUR BUDGET PICKS

Cosmos Cafe: Wander down the stone path to the cute cafe overlooking the beach for fresh home-cooked food and a traveller vibe. *8am-10pm* $

Bara Coco: Towards the western end of Pantai Bara, this welcoming alfresco restaurant serves local fish and cold beer just steps from the sand. *7am-10pm* $

Warung Bamboo: On the main street into Bira village, this is a reliable restaurant for staying open late and the seafood dishes are superb value. *8am-9pm* $

RM Claudya: Of the handful of warungs on the road leading to Pantai Bira, this one offers solid, low-cost takes on Indonesian staples. *8am-8pm* $

BOATS FROM BIRA

From Bira's harbour there are two or three ferries daily in each direction to Pulau Selayar (two hours, 34,000Rp), arriving at Pamatata port at the north end of Selayar. They usually depart at 8am and 1pm but schedules are fluid and often only finalised a day in advance – check with your accommodation or on Instagram (ASDP Selayar). There's a kiosk onboard where you can buy snacks and drinks. There's also a direct daily overnight bus-ferry combination from Makassar to Selayar with Aneka Transport (deluxe/sleeper bus 250,000/300,000Rp including ferry), which departs at midnight and arrives in Bira early morning to connect with the 8am ferry to Selayar.

PAUL HARDING/LONELY PLANET

Panorama Titik Nol

Mola-Mola Point, on the western side of Pulau Kambing, is best suited to advanced divers, where giant mola-mola (sunfish) are encountered. Over on the eastern side of Pulau Liukang Loe, **Shark Point** is a good place to spot visiting sharks, including 2m whitetips, blacktips and, occasionally, bull sharks, and it's an easier dive with a sloped profile.

Savour the Views from the Cape

Zero Point Sulawesi

The dramatic rocky promontory east of Pantai Bira marks the southernmost point of the Sulawesi mainland, and from here it's possible to see the sunrise, sunset, moonrise and moonset when conditions are right. **Panorama Titik Nol** *(Zero Point Lookout; 20,000Rp)* is an elaborate and colourful set of boardwalks and stairs on the east-facing cliffs, culminating in a mini replica *pinisi* half-ship overlooking the swirling ocean below, and representing Sulawesi's 'zero point' as its southernmost tip. **Jembatan Kaca** (Glass Bridge), on the west-facing side, is another series of sunset-viewing boardwalks down at sea level with a glass walkway leading to a viewing platform over the water.

Both viewpoints can be reached by road only a five-minute drive from Bira village or a 30-minute (2.5km) walk via Amatoa Resort (turn left at the resort). There are more spectacular clifftop viewpoints along the coast north of Bira at **Apparalang** and **Dego Dego**.

Beyond Bira Peninsula

Bulukumba
Bira Peninsula
Pulau Selayar
Benteng
Taka Bonerate Islands

Further south of the mainland lie some remote islands that are just beginning to land on the tourism radar.

While the Bira Peninsula has been attracting low-key travellers for years, Pulau Selayar and the little-visited islands beyond it are remote enough to have almost escaped tourism, but that's gradually changing. Still, only a relatively small number of adventurous travellers make it from the mainland and it's this untouristed atmosphere that makes these islands so alluring.

Selayar is a lightly populated island of fishing and farming villages with some fine east-coast beaches and a vibrant west-coast capital in Benteng. But it's the deserted islands further afield, reached only by chartered local boat, that will really wow beach-loving castaways. Even further away by slow ferry or liveaboard *pinisi*, the islands of Taka Bonerate reward intrepid DIY travellers with their isolation.

Places

Pulau Selayar

TIME FROM BIRA: **2HR**

Explore Selayar's islands and beaches

The long, skinny island of Selayar is inhabited by ethnic Bugis, Makassarese and Konjo, most of whom reside along the west coast and in the capital Benteng, making a living in fishing or agriculture. Harbourside Benteng has a decent range of accommodation, fish restaurants and an imposing new waterfront mosque, **Masjid Rahmatan Lil Alami**. Selayar's western coastline has the island's main road and some stretches of beach but suffers from tonnes of plastic and rubbish washed ashore. Much better, but harder to access, are the beaches on the southeastern side, such as **Pantai Pinang**, where there are three dive resorts (p607).

A motorbike or taxi is a good way to see a bit of the island's west coast, but bear in mind that it's almost 90km from north to south. A popular trip for island views and sunsets is to **Puncak Tanadoang** *(5000Rp)* in the inland hills, about

GETTING AROUND

Ferries (two hours) depart from Bira for Pamatata port on Pulau Selayar. There's no public transport from there to Benteng and a hard-to-find taxi costs at least 350,000Rp; try hitching with cars coming off the ferry. A cheap option is hiring a motorbike in Bira and bringing it on the ferry. Flights from Makassar to Pulau Selayar's Aroeppala Airport weren't operating at the time of writing. Ask your accommodation about motorbike hire on Selayar (100,000Rp per day).

SUNSETS & STREET FOOD

A popular evening tradition on Selayar's west coast is to watch the sun sink into the Flores Sea, and for many young people and families in Benteng that means a sunset snack of *pisang goreng* (banana fritters) and *sarabba* (a spicy coconut tea infused with ginger, cinnamon, cloves and palm sugar). A string of makeshift **cafes** set up on the waterfront sea wall in the late afternoon near Selayar Beach Hotel. As well as *sarabba,* they offer coffee and other snacks.

12km east of Benteng. Another sunset spot is **Sunari Beach Resort** (p638), 13km south of Benteng, where the beachfront restaurant welcomes nonguests with advance bookings.

Pulau Pasi, the large island directly across from Benteng, makes an excellent day trip for snorkelling, swimming and beach-hopping. The best beaches are around the southern section, so it's a much shorter and cheaper trip to charter a boat from Padang harbour near the airport, about 12km south of Benteng. Popular stops include Pantai Liang Kareta, Pantai Balo Jaha, Pantai Liang Tarrusu, and Balo Jaha Cave for swimming. Ask at your accommodation or contact local guide **Sulvi Sabinez** *(WhatsApp +62 852 4070 2970; sulvisabinez@gmail.com).*

Find your beach bliss

If you really want to go Robinson Crusoe, arrange a full-day boat trip to the near-deserted islands and stunning pristine beaches of **Pulau Bahuluang**, **Pulau Tambolongan** and **Pulau Gusung Polassi**, reached off the southern tip of Selayar. While they have small fishing settlements, the majority of the coastline and beaches here are uninhabited and only reached by small boat. Bahuluang is closest to Selayar, a relatively short ride west of the southern tip, while Tambolongan and Polassi are larger twin islands further south. All are surrounded by reefs with excellent snorkelling and diving, while Polassi offers spectacular hilltop hiking at **Bukit Nane**. For a visual experience of the islands, check out locally produced **Wonderful Selayar** *(wonderfulselayar.id).*

Although tourist infrastructure is still in its infancy on Selayar, there's a growing band of guides who are happy to give advice or arrange boat trips and other island activities. At Syafira Hotel (p638), Andi and the team behind Wonderful Selayar arrange three-island day trips for around 550,000Rp per person (with six people) including meals, transport and snorkelling gear. It may be possible for individuals to join with a group. Another recommended guide is Sulvi Sabinez; she speaks good English and works tirelessly promoting tourism and collaborating with local boatmen to get visitors to the islands.

Selayar for divers

Diving and snorkelling are exceptional here, with wall drop-offs and fringing reefs on the east side of the island, but it's highly seasonal and best from October or November to April when the sea is calm and sheltered from westerly winds. For

EATING ON SELAYAR: OUR PICKS

Sit upstairs with views of the street below.

Wisata Kuliner: The simple warungs next to the harbour in Benteng are the place for fresh seafood, with fish kept fresh in iceboxes. *9am-midnight* $

Oriental Resto & Cafe: There's good-value Chinese and Indonesian food at this clean, long-standing local Benteng restaurant. *7am-10pm* $

Dierra Cafe & Resto: In a modern cathedral-like space, Dierra is Benteng's best contemporary cafe-restaurant, serving Indonesian and Japanese dishes. *9am-11pm* $$

Mr Yess Coffee & Cafe: Locals rate this chilled cafe and restaurant for good coffee and Indonesian food, with occasional live music. *9am-11pm* $$

PAUL HARDING/LONELY PLANET

***Pisang goreng* (banana fritters) and *sarabba* (spiced tea)**

this reason, most of the handful of dive resorts are only open during the east-coast season or switch operations to the west at other times. Diving is low key, with small groups visiting the intimate resorts here, but it's well organised and you're likely to see plenty of turtles, rays and reef fish.

Taka Bonerate Islands

TIME FROM SELAYAR: **8HR**

Go remote at this coral atoll

Southeast of Pulau Selayar and north of Pulau Bonerate, the 2200-sq-km Taka Bonerate is the world's third-largest atoll, with some 500 sq km of coral reefs. Some of the islands and extensive reefs in the region are now part of **Taka Bonerate National Park** (Taman Nasional Taka Bonerate), a marine reserve with a rich variety of sea creatures and birdlife.

The main island here is Pulau Tinabo Besar, a tiny island with a national park post and a few basic bungalows. The beach here is famous for the baby sharks that mill around in the shallows. Most divers come here on a liveaboard boat, or on a package that will include lodging, food and diving centred around Tinabo. It is possible to arrive independently on the weekly slow boat (eight hours) from Benteng Harbour, but locals and national parks officials admit this boat is unreliable at best. Another option is to join a group in chartering a boat (for around 3,000,000Rp per person). Contact Sulvi Sabinez on Selayar, or check wonderfulselayar.id.

Public boats to populated Pulau Bonerate also leave irregularly from Selayar. Call into the Taka Bonerate National Park office in Benteng for a chat, though there's not much English spoken and staff can't make bookings.

SELAYAR'S ECO DIVE RESORTS

Selayar Eco Resort: Operates year-round but moves its base seasonally from the east (November to April) to west coast (May to November). Pantai Pinang has access to some of the island's best dive sites. *(selayar-eco-resort.sitew.fr)*

Selayar Dive Resort: Serious dive resort open only for the east-coast season, with a minimum one-week stay in thatched-roofed, sea-facing bungalows on a sandy beach. *(selayar-dive-resort.com)*

Pearl Beach Cottage: Ultra-stylish and secluded resort on a gorgeous east-coast beach with four Balinese-inspired villas. Activities include diving and snorkelling, paddleboarding and massage. *(pearlbeach cottage.com)*

Selayar Turtle Bay Resort: French-run dive resort with just five cottages on Pantai Pinang. *(selayarturtlebay.com)*

Tana Toraja

ANCIENT CULTURE | FUNERAL CEREMONIES | HILL TREKKING

TOP TIP
Most Tana Toraja tourist sites have an entry fee of 35,000Rp to 50,000Rp. There's usually a ticket booth and souvenir and drink stalls at each place. Most are open from 7am to sunset. Arrive early at the main sites to beat tour groups, saving the afternoon for funeral ceremonies (which usually start around noon).

Tana Toraja is the reason many travellers choose to visit Sulawesi and for good reason: this ancient culture is unique in Indonesia and isolated to a small but staggeringly beautiful highland region wedged between South and West Sulawesi. The Torajan people form a distinct ethnic group, with one of the most recognisable and compelling traditional cultures in Indonesia.

Tana Toraja offers some superb trekking, cycling and motorbiking through an evergreen landscape of cascading ricefields and soaring *tongkonan* (traditional Torajan houses). The culture is all-embracing: the Torajans proudly display their heritage through architecture, precipitous hand-carved cliff graves, otherworldly *tau tau* (carved wooden figures) and, famously, their elaborate funeral ceremonies.

In 1905 the Dutch began a bloody campaign to bring Central Sulawesi under their control, and by WWII many of the great Torajan ceremonies (with the exception of the *tomate* – funeral celebrations) were rapidly disappearing from local culture. Today, visitors are welcomed to these funeral ceremonies – a privilege and highlight while in Tana Toraja.

GETTING AROUND

Rantepao and Makale are the major transport hubs, with regular buses and shared taxis heading in all directions – the main routes are south to Makassar by luxury bus, north to Tentena and Palu by slow and uncomfortable bus or chartered taxi, or southeast to Bira via Sengkang by taxi.

For getting around the region it pays to hire a car and driver or rent a motorbike (from 100,000Rp per day) in Rantepao. There are many trekking routes linking villages, and mountain bikes can also be rented through Rantepao guesthouses.

Local public transport leaves from stops around central Rantepao and Terminal Bolu north of town; there are regular bemo (minibuses) and shared taxis to all main villages.

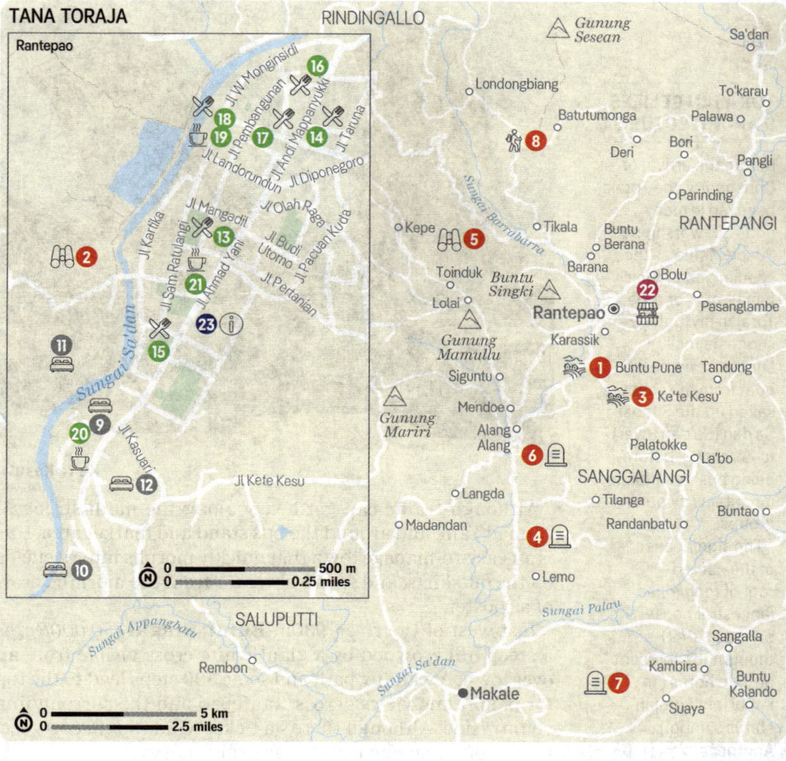

SIGHTS
1 Buntu Pune
2 Buntu Singki
3 Ke'te Kesu'
4 Lemo
5 Lolai
6 Londa
7 Tampang Allo
see 5 Tongkonan Lempe

ACTIVITIES
8 Gunung Sesean

SLEEPING
9 Pia's Poppies
10 Rosalina Homestay
11 Santai Toraja
12 Sulawesi Castle

EATING
13 Ayam Penyet Ria
14 Cafe Aras
15 Peleton Cafe Toraja
see 9 Pia's
16 Rumah Makan Saruran
see 11 Santai Toraja
17 Sop Ubi Ma'Uni
18 Warung Pong Buri'

DRINKING & NIGHTLIFE
19 Djong Coffee Roastery
20 Kaana Toraya Coffee
21 Kopi Toraja ToRi Coffee
see 11 Randan Uma Coffee

SHOPPING
22 Pasar Bolu
see 22 Pasar Hewan

INFORMATION
23 Government Tourist Office

Toraja's Urban Heart

A base in the hills

Rantepao is the busy tourist heart of Toraja and the best base for making forays into the hills, with a wide range of accommodation, restaurants, markets and guides on hand.

The town owes its existence to the Dutch, who tried (with moderate success) to bring the family-centred rule of the Torajan highlanders under centralised administration, creating two new seats of government: Rantepao and Makale. While that control shifted back and forth, Rantepao grew into a small centre of trade and commerce for the northern Torajan communities.

TORAJAN BELIEFS & ARCHITECTURE

Before the arrival of Christianity, the Toraja believed in many gods but worshipped Puang Matua as the special god of their family, clan or tribe. Torajan mythology suggests their ancestors came by boat from the south, sailed up the Sungai Sa'dan (Sa'dan River) to Enrekang, before being pushed into the mountains by other groups.

The significance of the curved roof of *tongkonan* (ancestral house or *rumah adat*) is thought to represent buffalo horns (an important Torajan status symbol). Another story is that it symbolises the boats they arrived on. When they became stranded on rocks they raised their boat on stilts and used the hull as a roof. While many roofs are tin or corrugated iron, you'll often see turf roofs made from bamboo and palm fibre.

PAUL HARDING 00/SHUTTERSTOCK

Ke'te Kesu'

Although traffic can get heavy along the main street, Jl Ahmad Yani, and around the bus stand and market area, this is an easy-to-manage town that quickly morphs into ricefields on the outskirts, and you're never far from the morning crow of a rooster.

Just west of the river, 930m **Buntu Singki** *(30,000Rp)* is a steep hill crowned by a giant white cross visible from all over town. A walking path and some 300 steps lead to the top for panoramic views across Rantepao and the surrounding countryside. Although there's a ticket window and entry fee, there's often no one here to take your money.

Abut 2km north of town near the bus stand, **Pasar Bolu** is a large covered market where Torajans come to buy and sell daily. Just south of here is the more famous water-buffalo market, **Pasar Hewan** – reputed to be the world's largest such market. The big event happens every six days (ask locally for timings), when water buffalo are brought in from all over Sulawesi and beyond to be displayed and traded. Most of the animals are destined for slaughter at funeral ceremonies and are very expensive – from 30 million to 100 million rupiah. It can be a depressing scene, with buffalo tethered to ropes via nose rings or herded into feed troughs. Even on non-market days there are buffalo on display and it's a much less chaotic scene.

Order two hours in advance for Torajan dishes

EATING IN RANTEPAO: OUR PICKS

Warung Pong Buri': This unassuming warung is a good place for lunch as the best dishes, such as pork *pamarrasan*, typically sell out early. *8am-9pm* $

Ayam Penyet Ria: Most come for the *ayam penyet* (smashed chicken, a tender spicy deliciousness), though Indonesian staples such as gado gado are available. *10am-10pm* $

Pia's: Popular for ambience and Torajan food, such as *pa'piong* (meat, veg and coconut cooked in bamboo tubes), plus decent pizza cooked to request. *7am-9pm* $$

Cafe Aras: Designed with Western palates in mind, though the mix of local and international dishes are tasty. Two locations on the same main street. *8am-10pm* $$

Tongkonan & Caves

Architecture near Rantepao

There are *tongkonan* all over Toraja but two of the easiest cultural sites to visit are just south of Rantepao. Turn left on Jl Buntupune Kesu to find hilltop **Buntu Pune** *(35,000Rp)*, with two fine *tongkonan* and four rice barns, some with ancient roofs covered in vegetation. According to local legend, one of the houses was built by Pong Maramba, an early 20th-century noble. During Dutch rule he was appointed head of the local district, but planned to rebel and was subsequently exiled to Ambon (Maluku), where he died. His body was returned to Tana Toraja and buried at the hill to the north of Buntu Pune. If you're on a budget you could skip this site.

About 2km further along, **Ke'te Kesu'** *(35,000Rp)* is a more impressive sight featuring four stately *tongkonan* and many granaries that were moved here in 1927 when the savvy family head noticed the Dutch government largely ignored anyone too far from their administrative centres. Later Kesu'ers got their village designated as the first official *objek wisata* (tourism site) in Toraja, and lobbied hard (with some success) for UNESCO World Heritage attention. Walk past the souvenir stalls to the cliff face behind the village, where you can climb up past cave graves and very old hanging graves – some reportedly 500 years old or more.

TORAJAN FOOD

Torajan speciality dishes include *pa'piong* – meat, usually pork, slow-cooked in a bamboo tube with pungent *miana* leaves, vegetables, shaved coconut and seasonings, often served with *balok* (palm sugar wine). *Pantollo pammarasan* is a heavy stew of pork, buffalo or chicken and vegetables cooked with herbs and spices into a thick blackened sauce, usually served with steamed rice. Look out for it at ceremonies or local restaurants.

Toraja's Finest Tau Tau

Visit Londa and Lemo on the southern circuit

Take the main road southwest towards Makale about 8km from Rantepao to find **Londa** *(35,000Rp)*, one of Toraja's most dramatic burial caves, located below a monumental cliff face. You can walk down through the scenic bowl of farmland and admire the entrance guarded by a balcony of *tau tau*, but to enter the cave you must be accompanied by a **lantern-wielding guide** *(50,000Rp for the lamp plus guide tip)*. Inside are piles of coffins and bones lying haphazardly on almost every ledge. If you're small enough, and don't suffer from claustrophobia, squeeze through the tunnel that connects the two main caves, passing some interesting stalactites and stalagmites. Members of the upper class are placed in hanging caskets on the cliff face, some at dizzying heights, while commoners are placed in the caves, often without caskets at all.

EATING IN RANTEPAO: OUR PICKS

Peleton Cafe Toraja: A suave place on three levels, with a rooftop terrace and views across Rantepao, this stylish bar and restaurant has great food. *11am-11pm* $$

Rumah Makan Saruran: Oodles of fried noodles and freshly prepared Indonesian-style Chinese food are served at this hopping restaurant on the main drag. *8am-10pm* $

Sop Ubi Ma'Uni: Local hole-in-the-wall soup-restaurant extraordinaire serving fried *ubi* (cassava) soup among other options. *9am-8pm* $

Santai Toraja: The stylish restaurant at this boutique hotel west of the river is worth visiting for its thoughtful Indonesian dishes and fresh ingredients. *7am-10pm* $$

TOP EXPERIENCE

Torajan Tomate

Of all Torajan ceremonies, the most important is the *tomate* (funeral; literally 'deceased'). Remarkably open to outside visitors, they include buffalo sacrifices, dancing, feasting and the procession of carrying the coffin. While tourists are usually welcome, observe local customs – a guide isn't essential but can help you understand the rituals and perhaps introduce you to the family.

JAFARSODIK/SHUTTERSTOCK

Tomate **procession**

TOP TIPS

- Wear black or dark-coloured clothing as a sign of respect, and bring shareable gifts such as sweets or cigarettes for the family of the deceased.
- Photography is allowed but show discretion.
- Most large funerals start around noon and are mostly on weekdays (starting Monday) not weekends.

What to Expect

The Toraja generally have two funeral ceremonies: one immediately after death, when the deceased is kept in the home, sometimes for years, while the family makes preparations (and saves up) for an elaborate, more public second funeral. The second funeral is usually scheduled during the dry months of July and August, but can be year-round.

Depending on the family's means and status, the second funeral is a big event that can be spread over several days and involve hundreds of guests, traditional dancing, lots of food, and ritual animal sacrifice.

The Importance of Water Buffalo

The Toraja believe that the souls of animals should follow their masters to the next life, hence the importance of animal sacrifices. Festivities may include a form of bullfighting. The number of buffalo to be sacrificed is carefully negotiated, and depends on status and means – a bufffalo can cost as much as a new car. The meat is then divided among the community as a one-off redistribution of wealth. Pigs are also sacrificed, hog-tied and carried in on a bamboo pole. While an integral part of funeral ceremonies, some will find the animal sacrifices very bloody and traumatic.

About 4.5km further south (look out for the signs and turn east on Jl Buntang) is **Lemo** *(50,000Rp)*, where a veritable village of *tau tau* stare down with unblinking eyes and outstretched arms from this impressive burial cliff riddled with tombs. The *tau tau* symbolise the continuation of the person's life after death, and it is forbidden to touch one outside of certain ceremonies. Unfortunately, this has not prevented looters from stealing them, so many families now keep them in their homes. The sheer rockface at Lemo has a series of balconies for statues of the deceased. According to local legend, these graves are for the descendants of a Toraja chief who built his house on top of the cliff into which the graves are now cut.

Among the souvenir and drink stalls here, expert craftspeople carve new *tau tau* used for funerals throughout the region. It's fascinating to watch, and they may have a few for sale in various sizes if you're looking for an offbeat souvenir.

Caves of the Dead

Hanging coffins and bones

The Torajan custom of burying their dead in caves is something you can observe firsthand while exploring the local sites open to visitors. The Toraja believe that you can take possessions with you into the afterlife, and the dead generally go well equipped to their graves. Since this historically led to grave plundering, the Toraja started to hide their dead in caves, hollowed out by specialist cave builders. Coffins are taken deep inside the caves, and *tau tau* are placed on balconies in the rockface in front of the caves to represent the departed.

Two of the best sites to admire an array of skulls, bones and hanging coffins are Londa (p611) and **Tampang Allo** *(50,000Rp)* in Sangalla village, a site that's far enough away from Rantepao (a 45-minute drive) that it sees relatively few visitors and tour groups. A short walk from the village and past *tongkonan* brings you to the main cave site, surrounded by paddy fields. There's not a souvenir stall in sight and – with its rows of *tau tau*, and an easily entered cave filled with piles of skulls and bones – this is one of the more evocative sites in Tana Toraja. The graves reportedly belong to the chiefs of Sangalla, descendants of the mythical divine being Tamborolangiq who introduced the caste system and death rituals into Torajan society.

LUXURY BUSES

The Makassar–Tana Toraja bus route is well travelled and famous among Sulawesi travellers, thanks to the luxury overnight buses (and less popular day buses). Deluxe buses are akin to business-class aircraft seats, while sleeper buses have upper and lower cots allowing about a 5ft stretch, with curtains, USB ports, reading light and blankets

Several companies, including Metro Permai and Bintang Timur, operate on this route, departing from the respective company offices, both in Makassar and Tana Toraja. Tell the driver where you want to get off – if it's along the route they'll stop for you, including at Makassar's airport.

There are plenty of buses (and bus companies) on this route but try to book a day in advance. Sleeper buses cost from 250,000Rp to 350,000Rp.

Excellent house-roasted coffee and great breakfasts.

DRINKING IN RANTEPAO: BEST FOR COFFEE

Kaana Toraya Coffee: One of Rantepao's original and best boutique coffee shops, tucked around the corner near Pia's. *6.30am-6.30pm Mon-Sat*

Kopi Toraja ToRi Coffee: Stylish cafe on the main street where the coffee is complemented by good service, good food and occasional live music. *11am-10pm*

Djong Coffee Roastery: Pop into this hole-in-the-wall place across from the river where you'll often find the owner roasting or brewing fine Torajan coffee. *8am-4pm*

Randan Uma Coffee: Overlooking the paddies on the west side of the Sungai Sa'dan, this open-air place is a sunset favourite. *10.30am-9pm*

DRIVING TOUR

Head for the Hills

North of Rantepao is where the hills and valleys unfold and villages full of *tongkonan* (traditional Torajan houses) appear around every turn. This is where you'll find those legendary views across verdant ricefields and into misty valleys. This scenic loop drive, ride or steep cycling trip starts and ends in Rantepao.

1 Sangkombong

From Rantepao, head north past the market and via Pangli village (with the Sungai Sa'dan on your right) to the traditional weaving village of Sangkombong, 12km northeast of Rantepao. Locals weave Torajan blankets, scarves and shawls on traditional handlooms beneath rows of *tongkonan*. It's a bit put on for tourists and the handicrafts are for sale, naturally, but it's still worth a look. On the way back, detour right on Jl Palawa for the turf-roofed *tongkonan* at **Palawa**.

The Drive: Backtrack to Pangli village and turn west through relatively flat scenic farmland and villages for 3.5km to Bori village. The roads here are rutted and at times unsealed: take it slow.

2 Bori' Kalimbuang

Bori should be on a postcard given its lush rice paddies surrounding an impossibly photogenic church. But the real attraction is **Bori' Kalimbuang** *(35,000Rp)*, a small

PAUL HARDING/LONELY PLANET

Bori village

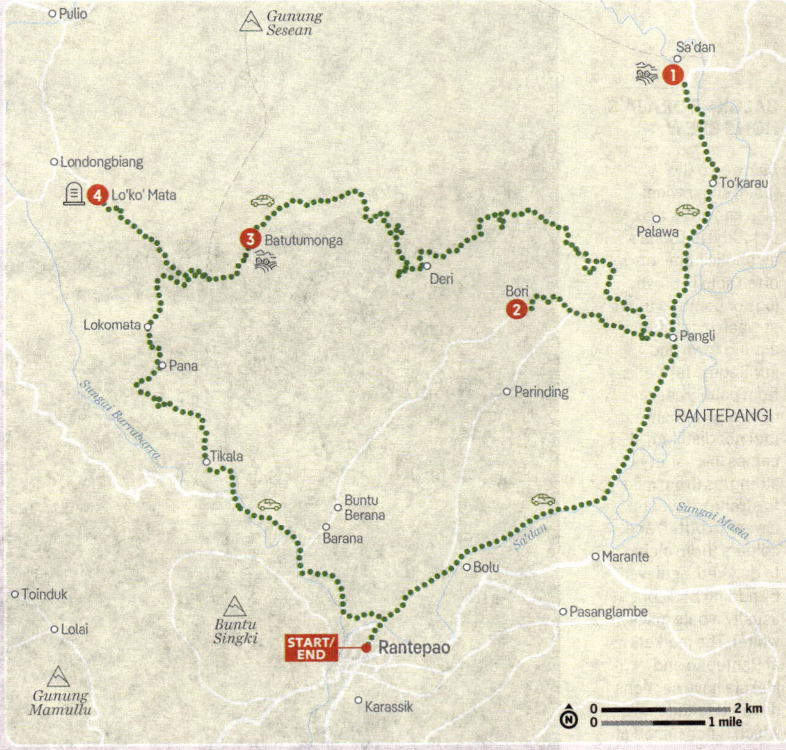

but incredibly evocative site of 102 standing stones, each representing a different funeral conducted here. It's humbling just to wander around the menhirs, some more than 2m tall.

The Drive: You'll need to backtrack again towards Pangli to find the shortest route to Batutumonga, where the road begins to climb and zigzag into the hills. If using a GPS or smart phone, type in 'Mentirotiku Guest House' to avoid getting lost, as there are numerous places with Batutumonga in their name.

3 Batutumonga

This is where to find iconic views from a ridge looking down on Rantepao and the surrounding fields and hills. Although there are viewpoints into and out of Batutumonga, this ridge has the most panoramic outlook and there are a couple of terrace cafes with homestays, plus the hillside **Mentirotiku Guest House**. The trailhead for Gunung Sesean (p617), a 3.5km hike to the summit, is near here – ask locally for directions.

The Drive: To make a loop drive, continue out the other side of Batutumonga village, past some lovely viewpoints to a junction. The left turn goes downhill to Rantepao; head right to continue on for about five minutes to the next stop.

4 Lokomata

Lokomata, 4km west of Batutumonga, is a fascinating collection of rock tombs bored into the sides of a giant round boulder. Look for the huge buffalo head carved under one and the intricate wood doors on others. Backtrack to find the road down to Rantepao that twists and turns for some 12km. On the outskirts of town, detour along Jl Penanian for a more scenic route through ricefields and traditional houses before crossing the Sungai Sa'dan just north of Hotel Luta Resort.

BALOK – TORAJA'S HOME BREW

Balok or 'ballo' (palm sugar wine; also known as *tuak* or toddy) is Toraja's alcoholic home brew, often sold in plastic jugs or bamboo tubes at small local shops around town and in villages. Tapped from palm trees and naturally fermented (but not distilled), it comes in a variety of strengths (from mild to strong), flavours (sweet to bitter) and colours (from clear to dark red, achieved by adding bark, but usually a pale milky white). The markets at Rantepao and Makale have sections devoted to the drink, which is consumed at room temperature.

Drinking alcohol isn't taboo in largely Christian Toraja. Beer and spirits are available in supermarkets and shops, and some restaurants, around Rantepao.

Finding a Guide

...or going it alone

Accredited guides in Tana Toraja hold a government-approved licence, obtained by undertaking a course in culture, language and etiquette. You can hire a guide with a car (for up to four people) for 600,000Rp per day (guide fee) plus 600,000Rp for the car, including attending a funeral if there is one on. Solo travellers with a motorbike can arrange a guide to ride along with. For trekking, guides also charge 600,000Rp per day plus any transport/food costs. All these rates are slightly negotiable but the 100 or so guides in the area try to keep their rates equal and fixed. Ask at your accommodation for recommendations (especially for trekking guides) or try the **Government Tourist Office**, open 9am to 4pm Monday to Saturday, which keeps a list of guides and calendar of events.

Trekking is the best way to reach isolated areas and to really get a feel for the Torajan countryside and its people. Historically settlements have revolved around family houses rather than 'villages', meaning civilisation is dispersed and

PAUL HARDING 00/SHUTTERSTOCK

Tongkonan Lempe

you're never far from the next family group, but with the rapid pace of development many of the backcountry treks now follow paved roads. It's highly advisable to take a good map or engage a local guide.

Popular short treks include the 8km walk from Rantepao to Londa via the villages of Siguntu' and Alang Alang-Londa, and the hike up **Gunung Sesean** from Batutumonga.

Above the Clouds

Misty views from Lolai

About 10km northwest of Rantepao, Lolai is another of Toraja's fabulous viewpoints and frequently lives up to its tagline 'village above the clouds'. The long north–south ridge line offers amazing views early in the morning when the valley below is often filled with fog that appears like a layer of cloud. There are numerous viewpoints but the best is **Tongkonan Lempe**, where there's a hotel and terrace with the bow of a replica ship poking out into the clouds, like a flying *Titanic*.

TORAJAN COFFEE

Famous for its earthy, full-bodied taste, Torajan coffee is one of Indonesia's most highly regarded regional brews. Tana Toraja is one of the few areas where the arabica bean dominates, accounting for 96% of local cultivation. Coffee was introduced to Toraja in the mid-19th century by the Dutch, who controlled production. In 1890, as coffee's value increased exponentially, a 'coffee war' erupted between Bugis and Toraja over trade routes.

Today most Torajan coffee is certified organic and produced by indigenous farmers: the volcanic soil, relatively cool climate and altitude (1400m to 1900m) is perfect for premium arabica production. Coffee from the cooperative Petani Kopi Organik Toraja (Toraja Coffee Farmers' Association) has fair-trade certification. The **Toraja Coffee Festival** is held in August.

Beyond Tana Toraja

It's a long way to anywhere from Tana Toraja, but most brave the slow road trip north through Central Sulawesi towards the Togean Islands.

Places

Central Sulawesi is a vast mountainous region that was almost abandoned by tourism due to a period of religious violence in the early 2000s, but is now regularly and safely traversed by travellers heading between Tana Toraja and the Togean Islands.

A stop on the shores of Danau Poso is more or less mandatory to break up the long bus or taxi ride to Ampana, Poso or Palu. Tranquil Tentena is more than just a stopover, though – it's the easiest place to arrange treks into the Lore Lindu National Park or Bada Valley, with their mysterious megaliths and wildlife-rich jungle. Southeast of Tana Toraja, on the long road to Bira, Sengkang is the halfway mark and jumping-off point for Danau Tempe.

GETTING AROUND

Most travellers pass through Central Sulawesi by bus or taxi from Toraja to Ampana via Tentena. Expect to pay 2,000,000Rp to charter a car between Rantepao and Tentena (10 to 12 hours). Palu-bound buses will drop you on the outskirts of Tentena, usually late at night, then continue on to Poso. An alternative is to backtrack to Makassar and fly to Luwuk (for Togeans) or Gorontalo or Manado.

Sengkang & Danau Tempe

TIME FROM TANA TORAJA: **6HR**

Silk-weaving villages

Roughly halfway between Bira and Tana Toraja, **Sengkang** is often used as a stopover by overlanding travellers. The lakeside town is known for its *sutera* (silk) weaving, and you can see the process at dozens of workshops in town and in the surrounding villages – listen out for the clacking of wooden handlooms down back streets. Showrooms in town have the finished product on display in everything from sarongs and head scarves to wedding outfits. The nearest silkworm farms are about 15km from Sengkang. Hotels can organise trips, or you can charter a *pete-pete*.

Stay in a floating house

A highlight of overnighting in this region is staying in a floating house on **Danau Tempe**, a large, shallow lake – the second-largest in Sulawesi after Poso – fringed by wetlands and fishing villages. More than 30 floating houses sit close to shore at the southern end of the lake across from land-based village **Salotenga**.

Hotels and guides can help charter a boat (200,000Rp for two hours), allowing you to speed along Sungai Walanae and visit the floating village for *kopi* (coffee) and *pisang goreng* (banana fritters), but a much better experience is to book a night at the **floating homestay** *(450,000Rp, incl meals and boat transport)*. The 'house' is basically a shack on a bamboo raft where you'll sleep on a mattress with mosquito net, but don't expect luxuries like plumbing or electricity. Wake at dawn to the sound of birds and, inevitably, roosters, then breakfast with the family and sunrise over the lake.

Tentena

TIME FROM TANA TORAJA: **6-12HR**

Danau Poso stopover

Tentena, a full-day drive from Tana Toraja, is an engaging little town at the northern end of Danau Poso, Indonesia's third-deepest lake, where it drains into the mouth of the Sungai Poso. Along with some good budget places to stay, Tentena is an excellent base for trips to the megaliths of Bada Valley and Lore Lindu National Park. You can also visit the fabulous multi-tiered waterfall **Air Terjun Saluopa** *(20,000Rp)*, which cascades down through the rainforest 15km west of Tentena. Local guides can take you deeper into the forest to spot tarsiers after dark.

In town is a photogenic 210m covered **bridge** across the Sungai Poso, from where you can view the V-shaped bamboo **eel traps** that snare the 2m giant eels for which the town is famous.

An alternative stopover is **Pendolo** at the southern end of the lake (and thus a couple of hours closer to Rantepao). There are some white-sand beaches and a few guesthouses, and it's usually possible to charter a fishing boat here to take you across the lake – even as far as Tentena.

Bada Valley

TIME FROM TENTENA: **4HR**

Discover ancient megaliths

Seemingly scattered haphazardly in the hills and valleys around the remote Lore Lindu National Park, the 400 or so ancient stone megaliths of unknown origin are estimated by some experts to be over 5000 years old. With the help of a guide/driver you can find a strange assortment of them in Bada Valley, 60km west of Tentena, including the striking 4m-tall leaning **Palindo**.

The origins of these Bronze Age megaliths are shrouded in mystery. The highest concentration is along Sungai Lariang in the Bada Valley, but there are others throughout the region, down to Tana Toraja in South Sulawesi. While you can see many of the statues in one long day from Tentena, several villages have homestays or guesthouses, including Bomba, Gintu and Tuare. To add even more adventure to your visit, consider a two-day trek over the mountains through the national park to **Behoa**, where even more megaliths are found (as well as onward transport to Palu or Poso).

WHY THE FLOATING HOUSES?

Danau Tempe's floating houses *(bola mawang)* and villages are unusual in Sulawesi and date back through several generations of fishing families likely descended from Buginese sailors. Many Southeast Asian fishing communities, including the Bajau, traditionally built their houses on stilts but the lake's changing nature meant the floating raft-like houses were more adaptable. When the water levels were high, families would stay close to the shore, houses tethered to a pole, while fishing and also farming on nearby land. When the lake lowered in the dry, the houses would float into the middle for the best fishing opportunities. The rafts use a basic rectangular layout with open bamboo decks for drying fish and socialising, and an enclosed 'house' for sleeping and family gatherings with a separate kitchen area.

RELIGIOUS TROUBLES

Central Sulawesi went through a dark period of Christian versus Muslim violence following the fall of President Suharto in 1998, leading to almost a decade where the region – particularly Tentena and Poso – was largely off limits to tourists.

It's still not clear what caused these communities to start fighting each other after generations of living peacefully together. An influx of Muslim immigrants from Java, under the transmigration program, abruptly shifted the balance of power in the region, but probably the biggest factors were the power vacuum resulting from Suharto's fall and the incendiary impact of extremist militias.

Today the region is peaceful again and Tentena is a popular tourist stopover between Toraja and Togean.

KHOLIK HANAFI/SHUTTERSTOCK

Megaliths, Lore Lindu National Park

The valley around Bariri village is abundant with megalithic objects, including statues of human forms as well as massive *kalamba* (stone pots) and *tutu'na* (stone lids). Trekking from here to Bada Valley (or vice versa) is possible and popular with adventure travellers – guides can be found locally or in Tentena or Palu.

Lore Lindu National Park

TIME FROM TENTENA: **4HR**

Wildlife and megaliths

The 2500-sq-km **Lore Lindu National Park** *(per person per day 150,000Rp plus guide fees)*, a UNESCO Biosphere Reserve, is barely touched by tourism and harbours tarsiers, hornbills and pygmy buffalo, among other wildlife. For national park trekking, a guide is compulsory and also necessary if you're intent on finding the megaliths. A full-day tour from Tentena with a guide and vehicle (for up to four people) costs about 2,500,000Rp. The guides in Tentena generally speak decent English and the trip will usually include a lunch stop at a family home.

If travelling independently, arrange a guide at Wuasa, Bomba, Badu or at the tourist office or national park office in Palu. Guides start at 250,000Rp for day trips, more for trekking; few speak much English.

EATING IN TENTENA: OUR PICKS

Ongga Bale: The tables on the riverbank are the main draw at this chicken-and-fish restaurant, and the food is fresh. *10am-11pm* $

Kayaku Foodshop: For some of the best *mie goreng* and nasi goreng in town try this little diner. *9am-8pm Mon-Sat* $

Dolidi Ndano Towale: There's a fine restaurant at this lakeside cottage resort 6km south of town. *8am-10pm* $$

Bukit Pamona: On the west side of the river it's hard to miss this elevated restaurant, serving all manner of Indonesian dishes with a view. *9am-9pm* $$

Togean Islands

ISLAND-HOPPING | BEACHES | DIVING & SNORKELLING

Swimming in the vast Gulf of Tomini that separates Central and North Sulawesi, the remote Togean Islands take a bit of work to get to, but they're oh so hard to leave. There's no airport here. There are no ATMs, little mobile-phone or wi-fi reception and no cars. Electricity is limited to generators and fresh water is a precious commodity. There's just a string of castaway islands, Bajau villages, gorgeous deserted golden beaches, crystal-clear bath-like water and hammocks swinging from verandas at secluded sea-front bungalows.

Then there's the rich diversity of marine life and astonishing coral formations that attract divers and snorkellers to the marine national park, with numerous dive resorts offering courses and recreational dives.

Getting here by boat from Ampana or Gorontalo is half the fun, but planning and flexibility are the keys to a successful Togean trip. And perhaps plan to stay a bit longer than you expected.

GETTING AROUND

The Togeans are reached by the fast boat from Ampana to Wakai (1½ hours), the overnight ferry from Gorontalo to Wakai (13 hours) or the slow public ferry from Ampana to Malenge (there are no stops at Kadidiri or Una Una). Private boat charters are pricey but easy to arrange on the main islands and your accommodation will usually arrange pickup from Wakai with advance notice. From Wakai by local boat it's 30 minutes to Kadidiri and two hours to Pulau Una Una. For more information see p628.

TOP TIP

Bring cash as there are no ATMs, though most resorts now accept credit card if they have a wi-fi connection. There's a one-time national park entrance fee (150,000Rp per foreigner), payable at the dock in Ampana or at Wakai if you're coming from Gorontalo.

Diving & Snorkelling

Atolls and reefs

The Togeans are the only place in Indonesia where you can find all three major reef environments – atoll, barrier and fringing reefs – in one location. Two atolls and their deep lagoons lie to the northwest of Pulau Batu Daka. **Barrier reefs** surround many islands at the 200m-depth contour (5km to 15km offshore), and **fringing reefs** surround all of the coasts, merging with sea grass and mangroves. There is also a well-preserved sunken WWII **B-24 bomber** (at a depth of between 14m and 22m). The **reefs** off volcanic Una Una offer some of the best visibility and most reliable diving in the islands.

Dynamite and cyanide fishing have damaged some reefs in the past but the marine park is protected and recovery is well underway, and many others remain untouched. Highlights

Continues on p625

HELP ME PICK:

Togean Island-Hopping

The biggest decision for most travellers to the Togeans is which island to stay on. Wherever you choose, it's easy enough (though not cheap) to charter a boat to hop between islands or, with more time, to use the public ferry.

Where to Go if You Love...

Diving & Snorkelling

Dedicated dive resorts are concentrated around the premier dive sites of Una Una, Kadidiri and Bomba.

Kadidiri Paradise Resort *(kadidiriparadise.com)* Togean's original dive resort and still one of the best.

Black Marlin Dive Resort *(blackmarlindiving.com)* Long-running PADI dive resort on the next beach across from Kadidiri Paradise.

Pristine Paradise Dive Resort *(pristine-paradise.com)* On volcanic Pulau Una Una, Pristine has a good dive school and satellite wi-fi.

Sanctum *(sanctumdiveunauna.com)* Pulau Una Una's original dive resort has all the facilities, pool, wi-fi and seafront bungalows.

Sera Beach Dive Resort *(serabeachdiveresort.com)* Occupying prime beachfront on Malenge, where you can snorkel on the house reef.

Araya Dive Resort *(arayadiveresort.com)* At Bomba, this boutique resort is the closest base for diving to the mainland and offers PADI courses.

Somewhere Easy to Access

Bomba, on the western tip of Pulau Batu Daka, is the first place you'll reach by ferry or speedboat from Ampana, so it's popular and convenient for short-stay travellers.

Poya Lisa Cottages *(poyalisa-bomba.com)* On its own narrow private island, this little paradise has two perfect beaches.

Poki Poki *(pokipoki.land)* On a sandy beach on Batu Daka's southwestern coast, with cosy wood-and-bamboo bungalows.

Island Retreat You can wave to passing ferries from your cottage on the beach at this popular place.

A Bit of Luxury

Harmony Bay Kadidiri *(hb-resort.com)* The most secluded and upmarket of Kadidiri's resorts, with stylish beachfront bungalows, excellent meals, yoga and a dive centre.

Bahia Tomini *(bahiatomini.com)* Facing a secluded Malenge beach, this wonderful castaway location features four beautifully created sea-facing wooden bungalows.

The Cliff *(theclifftogean.com)* Spectacularly located atop a Malenge cliff above Sera Beach, this is a full-service dive resort with king-size beds and wi-fi.

Remote Island Culture

Bolilanga Cottages *(bolilangaresort.com)* On a tiny speck of a white-sand-beach isle facing Katupat village, this family-run place is a slice of true tranquillity.

Fadhila Cottages *(fadhilacottage.com)* Wooden bungalows with terraces and hammocks line a palm-shaded beach facing either Katupat village or the ocean.

Sandy Bay Resort *(sandybay-resort.com)* Wooden bungalows with picture windows look out on a long, palm-fringed, sandy beach on Malenge island.

FROM LEFT: PAUL HARDING/LONELY PLANET, PAUL HARDING/LONELY PLANET

Left: Ampana-Gorontalo ferry; Above: Kadidiri Paradise Resort

HOW TO

When to go The dry months of April–October are the best time to visit. November–March sees fewer visitors and more rain, though ferry schedules are rarely affected.

Booking ahead While walk-ins (or sail-ins) may be possible, it's wise to book accommodation in advance or risk being stranded. Most places have websites and some are on booking sites.

Stay connected Phone reception (4G) works around the settlements of Wakai, Bomba and Katupat but it's patchy elsewhere. Most resorts offer satellite wi-fi.

Budgeting Resorts or homestays usually include three meals and charge per person for rooms. There are no ATMs beyond Ampana. Budget for boat trips and bring plenty of cash.

Togean Transport: Getting There & Around

The nearest useful airport is at Luwuk, with daily flights from Makassar. It's a five-hour car ride to/from Ampana. There's a small airport in Ampana that was receiving twice-weekly Susi Air flights from Palu when we visited but this could change. Gorontalo also has direct flights to Makassar and twice-weekly Susi Air flights to Manado.

Ampana is five to six hours by taxi (chartered or shared) from either Tentena or Luwuk. Public buses to Tentena or further south go via Poso (originating in Palu). It's a 20-hour journey if you want to get all the way from Ampana to Tana Toraja – our tip is to overnight in Tentena.

The 'fast' Hercules boat departs from Ampana to Wakai (1½ hours, 160,000Rp) via Bomba (one hour) daily at 9am, returning at 1pm (book ahead). The Ampana–Malenge slow public ferry (130,000Rp) takes all day to cover the journey, leaving Ampana at 10am on Monday, Wednesday and Saturday, returning from Pulau Papan on Tuesday, Thursday and Sunday. Boats meet passengers in Wakai and any homestay can arrange a boat with a day's notice (around 500,000Rp from Wakai to Kadidiri to Bomba or 1,200,000Rp for a full day trip). For more info see 3rhomestay.com/info-togian-islands.

A ferry departs twice a week between Gorontalo and Ampana/Wakai (see p628).

SIGHTS
1 Danau Mariona
2 Gunung Colo
3 Kabalutan
see 1 Karina Beach
4 Pulau Papan
5 Pulau Tangkian

SLEEPING
6 Araya Dive Resort
7 Bahia Tomini
8 Black Marlin Dive Resort
9 Bolilanga Cottages
10 Fadhila Cottages
see 8 Harmony Bay Kadidiri
11 Island Retreat
see 8 Kadidiri Paradise Resort
12 Poki Poki
see 6 Poya Lisa Cottages
13 Pristine Paradise Dive Resort
14 Reconnect Island Resort
see 13 Sanctum
see 7 Sandy Bay Resort
see 7 Sera Beach Dive Resort
see 7 The Cliff

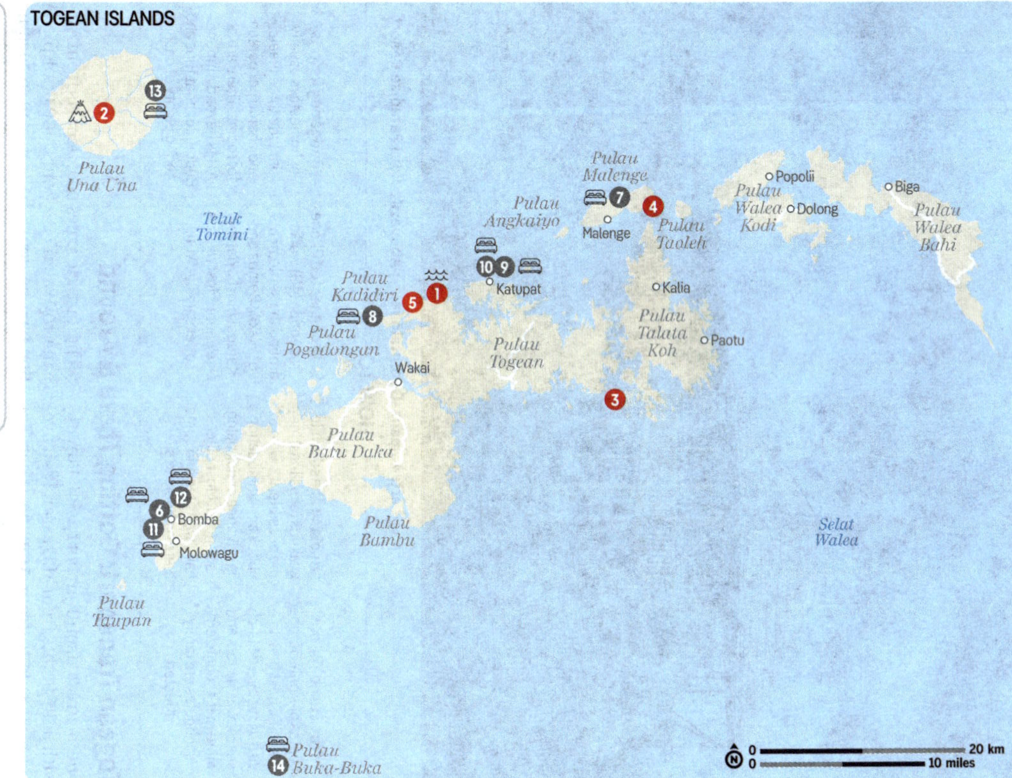

Continued from p621
include spectacular open-water topography, with coral canyons, plunging drop-offs, weird and wonderful pipe sponges and some truly giant gorgonian corals. Reefs teem with hundreds of species of tropical fish and macro life, including seahorses, painted frogfish and leaf scorpionfish.

For snorkellers, many islands have reefs accessible right off the beach, and some resorts claim their own house reef.

Visit Bajau Villages

Meet the sea gypsies

Nomadic Bajau (also spelt Bajo) 'sea gypsies' still dive for trepang (sea cucumber), pearls and spear fish, as they have done for hundreds, perhaps thousands, of years. The Bajau are historically hunter-gatherers who spend much of their lives on boats, travelling as family groups.

There are now several permanent Bajau settlements around the Togean Islands, and even some stilt villages on offshore reefs, but the itinerant character of Bajau culture survives. Newlyweds are put in a canoe and pushed out to sea to make their place in the world. When they have children, fathers dive with their three-day-old babies to introduce them to life on the sea. It's said the Bajau swim before they can walk and have a lung capacity greater than normal.

The easiest places to see and experience modern Bajau life are at the settlements on Palau Papan and Pulau Tangkian. **Pulau Papan** is famously connected to the eastern end of Malenge by a 1km-long wooden bridge (that's increasingly in need of repair). There's good snorkelling and corals around the bridge pylons. The stilt village is built on and around a rocky islet with a mosque, a couple of stores and even a small overwater resort. Smaller **Pulau Tangkian**, between Kadidiri and the Jellyfish Lake, has a fishing village and is the easiest to reach on the west side of the Togeans.

Kabalutan, part of the remote Kepulauan Kabalutan archipelago off the southern side of Togean Island, is one of the largest Bajau settlements, a tightly packed community of stilt houses linked by boardwalks with a local school, cottage industries and the community volleyball court. It's possible to arrange basic homestay accommodation here to really immerse yourself in Bajau life. Although the location's remote, a public boat between Ampana and Papan stops here on Monday, Wednesday and Saturday or you can charter a boat from Wakai for 500,000Rp.

Swim with the Jellyfish

Stinger-free lake

Danau Mariona *(25,000Rp)*, better known locally as Jellyfish Lake ('Danau Ubur Ubur'), is roughly halfway between Kadidiri and Katupat and is a popular trip where you can swim and snorkel with bright-orange stinger-free jellyfish – one of only a handful of places in the world where this is possible.

WHY I LOVE THE TOGEAN ISLANDS

Paul Harding, Lonely Planet writer

There's always a frisson of excitement when I board the fast boat at Ampana or slow boat from Gorontalo en route to the Togean Islands. It's usually the culmination of a long and tiring overland journey and it's a relief to relax as the boat threads its way through the island chain. The Togeans are one of those remote island destinations where the joy is in simply hanging out on the beach at a basic but somehow luxurious-feeling family resort. Communal meals with fellow travellers and new friends are a highlight. Diving, snorkelling, visiting Bajau villages are all bonuses but I just love the serenity.

TOGEAN MEALS

Apart from a few warungs (food stalls) around the harbour at Wakai or on Pulau Papan, there are no independent restaurants of note on the Togeans – everyone dines at their guesthouse or resort, with three daily meals included in the accommodation price. For this reason, most accommodation places charge per person, not per room, so check when booking to avoid a nasty surprise! Note that some resorts charge extra for meals if you book through a third-party online source, so again check the details. Meals are usually a communal affair of rice, fish or chicken and some vegetable sides, but variations such as pizza and pasta are common. Some resorts have a bar, but most can at least provide cold beer, snacks and free tea and coffee.

PAUL HARDING/LONELY PLANET

Pulau Papan (p625)

Local boats will take you to the main jetty from where you can walk through to the lake itself; there's a floating rubber pontoon with ladders to access the water (don't jump in as the jellyfish could be anywhere). Often the jellyfish are swimming around right next to the pontoon so you won't have to swim far. Most are only about the size of a fist, some as small as a thumb, but they're fascinating to watch and commune with. The jellyfish are harmless but avoid touching these fragile creatures (for their sake) and don't swim with fins.

Trips to the lake often include a stop for snorkelling at nearby **Karina Beach**, a delightful little sandy cove with some decent coral and marine life in shallow water starting about 20m off the beach.

Volcanic Una Una

Climbing and diving

Pulau Una Una is visible from a distance thanks to towering, active **Gunung Colo** (506m), which erupted in 1983, covering 90% of the island in ash and destroying all its houses and crops. Residents were safely evacuated, and many have since returned. You can climb to the crater rim on a half-day guided tour from the island resorts, which starts with a beach ride or drive to the trailhead, then a walk up through steaming vents, fumaroles and lava flows.

The offshore reefs at Una Una offer the best diving in the Togeans, with schooling barracudas, Napoleon wrasse, packs of jacks and large rays, as well as giant tubular pipe sponges. **Sanctum** (p622) and Pristine Paradise (p622) are two of the best dive resorts in the Togeans.

Beyond Togean Islands

Ampana, Gorontalo and Luwuk are key entry points to the Togean Islands and they're part of the adventure.

The journey between Central and North Sulawesi is a challenging and very long one by road – Ampana to Gorontalo is about 850km and roughly 20 hours straight along the shortest coastal road via Palu. This makes the Ampana–Gorontalo ferry, connecting the Togean Islands from the south and north, vital to overland travellers.

Places

Ampana

TIME FROM TOGEAN ISLANDS: **2-4HR**

Gateway to the Togeans

Ampana is the main gateway to the Togean Islands. It's far enough by road from the nearest major towns, such as Poso (four hours), Tentena (five hours) and Luwuk (five hours), that most travellers spend at least one night here. There's not a lot to see or do, apart from a busy market and some black-sand beaches, but Ampana is laid-back with some good accommodation choices catering to Togean-bound travellers. For up-to-date info on the islands and transport to/from Ampana, contact Dadang at Triple R Homestay (p639; he maintains the excellent website 3rhomestay.com/info-togian-islands) or Edy at Marina Cottages (p638). There's a tourist information office of sorts at the harbour but it's only open in the morning prior to the departure of boats to the Togeans; this is where you register and pay the national park fee (150,000Rp).

Gorontalo

TIME FROM TOGEAN ISLANDS: **13HR**

Swim with whale sharks

Gorontalo, the northern gateway to the Togeans, has some well-preserved Dutch houses but for most travellers it's a transit point between the Togeans and Manado or Makassar thanks to the overnight ferry. The other big attraction is seeing the whale sharks that come astonishingly close to shore almost year-round.

Whale sharks migrate to the Gulf of Tomini and hang around at **Botubarani** *(50,000Rp, plus 100,000Rp boat charge)*, 10km southeast of Gorontalo city, between June and September or later, as they're accustomed to being fed here. Many travellers

GETTING AROUND

There are daily shared minibuses between Ampana and Luwuk or Poso. Between Tentena and Ampana you'll need to charter a taxi. In Ampana and Gorontalo, harbourside motorcycle becaks *(bentor)* can take you to your accommodation. From Gorontalo there are daily flights to Makassar and twice-weekly Susi Air direct flights to Manado; minibuses and shared taxis to Manado take 10 hours.

THE GORONTALO FERRY

The 13-hour overnight ferry between Gorontalo and Wakai/Ampana in the Togeans operates twice a week so plan ahead. At the time of writing, the KM *Tuna Tomini* left Gorontalo heading to Wakai and Ampana at 5pm on Tuesday and Friday, returning to Gorontalo from Wakai on Monday and Thursday at 4pm.

The ferry has economy and business (air-conditioned) classes with seating (63,000/89,0000Rp). You can reserve a tatami mattress to sleep on. There are limited cabins that you may be able to upgrade to (600,000Rp) when buying your ticket or try to book in advance through your accommodation. Once on board, the ferry crew will often sell foreigners a bed in their cabin. There's an upper-deck snack kiosk, tables, a few airline-style seats and a kids' play area.

question the ethics of this operation but there are no nets here and the sharks are free to come and go. A prawn factory initially attracted the whale sharks and they're now fed prawns by boat captains, which keeps them coming back, but the government regulates activity to protect the great fish, limiting the numbers of boats or swimmers. Whatever your view, being able to swim with these magnificent, harmless creatures is a humbling experience and one of Sulawesi's most extraordinary wildlife encounters.

Luwuk & the Banggai Islands

TIME FROM AMPANA: **5HR**

Luwuk is a tumbledown port city on Central Sulawesi's remote eastern peninsula that has become a popular stepping stone to the Togean Islands thanks to its airport with direct daily flights from Makassar. It's a five-hour shared or chartered taxi ride to Ampana. It's also the harbour for boats to the Banggai Islands – a once-forgotten adventure that's back on the traveller to-do list.

Pristine lake and beach

Peleng is a large island in the Banggais, easily reached by daily ferry from Luwuk and home to an extraordinarily beautiful lake and some dreamy, deserted beaches. Although the main town is Salakan, most travellers are destined for the much closer Leme Leme port, just two hours away by **public ferry** *(54,0000Rp)*, departing from **Luwuk** at 2pm (returning around 10am). The star attraction here is **Danau Paisu Pok** *(5000Rp)*, an achingly beautiful lake in a bowl of rainforest just a five-minute walk from Lukpanenteng village, itself a half-hour taxi or motorbike ride north of Leme Leme. The deceptively deep water is incredibly clear – hire a snorkel and fins to the explore. You can also hire canoes, stand-up paddleboards and rubber tubes.

Also in Lukpanenteng is the smaller but no less photogenic spring-fed lagoon **Paisu Batango**. About 10km west of Lukpanenteng (the turn-off is clearly signposted) is **Pantai Poganda** *(10,000Rp)*, a beautiful stretch of palm-fringed sand abutting a dilapidated fishing village. A cafe here serves nasi goreng and fresh green coconuts.

There are a couple of budget homestays in Leme Leme (**Novpitri** is recommended) and Lukpanenteng (**Homestay Lukpanenteng 2** is closest to the lake). You can hire a motorbike or arrange a car and driver in Leme Leme.

EATING IN AMPANA: OUR PICKS

Warung Pangkep: Fish is grilled to perfection on barbecues out front of this local favourite; good *coto Makassar* (spicy beef soup) also. *8am-10pm* $

Marina Cottages: On the beach about 3km northeast of the harbour, this breezy, open-sided restaurant is a relaxing place for nasi goreng and cold beer. *7am-10pm* $

Triple R Cafe: Laid-back cafe at the homestay (p639) of the same name. Run by Dadang, it's a mine of Togean info and has a great traveller vibe. *7am-10pm* $

Lawaka Coffee: At the same-named hotel, this open-air cafe-restaurant offers a touch of style, with standard Indonesian fare. *8am-9pm* $$

Manado & Pulau Bunaken

FOOD & NIGHTLIFE | DIVING & SNORKELLING | ISLAND LIFE

Sulawesi's northern province covers a huge swathe of land but, for most travellers, it can be boiled down to the relatively small area in the far northeastern tip and the islands and reefs offshore. At the hub of this region is Manado, the prosperous coastal capital of North Sulawesi and Sulawesi's second city. Manado is a gateway by air and sea and the jumping-off point for Pulau Bunaken and its sister islands. A night in a comfy hotel, a bit of boutique shopping and exploring the city's decent collection of restaurants and rare Sulawesian nightlife may be on the cards before you disappear to the islands or highlands.

Christianity is the dominant religion (malls start selling Christmas decorations as early as October!) and the Dutch influence is stronger here than anywhere else in the country.

TOP TIP

The Zero Point monument is a city-centre landmark in Manado where *mikrolet* (small taxis) gather. From here it's about 700m north to the public ferry to Bunaken. South of here are the city's two main thoroughfares (one-way in each direction) and a string of shopping malls.

Spicy Cuisine & Nightlife

Bright lights of Manado

Manado's urban charms are hard to uncover, with few obvious sights and not much standout architecture other than a number of churches and the 19th-century **Kienteng Ban Hian Kong**, the oldest Buddhist temple in eastern Indonesia. The **Museum of North Sulawesi** *(5000Rp)*, closed Sundays,

GETTING AROUND

Manado's *mikrolet* (small taxis; 5000Rp) are everywhere. Those with 'Wanea' on the window sign heading south on Jl Sam Ratulangi will go to Terminal Karombasan. Grab rideshare works well in Manado and drivers will take you as far as Tomohon or Tangkoko. For a traditional taxi, call Bluebird.

A public boat (50,000Rp, one hour) leaves daily (except Sunday) at 2pm for Bunaken village from Manado's Dermaga Kalimas. They return at around 8am to 9am the next day. Smaller speedboats leave throughout the day, ferrying guests to accommodation on the islands, and will happily take you if there's room (usually around 100,000Rp, 30 minutes).

SIGHTS
1 Kienteng Ban Hian Kong
2 Museum of North Sulawesi

SLEEPING
3 4 Sisters Homestay
4 Aston Manado
5 Bastianos Bunaken Dive Resort
6 Bunaken Oasis
see 6 Happy Gecko
7 Hotel Minahasa
8 Ibis City Center Boulevard
9 Manado Green Hostel
10 Panorama Backpackers
11 Panorama Dive Resort
12 Two Fish

EATING
13 Carpe Diem
14 Deep Sea Tuna House
15 Raja Sate

DRINKING & NIGHTLIFE
16 Daebaq Resto & Korean Bar

SHOPPING
17 Manado Town Square

TRANSPORT
18 Majestic Kawanua

is worth a quick look for its extensive display of Minahasan, colonial and seafaring culture, and just to brighten the day of the staff.

The downtown waterfront boulevard is one nearly continuous shopping mall providing respite from the heat and an opportunity for some air-con retail therapy, with boutique shops, food courts and young Manado locals hanging out. One of the largest places is **Manado Town Square**, with a soaring arched ceiling painted as a cloud-filled sky.

Manado has some of the only noticeable nightlife in Sulawesi, of varying quality, with karaoke bars, beer bars and nightclubs with DJs playing into the early hours clustered around the waterfront on or just off Jl Laksda John Lie. There's a good range of restaurants serving spicy Minahasan cuisine such as *ayam rica-rica* (chicken with local spices) and *tinutuan* (Manado 'porridge'), a local breakfast rice dish. Jl Wakeke is a back street known for its street food.

Island Life

Dive into Bunaken

Tiny, coral-fringed **Pulau Bunaken**, less than an hour by boat from Manado, is North Sulawesi's top tourist draw for divers and snorkellers, but it retains a laid-back island soul and is certainly not overdeveloped. The majority of the island population lives in ramshackle Bunaken village at the southern end of the island, where boats dock and local homestays welcome budget travellers, while dive-oriented resorts are spread out along two beaches on either side of the island.

The island is part of the 891-sq-km **Bunaken Manado Tua Marine National Park** (Taman Laut Bunaken Manado Tua), which includes Manado Tua (Old Manado) and **Pulau Siladen**, which also has a few fine dive resorts. **Manado Tua** is a beautiful volcanic cone with some interesting **hiking**, including a steep marked route to the summit at 800m. Guides can be found on the island or see gunungbagging.com/manado-tua for information. Outrigger fishing boats to shuttle you to Manado Tua can be arranged through your accommodation or from the beach at Bunaken village.

Bunaken can be reached by public ferry (50,000Rp, daily except Sunday), departing from the main harbour at around 2pm. Alternatively, arrange a boat pickup with your accommodation, which may be from **Bahowo Mangrove Park**, the closest mainland point to Bunaken but a half-hour taxi ride north of Manado harbour.

ISLANDS PRESERVED

Divers looking to go beyond Bunaken can try the larger Bangka Islands to the northeast, reached from the mainland town of Likupang. Bangka was the scene of a controversial mining development bid in 2012, but a local environmental campaign was eventually successful in the courts and the permit was revoked. There are several dive resorts, including **Bastianos Bangka** and **Mimpi Indah** on the main island of Bangka and **Blue Bay Divers** on Pulau Sahaung.

If you really want to go remote, the volcanic islands of Sangihe-Talaud are strung out in the Celebes Sea between two and six hours by boat north of Manado. **Majestic Kawanua** *(majestickawanua.com)* has fast ferries from Manado to the main islands daily.

EATING & DRINKING IN MANADO: OUR PICKS

Raja Sate: Rightly renowned for its *sate* – you can't go wrong with a mixed plate that includes prawns, squid, chicken, beef and goat. *11am-3pm & 5-10pm Mon-Sat* $

Carpe Diem: Stylish modern restaurant with a broad menu of Indonesian and international dishes. Cocktail bar and live music on weekends. *11.30am-midnight* $$

Deep Sea Tuna House: Of the *ikan bakar* (grilled fish) huts popular along this stretch of the waterfront, this place is a favourite and is reliably fresh. *10am-11pm* $

Daebaq Resto & Korean Bar: This waterside rooftop bar and restaurant is perfect for watching the sunset with a Korean barbecue and Indo pop. *2-10pm* $$

TOP EXPERIENCE

Diving Bunaken & Siladen

Diving and snorkelling are the top draws for travellers to Bunaken and Siladen thanks to deep waters close to shore, dramatic vertical wall drop-offs and strong, nutrient-laden currents. Protected as a marine national park since 1991, the top dive sites and preserved coral ecosystem are easily explored given their proximity to land and the numerous experienced dive operators based here.

AL CARRERA/SHUTTERSTOCK

Biodiversity in Pulau Bunaken

TOP TIPS

- Boat dives cost from 500,000Rp with full equipment, and PADI courses are also available. Snorkellers can go along with the dive boats for around 100,000Rp per person.
- Diving on the east or west side of Bunaken will depend on where you're staying, and on currents and prevailing weather conditions.

PRACTICALITIES

- 150,000Rp national park fee for foreigners (usually collected by dive operators or your accommodation)

Dive Sites

The biodiversity in the marine park is extraordinary, with more than 300 types of coral and 3000 species of fish, caves and valleys full of brightly coloured sponges and large hawksbill and green turtles.

Likuan is a remarkable coral wall with three popular dive sites just south of Pantai Liang. Reef sharks and turtles are typically encountered. **Fukui Point** and **Mandolin** are outstanding for the numbers of fish, huge gorgonians and a forest of whip corals.

On the northern side, **Sachiko' Point** is a stunning wall dive with mild currents. Close to the mainland, **Molas Wreck** is a huge Dutch cargo ship sitting in 32m to 40m of water; for advanced divers only. On the northern side of Manado Tua, **Tanjung Kopi** entices with schools of barracudas, batfish and jacks; this is another advanced dive, due to strong currents.

Dive Resorts

- **Bunaken Oasis** *(bunakenoasis.com)* The most upmarket of Bunaken's resorts.
- **Bastianos Bunaken Dive Resort** *(bastianos.com)* High-quality dive outfit and boutique resort.
- **Panorama Dive Resort** and **Panorama Backpackers** *(bunakendiving.co)* Recommended family-run place.
- **Siladen Resort & Spa** *(siladen.com)* Top place on Siladen.
- **Two Fish** *(twofishdivers.com)* Top resort on Bunaken's east coast.

Beyond Manado & Pulau Bunaken

Pulau Bunaken
Tangkoko-Batuangas Dua Saudara Nature Reserve
Manado
Bitung
Pulau Lembeh
Tomohon
Tondano

Strike out into the Minahasa Highlands for trekking, volcano climbs and wildlife adventures.

There's plenty to see and do within easy reach of Manado, so don't be afraid to head inland from the coast. The highland region around Tomohon is speckled with photogenic, climbable volcanoes, lakes and rice paddies, and the Minahasan culture is on full display in Sunday church choirs, flower gardens and the stomach-churning 'extreme' meat market.

On the other side of the peninsula is Tangkoko, where the lowland nature reserve hugs the black-sand coast at Batuputih and harbours an astonishing range of birdlife and animals. The main industrial port town on this side, Bitung is the jumping-off point for Pulau Lembeh and the world-class muck diving in the Lembeh Strait.

Places

Tomohon

TIME FROM MANADO: **1HR**

Volcanic highs

The towering volcanic peaks of Gunung Mahawu and Gunung Lokon overlook Tomohon and, although notionally active, the craters can safely be climbed most of the time – ask locally about conditions and recent activity. **Gunung Mahawu** (1320m) is the easiest to summit, as you can drive almost all the way to the top, with steps to make the final five-minute ascent. An overgrown trail takes you around the 140m-deep crater in less than an hour, with fine views of Lokon, Tomohon and all the way out to Manado and Bunaken.

The perfect cone of **Gunung Lokon** (1580m) is visible from many parts of Tomohon. It's part of a twin volcano with Gunung Empung and the active crater Tompaluan in between. The standard hike goes to the crater rim and takes about an hour each way (not to the actual Lokon peak), starting just past Taman Wisata Pelangi viewpoint on the east side of the mountain, about 3km west of central Tomohon. Although you don't need a guide for this trek, check conditions before setting out and don't hike alone.

GETTING AROUND

Taxis (including Grab) will drive you from Manado to Tomohon (one hour), Tangkoko or Bitung (both two hours). *Pete-pete* (minivans) run regularly to Tomohon (30,000Rp), while buses and shared taxis operate to Bitung. Hotels and resorts in Tomohon rent out motorbikes for around 150,000Rp a day including fuel – a great way to explore the area. Boats to Lembeh can be chartered from near the ferry port or arranged through your dive-resort accommodation.

FULL BLOOM

Tomohon is known as the 'City of Flowers', with its highland winter climate ideal for flower gardens producing *krisan* (chrysanthemums), asters, marigolds and orchids, among others.

The **Tomohon International Flower Festival** (TIFF), held in early August, is one of the biggest community festivals in Sulawesi. As well as flower vendors and homes decked out with colourful blooms and garlands, there are food stalls, music and festivities over four days. The highlight is the street parade, where elaborate floats decorated with millions of fresh flowers wind down the main street of Jl Raya Tomohon, many of the floats celebrating a different country or culture. Book accommodation well in advance or brave the traffic and take a day trip from Manado.

PAUL HARDING/LONELY PLANET

For fine views of Lokon and the surrounding villages and ricefields, head to the hilltop **Kai'Santi Flower Garden** *(facebook.com/kaisantiflowergarden; 35,000Rp)* about 6km southwest of central Tomohon. The terraced gardens, decks and seating areas provide a great viewpoint. It's open from 10am to 6pm.

Near Lahendong, **Danau Linow** is a small, highly sulphurous lake that changes colours with the light, and is home to prolific birdlife. You can't swim in the lake but you might be able to hire a kayak from the main landing, while the terrace of the **Danau Linow Resort** is the place for coffee with a view.

Macabre market

Trigger warning! Tomohon's daily morning **meat and produce market** – the one you may have heard stories about – is one of those ghoulish cultural things that some travellers might want to view firsthand, but you wouldn't want to hang around long for. It's said that the Minahasan people will eat anything on four (or two) legs, apart from the table and chairs, and nowhere is this more evident than here. Most of the market is your usual fish, produce and household goods, but the 'extreme' section is devoted to the trade of various meats, such as rats, blowtorched bats and giant pythons, all on display in various states of slaughter or rigor mortis. While locals wander around choosing dinner, the market is likely to distress anyone with a weak stomach or the slightest interest in animal welfare. The trade of dog and cat meat was officially banned here in 2023 but on our latest visit that didn't appear to be the case. It's behind the *mikrolet* terminal on the eastern side of town.

Tomohon and Gunung Lokon (p633)

Record-breaking museum

Although inconveniently located 22km south of Tomohon, **Pa'Dior** *(Museum Pinawetengan; padior.org; 20,000Rp)* is a quirky museum and park that's offbeat enough to warrant the detour if you have your own transport. Where else could you see (and play) the world's largest trumpet, the world's largest *kolintang* (wooden xylophone) and the world's (formerly) longest silk sarong – all confirmed by the *Guinness Book of Records*? The open-air cultural and arts centre, open 9am to 5pm, also features an oddball collection of owls from around the world, a weaving workshop, an anti-narcotics exhibition, traditional Minahasan houses and a botanical garden. It's all the remarkable work of Benny Mamoto, a Java-born police general who is passionate about Minahasa culture and likes creating records – he also has the record for the largest orchestra playing bamboo instruments and the largest seashell ensemble to his name!

Anugerah is a recommended place

EATING & DRINKING IN TOMOHON: OUR PICKS

Kanzo: Cold beer and live music are the big draws at this bamboo hangout on the main drag. There's also a good selection of tasty fried snacks. *11am-11pm* $

Restoran Green Garden Tomohon: Slick Chinese restaurant with specialities such as roast pork and views of Lokon from the upper terrace. *7am-10pm* $$

Onong's Cafe: The laid-back traveller vibe and tasty Indonesian staples make this place a go-to. It's best accessed from the back road behind the guesthouse. *7am-10pm* $

Sate Stalls: Warungs on the main street fire up the charcoal braziers to barbecue delicious chicken, duck and pork *sate* skewers. *hours vary* $

MINAHASAN ADVENTURES

A recommended independent trekking guide is **Jotje Lala** *(WhatsApp +62 895 1550 7588; facebook.com/lovely.sulawesitour).*

Gunung Lokon Crater Hike: Follow an old lava flow to the rim of the crater (two to three hours).

Gunung Soputan Volcano Hike: Walk to the highest peak in North Sulawesi, another active volcano south of Tomohon (full day).

Gunung Klabat Volcano Hike: The ascent takes around five hours; wonderful views of Manado city (two days).

Whitewater Rafting, Sungai Nimanga: Start near Tomohon; 25 rapids, with a good chance of spotting wildlife (half-day).

Tekaan Telu Waterfall: Four separate drops of up to 60m; abseiling and canyoning is also possible (half-day).

Pulau Lembeh

TIME FROM MANADO: **1½HR**

Muck-diving magnet

While the Bunaken marine park is known for its wall dives, coral and turtles, the **Lembeh Strait**, between the industrial port of Bitung and the large island of Pulau Lembeh, is renowned for its muck diving. Scuba diving on the sedimentary bottom in search of macro creatures attracts hardcore underwater photographers searching for the tiny bizarre sea creatures that live here in profound numbers, so the diving is well organised across more than a dozen dive outfits.

As well as nudibranchs and sea slugs, some of the weird macro life you might see in the Lembeh Strait includes the hairy frogfish *(Antennarius striatus)*, the pygmy seahorse *(Hippocampus bargibanti)*, and the mimic octopus *(Thaumoctopus mimicus)*, which can convincingly imitate more than 15 other animals, including sea snakes, crabs, stingrays and jellyfish.

Most of the dive resorts are across water on the western side of Pulau Lembeh. It's easy enough to hire a boat to get across from Bitung, but your accommodation will arrange a pickup with advance notice. The following dive outfits are recommended.

Lembeh Resort *(lembehresort.com)* is a Balinese-style resort with a high level of service and nondive tours on offer. **NAD** *(nad-lembeh.com)* is well set up for dive photography; house reef dives are free. **Bastianos Froggies** *(bastianos.com/bastianos-lembeh)* is a Bunaken outfit established on Lembeh with stylish bungalows and a quality dive centre.

TOP EXPERIENCE

Tangkoko-Batuangas Dua Saudara Nature Reserve

Tiny tarsiers, crested macaques, cute cuscuses and endemic maleo birds can all be spotted on guided walks in the wonderfully accessible Tangkoko-Batuangas Dua Saudara Nature Reserve. Occupying 88 sq km of coastal forest two hours east of Manado, it's one of Sulawesi's most impressive and wildlife-rich nature reserves, and is bordered by black-sand beaches and overlooked by brooding volcanoes.

PAUL HARDING/LONELY PLANET

Spectral tarsiers

Stay the Night

The area of the reserve open to the public is known as the **Tangkoko Batuputih Nature Recreation Park** *(100,000Rp plus guide)*, and, while relatively small, it's big on wildlife experiences and easily reached from Batuputih village. Although long day trips to the park can be arranged from Manado, Tomohon or Bitung, there's a string of good-value guesthouses along the road to Batuputih, all with restaurants, air-con and guides or naturalists, so it's well worth staying overnight here to do both an evening walk and an early morning walk.

What to See

One-hour evening walks will usually reveal spectral tarsiers, tiny nocturnal primates with disproportionately large eyes and long legs and ears. They can be hard to spot in fading light (or darkness) but local guides know where to find them in the hollows of fig trees and most use high-powered telescopes rather than bright torches. Tree-dwelling tarantulas also emerge at night.

On two-hour morning walks you're likely to spot endemic black-crested macaques *(yaki)*, tree-dwelling marsupial cuscuses (often seen high in the forest canopy) and birdlife including maleo birds and red-knobbed hornbills. Bring water as well as a torch for evening walks.

TOP TIPS

- Given the mosquitoes and biting midges *(gonones)*, you'll need long pants, socks, covered shoes and insect repellent.
- Dolphin-spotting, snorkelling, birdwatching and fishing tours can be arranged for Batuputih Beach.
- Birdwatchers will find much to see outside the park, including in mangrove swamps reached by boat.

PRACTICALITIES

- park entry 100,000Rp plus a mandatory local guide (100,000Rp per person per hour)

Places We Love to Stay

$** Budget **$$** Midrange **$$$ Top End

Makassar & Around

MAP p691

Legenda Beril Hostel $ Reliable, long-running backpacker pad with good management in Chinatown, not far from Fort Rotterdam.

D'Prima Pattimurra $$ If you don't need features like a pool or gym, this high-rise near the fort is a bargain for midrange rooms with budget deals – frequented by airline crew.

Ge JacMart $$ Sparkling family-run homestay down a quiet lane near the seafront. The nine spacious 1st-floor rooms are elegant and supremely comfortable.

Swiss-Belhotel Makassar $$ The best of the high-rise midrange hotels with pool and rooftop bar and the only one on the waterfront. Online deals.

Harper Perintis by Aston $$ If you want to be near the airport, this flash Aston hotel is superb value with a fine pool and restaurant. Some promos include free airport transfers (a 15-minute ride).

Rammang Rammang Eco Lodge $$ Right on the river in Rammang Rammang and accessed by boat, the beautifully designed A-frame cottages here are fine places to relax but can get hot without air-con.

Aston Makassar $$$ Top-end stalwart with spacious rooms, pool, gym, sauna and spa and lavish buffet breakfasts – worth a splurge.

Bira Peninsula

MAP p621

Nusa Bira Indah $ Reliable budget bungalows near the end of the road to the beach; basic but with air-con and private bath.

Cosmos Bungalows $$ Rustic-chic, beautifully built bungalows (some with outdoor showers) descend down a narrow strip of land to the coastal cliffs at the north end of Pantai Bara.

Bara Coco $$ Sturdy wooden bungalows with fans and cold-water showers overlooking a coconut grove at the southern end of Pantai Bara.

Tevana House Reef $$$ Attention to detail is in everything, from the exquisitely landscaped cliff-side grounds to the four ironwood bungalows, rooftop sundeck and vegetarian restaurant.

Pulau Selayar

Syafira Hotel $$ Centrally located a couple of blocks from the waterfront, this is our favourite choice in Benteng, with immaculate air-con rooms and a cafe downstairs.

Sunari Beach Resort $$ Beachfront resort on the west coast, 13km south of Benteng, with sturdy wooden bungalows and a good restaurant.

Tana Toraja

MAP p609

Pia's Poppies $ This friendly budget lodge is popular with backpackers for its tidy rooms, tranquil gardens and social common areas. An excellent restaurant and all-round top choice.

Rosalina Homestay $ On the southern edge of town with views of rice paddies from the terrace. Torajan guide Enos heads this family-run homestay with free breakfast, plenty of local advice and motorbikes for hire.

Santai Toraja $$ Rantepao's newest boutique hotel, with modern touches, super-clean rooms, a good restaurant and a peaceful location overlooking rice paddies.

Sulawesi Castle $$ There are good views and clean rooms at this towering castle-like guesthouse, but the helpful and gracious owner is a highlight.

Tentena & Danau Poso

Victory Hotel $ Friendly family-run place popular with overnighting backpackers; there's a wide choice of rooms, motorbikes, and tour and guide recommendations.

Pendolo Cottages $ In the village of Pendolo at the southern end of Danau Poso, this is a rustic place where you can charter a boat for lake trips.

Togean Islands

MAP p624

For island resorts and guesthouses, see Togean Island-Hopping (p622).

Reconnect Island Resort $$$ Not part of the Togeans but nearby, this secluded island eco-resort on Pulau Buka-Buka is a half-hour private boat ride from Ampana. Luxurious rustic villas and all meals included.

Ampana

Marina Cottages $ Beachfront 'village' of well-maintained wooden cottages beside a smooth pebble beach about 3km north of Ampana harbour; deluxe cottages face the beach. Good restaurant and plenty of Togean info.

Triple R Homestay $$ Our favourite in Ampana, this is a comfy homestay in the true sense, with beautifully designed cabins in a soothing garden and travel-inspired decor everywhere. Charming host Dadang is a legend of the local tourism industry.

Lawaka Hotel $$ Lawaka is a modern, spotless midranger with hotel-style rooms, artsy decor and a good cafe facing a central garden.

Gorontalo

Harry & Mimin Homestay $ A true homestay with a lovely family. Rooms are simple but clean (the cheapest have shared bathroom) and Harry is a knowledgeable guide. It's popular with travellers to/from the Togean Islands; book well ahead.

Grand Q Hotel $$ For a bit more comfort, this is Gorontalo's best choice, with tip-top service and a rooftop pool, cafe and restaurant.

Manado

MAP p630

Manado Green Hostel $ Part of RedDoorz, this is Manado's only true hostel, with four-bed dorms (bunks) and lockers, shared bathrooms and a kitchen.

Ibis City Center Boulevard $$ Comfortable midranger well located across from the Town Square mall; good online deals.

Hotel Minahasa $$ Centrally located hilltop villa with a luxurious pool, city views and lots of stairs.

Aston Manado $$ Super-central business-class hotel. There's no pool but other facilities and buffet breakfasts are good.

Pulau Bunaken & Siladen

MAP p630

4 Sisters Homestay $ There are lots of good-value homestays in Bunaken village: this one is right on the beach with a good cafe and a full dive set-up.

Panorama Backpackers (p632) $$ Budget favourite on west-coast Pantai Liang; comfy cottages with verandas and meals included.

Happy Gecko $$ A full-service but intimate dive resort at the north end of Pantai Liang, with spacious bungalows and a beachfront restaurant.

Two Fish (p632) $$ Well-run dive resort with attractive cottages dotted around manicured grounds and a pool facing Pantai Pangalisang.

Tomohon

Onong's Homestay & Cafe $$ The main-street entrance beside an Alfamart gives way to a remarkable oasis of thatched bungalows, palm trees and a gurgling stream. There are cheaper rooms but we recommend the bungalows near the restaurant. Onong runs tours in his bright-red VW.

Highland Resort $$ Well-equipped wooden bungalows and a lush garden in the Kinilow region at the northern end of town; tours and trekking guides can be arranged.

Rimba Eco Resort $$ A calm oasis well off the main road; the beautifully designed bungalows here are well spread out in their own patch of rainforest. Food and service are top notch.

Tangkoko

Tangkoko Ranger Homestay $ Right opposite the park entrance, this is a budget choice but it's still clean and friendly, with the restaurant across the road.

Mama Roos Reborn $ Opposite the park entrance, Mama Roos has been around for decades and is in the process of renovating to put it on par with the area's best budget lodges.

Tangkoko Hill $$ A solid, comfortable, modern place with hyper-clean rooms, quality mattresses, desks and TVs.

Tangkoko Lodge $$ Spacious, clean rooms around a garden and a recommended restaurant.

PAUL HARDING/LONELY PLANET

Rammang Rammang Eco Lodge, near Makassar

TOOLKIT

The chapters in this section cover the most important topics you'll need to know about in Indonesia. They're full of nuts-and-bolts information and valuable insights to help you understand and navigate Indonesia and get the most out of your trip.

Nusa Penida (p217), Bali

BALNYES/SHUTTERSTOCK

Arriving

Most visitors arrive in Indonesia via Jakarta's Soekarno-Hatta international airport or Ngurah Rai international airport in Bali. International flights from Asia also arrive at Balikpapan, Lombok, Makassar, Manado, Medan, Padang and Surabaya. There are land and sea border crossings between Sumatra, Kalimantan and Malaysia, and from Papua to Papua New Guinea.

Visas

Citizens of 97 countries can get 30-day visas on arrival (VOA). These can be extended for a further 30 days. To skip the arrival queues, apply online (imigrasi.go.id) for a VOA or for a 60-day visa.

Onward Travel

Visitors are required to show proof of return or onward travel – normally a flight ticket – on arrival. Your passport should be valid for at least six months from the day of your arrival.

Wi-Fi

Almost all airports in Indonesia offer free wi-fi. At land borders, you'll need to find a nearby cafe or restaurant to get your online fix.

SIM Cards

Local SIM cards and data packages are cheap. They can be bought at any airport with international arrivals, and at phone and convenience stores everywhere. Make sure your phone is unlocked and bring your passport.

Airports to City Centres

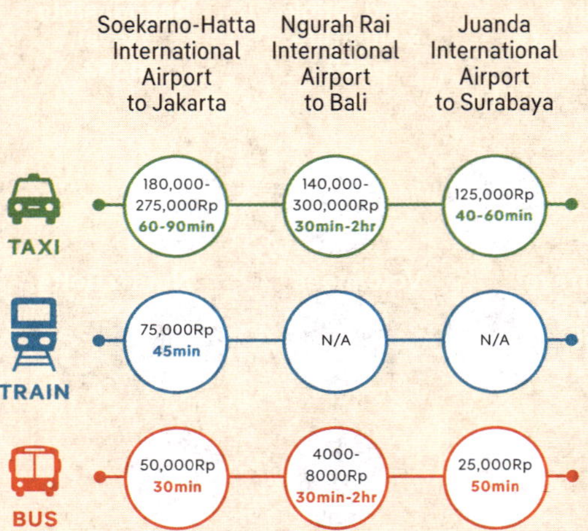

	Soekarno-Hatta International Airport to Jakarta	Ngurah Rai International Airport to Bali	Juanda International Airport to Surabaya
TAXI	180,000-275,000Rp 60-90min	140,000-300,000Rp 30min-2hr	125,000Rp 40-60min
TRAIN	75,000Rp 45min	N/A	N/A
BUS	50,000Rp 30min	4000-8000Rp 30min-2hr	25,000Rp 50min

AIRPORT TAXIS

Avoid the many unlicensed taxis that hang around Indonesia's busiest airports and be careful with the taxi firms inside the terminals, which often overcharge. If you're planning to take a taxi from Jakarta, Bali or Surabaya airports, the safest and most reliable company is **Bluebird**. But we advise downloading the **Grab** or **Gojek** ride-hailing apps, which are the best source of taxis and motorcycle taxis (helmet provided) in most Indonesian cities (in Jakarta, Green SM uses only electric cars). All major airports have Grab and Gojek pickup points, and the apps have English-language options. Just don't expect your driver to speak any English.

FROM LEFT: FUSE/GETTY IMAGES, WINFINITY/SHUTTERSTOCK

Getting Around

Planes, boats and buses are the principal ways to get around Indonesia, with trains available only in Java and parts of Sumatra and Sulawesi.

TRAVEL COSTS (MIN. PER DAY)

Car rental
200,000Rp

Motorcycle rental
80,000Rp

Bicycle rental
30,000Rp

Air

Air travel is the quickest and most convenient way of getting around Indonesia, and sometimes the only way. Numerous domestic airlines operate with varying degrees of efficiency, and tickets are relatively inexpensive. Flights to remote destinations are prone to cancellation, especially in periods of bad weather, while delays are common across the country. In remote but populated areas like Sulawesi, Kalimantan and Maluku, check flights with Susi Air's 10-seater planes.

Boat

A huge range of vessels sail Indonesia's waters. Low-cost airlines mean that far fewer travellers now use the large Pelni boats that visit 71 major ports across the archipelago on multiday journeys. Slow car ferries also link some big islands, while fast speedboats connect popular destinations like Bali and Lombok. Ferries and houseboats roam major rivers in Kalimantan. Small long-tail boats can be found anywhere there is water.

TIP

There are not many taxis roaming Indonesia's streets. Use the Grab or Gojek ride-hailing apps to get around cities and major towns. Jakarta's Green SM app has electric vehicles.

ROAD SAFETY

Indonesia's roads are crowded, chaotic and often in poor condition, especially on islands and in rural areas, while speed limits and road rules are routinely flouted. Many visitors to Bali rent motorbikes, but if you're not used to riding one, the island's busy roads are not the best place to learn. Always wear a helmet – you can be fined for not doing so – and expect the unexpected.

Bus & Shared Taxi

Local buses tend to be slow and uncomfortable, but some popular routes, such as Jakarta–Bali, use express, luxury or sleeper air-con buses. Book tickets a day in advance for these.

Train

Train travel in Indonesia is restricted to Java, a small network in Sumatra and a tiny stretch of track in Sulawesi. In Java, trains are inexpensive and among the most comfortable, fastest and easiest ways to travel.

Car & Motorcycle

Cars and motorcycles can be rented across Indonesia, but hiring a car and a driver is cheap, especially if you're in a group, allowing visitors maximum travel freedom.

DRIVING ESSENTIALS

Drive on the left

Speed limits: expressways and highways 60–100km/h; urban areas 50km/h; other roads 40–80km/h

21+

The minimum age to rent a car is 21; some companies charge more for drivers under 25

Money

CURRENCY: RUPIAH (RP)

Credit Cards

Visa and Mastercard are the most widely accepted credit cards, but aren't much use outside of major cities or areas with a big tourist presence.

Digital Payments

Local banks and digital wallets have embraced paying by phone, but Apple Pay and Google Wallet aren't currently accepted for making payments in Indonesia. The Dana app tends to work well.

ATMs

Most Indonesian ATMs accept cards affiliated with international networks. You'll be charged a fee by both the Indonesian bank and your bank. ATMs dispense money in 50,000Rp and 100,000Rp notes. The limit for a single withdrawal ranges from 500,000Rp to 3,000,000Rp. Note that some ATMs return your card after dispensing the money.

Tipping

Tipping is not standard in Indonesia – many restaurants and most hotels include a service charge in the bill – but leaving small change is always appreciated. It's customary to tip tour guides or houseboat crew, and also spa and massage therapists, as well as hotel staff who carry bags.

HOW MUCH FOR A...

Bicycle rickshaw
30,000Rp

Jakarta MRT ticket
4000–14,000Rp

Museum admission ticket
5000–25,000Rp

National park entry
150,000Rp

HOW TO... Use ATMs

Withdrawal limits at Indonesian ATMs vary widely. Some have a withdrawal limit of 500,000Rp, which is not very much in terms of foreign currency. Always choose an ATM that dispenses 50,000Rp notes, rather than one dispensing 100,000Rp notes (there's normally a sticker on the machine indicating what notes it dispenses). Bank Central Asia (BCA) is reliable and has a 2,500,000Rp withdrawal limit.

LOCAL TIP

Try to carry a fair amount of cash in bills of denominations 50,000Rp and under, as getting change for 100,000Rp notes can be a problem, especially in rural areas.

RUPIAH RE-DENOMINATION

Bank Indonesia – Indonesia's central bank – has spent the last decade considering whether to re-denominate the rupiah by removing three digits from the currency. The idea is to simplify the currency so, for example, the 20,000Rp note would become the 20Rp note, while retaining the same value as the old 20,000Rp note. The change was expected before the 2024 general election, and it remains just an idea at the time of writing. There's an expectation that re-denomination will occur in the future, and many Indonesians already quote prices using the shortened version.

Accommodation

Boutique Glam

There's an ever-increasing number of stylish boutique hotels in Bali, Lombok and Java, where there are also many excellent midrange and four-star resort choices. Outside touristed areas, hotel standards are variable, and slack maintenance and uneven service are common, although staff are usually pleasant. In Kalimantan, international chains such as Swissôtel and Mercure have excellent business-standard hotels. Indonesian hotels are generally a reasonable deal cost-wise.

Villa Life

Renting a villa is a popular option on Bali, although they're not without environmental costs in terms of water usage and placement amid once-pristine ricefields. Many come with pools, views, beaches and staff. Rates range from around US$200 per night for a modest villa to US$2000 per night and more. But several people sharing can make something grand affordable.

Experience a Homestay

Homestays are often possible in villages and in some towns. Ask the *kepala desa* (village head) about finding one (meals will usually be included). Homestays are a less commercial budget choice and an excellent way of experiencing Indonesian life close up. They're often more sustainable than other accommodation options, and benefit the locals directly.

Budget Digs

Hostels and budget hotels can be found in the most-visited destinations, but family-run guesthouses are still the main budget option in many parts of Indonesia. They often include the words losmen, *penginapan* or *pondok* in their name. Air-con is mostly standard now, but some guesthouses are still pretty basic, with squat toilets and a large water tank instead of a shower.

HOW MUCH FOR A NIGHT IN...

A boutique hotel
2,000,000Rp

A hostel
180,000–250,000Rp

A homestay
150,000–200,000Rp

Camping

Formal camping grounds with power and other facilities are rare. Some Kalimantan and Papua treks require camping, as do mountain and volcano treks, such as Gunung Rinjani on Lombok. Guides or operators usually provide gear.

ACCOMMODATION PRICE RANGES

Bali & Lombok

$ <450,000Rp

$$ 450,000Rp–1,400,000Rp

$$$ >1,400,000Rp

The Rest of Indonesia

$ <250,000Rp

$$ 250,000Rp–800,000Rp

$$$ >800,000Rp

BOOK AHEAD

It's wise to reserve rooms well in advance in the most popular destinations during the peak-season months of July and August, when visitor numbers surge across Indonesia and room rates can spike by as much as 50%. On Bali, Lombok and the Gili Islands, November and December are also busy months, especially around Christmas and New Year. Visit in the October–April low season for the best accommodation deals. There will be some daily rain, but you can travel without booking rooms in advance and prices drop dramatically.

CLOCKWISE FROM TOP LEFT: MELIMEY/SHUTTERSTOCK, SKYWING/SHUTTERSTOCK, J88 IMAGES/SHUTTERSTOCK

Monkeys, Bali (p183)

Family Travel

Indonesia is a child-loving archipelago. Indeed, many parents say they see much more of the country because their kids are so quickly whisked into everyday life. And with world-class wildlife and beaches, as well as mysterious temples to explore, there is no shortage of activities for kids.

Sights & Activities

Bali is by far the most family-orientated destination in Indonesia, with beaches galore and great spots for first-time snorkellers and surfers, as well as loads of child-friendly accommodation. The islands of Nusa Tenggara – Lombok, the Gilis and Flores – are more adventurous options and offer the chance to see the amazing Komodo dragons. Java, too, is kid-friendly, with plenty of theme parks, temples and beaches.

Getting Around

Pavements in Indonesia are often narrow and uneven, or just plain nonexistent, making them a challenge for pushchairs (prams) and strollers. A back carrier to transport tots is a good idea. If you're renting a car, note that car seats for kids are rarely available. Some cycle shops and bike-tour outfits on Bali and Lombok rent bicycles and helmets for children.

BEST ATTRACTIONS FOR FAMILIES

Waterbom Bali, Bali (p201)
Indonesia's best water park, with 26 water slides.

Komodo National Park, Nusa Tenggara (p306)
It's easy and safe to see the Komodo dragons here.

Tanjung Puting National Park, Kalimantan (p556)
Kids love cruising in a houseboat to see orangutans and other wildlife.

Bukit Lawang, Sumatra (p466)
River tubing, gentle jungle hikes and a good chance of spotting orangutans.

Yogyakarta, Java (p76)
Temples, palaces, museums and myriad cultural attractions.

Safety Standards

Safety standards in Indonesia may be slightly more lax than you're used to. Viewpoints probably have nothing to stop your kids falling over the edge, swimming pools are rarely fenced etc. But with proper precautions, children can travel safely.

Animal Encounters

Children love seeing Bali's many monkeys in action, but remember that they are wild animals and they do bite. Rabies is endemic in 26 of Indonesia's 38 provinces, including Bali, so keep kids away from stray dogs and monkeys.

STAYING SAFE & HEALTHY

Heavy traffic and poor pavements (sidewalks) are a risk to both kids and adults.

Check conditions for any activity carefully. Just because that rafting company sells tickets to families doesn't mean that they accommodate the safety needs of children.

Monitor the health situation, especially with regards to malaria and dengue fever.

Pharmaceuticals, sunscreen, mosquito repellent and baby supplies – disposable nappies (diapers), wipes, formula – are readily available in cities and large towns, but not elsewhere.

FROM LEFT: THEWANDERFULWAYFARER/SHUTTERSTOCK, NEW AFRICA/SHUTTERSTOCK

Health & Safe Travel

INSURANCE

Travel insurance that covers you for theft, loss and medical issues is an excellent idea. Get a policy that includes emergency evacuation by air. Some policies specifically exclude 'dangerous activities', which can mean scuba diving, hiring a motorcycle or even trekking. If your policy requires you to pay doctors or hospitals directly and claim later, make sure to keep all relevant documentation.

Mosquito-Borne Diseases

Malaria and dengue fever are two potentially fatal diseases that are carried by mosquitoes and present in many parts of Indonesia. The best protection is to avoid getting bitten, so wear long clothing at night and use repellent (bring hard-to-find DEET-free repellent from home). Cases spike during the October–April rainy season. Most travellers will experience nothing more than some itchy bites.

Keep Cool

Most people need a couple of weeks to adapt to the heat and humidity of Indonesia. Children are especially at risk from dehydration and sunstroke. Drink lots of water and avoid doing strenuous activity in the middle of the day. The sun is strong, even if there's cloud cover, so apply an SPF 50+ sunscreen and wear a wide-brimmed hat.

TAP WATER

Most locals don't drink the tap water. Stick to bottled or filtered water. Ice in restaurants and bars is generally safe.

Illegal Drugs

Indonesia has a zero-tolerance policy towards illegal narcotics. A number of foreigners have been executed in Bali for drugs offences over the last decade, while others remain on death row. Possession of a marijuana joint incurs a mandatory four-year prison sentence. Anyone caught with 5g or more of cocaine or heroin is looking at a life sentence.

POISONOUS SNAKES

There are over 70 species of venomous snakes in Indonesia and snakebite is a common cause of death in rural areas, not least because of a shortage of antivenom serum. Most poisonous snakes are shy or nocturnal – or sea snakes – and travellers rarely encounter them. If you're trekking in the rainforest, especially at night in Kalimantan, you're likely to see pit vipers and pythons.

CLOCKWISE FROM TOP LEFT: ALLSTARS/SHUTTERSTOCK, ALEXANDER SPATARI/GETTY IMAGES, DWI PUTRA STOCK/SHUTTERSTC

Fake Alcohol

High alcohol taxes have prompted a booming market for counterfeit booze. In popular destinations like Bali, Lombok and the Gilis, imported spirits are sometimes cut or replaced with locally produced *arak* (colourless, distilled palm wine) . But *arak* can contain poisonous methanol if it's not distilled properly, and a number of tourists have died or been hospitalised. Be cautious when imbibing cocktails and spirits.

Scams

Credit-card fraud, particularly the skimming of cards, is common in Bali. Be careful when paying by card and always use ATMs attached to banks, rather than standalone machines. Some moneychangers will short-change customers. Stick to large storefront operations or exchange counters at banks. Avoid moneychangers offering too-good exchange rates or ones in obscure locations: scores of travellers are taken in daily.

LGBTIQ+ TRAVELLERS

Indonesia doesn't have a dedicated law banning same-sex relationships and sexual activity, but equally there are no laws protecting LGBTIQ+ people from discrimination and hate crimes. LGBTIQ+ travellers in Indonesia should do the same as straight travellers and avoid public displays of affection. Although violence against LGBTIQ+ people is rare, visitors should note that same-sex relationships are illegal in Aceh in Sumatra, where Islamic sharia law is in operation, and same-sex sexual activity is punishable by public caning or a jail sentence.

Few LGBTIQ+ Indonesians would consider coming out to family and friends, and attitudes towards the LGBTIQ+ community are generally conservative. A September 2023 survey by the Pew Research Center in Washington, DC, revealed that 95% of Indonesians are opposed to same-sex marriage. The campaign for LGBTIQ+ acceptance has become more vocal in recent years, but powerful religious groups remain opposed to any legal recognition of LGBTIQ+ rights.

Bali is the most LGBTIQ-friendly destination, with plenty of LGBTIQ-friendly bars in south Bali. There are underground scenes in Jakarta and major cities. GAYa Nusantara is a useful resource covering Indonesia's LGBTIQ+ community. Bali-based Gaya Dewata offers medical advice and support.

Scan for GAYa Nusantara's website

SWIM SAFELY

Yellow flag
Potential hazards in the water

Green flag
Safe to swim

Red flag
Unsafe to swim

Black & white flag
Surfboard and watercraft zone

Yellow & red flag
Lifeguards on duty

Food, Drink & Nightlife

When to Eat

Breakfast (6am–8am) *Bakso* (meatball soup), *bubur ayam* (chicken rice porridge) and *nasi kuning* (yellow rice and sides) are popular choices.

Lunch (11am–2pm) Often the main meal of the day. Usually involves steamed rice, fish or chicken, a soup dish, vegetables and tempeh.

Dinner (6–9pm) Options include *mie goreng* (fried noodles) or *nasi campur* (Indonesian version of plate of the day).

Where to Eat

Warungs Simple places that provide a small range of staple dishes. Often known for cooking one type of dish in particular.

Rumah makan Literally 'eating house', these restaurants are a step up from warungs and serve a wider selection of food. Also known as *restoran*.

Masakan Padang These restaurants serve precooked meat, fish and vegetable dishes. Everything is on display, so just pick what you want.

Markets The best place to pick up delicious tropical fruit, as well as sweet and savoury snacks.

MENU DECODER

Air Water
Arak Alcohol distilled from palm sap or rice
Ayam Chicken
Ayam goreng Fried chicken
Bakar Barbecued or roasted
Bir Beer
Daging sapi Beef
Gado gado Steamed bean sprouts and vegetables served with a peanut sauce
Ikan Fish
Kopi Coffee
Lezat Delicious
Lombok Chilli
Mie goreng Fried wheat-flour noodles served with vegetables or meat
Nasi Rice
Nasi campur Steamed rice served with vegetables, meat or fish, fried shrimp, peanuts and egg
Nasi goreng Fried rice
Rendang Slow-cooked meat, usually beef
Roti Bread that's nearly always white and sweet
Sambal Spicy chilli sauce served as an accompaniment to most meals
Sate Grilled meat served on a skewer with peanut sauce
Soto Meat and vegetable broth: soup
Tahu Tofu
Teh Tea
Telur Egg

HOW TO... Eat Like an Indonesian

Hospitality is highly valued in Indonesia. If you're lucky enough to be invited to a local's home for a meal, you'll be treated warmly and any social hiccups will be ignored. But here a few tips to ensure that the experience is more enjoyable for everyone.

Wait until your host invites you to eat or drink before tucking in.

Indonesians rarely eat sitting at a table, preferring to sit on a mat on the floor with the dishes all around them.

If you're invited to someone's home for a meal don't be surprised if you are the only person eating. This is your host's way of showing that you are special. But don't eat huge amounts; the same dishes will be shared by the host and his family later.

Many Indonesians prefer to eat with their right hand rather than using utensils. But it's fine to ask for a fork and spoon.

KETUT MAHENDRI/SHUTTERSTOCK

HOW MUCH FOR A...

Noodle soup at a street stall
15,000Rp

Simple warung meal
15,000–30,000Rp

Seafood dinner for two
250,000Rp and up

Gourmet dinner for two
800,000Rp and up

Coffee
15,000–45,000Rp

Cocktail
80,000–200,000Rp

Small bottle of Bintang beer
20,000–40,000Rp

Cooking class in Bali
400,000Rp and up

HOW TO... Keep Kids Happy

Many parents worry that an unexpected chilli hidden in a dish will blow their kid's head off, but Indonesian food isn't as spicy as some other Southeast Asian cuisines, and sambal – the really hot stuff – is usually served on the side and added in by each diner. Restaurant proprietors, too, will often warn Westerners if a dish is spicy, or ask whether you like spicy food. Nevertheless, it's a good idea to learn the following phrases: *Tidak pedas* – literally 'not spicy' – and *Makanan tidak pedas ada?* – 'is there non-spicy food?'.

There are a number of staple Indonesian dishes that children often enjoy. Nasi goreng (fried rice), *mie goreng* (fried noodles), *bakso* (meatball soup), *mie rebus* (noodle soup), *sate ayam* (grilled chicken on a skewer in peanut sauce) and *pisang goreng* (banana fritters) are popular options for kids and available everywhere.

In major cities and heavily touristed places like Bali there are familiar fast-food outlets, as well as supermarkets and convenience stores selling international food and snacks. The sugar-rich iced drinks and fruit juices sold at street stalls are useful secret weapons when energy levels are low.

What you won't get, outside of Bali, are highchairs and kiddie menus. That doesn't mean children aren't welcome in eating establishments. On the contrary, almost all restaurant owners are delighted to see kids and staff will go out of their way to make them feel comfortable.

Chopsticks

Chopsticks are not commonly used in Indonesia, despite the many Chinese-style restaurants. You may see people eating noodles with them, but even in Japanese or Korean restaurants locals will often use a fork and spoon.

HOW TO... Celebrate With Food

All gatherings of Indonesians usually involve copious amounts of food. For special occasions the centrepiece will be a *tumpeng*: a pyramid of yellow rice surrounded by side dishes, the tip of which is cut off and offered to the VIP guest.

The biggest celebrations for the 87% of Indonesians who identify as Muslim are Ramadan and Idul Adha, the two main Islamic holidays. Each day of Ramadan, Muslims get up before sunrise to eat the only meal of the day until after sunset. Ramadan can be a challenging time for travellers, as many restaurants close for the holiday and you might have to skip lunch. However, when sunset does come, a good meal is easy to find.

The first thing Indonesians eat after fasting all day is *kolak* (fruit in coconut milk), a sweet dessert designed to reacquaint the body with food. Then, after prayers, there's the much-anticipated evening meal. In some places, like Bukittinggi in western Sumatra, food is set out on the street so that it can be enjoyed communally. Foreigners are always made welcome.

Following Ramadan, much of Indonesia goes on the road to visit family to celebrate Idul Fitri. During this period it's common to see *ketupat* – rice cakes wrapped up in palm leaves – hanging everywhere like seasonal ornaments. Seventy days after Idul Fitri is Idul Adha, when unfortunate goats can be seen tethered in cities, towns and villages waiting to be sacrificed. The meat is then distributed to the needy.

EATING PRICE RANGES

Bali & Lombok

$ <60,000Rp

$$ 60,000Rp–250,000Rp

$$$ >250,000Rp

The Rest of Indonesia

$ <50,000Rp

$$ 50,000Rp–150,000Rp

$$$ >150,000Rp

Responsible Travel

Climate Change & Travel

It's impossible to ignore the impact we have when travelling; Lonely Planet urges all travellers to engage with their travel carbon footprint, which will mainly come from air travel. While there often isn't an alternative, travellers can look to minimise the number of flights they take, opt for newer aircrafts and use cleaner ground transport, such as trains. One proposed solution – purchasing carbon offsets – unfortunately does not cancel out the impact of individual flights. While most destinations will depend on air travel for the foreseeable future, for now, pursuing ground-based travel where possible is the best course of action.

The **UN Carbon Offset Calculator** shows how flying impacts a household's emissions.

The **ICAO's carbon emissions calculator** allows visitors to analyse the CO_2 generated by point-to-point journeys.

Stay Raja Ampat (p421) in Papua helps locals open homestays in diving paradise Raja Ampat, which supports the local economy and empowers Papuans to preserve their environment and traditional way of life.

A number of tea plantations on the Dieng Plateau in Central Java, such as Kebun Teh Panama (p121), have been turned into responsible travel destinations, so visitors can now enjoy the stunning plateau panoramas.

Be a Trash Hero

Join the **Trash Hero** volunteers who clean up garbage across Indonesia, and who partner with communities on education and sustainability projects that aim to reduce and better manage plastic waste in particular.

Scan for more info about Trash Hero

Choose a Homestay

Consider staying with a family rather than in a hotel or guesthouse. Homestays are generally the most sustainable accommodation option, provide direct benefit to locals and are a great way to experience Indonesian life.

Diving Without Damage

Indonesia has some of the finest dive sites and is a magnet for underwater adventurers. But this means a higher risk of corals and reefs being damaged and marine life disturbed: watch those fins and never touch coral.

Get Involved in Wildlife Conservation

Help care for orangutans and sun bears (pictured above) at Samboja Lestari (p574) in East Kalimantan, a rehabilitation centre run by the Borneo Orangutan Survival Foundation *(orangutan.or.id)*, one of many wildlife conservation projects that welcomes volunteers.

Leave Sumatra's Elephants Alone

A number of so-called elephant sanctuaries operate in Sumatra, where local pachyderms are under threat from habitat loss, but none of them offer ethical elephant encounters. Avoid any place that offers elephant washing, rides or shows.

Respect Indonesia's Traditional Cultures

Experiencing different cultures is a highlight of any Indonesia trip, whether it's staying in a Dayak longhouse or trekking in Tana Toraja. But it's important to respect those cultures. Ask your guide about appropriate behaviour.

Water Bottles

Consider bringing a filtration device (or a reusable bottle to fill) rather than relying on single-use plastic bottles, which only add to Indonesia's waste crisis. It's also a good idea to bring your own reusable straw.

Travel by Train

Travelling across Java and parts of Sumatra by train is cheap, efficient and quick. Work on extending Indonesia's rail network is ongoing and using trains drastically cuts emissions compared to a flight or bus ride.

Volunteer

There are many volunteering opportunities in Indonesia, ranging from wildlife and marine conservation to sustainable agriculture projects and teaching in rural regions. Do some research before signing up to ensure you join a reputable organisation.

Simolap Wild Adventures in North Sumatra is a community-led initiative offering environmentally conscious trekking and more.

Conservation organisation ASRI (p552) operates in West Kalimantan's wildlife-rich Gunung Palung National Park and welcomes volunteers.

Social Forestry

Indonesia operates an ambitious **social forestry programme** that gives communities across the archipelago legal rights over 12.7 million hectares of forest, so they can be managed sustainably for the benefit of locals and the environment.

RESOURCES

Aliansi Masyarakat Adat Nusantara (aman.or.id) Works for a just and prosperous life for indigenous communities.

Idep Foundation (idepfoundation.org) Runs environmental and community improvement projects.

Profauna (profauna.net) Protects forests and combats the illegal wildlife trade.

CLOCKWISE FROM TOP LEFT: ANAN KAEWKHAMMUL/SHUTTERSTOCK, SURADECH PRAPAIRAT/SHUTTERSTOCK, KANITTHA BOON/SHUTTERSTOCK

Accessible Travel

Indonesia is a difficult destination for travellers with access needs, whether those with limited mobility, or vision or hearing impairments. Few buildings have disability access and public transport is mostly impossible for wheelchair users. But locals are normally quick to help people with accessibility issues.

Navigating Streets

Pavements (sidewalks) in Indonesia are either nonexistent or uneven, riddled with holes and jammed with all manner of street life. Wheelchair users will find it easier to use the roads.

Airport

Soekarno-Hatta international airport in Jakarta and Ngurah Rai international airport in Bali both have facilities for people with disabilities, including lifts, accessible toilets and air bridges for boarding/disembarking planes (let your airline know in advance).

Accommodation

A number of resorts and hotels in Bali are suitable for travellers with disabilities, but most Indonesian accommodation lacks wheelchair access or adapted rooms. As a poor alternative, staff will do their best to meet your needs.

ISLAND TRAVEL

The biggest challenge with accessing many islands is getting safely on and off the boats that dock at sometimes rickety piers or directly from the beach. Choosing an island with an airport is the most realistic option.

Blind Massage

Training as a massage therapist is a common option for the visually impaired in Indonesia. There are blind-massage places in all major destinations and they are well worth supporting.

Diving

A few operators on Bali and the Gili Islands offer diving for travellers with disabilities. If you can't meet the physical requirements to pass a PADI or SSI course, it's possible to do fun dives.

SHOPPING MALLS

New shopping malls are popping up all the time in Jakarta and major cities, and they are the places to head to for hassle-free shopping and eating, as well as an accessible toilet.

RESOURCES

Accessible Indonesia *(accessible indonesia.com)* Accessible Indonesia offers tours of Bali, Java and Sulawesi for wheelchair users.

Bali Access Travel *(baliwheelchairtravel.com)* Organises wheelchair-accessible transport and accommodation, as well as tours across Bali and Lombok.

Difa Bike *(instagram.com/difabike)* Unique in Indonesia, Difa Bike uses motorcycles with adapted sidecars for tours and transport for people with mobility needs in and around Yogyakarta.

Taxis

Most taxis are not suitable for people with access needs. But **Bluebird**, the most reliable Indonesian taxi company, does have a small fleet of vehicles in Jakarta and Surabaya that are wheelchair accessible. These cars can only be ordered by phone.

SYAHRUL HILDA/SHUTTERSTOCK

Fast-boat services, Nusa Penida (p217), Bali

HOW TO... Travel Safely by Boat

Boat safety is an important consideration across Indonesia, where fatal accidents involving ferries and speedboats are sadly commonplace. In 2024 alone there were 128 maritime accidents. Travellers are often confronted with vessels that appear barely seaworthy, but which may be the only option to travel between islands.

The busy routes linking Bali, Nusa Lembongan, Lombok and the Gilis have all seen accidents involving fast tourist boats and public car ferries. Given Indonesia's lax safety regulations, it is essential that you take responsibility for your own safety, as no one else will. Consider the following points for any boat travel in Indonesia.

Avoid Fly-by-Night Vessels

Beware of sole operators who have converted a fishing vessel into a speedboat by attaching a few engines to its stern in an effort to cash in on the tourist boom. Always use boats run by companies rather than accepting a ride from someone you met on the beach.

Bigger is Better

Travelling on a larger boat is generally always safer, even if your journey is likely to be longer, as it will handle the open ocean much better than small and overpowered speedboats, which are especially prone to capsizing in rough seas.

Overcrowding

At busy times such as Idul Fitri, boats can have more people on board than there are seats, and aisles are jammed with luggage. Try to avoid travelling during holidays and peak periods to minimise the chance of being on an overloaded boat.

Safety Equipment & Exits

Make certain your boat has life jackets and that you know how to locate and use them. Don't expect a panicked crew to hand them out in an emergency. On larger vessels confirm that there are sufficient life rafts. Make sure you know where the nearest exit is: some boats will have only one exit, which can turn them into deathtraps in the event of an accident.

PELNI SHIPS

The large vessels operated by Pelni (Pelayaran Nasional Indonesia; the national shipping line with a fleet of passenger ships) that link major ports across the archipelago are by far the safest boats to travel on; there hasn't been a deadly accident involving a Pelni ship since 1981. Nevertheless, Pelni vessels present their own challenges. They're often overloaded with passengers crammed into every available space and conditions (toilets especially) can get grim. They lack lockers, so travellers need to keep an eye on their gear. On-board food is mostly restricted to instant noodles. And watch for pickpockets during the mad rush to board and disembark.

Volcanoes

Much of Indonesia is defined by its many volcanoes, 129 of which are active and 65 of which are classified as dangerous. These spectacular peaks tower above the forests and oceans and draw hikers to their steaming summits, while others flock to their colourful lakes and bubbling mud pits.

Active Volcanoes

On 3 December 2023 Gunung Marapi in Sumatra erupted, killing 23 local hikers trekking near the crater. Marapi is Sumatra's most active volcano, along with Gunung Kerinci and Gunung Sinabung, but it's not the most active volcano in all Indonesia. That honour goes to the namesake Gunung Merapi in Java, which has been erupting regularly since 1548. It's common to see smoke emerging from the volcano. Gunung Semeru, also on Java, is another very active volcano and has been in a state of near-continuous eruption since 1967.

Climb a Volcano

Climbing volcanoes is a popular option for both locals and travellers, despite the threat of eruptions. Gunung Agung on Bali, Gunung Rinjani on Lombok and Gunung Bromo in East Java are among the most visited volcanoes. But Indonesian volcanoes don't come much smaller or more well-shaped than the 656m-high Gunung Api, a pocket Mt Fuji overlooking the Banda Islands that can be climbed in three strenuous hours.

Historic Eruptions

Some volcanic eruptions in Indonesia have had a terrifying effect on the world. Ash from the cataclysmic 1815 eruption of Gunung Tambora in Sumbawa killed 71,000 people and caused crop failures in Europe. The climax of the 1883 eruption of Krakatau between Java and Sumatra resulted in explosions that could be heard as far away as Australia and generated tsunamis that killed tens of thousands. And when super-volcano Toba on Sumatra erupted 74,000-odd years ago, it decreased the global temperature by between 3°C and 5°C.

Religious Significance

Volcanoes play a pivotal role in most Indonesian cultures and almost all of them are associated with ancient deities. In Bali, Lombok and Java, major places of worship grace the slopes of prominent volcanic cones, and eruptions are taken as demonstrations of divine disappointment or anger. Perhaps the most worshipped volcano is Gunung Bromo in East Java. Every year, thousands of locals climb Bromo to throw offerings in its crater as a way of expressing their appreciation to their traditional gods.

RING OF FIRE

Indonesia is stretched along part of the Pacific Ring of Fire, a tectonic belt that circumscribes the Pacific Ocean. Two-thirds of the earth's volcanoes lie along the Ring of Fire and 90% of all earthquakes occur in this region. The 2004 tsunami in Sumatra was caused by an offshore earthquake, the third-largest ever recorded, and generated waves up to 10m tall. The tsunami killed over 160,000 Indonesians and displaced half a million more.

MARTI BUG CATCHER/SHUTTERSTOCK

Nuts & Bolts

OPENING HOURS

These opening hours may vary during Ramadan.

Banks 8am–3pm Monday to Friday, 8am–1pm Saturday

Government offices 8am–4pm Monday to Friday

Restaurants 11am–10pm every day

Shops 7am–9pm and malls 10am–10pm every day

Smoking

Around one third of adult Indonesians smoke, with clove-flavoured *kretek* cigarettes the weed of choice. Smoking is banned in hotels and restaurants, as well as other indoor environments, but the law is not always enforced. Vaping is also widespread.

Toilets

Kamar kecil is Bahasa Indonesia for 'toilet', but 'way-say' (WC) is also understood. In untouristy/rural areas expect squat toilets, which are flushed with water scooped out of a tank. Toilet paper goes in a wastebasket by the side. Shopping malls, petrol stations and convenience stores have public toilets.

Electricity

230V/50Hz

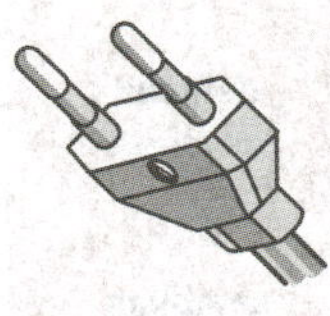

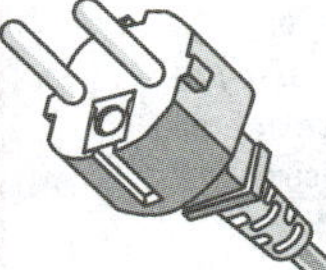

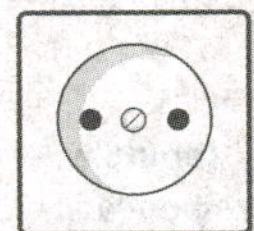

Type C
220V/50Hz

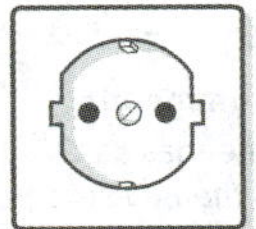

Type F
230V/50Hz

GOOD TO KNOW

Time zone
GMT/UTC plus seven to nine hours

Country calling code
+62

Emergency number
112

Internet Access

Most accommodation offers free wi-fi. Internet access can be patchy or nonexistent in remote areas.

Weights & Measures

The use of the metric system has been compulsory since 1938.

PUBLIC HOLIDAYS

Tahun Baru Masehi (New Year's Day) 1 January

Isra Miraj Nabi Muhammad (Ascension of the Prophet Muhammad) 16 January 2026

Tahun Baru Imlek (Chinese New Year) 17 February 2026

Nyepi (Balinese Hindu New Year) 19 March 2026

Idul Fitri (Lebaran) 20–21 March 2026

Wafat Yesus Kristus (Good Friday) 3 April 2026

Hari Buruh (Labour Day) 1 May

Kenaikan Yesus Kristus (Ascension of Christ) 14 May 2026

Idul Adha (Islamic feast of the sacrifice) 27 May 2026

Hari Waisak (Buddhist Holiday) 31 May 2026

Muharram (Islamic New Year) 26 June 2026

Hari Proklamasi Kemerdekaan (Independence Day) 17 August

Maulud Nabi Muhammad (Birthday of the Prophet Muhammad) 25 August 2026

Hari Natal (Christmas Day) 25 December

Language

Bahasa Indonesia is the official language of Indonesia. It has approximately 220 million speakers, although it's the mother tongue for only about 20 million. Most people in Bali and on Lombok also speak their own indigenous languages, Balinese and Sasak, respectively.

Basics

Hello. Salam. *sa·lam*
Goodbye. Selamat jalan. *se·la·mat ja·lan*
Yes. Ya. *ya*
No. Tidak. *ti·dak*
Please. Tolong. *to·long*
Thank you. Terima kasih. *te·ri·ma ka·sih*
Excuse me. Permisi. *per·mi·si*
Sorry. Maaf. *ma·af*
What's your name? Siapa namanya? *si·a·pa na·ma·nya*
My name is ... Nama saya ... *na·ma sa·ya ...*
Do you speak English? Anda bisa Bahasa Inggris? *an·da bi·sa ba·ha·sa ing·gris*
I don't understand. Saya tidak mengerti. *sa·ya ti·dak meng·er·ti*

Directions

Where's (the station)? Di mana (stasiun)? *di ma·na (sta·si·oon)*
What's the address? Apa alamatnya? *a·pa a·la·mat·nya*
Can you show me (on the map)? Bisa tunjukkan kepada saya (di peta)? *bi·sa toon·joo·kan ke·pa·da sa·ya (di pe·ta)*

Signs

Buka Open
Tutup Closed
Dilarang Prohibited
Kamar Kecil Toilets
Keluar Exit
Masuk Entrance
Pria Men
Wanitai Women
Polisi Police
Rumah Sakit Hospital

Time

What time is it? Jam berapa? *jam be·ra·pa*
It's (10) o'clock. Jam (sepuluh). *jam (se·poo·looh)*
Half past (10). Setengah (sebelas). *se·teng·ah (se·be·las)*
morning Pagi *pa·gi*
afternoon Sore *so·re*
evening Malam *ma·lam*
yesterday Kemarin *ke·ma·rin*
today Hari ini *ha·ri i·ni*
tomorrow Besok *be·sok*

Emergencies

Help! Tolong! *to·long*
Go away! Pergi! *per·gi*
Call ...! Panggil...! *pang·gil*
...a doctor dokter. *dok·ter*
...the police polisi. *po·li·si*

Eating & Drinking

What would you recommend? Apa yang Anda rekomendasikan? *a·pa yang an·da re·ko·men·da·si·kan*
Cheers! Bersulang! *ber·soo·lang*
That was delicious. Ini enak sekali. *i·ni e·nak se·ka·li*

NUMBERS

1 **satu** *sa·too*
2 **dua** *doo·a*
3 **tiga** *ti·ga*
4 **empat** *em·pat*
5 **lima** *li·ma*
6 **enam** *e·nam*
7 **tujuh** *too·jooh*
8 **delapan** *de·la·pan*
9 **sembilan** *sem·bi·lan*
10 **sepuluh** *se·poo·looh*

DONATIONS TO ENGLISH
Orangutan, dugong, bamboo, papaya, satay, sarong, gong

PRONUNCIATION

Pronunciation is easy to master in Bahasa Indonesia. Each letter always represents the same sound and most letters are pronounced the same as their English counterparts.

Origins

Bahasa Indonesia, and its closest relative Malay, both developed from Old Malay, an Austronesian language spoken in the kingdom of Srivijaya on the island of Sumatra.

Official Language

With the Declaration of Independence in 1942, Bahasa Indonesia was proclaimed the country's official language.

Street Talk

Blend in with the cool kids with the following sentences.

Alay – Tacky, garish, drama queen
Basian – Hangover
Jijay – Disgusting, grotesque
Kimpoi – Sexual intercourse
Koplak – Silly
Ndakik-ndakik – Words or phrases too hard to understand
Pansi – What the hell?

WHO SPEAKS BAHASA INDONESIA?

Bahasa Indonesia is the official language of the Republic of Indonesia. It's used in administration, education, business and the media, although less than 10% of the population claim it as their mother tongue. For the majority of speakers it's the second language, but it is a uniting force for the hundreds of ethnic groups scattered across the world's largest archipelago.

ERIC ISSELEE/SHUTTERSTOCK

THE INDONESIA

STORYBOOK

Our writers delve deeply into different aspects of Indonesian life.

Pura Besakih (p246), Bali

PHRAISOHN SIRIPOOL/SHUTTERSTOCK

A HISTORY OF INDONESIA IN 15 PLACES

The story of Indonesia is a colourful dance of migrants and invaders, rebels and religions, kingdoms and empires, choreographed by the country's island backdrop and its location on millennia-old Asian trade routes. It's also a story of remarkable resilience. Amid wars, natural disasters and colonial rule, Indonesians have weathered it all. By Anthony Ham

OVER THE MILLENNIA, humans have left their mark in countless ways on the islands of Indonesia. Some 40,000 years ago, unknown painters created realistic paintings – among the oldest on earth – in caves in Sumatra, the same island where you'll find some of Southeast Asia's most impressive megaliths.

Java, meanwhile, could be an island nation unto its own. It was here in 1892 that a paleoanthropologist unearthed bones of the so-called Java Man – one-million-year-old fossils of an early hominid that led to a groundbreaking discovery in the history of human evolution. The world's most populous island has been at the epicentre of major events in Indonesian (and world) history – from the building of magnificent temples by powerful Hindu and Buddhist kingdoms to the bloody fight for independence in the aftermath of WWII.

Other parts of the archipelago have seen the rise and fall of empires. On Bali, elaborate centuries-old holy sites dot the mountains and valleys, while the so-called Spice Islands of Maluku still contain the ruins of 17th-century fortresses – vestiges of more than three centuries of brutal Dutch rule. Indonesia's location on the Pacific Ring of Fire has also deeply affected the nation, due to devastating earthquakes, volcanic eruptions and tsunamis.

1. Leang Leang

PREHISTORIC CAVE PAINTINGS

On the island of Sulawesi, in the karst mountains north of Makassar, prehistoric peoples left behind visible signs of their presence in hundreds of caves. Tens of thousands of years ago, these rock walls became a sprawling canvas for handprint stencils and images of animals. The works were first spotted in the 1950s, though in 2017 researchers stumbled upon a surprisingly realistic depiction of the Celebes warty pig. The purple-hued painting was made from pulverised ochre turned into powder and mixed with water. It was later estimated to be over 45,000 years old – making it the world's oldest-known example of figurative art.

For more on Leang Leang, see p598.

2. Bada Valley

LAND OF MEGALITHS

Hidden among the rolling hills of Central Sulawesi, prehistoric carvings inspire wonder like few other places in Indonesia. Among several hundred megaliths, more than two dozen have minimalist, human-like features – oversized round heads, hands, and even prominent genitals. Precise dating of these works has proved elusive, with estimates ranging from 1000 to

5000 years ago. Little is known of who created them. Vaguely reminiscent of Polynesian Moai and Korean Dol Hareubang statues, these megaliths are unlike any prehistoric art found elsewhere in Indonesia and serve as symbols of a mysterious and organised civilisation that left no other traces of their presence.

For more on the megaliths of Bada Valley, see p619.

3. Pura Besakih

ANCIENT HOLY PLACE

High on the slopes of Gunung Agung, Pura Besakih has stood for centuries, surviving earthquakes, volcanic eruptions and large numbers of pilgrims drawn to one of Bali's holiest Hindu sites. Some scholars suspect it was founded in the 9th century by Mpu Kuturan, a Javanese priest who brought Hinduism to Bali. Others liken the stone bases on which the six-level complex stands as similar to prehistoric megalithic sites over 2000 years old. The so-called Mother Temple is not really a single temple, but over 20 separate temples, set with stone carvings, imposing gates and elaborate shrines dedicated to Hindu deities.

For more on Pura Besakih, see p246.

Megalith, Bada Valley (p619)

ALVAROBUENO/SHUTTERSTOCK

4. Borobudur

BUDDHIST GRANDEUR IN JAVA

On the outskirts of Yogyakarta, the world's largest Buddhist temple attests to the astonishing reign of the Shailendra dynasty, which built this colossal wonder back in the 8th century. Borobudur was conceived as a Buddhist vision of the cosmos. From above, the structure resembles a 3D tantric mandala through which Buddhist pilgrims could thread a path from the everyday, represented in stone relief, towards a contemplation of nirvana at the monument's crowning stupa. Paralleling the spiritual journey towards enlightenment, the corridors lead past rich sequences of stone reliefs that can be read as a textbook of early Javanese culture and Buddhist doctrine.

For more on Borobudur, see p88.

5. Prambanan

CENTURIES OF HINDU RULE

The magnificent temple complex of Prambanan dates to the 9th century – around 50 years after Borobudur. Little else is known about its early history, although it may have been built by Rakai Pikatan to commemorate the return of a Hindu dynasty to sole power in Java. The whole Prambanan Plain was abandoned when the Hindu-Javanese kings moved to East Java and, in the middle of the 16th century, a great earthquake toppled many structures. Today the majority of these 240-plus temples have been restored, highlighting the incredible artistry of centuries ago, with exquisite reliefs of Vishnu, Brahma and other important Hindu deities.

For more on Prambanan, see p86.

6. Masjid Wapaue

THE SPREAD OF ISLAM

Muslim Arab traders had appeared in Indonesia as early as the 7th century. By the 13th century Arabs had established settlements in major Indonesian ports, and it was then that the first local rulers adopted Islam. Gradually over the next two centuries, then more rapidly, other Indonesian ports with Muslim communities switched to Islam. On the island of Ambon, the thatch-roof Masjid Wapaue attests to the spread of Islam to far-flung corners of Maluku. Originally constructed in 1414, the mosque was moved several times over the centuries and is still actively used by the local community.

For more on Masjid Wapaue, see p395.

7. Pura Rambut Siwi

LEGENDARY PILGRIMAGE SITE

On Bali, Hinduism had roots dating back more than six centuries by the time the Shaivite priest and famous traveller Nirartha came to the island in 1537. He had left the royal courts of Blambangan, Java, and became the advisor to Dalem Baturenggong, who ruled during the golden age of the Balinese kingdom of Gelgel. Nirartha also established a handful of temples, including Pura Rambut Siwi, which has a magnificent coastal setting overlooking a black-sand beach. Many miracles were attributed to the celebrated holy man. According to one legend, Nirartha repaired Pura Rambut Siwi after a devastating earthquake, using a lock of his hair.

For more on Pura Rambut Siwi, see p281.

8. Kota Tua

EUROPEAN VESTIGES IN THE TROPICS

In the early 17th century, the Dutch and English jostled for power in present-day Jakarta. The Dutch ultimately emerged victorious, and in 1619 began building the stout walls and towers that would protect Batavia, the newly christened capital of the Dutch East Indies. Vestiges of that European settlement survive in Kota Tua ('old town'), including Kali Besar, an 18th-century canal built along the Sungai Ciliwung (Ciliwung River) that connects the port to the old city of Batavia. The narrow waterway once thrived with commerce, as boats shuttled goods to and from the port past the houses of Batavia's rich and famous.

For more on Kota Tua, see p68.

9. Benteng Hollandia

BATTLES OVER THE SPICE TRADE

Nutmeg, mace and cloves once grew almost exclusively in a tiny smattering of islands across Maluku. When Europeans discovered the source of these rarities, chaos ensued, as Portugal, Spain, England and the Netherlands fought for control over the newly dubbed 'Spice Islands'. As elsewhere in Indonesia, the Dutch gained the upper hand, thanks to the building of huge fortresses like Benteng Hollandia in the 17th century. The English held out until the 1660s and were finally convinced to leave Maluku for good when they traded the tiny island of Run for an island in North America by the name of Manhattan.

For more on Benteng Hollandia, see p403.

10. Kebun Raya (Bogor Botanical Gardens)

TROPICAL BLOOMS OF THE 19TH CENTURY

Founded by the German-born botanist Caspar Georg Carl Reinwardt in 1817, Bogor's pride and joy are the oldest botanical gardens in Southeast Asia. Apart from nurturing myriad flowering species, the gardens played an instrumental role in the development of economically viable species and culturing new varieties of coffee,

Kebun Raya (Bogor Botanical Gardens; p153), Java

DEAN31/SHUTTERSTOCK

rice, rubber and even cinchona – used to make quinine for malaria treatment. The on-site Zoological Museum, added in 1894, has an atmospheric collection of various specimens, from iridescent butterflies to a replica of Java Man, a breakthrough in the study of human evolution when it was discovered in 1891.

For more on Kebun Raya (Bogor Botanical Gardens), see p153.

11. Krakatau

ERUPTION THAT CHANGED HISTORY

In May 1883, Krakatau – located off the west coast of Java – erupted in one of the most powerful volcanic events in recorded history. The eruptions continued over the next few months, culminating in a great explosion in August that was so powerful it could be heard thousands of kilometres away. Tragically, over 36,000 people lost their lives, with scores of villages destroyed by the tsunamis created in the wake of the eruption. It affected the entire earth: dust clouds circled the globe, creating a volcanic winter, and global temperatures fell an average of 1.2°C for five years.

For more on Krakatau, see p178.

12. Pantai Base G

TRAUMAS OF WWII

When Japan invaded the Dutch East Indies in 1942, Indonesians initially welcomed the Japanese as liberators. Feelings changed as they were subjected to slave labour and starvation, which led to a staggering loss of life – upwards of four million Indonesian deaths, by some estimates. The Allies made little attempt to dislodge the Japanese from Java or Sumatra. Instead, US General Douglas MacArthur focused on New Guinea, and in 1944 spearheaded the landing of 80,000 Allied troops near Jayapura during the Battle of Hollandia. Serving as their administrative headquarters was Pantai Base G, today a scenic stretch of beachfront.

For more on Pantai Base G, see p437.

13. National Monument (Monas)

THE FIGHT FOR INDEPENDENCE

After the Japanese surrender in 1945, Indonesians seized the moment and declared independence from the Netherlands. The Dutch deployed over 200,000 soldiers to crush the rebellion. The war raged for four years, and an estimated 100,000 Indonesians died. In 1954, Sukarno, one of the leaders of Indonesian independence and the nation's first president, hosted a design competition for a monument commemorating Indonesia's independence. Construction began in 1961, though lack of funding caused years of delays, and it wasn't until 1975 that the public finally saw the opening of the monument.

For more on the National Monument (Monas), see p64.

14. Museum Konferensi Asia Afrika

UNITING ASIA AND AFRICA

The past seems ever present on the streets of Bandung, with its Art Deco architecture that once held grand hotels, high-end restaurants and artfully designed cinemas. These buildings – mostly from the 1920s – were given new life following Indonesia's independence in 1949. The 1926 Concordia dance hall would be rebranded as Gedung Mederka (Freedom Building) when Sukarno, Indonesia's first president, hosted the Asia-Africa Conference – a groundbreaking event that bought together countries both newly freed from colonialism and those still struggling under oppressive foreign regimes. The gathering served as a great symbol of equality for all races and respect for human rights.

For more on Museum Konferensi Asia Afrika, see p166.

15. Museum PLTD Apung

INDONESIA'S WORST NATURAL DISASTER

On 26 December 2004, the city of Banda Aceh experienced a 9.1-magnitude earthquake off the west coast of Sumatra. Around 15 minutes later, a towering wall of water – the first of three waves – flooded the city, destroying nearly everything in its wake. Over 60,000 people in the city died (a quarter of the population). The *PLTD Apung* is a visible monument from that horrific event. This 2500-tonne vessel was carried several kilometres inland by the tsunami and was later turned into a museum to document the devastation that killed more than 160,000 Indonesians and over 230,000 people worldwide.

For more on the Museum PLTD Apung, see p501.

MEET THE INDONESIANS

Home to 17,000 islands, there are both fascinating cultural differences and similarities that unite this food-loving nation. Leyla Rose introduces her people.

DESPITE BEING THE fourth-most-populous nation on earth, Indonesia has continued to fly under the radar for many. That perception may well be changing.

You can easily spot an Indonesian name – hospital records are overwhelmed with 'Budi' and 'Ayu', typical names for boys and girls. Many Indonesians, particularly the older generations, only have one given name – easy to remember, but a little more difficult to pinpoint the exact Budi you're looking for. There are island variations, too. For example, in Bali, the firstborn son is always called Wayan, Putu or Gede. There are also set names for the second son, third son etc. Honorifics continue to be used, with each region having its own way of addressing someone, whether they're older or younger, male or female. As a general rule, *pak* (father) is used when politely greeting an older male, *ibu* (mother) for older females – even when they're not your parents.

In recent years, the birth rate has been on a steady decline. Meanwhile, labour migration is high, with many Indonesians seeking more lucrative work opportunities in other Asian countries, as well as the Middle East.

Indonesia is home to 1340 ethnic groups and over 700 languages, so the regional differences are astounding. Someone from the west of Lombok will struggle to understand people living in the south – completely different languages are used, despite being just an hour's drive apart. It's no surprise then, to find that Indonesia is home to the highest percentage of trilingual speakers in the world. The 'standard' Indonesian accent that you'll hear on TV or in movies is from Jakarta, but accents will vary depending on which island you go to. Formal Indonesian and colloquial Indonesian are almost completely different languages.

There are also religious differences. Indonesia is the world's largest Muslim nation, with approximately 87% of the population following Islam. Bali is the only province with a Hindu majority, where people practise Balinese Hinduism. The further east you go, Christianity begins to dominate.

Despite these differences, there are many commonalities that unite the world's largest archipelago; the major one is food. It's the nucleus of any social gathering, and you'll often find restaurants and street-food places open until late. 'Have you eaten yet?' is a common greeting, so don't be surprised when someone you just met invites you to their house to eat.

But things run a little slower in Indonesia (we call it 'island time'), and it's normal to have people show up late. Very late. You can't stay upset for too long though, as Indonesians are some of the most generous people you'll ever meet. In fact, the country had retained top position for the sixth year running in the 2023 World Giving Index.

Population

Indonesia has a population of 283.5 million. There are 1340 recognised ethnic groups, the largest being Javanese, who account for 40% of the total population. While it's not the largest island, Java is certainly the most populated, home to 56% of the country's people.

CLOCKWISE FROM TOP LEFT: ARTEM BELIAIKIN/SHUTTERSTOCK, IZLAN SOMAI/SHUTTERSTOCK, AJILHAMPRATAMA/SHUTTERSTOCK, GUDKOV ANDREY/SHUTTERSTOCK

I'M INDONESIAN, BUT WHAT DOES THAT MEAN?

I was born in Lombok. My birth mother was from Sumbawa and my birth father was from Germany. I was adopted, and my adoptive mother is from England, while my adoptive father was from Sumatra. This duality has given me a unique perspective in understanding the country's language and culture, while being exposed to the rest of the world through the tourists staying at my parents' hotel. People travel from far and wide to visit Indonesia.

Mixed marriages are common, whether that's among different islands or out of the country. People also travel among islands to live and work. On tourist islands like Bali and Lombok, there are large expat populations from Australia and Europe, many of whom have set up businesses or work remotely.

Equally, there are many Indonesians who choose to leave – the Indonesian diaspora is over nine million people, with Malaysia, the Netherlands, Australia and China being the most common destinations.

THREADS OF TRADITION

Indonesia's ancient textile art form is still a style staple today.

By Leyla Rose

IT'S ALMOST IMPOSSIBLE to visit Indonesia and not encounter batik fabric, whether being worn as a piece of clothing, used in handicrafts and decorative items such as purses and bags, or in furnishings like tablecloths and cushion covers. These intricate, UNESCO-listed fabrics are an integral part of the Indonesian nation's culture and history.

Early examples of batik and wax-resist dyeing techniques have been found across Central Asia, India and the Middle East, dating back 2000 years ago. It's thought that the craft was brought to Indonesia via maritime trade routes, and although there are no definitive dates, it really burgeoned between 13 CE and 15 CE in Java during the Majapahit Empire – a Hindu-Buddhist kingdom in which art and culture including literary works, decorated temples, ornate sculptures and batik textiles, all flourished. The word 'batik' itself originates from the Javanese term *ambatik,* a combination of two words meaning 'painting' and 'dots' – a reference to how this particular type of textile is made.

The most traditional batik-making techniques in Indonesia are *batik tulis* and *batik cap. Batik tulis* is where a canting (a type of copper tool) is dipped in hot wax

Batik tulis

and traced over the pattern on the cloth. Meanwhile, *batik cap* is where patterned stamps made of copper are dipped into the wax and pressed onto the fabric repeatedly to create a uniform pattern. Once the patterns have been traced or stamped with wax, the fabric is dyed. The waxed areas don't absorb the dye, and these are subsequently removed to reveal the motif underneath. The fabric can be dyed multiple times to create multicoloured, multipatterned pieces. Alternative methods include *batik kombinasi,* a combination of *batik tulis* and *batik cap,* as well as tie-dyeing and digital printing using machines.

The patterns depicted on batik fabrics always have a symbolic meaning, representing prayers, hopes and dreams, noble values and moral lessons passed down from ancestors. While batik was originally reserved for and worn by only the royal courts, it soon became mass produced for the general population.

THE PATTERNS DEPICTED ON BATIK FABRICS ALWAYS HAVE A SYMBOLIC MEANING, REPRESENTING PRAYERS, HOPES AND DREAMS, NOBLE VALUES AND MORAL LESSONS PASSED DOWN FROM ANCESTORS.

Batik cap

FROM LEFT: WILLIAM REINALDY/SHUTTERSTOCK, REEZKY PRADATA/SHUTTERSTOCK

Motifs vary depending on the area. Batik from coastal areas such as Cirebon and Pekalongan in north Java are known for their bright blues, reds, yellows and oranges. These cities were once popular ports of call for Indian, Chinese and Arab traders, which meant that a wider choice of dyes and inks was available. Trade with these different cultures also influenced the patterns on the batik made in these areas, such as Chinese-influenced dragons and phoenixes, and Indian-influenced geometric patterns. Meanwhile, batik from inland areas like Yogyakarta and Solo feature more earthy colours such as brown, beige and black. They tend to take on a more spiritual meaning too, often featuring symbols from Javanese-Hindu beliefs, such as *sidomukti* (the hope that the wearer will always be happy) and *truntum* (the wearer will receive endless love).

Batik fabrics are still a large part of everyday life in Indonesia, from slings that mothers use to carry their babies, to the shrouds used to wrap the dead, and everything in between: weddings, ceremonies, even workwear – many offices in Indonesia have a mandatory 'Batik Friday' policy.

And batik is experiencing a new evolution. There's a current movement amongst Indonesia's youth called *berkain,* or 'to cloth' (*kain* means cloth, and *ber* is an action suffix). It's about celebrating traditional fabrics such as batik or ikat, wearing them in everyday life and not just as formal attire. It's a way for young people to express pride in cultural heritage in their own, creative way by pairing traditional fabrics with modern fashion and accessories. The *berkain* movement is driven by a resurgence of interest in traditional crafts, with young, innovative designers incorporating batik into contemporary styles including T-shirts, chic jumpsuits and trendy culottes. Batik can even be seen hitting the runways in Indonesia and abroad, with high-end designers utilising the textiles in their collections. Despite being over 2000 years old, batik is clearly here to stay.

Melissa's Garden (p428), Raja Ampat

PURWANTO NUGROHO/SHUTTERSTOCK

THE LOCAL FIGHT TO SAVE INDONESIA'S 'LAST PARADISE'

Raja Ampat's deeply interconnected ecosystem faces threats from tourism and now nickel extraction. Here's what locals are doing to preserve its delicate balance. By Tiara Maharani

RAJA AMPAT IS home to more than 1300 species of reef fish and 75% of the world's coral species, making it a true bucket-list destination for nature lovers. However, the effects of tourism and now nickel extraction threaten its otherworldly beauty, and locals are spearheading efforts to preserve this 'Amazon of the Seas'.

A Biodiversity Hot Spot

Located off the northwest coast of Southwest Papua Province, the over-1500 islands of the Raja Ampat archipelago are home to mangrove forests, coral reefs and seagrass beds that provide critical habitat for a trove of marine biodiversity, from whale sharks to pygmy seahorses.

Designated a UNESCO Global Geopark in 2023 and a Biosphere Reserve in 2025, Raja Ampat draws over 30,000 travellers yearly, with visitors bringing vital income but also the potential to disturb delicate reefs and forests. Research and local experience suggest the ever-increasing visitor numbers are already a third more than what the reefs can sustainably accommodate.

Local Guardians

Thankfully, local residents have played their part in protecting this remote corner of West Papua since long before the arrival of tourism.

Local communities are guided in daily life by a culture and beliefs that involve deep respect for their environment, and one way they safeguard their home is through *sasi,* a traditional practice that temporarily pauses fishing and harvesting to allow ecosystems to recover.

In 'closed' *sasi,* fishing is completely off limits anywhere from a week to two years, depending on how local elders read the rhythms of nature. When the area reopens ('open' *sasi*), the community is free to harvest the bounty of the sea but with strict conditions in place. Catches must be taken sustainably using traditional tools rather than modern methods.

This has proven effective: when dynamite fishing severely damaged coral reefs and seagrass beds in the waters of Misool in the 1980s and '90s, it was the reinstatement of *sasi* that allowed these ecosystems to heal.

A New Threat

However, Raja Ampat faces a potentially more damaging threat in the form of nickel mining, with more than 22,000 hectares of nickel-mining concessions found within the archipelago.

Large-scale nickel mining commenced here in the late 1960s, primarily concentrated on Gag Island, followed by Kawei and Manuran. Operations continued sporadically, but between 2020 and 2024, land use for mining grew by nearly 500 hectares, triple the pace of the previous five years, according to data from conservation NGO Auriga Nusantara.

This sparked outrage among local communities in Indonesia, and also drew global concern. After mounting public pressure, the Indonesian government revoked four nickel-mining licenses, leaving just one operation on Gag Island.

But the damage has been done. Environmental groups have documented at least three major impacts from mining in Raja Ampat: heavy sedimentation, extensive coral breakage and widespread coral bleaching. Of these, only bleaching offers any real chance of recovery, but even then, restoration can take decades.

Local Impact

The deepest wounds are felt by the same local communities that have protected these islands for generations. On Gag Island, contaminated water prevents villagers from swimming, while mangroves and coastal vegetation have been damaged, leaving homes exposed to waves and storms.

As forests are cleared and shores darken with sediment, traditional fishing grounds shrink and the ancient biocultural practices are at risk of extinction. In some places, fish have become scarce, forcing villages that once relied entirely on the ocean to supplement their income with small-scale tourism.

But even this lifeline is fragile. If the environment falters, will travellers still come to Raja Ampat?

An Uncertain Future

Some residents reassure themselves that the last active mining operation on Gag Island is far from tourist areas and village life. But that comfort is thin, considering there are plans to build Papua's first nickel smelter, a 500-hectare project inside the Sorong Special Economic Zone that's expected to process up to 160,000 tonnes of nickel each year. The main gateway to Raja Ampat, Sorong is just 35km by sea from the Dampier Strait, where most dive sites are located, and the smelting project raises serious environmental concerns.

Unlike the existing sites on Gag Island, the smelter could turn quiet waters into busy shipping lanes. Increased marine traffic brings the risks of oil spills, sediment runoff and noise pollution, which could stress coral reefs and fragile ecosystems, threatening the traditional livelihoods of local fishing communities.

The concern isn't limited to the Sorong project: without clear rules and consistent oversight, new mining operations could pop up elsewhere.

The Local Fight

While these threats loom, local communities are taking action to protect their islands' ecosystems. In villages across Southwest Papua, homestays are now more than places to sleep. With training through NGOs and government bodies, homestay owners teach visitors how to protect the ocean through traditional beliefs and practices.

Dive operators also instruct their guests how to avoid damaging corals, and plan trails to avoid damaging mangroves and forest floors. Even small measures, like limiting visitor numbers in sensitive spots or coordinating boat departures, help reduce pressure on the islands' resources.

Locals know that tourism brings many challenges, but they say these issues are manageable and reversible. The extraction industry is not. The tension is no longer framed as development versus conservation. It's about whether Raja Ampat's future will be shaped by decisions made in boardrooms or by the communities who have cared for these ecosystems for generations.

The choices made today will determine whether the next generations inherit thriving ecotourism economies and intact forests, or the long shadow of industrial scars.

BALINESE HINDUISM: A SPIRITUAL BLEND

Unique rituals and ceremonies to live in harmony on the Island of the Gods. By Christine Gilbert

NINETY PERCENT OF Bali's population identifies as Hindu, according to Indonesia's Ministry of Religious Affairs. However, Hinduism in Bali has its own history and practices, making it distinctive from Hinduism in India. Elements of Balinese Hinduism incorporate indigenous Balinese paradigms, traditions and rituals. It also has parallels to Buddhism, Shinto and Taoism.

What is Balinese Hinduism?

Balinese Hindus believe in god, the soul, the law of karma, reincarnation and nirvana. To unite with god at the end of life, followers practice different types of yoga. I Made Gunarta, a founder of the Bali Spirit Festival who comes from a long line of Balinese temple and sarcophagus builders, describes the four types in this way: '*Bhakti yoga,* simply you [are a] devotee. Second one is...*kriya yoga,* you use your skill. Third one [is] *jnana yoga,* you use your knowledge...and *raja yoga*...when you [are] leading people with spirituality.'

While these tenets cross over with Indian Hinduism, Balinese Hinduism adds to them by incorporating animism (the indigenous belief that animals, objects and places have their own spirits). The ocean, mountains, rivers and houses all have spirits to be recognised, and one should attempt to live in harmony with them via shrines and offerings.

Bali has its own symbols and stories apart from Indian lore, like the figures of Barong and Rangda, representing good and evil respectively. The struggle between these two entities is shown in dances with performers wearing ornate masks blessed with holy water. Barong is often depicted as a lion, while Rangda's mask incorporates huge teeth and matted hair.

History of Hinduism in Bali

The beginnings of Hinduism in Bali can be attributed to Indian traders and priests visiting in the 1st century CE, bringing their regional religions with them. Hinduism's spread greatly increased when Java's Majapahit Empire took over Bali in 1343, prompting a huge wave of Javanese Hindus to migrate. At the turn of the 15th century, when Java became increasingly Muslim, even more Javanese Hindus moved to Bali. Yet it wasn't until Indonesia gained independence from the Dutch in the 1940s when some Balinese started to strongly identify as Hindu. They recognised that their type of Hinduism was specific to Bali and by claiming it, they could protect themselves against Dutch influence and proselytisation by both Muslims and Christians.

Galungan, Penglipuran (p241)

HENRI FITRIADI/SHUTTERSTOCK

Important Balinese Religious Days

Bali has two calendar systems that affect significant religious holidays' dates. The lunar Saka calendar, made up of 12 months, determines the date on which Nyepi, the annual Day of Silence falls. The other calendar, Pawukon, runs for 210 days, and is based on rituals, not solar or lunar cycles. Consisting of 10 weeks running concurrently, it determines the date when most of the island's religious festivals will land, as they change yearly.

Nyepi begins the Saka calendar year. To observe it, silence falls throughout the island for 24 hours. The Balinese take time to reflect and observe rituals tied to self-control, release of attachment, stillness and abstaining from entertainment. Everyone stays indoors, and everything closes. Malevolent spirits are believed to roam the island, and its deserted appearance is a strategy to prevent them from bringing harm.

This prevention begins prior to Nyepi, when neighbourhood groups make ogoh-ogoh, massive sculptures representing evil spirits or sometimes gods and goddesses. Made of polystyrene and bamboo covered in painted paper, ogoh-ogoh are paraded through the streets the day before Nyepi and then burned.

Another auspicious holiday is Galungan, a celebration of good triumphing over evil, coupled with the visit of ancestral spirits. The origin of Galungan is tied to King Mayadenawa, said to be an ancient king in Bali. He forbade worship of the island's gods and destroyed its temples. Indra (the God of War) began a war against the king, who in turn poisoned the well of Indra's army. Indra responded by creating a new spring to heal those who'd drunk from the poisoned one. Indra's army then defeated the king. Galungan is the anniversary of their victory.

From the beginning of Galungan until Kuningan (the 10th day after Galungan), spirits of deceased ancestors are said to visit Bali. Festivities include feasting, temple visits and streets filled with bamboo poles decorated with offerings for ancestors.

Offerings, Rituals & Blessings

Walk down the streets of Bali and you'll see Canang Sari, a popular offering adorning the entrances to homes, storefronts, temples and even the handlebars of motorbikes. Made of small boxes of banana or coconut leaves, *Canang Sari* contain flowers, betel and pandan leaves, incense, rice and other tokens of devotion. All parts of the offering symbolise various things: different flower colours for certain gods and rice for prosperity. The incense is thought to usher prayers between the physical and spiritual worlds. Canang Sari is believed to bring spiritual balance and protection – meaning it can be and usually is placed virtually everywhere.

For temple visits and ceremonies in Bali, the ritual dress is that of a sarong paired with a sash. The sarong represents the idea of duality in Balinese Hinduism, known as *rwa bhineda* (literally meaning 'two opposites'). This concept applies not only to good and evil, but to all aspects of life, such as birth and death – states and emotions' opposites are needed to find harmony and balance throughout the universe. The sash symbolizes a 'tying off' of emotions to control them in sacred spaces and ceremonies, as well as the desire for purity.

One of the most famous Balinese rituals is Melukat, a bathing ritual for spiritual and physical purification. The significance of holy water in Hinduism dates back to the *Bhagavad Gita*, an epic poem in which the Hindu deity Krishna says he accepts water offerings. Holy water features prominently in ceremonies, temples, blessings and household shrines. Holy water's potency depends on several factors: its source, the mantras used to bless it and the type of priest performing the blessing. One of the most accessible ways to experience Melukat is to go to the Tirta Empul Temple, the very one Indra was said to have created in the Galungan origin story.

Graffiti and public murals, Canggu (p188)
(p188)

TOM HENTY/SHUTTERSTOCK

IN INDONESIA, CONTEMPORARY ART BLOOMS & BOOMS

Well known for traditional and indigenous art, Indonesian artists are now stepping into the 21st century with daring new contemporary works. By Ian Lloyd Neubauer

TAKE A STROLL through any tourist area in Indonesia and you might think Indonesian art is all about the past: intricate batik fabrics and paintings of bucolic ricefields by colonial-era artists of the Ubud style. But when it comes to modern and contemporary art, Indonesia has traditionally been a laggard – and with good reason.

From Traditional to Modern

From independence in the 1940s through to the late 1990s, the country was mostly under military rule. Critical voices that drive dialogue and debate – one of the cornerstones of contemporary art – were heavily censored. By the time democracy was restored at the turn of the century, Indonesia was a cultural wasteland as far as contemporary art was concerned.

However, the new era of openness that followed let a young, tech-savvy population (around one in four Indonesians are young adults) harness the nation's long tradition of visual culture and apply it to modern styles with such vigour and lack of subtlety that Indonesia is now a Southeast Asian hot spot for contemporary art.

'Indonesia has one of the strongest markets in Southeast Asia because it has a community that gathers together to support the art scene and that is what I see is lacking in many other countries in the region. Economically, it is very strong,' says Joel Harumal, the Singaporean owner of Kotak Art Collective, a gallery in Jakarta. 'The whole world can learn from Indonesia about how to successfully share culture. It's the only country I know of that has a Ministry of Creative Economy.'

Bolthole for Artists

In the capital Jakarta, the opening of MACAN (Museum of Modern and Contemporary Art) in 2017 has led to a proliferation of galleries, artist collectives, collectors groups and nonprofits: a comprehensive art ecosystem rivalling that of Indonesia's cultural capital Yogyakarta.

But it is the neighbouring island of Bali – a bolthole for international artists for more than 100 years and now a global tourism hub flush with cash and crypto – where Indonesia's burgeoning contemporary art scene can be most easily accessed by visitors.

From the ramshackle capital Denpasar to the island's hipster headquarters Canggu, alleyways, breakwaters and sometimes entire buildings have been tagged

with graffiti and public murals that mix ancient Balinese culture and contemporary themes. Take, for example, the work of Slinat, a Balinese artist who spray paints large-scale reproductions of black-and-white photographs of Balinese dancers with biohazard masks juxtaposed across their faces.

'These old photos were the first imagery used to promote tourism in Bali and convey that it is an exotic place. They kick-started tourism in Bali,' Slinat says. 'But then we had too much tourism and it ruined the exoticness of Bali. So I created this parody to express how much things have changed here since those photos were taken.'

Galleries are a dime a dozen in beachfront tourist areas and also in Ubud, a small city in the lush green riverlands of central Bali. The majority focus on traditional art because it's what tourists come to Bali ready to buy. But contemporary art is gaining ground, particularly in the busy beachside strip running from Kuta to Canggu.

The island also boasts a calendar chock-a-block with art and cultural events: the Ubud Readers & Writers Festival, the largest literary event in Southeast Asia; the Bali Spirit Festival, which combines art, yoga, healing and music; and the Bali Art Festival in July, an event dedicated entirely to preserving and promoting traditional handicrafts.

Last year, the island also got its first event dedicated to contemporary art. Art & Bali takes place in September at Nuanu, a visionary entertainment and residential project on Bali's west coast, featuring a beach club, luxury residential villas, a day school, a hotel, galleries, and an abundance of art, including giant sculptures that resemble those from the Burning Man festival in the US. In fact, they were designed by Daniel Jonathan Popper, the South African sculptor whose large-scale flammable sculptures define the Burning Man zeitgeist.

The Fair Comes to Town

A two-day event, Art & Bali features performances, talks, workshops, after-dark celebrations of art and more. However, its epicentre is the Labyrinth Convention Centre where, last year, 17 galleries and collectives representing 150 local and international artists from Indonesia and the region peddled their wares. The contrast in the utility of the works created by these two groups was well pronounced, though not in favour of the international artists as one might imagine.

Contributors, including Ubud-based Australian contemporary artist Rodney Glick and South Korean fashion designer Consteller DL, exhibited works at the event to varying degrees of success and originality.

Things got much more interesting at the Kotak Art Collective booth. The centrepiece here was a statue of a tall, squashed, canary-yellow double-decker bus made from resin, acrylic and automotive paint with playful plastic animal characters in the seats and cartoon-cloud-like smoke belching from the exhaust. Created by Yogyakartan sculptor Sumbul Pranov, it represents 'the way we see things as children, bigger and more colourful as they are,' said gallery director Joel Harumal.

At the Laku Art Space booth, I was drawn to three paintings by another heavy hitter from Yogyakarta, Valentino Febri. The second-generation artist paints scenes from his home town, like a woman patting her dog and lovers sitting by a canal. The fair complexions and plus-size bodies of the models combined with pastel-coloured backgrounds make me think the artists borrowed heavily from European impressionists like Claude Monet who emphasise light and colour, and the famous fat women of Colombian artist Fernando Botero.

But Febri's inspiration came much closer to home. 'I based the subjects in these paintings on the skinny figures in the *wayang*,' he said, referring to the famous puppetry of Indonesia, the country's most iconic art, which originated in his home island, Java. 'I just gave them rounder faces.'

INDEX

Map Pages **000**

Map Pages **000**

N

T

Map Pages **000**

Y

"The first time I heard Gunung Dukono (p387) rumble, I thought a jet plane had just landed by the lava flows behind me."

MARCO FERRARESE

"That time a monkey swam 50m across a fast-flowing mountain stream just to steal my biscuits."

MARK EVELEIGH

Mapping data sources:
© Lonely Planet
© OpenStreetMap http://openstreetmap.org/copyright

FROM LEFT: LABETAA ANDRE/SHUTTERSTOCK, JORGE SANCHEZ PHOTOS/SHUTTERSTOCK

THIS BOOK

This 15th edition of Lonely Planet's Indonesia was researched and written by Anthony Ham, Ray Bartlett, Jade Bremner, Mark Eveleigh, Narina Exelby, Marco Ferrarese, Christine Gilbert, Paul Harding, Tiara Maharani, Ian Neubauer, Sarah Reid and Leyla Rose.

The previous edition was written by Jayne D'Arcy, David Eimer, Mark Johanson, Jason Lee, Regis St Louis and Ryan Ver Berkmoes.

This edition was produced by the following:

Destination Editor James Pham

Production Editor Amy Lysen

Image Researcher Eoin Loughney

Cartographer Corey Hutchison

Coordinating Editor Christopher Pitts

Assisting Editors Soo Hamilton, Jenna Myers, Gabrielle Stefanos, Jeremy Toynbee

Cover Researcher Giada de Agostinis

Thanks Fergal Condon, Melanie Dankel, Darren O'Connell, Saralinda Turner

Paper in this book is certified against the Forest Stewardship Council™ standards. FSC™ promotes environmentally responsible, socially beneficial and economically viable management of the world's forests.

Published by Lonely Planet Global Limited
CRN 554153
15th edition – Aug 2026
ISBN 978 1 83869 803 4

10 9 8 7 6 5 4 3 2 1
Printed in Italy